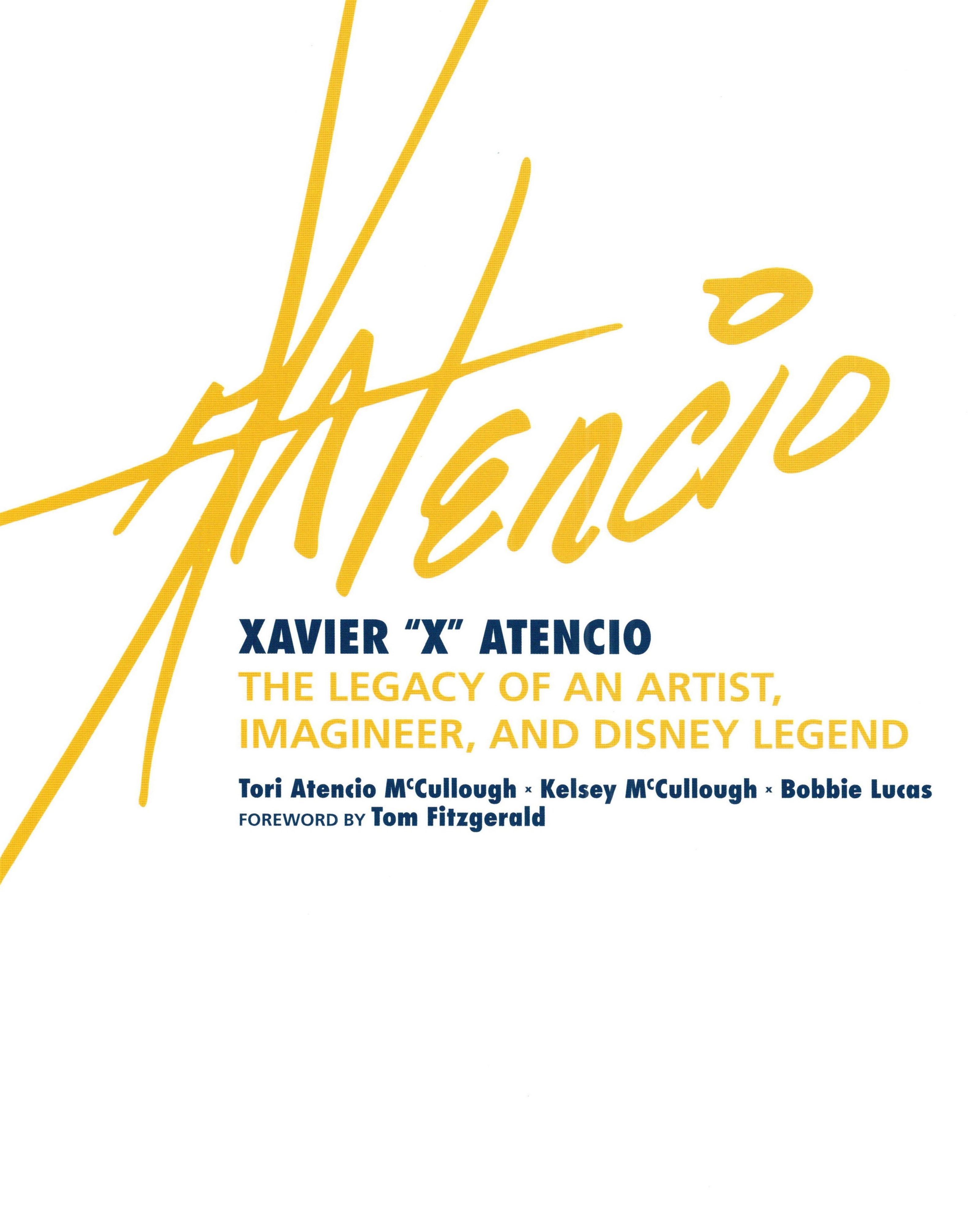

XAVIER "X" ATENCIO

THE LEGACY OF AN ARTIST, IMAGINEER, AND DISNEY LEGEND

Tori Atencio McCullough × Kelsey McCullough × Bobbie Lucas

FOREWORD BY **Tom Fitzgerald**

XAVIER "X" ATENCIO

THE LEGACY OF AN ARTIST, IMAGINEER, AND DISNEY LEGEND

Tori Atencio McCullough × Kelsey McCullough × Bobbie Lucas

FOREWORD BY **Tom Fitzgerald**

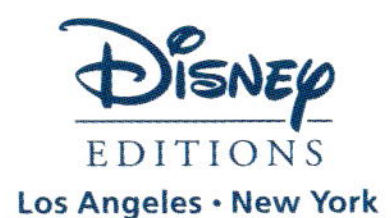

Los Angeles • New York

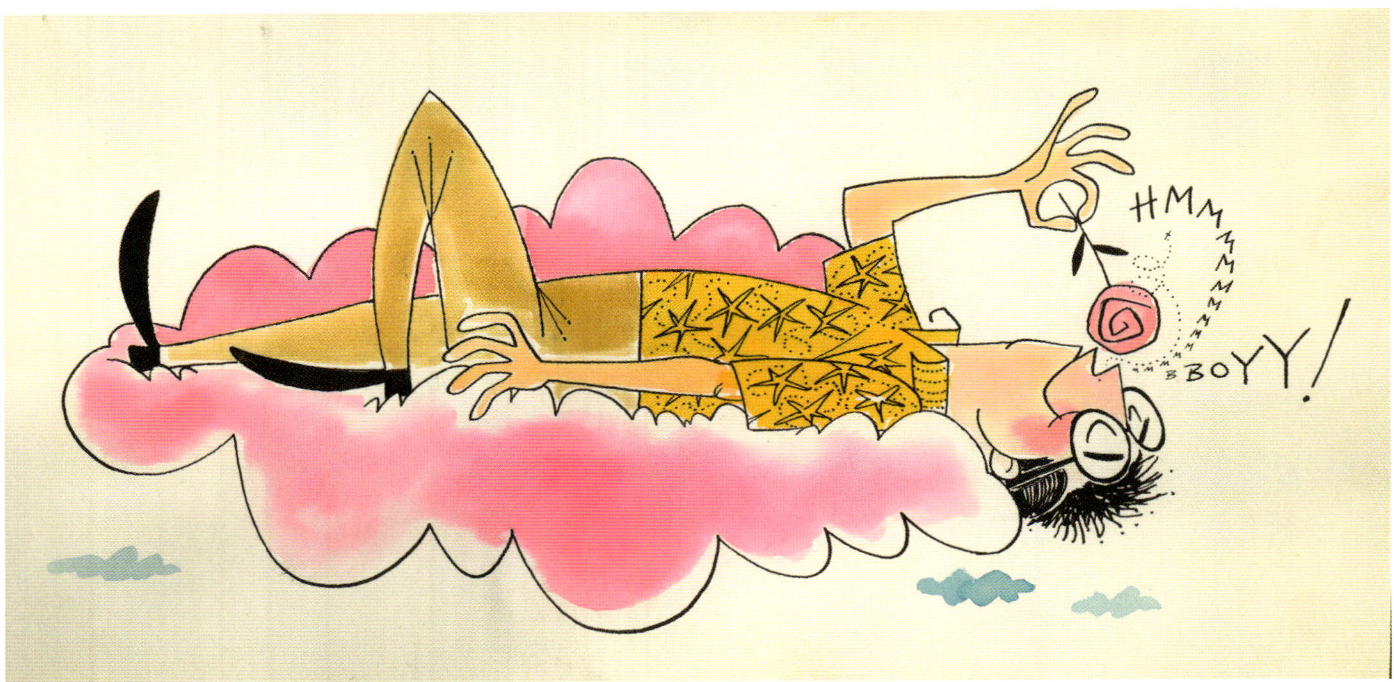

The following are some of the trademarks, registered marks, and service marks owned by Disney Enterprises, Inc.: Adventureland® Area; Audio-Animatronics® Figures; Big Thunder Mountain® Railroad; Disneyland® Park; Disney's Animal Kingdom® Theme Park; Disney's Fort Wilderness Resort; Disney's Hollywood Studios; EPCOT®; Fantasyland® Area; FASTPASS® Service; Frontierland® Area; Imagineering; Imagineers; "it's a small world"; Magic Kingdom® Park; Main Street, U.S.A.® Area; Mickey's Toontown®; Monorail; Shanghai Disneyland; Space Mountain® Attraction; Splash Mountain® Attraction; Tokyo Disneyland; Tomorrowland® Area; and Walt Disney World® Resort.

Academy Award® and Oscar® are registered trademarks of the Academy of Motion Picture Arts and Sciences.

Published by Disney Editions, an imprint of Buena Vista Books, Inc. For information address Disney Editions, 7 Hudson Square, New York, New York 10013.

Printed in China
First Hardcover Edition, November 2025
10 9 8 7 6 5 4 3 2 1
ISBN 978-1-368-10129-5

FAC-025393-25156

Contents

Dedication

Our eternal gratitude goes to Judianne Atencio, X's younger daughter, and the true Atencio family historian and inheritor of X's storytelling talents. It is an understatement to say that this book would not have been possible without her and her many years researching and documenting our family's history.

Her records, photos, recollections, and detailed accounts were invaluable in crafting the full narrative of X's life story and legacy. Additionally, Judianne is a tireless advocate of X's legacy across social media, continuing to keep his story alive and connected to Disney fans worldwide.

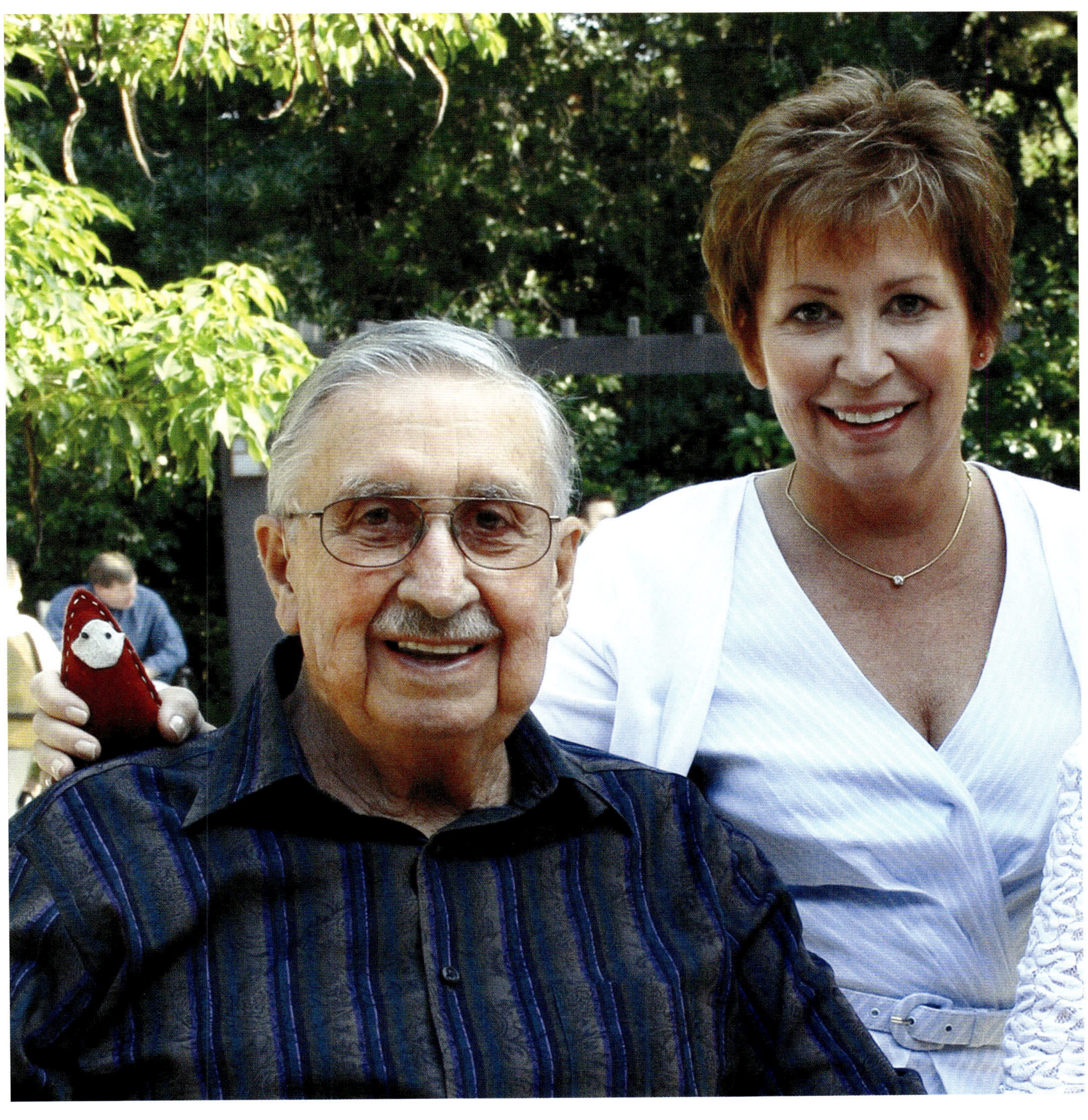

ABOVE: Judianne with X at his ninetieth birthday party.

Tori Atencio McCullough

I GREW UP IN A DISNEY FAMILY. I DON'T MEAN *the* Disney family, of course. Still, I can attest that when your dad worked for *the* Walt Disney, you were surrounded by some pixie dust. There were things we often took for granted, such as family excursions to Disneyland, where we parked backstage behind Main Street, U.S.A.; a tour of the Mary Poppins set, where Walt just magically appeared as if summoned by Mary herself; and holiday parties at the studio, where Wally Boag entertained us. We were used to our dad's bringing home the Disney animated classics to show on a borrowed projector for our birthday parties. And although we didn't realize it then, the family Christmas cards, which my dad designed each year, reflected the styling of his latest project at work. The one thing we didn't ever take for granted as we got older was the fact that he could get us a summer job at WED or the studio.

That is how my Disney story began. I started working at WED Enterprises during the summer of 1972, and that was when my relationship with my father, X Atencio, really changed.

As was typical in the 1950s and 1960s, the day-to-day child-rearing responsibilities belonged to my mother. Dad arrived home for dinner at the same time every night before heading to his home studio to do whatever freelance drawing work he could pick up to support his growing family. He was always supportive, especially if we had an art project to do. Still, I spent almost no one-on-one time with him in my early years. When we went on family outings, there were four kids vying for his attention. Just once, he took me to a movie screening on a Saturday afternoon, because he was a voting member of the Academy of Motion Picture Arts and Sciences and the movie was child friendly. The memory of that is so vivid to me, because it was unbelievably special.

So imagine the thrill of going to work with him every day for three months! We'd jump into his little white Porsche with the red interior, and the two of us would brave the San Fernando Valley freeway traffic. I had him to myself five days a week! Now we had something we could share. After work I would tell him what I had done that day, and who I had met, and he in turn would tell me what he was working on.

After four years of being a "summer hire," I graduated from college, where I had traded my interest in studio arts for a passion for interior design. I had developed a real love for the Imagineering life by then, so I applied for an interior designer position in the Interiors department. From 1976 until 1984, when my dad retired, we were in the same orbit. We were both very involved in the design of EPCOT, but the interesting thing is that we were involved in completely different aspects. He, was working on the show design of the Mexico pavilion and the production of all the scripts and audio for the attractions, while I was focused on the design of the shops and restaurants. The closest we came to working together was when I designed the restaurant in the Mexico pavilion, San Angel Inn, which overlooked "his" attraction El Rio del Tiempo. But even though we didn't work together directly, we knew all the same people. Back then, it felt like everyone knew everyone, or pretty darn near it. After he retired, whenever we joined him for the family Sunday dinner, he would ask, "What's new at the Mouse Factory?" Eventually he stopped asking that question, because he no longer recognized the names, he didn't know the projects, and he could no longer relate to Imagineering. Now, in my eighth year of retirement from WDI, I understand that feeling.

I learned a lot from my dad throughout my life, but it wasn't until I went to work with him that I learned the real-life lessons. He was incredibly well liked by everyone, from his longtime colleagues to the newest Imagineers. Everyone was equal in his book. He and my mom held a Christmas party at their home every year. The guest list didn't include WED executives. The ones who made that list were their executive secretaries. Longtime friends, like Claude Coats, Harriet Burns, Herb Ryman, and Bill Justice, rounded out the partygoers. For many years he hosted the audio department's summer party at

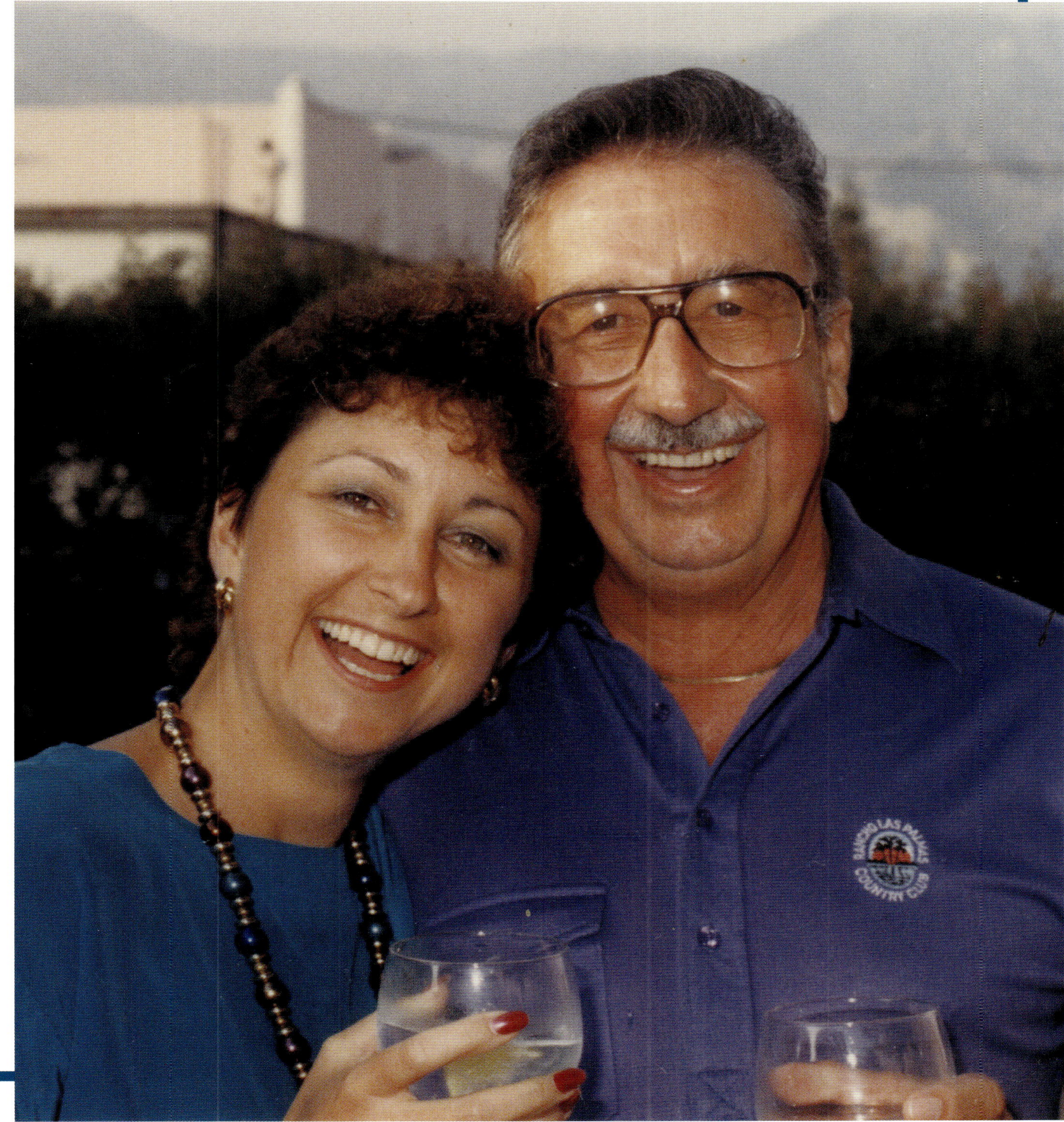

his home, because he had a swimming pool. There was no caste system in his eyes.

His innate generosity was clear when every Christmas he would buy a case of wine and pass the bottles out, not to his bosses but to the cafeteria staff, the custodial staff, and the security guard who greeted him every morning at the gate. That was the kind of man X Atencio was. I learned from him by observing how he treated everyone, and I carried that through my entire career. I always tried to treat my team with respect, compassion, and empathy.

When he passed away in 2017 at the ripe old age of ninety-eight, many Imagineers sent my family their condolences, in cards or through social media. Every one of them said the same thing: "I loved X. He was always so good to me. He was always so nice to me."

Sure, Disney fans will remember him fondly for all the great work he did and the magic he left behind, but to me his kindness is his most incredible legacy.

ABOVE: Tori and X at a party at WED.

Kelsey McCullough

WHILE PUTTING TOGETHER THIS book, I repeatedly asked myself, "Why didn't we think of doing this while Papa was still alive?" I longed for just one more lunch sitting in the red leather booth at Ruby's Diner, where I could pepper him with questions about his extraordinary life while pocketing bits of inspiration and life lessons.

Growing up in Los Angeles, I was a thirty-minute drive from my grandparents for most of my life. This proximity allowed me to spend extended periods of time with Papa, as I called my grandfather. As I got older, the things I cherished most about that time evolved.

When I was a small child, the highlight of any day spent at his house was sitting at his drawing board in his art studio while he taught me to draw my favorite Disney characters. In my early years, I watched him draw Mickey Mouse and Goofy with such ease that I assumed drawing a perfect Mickey was something all adults could do as easily as writing their own name. The way he brought these characters to life combined with the smattering of Mickey Mouse paraphernalia across his house led me to believe that these were not just fictional characters but real friends—and, in the case of Mickey Mouse, the favorite child of the family. Of course, when I became older, I understood that his knack for capturing the perfect character on the page was not a basic life skill but a rare talent. Over time, I also discovered that there was much more to admire about him than his artistic skills.

I felt that I learned the most about my grandfather when I got my driver's license at sixteen and began a tradition of taking him out to lunch at Ruby's Diner. I had always known Papa to be a man of tradition, after watching him prepare posole (a New Mexican pork-and-hominy stew) and Tom and Jerrys every Christmas morning, as his parents and grandparents had done. I was thrilled to have a tradition that we could share together. I would drive out to his house to pick him up, and we would squeeze into my charcoal-gray Volkswagen Beetle and head off to the Woodland Hills Promenade mall, just the two of us. Until this point, most of my time spent with him was also full of other family members, so this became the time when we got to really know each other and I came to understand him better through what he said—and, just as important, what he didn't say. Despite usually having the best stories and the most interesting history of anyone in any social situation, he let others take the lead on talking. He was a listener and an observer—two traits that I find to be key in why he and his work connect so deeply with so many people. While I would have loved for him to regale me with stories of his legendary career, I found that those stories came in response to my questions. When asking him about a part of his life revealed a previously unheard story or especially colorful tale, it felt like hitting the jackpot.

And in my journey to better understand our family's North Star and patriarch during that time, I got the ultimate windfall when one night after dinner at his house, he gave me an old wooden art box his grandfather had built for him when he was in high school. When we opened the box, a musty smell emerged, and as if it were a time capsule, I began to sift through its contents—a diary from his time in the war; his drawings of Pacheco the Colorado Cowboy that got him his first job at Disney; memorabilia from the Pinocchio premiere in 1940; and sketchbooks with drawings from his high school years, his one semester of art school, and his early days at Disney. I felt transported back in time, like I was getting to know my grandfather as a young adult—eager to take on the world, unsure of what lay ahead of him—rather than as the eighty-seven-year-old man sitting across from me in his forest-green recliner. But once again, I came to realize that he chose to share this part of his life with me by showing rather than telling.

Now, more than ten years into my own Disney career, I can't help thinking of my grandfather and his forty-six years at the company. Every day on my drive to work, I turn left off Hyperion Avenue at the spot where the Disney Studio was located when Papa got the job offer that would change the course of his

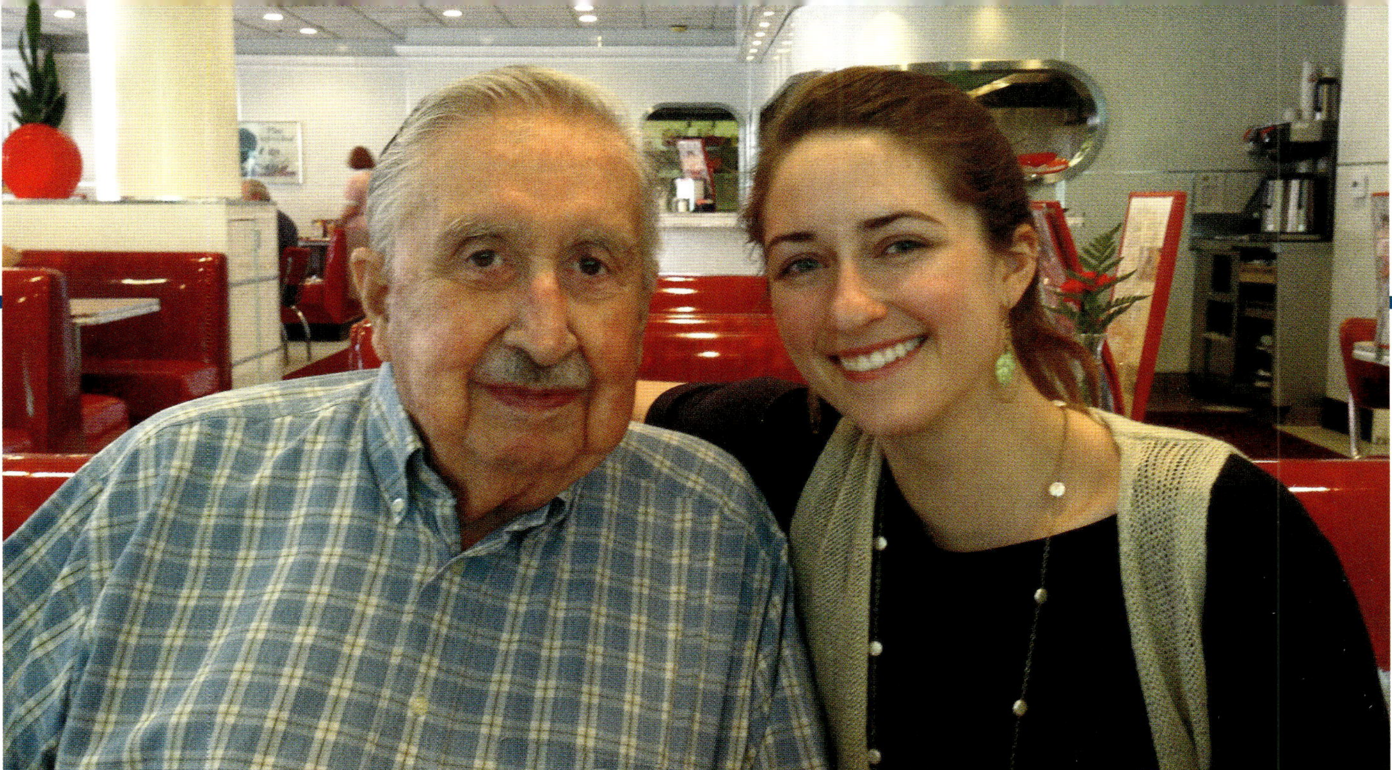

life. When I arrive at the studio in Burbank, I exit the parking structure into Legends Plaza and walk past his handprints on my way to the old Animation building, where he once sat with a pipe in his mouth while cleaning up the dinosaur drawings on *Fantasia*. And I eat lunch—albeit with a much less exciting menu—at the same commissary where he shared meals and learned from his colleagues. While The Walt Disney Company of today is vastly different from the one he started at in 1938 and even the one he retired from in 1984, similar challenges and opportunities still exist at the company. The Walt Disney Company is still a place where incredibly talented people come together to create stories and experiences much greater than what any one person could achieve on their own. In that environment, I continue to be inspired by Papa's approach, most famously with the Haunted Mansion, of figuring out how to bring the best ideas together seamlessly rather than trying to force through his own singular vision or opinion. The company still has periods of great success followed by times of great struggle. When it feels like the road ahead is uncertain, there is comfort in thinking about the times he may have felt the same way—on his return from the war, after Walt's death—and knowing that in the end it all worked out beyond his wildest imagination. In the time I've spent reflecting on his life and putting together this book, what I've come to admire most about my grandfather's career is not the output itself (while it's undeniably brilliant) but how he went about doing it—always with an open mind, an easygoing demeanor, and a collaborative approach that maximized the power of bringing people together rather than a chase for individual credit.

The one way in which he most frequently did talk about himself and his storied career was through various speaking engagements he participated in for Disney, especially after his retirement. While I watched hours of these interviews, one thing that jumped out to me was that he would often say he was being asked to speak because people wanted to hear "what it was like working with Walt Disney." Ever humble and deeply committed to the belief that there was one name on the door when working for The Walt Disney Company, he saw those speaking engagements primarily as a way of sharing a perspective from a supporting role on working with a genius. He never imagined that his story, his wild and diverse talents, and the sharp sense of humor he carried through his ninety-eight-year life could be as inspiring to people in their own right. I can hear him now saying, "Who the hell would want to read that?" if we had even suggested the idea of writing a book about his life. And here is where his wisdom ends. I am constantly amazed by how many people I meet who feel strong connections to and admiration for Papa's work. My hope is that after reading this book, those who were not lucky enough to know him see that there is as much to admire about the man behind the work as there is to admire about the work itself. So while I would love to be able to ask him all the questions that have come up in putting his story together, I know that by doing it now we are able to give him the spotlight he deserves.

ABOVE: Kelsey and X during one of their cheeseburger lunches at Ruby's Diner.

Bobbie Lucas

I'M NOT ONE OF X'S NINE GRANDCHILDREN. I could most closely be defined as a grandchild-in-law, if there is such a thing. My mom's brother is Tori's husband, Mike McCullough, making Tori my aunt and X either my grandfather-in-law or nothing! But he wasn't nothing; that's for sure. I grew up twenty-five hundred miles away from X, Tori, Kelsey, and Disney, in the magical land of suburban New Jersey, but X was still a legend to my family. "He wrote the 'Yo Ho' pirates song," my mother and grandmother would state proudly and repeatedly to all who would listen. We'd go out to California to visit, and the whole McCullough family would spend the day at Disneyland. In addition to the usual family memories of wonderfully chaotic days spent en masse with your eleven or so closest relatives, my earliest memories at Disneyland were of being lightly ridiculed by my family for being scared on the Pirates attraction. "Of course! X created it, and you're scared." Well, they were right; he did create it, and I was scared. With the darkness, the drop into the waters below, and the eerie warning that "dead men tell no tales," my childhood self didn't react well to the ride, which we always had to go on, no exceptions!

I knew X had worked on the original Parent Trap and I remember watching it once with my parents and seeing his name in the credits, something I found particularly impressive. Though I must admit that I only saw the original 1960s movie that one time until I rewatched it as research for this book, because as a child of the 1990s, I am forever loyal to the Nancy Meyers/Lindsay Lohan adaptation. (Sorry, X.)

X and Maureen stopped by our home in New Jersey once with their daughter-in-law Kathy when they were in town visiting. Joe and Kathy lived in northern New Jersey at the time, and Kathy drove them down to see us before they embarked on a cruise, leaving from some nearby port. We took them to lunch, and everyone, had a lovely day.

The most exciting aspect of X's career to McCullough side of the Disney family lore was that X had worked on Pirates of the Caribbean, which is unsurprising, since this was during the peak of the international box office reign of the Pirates of the Caribbean franchise films. X had gotten to go to set, and my cousin Kelsey had gone with him. The resulting photo of X, Johnny Depp, and Kelsey became the McCulloughs' Christmas card that year. My mom hung it on our fridge for a very long time. While my friends would freak out anytime they saw it, my favorite memory of the card is when my grandmother called to ask if the older man in a pirate costume in the photo was Kelsey's boyfriend. Attempting to explain that the international star in the photo was not in fact Kelsey's boyfriend took more time than one would expect.

In my early twenties, I moved to Los Angeles and, in doing so, was beyond fortunate to get to spend more time with Tori, Mike, Kelsey, X, and Maureen. I've spent multiple holidays—Thanksgiving, Christmas, and Easter—at their home. X was always sweet and welcoming, seated in his chair by his bar, awaiting his happy hour drink. He raved about his love of martinis and bacon cheeseburgers. He was quiet, but he always listened, somehow able to really see you. He cared and accepted you—even with his silence. Going to his house was like stepping through time: a mid-century modern Disney mecca—with statues commemorating his years at Disney, drawings, black-and-white photos, a bar that was reminiscent of the Tiki Room, and a Haunted Mansion gravestone in his backyard by his pool. People flowed in and out as the holidays went on: friends, family, family of friends, friends of family, priests, former colleagues—you named them, and they were either present or would probably be arriving soon.

As far as I'm aware, there are only three photos capturing my time spent at X and Maureen's home, only one with X and me both in the photo. The two without X are an Easter photo of me taking an after-brunch nap in a chair after a few too many mimosas, a classic X-approved activity, and a family photo that is its own story for another time. However, the one with X, while not perfect, given the side profile of each of our faces, does indeed capture the essence of X's memory: a Christmas gathering filled

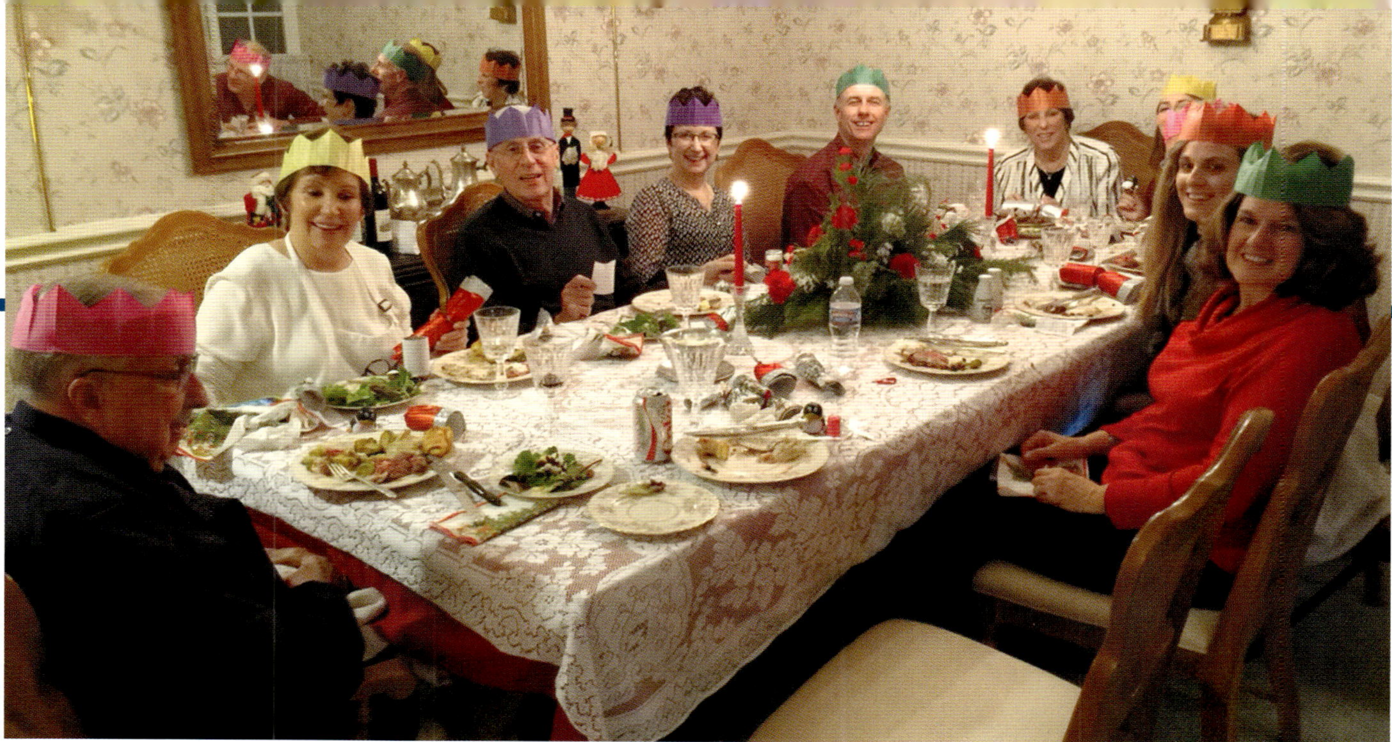

with good food, great family and friends, and much love.

While X wasn't my grandfather, it felt like he was a grandfather to me and to so many others. His warmth, humor, and presence made you feel welcomed, and perhaps because he spent his life creating worlds, characters, and spaces for children of all ages, he saw your emotions, fears, and hopes, and with a little smile and a joke, he made you believe your dreams were possible to achieve.

Working on this book has been an honor and a privilege, and in addition to being thankful to Wendy, Tori, Kelsey, Judianne, and the rest of the Atencio family for making me an "honorary Atencio" and entrusting me with this incredible responsibility, I'm grateful for the opportunity to have gotten to know X better and explore the inner workings of his entire life and career. For someone who moved to Los Angeles at a similar age as X, to pursue a career in film and television entertainment during what at times has felt like worldwide upheaval, studying X's life and the cyclical nature of society and entertainment has been reassuring. Furthermore, X's drive and willingness to try new things, always accepting possibilities as they were offered to him, have been inspiring. His No Dough Productions parallels my own ironically named production company with a trusted colleague. And since agreeing to write this book in 2020, I've found myself somehow pulled into this Disney family business, working in television development at ABC Signature on the Disney Studio lot in the old Animation building, just one floor below Walt's old office, and on hallowed ground X walked many, many times.

Finishing the first draft of the final chapter and this reflection on Sunday, September 10, 2023, I realized that today marks the six-year anniversary of X's death. Moreover, it's the first time since then that September 10 has fallen on a Sunday. I can't help being struck by the coincidence. While I've felt X's presence throughout the writing of this entire book, he has never seemed closer than today. As the lit candle flickers on my dresser, the September Los Angeles "deathly still" air is moved around my apartment only by the help of a small portable fan—reminding me, as X wrote in his Haunted Mansion script, "that is the time when ghosts are present."

Ultimately, unpacking the man and the legend of X Atencio that tangentially impacted my childhood did not disappoint. His ethos as a person matched the level of his work, making him a rare, wonderful, authentic sight to behold and an inspirational legend worthy of that lofty title.

While X's booming caution in Pirates that "dead men tell no tales" might have frightened me as a child, it's only now as an adult reflecting on his life, career, and legacy that I realize a new meaning for this phrase. Dead men may tell no tales, but the work you create and the legacy you forge in life will remain even after you're gone; and if you happen to write it all down or leave enough treasures for those who remain "foolish mortals" "seeking adventure," your legend will live on in the hearts, minds, and coffee table books of loved ones, trusted colleagues, and Disney admirers.

As X would say, "it's too good for them. Ship it!"

ABOVE: The only picture Bobbie has with X, from a Christmas Eve dinner in 2015.

Foreword

WHEN IT CAME TO TALENT, WALT Disney had X-ray vision. He could see skills in individuals they never knew they had—and he knew how to deploy that talent to get exceptional results. As Disney Legend Rolly Crump said, "he was the best casting director that was ever put on this planet!"

X Atencio had already had an illustrious career at the Disney Studio when Walt brought him to WED Enterprises (now Walt Disney Imagineering). At the time X didn't understand why he brought him over, but Walt knew. Disney Legend and longtime Imagineering leader Marty Sklar agreed that "the people that Walt brought over from the studio all had a purpose. He understood what he could get out of almost every one of the people that he had here at Imagineering in those early days." It wasn't long before X was helping bring to life Walt Disney's vision for attractions for Disneyland in ways X likely never would have imagined—writing shows and scripts, penning song lyrics, developing characters, and more.

I knew and loved X Atencio's writing long before I knew who the author was. It began with the vinyl records of Pirates of the Caribbean and the Haunted Mansion, which my father had bought me on a business trip to California. Then came my first trip to Disneyland in 1969, when I got to experience the magic in person. And in 1977, working as a cast member at "the Mansion" at Walt Disney World, I ushered thousands of "foolish mortals" through the attraction and heard X's classic and clever Ghost Host narrations all day, every day. I was in spiritual heaven!

Two years later, I was hired as a writer at WED in California. Within the first week, I was assigned to write a safety spiel for Big Thunder Mountain Railroad, then under construction at Disneyland. My boss told me to head to the WED recording studio and added, "X Atencio will help you out."

When I arrived, X was directing the talented actor Dallas McKennon, who was playing Benjamin Franklin for some early voice tests for what would be the American Adventure at EPCOT Center. As soon as he was done with "Ben," X introduced me to Dallas and set up the tone and character for the safety spiel. In an instant, Ben Franklin turned into a crusty old miner, and in just a few readings—under X's direction—the wildest ride in the wilderness had its recording.

X became a mentor to me, providing guidance not only on how to direct talent but how to write for different types of attractions, how to tell a story in the unique format of the parks, and so much more. When I needed help with anything—from character designs for a roller-coaster-building beaver or the "SMRT-1" robot for EPCOT to a Mickey Mouse logo for Imagineering's Theme Park Media department—X was always there. And it was always an honor to have his art and artistry added to a project.

He was also a good and treasured friend. When I was new to Los Angeles, X never wanted me to be alone on holidays and would invite me to join his family for Easter, Thanksgiving, and Christmas dinners. Always the mentor, he taught me how to properly carve a turkey, a skill that to this day I am happy to show off to friends and family. That thoughtfulness and kindness was X to a T!

Though he is perhaps best known for the iconic song lyrics and scripts he penned for Pirates of the Caribbean and the Haunted Mansion, his contributions span decades of Disney history, from animated

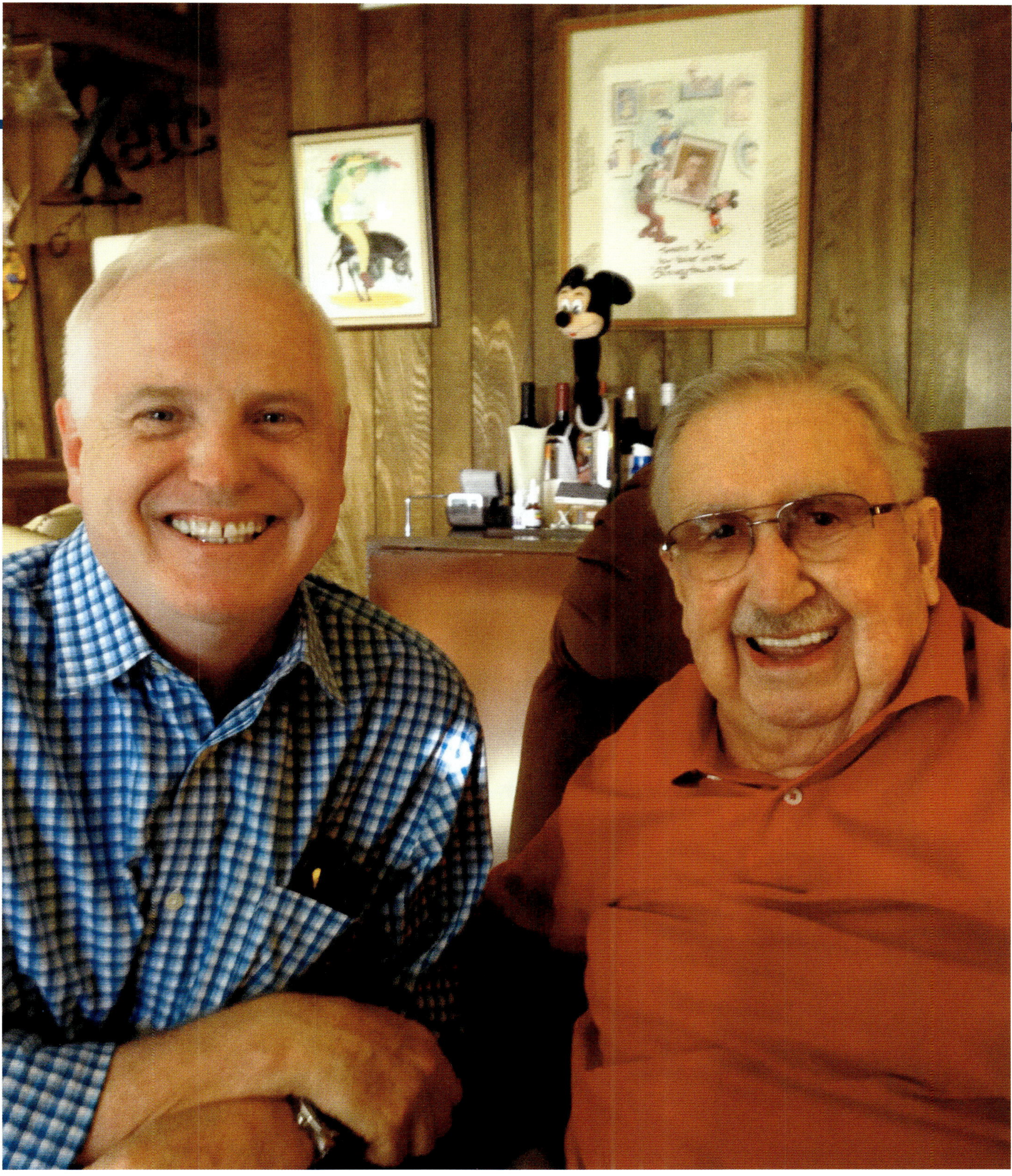

classics to global theme parks. X Atencio truly embodied what it means to be a Disney Legend. He was massively talented, curious, passionate, kind, generous, fearless, and a team player, and he always sought to create an atmosphere of fun while working. "After all," as Marty Sklar used to say, "if you're not having fun, you're in the wrong business!"

So to quote the master, if "ye come seeking adventure . . . you've come to the proper place!" Bobbie Lucas and the Atencio family have crafted a beautiful story of a beautiful man. With that, your "tour begins here . . . There's no turning back now!"

Tom Fitzgerald

CHIEF STORYTELLING EXECUTIVE
WALT DISNEY IMAGINEERING

ABOVE: Tom and X at X's home.

Prologue

IT WAS ANOTHER BEAUTIFUL DAY IN BURBANK, California in 1965, as X Atencio prepared for a meeting with his boss, Walt Disney, to discuss the progress X had made on exploring how to turn Walt's doodles into a short film. Though there had been a few meetings on this topic, X felt he wasn't getting any closer to nailing down the story concept. And yet, when your boss is Walt Disney, you work your hardest to make his vision a reality.

As the meeting got underway, X began his status update to Walt, eventually pausing his appraisal to look up at Walt and admit, "You know, Walt. I don't think we know what the hell we're doing here." Walt arched his eyebrow in response before reaching out across the table and shaking X's hand. Without missing a beat, Walt replied, as X remembered, "I appreciate an honest man. I think now is the time to scrap the whole thing." And with that, Walt got up and walked out of the room.

The next day X received a call summoning him up to Walt's office. Upon X's arrival to the third floor of the old Animation Building office, Walt proclaimed, "X, I've been wanting to get you over to WED for some time, and I think now would be a good time to go." Now known as Walt Disney Imagineering, WED (Walter Elias Disney) Enterprises was established by Walt in 1952 as a place where he could develop new ideas beyond the work at the Disney Studio. X was familiar with WED, as he had worked with them on several projects such as Walt Disney's Enchanted Tiki Room during his time at the studio, but he had no idea why Walt wanted him to move divisions. The studio had been his home since he was hired as an in-betweener at age eighteen, and now, called upon by Walt himself, X was moving two and a half miles down the road to WED and to an uncertain future.

Leaving his Disney studio friends behind and having to trade in his very comfortable animation desk for a plank of wood and two sawhorses at WED left X so heartbroken that every day when he drove past the studio on his way home from work, he grew teary-eyed. And if that wasn't enough, he spent every lunch hour for the first month running from WED back to the studio to dine with his old friends. What he didn't know during this adjustment period was that moving to WED would open another chapter of his life, one beyond his wildest imaginations—filled with pirates and ghosts, trips around the globe, and a legacy that would last for generations to come. And while X may not have known why he was at WED or what Walt had in mind for him, he was about to find out.

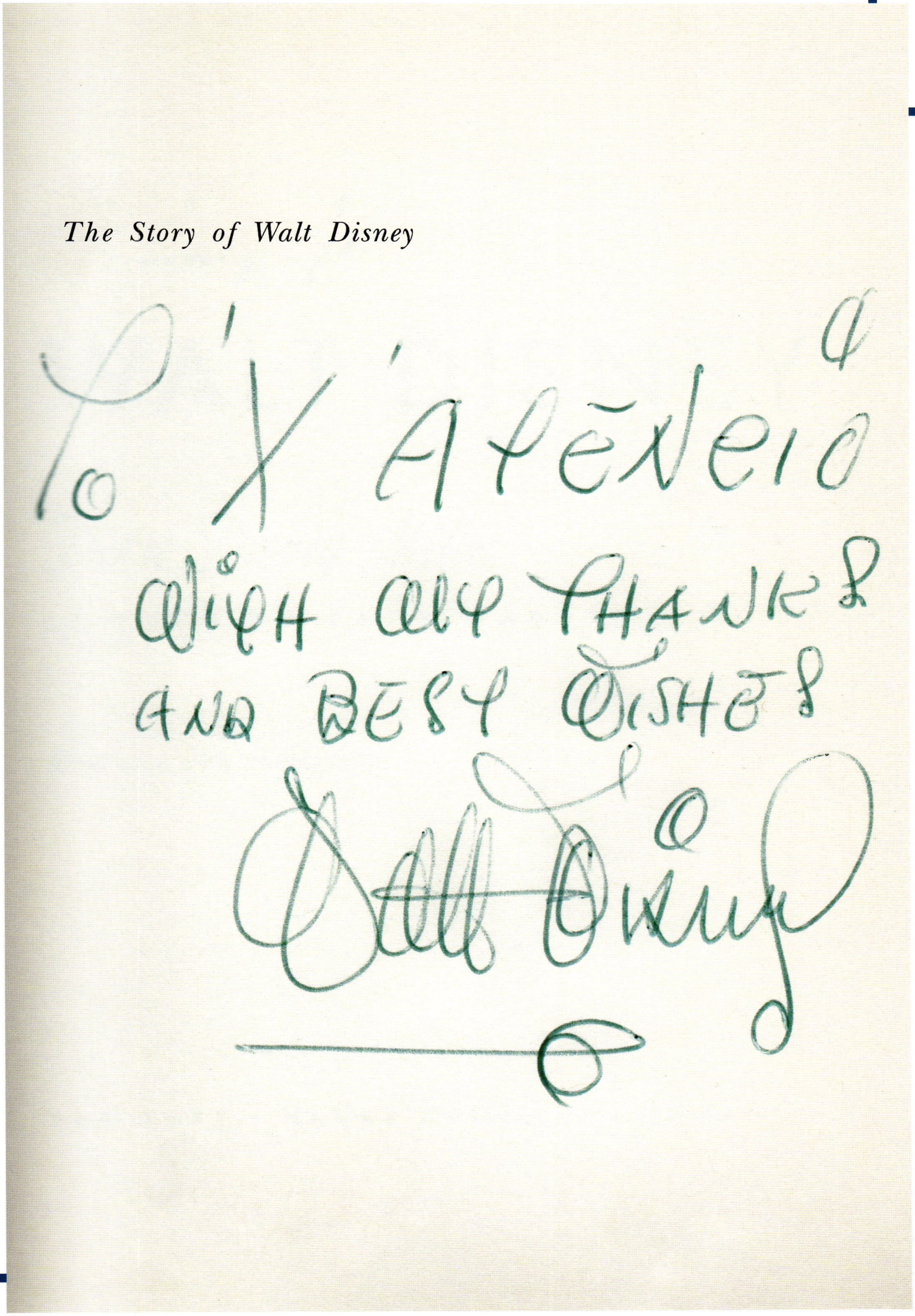

The Story of Walt Disney

To X Atencio
With my Thanks
and Best Wishes
Walt Disney

ABOVE: Book inscribed by Walt to X.

1

Growing Up in Colorado

FRANCIS XAVIER ("X") ATENCIO WAS born on September 4, 1919, into a world just emerging from the maelstrom of the Spanish flu and World War I.

X was born in Trinidad, Colorado, but spent his childhood living in the nearby southern Colorado town of Walsenburg, population approximately 3,500. As was the practice in the 1910s, X's mother, Ida Abeyta Atencio, traveled to her parents' home to give birth to each of her four children. Meanwhile, X's father, Agapito Atencio, stayed at home. This tradition allowed Ida to benefit from her female family members' help and return home when she had recovered enough to care for the children on her own.

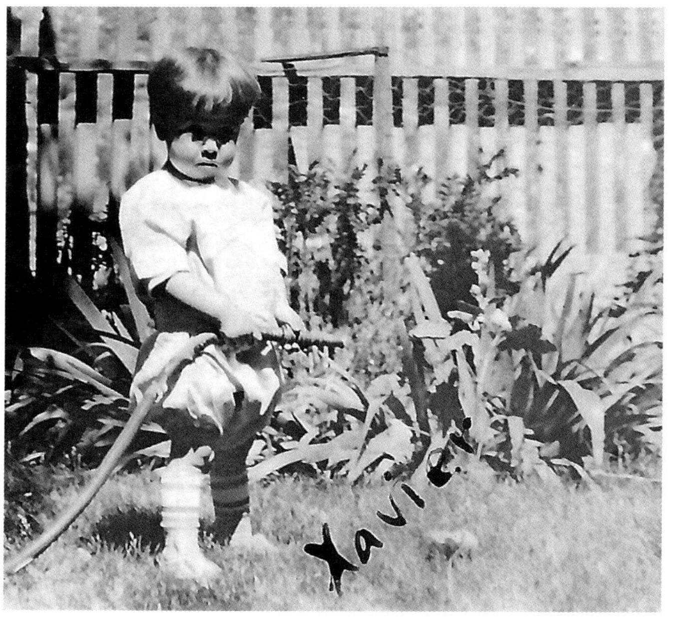

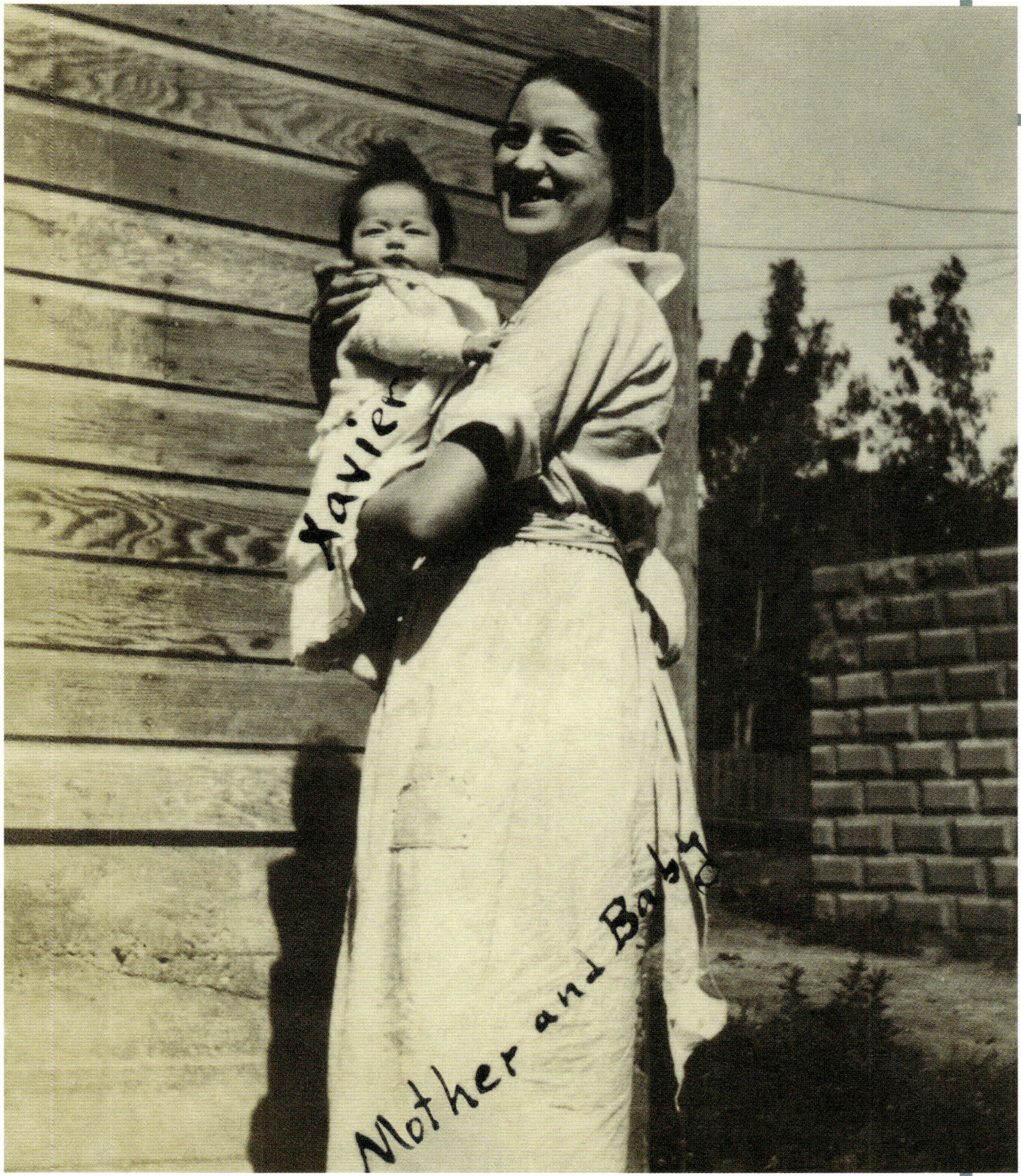

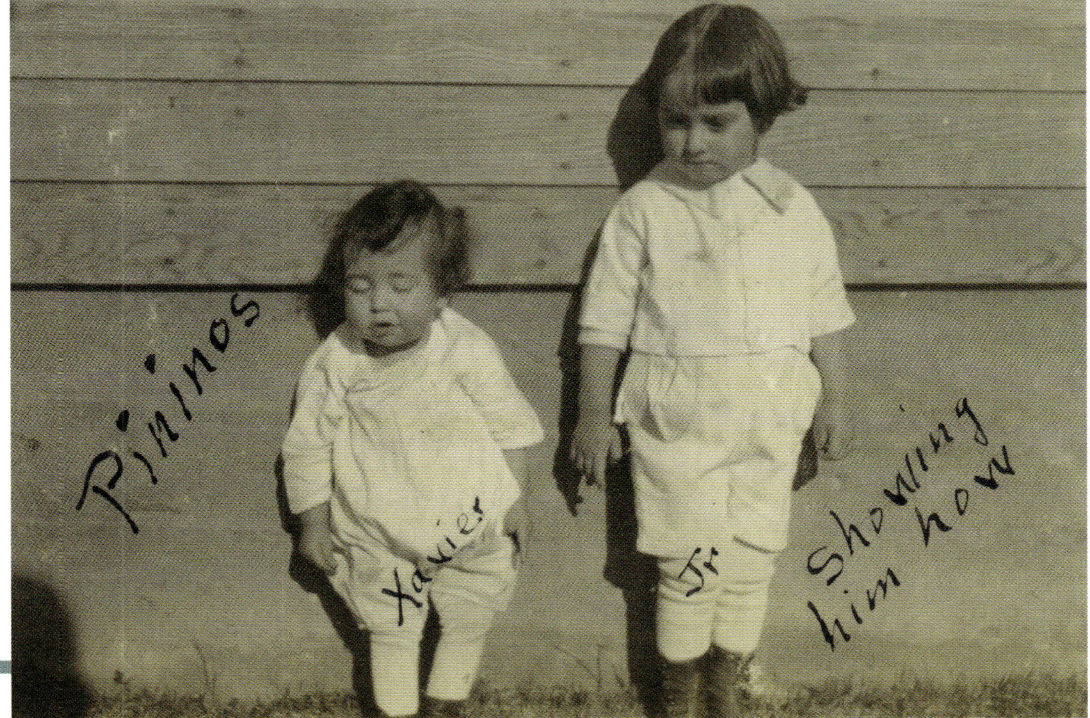

OPPOSITE: X as a toddler in the yard; ABOVE (TOP): X and his mother, Ida, in Trinidad, Colorado, 1919; ABOVE (BOTTOM): X taking his first steps with his brother, Pete, 1920.

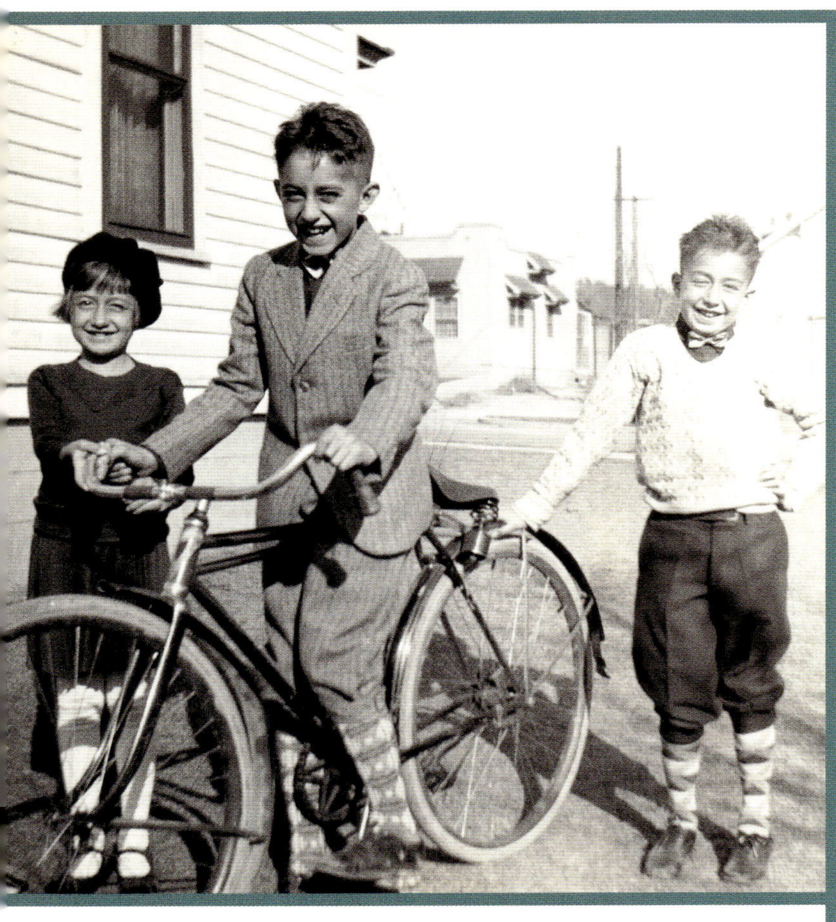

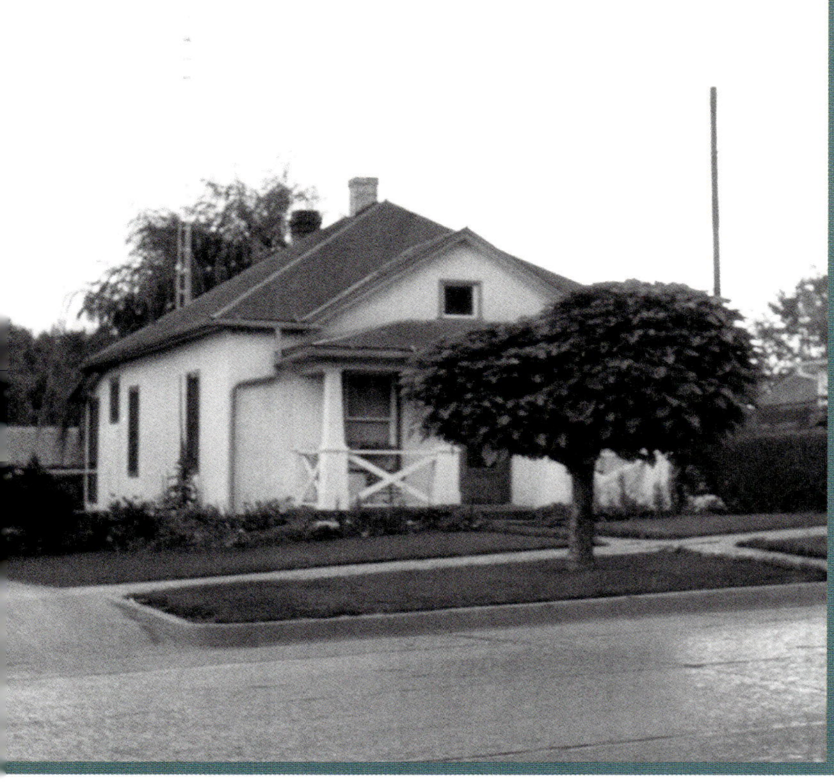

X loved living in Walsenburg and considered it a delightful small town where everyone knew each other. As the second child and son born to Agapito and Ida within the first two years of their marriage in 1917, X and his older brother, Agapito Peter ("Pete"), soon found their family growing with the birth of a sister, Loretta Constance ("Connie") in 1921, and later a baby brother, Theodore Abeyta ("Ted"), in 1932. The family's modest two-bedroom Walsen Avenue home was cramped for a family of six, but they adapted and made the best of their dwelling. How? The oldest two boys, X and Pete, would use bedrolls and sleep in the kitchen.

While the boys could have found fault with this setup and bemoaned it, X always looked on the bright side. He described one of his fondest childhood memories as lying on his cot in the kitchen in front of the warm stove, staring out the window at the streetlamp and watching as the snow fell, turning the world into a peaceful and magical winter pastoral. Likewise, X fondly recalled their Christmas traditions and how their grandparents would take the bus from Trinidad to Walsenburg and stay with them for the holidays, resulting in an even more stuffed home, filled wall-to-wall with mattresses, as well as a Christmas tree in the corner and the feeling of familial Yuletide bliss.

X's first language was Spanish, the main language spoken in Trinidad and Walsenburg in the 1920s and the primary language in his household. In fact, X and his siblings didn't learn English until they enrolled in school. X's family also spoke a particular regional dialect of archaic Spanish that was native to and existed only in northern New Mexico and southern Colorado. This version of the language originated from the classic Spanish that was brought by the conquistadors into Mexico, then merged into a rural Castilian sixteenth-century Spanish that the original settlers pushed into New Mexico, before finally coming north to Colorado where it found itself infused over the years with words from various Native American tribes, French fur trappers, and American settlers—the very same groups that populated X's family tree.

ABOVE (TOP): Connie, Pete, and X playing outside the house; ABOVE (BOTTOM): X's childhood home in Walsenburg, Colorado; OPPOSITE (TOP): X as a young boy with his father; OPPOSITE (BOTTOM): X goofing off in a family photo, 1933.

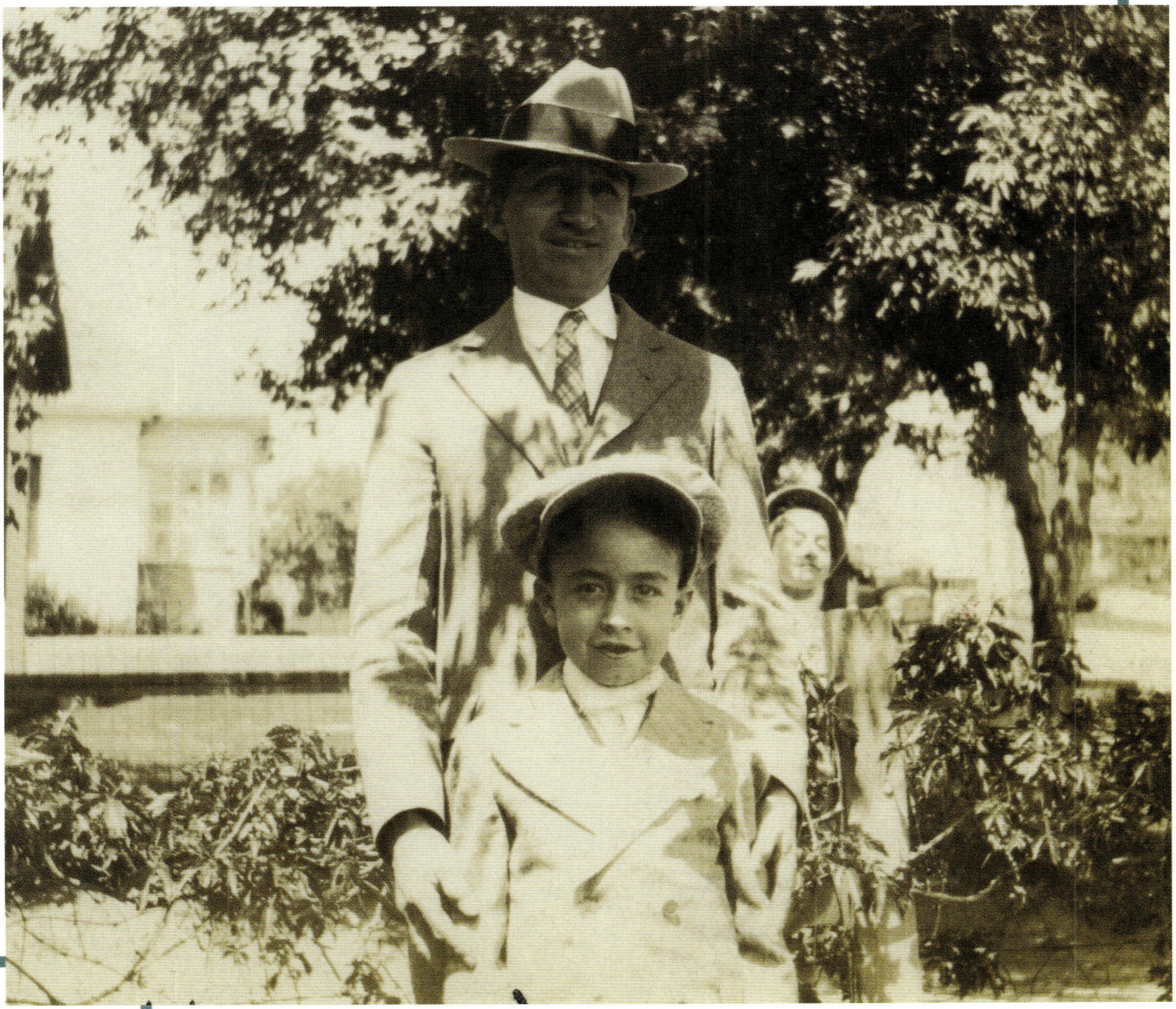

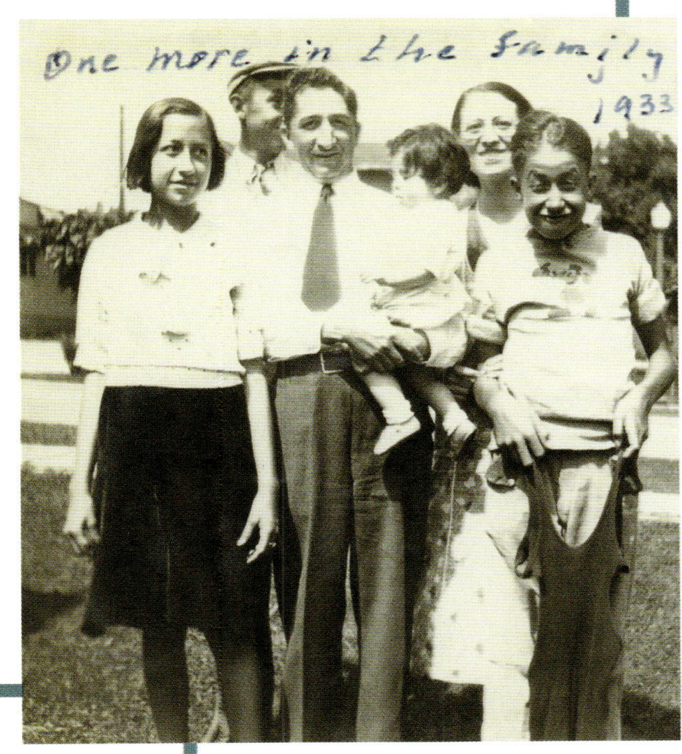

Descending from the famed Spanish conquistadors and colonists, the Atencio-Abeyta family has North American roots that run deeper than one would expect. In 1598, nine years before the initial English settlement at Jamestown (in what's now Virginia), the first Spanish village in what would eventually come to be known as New Mexico was established a few miles south of the present-day Colorado border. The migration was aided by the future founder of Trinidad, Felipe Baca, who in 1860 brought back to New Mexico produce that he had farmed while living in Colorado. The locals were astounded by the variety of crops, as well as the fertility of the land and more favorable climate conditions. Shortly thereafter, in March 1862, twelve heads of families, all Spanish Americans, including X's maternal great-grandfather, Jesus Maria Abeyta, prepared to leave New Mexico and move to Trinidad, Colorado.

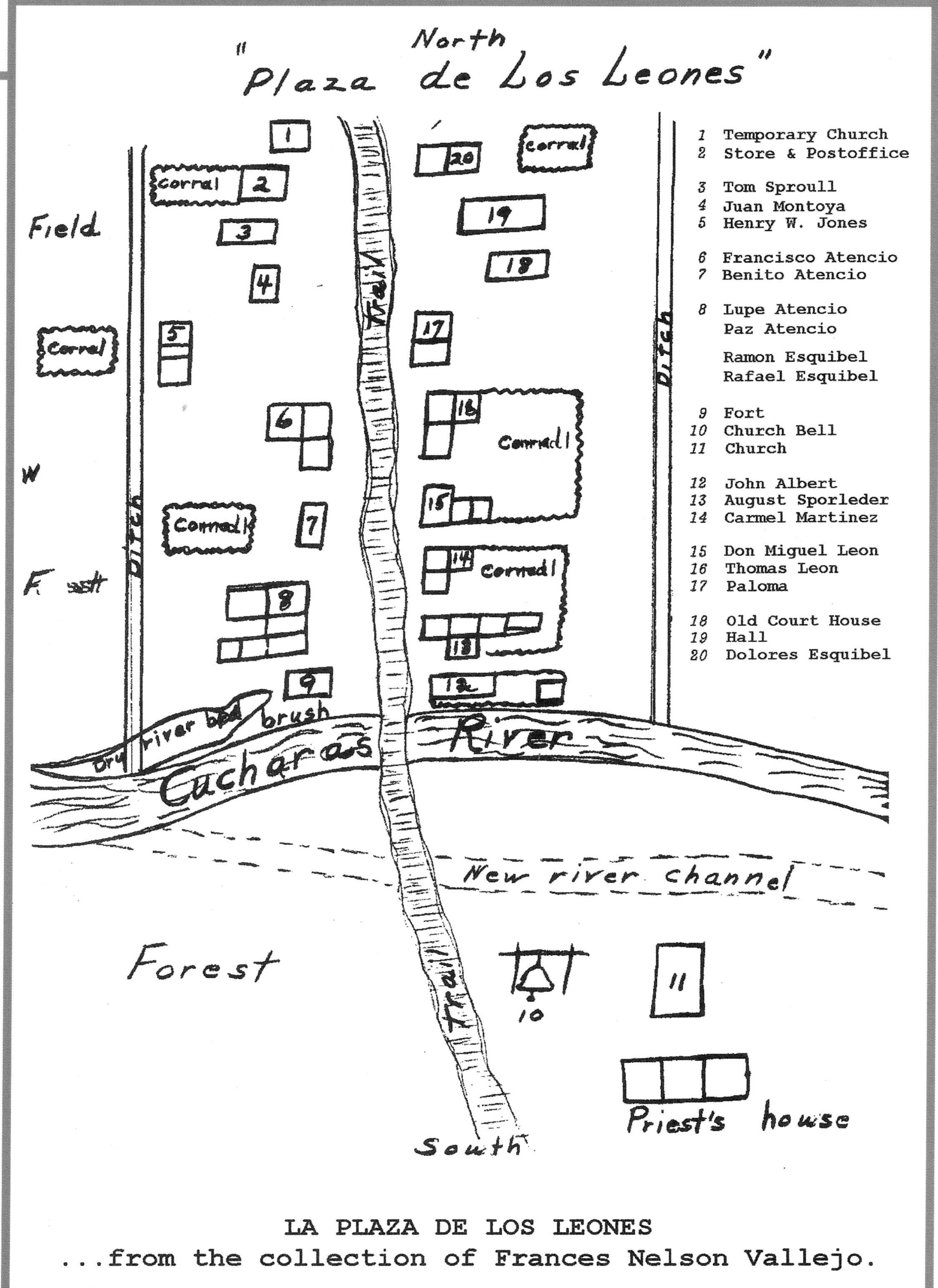

ABOVE: A map depicting the 1875 Plaza de los Leones, where X's ancestors settled; OPPOSITE: St. Mary School in Walsenburg, which X attended.

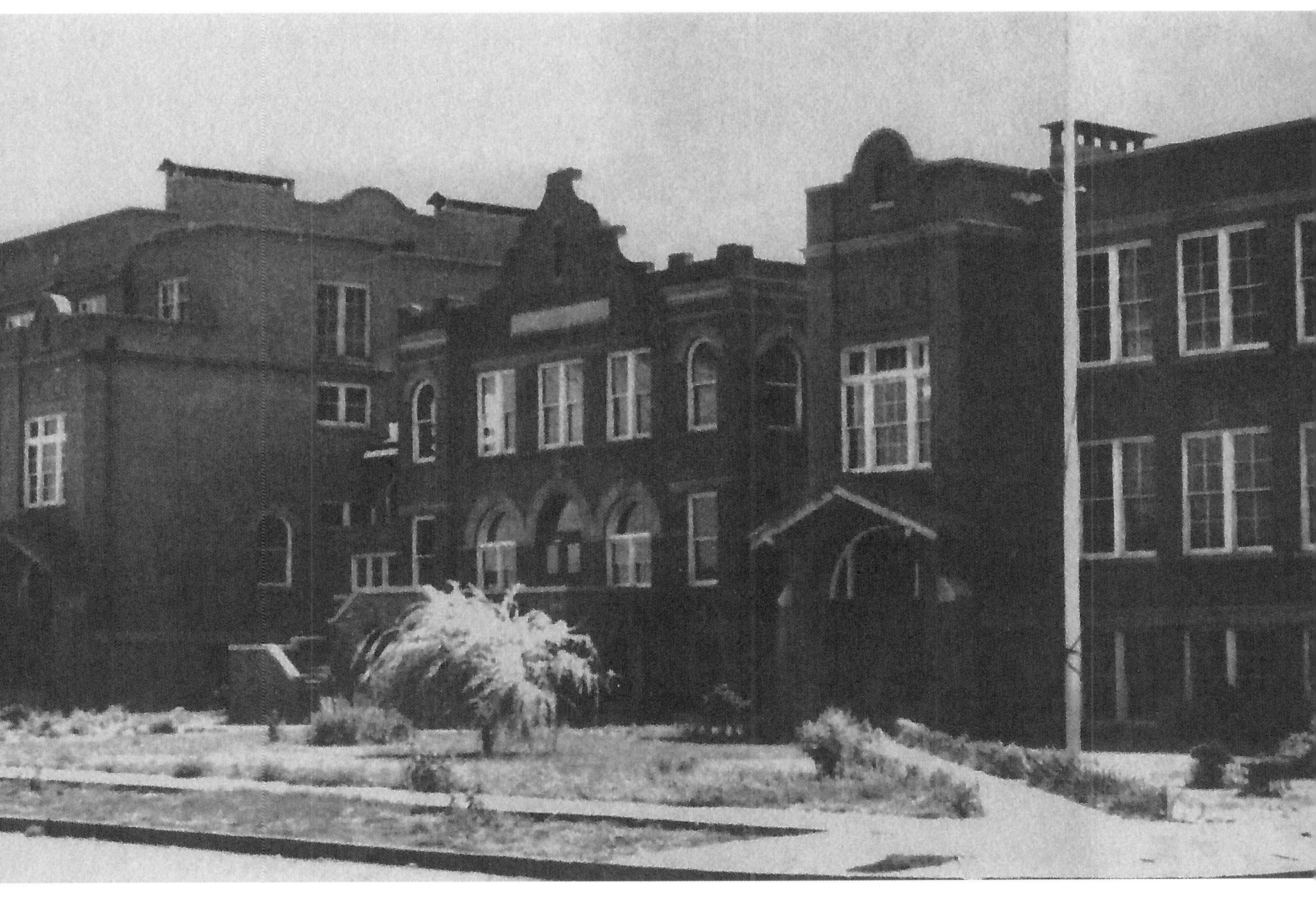

As their history was told to X, his paternal great-grandfather, Francisco Antonio Atencio, and his brother Miguel Antonio Atencio came to Colorado slightly earlier in 1859 and erected wick-iups, indigenous semipermanent arched teepee-like structures with poles covered by brush, grass, and other materials, making Francisco and Miguel two of the original settlers of what was first called La Plaza de los Leones and is now known as Walsenburg. Likewise, his great-grandfather Jose Agapito, one of the original settlers, was known as the "Patriarch of Bear Creek." With this expanding migration still in its nascent stage, Colorado officially achieved statehood in 1876, becoming the thirty-eighth U.S. state.

Growing up in such a small community, but with a large extended family, X found himself surrounded by a cast of lively characters who weaved together the tapestry of his youth. His grandparents and uncles lived nearby and frequently visited; many of them had spent their own upbringings surrounded by Native Americans from the region and now lived as nomadic shepherds and farmers. They would stop by for a warm meal and a place to shower and change, and to exchange riveting stories of their own escapades, before leaving to return to the fields.

Many of X's childhood memories included the usual activities: playing school sports, biking around his neighborhood, and sledding in the winter. That didn't mean X's childhood wasn't impacted by the realities of life. One month before X's tenth birthday, the Great Depression began. With hard times hitting the family of six, X and Pete, the two oldest children, found part-time jobs to help provide extra income. In the early mornings before school, the boys would deliver the local newspapers and run the job press. They worked quickly and efficiently, knowing that any mistakes or forgotten deliveries would get them in trouble with their mother; for as anyone who has ever lived in a small town knows, the news would travel fast and get back to Ida, in this case through the town's telephone party line.

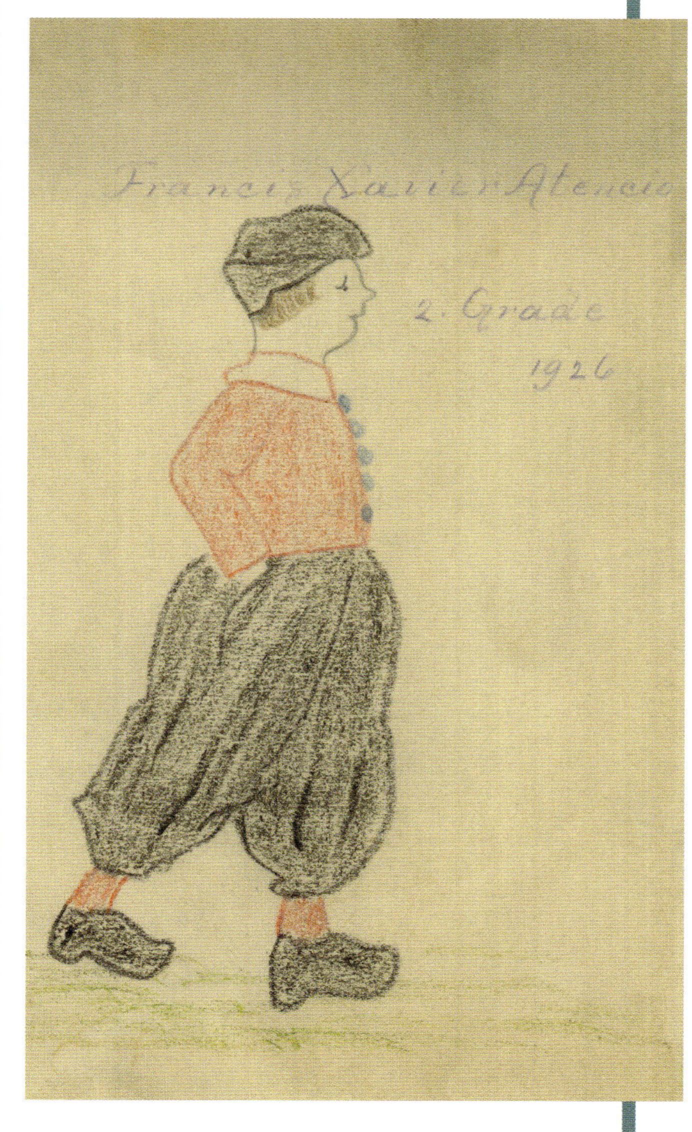

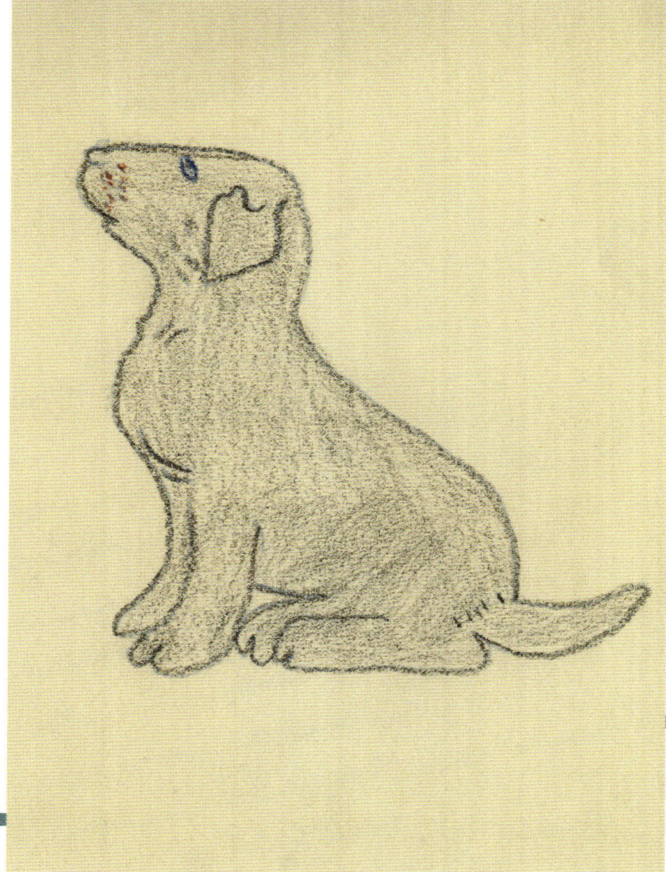

In the summers, Agapito and Ida sent X and his siblings back to Trinidad to stay with their maternal grandparents. In Trinidad, which was much more rural than Walsenburg, X spent most of his time around animals observing them and their behaviors: chickens clucking in the yard, sheep and goats grazing in the field. X, a self-taught artist, watched these animals and used them as his first models for drawing. His eye picked up the movements and mannerisms of the animals, a skill of observation that continued in his later career at Disney when he found himself frequently animating animal characters for the studio's features.

X also enjoyed spending time with his grandmother Victoria and great aunt Elisa. Every year at the end of summer, Victoria and Elisa sent X and Pete out to find prized piñon nuts for roasting. X often recounted a humorous anecdote tied to the first time he took on this harvest. Having been sent off with an old steel bucket and a general knowledge of what the round piñons looked like, X filled his pail, eager to impress Victoria, his abuela. Upon returning to the house and excited by the prospect of eating some of the roasted piñon nuts "delicacy," X shockingly discovered a rather large oversight. To the hilarious delight of his grandmother and great aunt, X and Pete had actually only brought back about ten piñon nuts, and instead had collected two full buckets of cagadas de conejos, or what are known in English as rabbit turds. These relationships, childhood exposures, youthful misadventures, and the larger Southwestern culture that X experienced provided him with a treasure trove of life events and ultimately became lasting influences on his creative work and career.

X also spent a lot of time around newspapers. His father, Agapito, was well known in social, religious, fraternal, and political circles throughout their hometown's Huerfano County and had many different jobs during X's upbringing—such as bank cashier, insurance salesman, postmaster—plus served as an active member of the Knights of Columbus. These activities further stoked his interest in politics and led to an unsuccessful run for local political office. Yet it was his 1932 founding of *El Clarin*, a local well-respected weekly Spanish language newspaper, that

LEFT: X's early drawings completed in 1926, when he was in second grade; OPPOSITE: X with a goat during one of his summers in Trinidad.

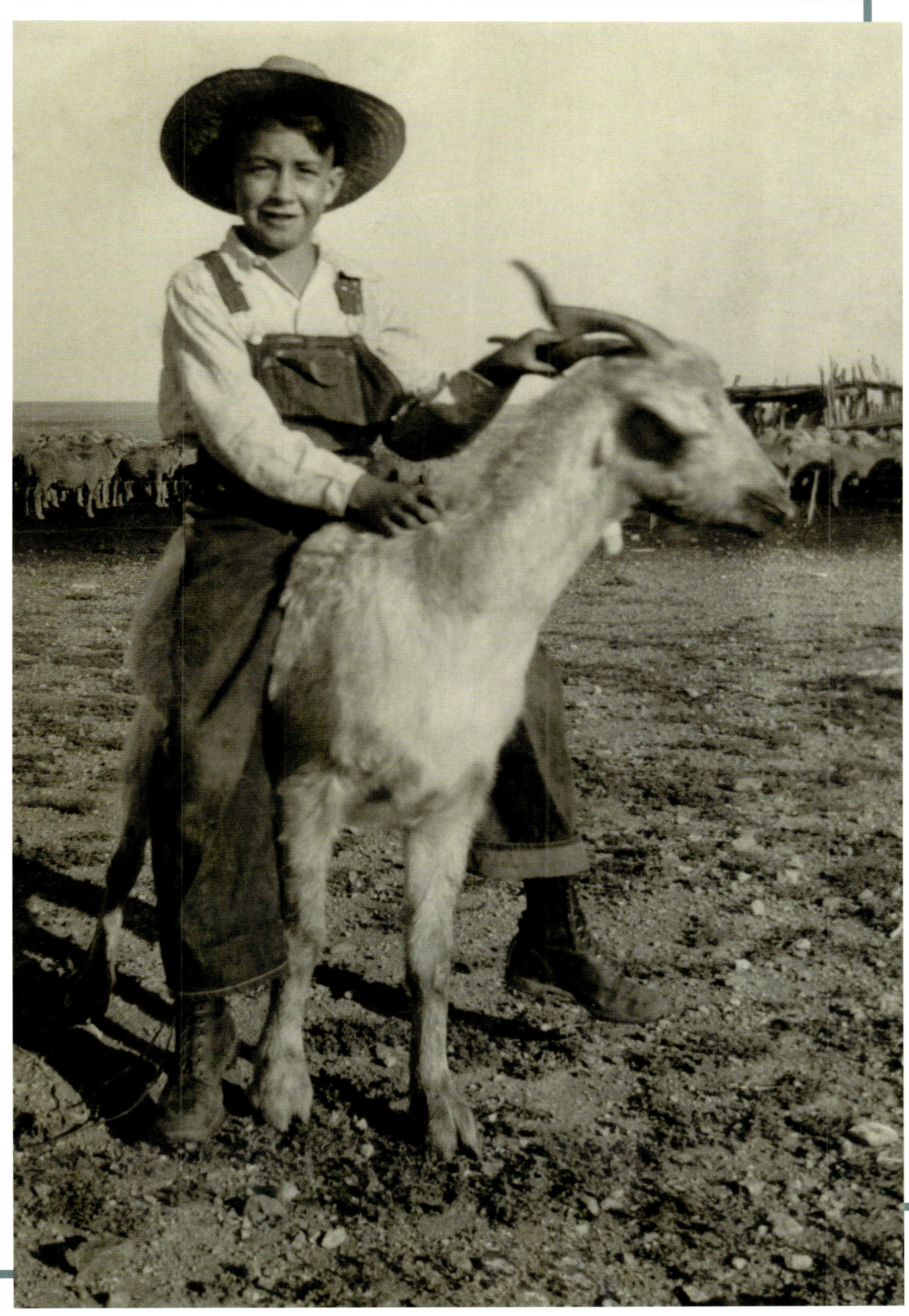

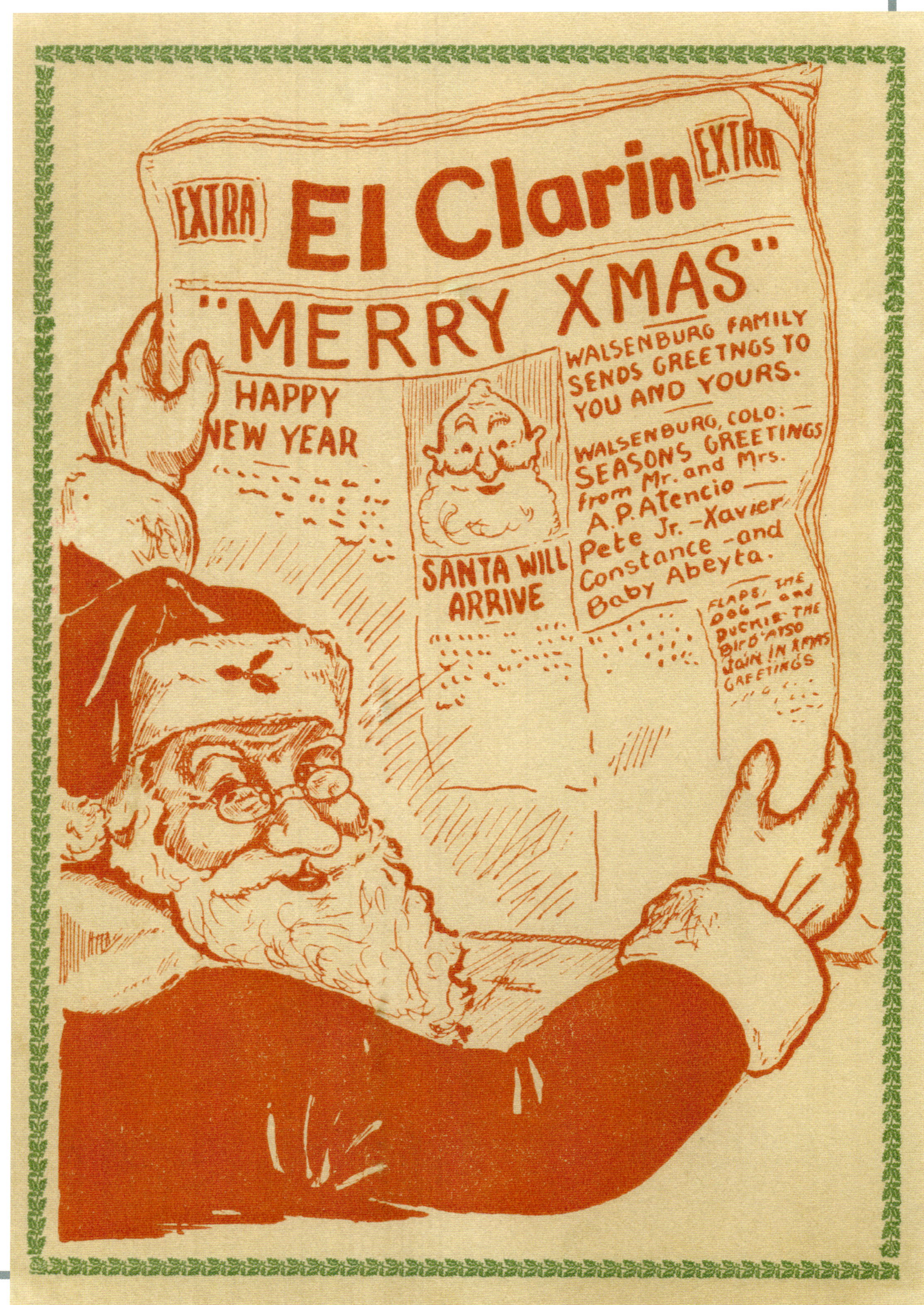
EXTRA
El Clarin
EXTRA
"MERRY XMAS"
HAPPY NEW YEAR
SANTA WILL ARRIVE
WALSENBURG FAMILY SENDS GREETNGS TO YOU AND YOURS.
WALSENBURG, COLO: — SEASONS GREETINGS from Mr. and Mrs. A. P. Atencio — Pete Jr. - Xavier Constance - and Baby Abeyta.
FLAPS, THE DOG — and DUCKIE THE BIRD ALSO JOIN IN XMAS GREETINGS

FAIR TO ONE----FAIR TO ALL

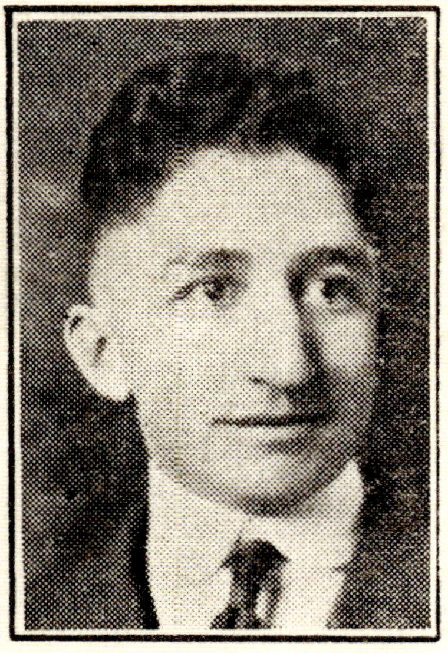

VOTE FOR

A. PETE ATENCIO

REPUBLICAN CANDIDATE FOR

COUNTY ASSESSOR

HUERFANO COUNTY

ELECTION NOVEMBER 4, 1930

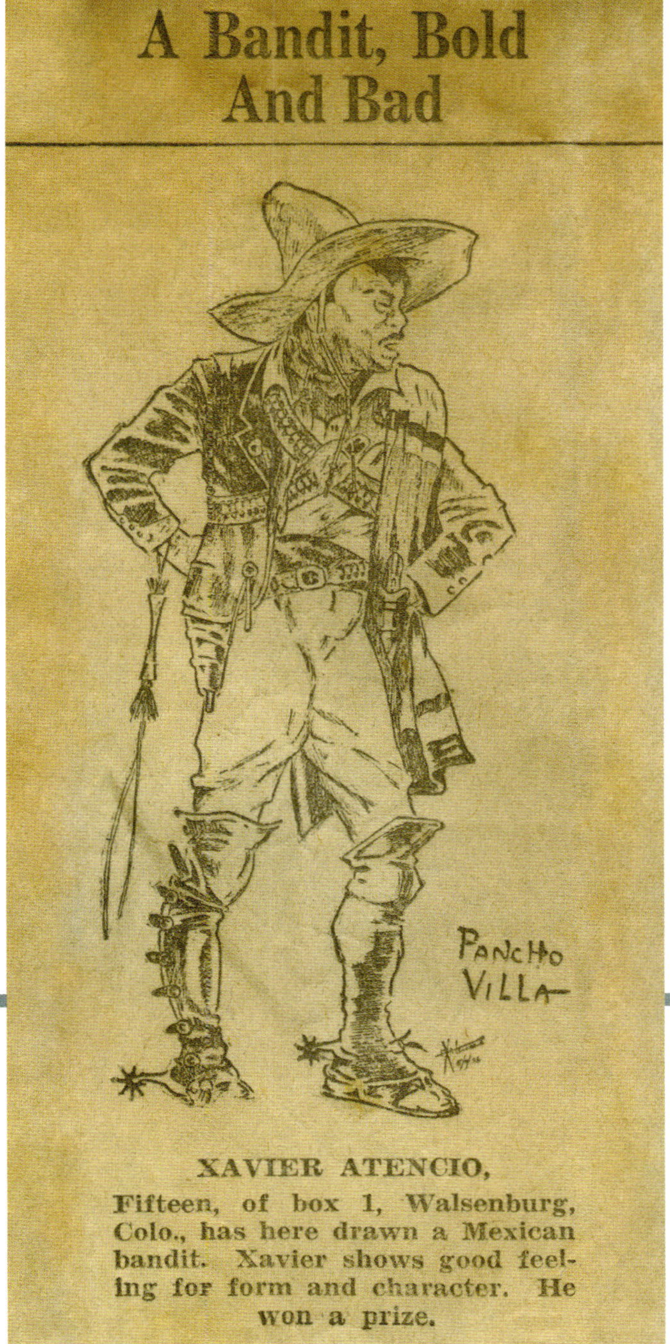

A Bandit, Bold And Bad

XAVIER ATENCIO, Fifteen, of box 1, Walsenburg, Colo., has here drawn a Mexican bandit. Xavier shows good feeling for form and character. He won a prize.

caught X's full attention. Like his father's blending of politics and journalism, X mixed his own love of writing with his artistic abilities: he served as the editor of his high school newspaper, the *Paladin*, plus designed background art for the paper's header, and drew pictures for local town newspapers, such as the *Walsenburg World*, even winning a prize for one of his Pancho Villa drawings in 1936 (which then appeared in the *Denver Post*). In another local newspaper clipping, X was described as "one of the most talented young artists ever to attend the school [Saint Mary's High School]."

In addition to being recognized early in life for his creative talents, X was also voted the most popular boy at school during his senior year. That year, X played on the state champion St. Mary's High School basketball team and traveled to Denver for a game against St. Joseph's. Knowing how far the team was from home, Cecelia O'Byrne and another local mother each invited half of the St. Mary's team to their homes for dinner. Before the eight extra teenage boys, one coach, and two priests arrived, Cecelia sent her daughter Mary (one of St. Joseph's

OPPOSITE: X's hand-designed 1936 Christmas card, commissioned for *El Clarin*; ABOVE (TOP): Agapito's campaign card for county assessor; LEFT: X's prizewinning drawing of Pancho Villa.

cheerleaders) to the store to buy more groceries. Upon arriving back at the house, Mary met X, who immediately introduced himself: "Hi . . . I'm Xavier Atencio," he said with confidence. They immediately hit it off, and when X returned home, he wrote her a thank-you note in study hall, establishing the start of a long-distance relationship between the two. They continued to send mail back and forth with X's letters to Mary consisting more of drawings with brief notes, as evidenced in his November 1937 portrait of Mary with the wording *Her Royal Highness* on one side and the one sentence *Dear Mary, May this little sketch remind you, occasionally, of someone who thinks a great deal of you* on the other. When X asked her to send him a photograph of herself that he could have,

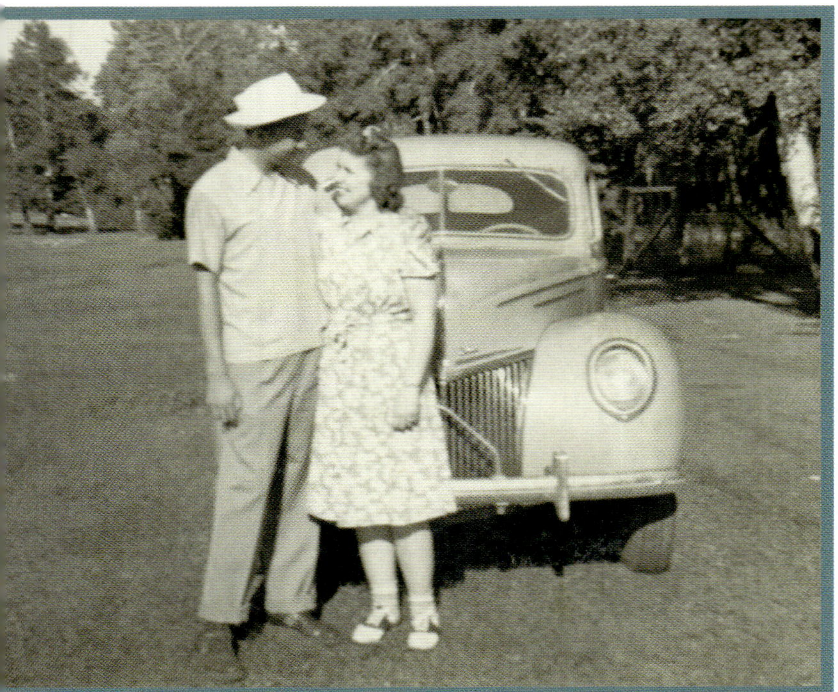

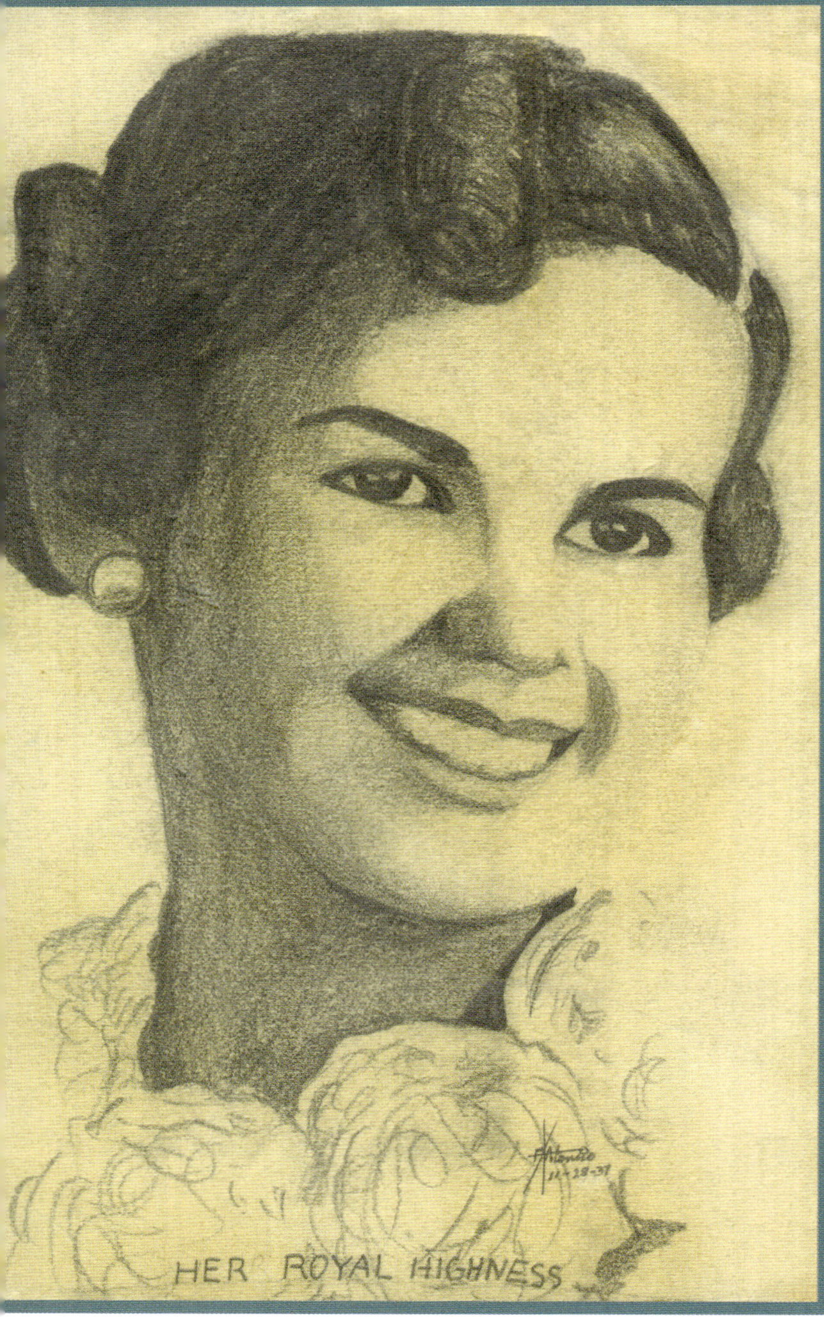

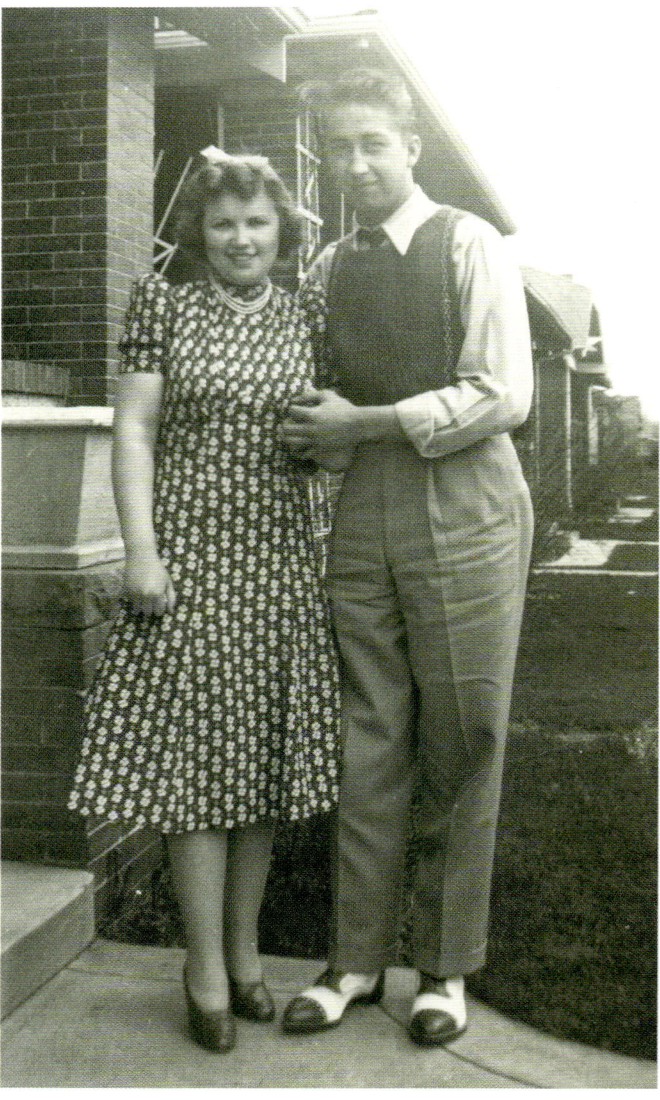

TOP LEFT AND ABOVE: X and Mary in 1937, shortly after they began dating; LEFT: A drawing of Mary O'Byrne that X sent to her inscribed with a note on the back shortly after they met; OPPOSITE: X's 1960 Valentine's Day card to Mary illustrating their first meeting.

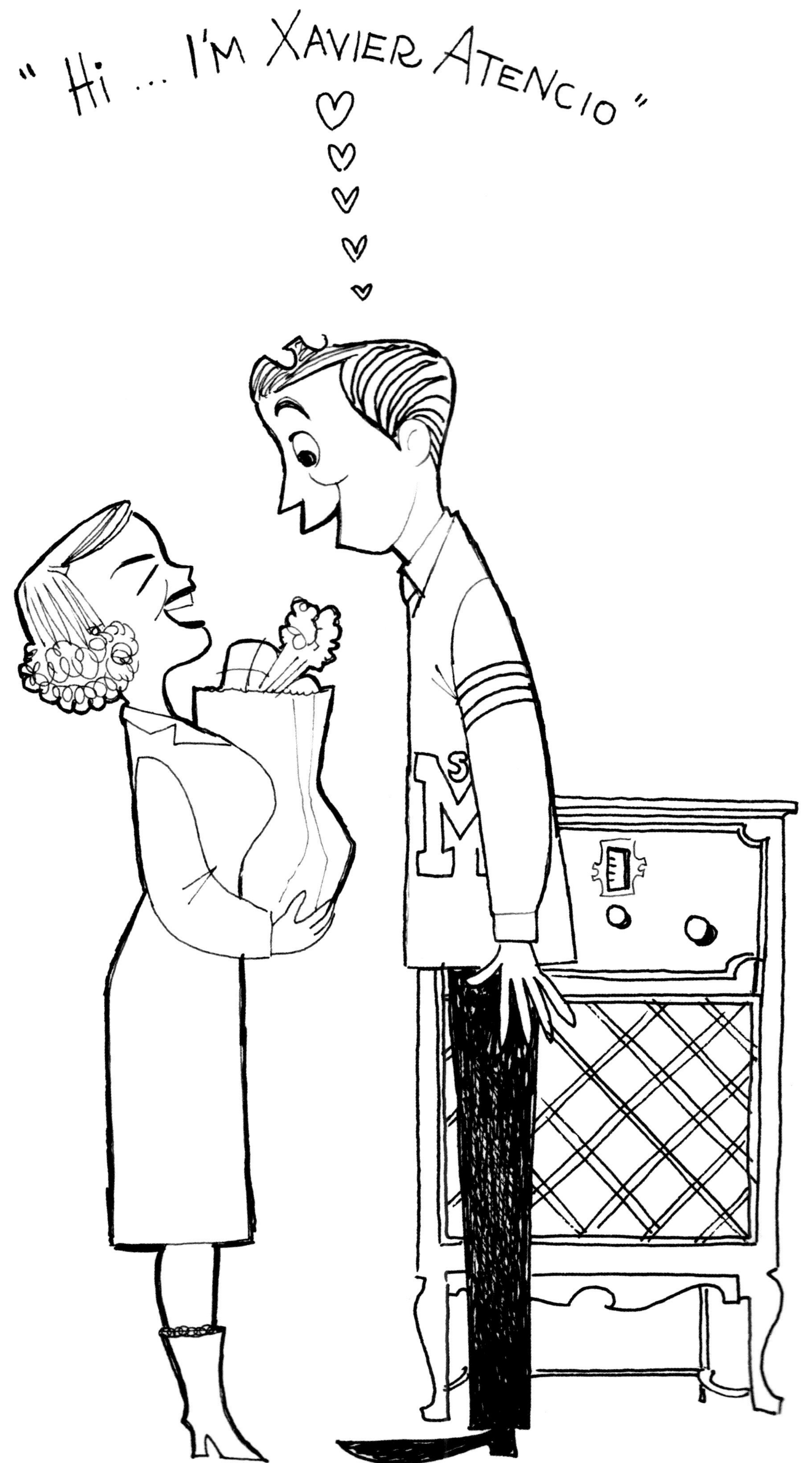

HAPPY ANNIVERSARY MY DARLING... Y.A.A. ONLY FOREVER.

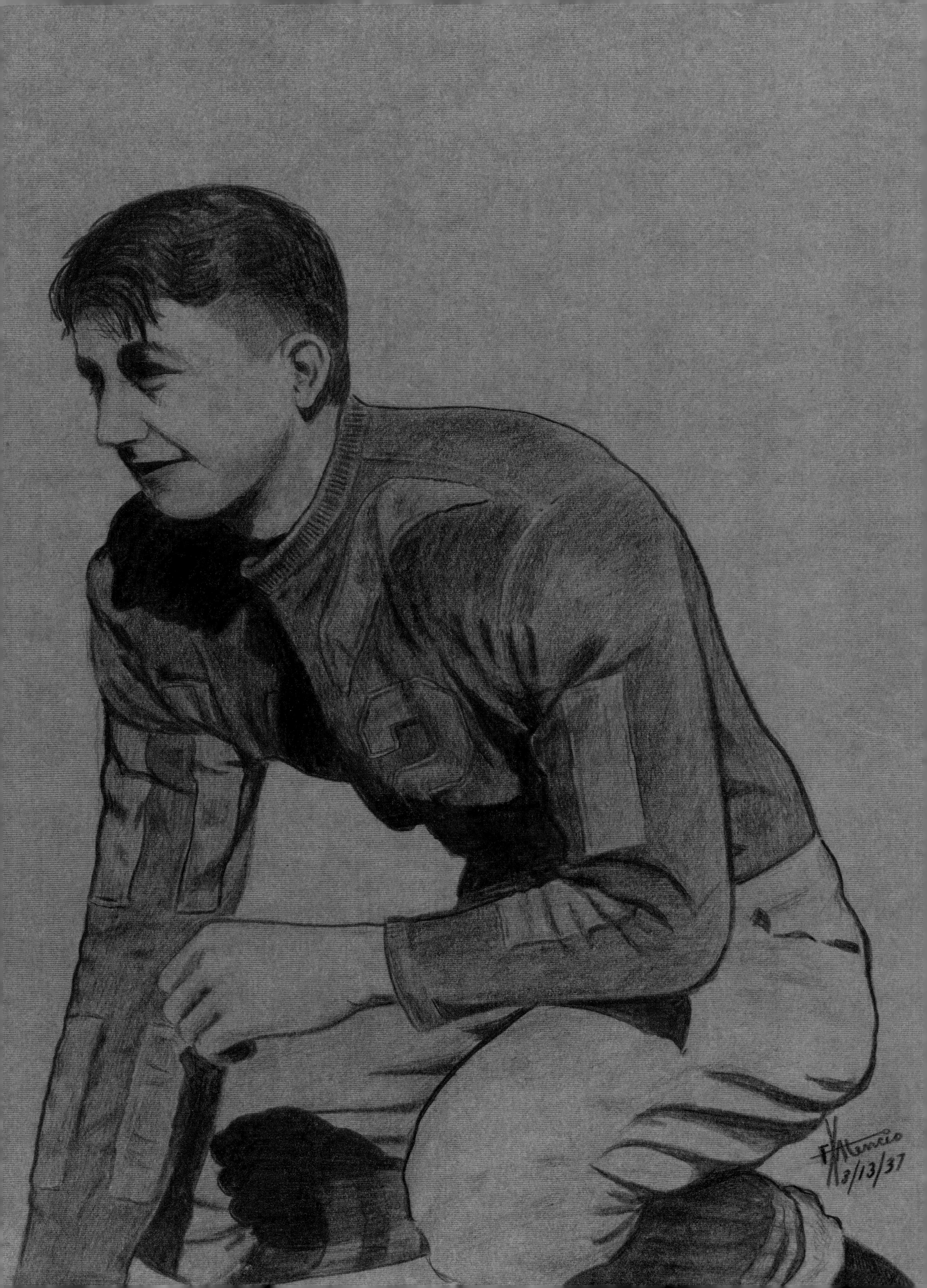
F. Atencio
3/13/37

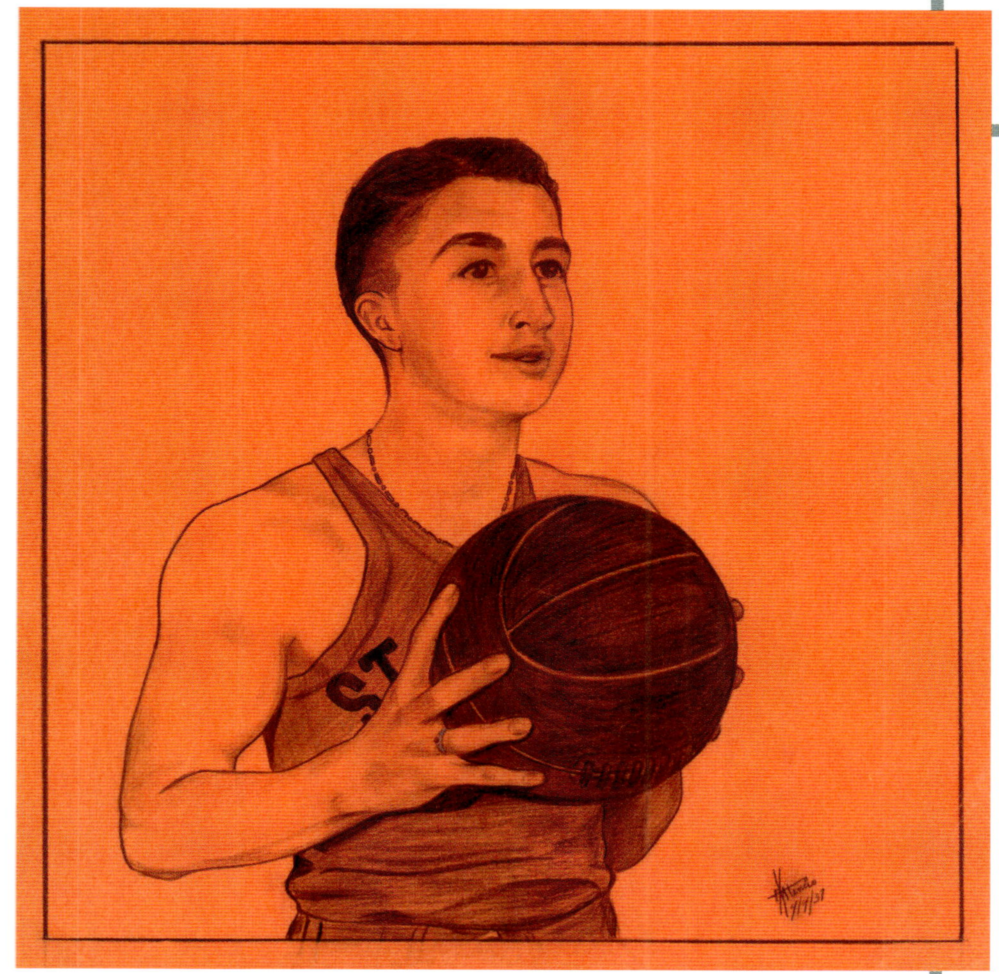

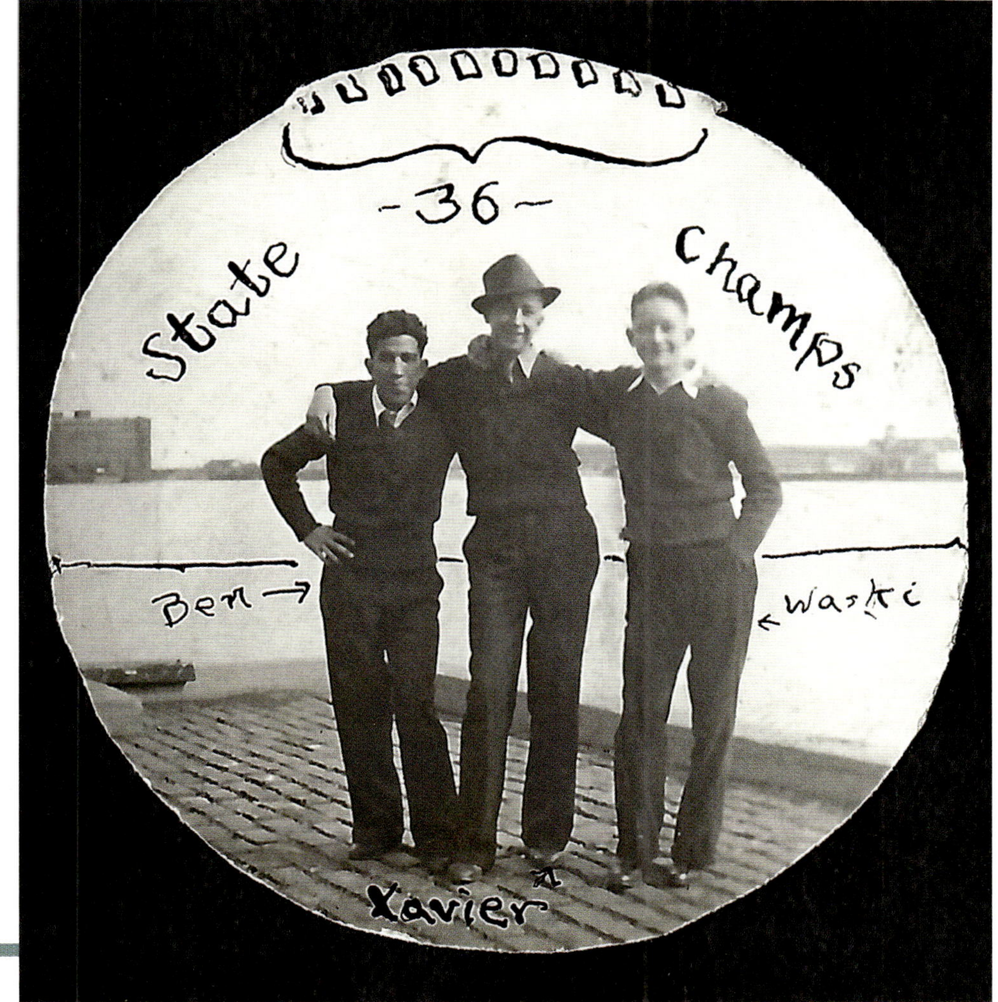

OPPOSITE: A 1937 self-portrait of X in his football uniform; ABOVE (TOP): A 1937 self-portrait of X playing basketball; ABOVE (BOTTOM): X with his friends and basketball teammates Ben Maes and Ray Waski, in 1936.

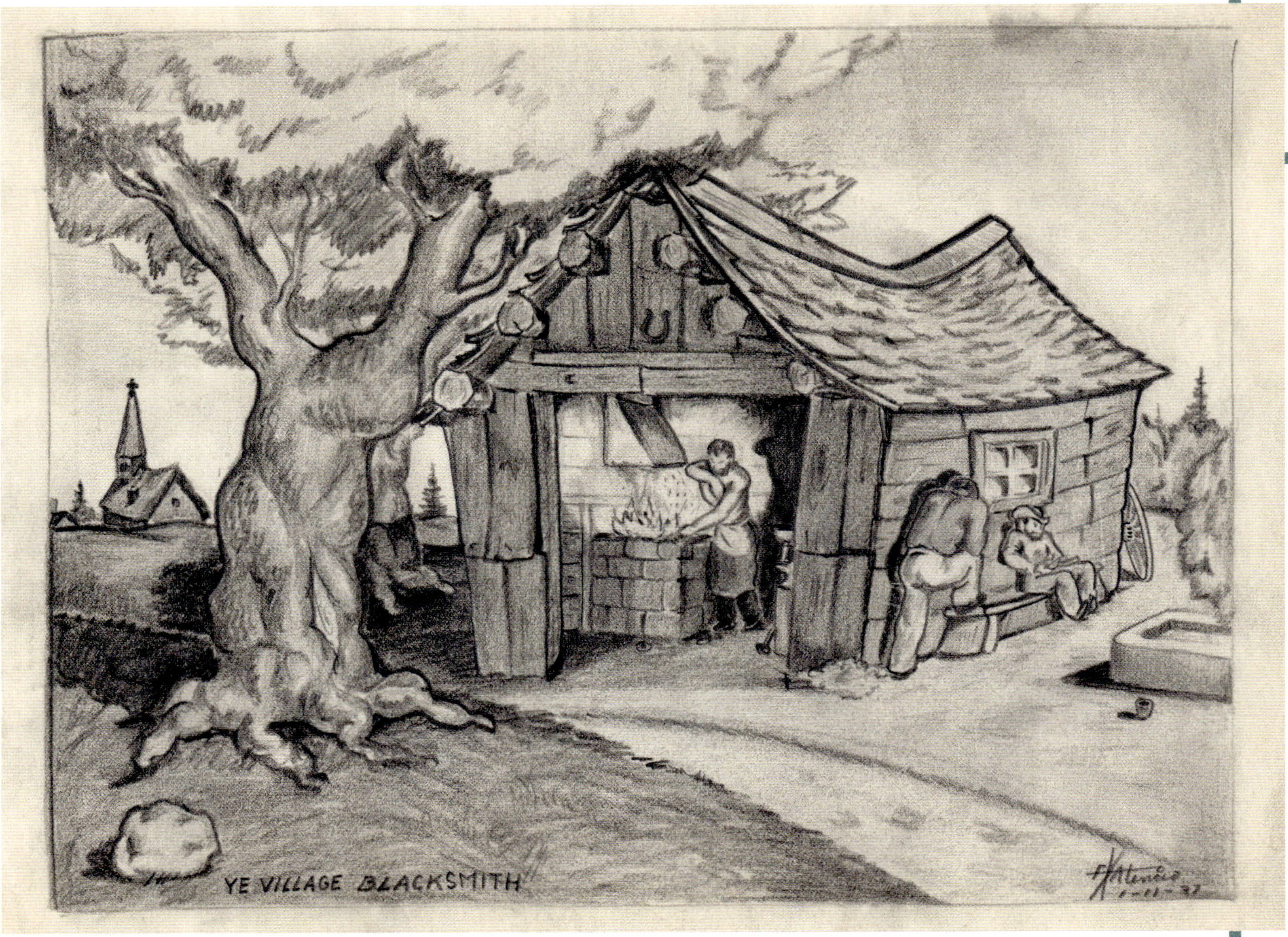

YE VILLAGE BLACKSMITH

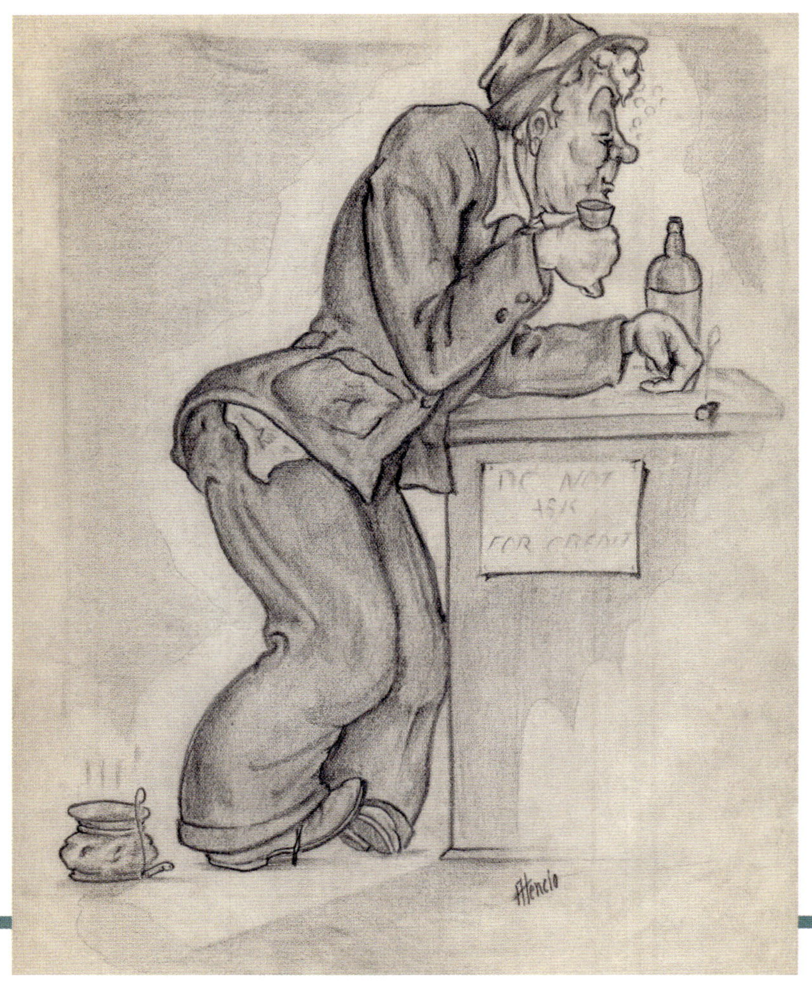

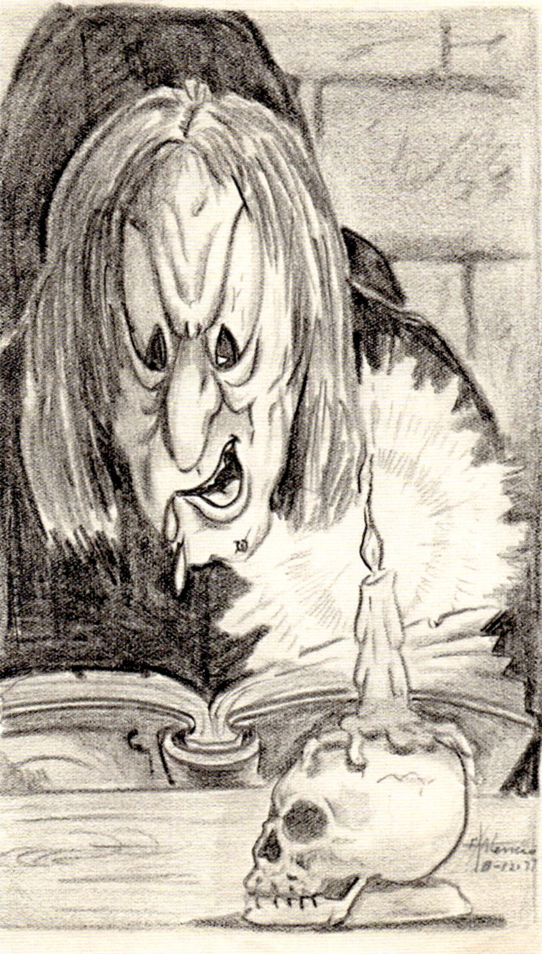

ABOVE: X's high school pencil drawings from 1937; OPPOSITE (TOP): X drawing at his grandparents' home in Trinidad, 1937; OPPOSITE (BOTTOM): X's 1937 high school senior portrait.

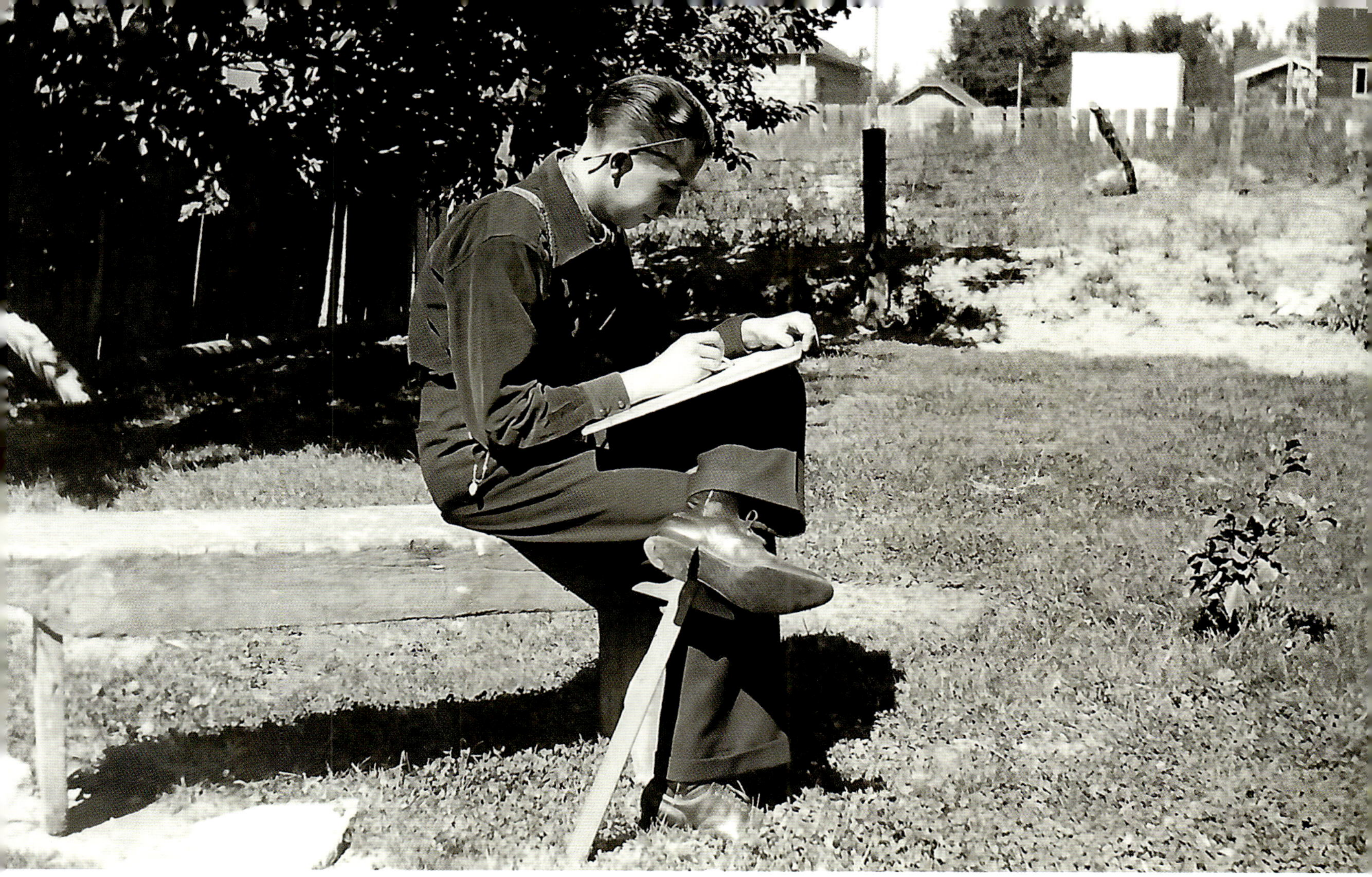

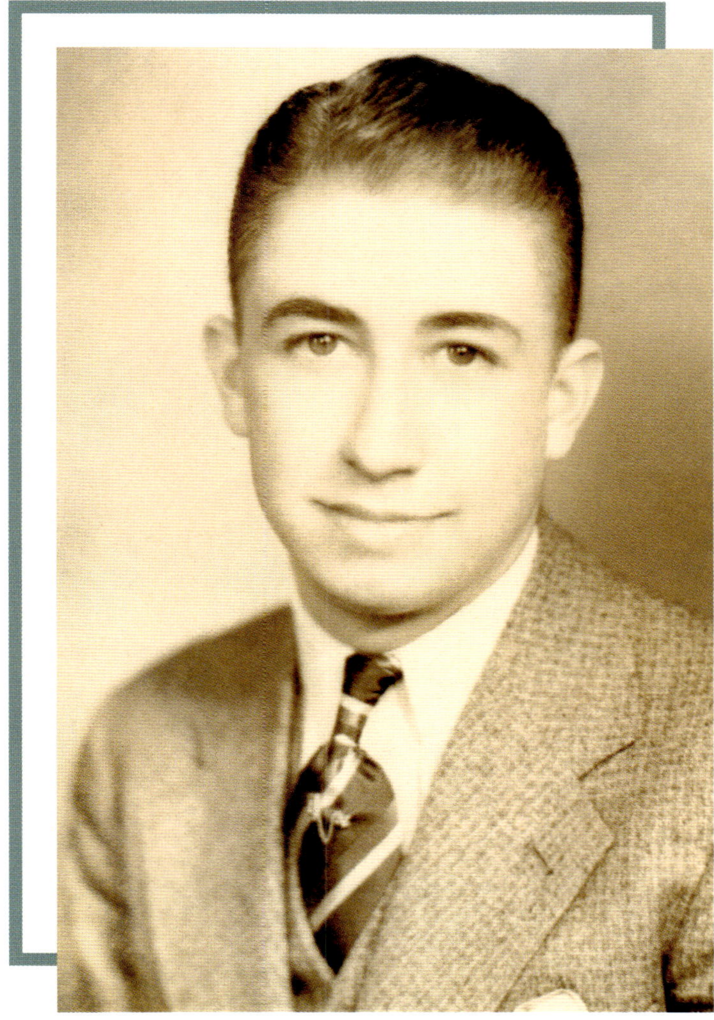

she did. Years later, X would joke that Mary talked to and fell for him because he "was the only boy there that night who spoke English," but more realistically, this was a humorous, slightly self-deprecating claim made by a man who had been lucky enough to find love.

During X's senior year of high school, he also decided to pursue his passions and follow in his father's footsteps by applying to journalism school at the University of Denver. But after his application was rejected by the university, X needed to come up with a plan B. Trusting in his artistic abilities and acknowledging the practicality that he had family (his grandmother and a few aunts) with whom he could stay while he established himself, X decided to leave Walsenburg and head to Southern California, where he would apply to art school with a new career goal: if he couldn't write for the newspapers, he could hopefully parlay his artistic talents into drawing cartoons for those very same papers.

In the fall of 1937, X left behind his family, friends, and life in Colorado. Moving in with his aunt and uncle, X officially enrolled in the Chouinard Art Institute in Los Angeles.

2

Early Days at the Walt Disney Studios

DURING HIS FIRST SEMESTER AT the Chouinard Art Institute, X enrolled in a pre-animation course. Toward the end of the class, his instructor asked him to critique several Disney cartoons. X completed the assignment and impressed his teacher with his work and analysis, prompting the instructor to encourage X to submit his portfolio to The Walt Disney Studios so that he and other like-minded students could have working animators and artists critique and provide constructive criticism on their materials. This connection with Disney was possible because some of the art-school teachers also taught night classes for the animators at the studio once or twice a week.

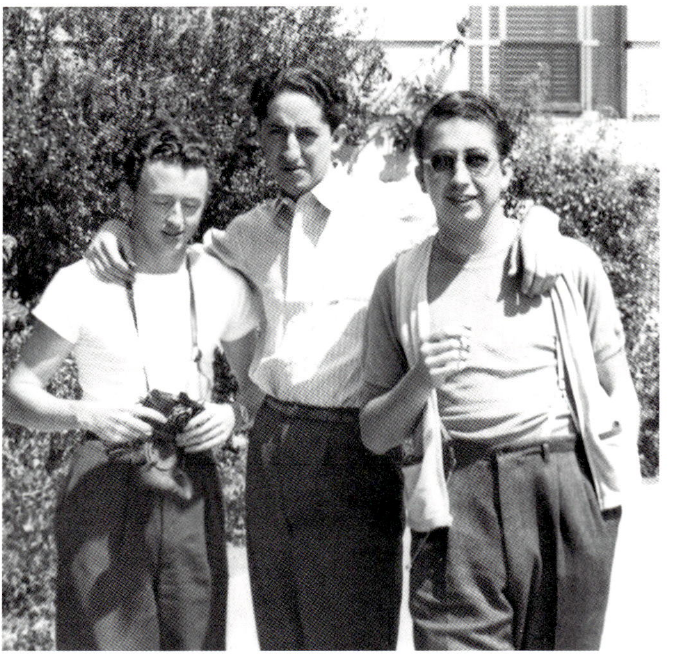

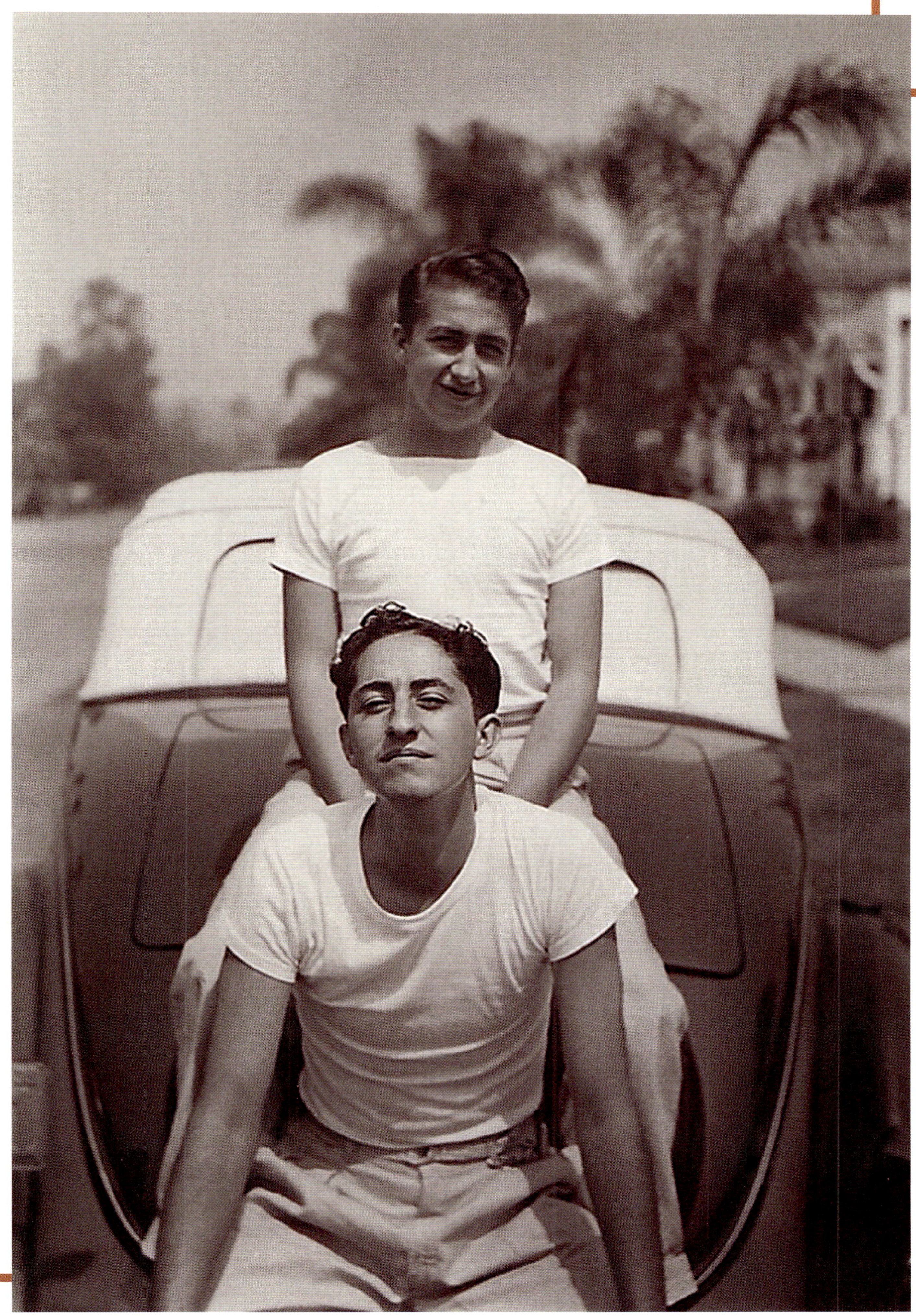

OPPOSITE: X (right), his brother Pete (center), and a friend after arriving in Hollywood; ABOVE: X (background) and his brother Pete, shortly after moving to Los Angeles.

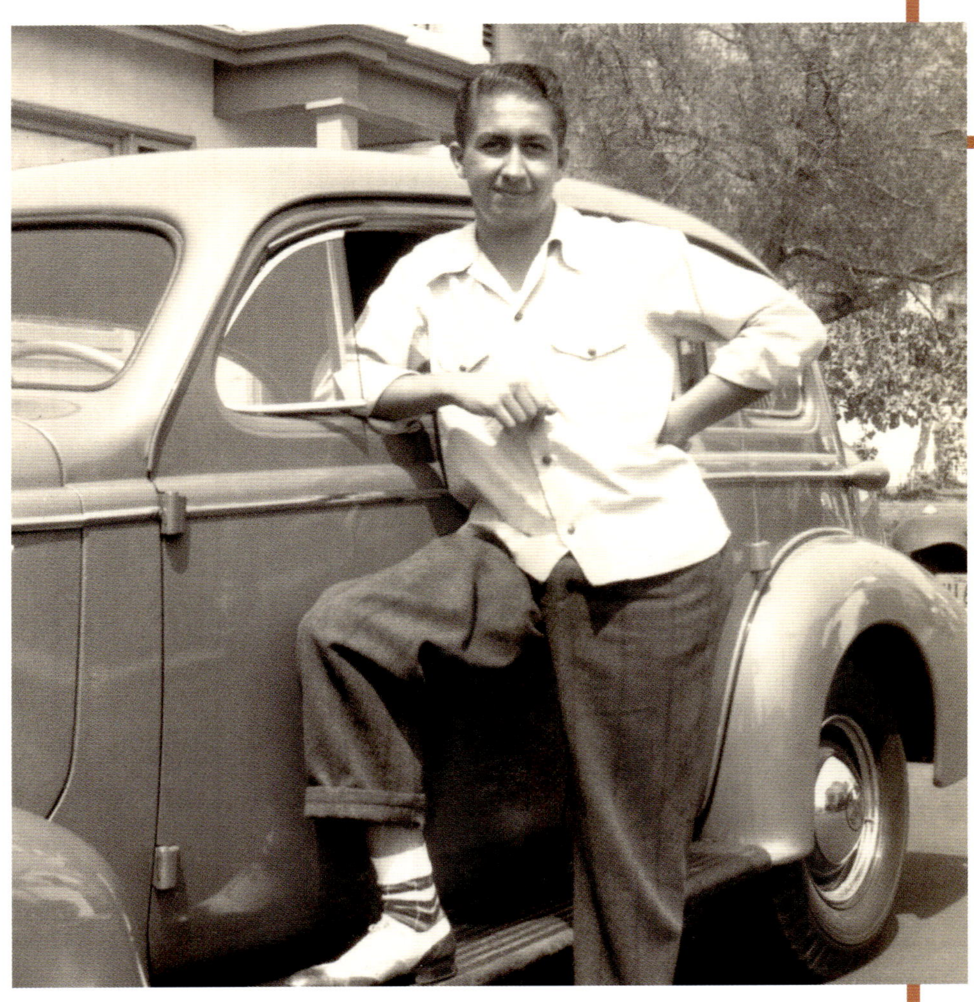

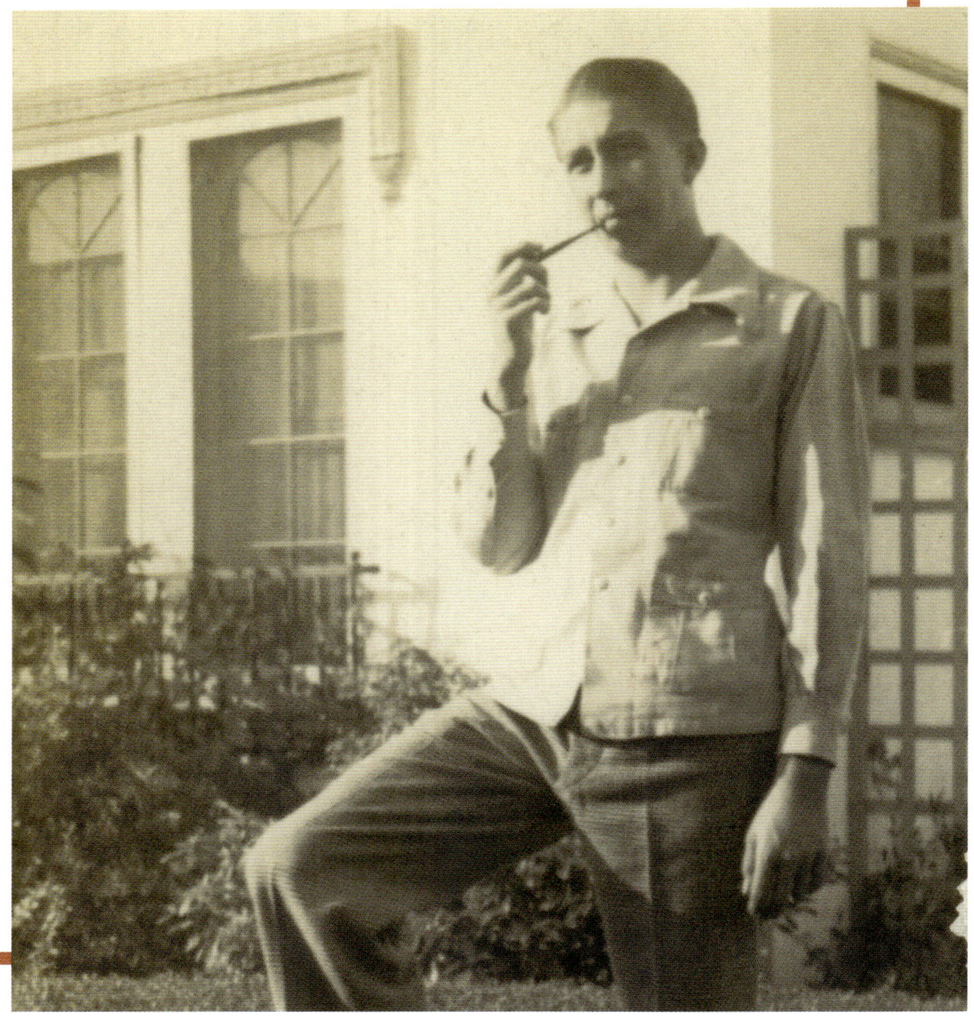

TOP AND BOTTOM: X in Los Angeles, 1939, shortly after moving there; OPPOSITE: Drawings from X's first semester at Chouinard Art Institute.

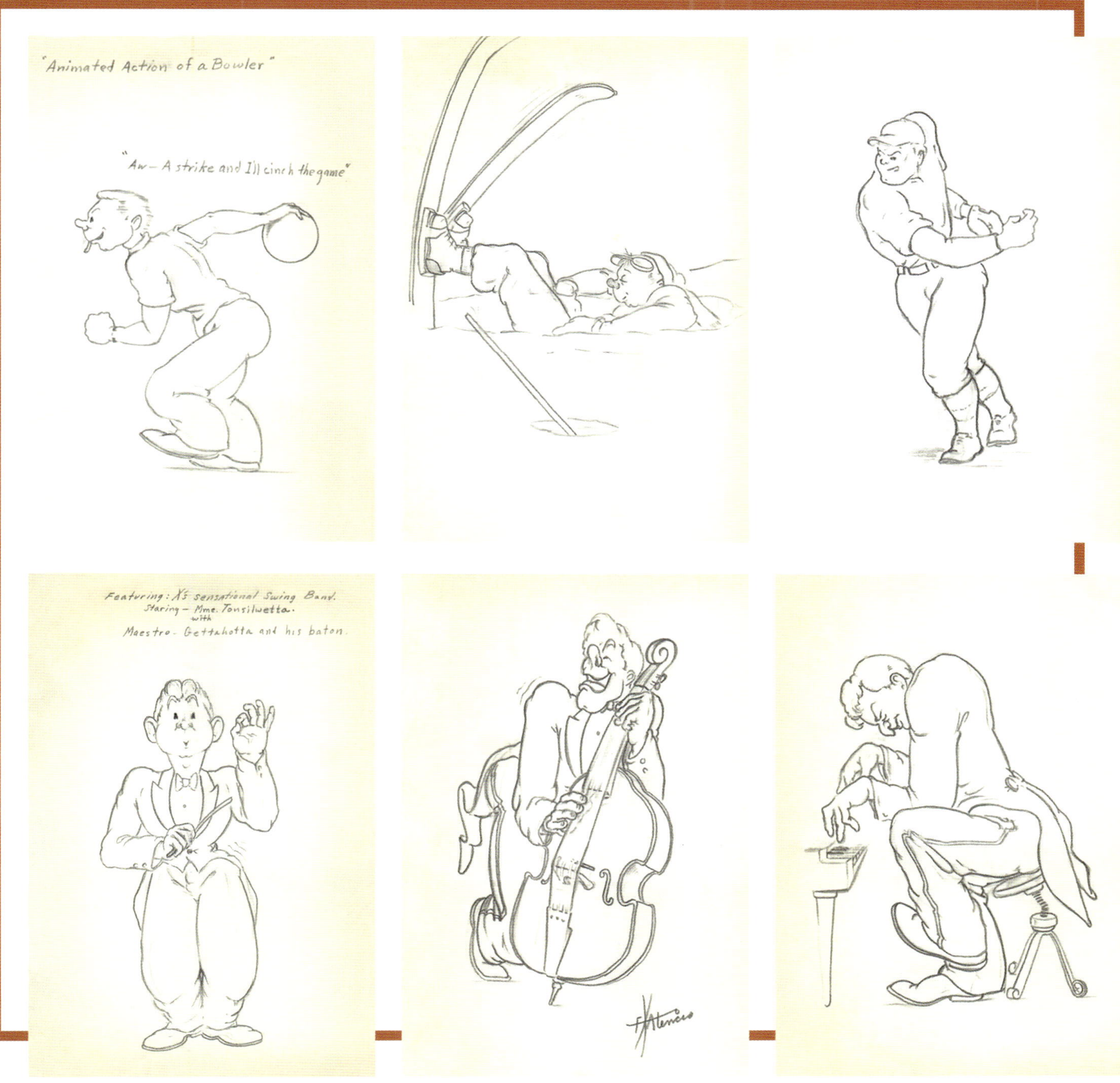

X doubted that he had the required artistic background to warrant feedback from professional animators, but his teacher insisted that he put something together. While X acquiesced, he was also a self-described procrastinator and waited until the night before the due date to start the assignment. As instructed, X turned in his portfolio, a storyboard of an original creation, *Pacheco the Cowboy*. The storyboard illustrated Pacheco, the Colorado cowboy, reading about a horseshoe-throwing competition in Walsenburg. Determined to win, Pacheco boldly enters the competition. However, on the day of the event, Pacheco finds himself feeling very nervous as his turn arrives. He calls his horse over and prepares to throw the horseshoe, but he's sweating, breathing deeply, and trying to calm himself down. Then, as he finally goes to throw the horseshoe, his horse surprises him and gives him a kiss on the cheek. Despite this pleasant disturbance, Pacheco throws a ringer and wins the competition. X's storyboards clearly demonstrated the inspirations for his early work: the story's setting in his hometown of Walsenburg, the horseshoe-throwing competitions and cowboys stemming from the Spanish and Southwestern influences of his childhood, and the loving portraits of animals with character and depth that he knew from his youthful experiences visiting his grandparents' home in Trinidad. He even went so far as to have Pacheco reading an issue of his father's newspaper, *El Clarin*.

Pleased with his work and awaiting feedback,

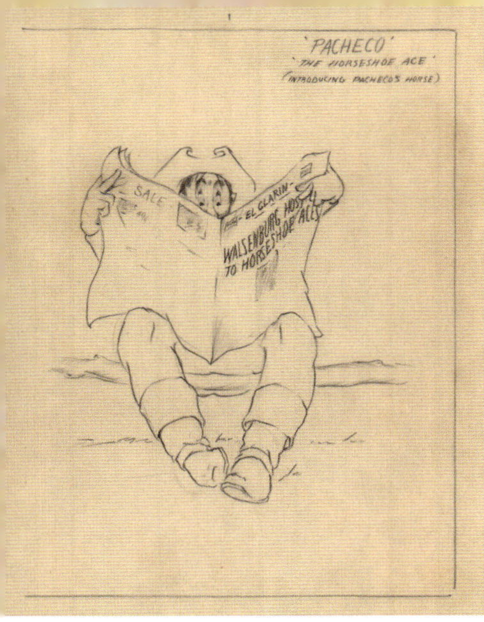

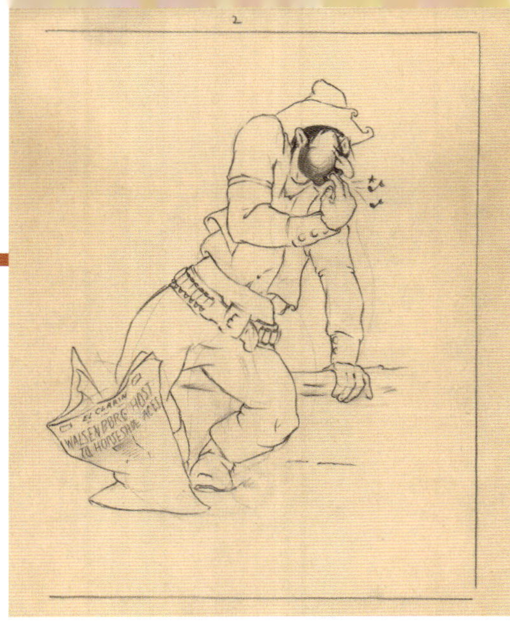

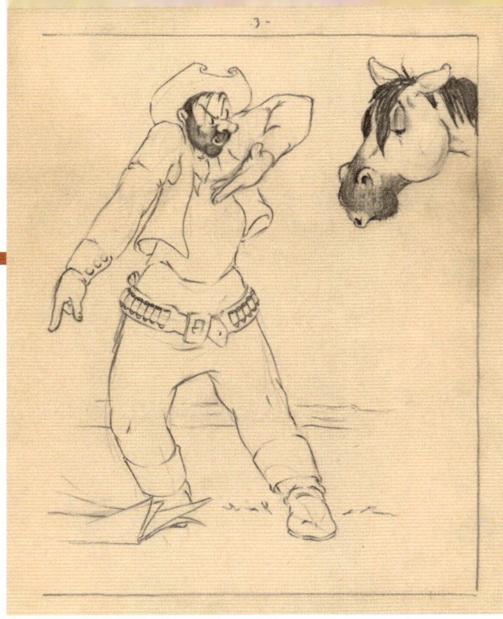

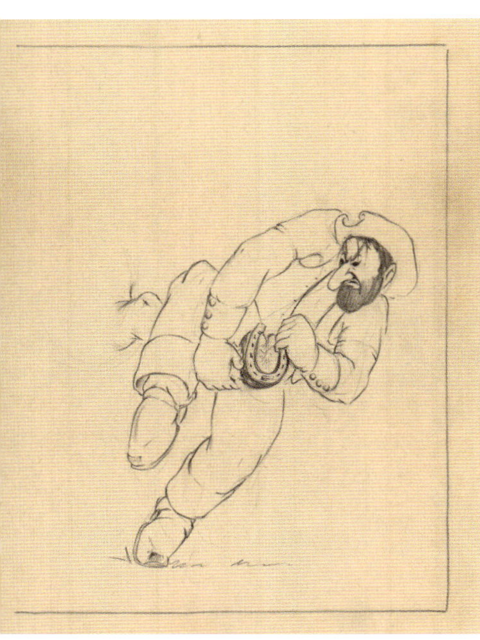

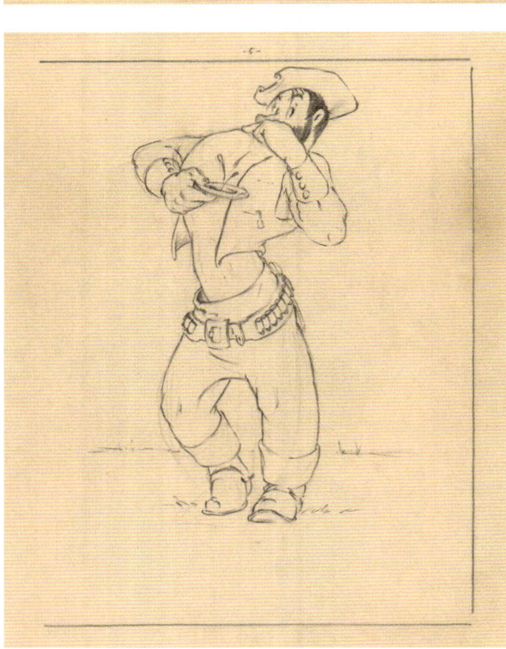

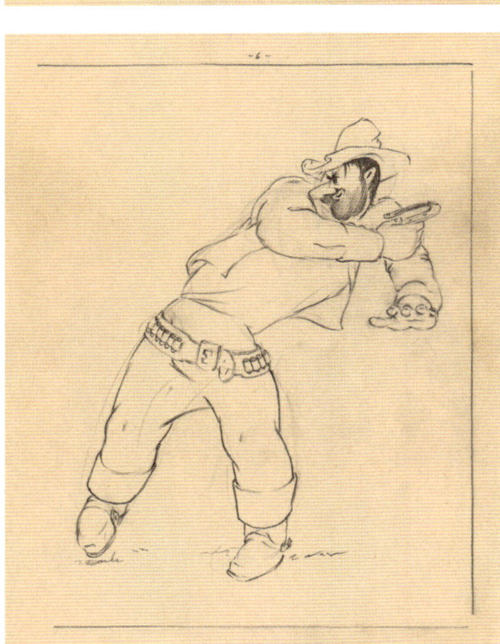

X was realistic in his expectations. With only a few months of formal art training under his belt, X expected criticism that would help to elevate his artwork but wasn't anticipating a life-changing experience. With his assignment behind him, X turned his attention to a more immediate need: attempting to obtain a summer job at Disney so he could pay for another year of art school. Always practical and humble, X thought he would perhaps attain a job in the "traffic department," the term then coined for being a messenger boy in the studio's mail division.

In an ironic twist of fate, X received a call to come in for a job interview based on his portfolio, but he missed it as he had already headed out to the studio, located then on Hyperion Avenue in the Silver Lake neighborhood of Los Angeles just east of Hollywood, to inquire about the messenger job. Upon arriving at the studio, X was surprised to find himself face to face with his "competition"—three classmates from Chouinard. While X saw his job prospects

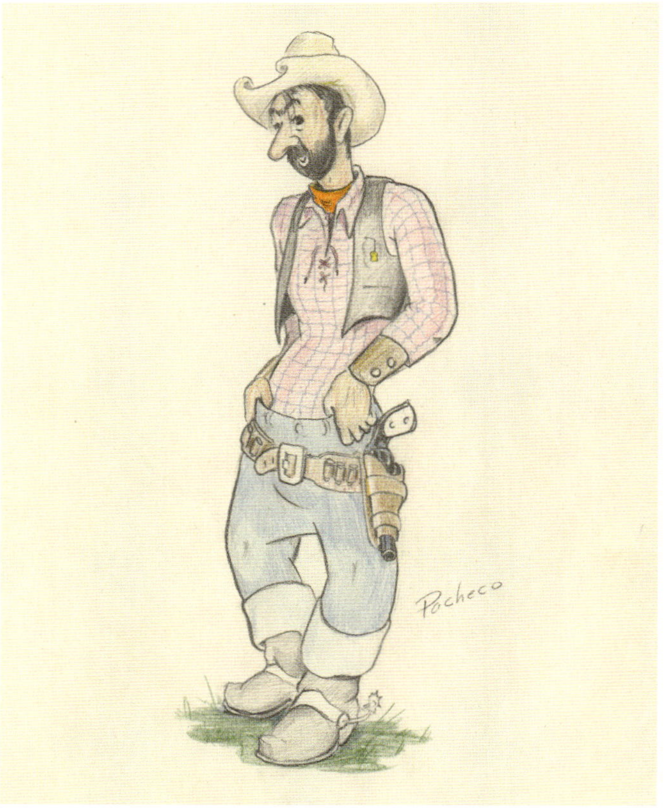

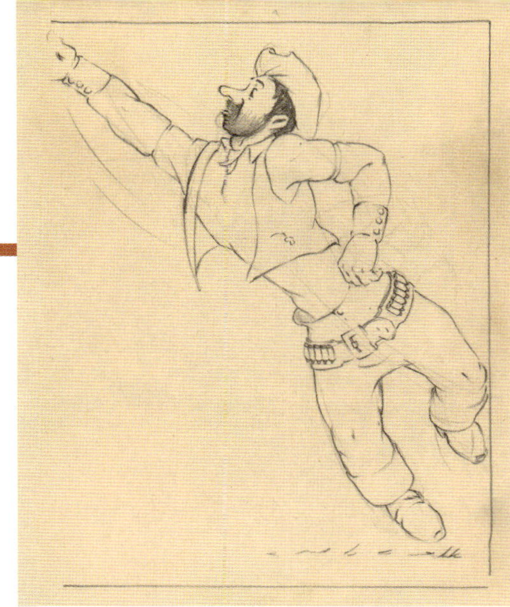

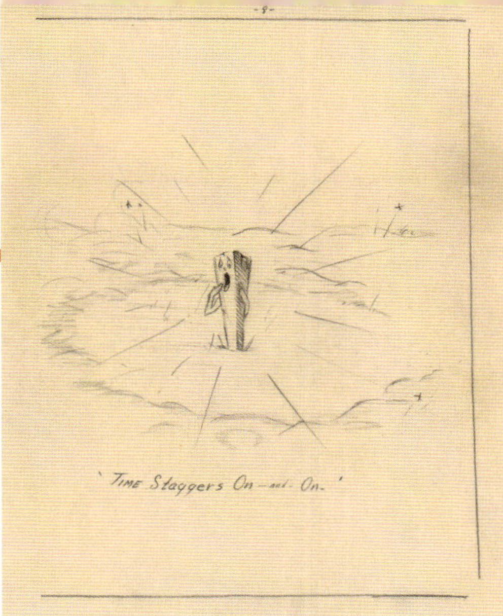

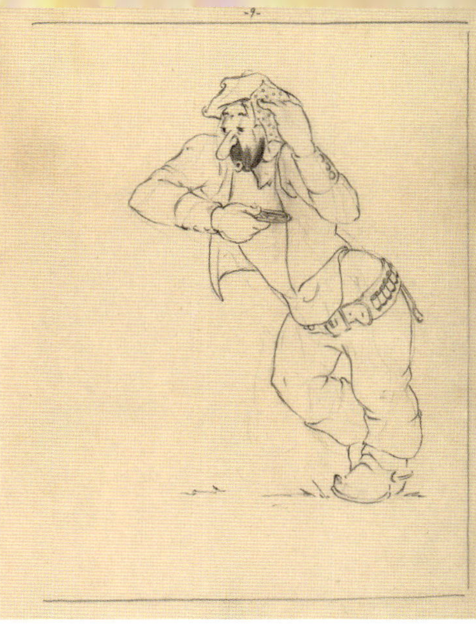

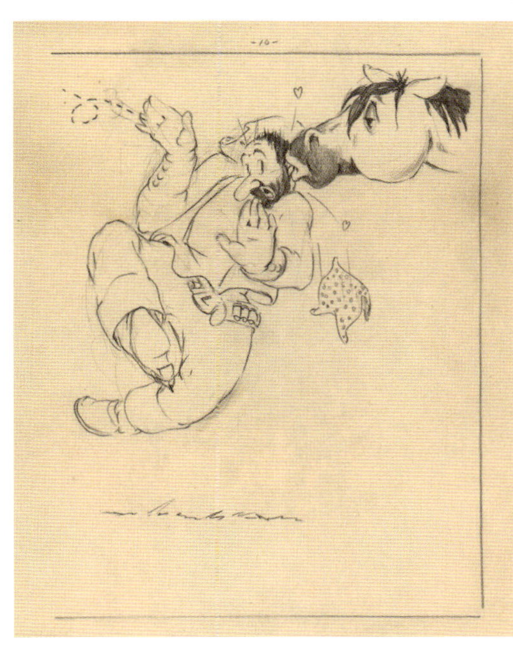

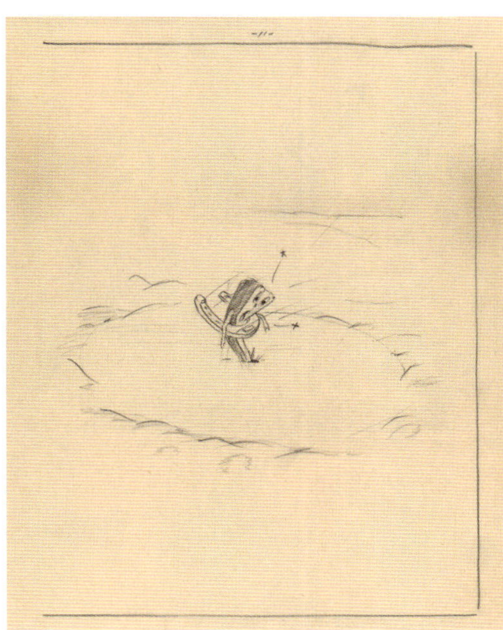

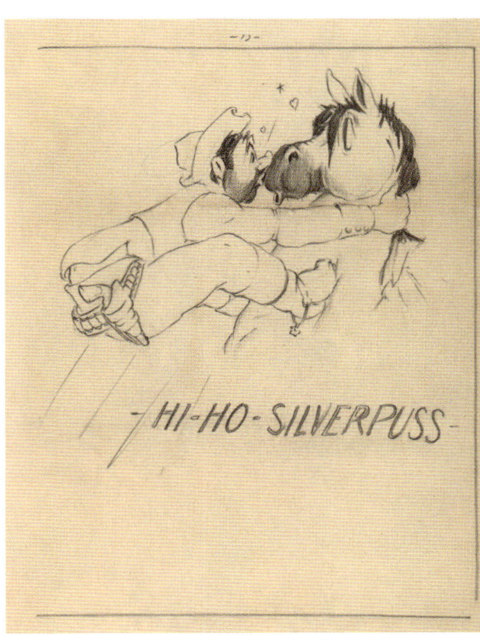

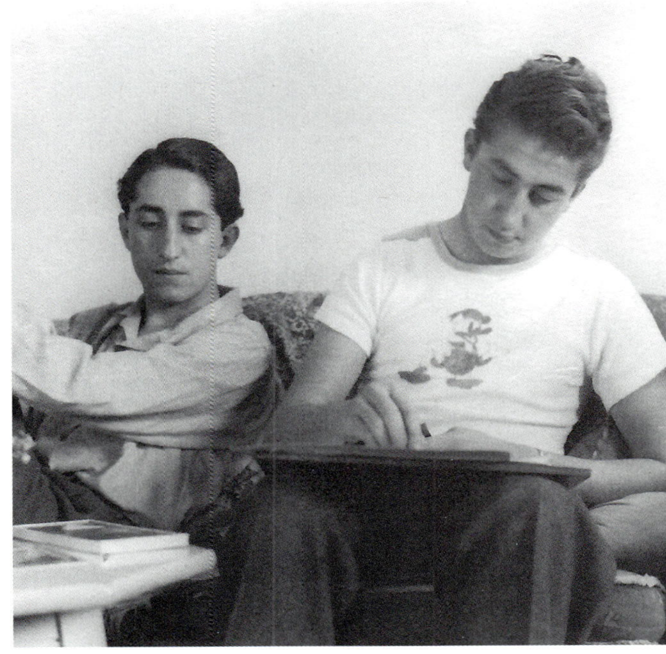

OPPOSITE AND TOP: X's 1938 job application drawings for Disney; ABOVE: X, sketching next to his brother Pete.

diminishing before his very eyes, he went in alone to interview with the hiring manager, George Drake, who held X's illustrations and told him, "I looked through your portfolio and I like what you've got. Would you like to come work for us?" Shocked and thrilled, X replied, "Holy Toledo, would I ever!"

Elated by his good news, X channeled his frenetic energy into running all the way home to his grandmother's house (an approximately three-mile trip to where she lived on Western Avenue), yelling, "I got a job at Disney! I got a job at Disney!" the entire way. As it turns out, X's timing was perfect. Disney, buoyed by the success of *Snow White and the Seven Dwarfs* (1937), was looking to expand its workforce and hire new animators. Tapping into talent, proximity to the Disney studio, and connected professors, X had landed a dream job in 1938 at age eighteen.

Local newspapers in Colorado picked up the story, publishing headlines such as "Local Boy to Join Walt Disney Staff of Animators: Xavier Atencio

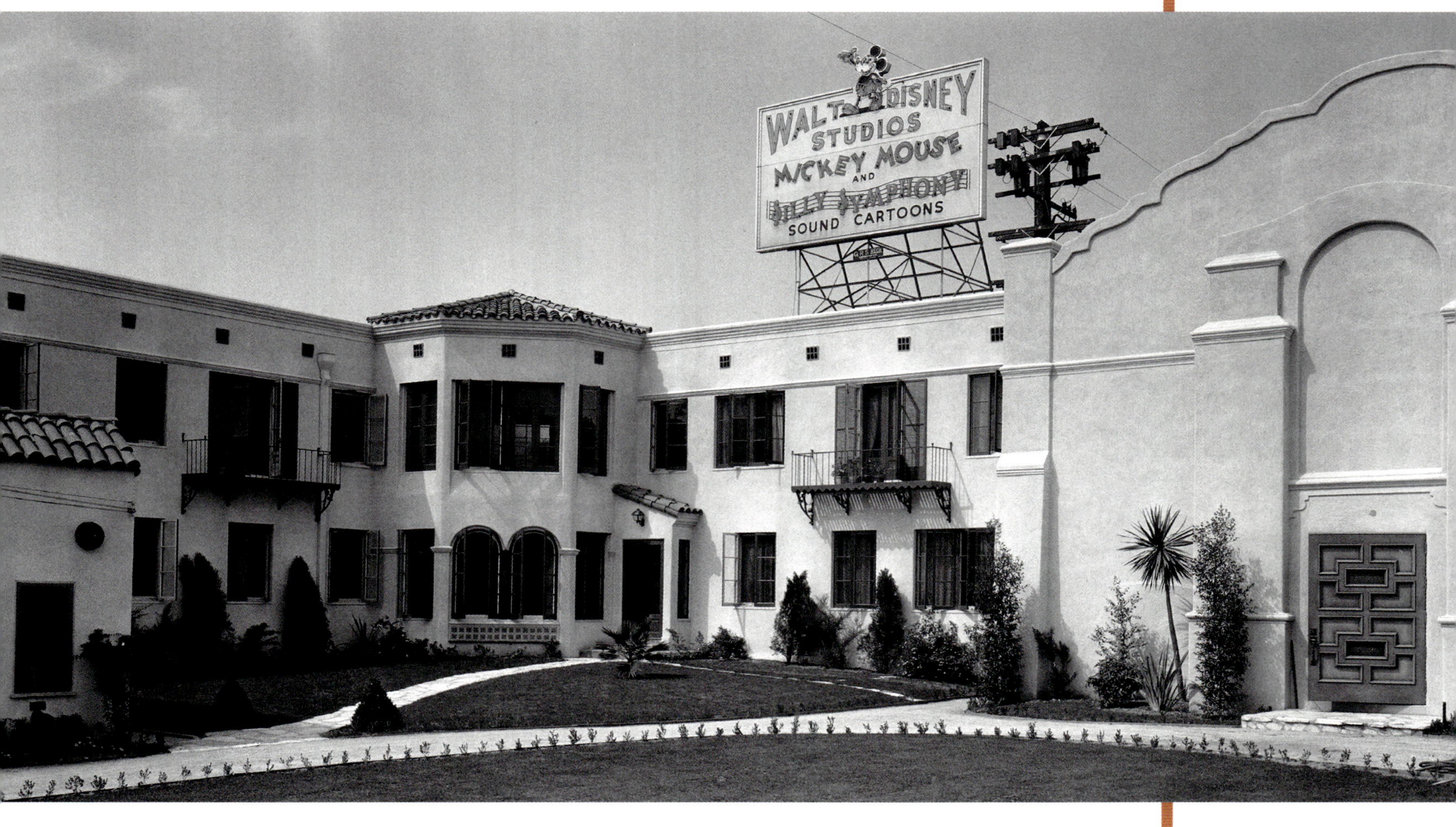

Makes Good After Only Few Months." They noted that X Atencio "had been chosen [as] one of the four new animators in Hollywood to join the staff of Walt Disney. . . . Disney, who has become so well known in recent months by his marvelous production of *Snow White and the Seven Dwarfs*, made his appointments Wednesday, and young Atencio . . . with three other Hollywood animator students was chosen. Disney also selected 16 others from over the United States, increasing his present staff by 20." Their pride in X's personal accomplishments embodied the community's belief in and love for X, sounding almost like familial praise.

One local Colorado paper even ventured to write, "Xavier, who is a graduate of St. Mary's high school of 1937, starts work for Disney Monday morning. One of the other three in Hollywood who was chosen has been receiving instruction in animation for six years, while young Atencio has had less than

ABOVE: Disney Brothers Studios on Hyperion Avenue; ABOVE (RIGHT): X hard at work as an in-betweener on *Pinocchio*, 1939; RIGHT: X's self-portrait, shortly after starting at Disney; OPPOSITE: Various articles from the local Colorado newspapers heralding X's new job at Disney.

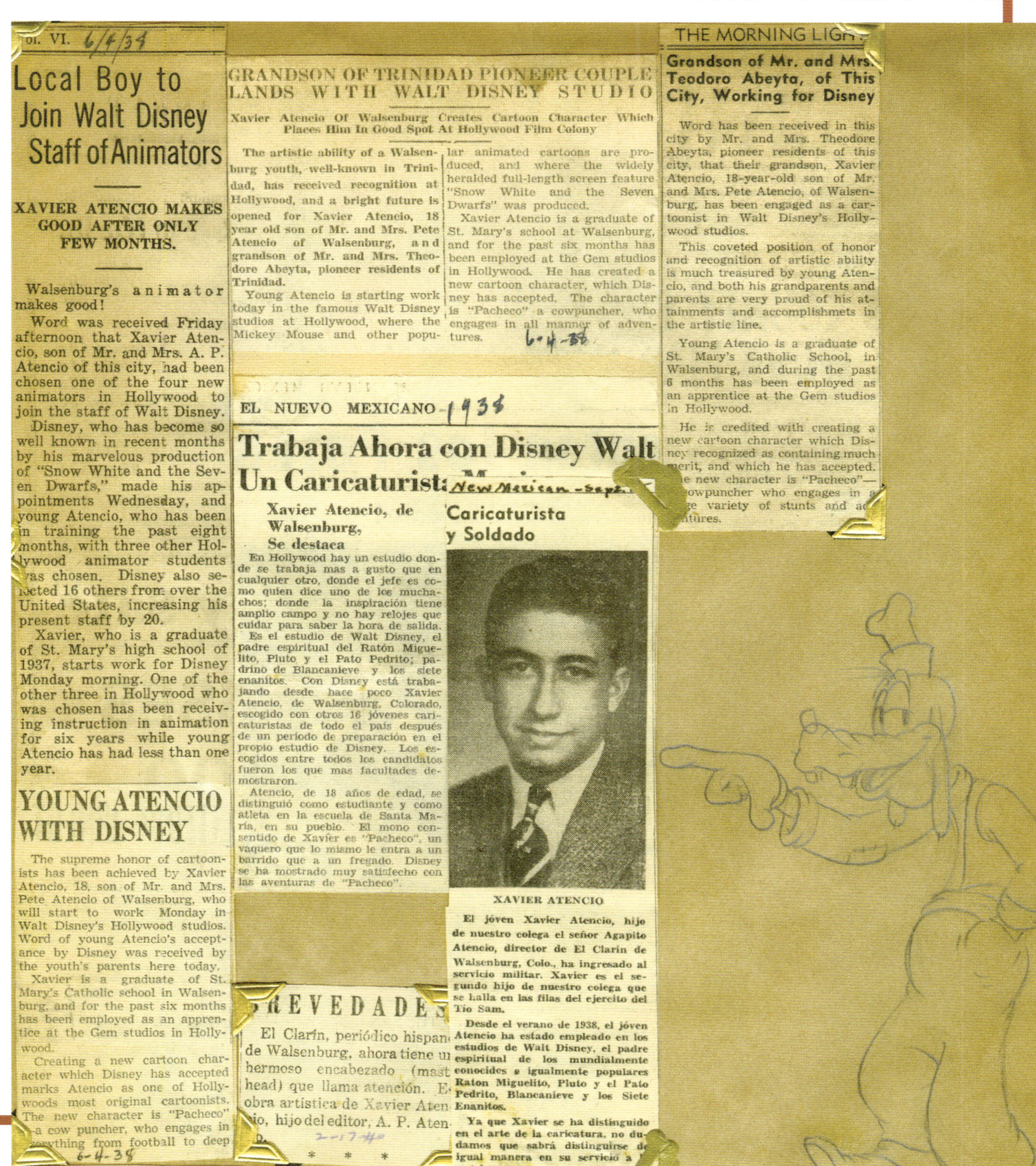

Vol. VI. 6/4/38

Local Boy to Join Walt Disney Staff of Animators

XAVIER ATENCIO MAKES GOOD AFTER ONLY FEW MONTHS.

Walsenburg's animator makes good!

Word was received Friday afternoon that Xavier Atencio, son of Mr. and Mrs. A. P. Atencio of this city, had been chosen one of the four new animators in Hollywood to join the staff of Walt Disney.

Disney, who has become so well known in recent months by his marvelous production of "Snow White and the Seven Dwarfs," made his appointments Wednesday, and young Atencio, who has been in training the past eight months, with three other Hollywood animator students was chosen. Disney also selected 16 others from over the United States, increasing his present staff by 20.

Xavier, who is a graduate of St. Mary's high school of 1937, starts work for Disney Monday morning. One of the other three in Hollywood who was chosen has been receiving instruction in animation for six years while young Atencio has had less than one year.

YOUNG ATENCIO WITH DISNEY

The supreme honor of cartoonists has been achieved by Xavier Atencio, 18, son of Mr. and Mrs. Pete Atencio of Walsenburg, who will start to work Monday in Walt Disney's Hollywood studios. Word of young Atencio's acceptance by Disney was received by the youth's parents here today.

Xavier is a graduate of St. Mary's Catholic school in Walsenburg, and for the past six months has been employed as an apprentice at the Gem studios in Hollywood.

Creating a new cartoon character which Disney has accepted marks Atencio as one of Hollywoods most original cartoonists. The new character is "Pacheco"—a cow puncher, who engages in ...ything from football to deep

6-4-38

GRANDSON OF TRINIDAD PIONEER COUPLE LANDS WITH WALT DISNEY STUDIO

Xavier Atencio Of Walsenburg Creates Cartoon Character Which Places Him In Good Spot At Hollywood Film Colony

The artistic ability of a Walsenburg youth, well-known in Trinidad, has received recognition at Hollywood, and a bright future is opened for Xavier Atencio, 18 year old son of Mr. and Mrs. Pete Atencio of Walsenburg, and grandson of Mr. and Mrs. Theodore Abeyta, pioneer residents of Trinidad.

Young Atencio is starting work today in the famous Walt Disney studios at Hollywood, where the Mickey Mouse and other popular animated cartoons are produced, and where the widely heralded full-length screen feature "Snow White and the Seven Dwarfs" was produced.

Xavier Atencio is a graduate of St. Mary's school at Walsenburg, and for the past six months has been employed at the Gem studios in Hollywood. He has created a new cartoon character, which Disney has accepted. The character is "Pacheco" a cowpuncher, who engages in all manner of adventures.

6-4-38

THE MORNING LIGHT

Grandson of Mr. and Mrs. Teodoro Abeyta, of This City, Working for Disney

Word has been received in this city by Mr. and Mrs. Theodore Abeyta, pioneer residents of this city, that their grandson, Xavier Atencio, 18-year-old son of Mr. and Mrs. Pete Atencio, of Walsenburg, has been engaged as a cartoonist in Walt Disney's Hollywood studios.

This coveted position of honor and recognition of artistic ability is much treasured by young Atencio, and both his grandparents and parents are very proud of his attainments and accomplishmets in the artistic line.

Young Atencio is a graduate of St. Mary's Catholic School, in Walsenburg, and during the past 6 months has been employed as an apprentice at the Gem studios in Hollywood.

He is credited with creating a new cartoon character which Disney recognized as containing much merit, and which he has accepted. The new character is "Pacheco"—a cowpuncher who engages in a ...ge variety of stunts and adventures.

EL NUEVO MEXICANO 1938

Trabaja Ahora con Disney Walt Un Caricaturista

Xavier Atencio, de Walsenburg, Se destaca

En Hollywood hay un estudio donde se trabaja mas a gusto que en cualquier otro, donde el jefe es como quien dice uno de los muchachos; donde la inspiración tiene amplio campo y no hay relojes que cuidar para saber la hora de salida.

Es el estudio de Walt Disney, el padre espiritual del Ratón Miguelito, Pluto y el Pato Pedrito; padrino de Blancanieve y los siete enanitos. Con Disney está trabajando desde hace poco Xavier Atencio, de Walsenburg, Colorado, escogido con otros 16 jóvenes caricaturistas de todo el país después de un periodo de preparación en el propio estudio de Disney. Los escogidos entre todos los candidatos fueron los que mas facultades demostraron.

Atencio, de 18 años de edad, se distinguió como estudiante y como atleta en la escuela de Santa María, en su pueblo. El mono consentido de Xavier es "Pacheco", un vaquero que lo mismo le entra a un barrido que a un fregado. Disney se ha mostrado muy satisfecho con las aventuras de "Pacheco".

New Mexican - Sept.

Caricaturista y Soldado

XAVIER ATENCIO

El jóven Xavier Atencio, hijo de nuestro colega el señor Agapito Atencio, director de El Clarin de Walsenburg, Colo., ha ingresado al servicio militar. Xavier es el segundo hijo de nuestro colega que se halla en las filas del ejercito del Tío Sam.

Desde el verano de 1938, el jóven Atencio ha estado empleado en los estudios de Walt Disney, el padre espiritual de los mundialmente conocidos e igualmente populares Raton Miguelito, Pluto y el Pato Pedrito, Blancanieve y los Siete Enanitos.

Ya que Xavier se ha distinguido en el arte de la caricatura, no dudamos que sabrá distinguirse de igual manera en su servicio a ...

...REVEDADES

El Clarín, periódico hispan... de Walsenburg, ahora tiene u... hermoso encabezado (mast head) que llama atención. E... obra artística de Xavier Atencio, hijo del editor, A. P. Aten...

2-17-40

* * *

one year." This commentary not only touted X's accomplishment but noted the speed with which his success had occurred, underscoring his quick and natural talent, and boasting in a way that reflected well on the entire Walsenburg community.

X officially started work at Walt Disney Productions on June 6, 1938, as a trainee animator, earning a salary of twelve dollars a week. While it was a far cry from today's salaries, the cost of living was also much lower. According to X, on average at that time haircuts cost approximately thirty-five cents, and gas was fourteen cents a gallon. X and the rest of his incoming class of twenty hopeful animators from around the country went through a month of training where they were taught all the animation basics—from flag waving to ball bouncing—and then completed little tests to prove their proficiency and understanding.

Those who had proven their abilities were put on contract and offered jobs to continue at the studio, and their salaries were increased to eighteen dollars a week. Included in this group was X, who officially dropped out of Chouinard to pursue a career at Disney, occasionally still taking night classes through the art school along with the other Disney animators. X received his first official assignment working under noted animator and eventual director/producer Wolfgang "Woolie" Reitherman as an in-betweener on *Pinocchio* (1940). Woolie was one of Walt's core animators, humorously known as the "Nine Old Men," and he took X under his wing. X and three others—Bill Justice (Woolie's first assistant and a colleague with whom X would repeatedly work in the future), Louis Terri, and Gerald James—made up the self-named "Woolie Unit." Woolie's assignment was to work on Monstro the Whale, while X cleaned up Woolie's sketches and handled the traditional in-betweener duties of creating the series of new animations, usually the easiest and simplest actions, that existed in between the main frames and the extreme drawings done by the animators.

X found Woolie to be a relentless perfectionist who wanted the animation done properly and to his specifications. Animators passed their rough drawings off to the assistant animators and in-betweeners, who took clean pieces of paper and started over based on the animators' work. Woolie, however, used blue, red, and black pencils to continually draw over his illustrations on the same sheets of paper until they looked like rags and only then handed them over to the Woolie Unit. Although erasing and cleaning up were made much harder by Woolie's working style, X always acknowledged that it did work well and ultimately gave the character more form and, as Woolie wanted, "guts." X's beginner-level work was very mechanical and technical, lacking the creativity one assumes when they think of animation, but it was also essential training that reinforced the artistic basics and taught X the importance of discipline and timing. Ultimately, X's work cleaning up the drawings was vital to ensure that the women (and they were usually women) from the Ink and Paint Department could ink them onto the cels.

According to *An Introduction to The Walt Disney Studios*, circa 1939, the in-betweener handled all of the rough and cleaned-up drawings that were not the responsibility of the assistant animator, meaning that he was responsible for more than half the drawings though was less concerned about the larger creative vision. Both the assistant animators and the in-betweeners had to have the innate abilities required of an animator and use those

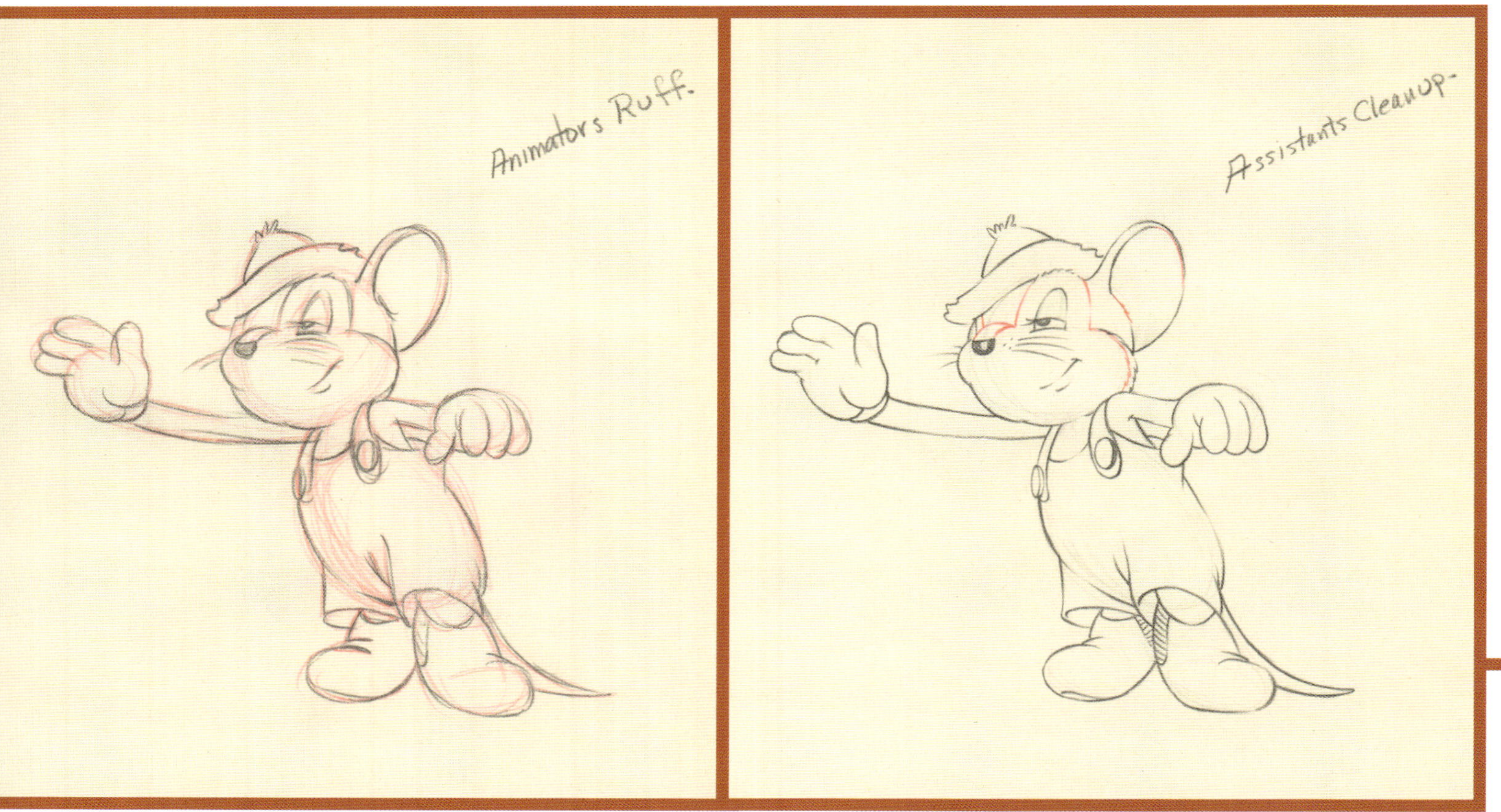

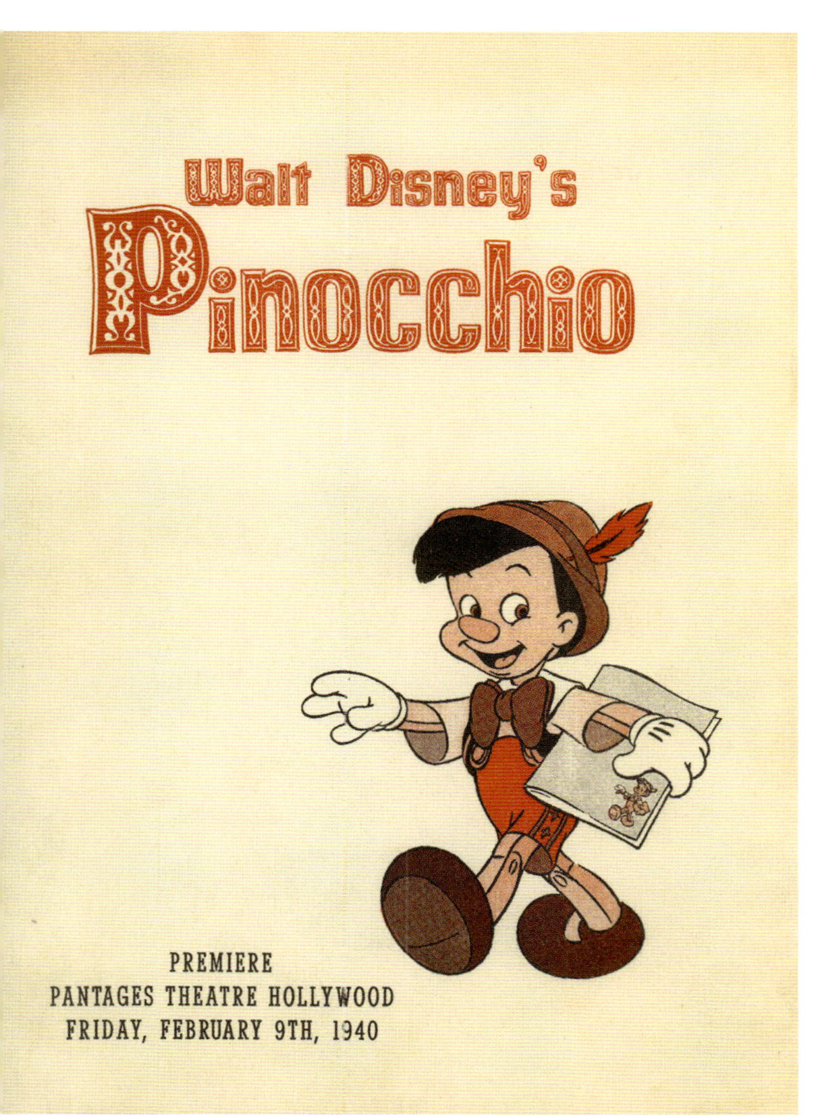

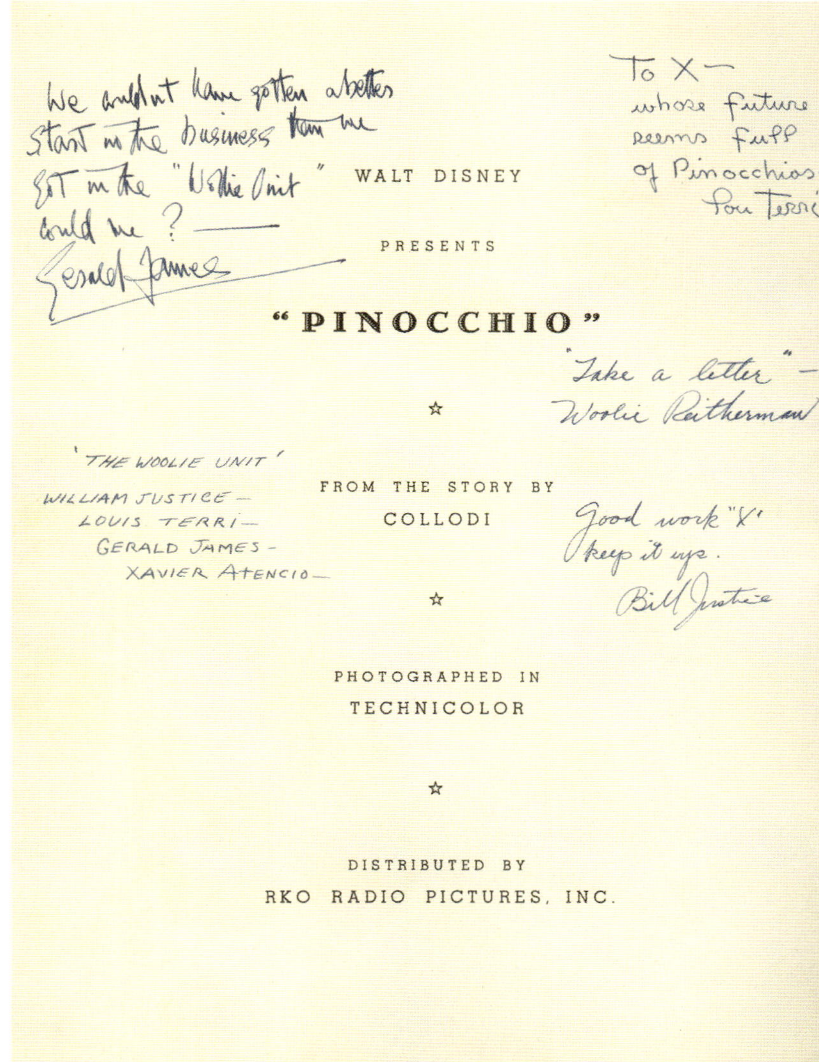

We couldn't have gotten a better start in the business than we got in the "Woolie Unit" could we? — Gerald James

To X— whose future seems full of Pinocchios— Lou Terri

WALT DISNEY

PRESENTS

"PINOCCHIO"

"Take a letter"— Woolie Reitherman

☆

'THE WOOLIE UNIT'
WILLIAM JUSTICE—
LOUIS TERRI—
GERALD JAMES—
XAVIER ATENCIO—

FROM THE STORY BY
COLLODI

Good work "X" keep it up. Bill Justice

☆

PHOTOGRAPHED IN
TECHNICOLOR

☆

DISTRIBUTED BY
RKO RADIO PICTURES, INC.

opportunities as stepping stones and learning experiences on the path to becoming an artist and full animator. Likewise, in such a collaborative environment, establishing one central creative vision and style for characters, tone, and action was key. Thus, in-betweeners and assistant animators needed to easily adapt to different working styles, be skilled at drawing, and inherently understand story and caricature.

The assumption was to do your job well and keep advancing little by little up the chain until you were allowed to do animating of your own. From the animator's perspective, relying on your team and trusting them to carry out your vision quickly and efficiently was necessary for success. When animators found people that they worked well with, it made sense for them to continue together project to project, with the lower-level employee gaining mentorship and trust, and the animator acquiring a trusted confidant capable of understanding their working methods through an unspoken shorthand.

And while some would dislike working for a highly particular boss, X loved working for Woolie, who also became a close friend over the years. He thought Woolie was a very good boss and continued to work with him as they moved together from *Pinocchio* to *Fantasia* (1940). After the completion of *Pinocchio*, Bill Justice, Woolie's first assistant, moved into animation and left the Woolie Unit. Bill's promotion and X's hard work on *Pinocchio* left room for X to move into Bill's previous role as Woolie's first assistant animator on *Fantasia*, where they worked on

OPPOSITE: X's sketchbook drawings demonstrating the animator's rough versus the assistant's cleanup, featuring a character from the 1936 short *The Country Cousin*; ABOVE (LEFT): X's *Pinocchio* premiere booklet, 1940; ABOVE (RIGHT): Title page of the *Pinocchio* premiere booklet, signed by members of the Woolie Unit.

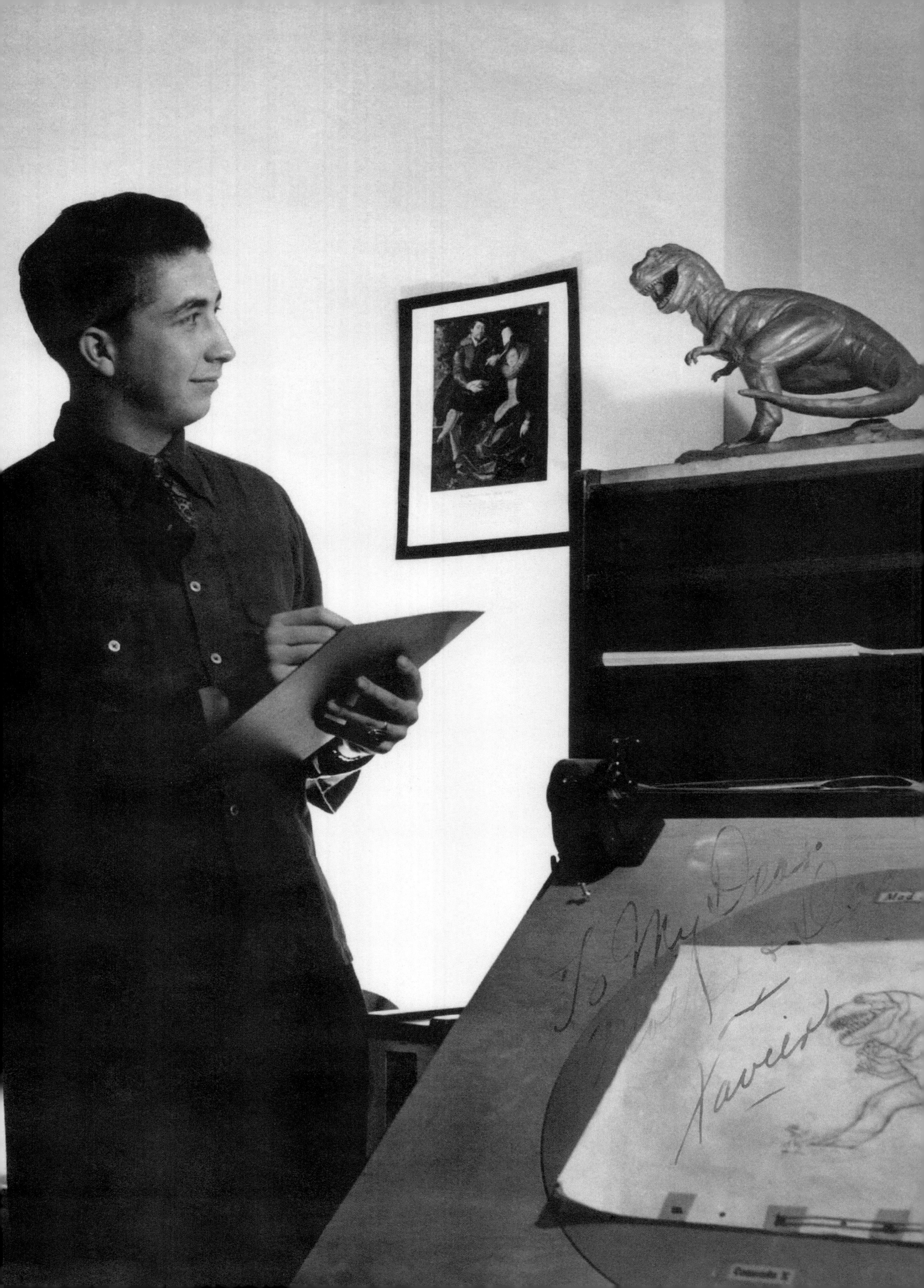
To My Dear
Xavier

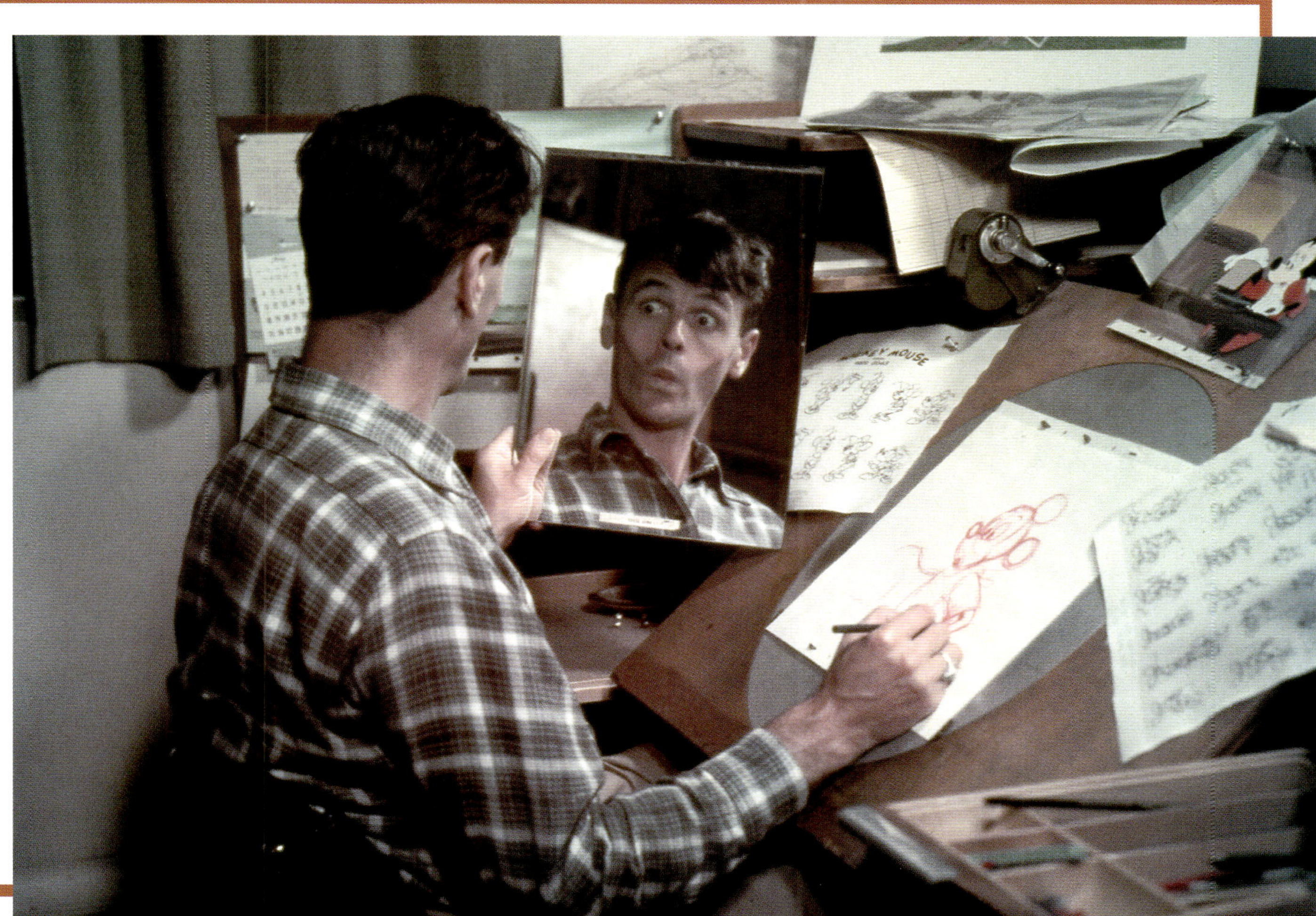

the battle between a Tyrannosaurus rex and a stegosaurus in the "Rite of Spring" segment set to music by Igor Stravinsky. Although there were two assistant animators assigned to Woolie, one was solely responsible for doing the rough animation with him. Woolie would indicate just the extreme drawings, and then the other assistant would finish the action. X was in charge of the clean-up phase and continued with those same responsibilities working for Woolie on *Dumbo* (1941).

X always said that his favorite Disney movie was *Pinocchio* and that he had a "soft spot in his heart for that picture." Observers note "firsts" often leave long-lasting impressions, and *Pinocchio* was in progress during X's most formative time. And like Pinocchio, X was embarking at this point on his own bildungsroman-esque journey of self-discovery. Both Pinocchio and X figured out who they wanted to be and made conscientious choices; Pinocchio longed

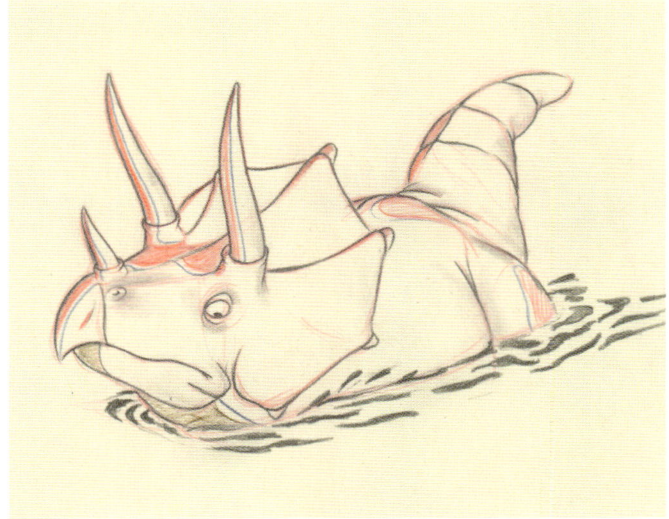

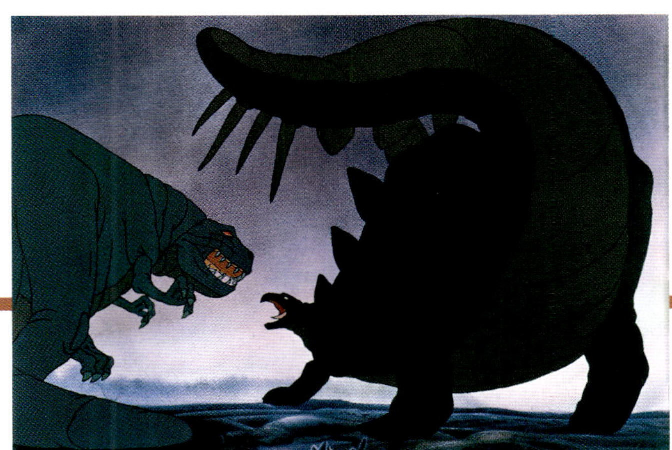

OPPOSITE: Photo of X working on *Fantasia*, which he sent to his mother, signing it, "To My Dear Mother"; TOP: Wolfgang "Woolie" Reitherman; RIGHT (TOP): X's drawing of a triceratops for *Fantasia*; RIGHT (BOTTOM): A finished scene from *Fantasia* that X worked on.

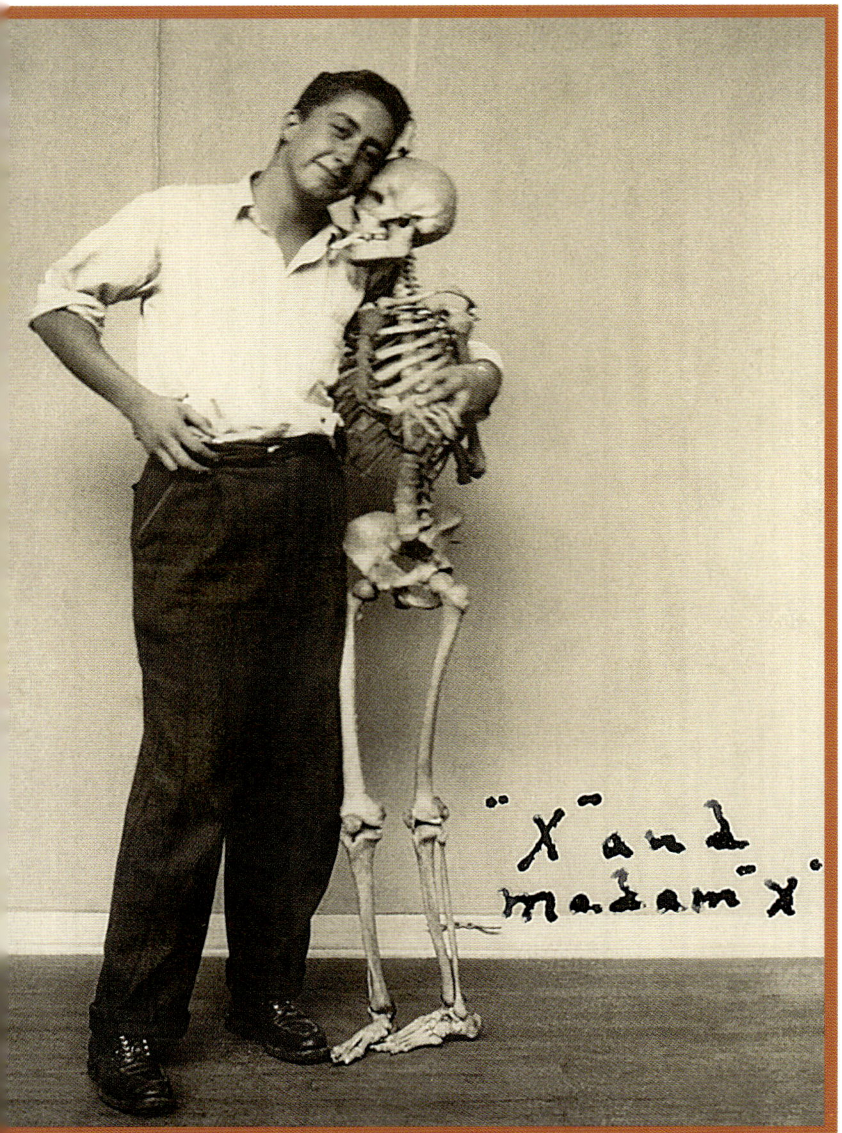

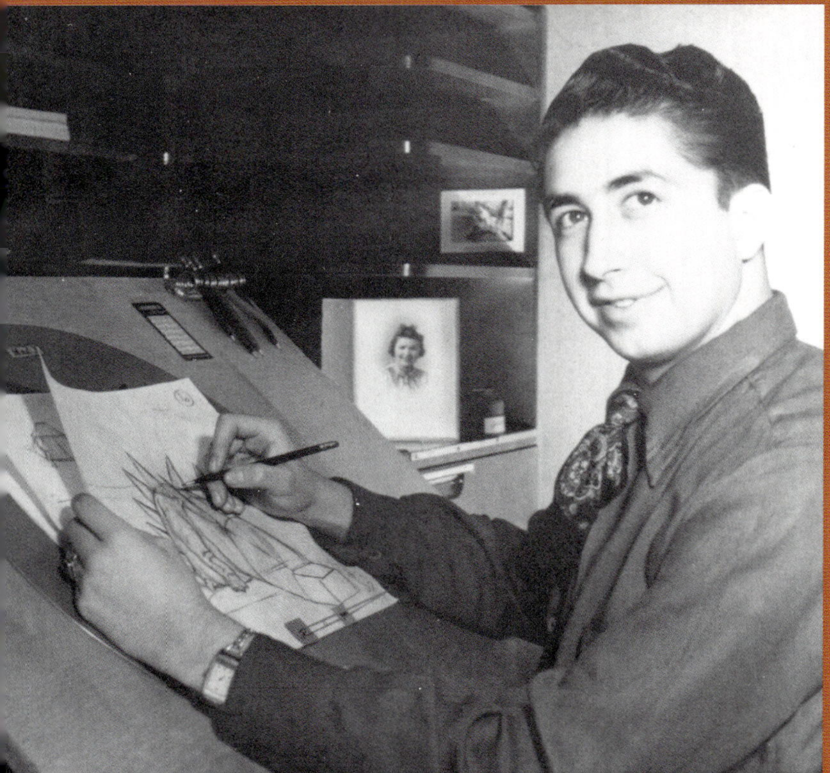

to become "a real boy," while X's growth was twofold. In addition to learning the artistic and other requirements of his job, X also discovered how to be an adult. X's work on *Pinocchio*, during his late teens, served as "college" and gave him the freedom and time to try new things—both creatively and otherwise (à la his brief stint smoking a pipe while trying to blend in with many of the other animators). His job as an in-betweener learning from one of the best animators might have been the deep emotional crux of his love for this film, having offered him an early glimpse of what it was like to find purpose and joy in your job. Rarer still was the true camaraderie the Woolie Unit had on *Pinocchio*, as depicted in the signatures on the premiere film program that X planned to send as a keepsake for Mary, in particular the loving, joking quality of Woolie's message and X's equally cheeky but friendly reply. Regardless of the reasoning, his first Disney project clearly had an indelible impact on him.

X's satisfaction with his work was further evidenced in the ways it began to show up in his personal drawings. First, there were the signed drawings he had worked on that he sent home to show his family his growing artistry and the day-to-day fruits of his labors. On one photograph that he sent home of himself drawing a dinosaur from *Fantasia*, he wrote, "To my dear mother —Xavier," exemplifying both the pride he had in his work and the deep bonds that remained even across great distances and his growing independent life in California. From there, his own

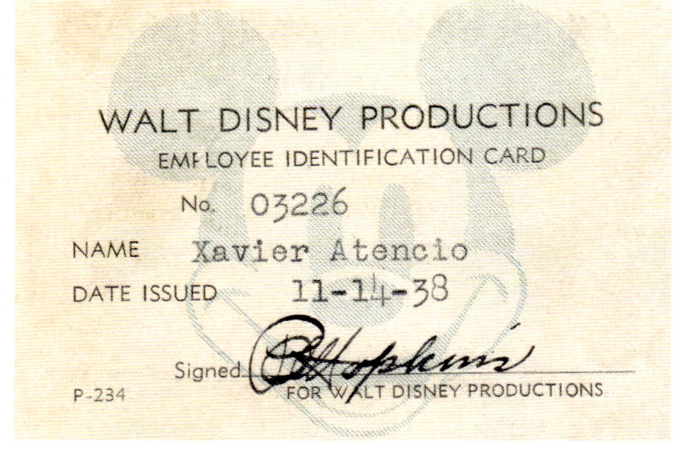

WALT DISNEY PRODUCTIONS
EMPLOYEE IDENTIFICATION CARD
No. 03226
NAME Xavier Atencio
DATE ISSUED 11-14-38
Signed [signature] FOR WALT DISNEY PRODUCTIONS
P-234

TOP: X, in his early days at the studio; LEFT: X at his desk drawing dinosaurs for *Fantasia*; ABOVE: X's employee ID card from his early days at Walt Disney Productions; OPPOSITE: Another signed page from the *Pinocchio* premiere booklet, one that X acquired and sent to Mary.

Supervising Directors

BEN SHARPSTEEN
HAMILTON LUSKE

Sequence Directors

BILL ROBERTS
JACK KINNEY
NORMAN FERGUSON
WILFRED JACKSON
T. HEE

Animation Direction

FRED MOORE
MILTON KAHL
WARD KIMBALL
ERIC LARSON
FRANKLIN THOMAS
VLADIMIR TYTLA
ARTHUR BABBITT
WOOLIE REITHERMAN

Story Adaptation

TED SEARS
WEBB SMITH
JOSEPH SABO
OTTO ENGLANDER
WILLIAM COTTRELL
ERDMAN PENNER
AURELIUS BATTAGLIA

Character Designs

JOE GRANT
ALBERT HURTER
CAMPBELL GRANT
JOHN P. MILLER
MARTIN PROVENSEN
JOHN WALBRIDGE

Music and Lyrics

LEIGH HARLINE
NED WASHINGTON
PAUL J. SMITH

Art Direction

CHARLES PHILIPPI
HUGH HENNESY
DICK KELSEY
TERRELL STAPP
JOHN HUBLEY
KENNETH ANDERSON
KENDALL O'CONNOR
THOR PUTNAM
McLAREN STEWART
AL ZINNEN

Backgrounds

CLAUDE COATS
ED STARR
MERLE COX
RAY HUFFINE

Animation

JACK CAMPBELL
BERNY WOLF
DON LUSK
NORMAN TATE
LYNN KARP
ART PALMER
DON TOBIN
GEORGE ROWLEY
DON PATTERSON
LES CLARK
HUGH FRASER
OLIVER M. JOHNSTON
DON TOWSLEY
JOHN LOUNSBERRY
JOHN BRADBURY
CHARLES NICHOLS
JOSHUA MEADOR
ROBERT MARTSCH
JOHN McMANUS
PRESTON BLAIR
MARVIN WOODWARD
JOHN ELLIOTTE

Dear Mary:
Have heard lots about you
Love and
xxxxxxxx
xxxxxxxxx
xxxxxxx
Woolie Reitherman
P.S. This guy "X" ain't so hot - Howza about sitting this one out.

Don't believe a word of it — but he is a swell boss!!
"X"

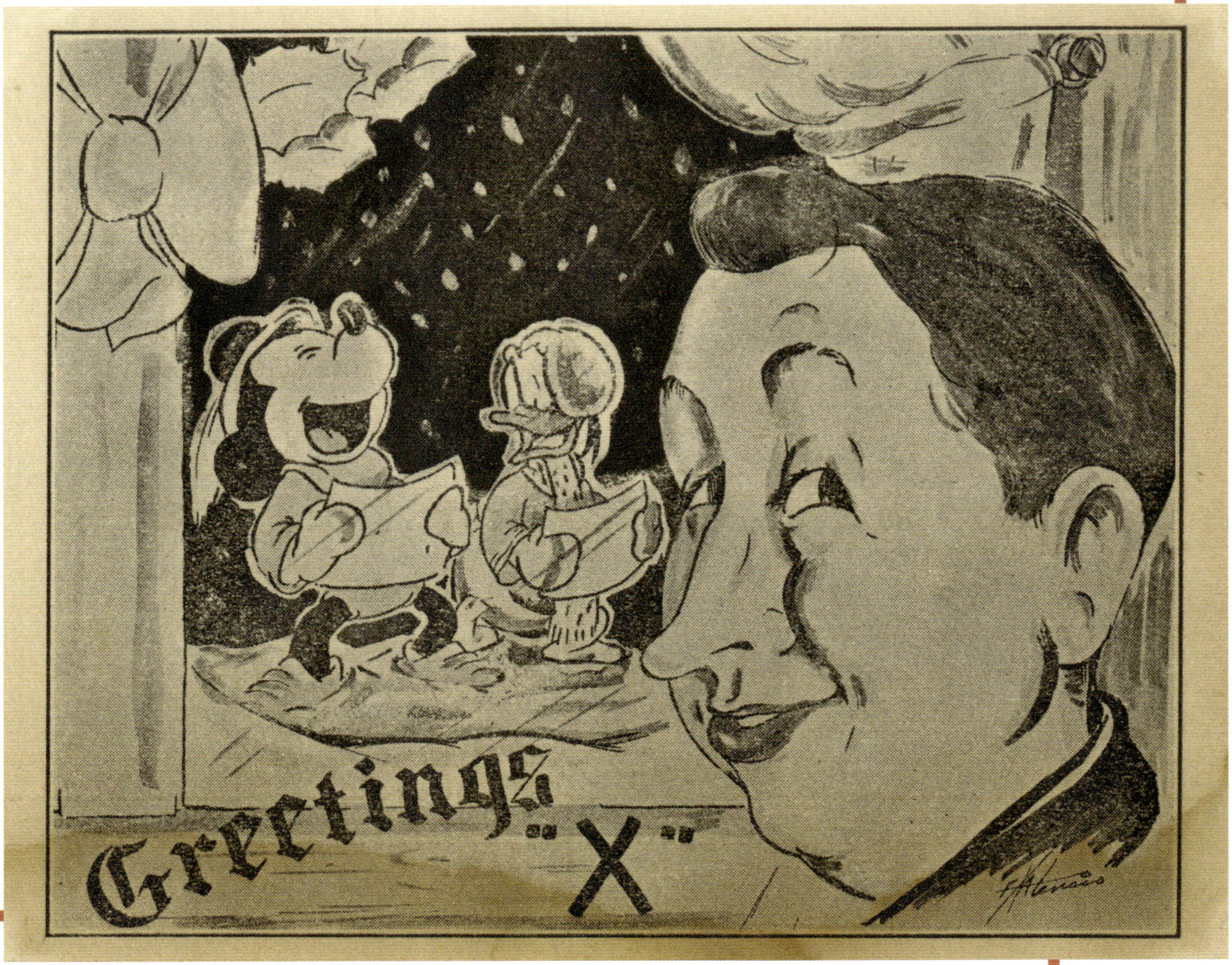

Greetings "X"

personal artwork became synonymous with that of his work at Disney. His holiday card, a lasting tradition, illustrated a self-portrait of X with Mickey and Donald caroling behind him.

Meanwhile, a card sent back home to his long-distance girlfriend, Mary, featured a sweet note of affection delivered by Jiminy Cricket. As X pursued his career in California, Mary had enrolled in college back at Loretto Heights College in Denver, and their letter writing was the only affordable way to consistently stay in touch, deepen their relationship, and fully express themselves. X's use of Disney characters in these notes demonstrated how important and enduring the characters had become to his own art and identity.

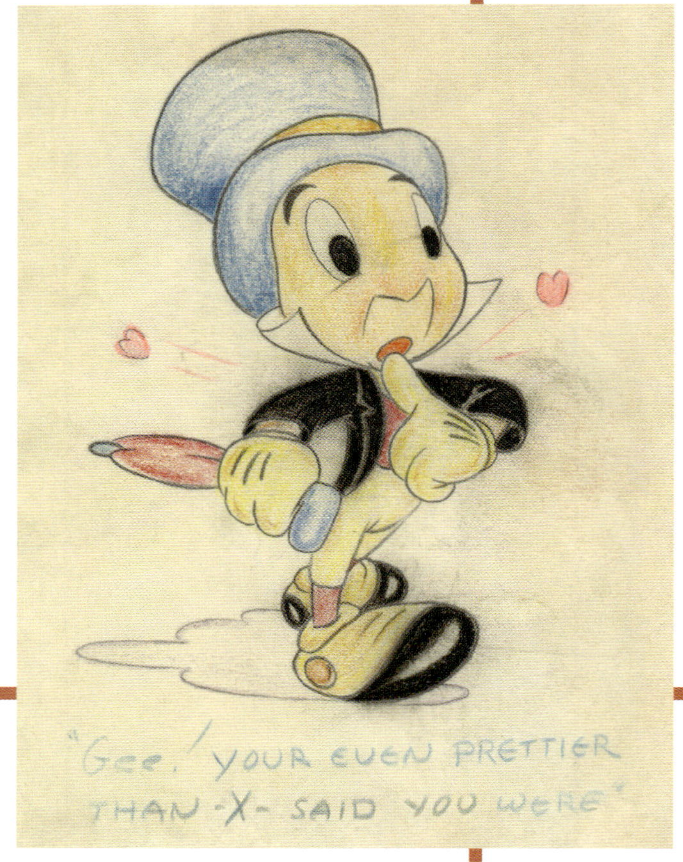

TOP: X's personal Christmas card, 1938; RIGHT: A 1938 card to Mary from X; OPPOSITE: Two 1940 cards X sent to Mary.

X rose through the ranks as Disney was enjoying great success. The studio moved from its fledgling Hyperion Avenue location in Los Angeles proper to a new, expansive campus in Burbank in early 1940. Unfortunately, with success came rising tensions, and Disney soon found itself at the center of a 1941 animator's strike during production of *Dumbo*, in which the eligible nonunionized Disney employees, led by animator Art Babbitt, picketed and stayed off the job for over three months. While X didn't consider himself a rabble-rouser, and it was early enough in his career that he didn't necessarily understand everything he was fighting for, X went out on strike to support his colleagues and "buddies," often one and the same, trusting in their reasoning for demanding change. His drawings of his colleagues and fellow picketers during the strike conveyed the seriousness of their demands but also the solidarity they displayed marching on the picket lines. X's drawings captured the essence of the times, and along with caricatures of himself and his fellow animators during the early Disney days, reinforced that X's artistic inspiration came from the people and world around him.

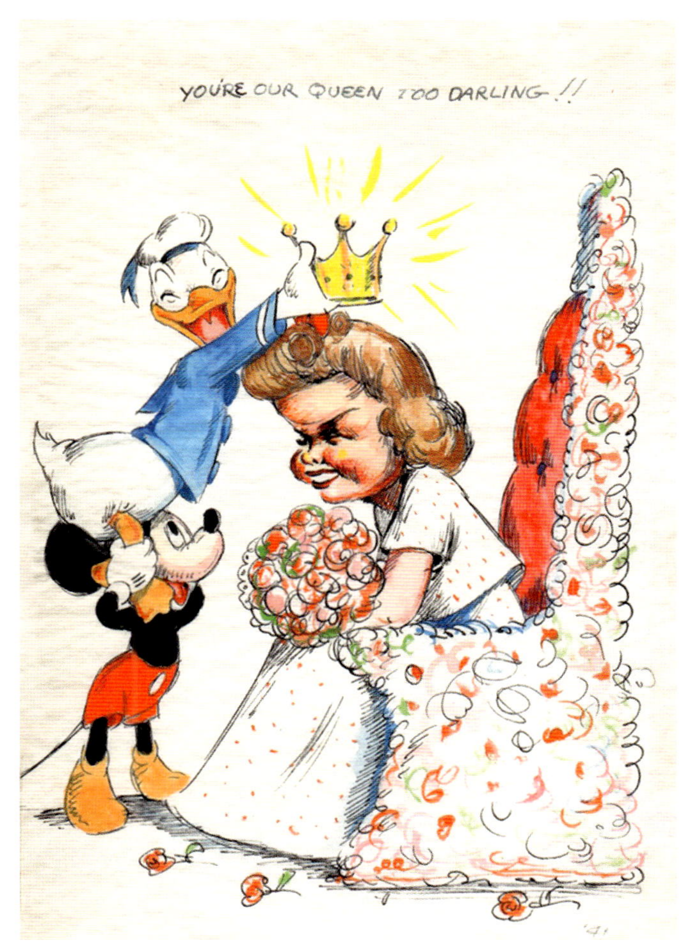

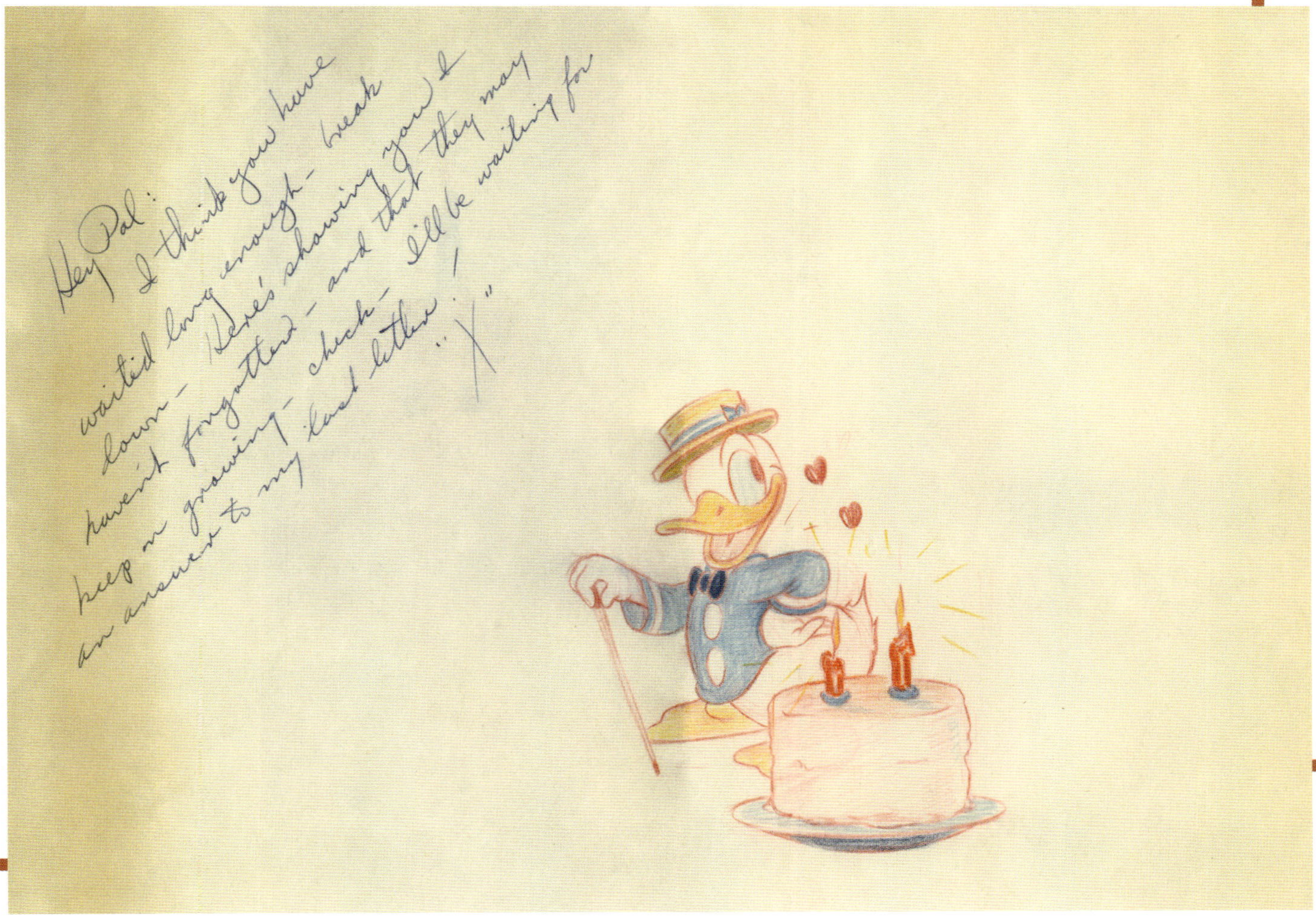

Hey Pal:
I think you have
waited long enough - break
down - Here's showing you I
haven't forgotten - and that they may
keep on growing - check - I'll be waiting for
an answer to my last letter!
"X"

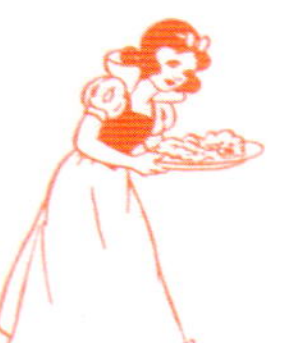

snow white special
Tasty Chicken Salad on Lettuce, with Avocado, Tomato and Egg
40c

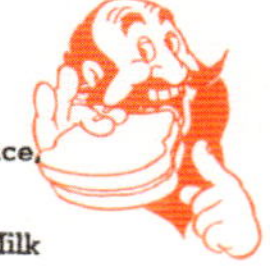

artist's special
Fried Ham with Country Gravy, Apple Sauce, and Special French Fried Potatoes
Rolls and Butter — Coffee or Milk
40c

stromboli's favorite sandwich
Hot Roast Prime Ribs of Beef with Gravy, Mashed Potatoes and Vegetables
35c

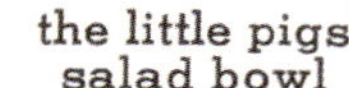

the little pigs' salad bowl
Made with Crisp Lettuce, Romaine Chicory, Watercress, Celery, Garnished with Tomatoes, Egg and Julienne of Ham and Cheese
Your Choice of French, Mayonnaise or 1000 Island Dressing
35c

cocktails and appetizers
Crab, Shrimp or Lobster Cocktail Supreme 35
Chilled Celery 20
Ripe or Green Olives or Burr Gherkins 25
Radishes 10
Green Onions 10
Filet of Marinated Herring 25
Fruit Cocktail Supreme 30
Tomato, Orange, Grapefruit or Pineapple Juice 10

soups
Consomme or Chicken Broth, Cup 10; Bowl 15

salads
Victor's Special Seafood Salad Bowl 45
Mixed Green wih Vegetables 35
Health Salad, Shredded Vegetables with Cottage Cheese 40
Lettuce, Pineapple, Peach, Pear with Cottage Cheese 35
Combination Vegetable Salad 40
Crab, Shrimp or Lobster 50
Mayonnaise, French or 1000 Island Dressing Served with Above Salads

steaks, chops, etc.
New York Cut (20 minutes) 1.25
Filet Mignon (20 minutes) 1.25
Top Sirloin (20 minutes) 90
French Lamb Chop (15 minutes) 65
Pork Chops (15 minutes) 65
English Mutton Chop with Kidney (25 minutes) 90
Calf's Liver with Bacon (15 minutes) 70
Ham or Bacon and Eggs 45
Half a Fried Chicken with Currant Jelly (20 minutes) 90
French Fried or Hashed Brown Potatoes Served with Above Orders

fresh vegetables and potatoes
New Peas 15
Buttered Spinach 15
New String Beans 15
Baby Lima Beans 15
French Fried Potatoes 15
Hashed Brown Potatoes 15

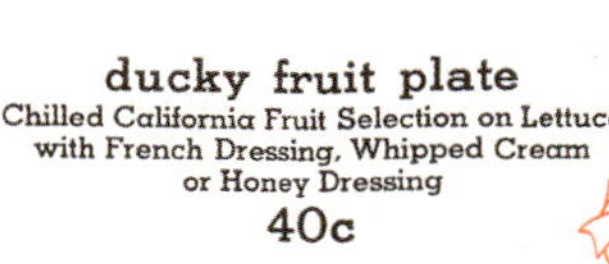

ducky fruit plate
Chilled California Fruit Selection on Lettuce with French Dressing, Whipped Cream or Honey Dressing
40c

minnie's delight
Bubbling Melted Cheese with Poached Egg, Bacon, and Melba Toast
45c

monstro's morsel
Fish Plate (Fried Oysters, Scallops, Shrimp and Sole) Special Fried Potato, Peppy Dressing and Cold Slaw
55c

hot roast turkey sandwich 35c
Served with Mashed Potato and Cranberry Sauce

daily specials
monday 45c
Brisket of Corn Beef with Cabbage and Boiled Potatoes, Pie, Cake, Ice Cream, Sherbet or Pudding

tuesday 45c
Chicken Pot Pie, Family Style, Pie, Cake, Ice Cream, Sherbet or Pudding

wednesday 45c
Spring Lamb Stew in Casserole, with Vegetables
Pie, Cake, Ice Cream, Sherbet or Pudding

thursday 45c
Enchiladas Veracruzana Served with Mexican Sauce and Frijoles, Topped with Melted Cheese
Pie, Cake, Ice Cream, Sherbet or Pudding

friday 45c
Deviled Crab Meat in Shell, with Potatoes and Vegetable, Pie, Cake, Ice Cream, Sherbet or Pudding

Tea, Coffee or Milk, with Above Orders

Minimum Service in Dining Room 25c
VICTOR WILL APPERCIATE SUGGESTIONS TO IMPROVE OUR SERVICE
3% Sales Tax will be added to all Taxable Items

sandwiches
(Served on White, Whole Wheat or Rye)

Deviled Ham 20
Cold Ham 20
Deviled Egg 20
Tuna and Egg 20
Lettuce and Tomato 20
Liver Sausage 20
Mickey Hamburger with Cheese 20
Sardine 20
Peanut Butter and Jelly 20
American or Swiss 20
Imported Swiss 30
Corn Beef, Lamb, Beef or Pork 25
Chicken Salad Sandwich 30

combination sandwiches
CHEF'S SPECIAL: Avocado, Cheese, Tongue, and Lettuce on Toast 40
SPECIAL: Bacon, Tomato, Lettuce and Tongue, Thousand Island Dressing (on Toast) 40
CLUB HOUSE: Chicken, Lettuce, Bacon, Tomato with Mayonnaise on Toast 50
MONTE CRISTO: Chicken, Ham, Swiss Cheese, Dipped in Egg, Fried in Butter 50

desserts and cheese
Choice of Pie 10; with Cheese or a la Mode 15

Layer Cake	10	Choice of Sundae	15
Pastry	10	Choice of Parfait	20
Coffee Cake	10	Doughnuts, each	05
Ice Cream or Sherbet	10	Pound Cake	10
Jell-O	10	Roquefort Cheese	25
Cup Custard	10	Camembert	25
Baked Apple	10	Imported Swiss	25
with Cream	15	American Swiss	15
Fresh Fruit Compote	15	Martin New York	20

beverages

Coffee	05	Chocolate 10; Pot	15
Tea	10	Postum 10; Pot	15
Milk	10	Ovaltine 10; Pot	15
Half and Half	25	Iced Coffee or Tea	10
Buttermilk	05		
Heineken	35	Eastside	15
Budweiser	20	Rainier	15
Schlitz	20	Canada Dry Water	20
Miller's High Life	20	White Rock, pts.	20
Pabst Blue Ribbon	20	Canada Dry Ginger Ale	20
Acme	15		

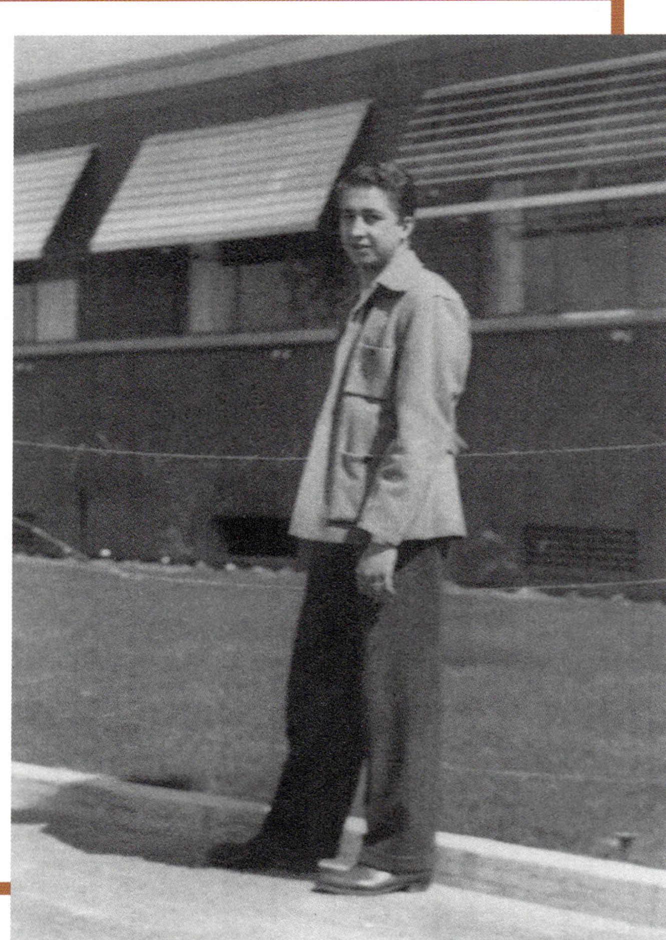

When the strike ended and Disney agreed to sign the Screen Cartoon Guild contract, X was asked to come back to work, an offer that didn't extend to every employee. Unfortunately, he was forced to turn down Disney's offer, as he had just been drafted. That's because, twelve days after X's twenty-first birthday, the United States had instituted the Selective Training and Service Act of 1940 (the country's first-ever peacetime draft) in response to France swiftly capitulating to Nazi Germany as World War II raged and growing concerns that Great Britain alone would not be able to defend itself against Germany and its Axis allies.

Aware of the news—overseas in Europe, Africa, and Asia—X had long feared it would only be a matter of time before he was required to serve, even though the United States had yet to enter the war. X had

TOP: A Disney commissary menu from the early 1940s that X held on to for more than sixty years; LEFT: X in his early days with Disney at the studio in Burbank; OPPOSITE: X's 1941 communication from the Screen Cartoon Guild.

Screen Cartoon Guild 1441 North McCadden Place.

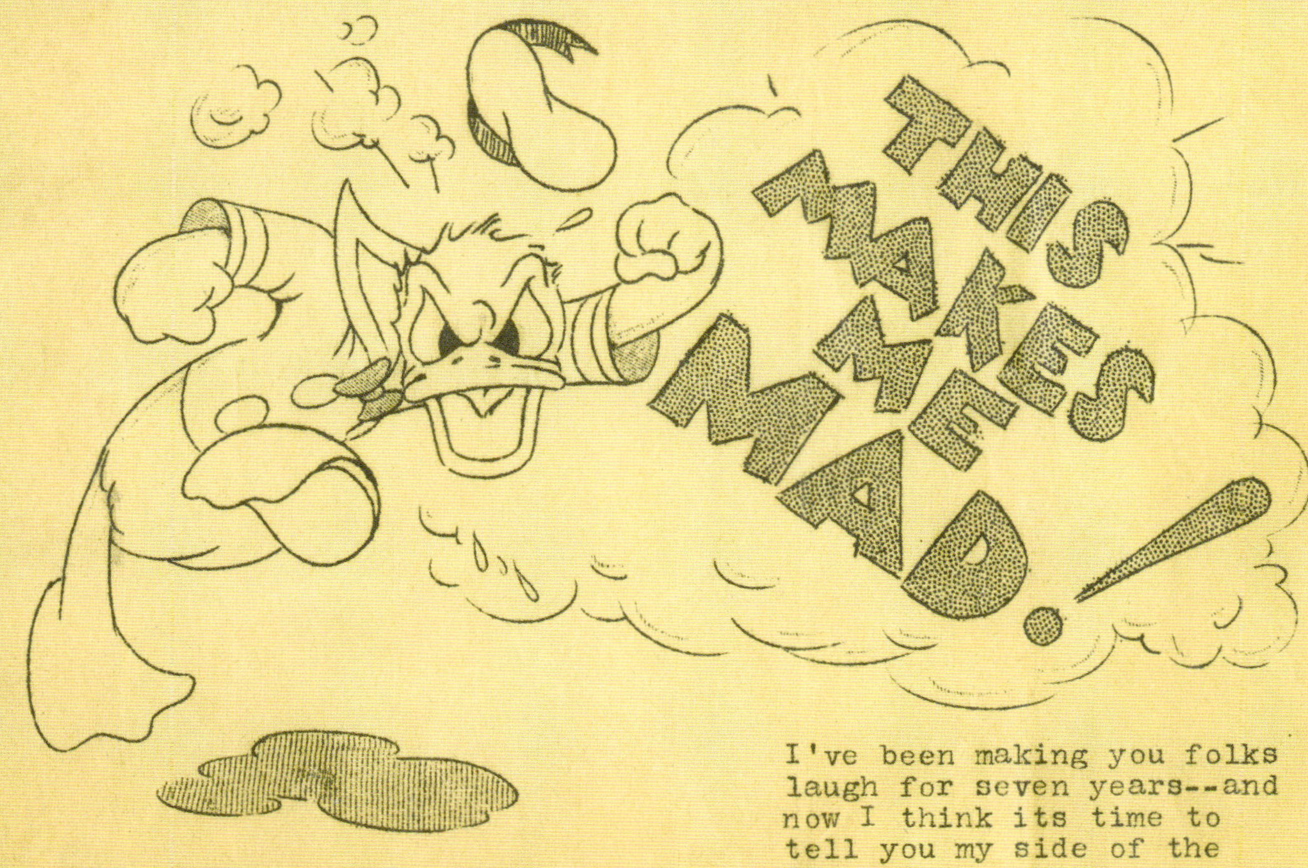

I've been making you folks laugh for seven years--and now I think its time to tell you my side of the story.

DO YOU KNOW THAT:

The fellows and girls who draw me make less than house painters.

The girls are the lowest paid in the entire cartoon industry (They earn from $16. to $20. a week.

And dont forget that these kids are the ones who make me move and write my lines.

On SNOW WHITE the muchly-publicized bonuses didn't even compensate them for the two years of overtime they worked. (Snow White grossed more than $10,000,000.00)

On PINNOCHIO ditto

On FANTASIA ditto

These kids are as proud of their product and their profession as Walt.

All they want is a living wage and the right to have a voice in determining their own futures.

The studio however, has refused to either recognize or even to talk to them.

The Studio <u>IS NOT</u> a defense industry.

ALL THEY WANT IS FOR YOU FOLKS TO UNDERSTAND THEIR SIDE OF THE CASE

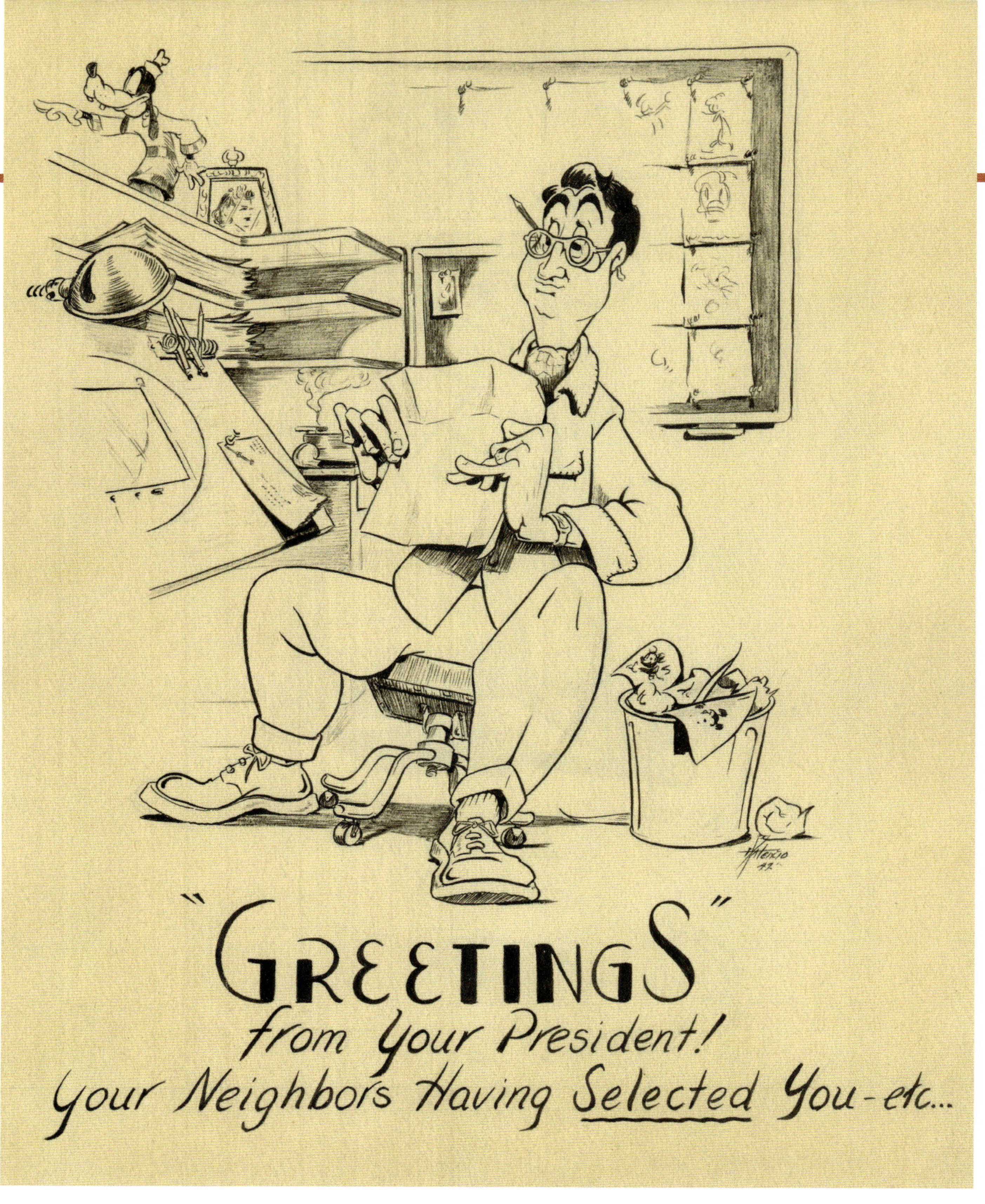

already seen the first crack in the Woolie Unit when his colleague Gerald James enlisted in December 1940 with the British Commonwealth forces. Nine months later, X followed in Gerald's footsteps, and correspondingly his official Disney resignation was dated September 15, 1941. He was an assistant animator when he left.

Even harder than saying goodbye to Disney and his friends and colleagues, many of whom would also end up leaving to serve in the war (which America officially entered before the end of 1941), was saying goodbye to Mary. While their relationship had been long distance, save for the occasional visit on X's trips home to see his family, their mutual dedication, Disney-infused letters, and affections had allowed their love to blossom. However, X's "letter from Uncle Sam," as he liked to call it, put any plans for a future with Mary indefinitely on hold.

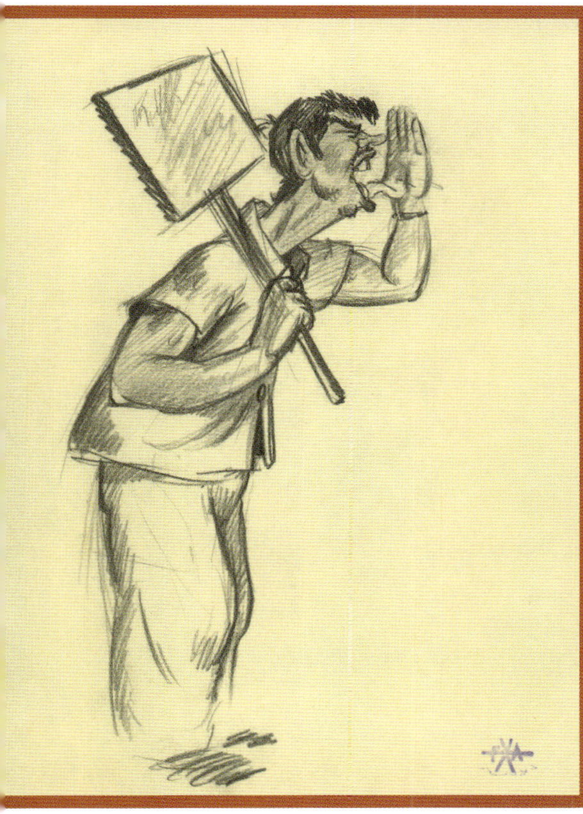

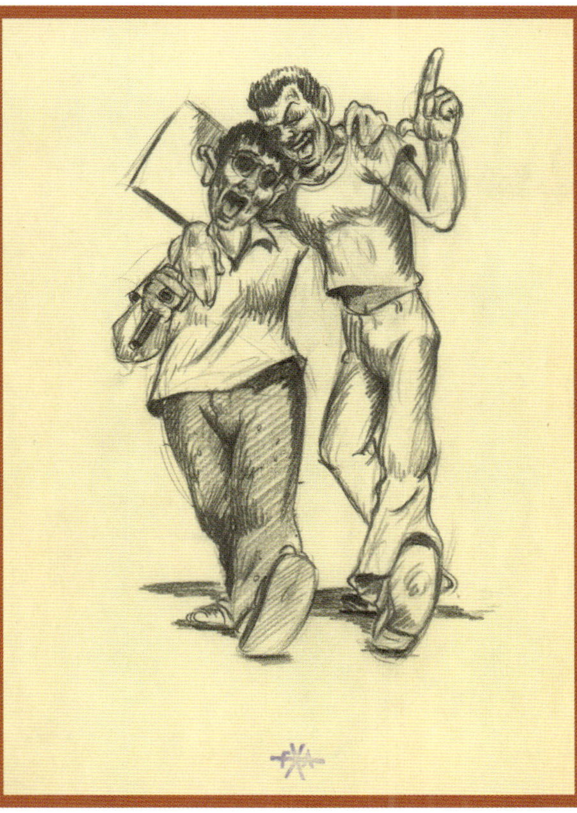

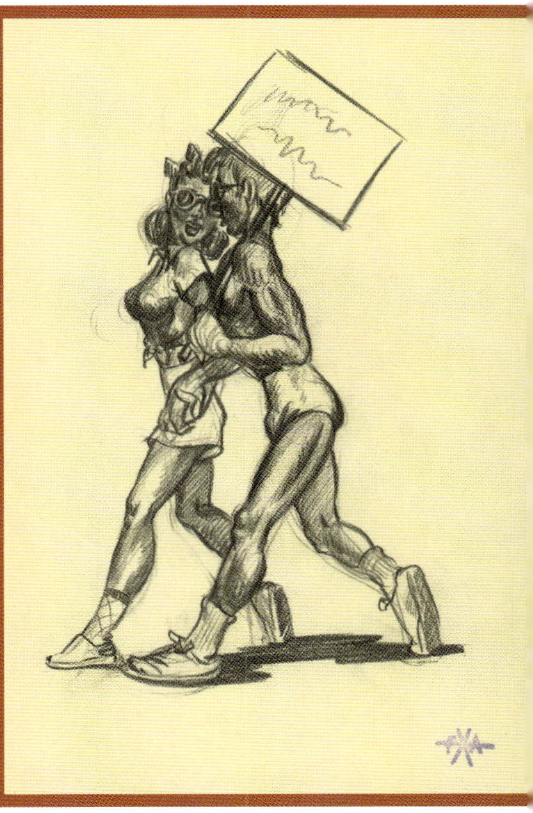

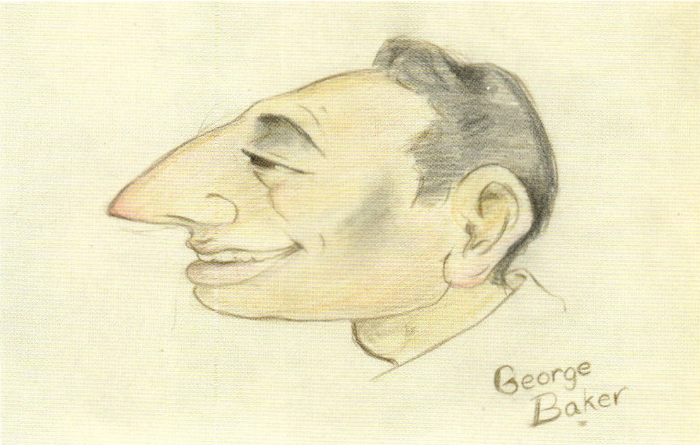

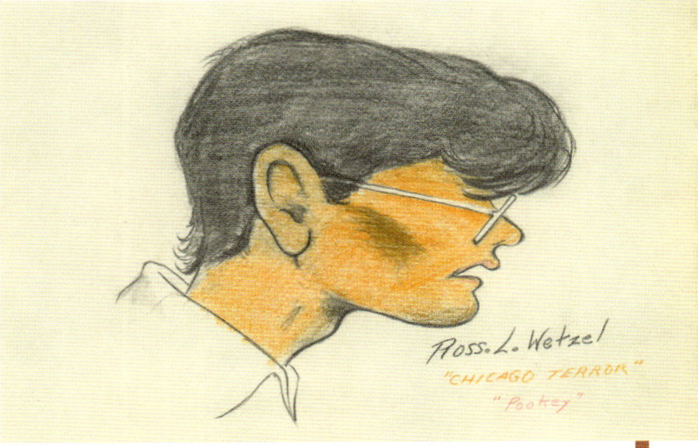

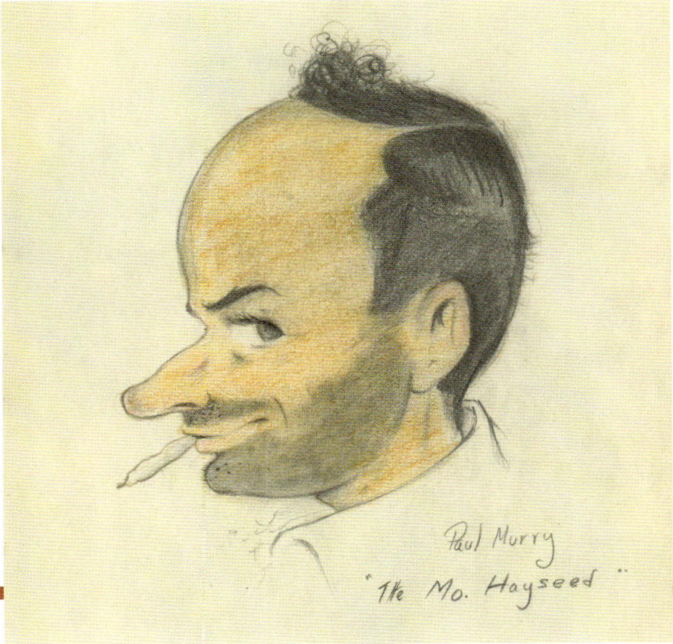

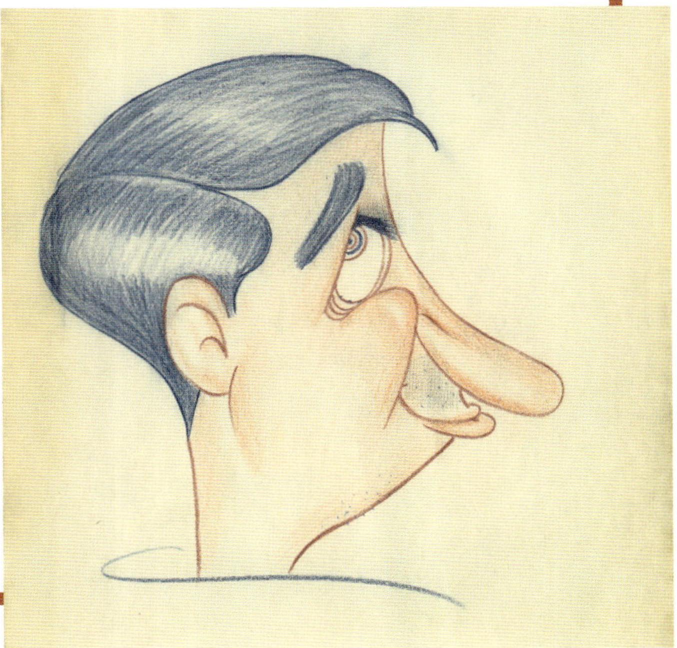

OPPOSITE: A drawing from X's sketchbook in 1941, showing his disappointment with having to leave Disney due to the draft; TOP: X's drawings of picketers during the 1941 animators strike; MIDDLE AND BOTTOM: Caricatures X did of himself and some of his friends from his early days at the studio.

3

The War Years

IN SEPTEMBER 1941, X LEFT HIS LIFE IN Los Angeles behind and shipped off to the faraway land of Fort Monmouth, New Jersey, for what he believed would be one year of military service. X was officially stationed at Fort Monmouth's Training Film Production Laboratory, where he was assigned to serve after having been drafted into the Signal Corps, a department under the motion picture group that made films for the U.S. Army. (Fort Monmouth is now owned by Netflix and is in the process of being turned into a large film and television production facility.) While the films were mainly for military training and recruitment purposes, the army had specifically assigned personnel to this unit from different studios, ensuring that their films were being made by people with experience in entertainment.

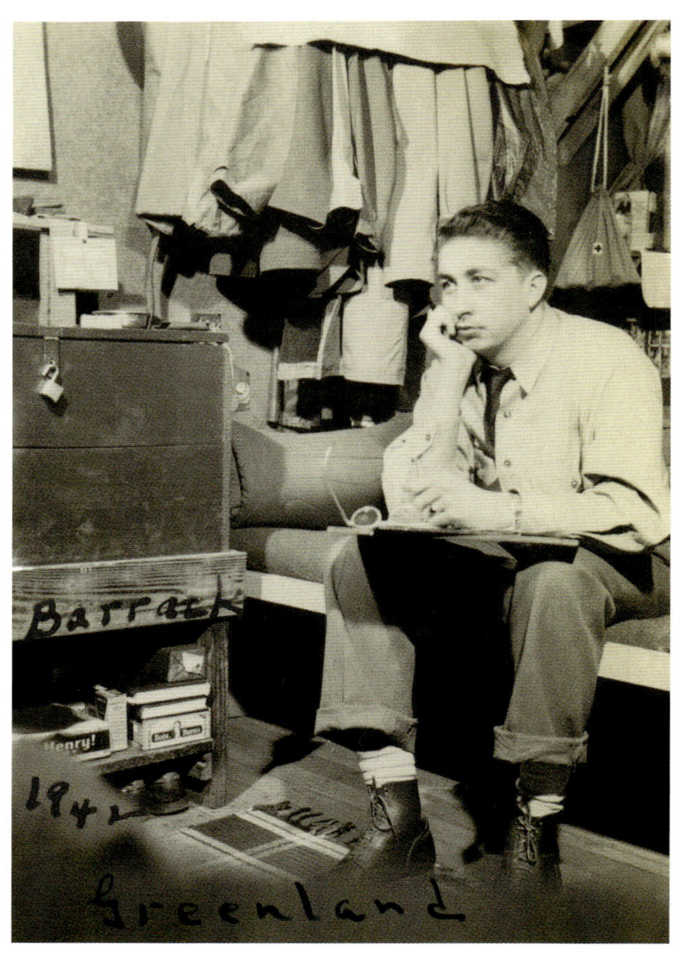

Although no longer a Disney employee, X still had Mickey and friends as a part of his life and art. On October 23, 1941, Walt sent twenty enlisted men who were stationed at Fort Monmouth—nineteen of whom were former Disney Studios animation

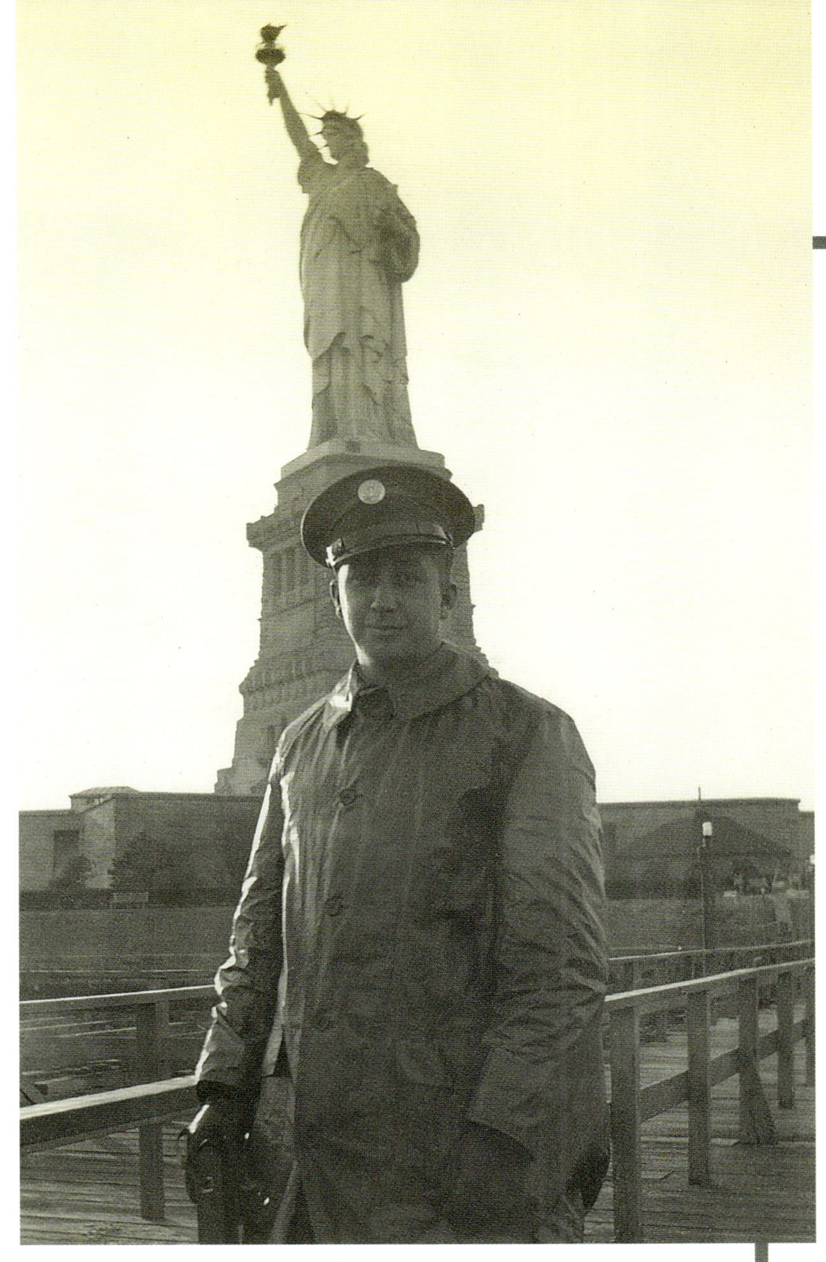

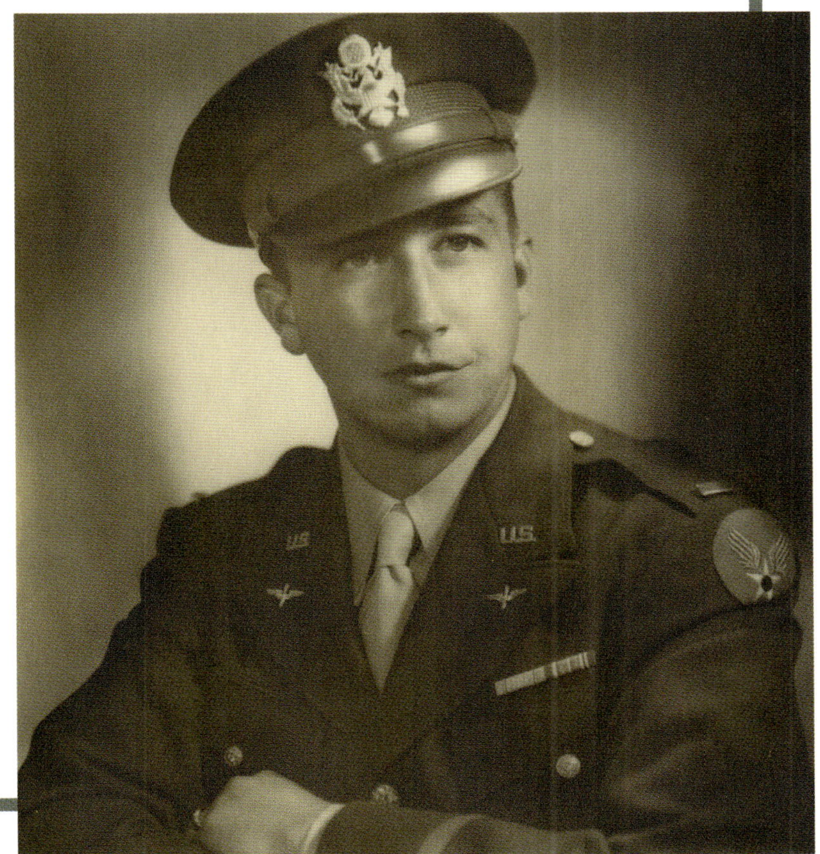

OPPOSITE: X in his barracks in Greenland in 1942; ABOVE (TOP): X in New York City at the Statue of Liberty in 1941; ABOVE (BOTTOM): X's portrait from New York City in 1941.

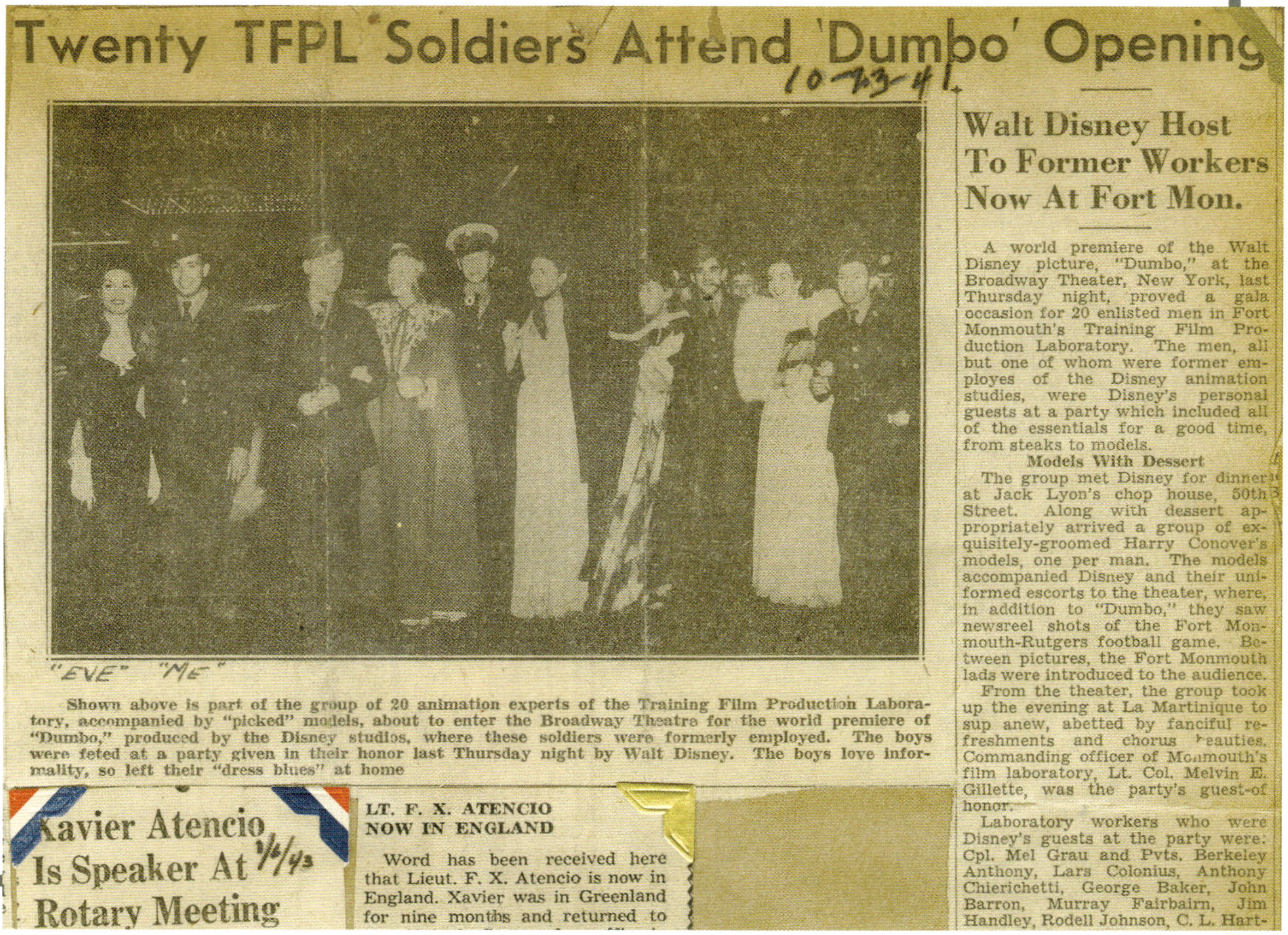

Twenty TFPL Soldiers Attend 'Dumbo' Opening

10-23-41

"EVE" "ME"

Shown above is part of the group of 20 animation experts of the Training Film Production Laboratory, accompanied by "picked" models, about to enter the Broadway Theatre for the world premiere of "Dumbo," produced by the Disney studios, where these soldiers were formerly employed. The boys were feted at a party given in their honor last Thursday night by Walt Disney. The boys love informality, so left their "dress blues" at home

Walt Disney Host To Former Workers Now At Fort Mon.

A world premiere of the Walt Disney picture, "Dumbo," at the Broadway Theater, New York, last Thursday night, proved a gala occasion for 20 enlisted men in Fort Monmouth's Training Film Production Laboratory. The men, all but one of whom were former employes of the Disney animation studies, were Disney's personal guests at a party which included all of the essentials for a good time, from steaks to models.

Models With Dessert

The group met Disney for dinner at Jack Lyon's chop house, 50th Street. Along with dessert appropriately arrived a group of exquisitely-groomed Harry Conover's models, one per man. The models accompanied Disney and their uniformed escorts to the theater, where, in addition to "Dumbo," they saw newsreel shots of the Fort Monmouth-Rutgers football game. Between pictures, the Fort Monmouth lads were introduced to the audience.

From the theater, the group took up the evening at La Martinique to sup anew, abetted by fanciful refreshments and chorus beauties. Commanding officer of Monmouth's film laboratory, Lt. Col. Melvin E. Gillette, was the party's guest-of honor.

Laboratory workers who were Disney's guests at the party were: Cpl. Mel Grau and Pvts. Berkeley Anthony, Lars Colonius, Anthony Chierichetti, George Baker, John Barron, Murray Fairbairn, Jim Handley, Rodell Johnson, C. L. Hart-

Xavier Atencio Is Speaker At Rotary Meeting

3/6/43

LT. F. X. ATENCIO NOW IN ENGLAND

Word has been received here that Lieut. F. X. Atencio is now in England. Xavier was in Greenland for nine months and returned to

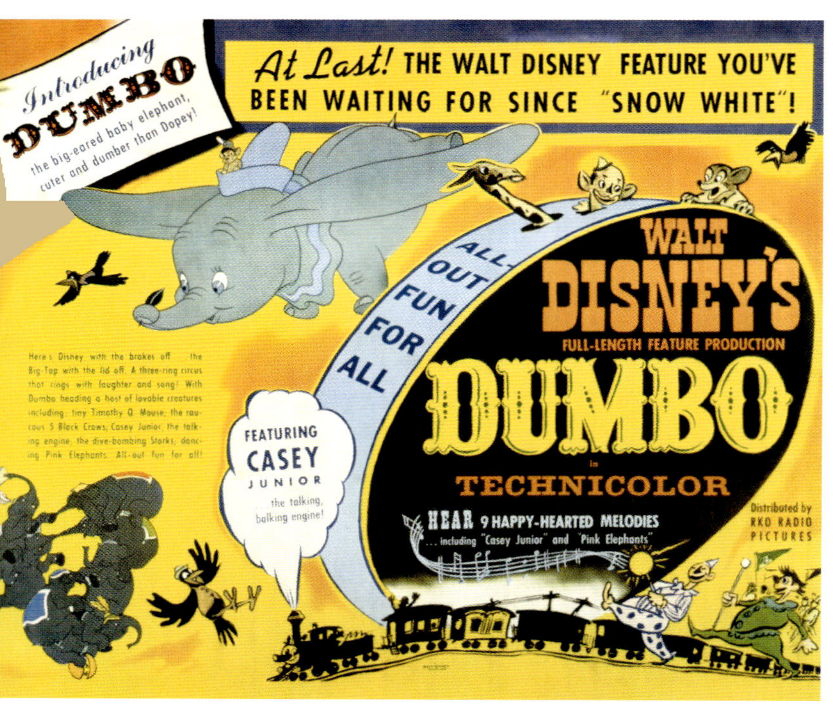

employees—to the New York City world premiere of *Dumbo* at the Broadway Theatre. Treating them to a special evening off as Walt's personal guests, the men, dressed in their uniforms, went with their commander on a chartered bus to New York City, where they had dinner at the Jack Lyons Chop House across from Radio City Music Hall. The guests were treated to steaks, scotch and sodas, and dessert, all on the house ("of Mouse," aka Walt). Harry Conover models had arrived for the evening to accompany the soldiers as their dates to the premiere. X was paired with Eve Whitney, a model who had repeatedly appeared in *Life* magazine. As was common practice at the time, newsreel shorts were shown before the main feature, though instead of the usual army recruitment and patriotic shorts that played, these newsreel shots were from the Fort Monmouth–Rutgers football

ABOVE: A 1941 newspaper clipping showing X (SECOND FROM LEFT) photographed at the *Dumbo* premiere in New York City; LEFT: Original *Dumbo* movie poster; OPPOSITE (TOP): X's 1941 drawing after the bombing of Pearl Harbor; BOTTOM: X with his U.S. Army Signal Corps sign featuring Donald Duck.

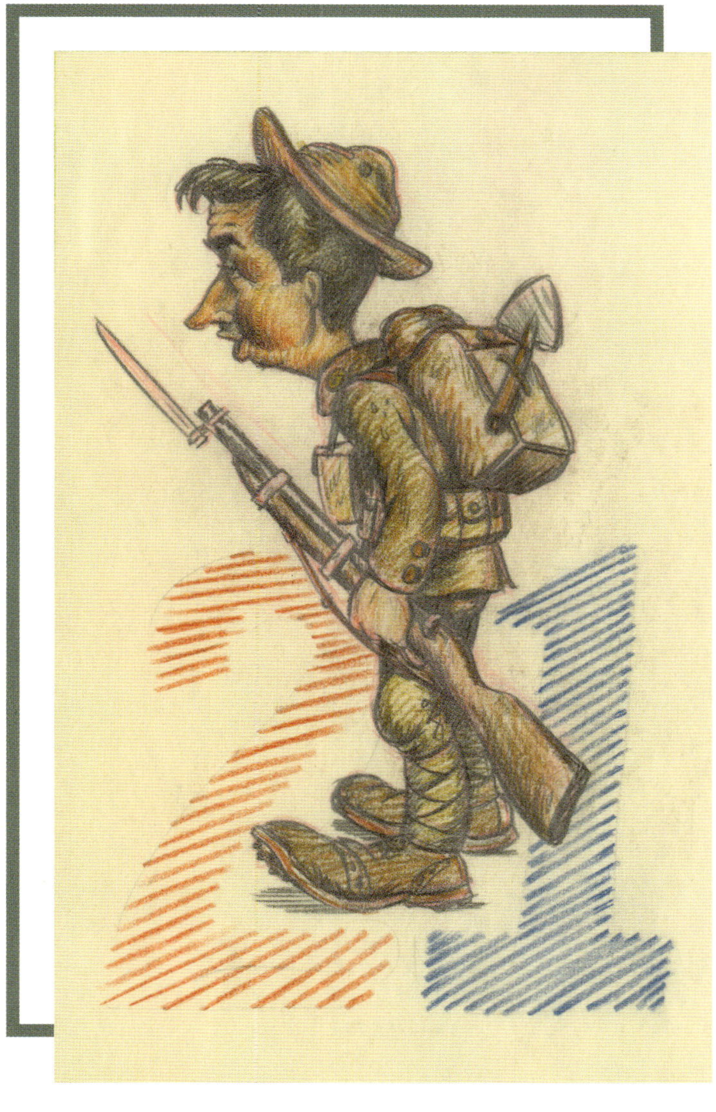

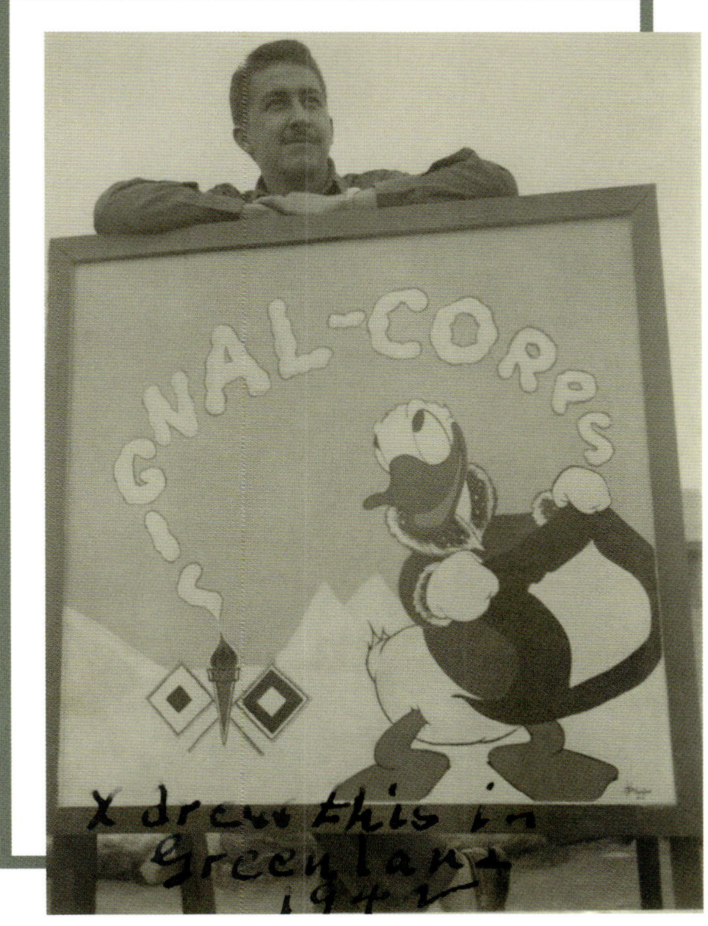

game. Between the reels, the soldiers, including X, were introduced to the audience, and then they all settled in for the first public unveiling of *Dumbo*.

After the film, the group went to La Martinique, a popular nightclub in the 1940s, located in a basement of a structure at 57 West Fifty-Seventh Street, for more refreshments. In addition to providing an uplift in morale during a comparatively lower stakes period of the U.S. draft, the evening also served to remind these men about the joys and power Disney offered and wielded, respectively. Keeping up with X's career and activities the Walsenburg newspaper reported on the evening's fun and fanfare, while also astutely commenting on the subliminal reasoning for the evening's activities: "Any one [sic] with half a mind could see that Disney is just being nice to those boys so they will come back and work for him after the duration and not stay in the army."

Walt's intention to remind the enlisted men of the magic, joy, and comradery of Disney worked. Throughout his time in Fort Monmouth, X had enough downtime to keep honing his artwork. Always one to draw what he knew, X sketched himself, his fellow soldiers, and illustrated brochures and menu covers for his unit. In addition to the military influence in his artwork, his foundational Disney drawings of Mickey and his cartoon friends remained present in his art at this time, as evidenced by the signage X designed for the military base and his 1941 Christmas cards, which included Mickey and Donald looking a little more serious than usual and wearing their own army hats.

It's worth noting that throughout his life, X's artwork usually had such a vibrant essence, with upbeat characters and drawings whose joy often radiated off the page. In keeping with his true-to-life and emotive drawings, it is only during his war years where X's art felt a little more somber, reflecting both the gravity of the times and his own palpable disappointment in the war's impact on his life and career.

Outside of his Disney premiere experience, drawing practices, and daily Signal Corps work, X spent this time trying to be reassigned to cryptography training so that he could move to an army base located in Missouri, putting him a little closer to his family and Mary in Colorado. X had returned to Colorado for brief visits with Mary and his family before heading to New Jersey, but he soon wanted to transition to a base closer in the hopes of being able to get away for weekend visits. However, any efforts

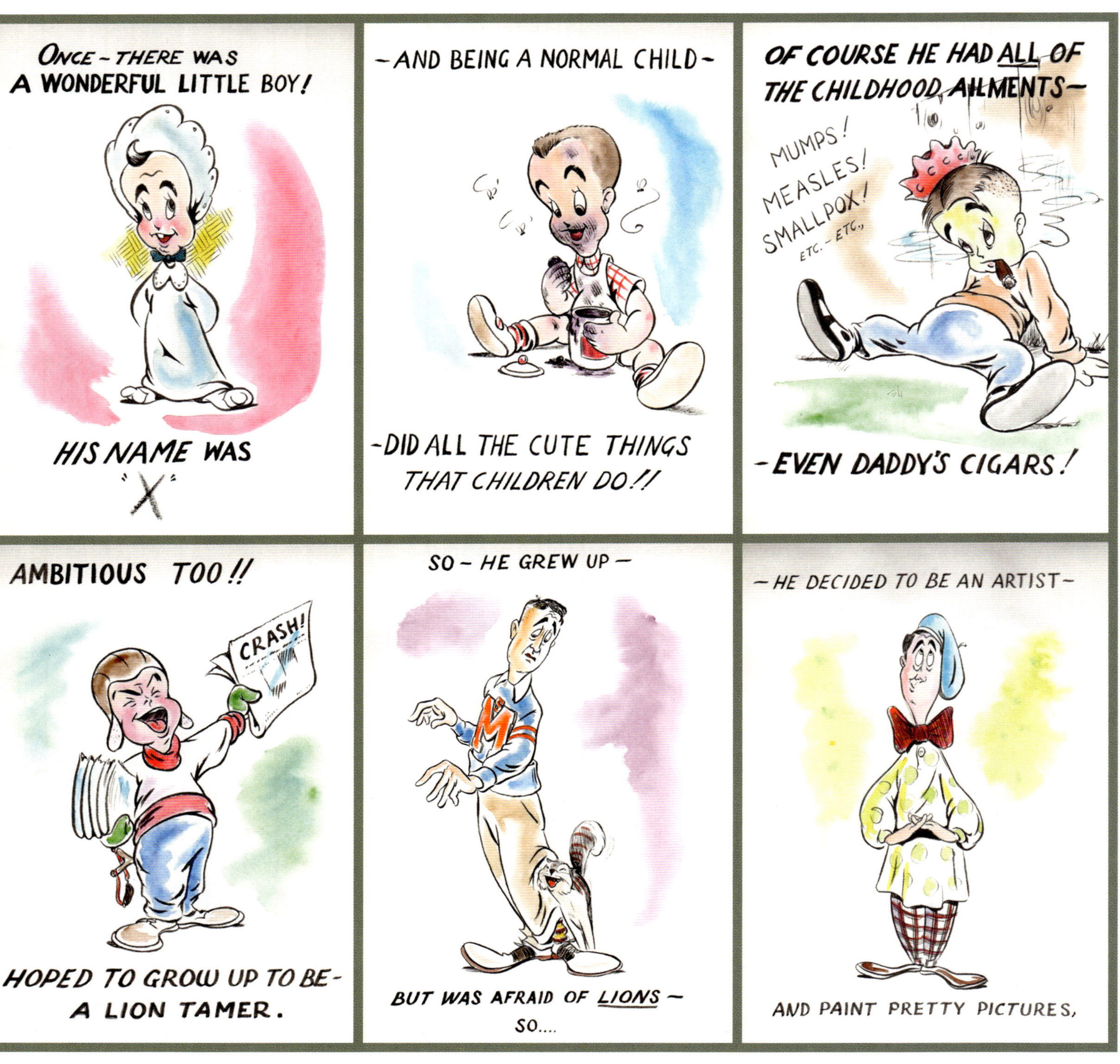

ABOVE AND OPPOSITE: X's illustrated life story, painted while he was stationed in Greenland.

to move to the middle of the country were dashed on December 7, 1941, when the Japanese attacked Pearl Harbor, and the United States responded by declaring war on Japan. On December 11, Germany and Italy declared war on the United States, and America responded by counter-declaring war on Germany and Italy, officially and fully entering World War II, crushing many drafted and enlisted men's hopes of being home within the year by extending draft terms indefinitely.

After five months at Fort Monmouth, X finally received some "welcome" news—to an extent. He was being sent to cryptography school! However, this new assignment put him more than a thousand miles farther away from Colorado than New Jersey was, on the icy, isolated island of Greenland.

Corporal X Atencio arrived in Greenland on February 26, 1942. Even before entering the war, the United States had, as a neutral party, taken over Greenland in 1940 after Denmark, which had con-

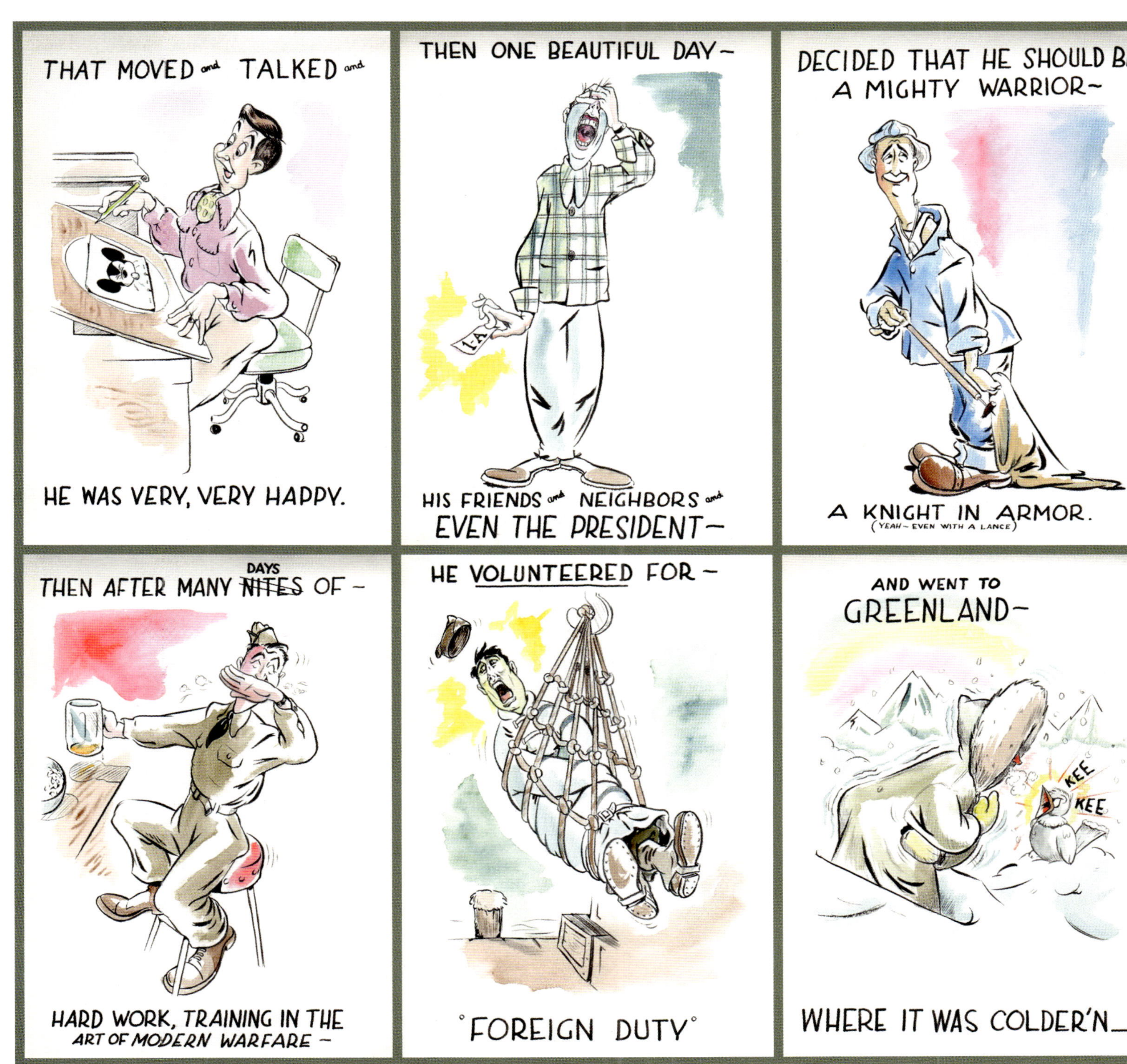

trolled the territory, had fallen to Germany. Upon arrival in Greenland, X was sent to his new base, Bluie West One, one of the code-named U.S. established bases; another was, not surprisingly, code-named Bluie East One. The influx of thousands of U.S. soldiers before and during the war was the most exciting thing that had happened in Greenland in quite a while, given that the locale's population was under twenty thousand. And although he was "at war," X found his ten months in Greenland to be less than riveting. Often, he and his fellow soldiers were so bored that to pass the time, the other men encouraged X to sketch them. X wrote home to his parents, telling them that he was "entertaining many of his buddies with his original army-life drawings." X recounted one experience in which the sergeants wanted him to do a drawing of them. He set to work but stopped when he realized it was his turn to go on guard duty. The sergeants told X to wait, called over the next corporal, and, when he arrived, ordered him to serve

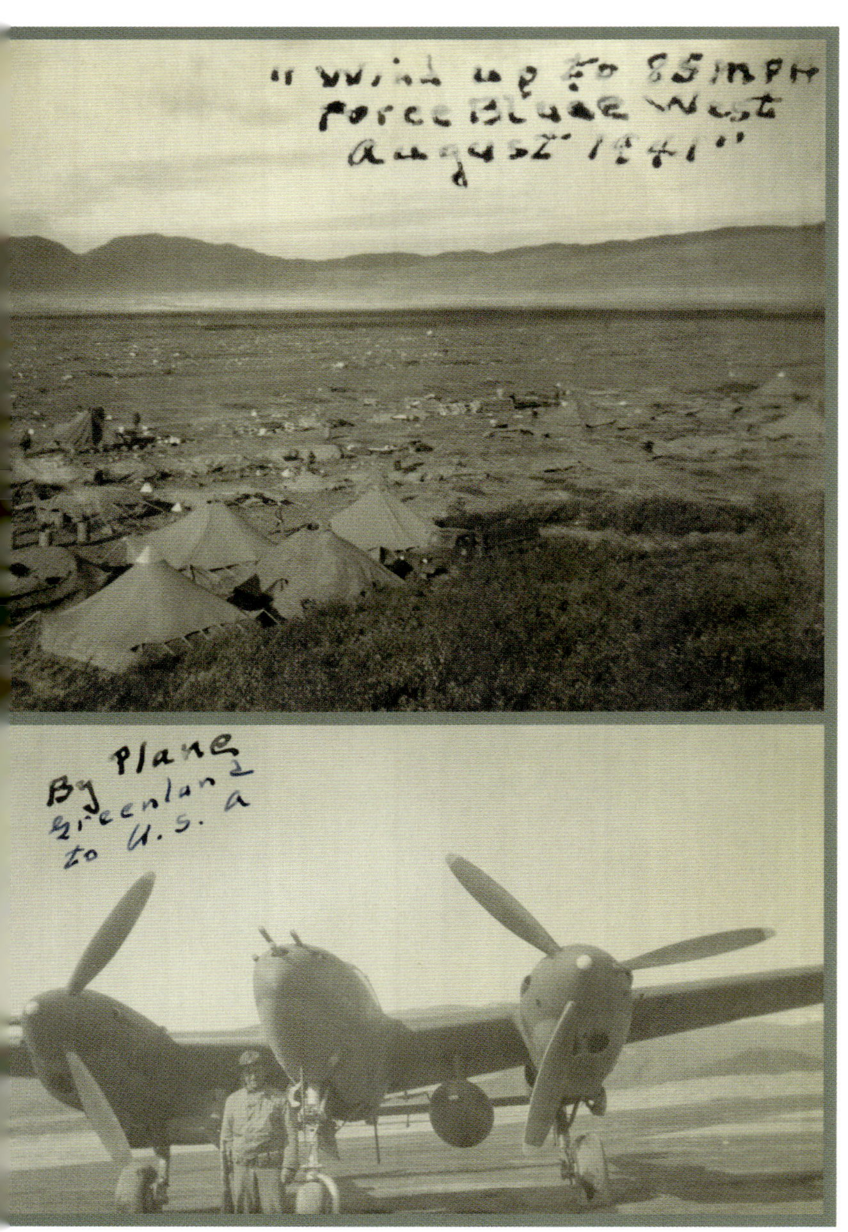

guard duty in X's place, thus allowing X to finish his illustrations. When X wasn't drawing his compatriots, he was illustrating his own life story, in a series of drawings, depicted through simple captions that leave no room for confusion or misinterpretation: he clearly had been happy with his life's trajectory until he found himself in the war, and especially since he found himself trapped in frigid Greenland.

X's older brother, Pete Jr., was also in the army, first in the San Francisco Coast Artillery, before moving over to the Air Corps. Now a navigator, Pete sent X pictures of himself in his flying suit announcing he had been moved to Officer Candidate School in Miami. The warmth of a tropical Florida beach was much more appealing than the frozen tundra of Greenland, so X followed suit and applied to the Air Corps. Once accepted, X was finally out of Greenland and on his way to Miami Beach, for training. Back on U.S. soil, X excelled in and completed his training, earning his gold bars.

His first official commission with the Air Corps was in England, but before being shipped off, he briefly returned home to visit his family. It was the Fourth of July weekend, and on the evening of July 3, 1943, X took Mary out to the Trocadero Ballroom at Elitch Gardens park in Denver; the big band and dancing venue was the spot where the younger residents flocked to escape, albeit briefly, from their troubles and worries. However, on that evening, X and Mary weren't dancing. Instead, X proposed to Mary, and

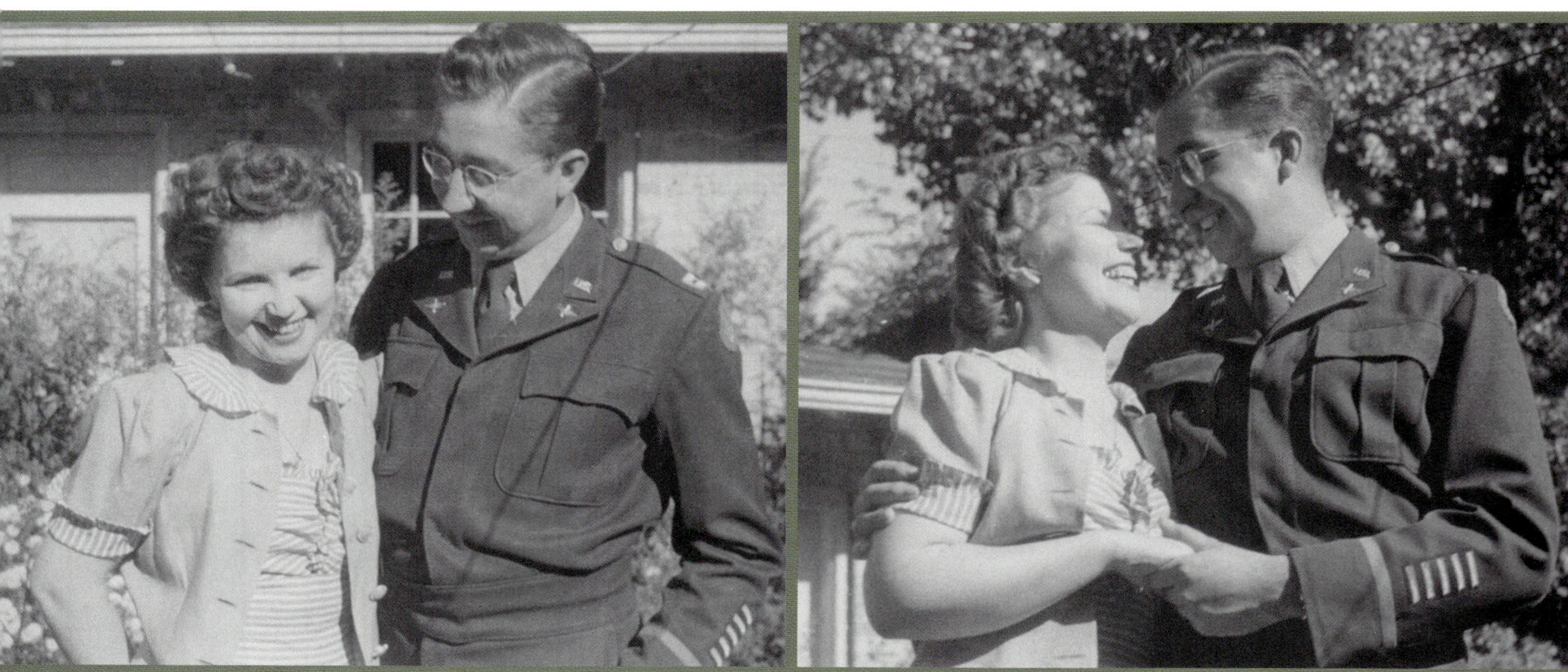

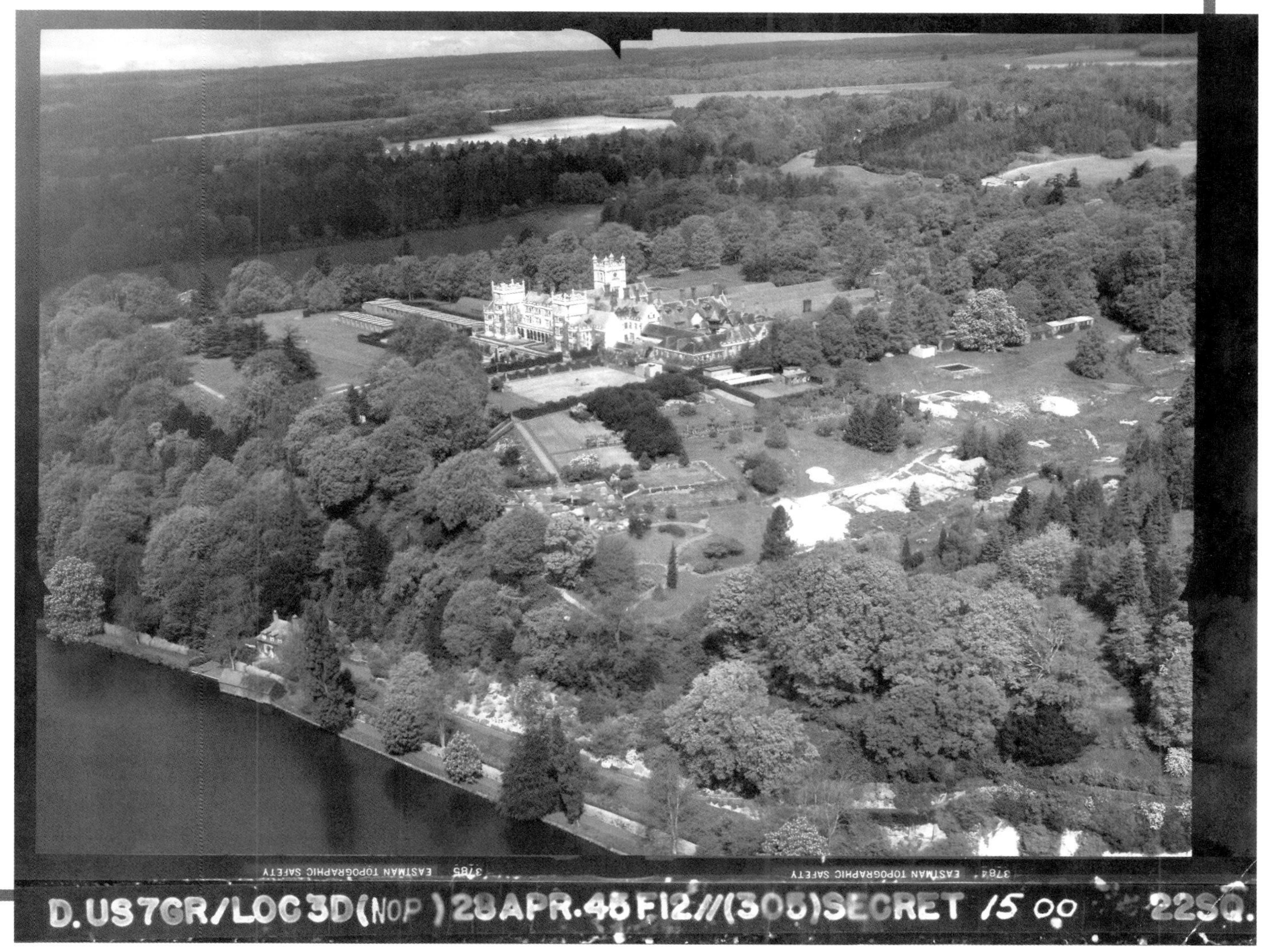

Mary said yes. Like many couples of that era, their engagement was met with joy, but also trepidation, as they didn't know how long X would be away or even if X would ever return home. Apart for so long, X described their engagement, as well as much of their dating relationship, as a "courtship by U.S. mail."

Upon arriving in the United Kingdom, X was stationed thirty-five miles west of London at Danesfield House, a requisitioned country house. It was renamed RAF Medmenham, the home and working military base for the Royal Air Force unit responsible for interpreting aerial photography, a group that ultimately analyzed tens of millions of aerial photos taken during the war. Danesfield House was a nontraditional choice to house Britain's top secret photo-intelligence unit. Its white stone exterior, red-tiled roof, and distinct chimneys made it actually stand out, as if it didn't already residing isolated and atop the highland landscape! These were not exactly the most deceptive ways one would think to keep such a vital place safe, hidden, and free from enemy attack. And yet, on the upside, it was a large house without leaks that had workable plumbing and central heating. While many of the locals found it outlandish, nicknaming the house "The Wedding Cake," British Prime Minister Winston Churchill had a fondness for it, instead coining it with the less pithy moniker, the "Chalk House with the Tudor Chimneys." Regardless of the derisive comments, Churchill had enough faith in the house to allow his daughter Sarah Oliver to also be stationed at Medmenham.

X was first assigned to Medmenham Airfield

OPPOSITE (TOP AND MIDDLE): X's photos from his time in Greenland; OPPOSITE (BOTTOM): X and Mary's engagement in 1943; ABOVE: Aerial photo of RAF Medmenham.

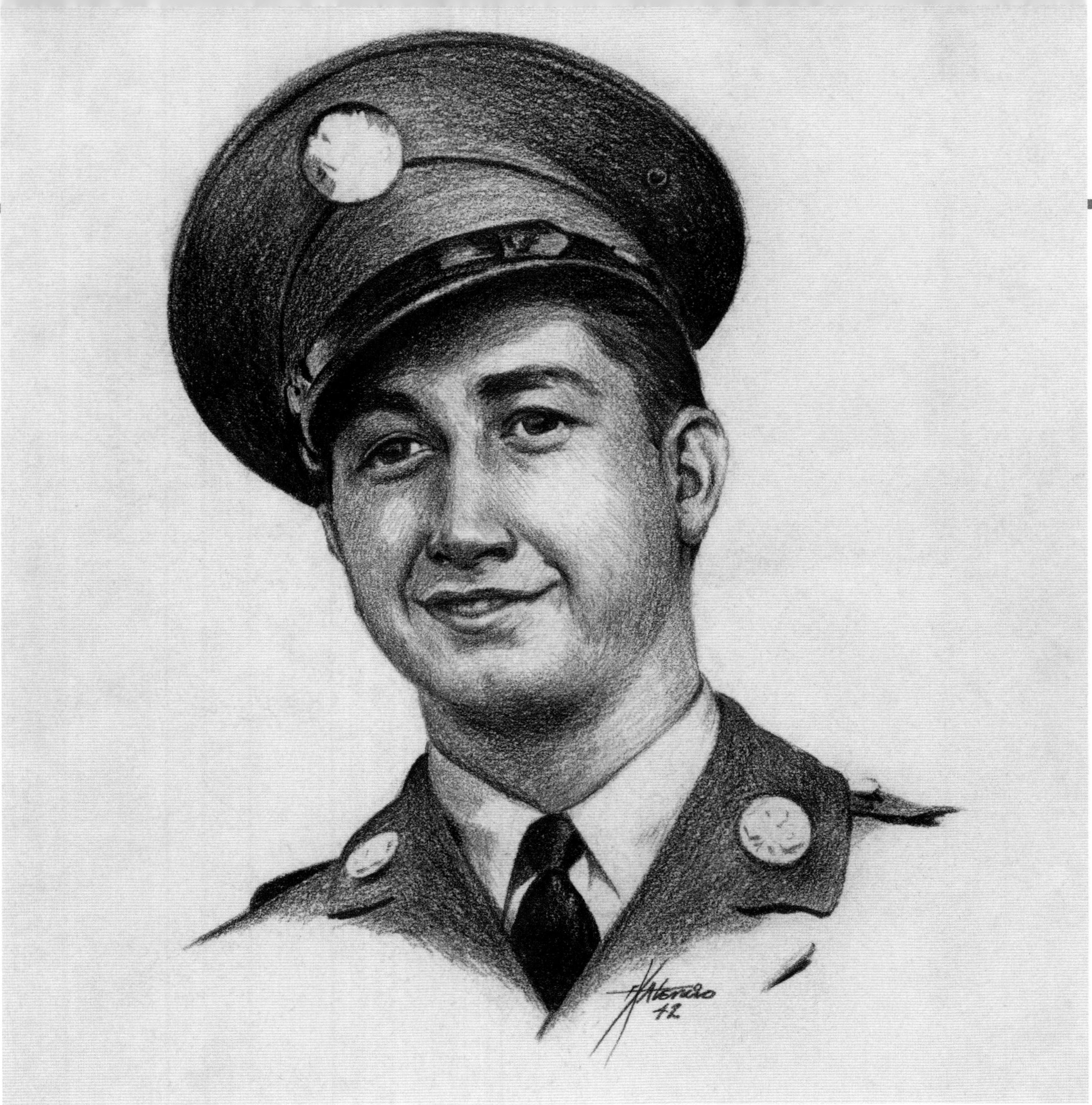

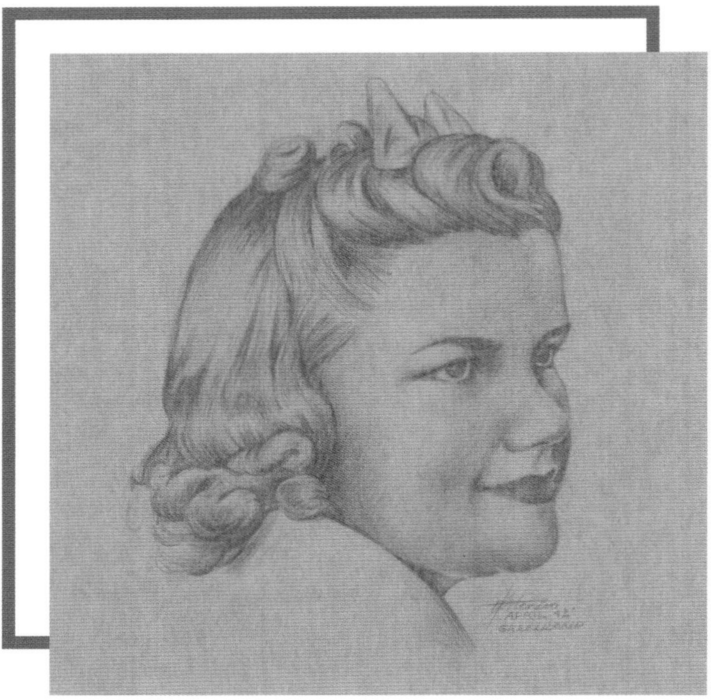

Section C in August 1943. At this point in the war, the Third Reich was attempting to remain in control after their catastrophic February defeat on the Eastern Front at the Battle of Stalingrad in Russia, Germany's first major loss in the war, at least on the Continent. German troops had also flooded into Italy around this time to take over their former ally's defenses after the Allied forces' victory in North Africa, which was followed by the launch of the invasion of Italy and Italy's technical surrender soon after. Meanwhile, British, Australian, and Indian forces continued to fight the Japanese in Burma (now known as Myanmar), while American forces battled to wrest control back from them in the Pacific; China was attempting to stem the Japanese offensive in their country; war continued to rage in the Atlantic; and German concentration

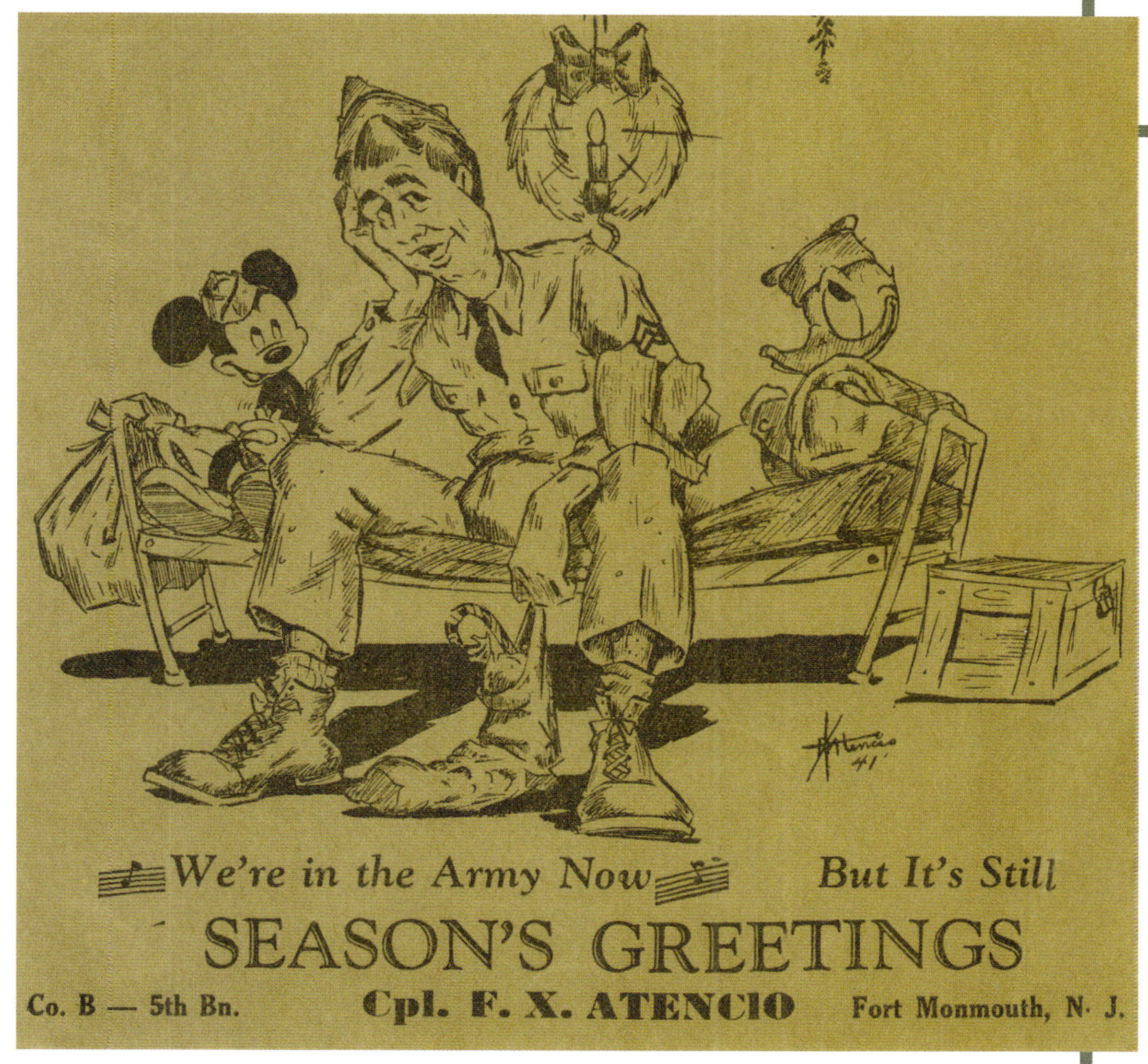

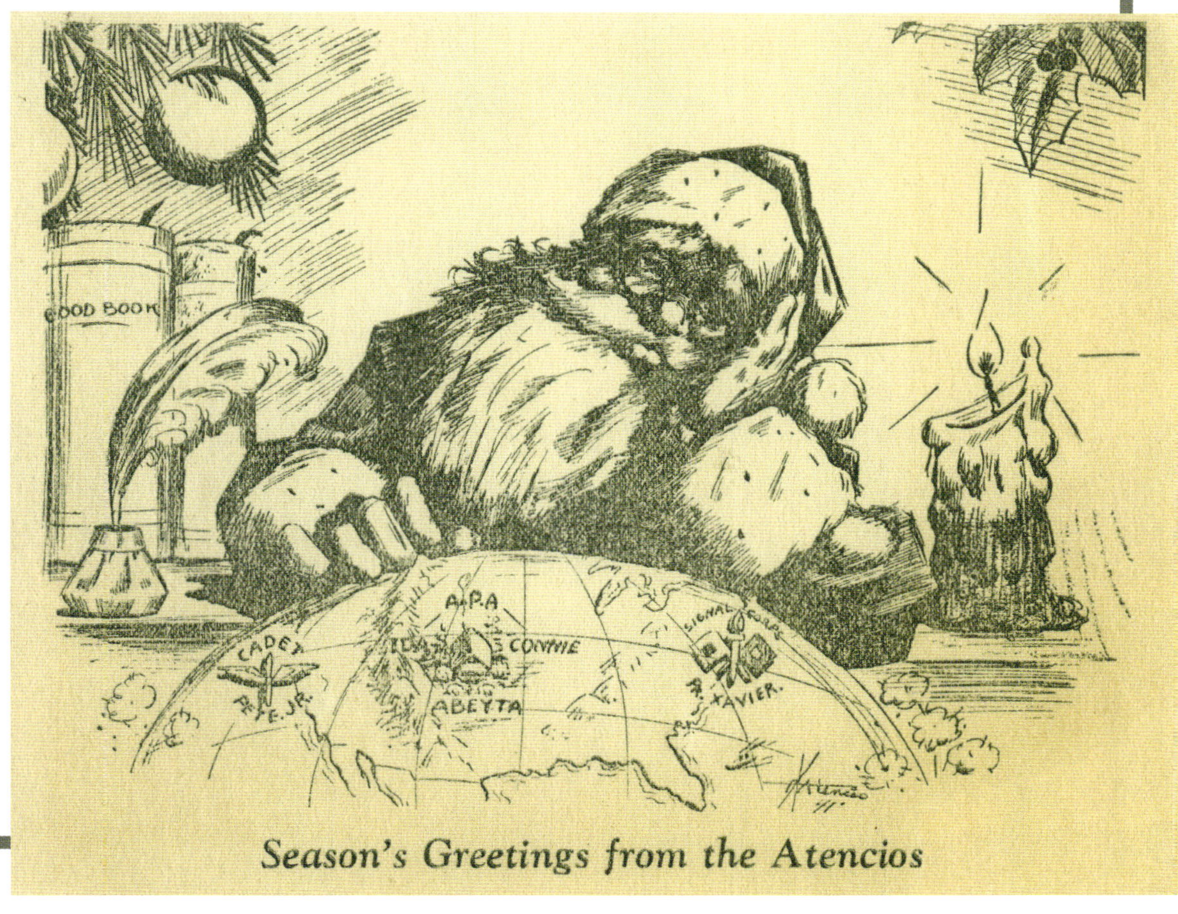

OPPOSITE (TOP): X's self-portrait, drawn while he was stationed in Greenland; OPPOSITE (BOTTOM): X's 1942 drawing of Mary, which he drew on the back of his sketchbook while stationed in Greenland; ABOVE (TOP): X's Christmas card from 1941; ABOVE (BOTTOM): The Atencio family Christmas card, which X drew in 1941.

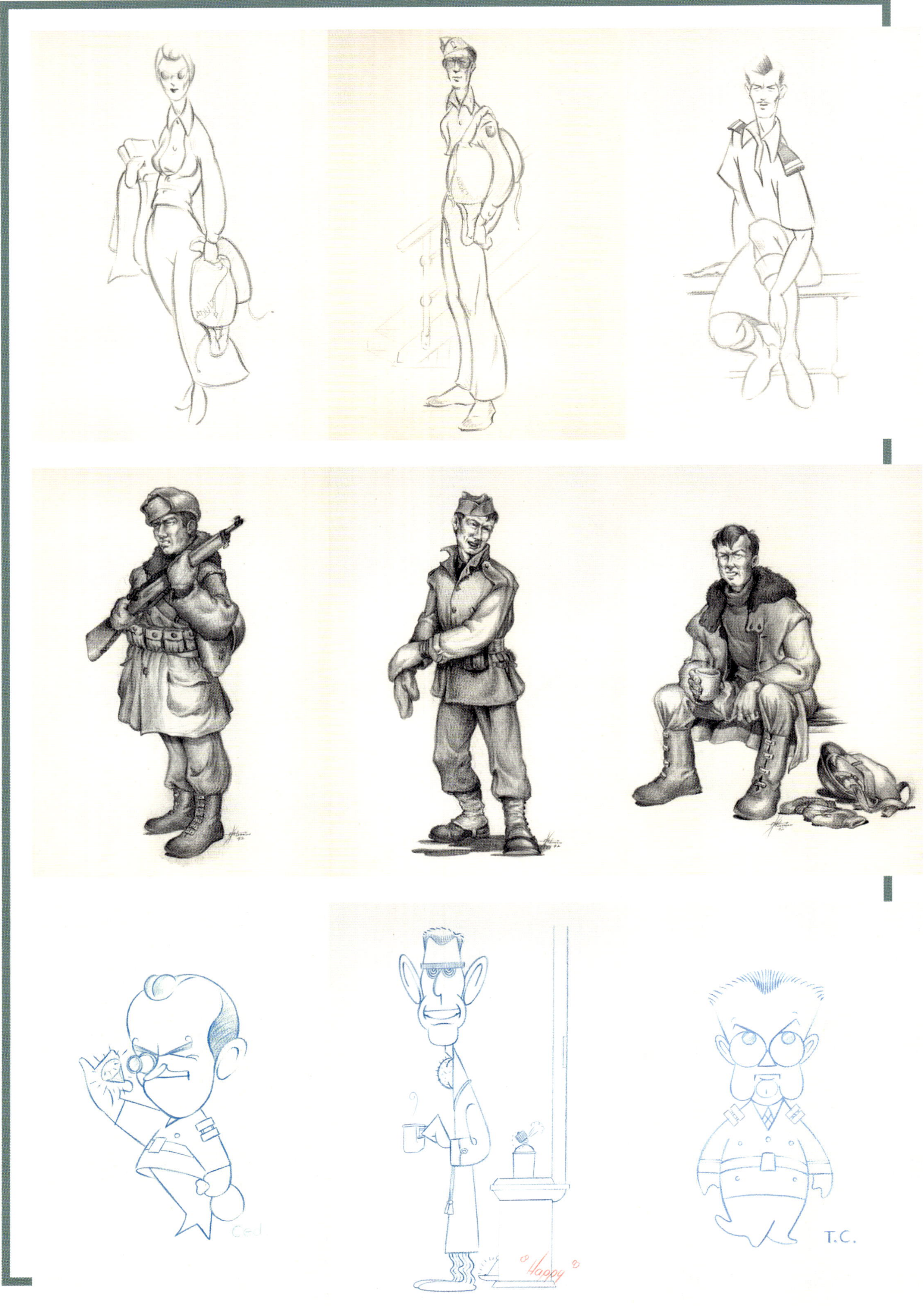
Cel
Happy
T.C.

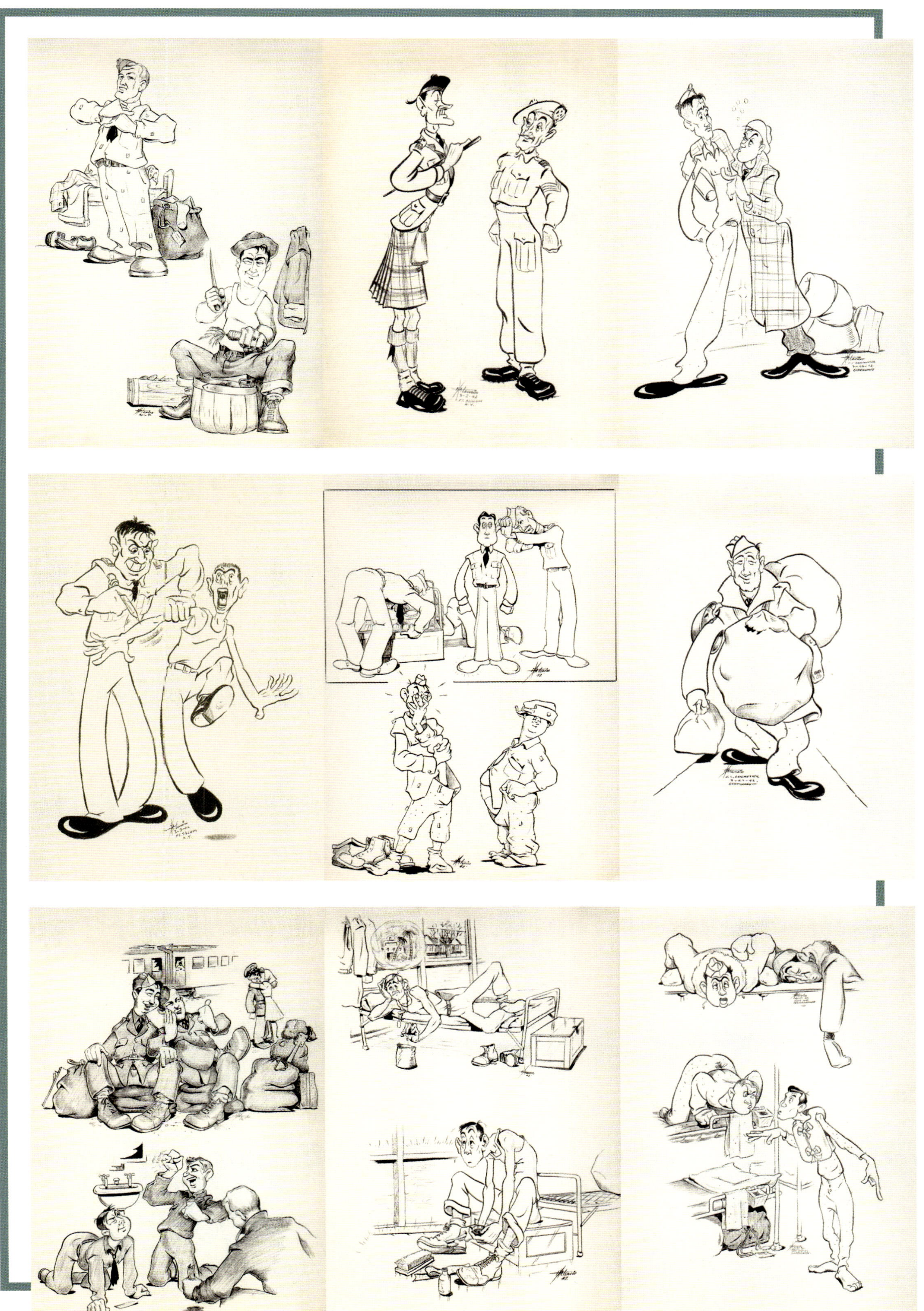

OPPOSITE AND ABOVE: X's varied drawings of his fellow service members and life on base during his time in the army.

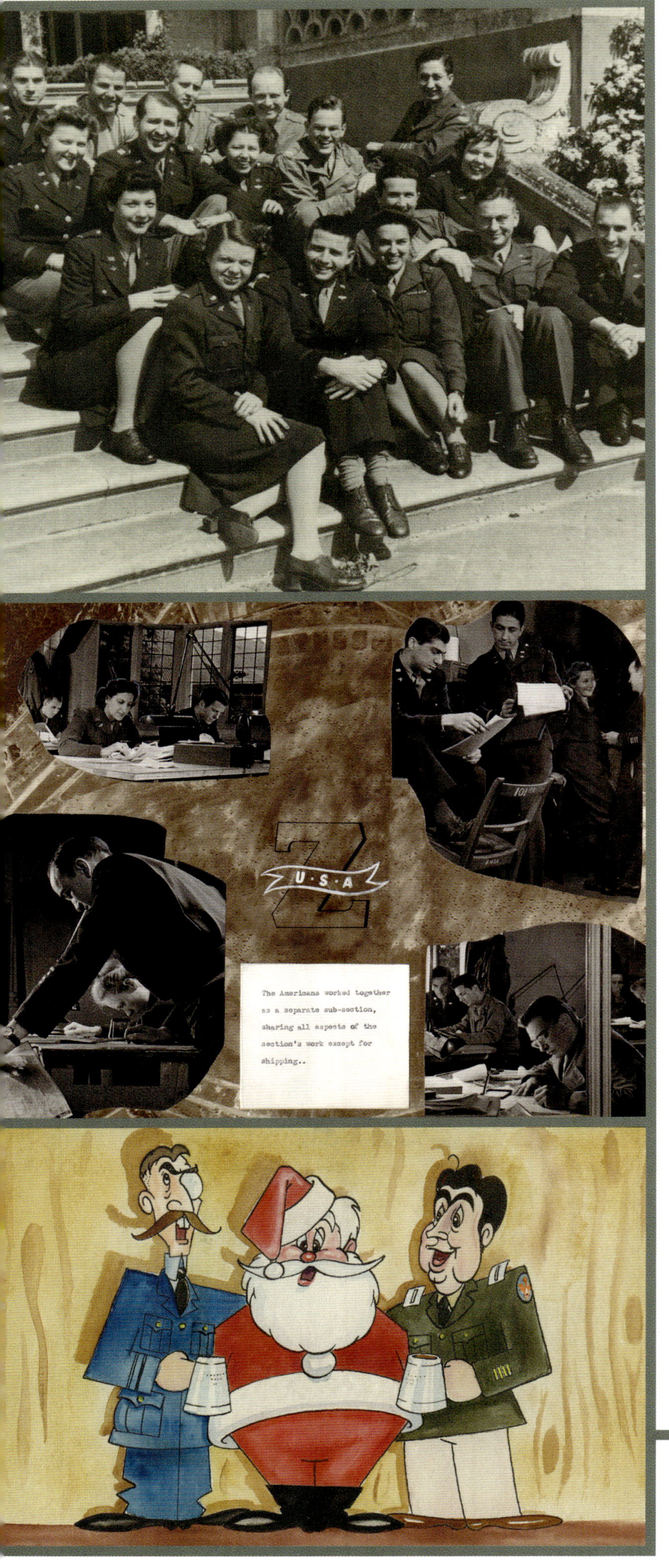

camps were operating at their full capacity, accounting for the deaths of millions. Even Britain was continuing to defend the homeland and secure itself against the threat of a German invasion at this point, as the Nazis (and their Vichy French supporters) occupied and controlled all of France and practically all of Europe just on the other side of the English Channel.

Combining his Air Corps and cryptography training with his artistic attention to detail, X and his unit, which was comprised of both British and American personnel, were carrying out photo-intelligence operations and seeking to identify locations where German forces had built or were suspected of developing weapons for pilotless rockets and long-range missiles that could be used to drop bombs and hit military and civilian sites far from the battlefields. From there, the team would alert their aerial bombers to the locations so that they could attack the correct targets. In addition, new R & D was in the works, such as stereoscopes, which were being used to analyze the Nazis' plans and even get a clearer image of them. This 3D technology allowed the aerial intelligence unit to identify the Nazis' weapons and better observe what they were building. Dr. Allan Williams, head of Britain's National Collection of Aerial Photography (NCAP), described in his book *Operation Crossbow: The Untold Story of the Search for Hitler's Secret Weapons* how "a built object or a topographical feature, instantly recognizable when viewed on the ground, very often becomes quite unfamiliar when seen from above. It was this ability to recognise features from a new angle that was essential . . . it required a particular mentality, 'a kind of super-jigsaw mind' that someone, irrespective of their natural-born intelligence, either did or didn't have." The stereoscopic/3D nature of the work was a large part of the reason why intelligence wanted to recruit artists, who, in addition to their attention to detail, were more easily able to understand slope grades and visualize how things usually observed from the ground might look different from other angles.

Approximately 80 percent of British intelligence came from this type of photo analysis work. While the British recruits tended to rely on academics

LEFT (TOP): X with some of his fellow photo interpreters at Medmenham; LEFT (MIDDLE): X (top right) in the Z Section page of *Medmenham U.S.A.*; LEFT (BOTTOM): The inside of X's Christmas card to Mary in 1944, complete with Santa and celebratory army officers; OPPOSITE: X at his desk at Medmenham.

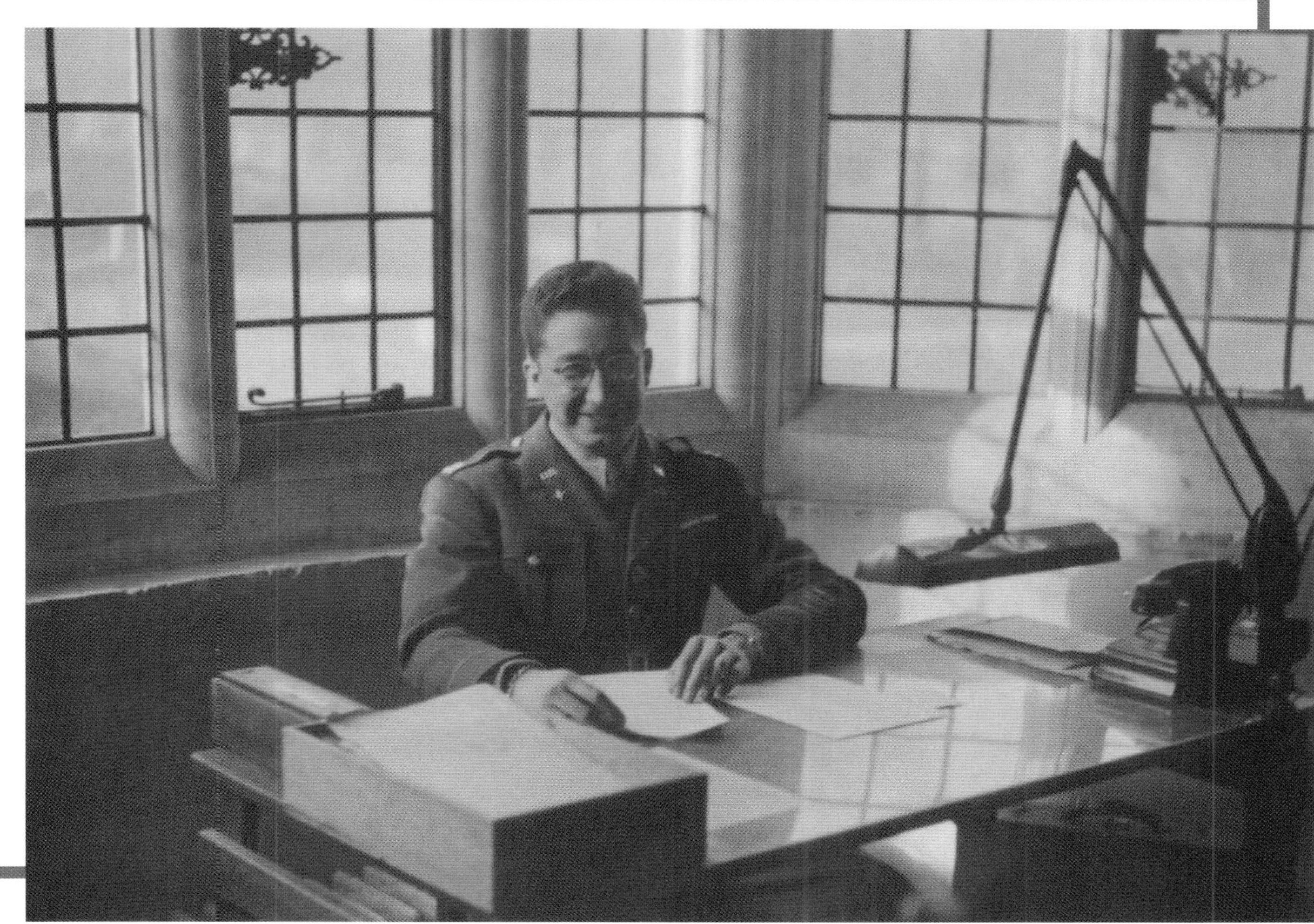

(mathematicians, archaeologists, geologists, and others from their top schools, Oxford and Cambridge) to be interpreters, they integrated Americans into the process as well. Instead of separating the operations by nationality once the Americans joined the war, they kept the teams as they were, mixing and combining new recruits from both countries as they arrived. The mixture of science and art created an environment of highly focused, intelligent, and detail-oriented observers, capable of successfully channeling their efforts both to civilian and military endeavors. Interestingly, this focus on combining people who have a particular expertise in artistry, technology, or engineering mirrors X's later work at WED, perhaps providing X's foundational understanding of how to adapt, communicate, and work with all types of individuals in many different high-pressure situations.

While one can imagine the importance of this work, it is only recently (between 2004 and 2008) that the largest portion of these aerial photographs were declassified, revealing to the world the true influence on strategy and impact the intelligence that was gathered at Medmenham had on the ending of the war. According to Wing Commander Mike Mockford, a veteran photo interpreter, without their work, the war would have been extended by another year or two, with a much longer corresponding casualty list. Hitler and the Germans were building the first weapons of mass destruction—rockets and pilotless drones known as V-1 bombs and V-2 missiles. In 1944 and 1945, during just two years of the war, nearly nine thousand people were killed by these advanced German weapons, and Hitler knew they were the key to turning the tide of the war back in his favor. This technology proved to be a huge risk to the Allied forces, even as they were nearing victory, and especially a year earlier to the success of the long-planned seaborne Allied invasion of France's coastline early June 1944, more commonly known as D-Day.

The intelligence from Medmenham was also used in Operation Crossbow, the hunt for Germany's V-1 launch sites for flying bombs, a critical operation that needed to be completed ahead of D-Day to ensure the Germans couldn't issue a counter aerial attack during the Allies' invasion of Normandy. Most likely, without Operation Crossbow, D-Day would have needed to be delayed. But thanks to the gathering

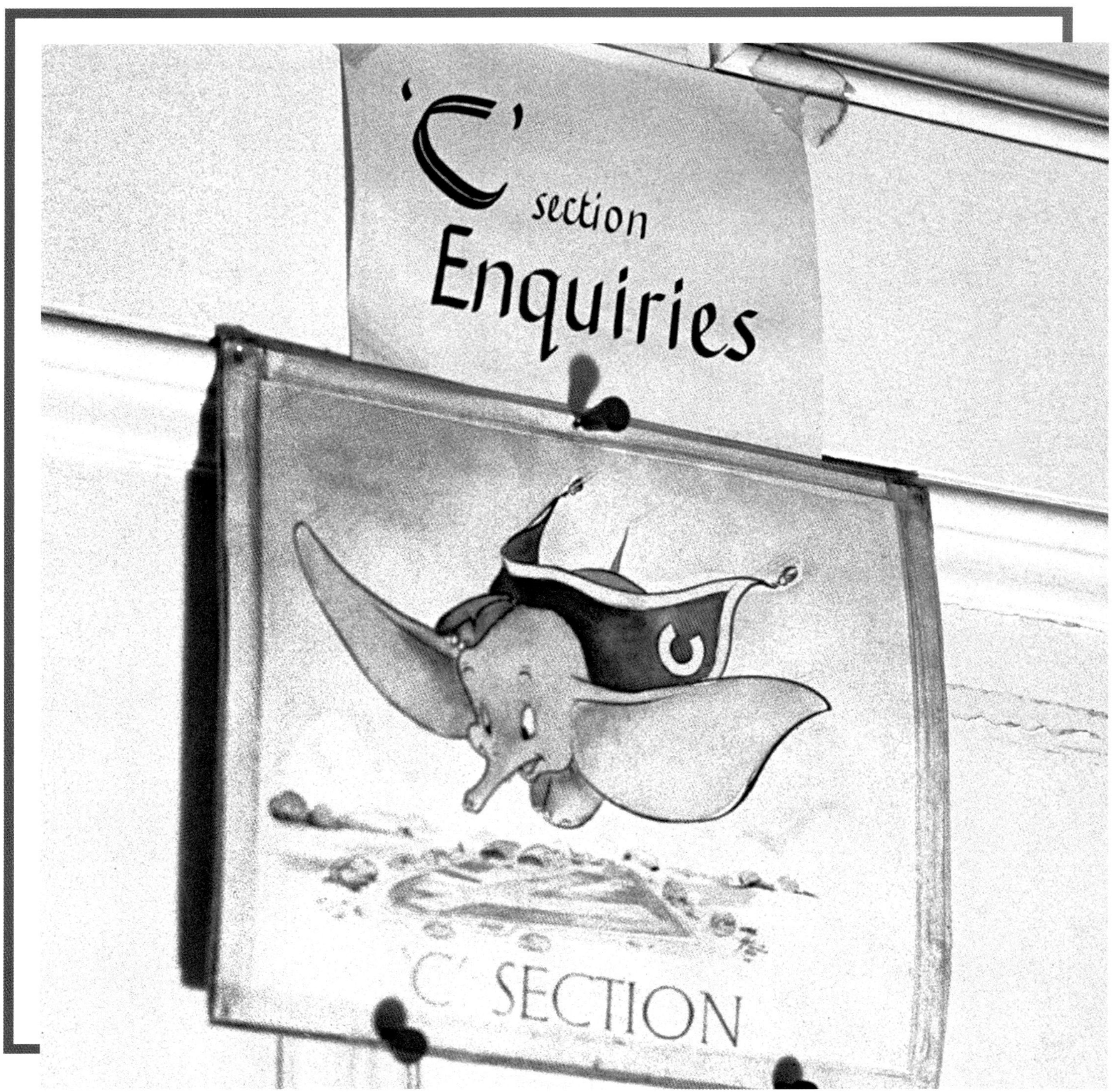

of this vital intelligence and corresponding physical destruction of the launch sites uncovered, the number of potential V-1 launches was reduced by 99 percent, and ultimately not one German V-1 rocket was effectively fired on D-Day at Allied forces already under intense fire.

For the first time in the war, in England, X was actually very busy. The photo-intelligence work took more time, attention to detail, and energy than had X's prior responsibilities and came during a period when the war was speeding up. Time was of the essence, and every minute truly counted. X's demanding "day job" schedule is easily reconfirmed when one looks at the lack of "fun" artwork he was producing at this time, especially in comparison to the art he had had time to create while stationed

ABOVE: X's drawing of Dumbo on the entrance building to Section C of RAF Medmenham; OPPOSITE (TOP): X's officer ID card from 1943; OPPOSITE (BOTTOM): X on the grounds of RAF Medmenham in 1943.

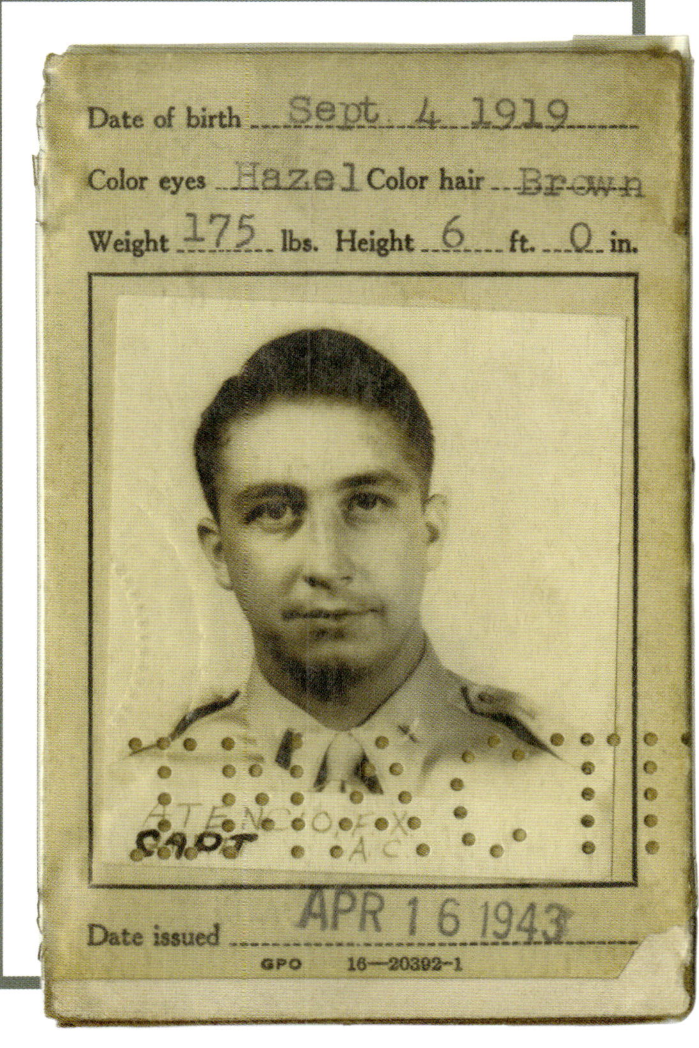
Date of birth Sept 4 1919
Color eyes Hazel Color hair Brown
Weight 175 lbs. Height 6 ft. 0 in.
ATENCIO, F X
CAPT A C
Date issued APR 16 1943
GPO 16—20392-1

in Greenland. Though when X did find occasions to draw in England, it was yet again Disney artwork that inspired him, as demonstrated by X's drawing of Dumbo that adorned the building and greeted visitors to Section C.

X's time at Medmenham also gave him the opportunity to revisit his journalistic abilities. American service members heading home created a publication to commemorate their time in England called *Medmenham U.S.A.*, of which X was the editor in chief. The opening read:

> This is a sentimental dossier. It is a record of all the people, all the work, all the living that made RAF Medmenham so memorable. It is a personal history of the Americans who lived and worked here with the British Allies. All of us in years to come will seek to recall the flavor of our unique experience. This dossier is your source of comparative cover for future reminiscing.

Likewise, upon the retirement of Wing Commander Hugh Hamshaw Thomas, the commander was gifted with an album of memories, including a

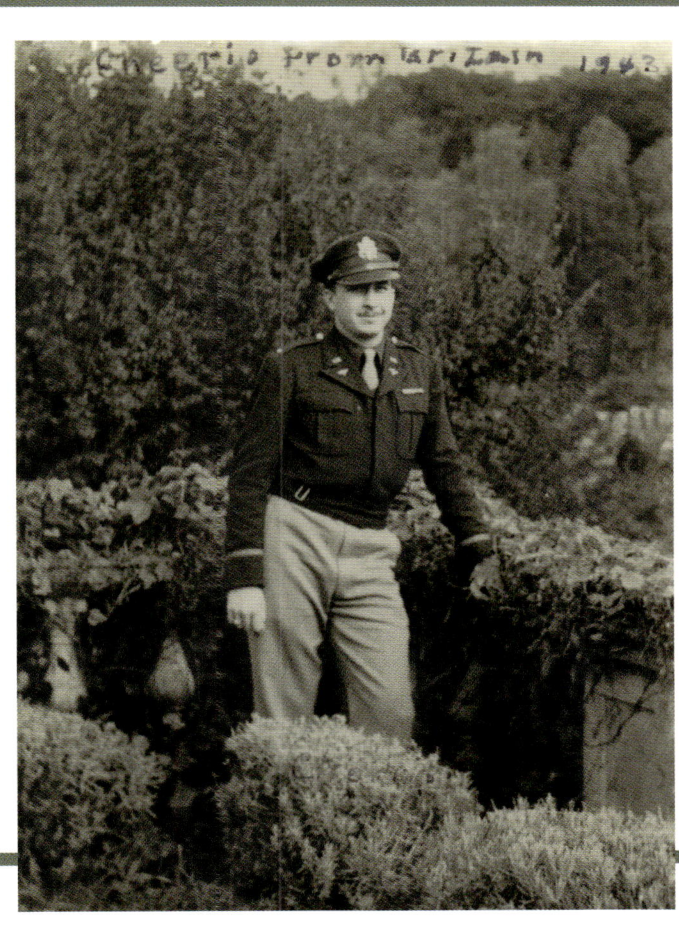

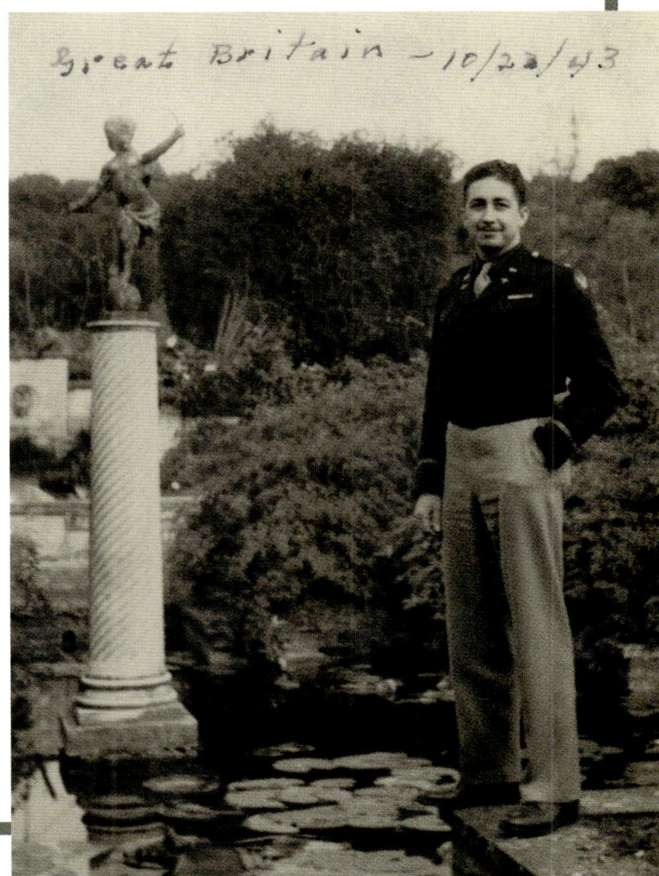

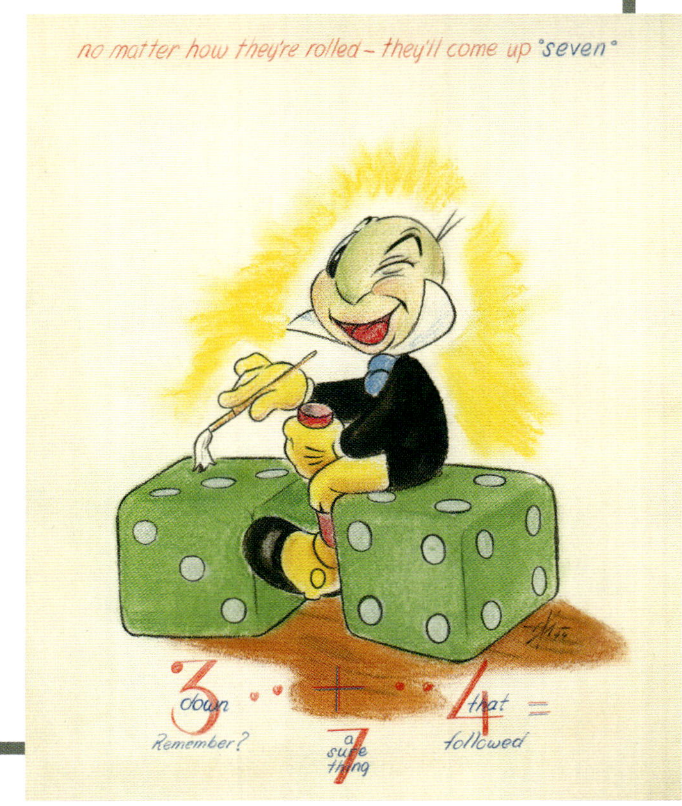

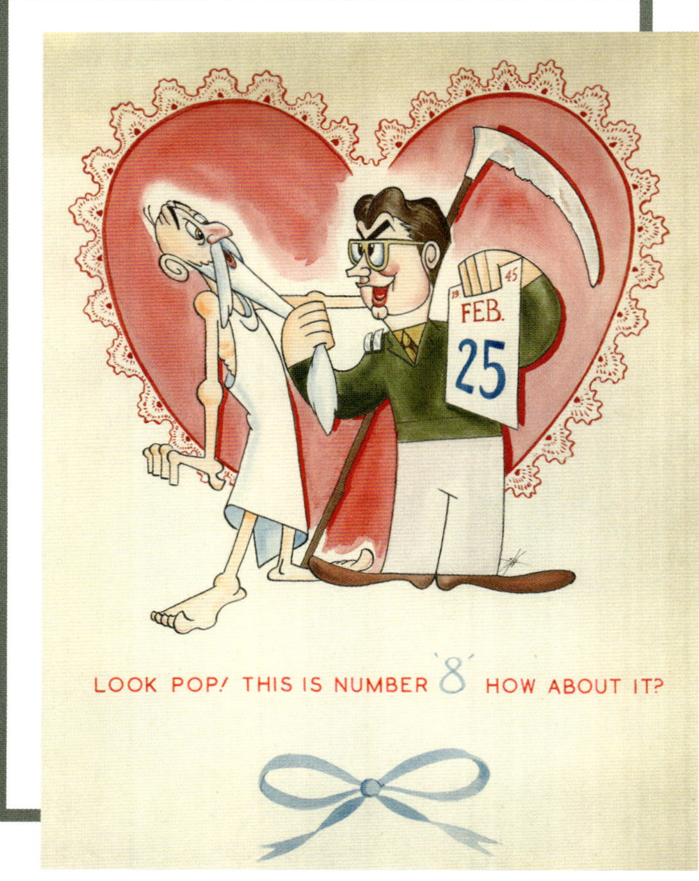

TOP: X's card to Mary in 1944 for the seventh anniversary of their first date; ABOVE: X's Card to Mary, celebrating the eighth anniversary of the start of their relationship, depicts his frustration with Father Time; OPPOSITE (TOP): X's retirement card for Commander Hugh Hamshaw Thomas from Medmenham; OPPOSITE (BOTTOM): X's painting of a little demon spraying clouds, the greatest enemy of the intelligence unit, over an aerial photograph.

drawing from X, showing both X's notable artistry and foreshadowing his later reputation for creating memorable retirement cards in addition to the rest of his artistic prowess.

Finally, Allied victory in Europe over Germany was declared on May 8, 1945, and while the war had officially ended on the Continent, there were not enough ships to bring everyone in the armed forces back immediately to America. So X traveled with some of his fellow service members around Europe, waiting for his turn to go home. That happened on August 21, 1945, almost four years to the day after he had left for Fort Monmouth, in New Jersey. But now X was returning home aboard the famed *Queen Mary* luxury liner (which had been turned into a troop carrier during the war), traveling from Southampton, England, to New York. While X's elongated war years weren't what he expected, he had grown as an independent adult, fought against tyranny in a world war, and still maintained his status as an artist. And it was that very status as a Disney artist that X upheld while abroad in trying situations.

Although hard to pinpoint, X believed that Disney's influence and acceptance around the world stemmed from an intangible "Disney magic." He stated in an interview that during his three years overseas, "I remember during the war when I was in England the fact that I worked for Walt Disney had a magic side effect. I got out of more lousy details as a GI just because I was a Disney animator." Though other animators were in the same New Jersey film lab groups as X, making training films, "[including] animators from Warner Brothers, MGM, etc., [nobody] paid any attention to them. But the mere fact that I worked for Walt Disney was magic."

While hard to describe, the Disney essence had remained with X and had gotten him through the war. Now, heading home to America as a veteran, X could look to the future with his fiancée and his career at Disney, finally ready and able to embark on the next chapter of his life.

After the war, X never talked about what he had done during his time in England. It wasn't until many years later, during a visit to his granddaughter Kelsey's high school class on Grandparents' Day, that

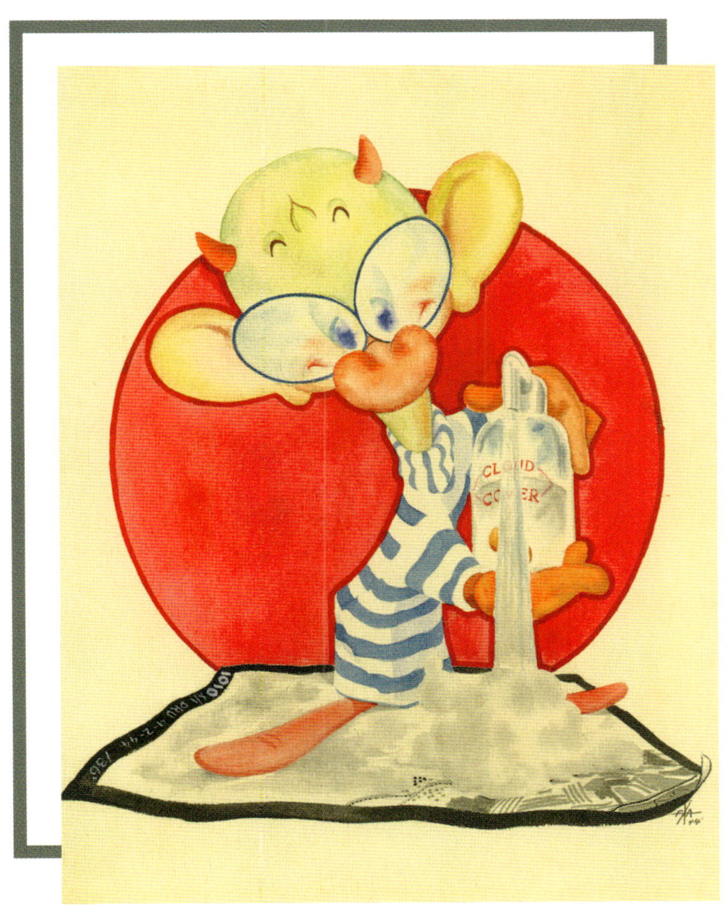

his family first heard more details of what had happened fighting the Axis powers. During the class discussion, X was asked to describe his involvement in World War II. He explained he was "in the aerial-intelligence unit. So, the pilots would go out and take pictures, which they would send back to us to search for German rocket launch sites. And if we found one, we'd radio over, let them know where it was, and tell them to bomb the suckers." This was a humorous and nationalistic retelling for a group of teenage girls at least sixty years after the war had ended, but one that still recounted the seriousness of their work. In true familial fashion, this fascinating tale was taken home by Kelsey and quickly spread in many second- and third-hand retellings throughout the family, as it was the first time X's family truly heard what he had done in the war.

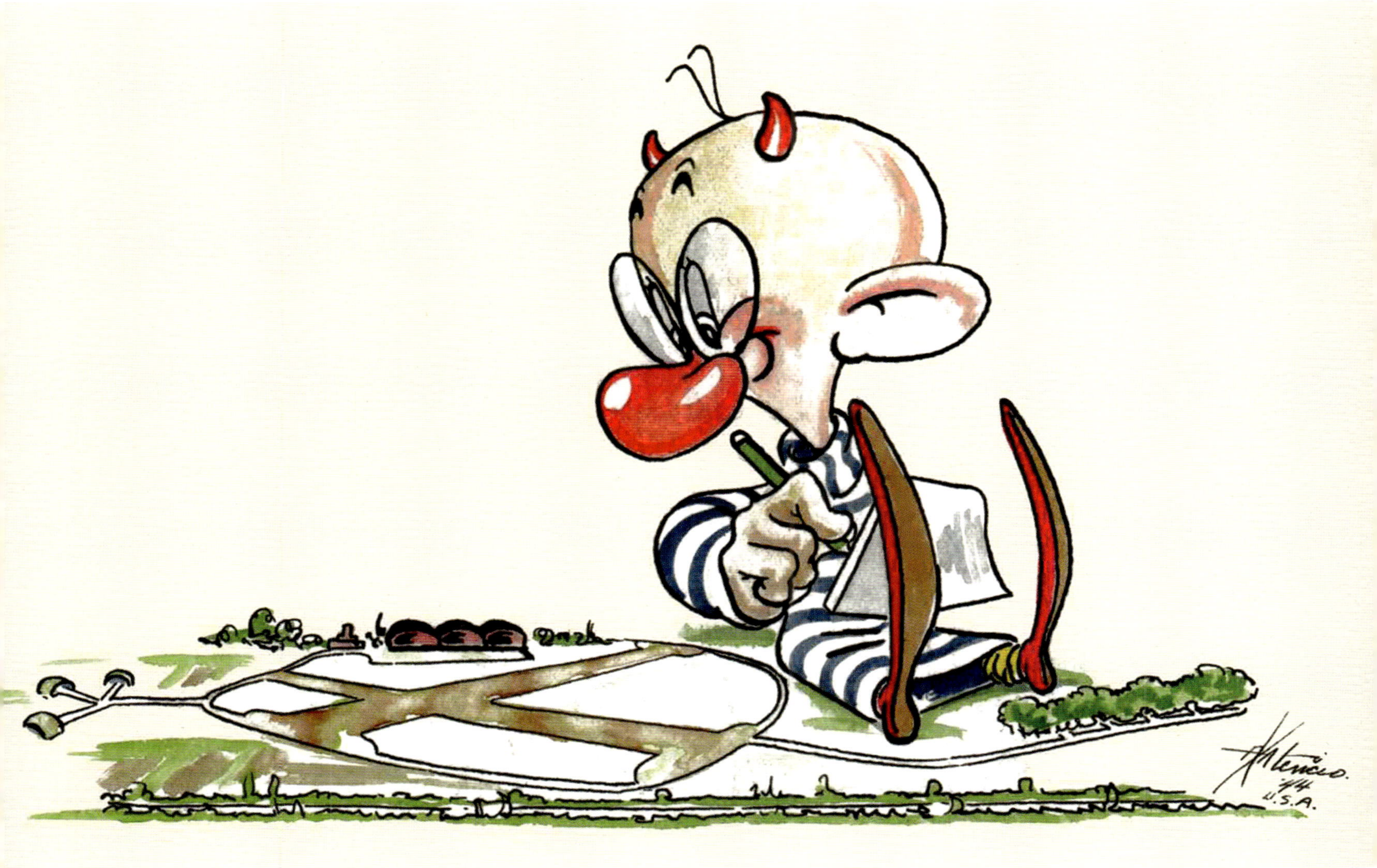

While they had known he was stationed in England, it was only through this Grandparents' Day reveal that X's own children, Tori (Kelsey's mother), Judianne, and Joe, started to understand that X's

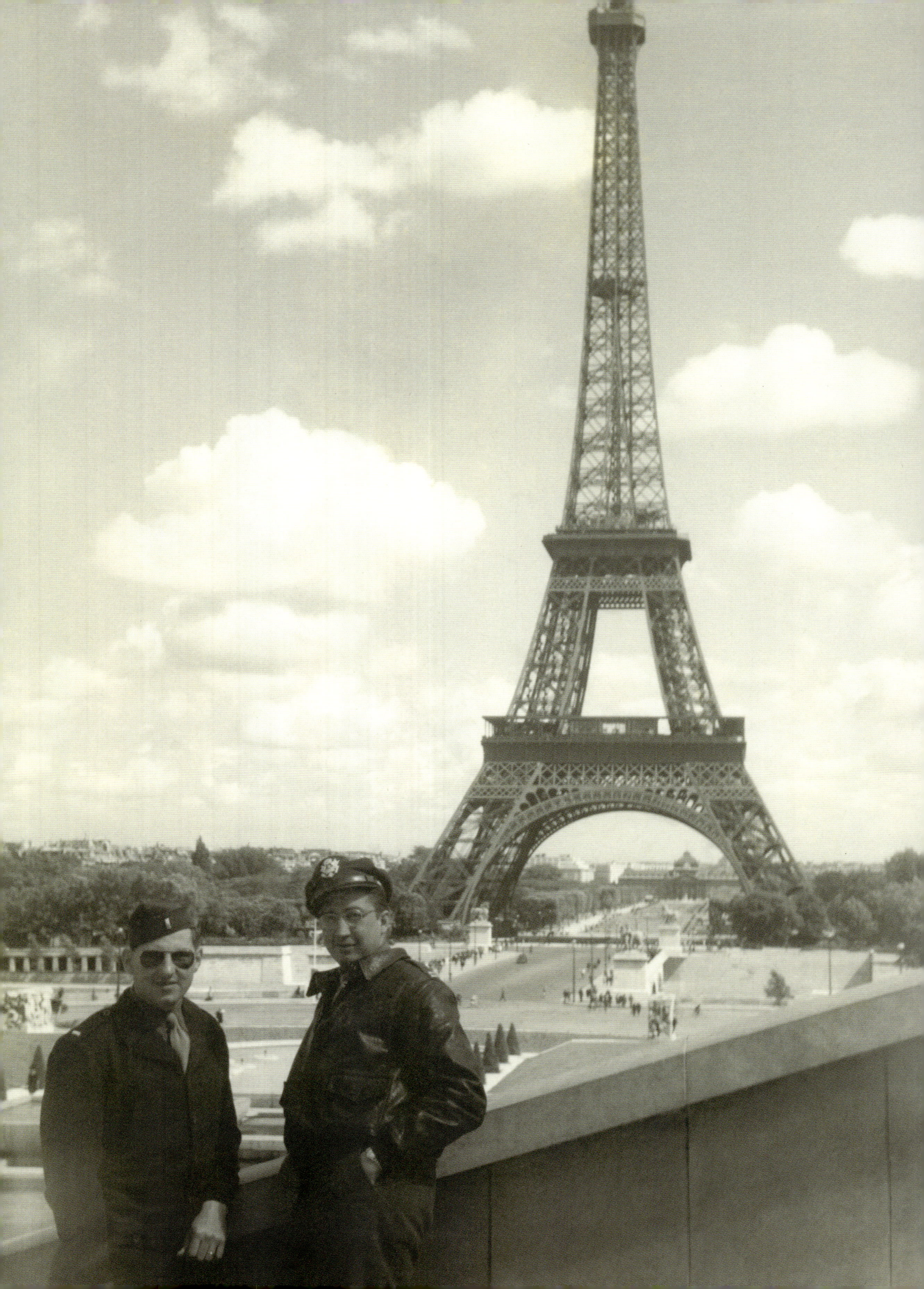

humbleness regarding his role in the war might have been hiding deeper stories far more of consequence than what he had shared with them about his time in Greenland.

During a 2012 PBS *NOVA* episode entitled "3D Spies of WWII," X's family finally saw the full impact of the work he and his team had on the outcome of the war. X was interviewed for this episode of the documentary series and discussed the group's contributions but never boasted about his own work. Although one might think that X himself didn't realize his own impact, given the isolation at Medmenham house, lack of modern-day technology, media, and communication—all valid reasons for the time—NCAP's Dr. Allan Williams asserted that X and his colleagues did understand the importance of what they were doing, yet again reaffirming that X's humbleness was more of the reason for downplaying his own influence—and contributions during the war.

—ROCKY MOUNTAIN NEWS—3

84 Colorado Soldiers Are Coming Home

Eighty-four Colorado soldiers, including 25 from Denver, are scheduled to arrive Wednesday in New York from Europe on the liner Queen Mary, the Associated Press reported last night. The list of men is tentative and has not been corrected as of the sailing date. Those listed are:

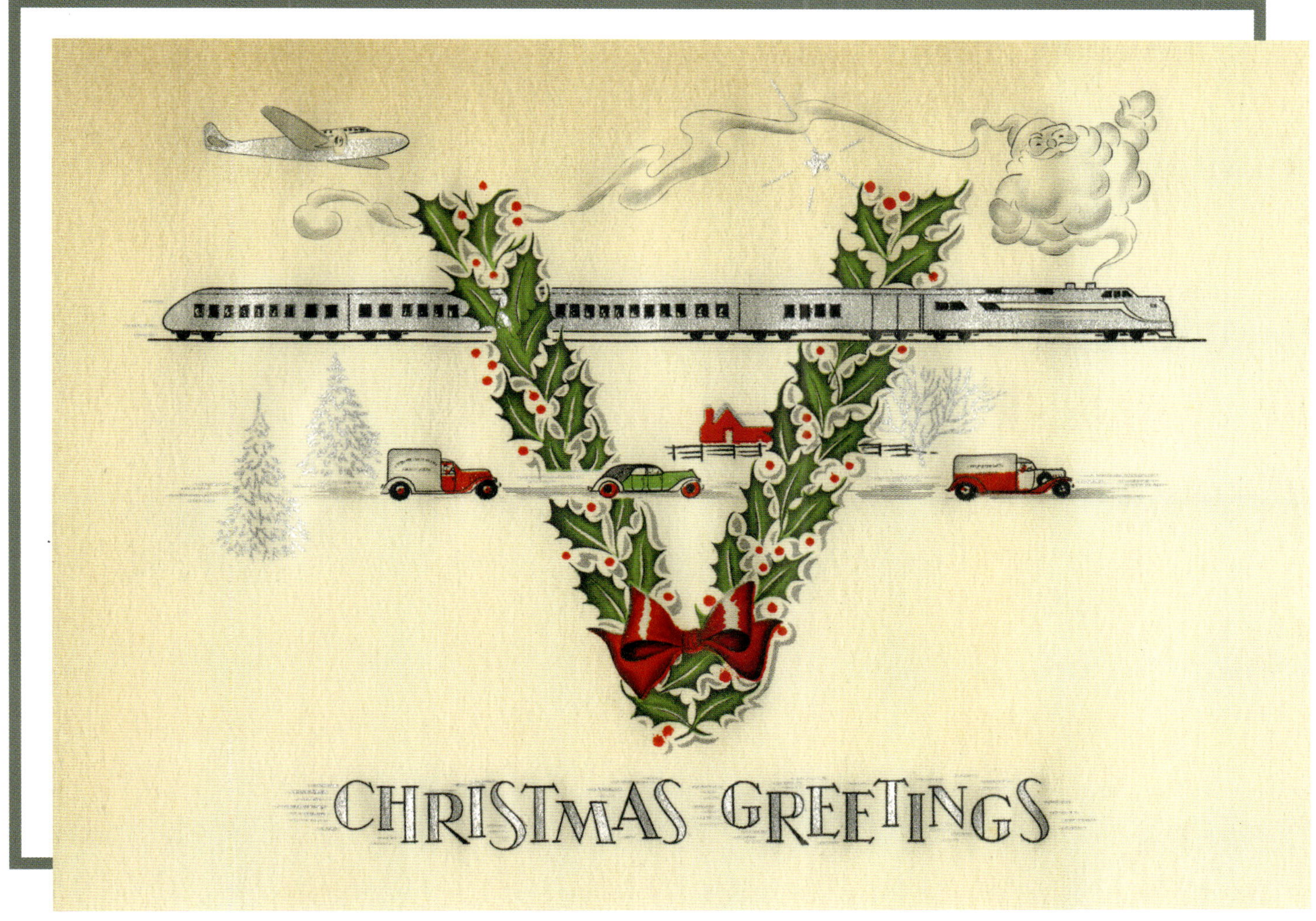

OPPOSITE: X in Paris after the Allied victory before he could get home to America; TOP: A newspaper clipping from the *Rocky Mountain News* announcing X's return home from the war, aboard the *Queen Mary*; ABOVE: The 1945 Atencio family Christmas card.

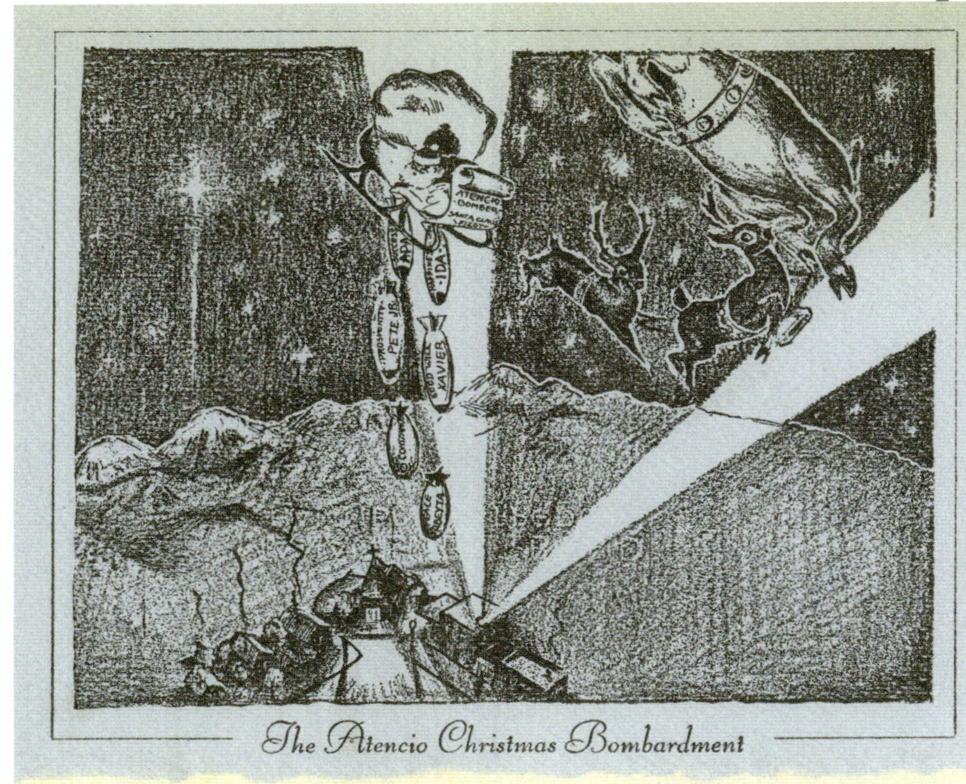

The Atencio Christmas Bombardment

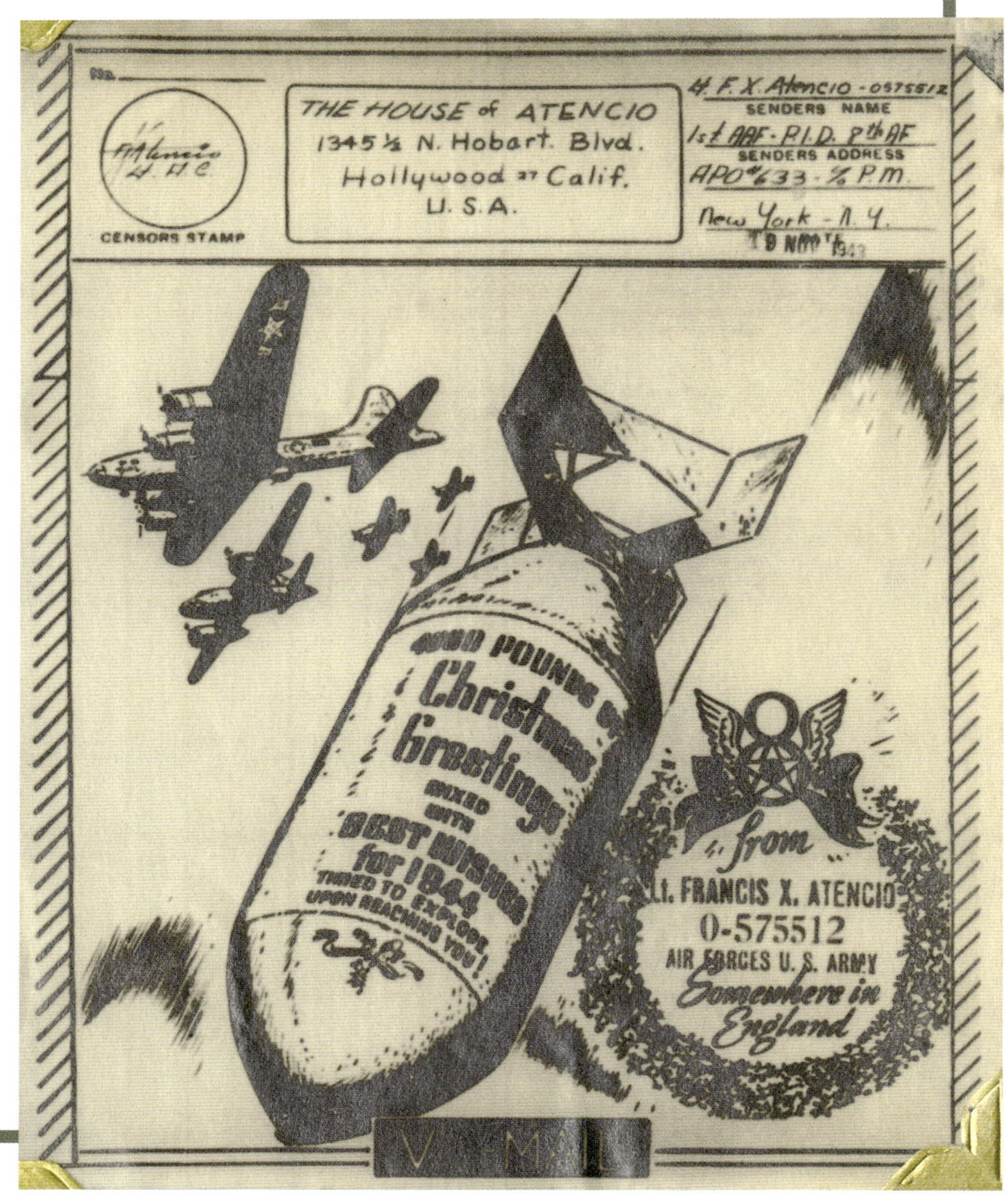

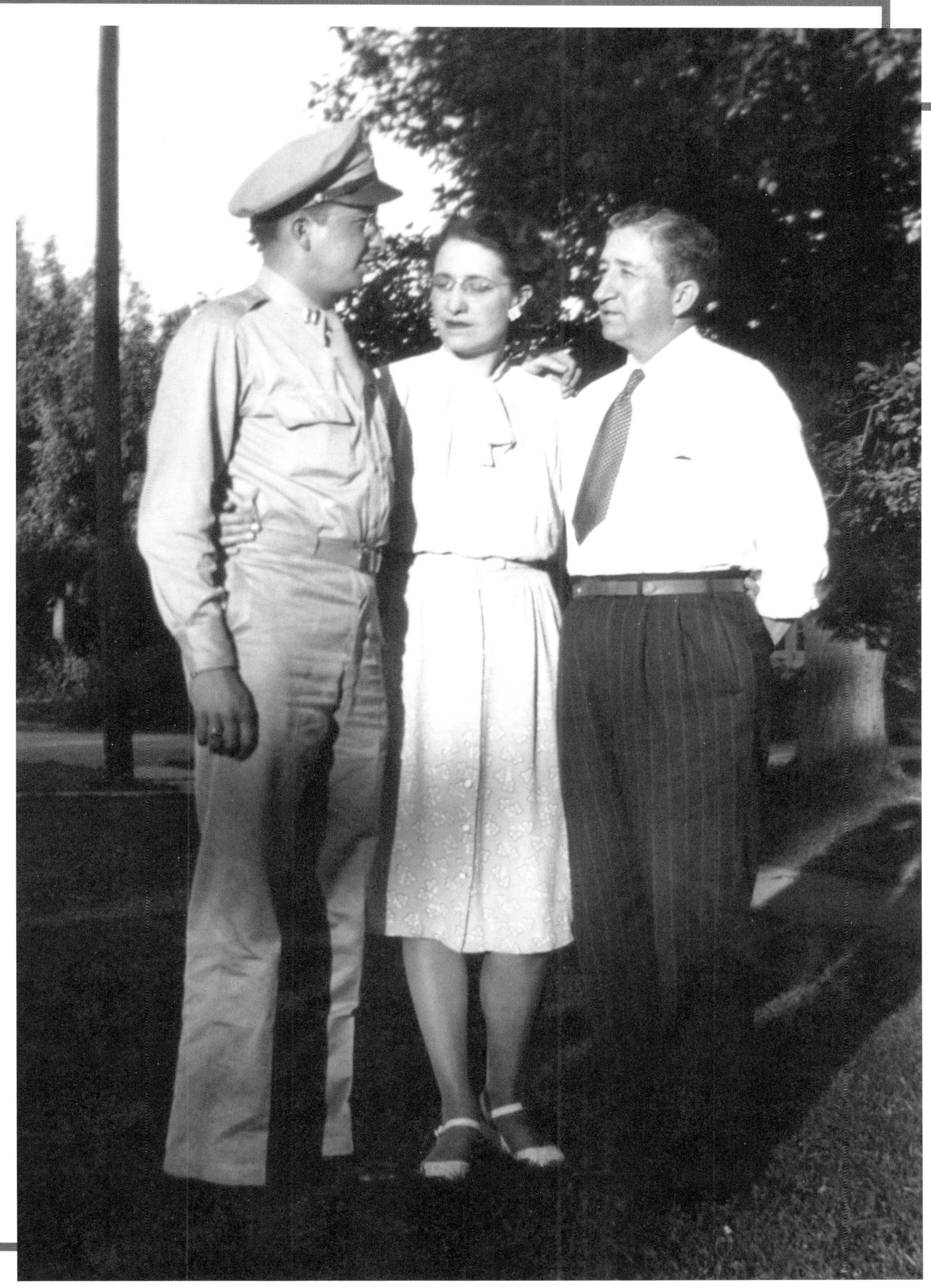

OPPOSITE: Atencio family Christmas cards designed by X for 1942 (TOP) and 1943 (BOTTOM); ABOVE: X with his parents upon his return home from the war.

4

Back to the Studio

AFTER FOUR YEARS SERVING IN A six-year war, X was officially heading home. He sent his father a telegram on August 22, 1945, saying, WILL ARRIVE IN DENVER ON OR ABOUT SUNDAY. HOPING TO SEE YOU SOON. One from Mary to X's family soon followed, stating that she had spoken to X after he had disembarked the *Queen Mary* in New York, and that they should prepare to travel, for X and Mary's wedding would take place within the month.

On September 15, 1945, X and Mary were officially married at the Cathedral Basilica of the Immaculate Heart in Denver. Mary had somehow managed to successfully plan a wedding in just a few weeks. However, with such short notice came some sacrifices— for while X's brother Pete was able to make it back to Colorado for the wedding, most of X's friends were still returning from Europe or were scattered around the United States after the war and unable to attend. Having no groomsmen next to Mary's bridal party presented an untraditional challenge, but a corresponding unconventional solution was offered. X's future brother-in-law, who happened to be a Denver police detective, rounded up a few fellow detectives to stand in as X's groomsmen.

While X was grateful for their help and comradery, the whole event happened so quickly that he never even learned their names. Regardless of this unique twist, X and Mary had a wonderful wedding, surrounded by those close family, friends, and distant detectives that were witnesses to the happy couple's union, able to celebrate finally starting their life together after eight years of a long-distance courtship.

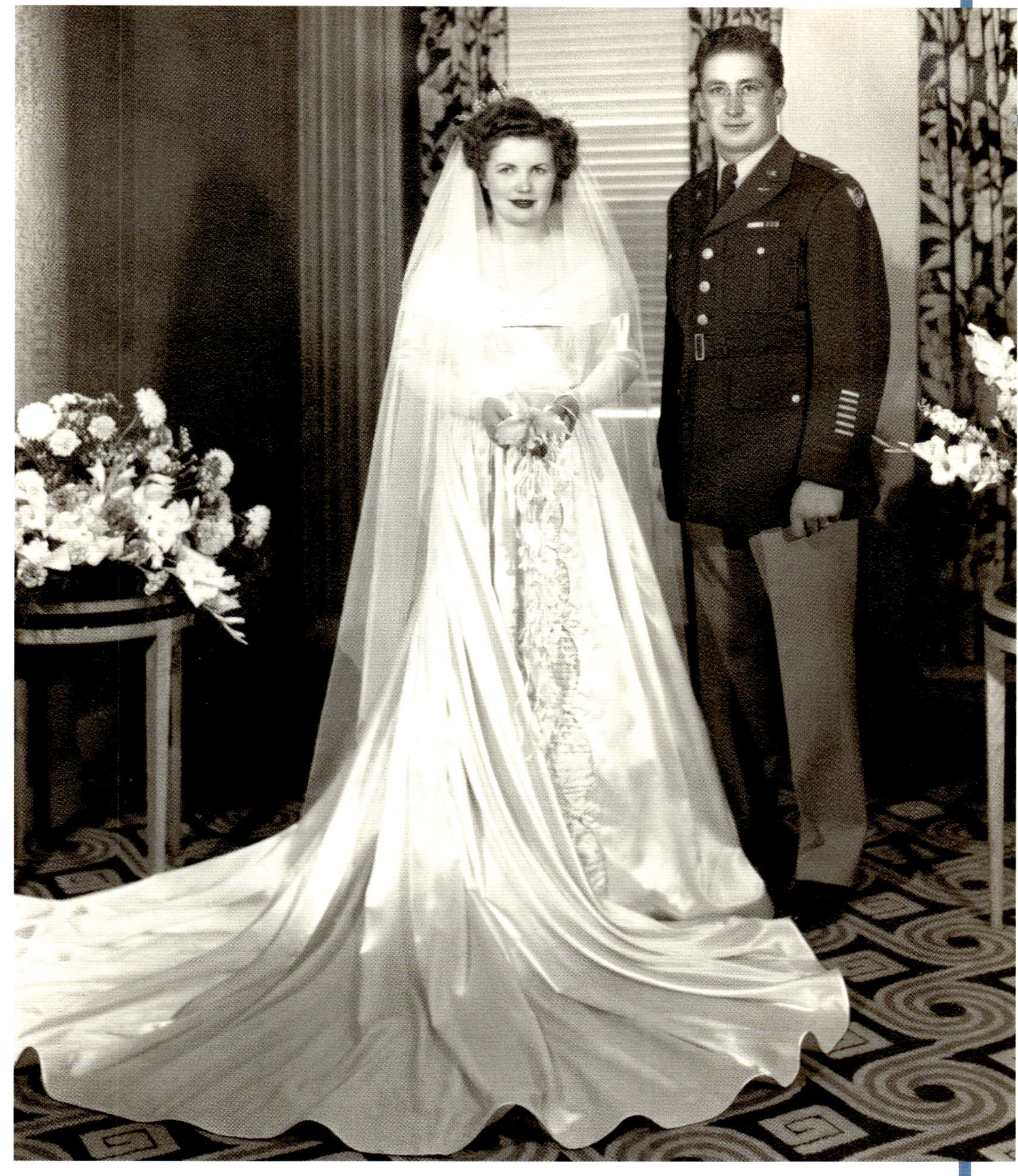

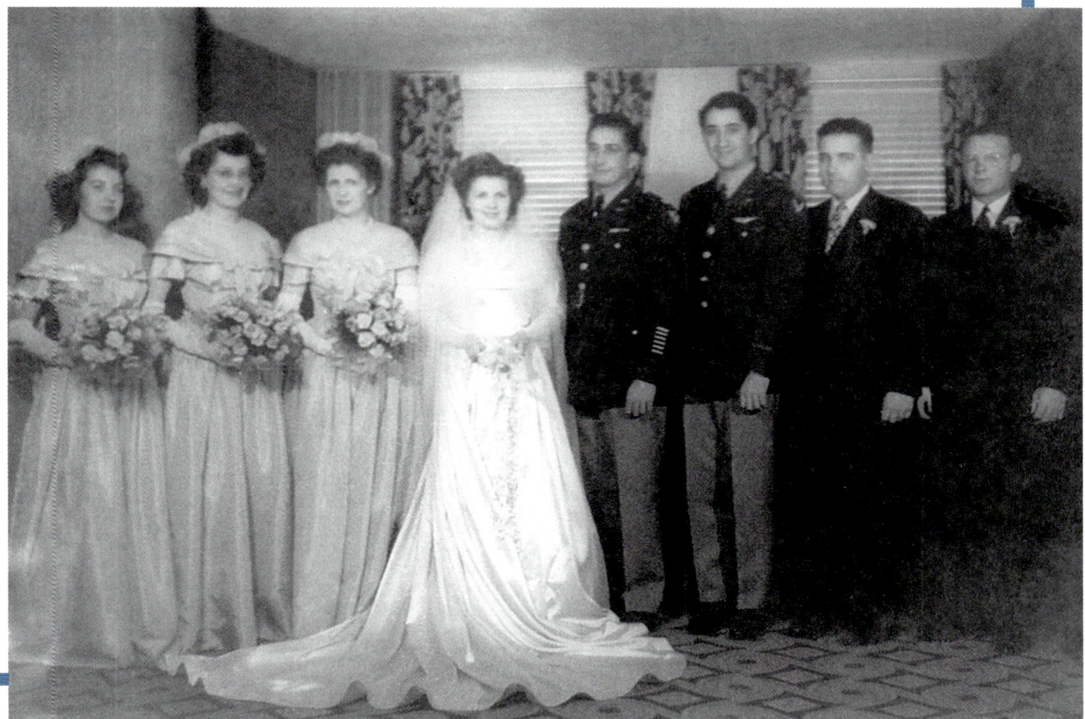

TOP: X and Mary on their wedding day, September 15, 1945; BOTTOM: X and Mary with their wedding party, including the two fill-in Denver policemen who served as groomsmen.

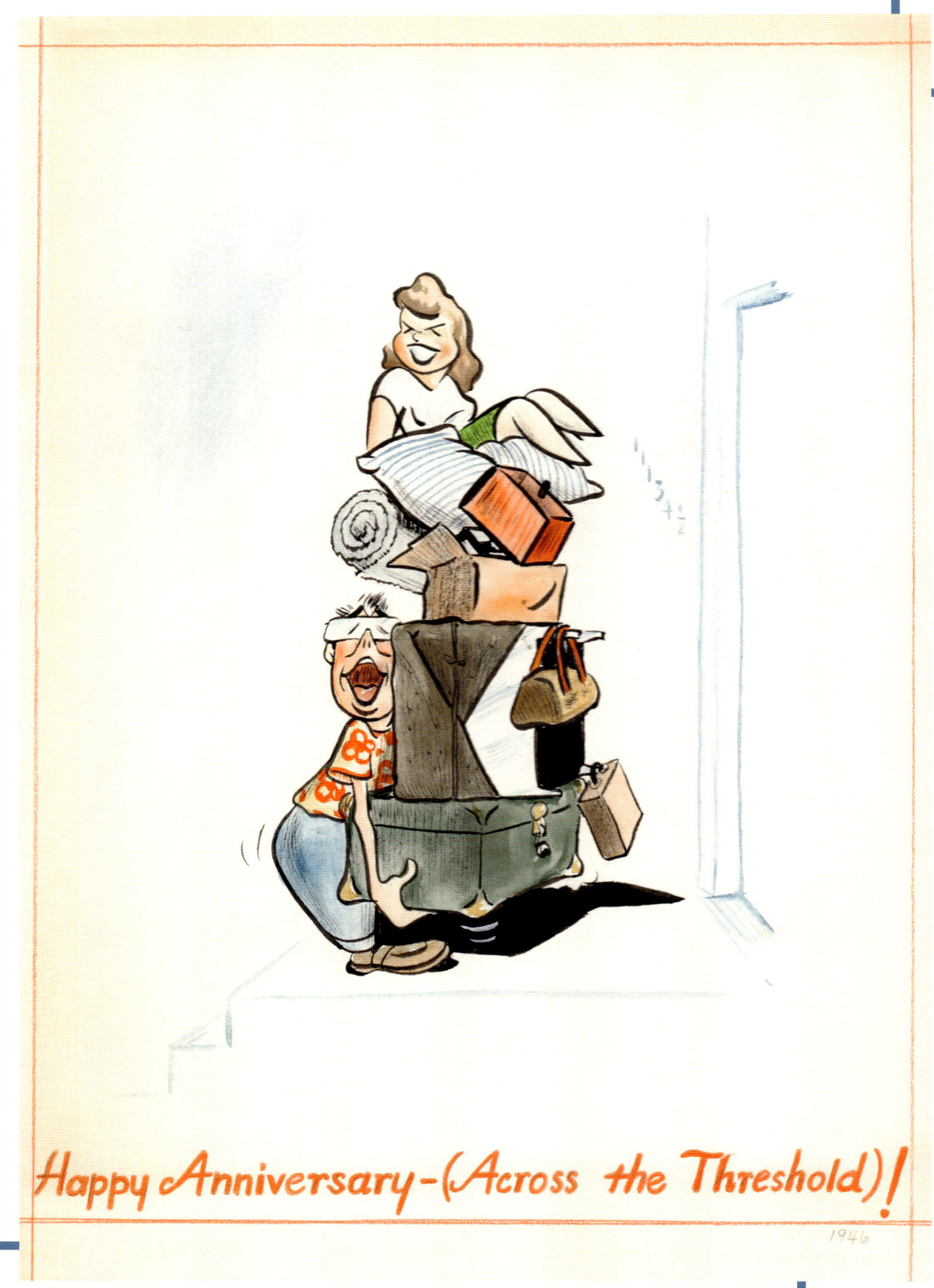

ABOVE: X's card to Mary, from 1946, celebrating their success in finally finding an apartment; OPPOSITE (TOP LEFT): X's first wedding anniversary card to Mary; OPPOSITE (BOTTOM LEFT): X's card to Mary for the ninth anniversary of their courtship; OPPOSITE (RIGHT): X's Valentine's Day card to Mary, from 1946, lamenting their frustration over their inability to find their own apartment.

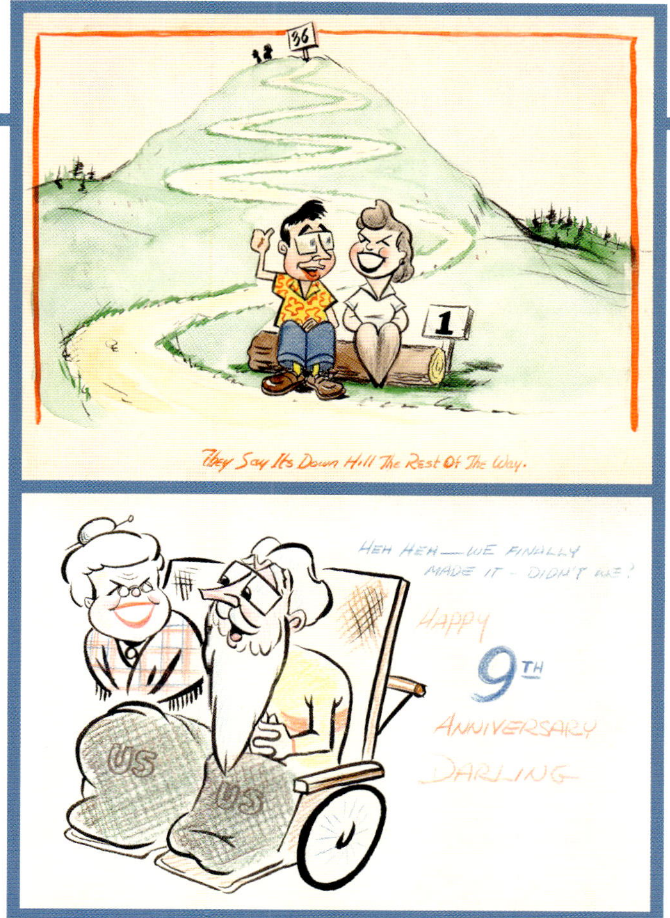

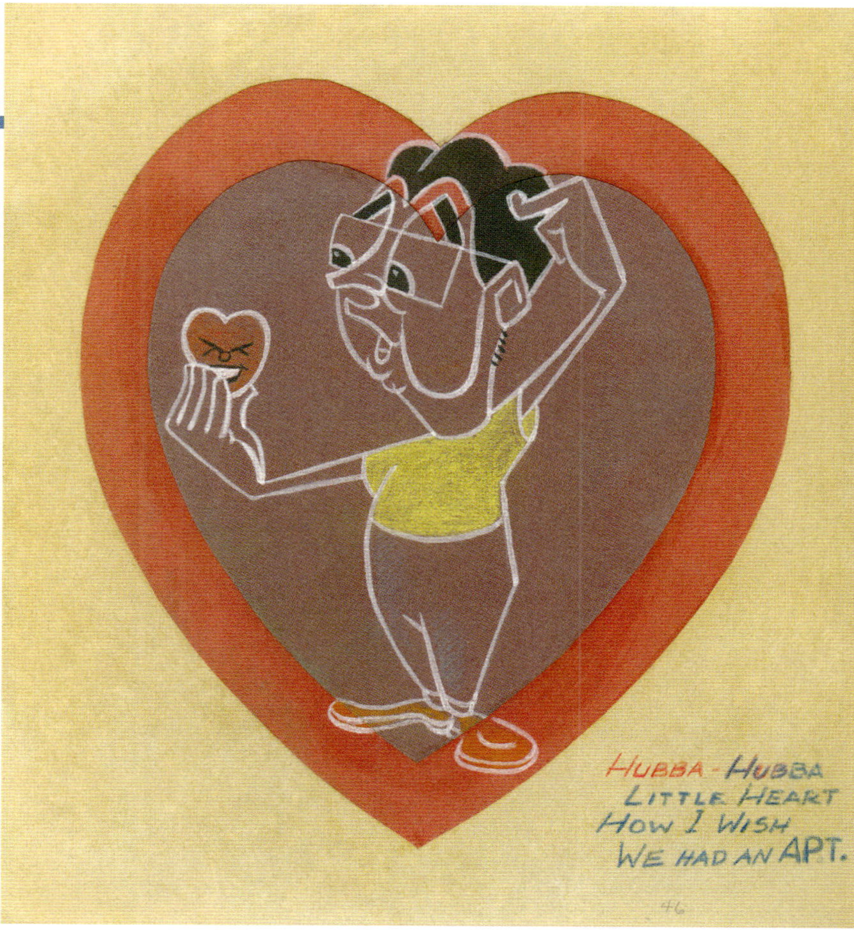

X and Mary honeymooned in Estes Park, Colorado, and then headed west, returning to California. Domestic bliss was short-lived upon arrival in Los Angeles as they, like many others around the country, found themselves facing a housing shortage for returning war veterans. Adapting to the less-than-ideal circumstances, X and Mary moved into an apartment in Los Angeles' North Hollywood neighborhood with an older couple who were willing to rent them a bedroom in their shared space. They would live in this transitory space with their older "roommates" for a few years before finally getting their own apartment in the city's Westwood section.

California was now truly home for X. In addition to Mary joining X and his aunts and grandmother in Los Angeles, X's parents and siblings had also all moved to California during the war. Even Mary's family would eventually move west to California, though not until the 1960s.

Having settled back into life in Los Angeles, X wrote to Disney Studios saying that he had returned from the war and was ready to resume work. They replied, saying that they were ready to have him back, and on November 7, 1945, X was officially reinstated as an assistant animator. While X was thrilled to resume his job, he started to recognize that returning to life at Disney would be more of an adjustment than he had expected.

The main reason for this difficult transition was the slow realization that while four years had passed for X at war, four years had also passed for those left behind. And while his relationship with Mary had endured, not every person was so blessed. X learned that Gerald James, his close friend and fellow Woolie Unit colleague, had been killed when his plane was shot down. This loss, especially of one of his Disney brothers, left an indelible mark on X, and in Gerald's memory, X kept a photograph displayed for the rest of his life of him and Gerald sitting outside the Disney Animation Building. The photograph was inscribed with a note from Gerald that read, WE'LL MEET AGAIN. TILL THEN.

Shortly thereafter, in 1947, X's father, Agapito, passed away. The profound loss was devastating to the entire Atencio family. X had just settled back into life in America, finally living near his parents and most of his family, sans his older brother, Pete, who was again living in Colorado. In addition to dealing with his own grief, X now found himself the acting patriarch of the California Atencio clan, at just shy

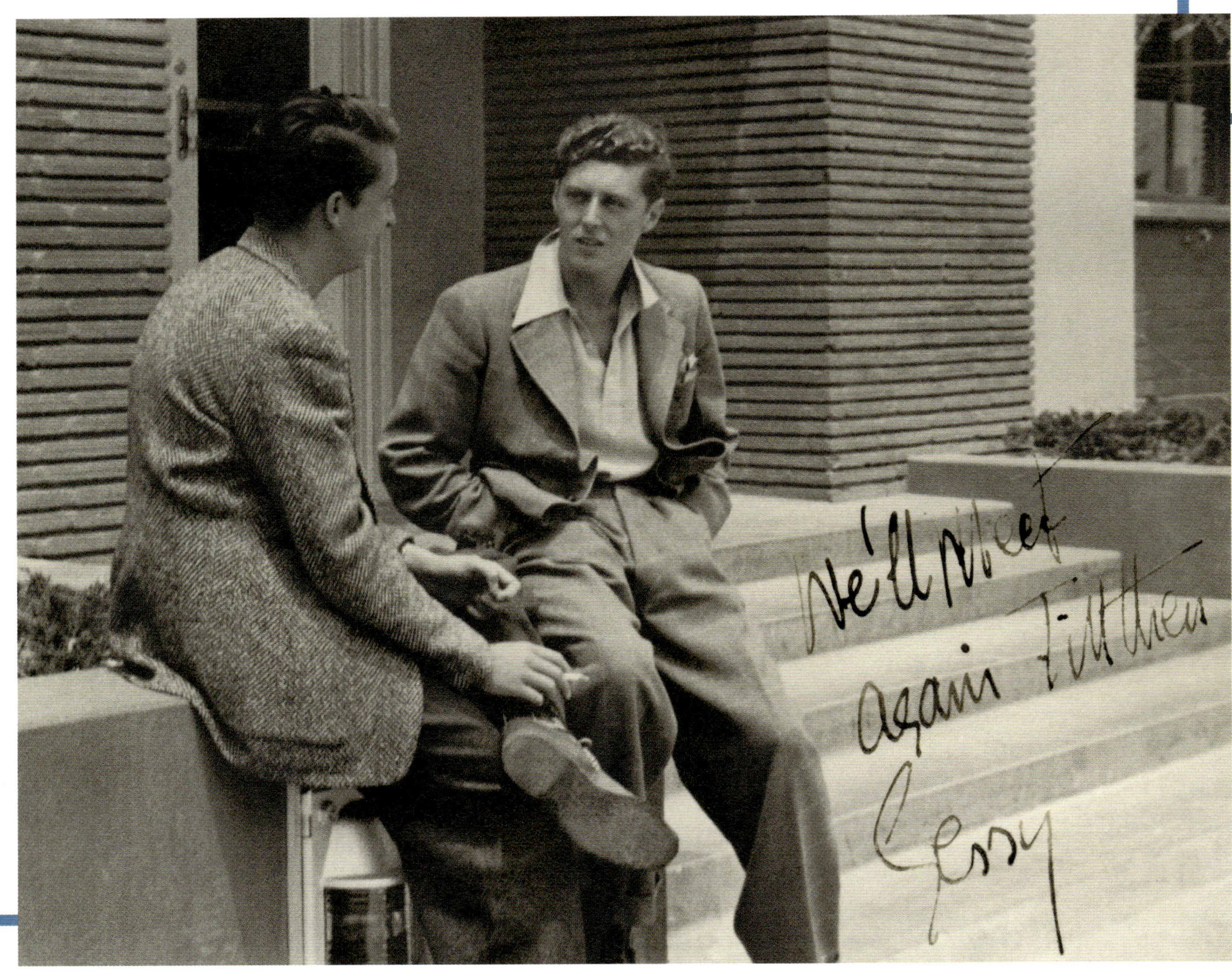

of thirty years old. Given that X's brother Ted was thirteen years younger than X, just having reached the age of fifteen, X became a father figure to Ted through his teens and twenties. X lent Ted his car to go out on dates, and upon his high school graduation, X even paid for Ted's college tuition at Loyola University. The family had grown even closer, supporting each other through their grief and navigating daily life without Agapito.

Like X and the other returning veterans, Disney itself was also going through a postwar readjustment as it tried to find and reclaim its identity while adapting to the changing times. Right from the get-go, there were the physical changes at the studio, including the termination of the government-required identification cards and the removal of the military guards at production doors. Likewise, the mass production of low-cost training films and other patriotic war films ceased. Hollywood found its industry shifting as the postwar period of regrowth in Europe focused on internal production and less on American exports. Financially and economically, European markets pulled back on the number of Hollywood movies they were requesting, drastically affecting the American studios, and Disney in particular. France limited their release of American imports to 110 films per year, and Great Britain established a governmental rule that 45 percent of all films shown in England must be domestically produced.

Without the ability to rely on the international market, and with the decline in both demand and profits, Hollywood, now also struggling with its own collapse of the studio system, once again had to readjust its business model to survive. Each studio, offering different products, altered its films accordingly. For Disney, this meant developing more inexpensive package features and focusing on films that blended live action with short sections of animation such as *Song of the South* (1946).

The inexpensive package features had two different variations, though both focused on stringing together one narrative from a ranging number of

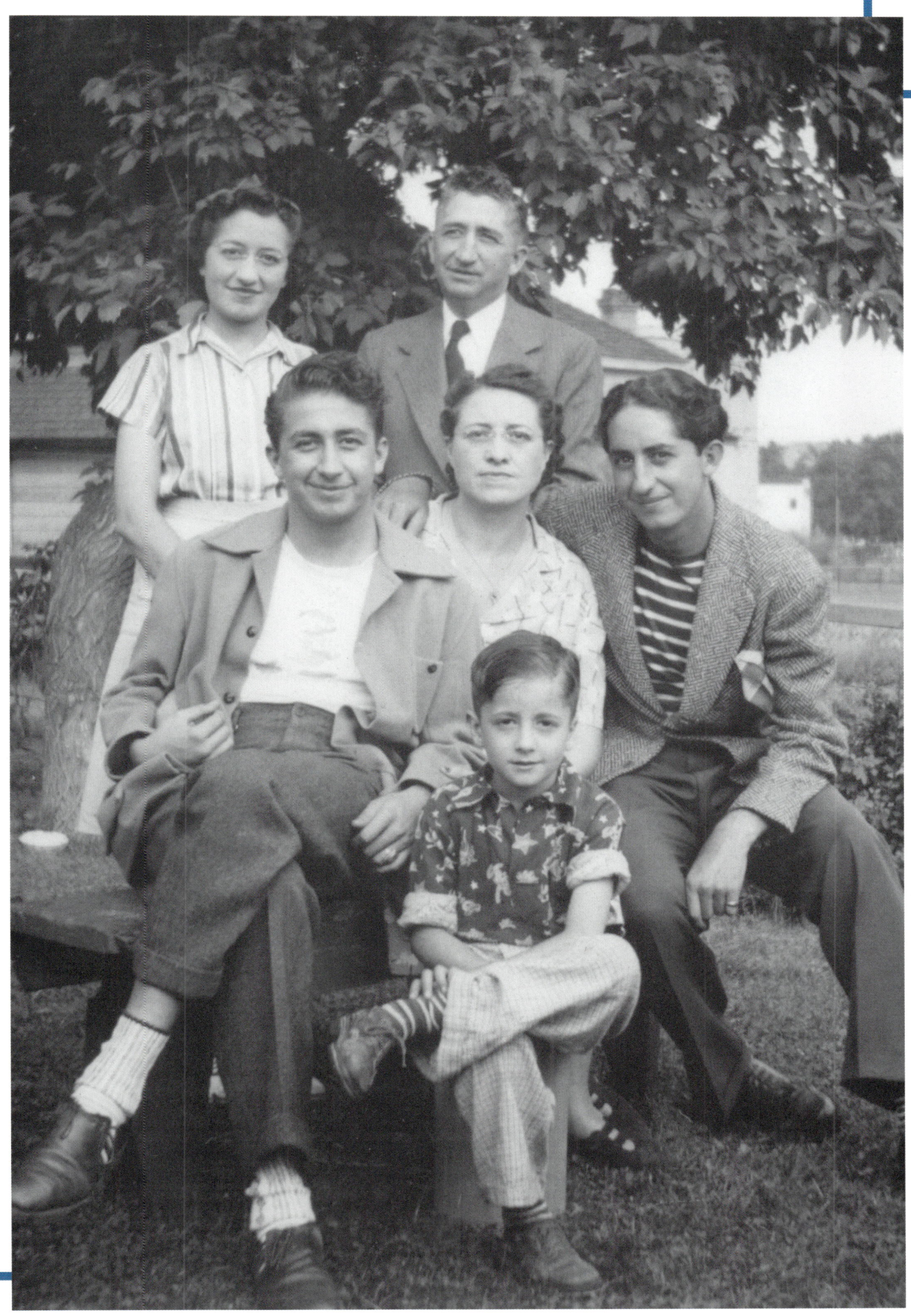

OPPOSITE: X and Gera d James sitting outside the Disney studio's Animation Building in 1940. The photo has an inscription from Gerald before he went to war; ABOVE: X with his parents and three siblings in Colorado.

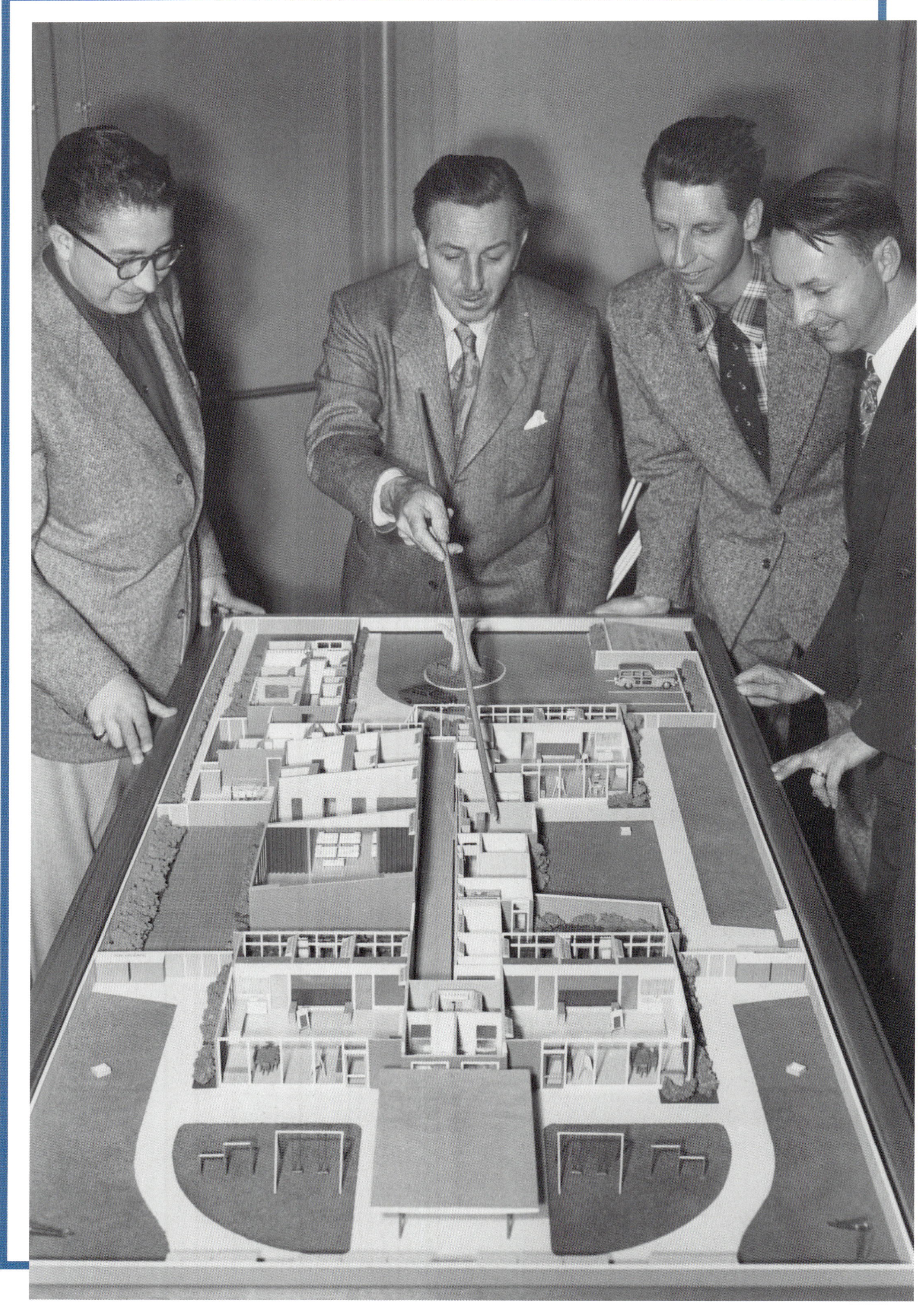

ABOVE: X, Walt, Eric Cleworth (writer and director), and Wathel Rogers in 1951, working on the model of the John Tracy Clinic; OPPOSITE: X and Walt Disney in 1951, photographed during a presentation of the John Tracy Clinic model.

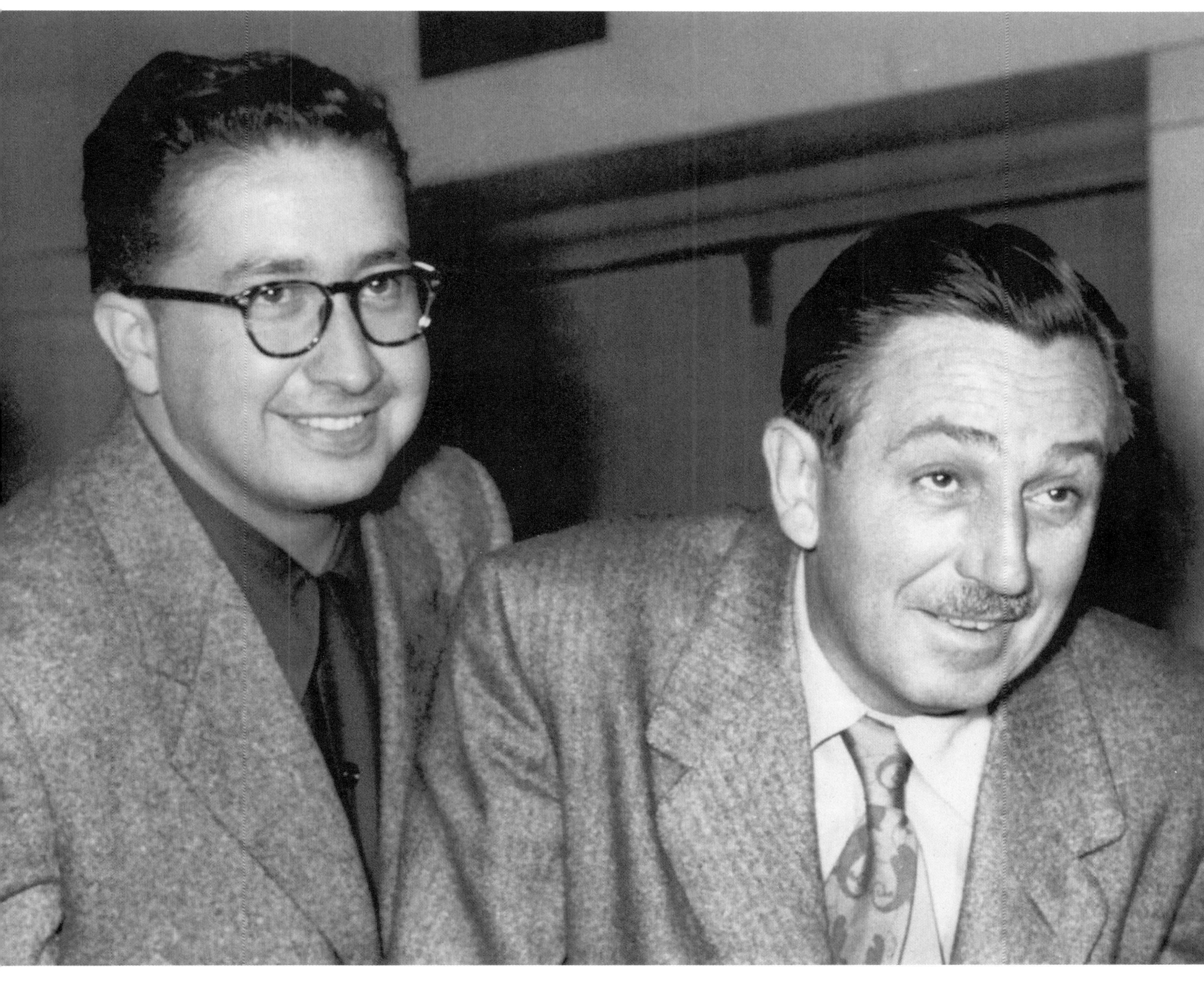

short subjects to create a feature-length production. While many of these films showcased some wonderful, creative work, none ultimately produced strong box office results or critical praise at the time. Walt continued to push tirelessly to adapt to the changing audience demands while maintaining the animation legacy on which his company had been built. And yet, by 1953, even Walt would be willing to admit—internally—that animation was currently being sustained at the studio more for tradition than profits. This point was further evidenced by the fact that while animated films continued being produced at Disney during this period, Walt himself ceded some control and instead turned his attention to other more important and large-scale endeavors, such as television productions and the opening of Disneyland.

Due to the decline in animation, it wasn't unusual for animators to get assigned to other special projects to maximize their work and minimize their downtime between features. In 1951, X was asked to work on one such endeavor for a nonprofit that earned him some face time with Walt. It involved the John Tracy Clinic, a nonprofit education center for children with hearing loss founded in 1943. The clinic was started by Louise Tracy, wife of Spencer Tracy, and named after their son, who was diagnosed as deaf as a very young child. Walt Disney was a good friend of Spencer Tracy's and, in addition to becoming

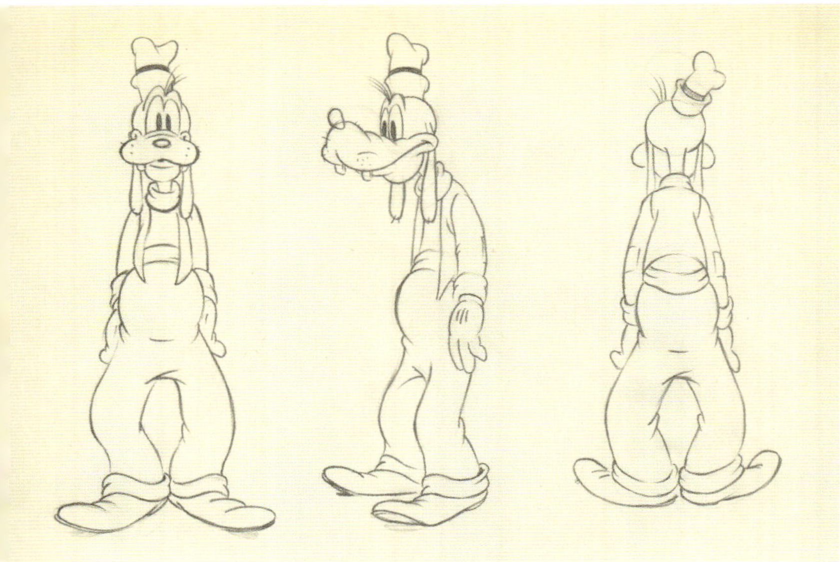

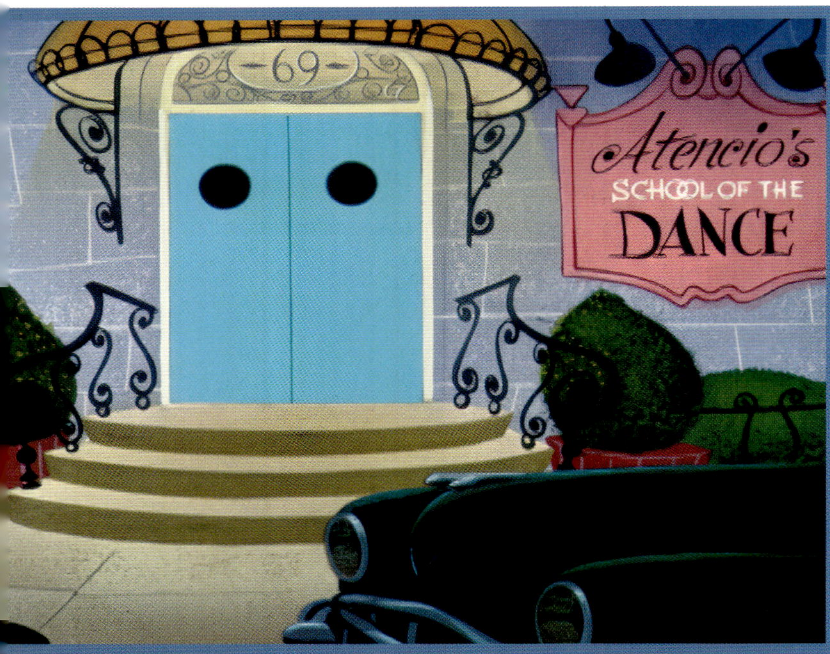

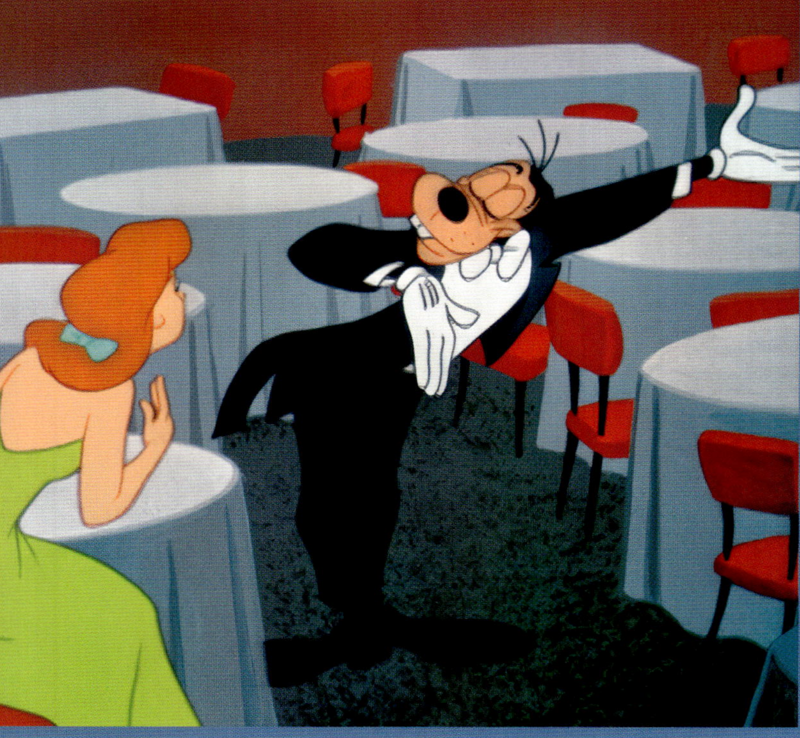

one of the first board members of the organization, agreed to enlist some of his studio employees to create a scale model of the new modern building they were planning to construct to help establish more attention and buzz around the organization. This in turn would help increase enthusiasm for their fundraising efforts. X was asked to join Wathel Rogers on the project. Walt knew that Wathel made scale models of railroads and commissioned him for the job; and Wathel, who had worked in animation with X, brought him on board. While it was a short-term project, the goodwill X established with Walt, the Tracys, and Wathel, with whom he would go on to work on Walt Disney's Enchanted Tiki Room, was worth the efforts. Louise Tracy even wrote X a note at the completion of the project, saying:

> My dear Mr. Atencio: Last Saturday the Parents' Auxiliary of the Clinic held its Bazaar—its annual fundraising event for the benefit of the Clinic. On display prominently was the little model of the building you helped to make. . . . I know it was part of your job at the Studio to build the model but, somehow, I feel that something special went into it and it is for this 'extra-special' touch that I want to thank you.

X also had to come to terms with the reality that his fellow assistant animators and colleagues who had not gone to war were now full-fledged animators. Meanwhile, not only was X still an assistant animator working with Woolie, but he also actually felt as though he had to start all over again. So X completed many more storyboards and layouts, doing very little traditional animator work. Moreover, at a time when Disney itself was grappling with its animation roots and a decreased global demand for its content, X's prospects for promotion most likely looked even grimmer.

X began working with Art Babbitt, who had been one of the leaders of the 1941 labor strike, as his assistant. While Art was a great animator, the studio hadn't been particularly keen to hire him back.

LEFT (TOP TO BOTTOM): X's 360-degree Goofy drawings; A still of "Atencio's School of the Dance" from *How to Dance*, released in 1953; An example of X's finished standardization of "the Goof" in *How to Dance*; OPPOSITE: An example of United Productions of America's modern design aesthetic.

However, they were forced to offer Art his job back after the war because he was a serviceman, which by requirement meant they had to employ him for a year after he returned from war. X learned a lot from Art but found his growth stymied as he was again in charge of doing clean-up work. But after Art left the studio, X became clean-up supervisor and worked with Jack Kinney, the director of the Goofy shorts. Although still technically an assistant, X would take all the scenes for the short subjects and key them, making two or three drawings per scene in which he arranged the costume and style of the character before passing it on to the other assistants to use as a model for their remaining work and drawings. This ensured a consistency in tone and style throughout the entire project.

For each short, there were approximately four to five animators animating, each with their own drawing styles and often their own proportions for their drawings, so X also oversaw and maintained the uniformity in and across all scenes. While some animators were good draftsmen and animators whose work could easily be used as the baseline for uniformity, others were less adept, and more effort was required to correct their drawings to match the work of the larger group. Spending so much time focused on specializing in the art of drawing Goofy and ensuring Goofy's standardization in all short creations, X said that he felt that he "knew 'the Goof' better than anybody." Ultimately, X continued coordinating and overseeing the clean-up work and corresponding uniformity until 1953 when he went to work with Ward Kimball.

Ward, another one of Walt's "Nine Old Men," recruited X to work in his unit. A new style of animation that was tied to the launch of the United Productions of America (UPA) studio had gained more popularity in recent years. This UPA studio was started by former Disney animators who left Disney after the strike and had launched their own animation studio, founded as a direct reaction to the principles and realist aesthetics of Disney animation. Unlike Disney's classic style, UPA instead focused on a minimalistic and painterly approach that was crafted by artists who knew how to draw and control a flat surface, using the materials to create an intricate but minimalist design that spoke to audiences and reflected the changing times.

According to X, the animators called them "pointy nose characters as opposed to little fat bunnies," to give a specific visualization to the drastically

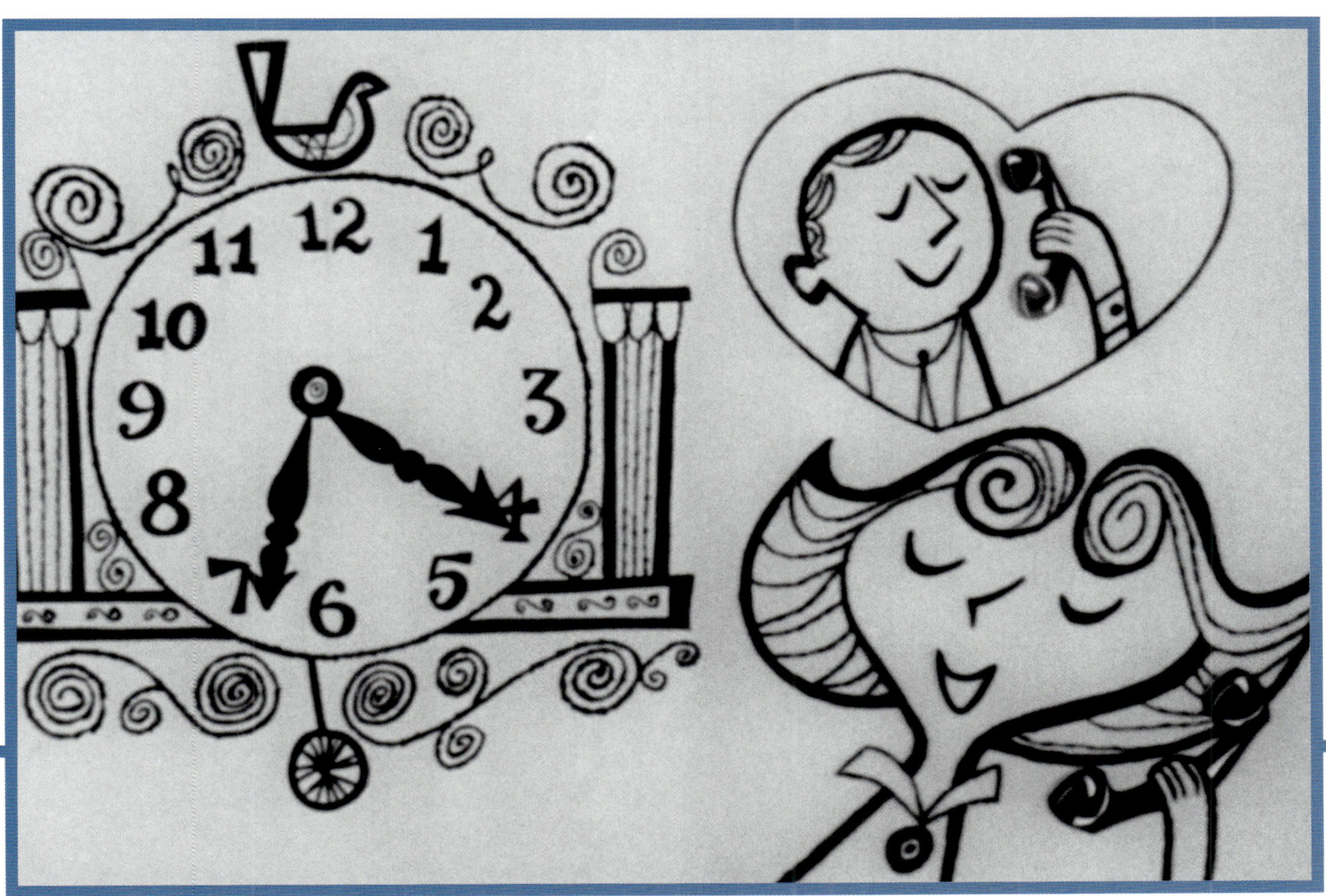

different designs. Aware of both styles and the rival studio that had been started by former colleagues, X, and others, were willing and excited by the prospect of working on both. One time X asked Walt, "Why don't we do something like [what] UPA has been doing?" before further admitting to Walt that he liked UPA's stylized characters. Engaged in both an ideological and box office battle, Walt replied, "They're making pictures for the intellect; we're making pictures for the heart. And there's a hell of a lot more heart than there are intellects."

While Walt publicly admonished the other studio and their "un-Disney-like" style, he was open to trying to produce some like-minded films, given Ward's advocacy, and since their style of animation was cheaper, faster, and slowly gaining popularity with audiences. Needing more volume and lower cost content in a style that spoke to the audiences' changing tastes, Walt ultimately listened to the suggestions of his artists and took a lower-risk chance, putting Ward in charge of such productions that melded traditional Disney animation with the newer UPA style.

Ward wanted to make films with a more modern aesthetic, and he knew X drew "pointy nosed characters" that would match his artistic sensibilities. X agreed and went to work with Ward on the shorts *Adventures in Music: Melody* and *Toot, Whistle,*

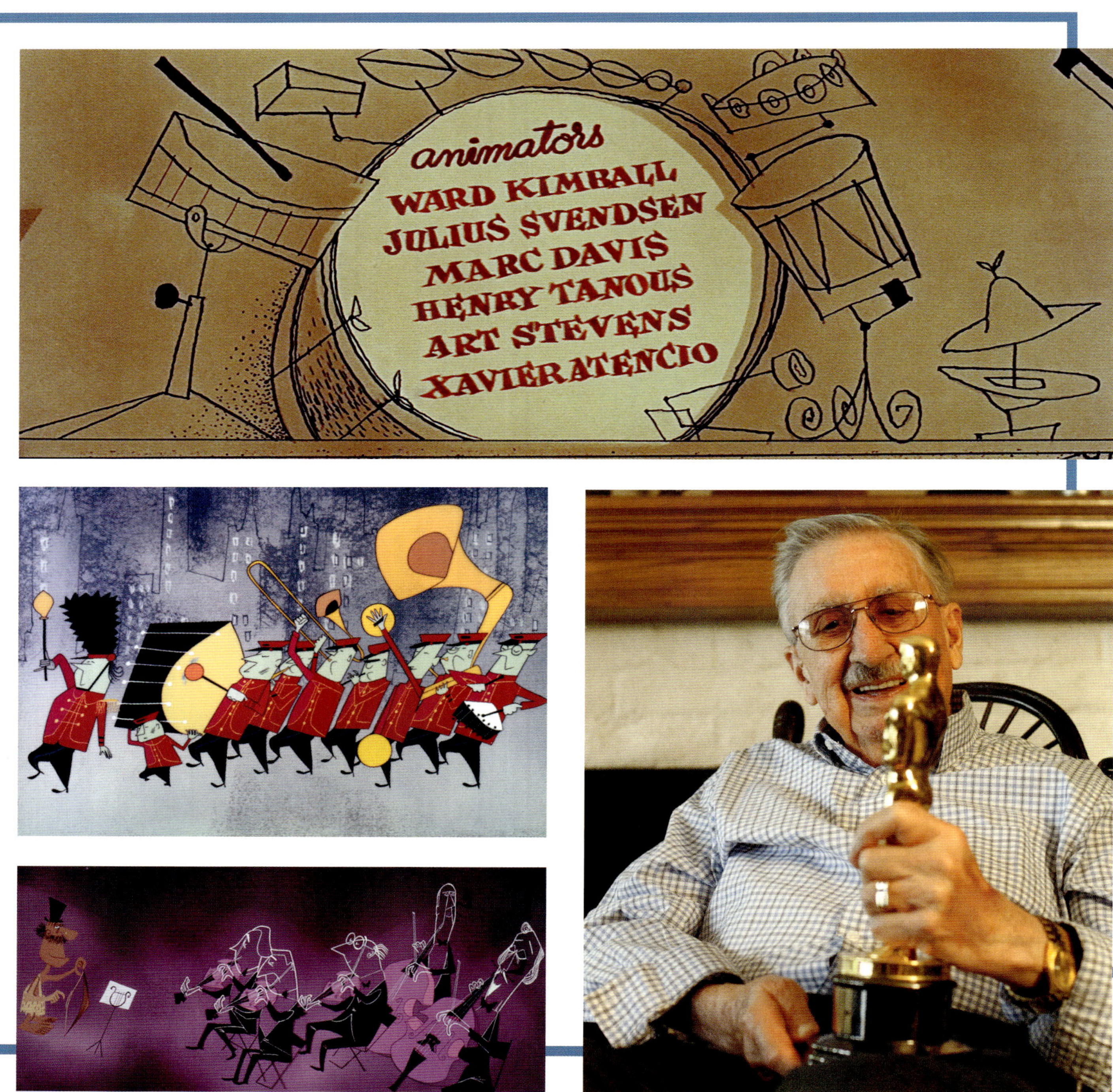

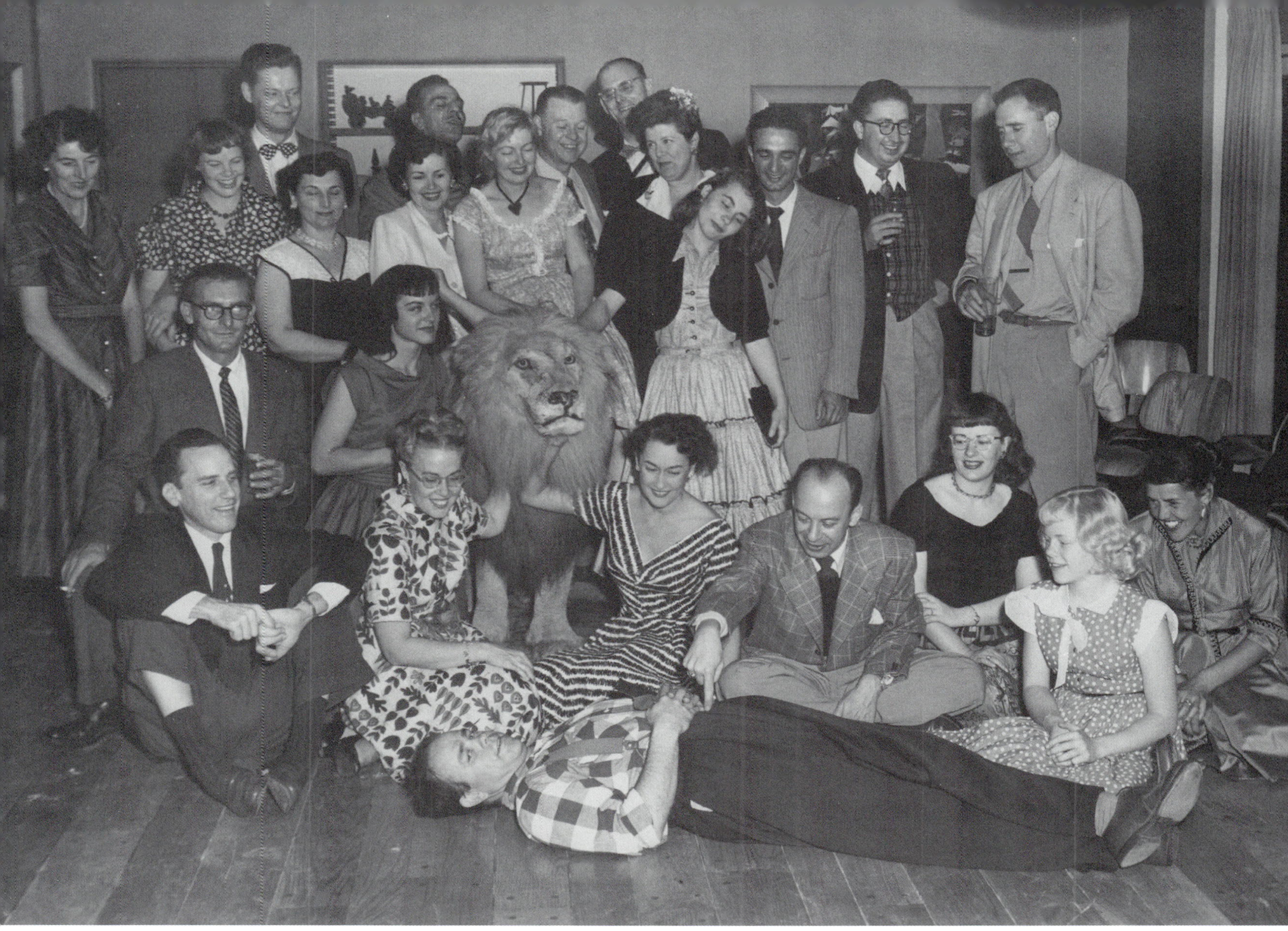

Plunk and Boom (both 1953). *Toot, Whistle, Plunk and Boom* ultimately became X's first official screen credit as an animator. Ward set up a style on the project with another artist, and X was again in charge of cleaning up and ensuring they kept to the style guide and consistently applied the aesthetic throughout all hands and phases of the project.

For *Melody*, Ward took a greater risk, wanting to consciously break with Disney traditions and by bringing in designers from outside the studio who didn't adhere to its usual style. The first designer was Eyvind Earle, who was a fine arts painter already working in the Disney ecosystem but gaining a growing reputation for causing problems, as his backgrounds were so detailed that people felt they detracted from the frame's main foreground action. The second was Tommy Oreb, a layout man who wanted to push boundaries by using a New York advertising style of flat, graphic characters. As the short was pegged as an educational picture not for theatrical release, Ward was able to have more control over the piece and successfully depart from the Disney norms. And since the film was deemed too small and low profile, management didn't have the picture on their radars, and senior animators were too busy working on features, Ward had to rely on longtime assistants for the lead roles on it.

The assistants were thrilled to be given more creative freedom and higher positions than usual and worked together to experiment artistically on

OPPOSITE (TOP): X's first screen credit, along with those for Ward Kimball and his fellow animators, on *Toot, Whistle, Plunk and Boom*; OPPOSITE (MIDDLE AND BOTTOM LEFT): Stills from 1953's *Toot, Whistle, Plunk and Boom*; OPPOSITE (BOTTOM RIGHT): X holds the Best Short Subject Oscar the studio garnered for *Toot, Whistle, Plunk and Boom*; ABOVE: The *Toot, Whistle, Plunk and Boom* wrap party in 1953, with X standing second from right among his colleagues and a stuffed lion.

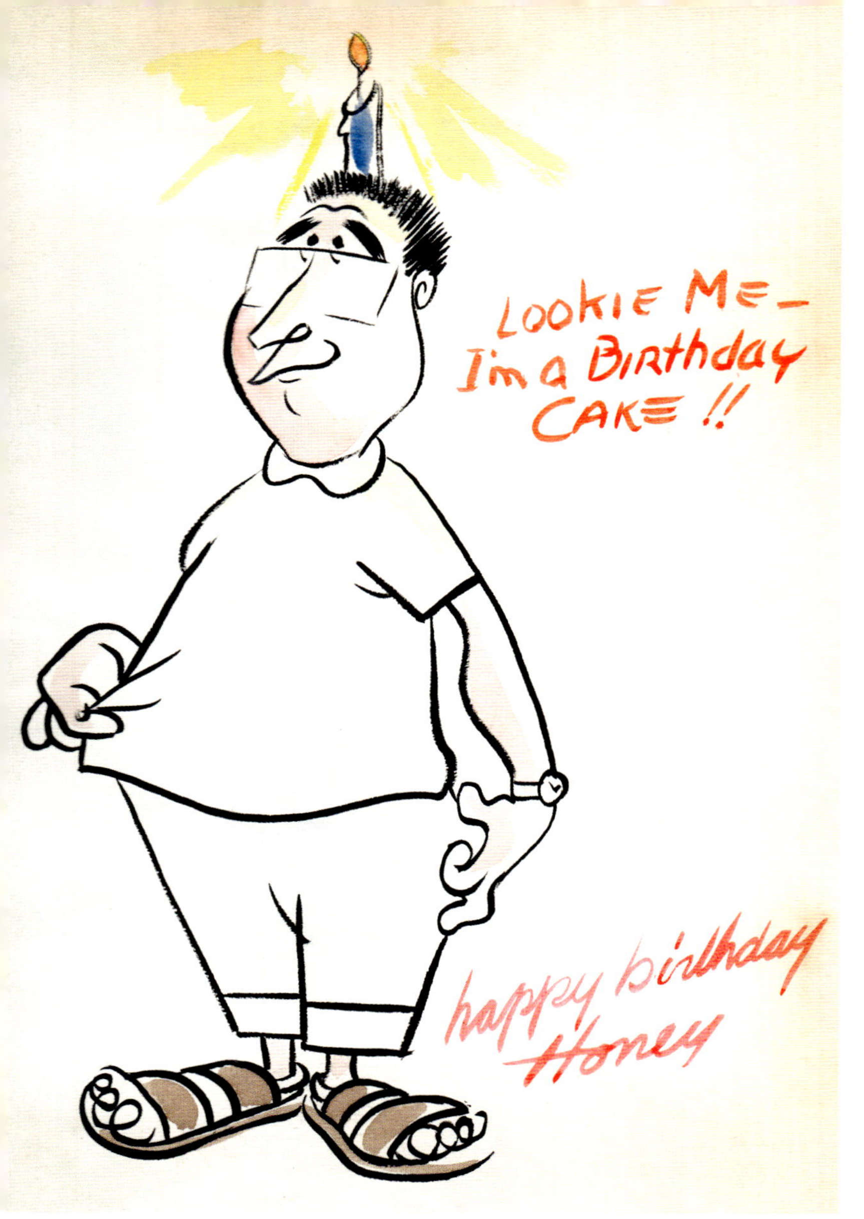

the bounds of animation. These bold choices excited Ward, who wanted to be anti-realistic in his animation style, often opposing the visual style established in traditional Disney animated films, which focused on realism and intricate, lifelike designs that helped to craft the believability of the world and story. Although his style was a departure, with not much support from higher-level animators, Ward had Walt's favor and trust and was given free rein on what he wanted to do (at least for lower-cost shorts), which ultimately benefited X and other rising, experimentally stylistic artists at Disney. This freer experimentation under an encouraging artist like Ward

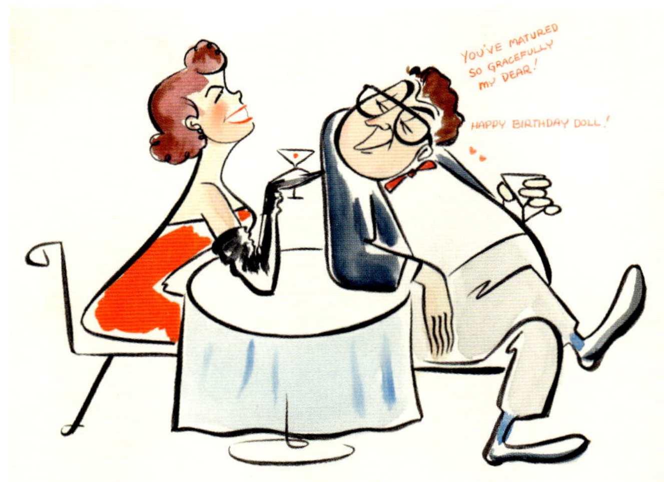

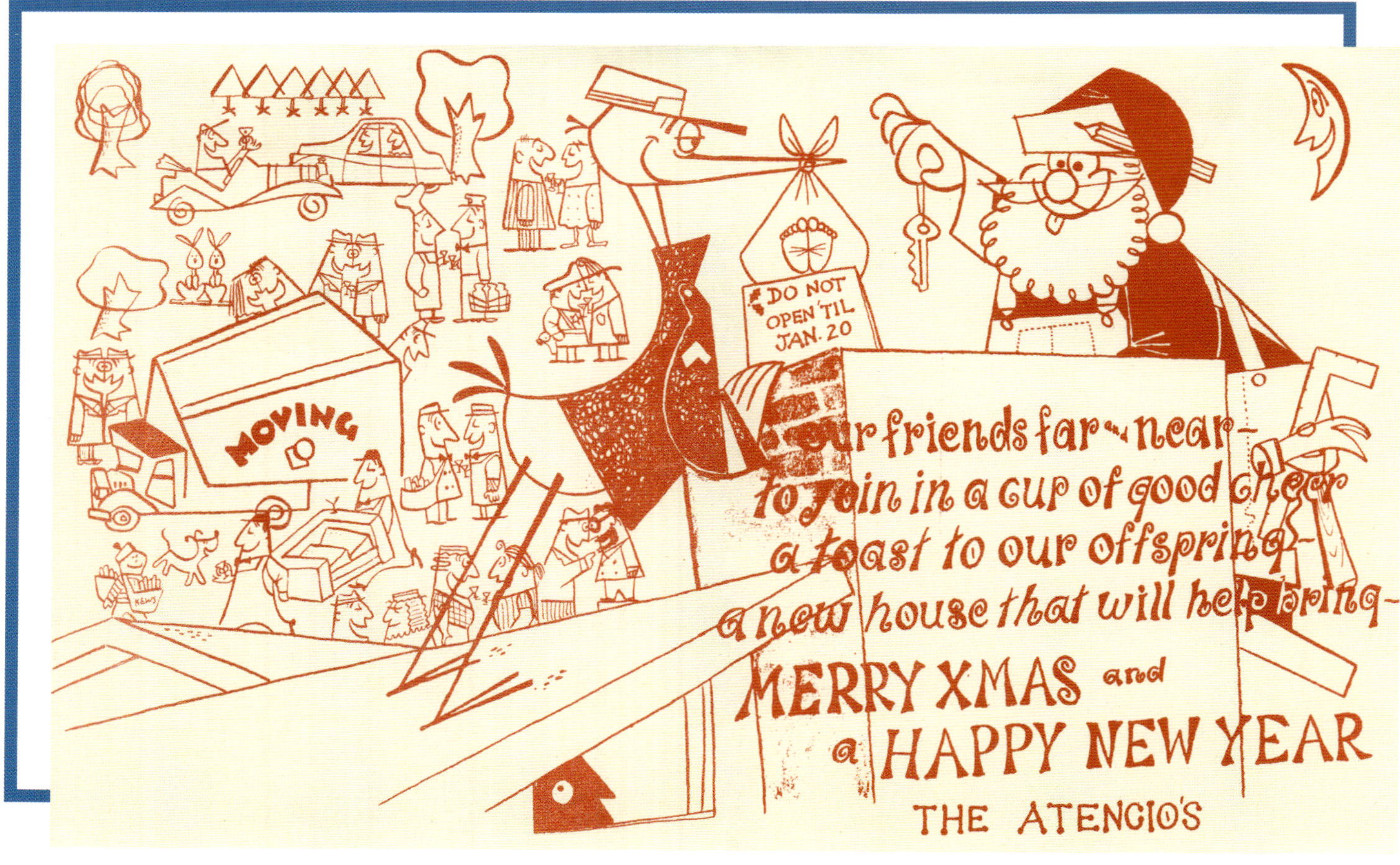

TOP: X's birthday cards to Mary, from 1951 and 1952, showing the "slightly pointy nosed characters" that caught the attention of Ward Kimball; ABOVE: Atencio family Christmas card, December 1953, reflecting the modern style of *Toot, Whistle, Plunk and Boom*; OPPOSITE: Letter from the Academy of Motion Picture Arts and Sciences in 1956 inviting X to join.

ACADEMY OF MOTION PICTURE ARTS AND SCIENCES

HOLLYWOOD, CALIFORNIA

GEORGE SEATON
PRESIDENT

December 18, 1956

Mr. F. Xavier Atencio
5223 Canoga Avenue
Woodland Hills, Calif.

Dear Mr. Atencio:

Membership in the Academy is offered to those who have contributed to the arts and sciences of motion pictures. Your name has been submitted by qualified sponsors, and the Board of Governors has authorized me to extend you an invitation to become a member of the Short Subjects Branch of our organization.

The Academy is an honorary association of artists and craftsmen employed in the film industry, and our purpose is to foster co-operation among the creative leaders of our profession. The nominal dues ($3.00 per month) are tax deductible. If you wish additional information about membership, please telephone Mrs. Margaret Herrick, Academy Executive Director, Crestview 51146.

An acceptance card is enclosed for your convenience.

Cordially,

George Seaton

George Seaton

GS:cc
Encl.

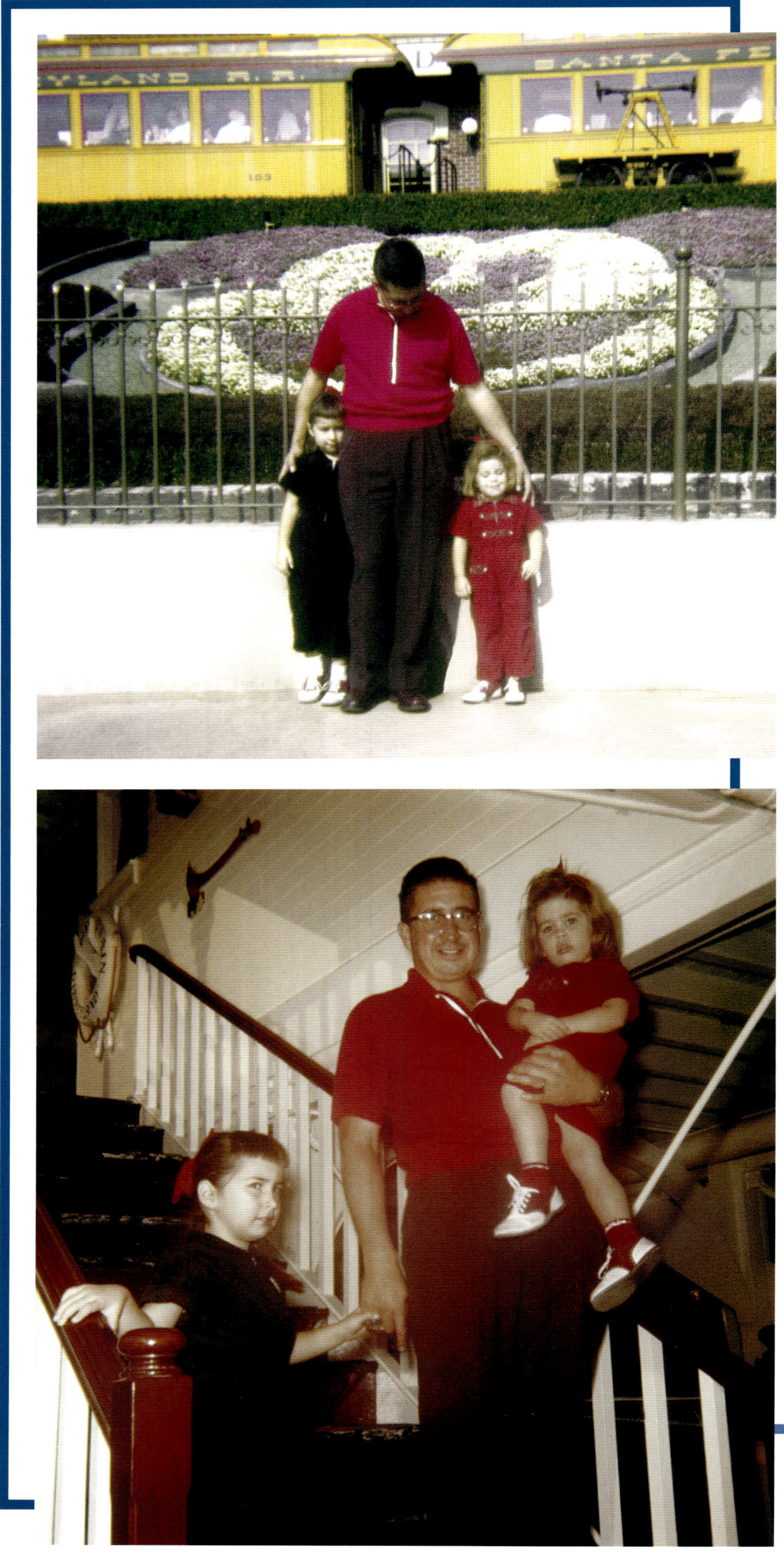

led to changes in X's own style. In looking at X's personal work at this time, including his 1953 Christmas card, X's pre–*Toot, Whistle, Plunk and Boom* "slightly pointy nosed characters" had evolved into "very pointy nosed characters."

While Walt never really warmed to *Melody*, he did like *Toot, Whistle, Plunk and Boom*, which went on to win the Academy Award for Best Short Subject (Cartoons), the first award for a Disney animated short in over a decade. Though *Toot, Whistle, Plunk and Boom* represented X's first official screen credit, industry standard at the time dictated that the Oscar go to the whole studio and not to the individual artists involved. While X attended the wrap party for the film, he wasn't given an Academy Award for his individual efforts. Instead, Walt accepted the award, and X never even saw the Oscar statue until decades later when he was offered the chance to hold it during a D23 interview. Likely as a result of the success of *Toot, Whistle, Plunk and Boom*, X was invited to join the Academy of Motion Picture Arts and Sciences as a member of the Short Subjects branch on December 18, 1956.

X took pride in a job well done and basked in the critical praise. According to *Time* magazine, "*Toot* takes Disney in one jump from the nursery to the intellectual cocktail party." *Toot, Whistle, Plunk and Boom* was also the first animated cartoon to appear in wide-screen CinemaScope, and given its successes, it officially "began the inevitable turn toward stylistic modernism." Although Walt would ultimately agree to make both UPA-style and traditional Disney pictures, Disney's legacy lies in its heart and "fat bunny"–style productions, proving that even while adapting to changing design preferences and audience tastes, Walt knew his brand and stuck to it, asking the same from his artists and animators. However, particularly in the short-form space, where it was faster, cheaper, and easier to experiment, Walt gave leeway to those he trusted to play around with what Disney could create.

Perhaps the largest change in the history of Disney, though, was the July 17, 1955, opening of Disneyland, which revolutionized American pop culture and themed entertainment. Disneyland changed Americans' vacation patterns and leisure activities; it established the idea of high-concept and synergistic "theme parks" beyond the previously existing perception of what constituted an amusement park—and ultimately forever altered the way global audiences and creators engaged with films and interactive storytelling. X and many other employees were invited to opening day in Anaheim, just down Interstate 5 from Burbank. They headed to the park in the July heat the day of the park's premiere and were seated in the railroad cars near Adventureland. The plan was that the cameras would pan around, and the employees would wave and smile, providing great marketing

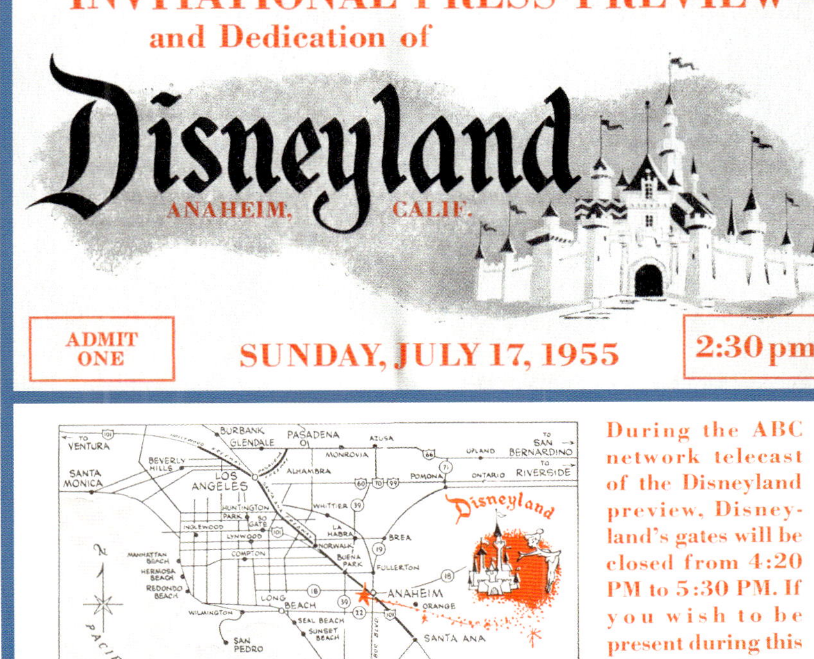

OPPOSITE (TOP): Tori, X, and Judianne in front of the Santa Fe & Disneyland Railroad. OPPOSITE (BOTTOM): X and his daughters on the *Mark Twain*; LEFT: X's ticket for the Santa Fe & Disneyland Railroad on Disneyland's opening day; ABOVE: The front and back of X's ticket to the Sunday, July 17, 1955, press preview and dedication of Disneyland.

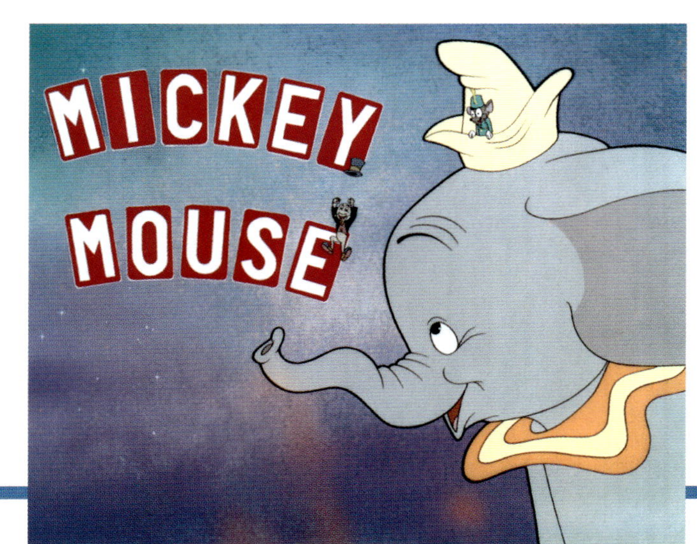

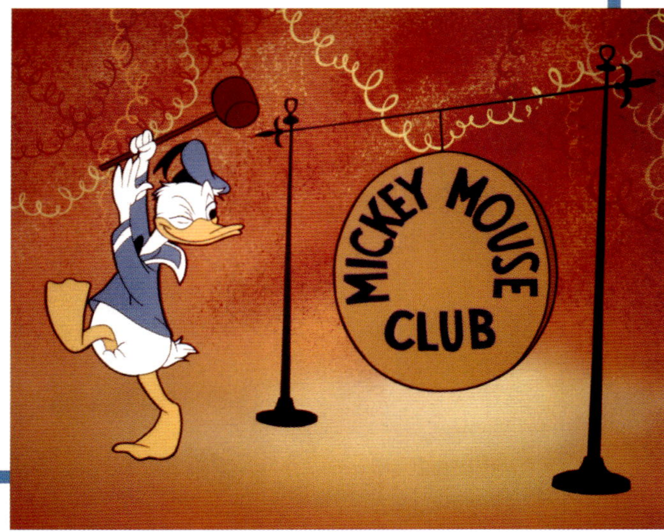

and promotion for the company. However, the plan failed, and according to X, "Well, hell, they never showed up, and we're sitting on the boxcar. So that's all I saw of opening day at the park." Between his day of waiting and his attending alone (due to a member of his family being ill), X's opening day at Disneyland was hardly the "magical day" he had envisioned. Still, X fondly remembered getting to be a small part of this culture-shifting phenomenon.

As the 1950s continued and audiences started to pursue the new suburban ideal—larger families, bigger homes with yards, and the massively growing appeal of television—movies suffered at the box office. For Disney, this meant the end of the traditional Disney short films, particularly as theaters closed or focused on double features to attract audiences. The shorts had for years been facing continued budget cuts and curtailment to keep them profitable, but with ever-changing tastes and demands by the audience being marketed to, further budget cuts weren't going to make a difference, profits were sinking fast regardless, and the shorts themselves could no longer be justified. Without the shorts, changes came to the studio's animation department. In the past, when the animators were between features, they would pick up quick work on one of the shorts, but now they often found themselves worried they would be laid off between projects or hired on a project-by-project basis.

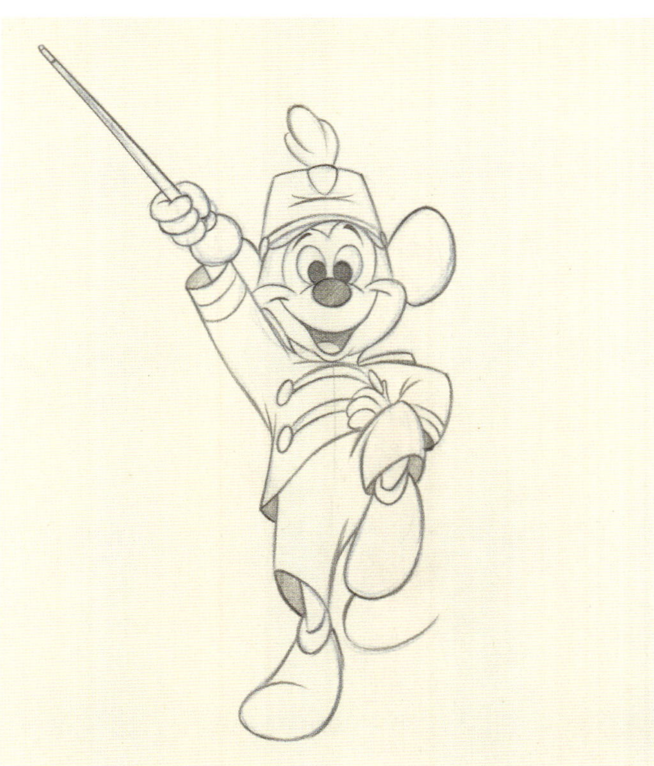

To counter these trends—and to take full advantage of a new medium, Walt began broadcasting *Disneyland* (later renamed *Walt Disney's Wonderful World of Color*) in 1954, a weekly television show that helped both to market Disney and, soon after, premiere the newly opened Disneyland Park directly into the homes of families around America. Particularly for Disney, which sought first and foremost to appeal to families with children, the television medium provided a more economical and accessible means of attracting viewership and offering content. Disney's strategy and product needs expanded and changed rapidly to successfully capture this new market and interest, and during what was by now considered

ABOVE: Stills from the title sequence for the *Mickey Mouse Club* using colored background cards; LEFT: X's pencil drawing of Mickey Mouse for the *Mickey Mouse Club* title sequence; OPPOSITE: A still from *Jack and Old Mac*.

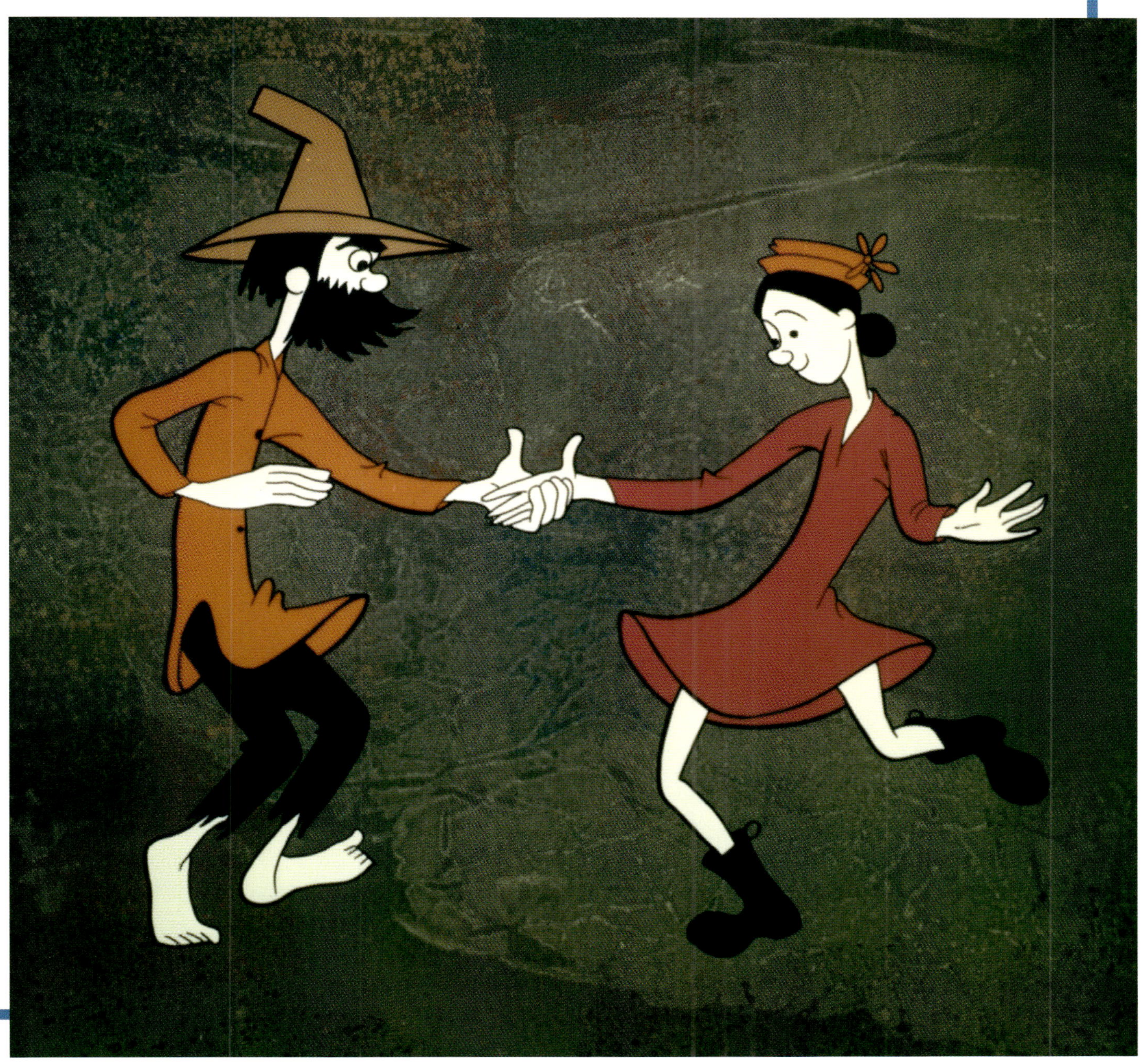

television's heyday, the studio was at the point where it produced as much film in a week as it used to produce in a year.

With these new needs came more responsibility and opportunity for those working at the studio. Walt gave Bill Justice, X's old colleague and friend from the Woolie Unit, the chance to be a cartoon director. When Bill Justice agreed, he constructed a small team with a trusted assistant at its core, offering X the role as his right-hand man. Bill had always been impressed by X's talent and felt he had a "unique ability to do most anything he wanted." Likewise, it didn't hurt that Bill also felt X was "one of the finest people he had ever known." Bill and X started off being given small projects, meaning that they were able to be nimble and get the work done quickly and by themselves without relying on the other studio divisions, which were already overburdened by the rapidly growing output of work the studio was being tasked with producing. They designed the backgrounds and the characters, animated the projects, and did the whole production as opposed to having a specialized labor "assembly line" do it. X and Bill were also tasked with increasing their productivity without increasing costs, the endless plight of the Hollywood artist.

However, X had always been a visionary, plus a practical thinker. He came up with his first "radical idea for the time" when developing the title sequence for television's *Mickey Mouse Club* (which premiered in 1955). To save time on developing backgrounds, X suggested using colored cards for the backgrounds.

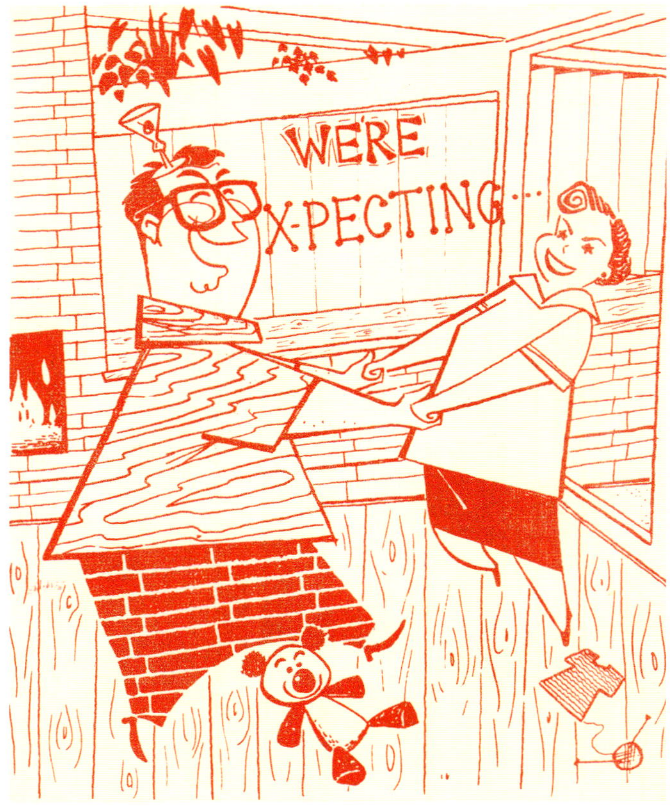

Bill agreed to his proposal, and together they built a cost-effective opening sequence that became one of the most used pieces of film in studio history. X went further in adding his own personal mark to the titles with a sequence of instruments and music notes that was distinctly in the modern style he had developed while working with Ward. And to really entice audiences, they created several different endings to the opening, ensuring that it remained fresh and interesting. When audiences realized this, they would watch the opening and wait in anticipation to see which ending they were going to get, offering what is now an early form of direct audience interaction between the creative teams and their fans.

X continued working with Bill on more short films, including *Jack and Old Mac* (1956), an unusual two-part film that based the first section's title and narrative on the nursery rhyme "The House That Jack Built," and the second part on the song "Old MacDonald Had a Farm," though the second part of the short was titled "Old MacDonald Had a Band." *Jack and Old Mac* diverged from Disney's usual animation style, focusing on X and Bill's pioneering inexpensive yet effective style of simplified television animation with minimum backgrounds like they had constructed for the *Mickey Mouse Club*. Bill Justice directed *Jack and Old Mac*, and X designed the characters. Another partner for this project was prolific composer George Bruns, who wrote the music for the short and would later go on to write the music for the Pirates of the Caribbean attraction in partnership with X.

In 1952, meantime, outside of work, X and Mary bought two adjoining lots of land in a new sleepy San Fernando Valley part of Los Angeles called Woodland Hills. The properties on the corner of Canoga and Ventura Avenues afforded views of orange groves and a dairy farm with grazing cows. X designed a small two-bedroom, one-and-a-half-bathroom home, inspired by the popular mid-century modern style. The house also had an art studio for X, specifically planned with no access from the inside of the home in anticipation of being able to work without interruptions and distractions from anyone, including his future children.

And in a stroke of fortuitous timing, after eight years of trying to have children, X and Mary found out that Mary was pregnant soon after construction started on the house. In January 1954, Victoria ("Tori") Atencio made her official entrance into the world, just months before they officially moved into their newly constructed Woodland Hills home. Almost two years later, in December 1955, their second daughter, Judianne, was born. While raising two daughters, the family was able to fit easily into their two-bedroom

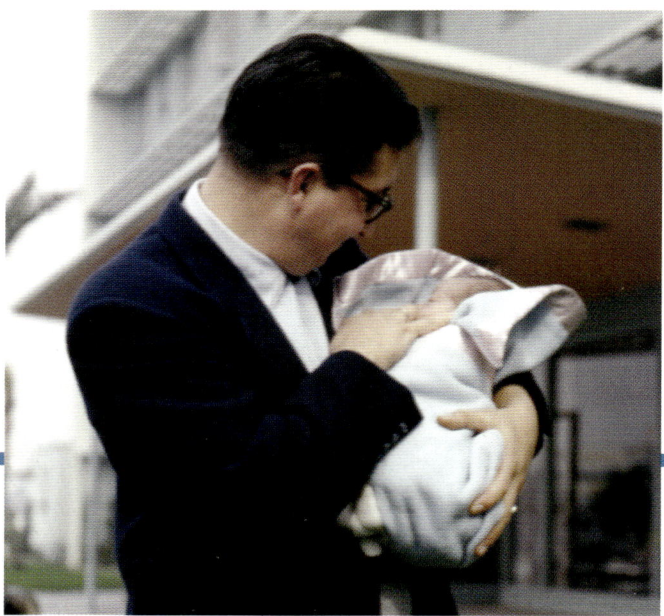

ABOVE: X's 1953 Christmas card announcing Mary's pregnancy and their upcoming move; RIGHT: X holding Tori at St. Joseph's Hospital in Burbank shortly after her birth.

home. But the arrival of their third child and first son, Gerald ("Jerry"), in 1957, and then their fourth and final child, Joseph ("Joe"), in 1959, tested the true limits of the house. At first, all four children lived together in the house's second bedroom, but the siblings soon started to outgrow the practicality of sharing the space. Instead of moving into a larger home, X designed and built an addition to the house that included a family room and an extra upstairs bedroom and bathroom. In 1960, Tori and Judianne officially moved into the new room upstairs.

With a household of six, X and Mary were always busy. Mary was a full-time mother keeping up with four young children. Meanwhile, X would leave for work at Disney every morning and come home

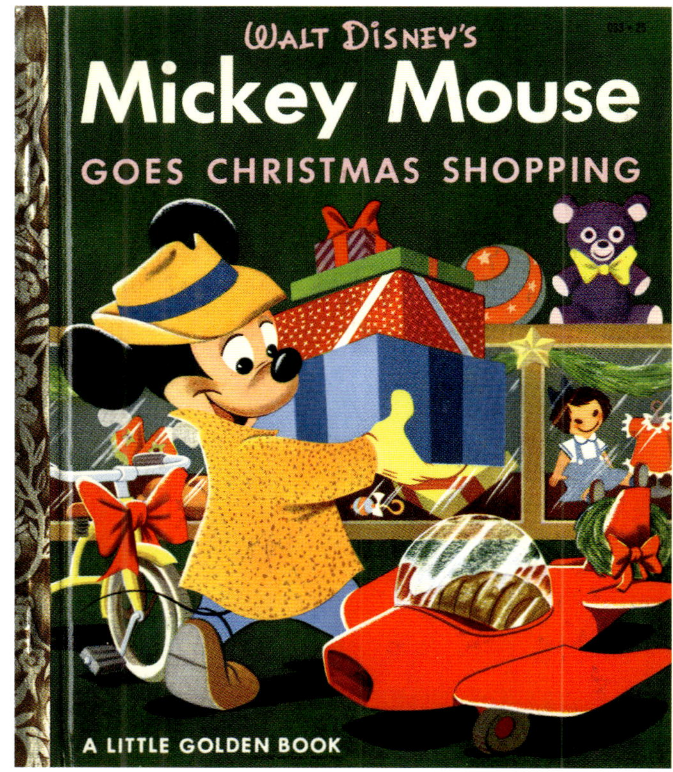

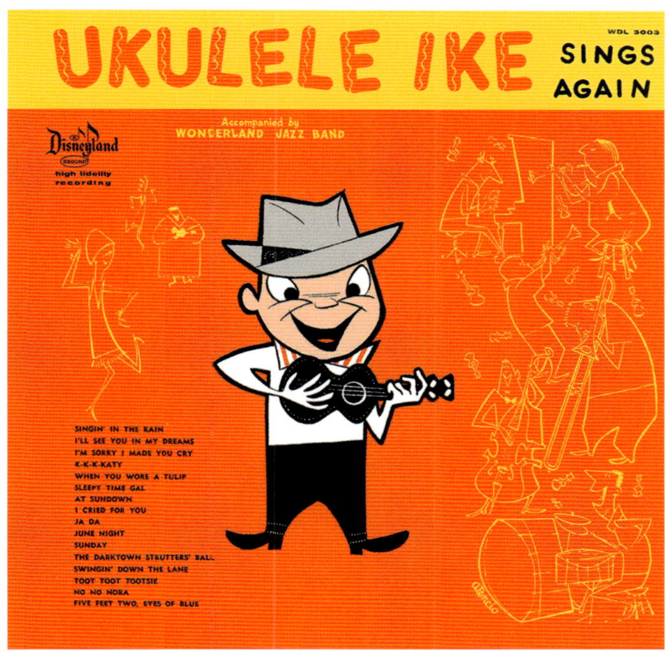

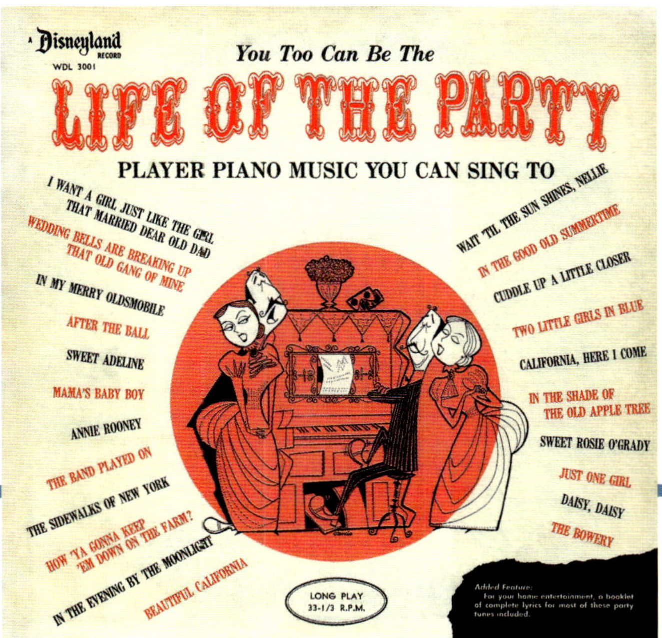

dutifully around 5:30 p.m. every evening for dinner and to spend time with his family. However, after work and dinner there was no time for X to relax and watch television or read the paper. Instead, X was back to work, for while he loved his job at Disney, the studio wasn't paying him enough to support such a large family, a reality for many of the artists and animators working at that time at the company. X would finish dinner and head out to his home studio and begin to draw. Mary would get the children ready for bed and then send them out in their pajamas to say good night to their dad.

In sticking with his strengths and mirroring his own father's balancing of creative pursuits with work in order to support his family, X channeled his artistry and his drive into his side work. Outside of his ever-growing generous list of free-card recipients for any and all occasions—birthdays, anniversaries, birth announcements, Mother's Day, Christmas—X had many paying clients over the years seeking his artistry on a freelance basis, including Walt Disney Productions. X worked for Disney's merchandising

(Continued on page 84)

LEFT: X's Disneyland Records album-cover designs, featuring his modern styling; ABOVE: One of the Little Golden Books illustrated by X.

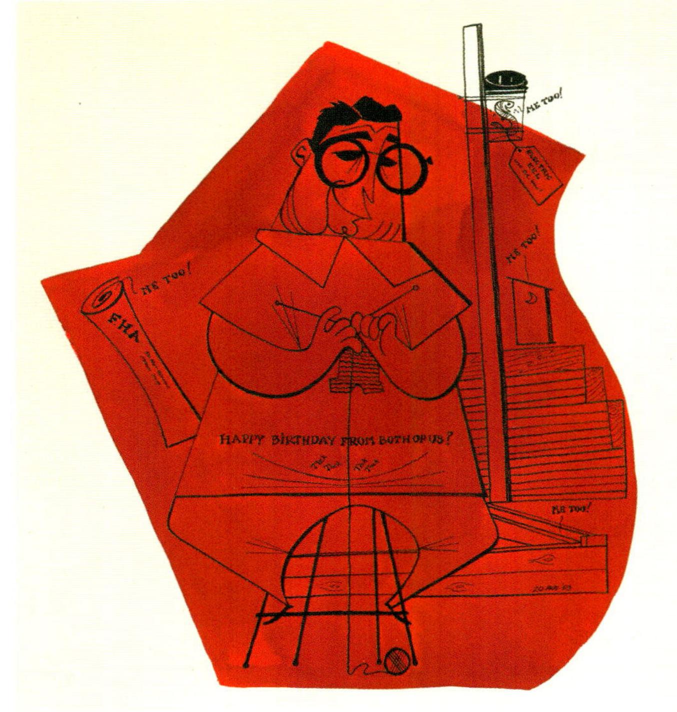

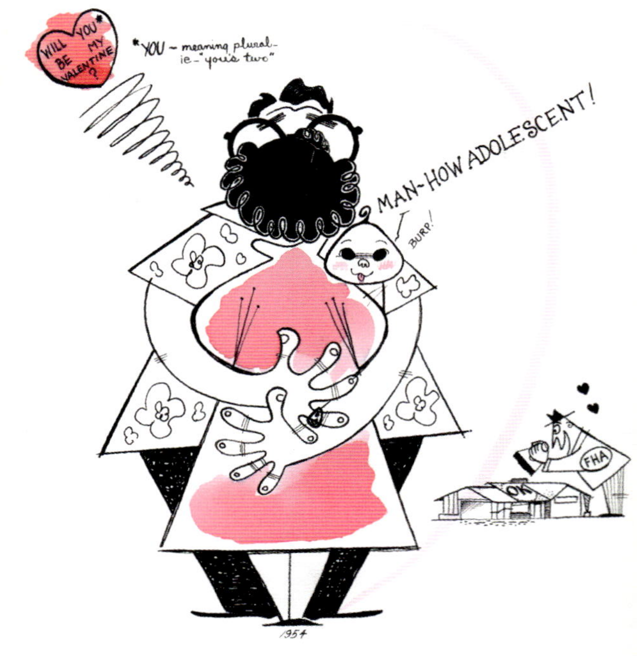

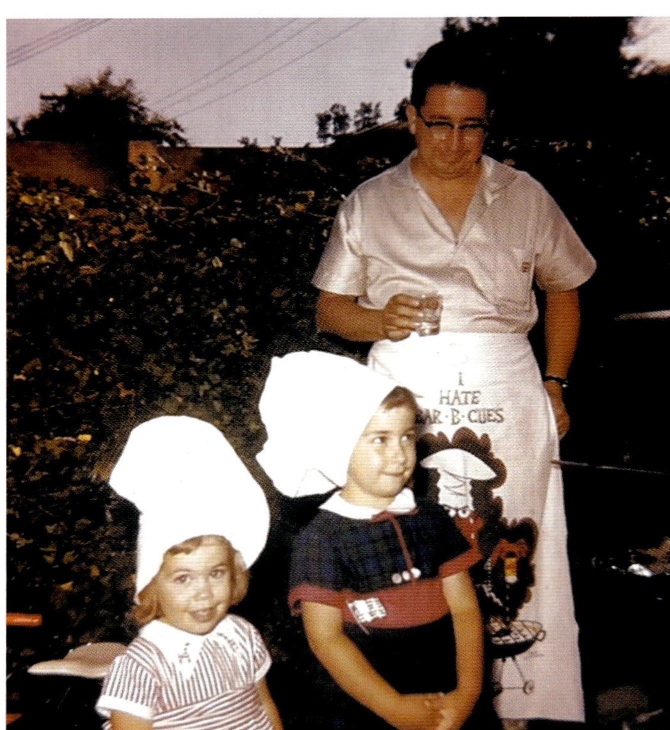

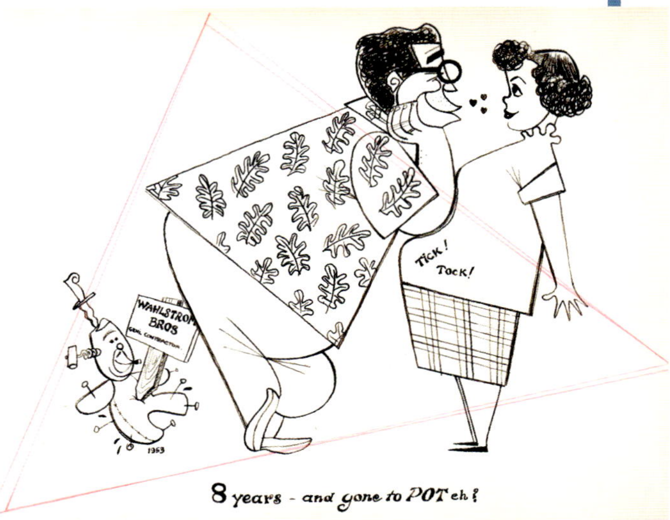

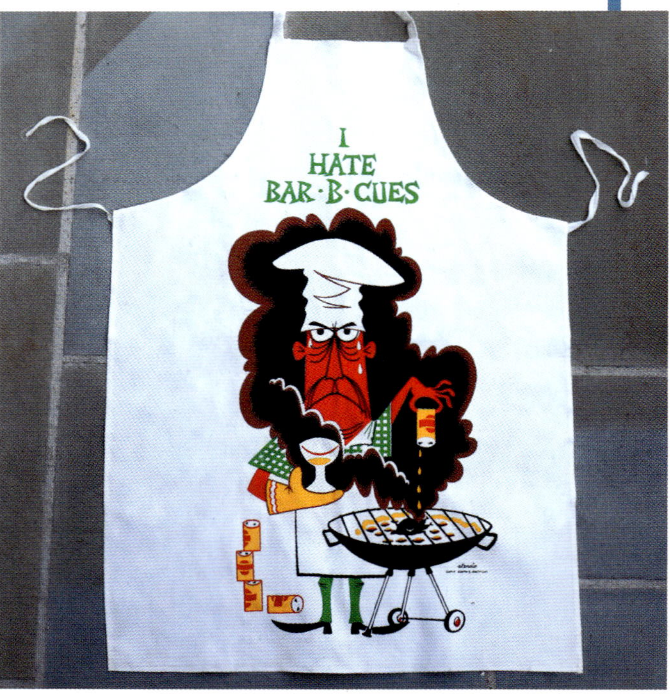

ABOVE (CLOCKWISE FROM TOP LEFT): X's birthday card to Mary in 1953 depicting their home-building process and preparations for the arrival of a baby; X's 1954 Valentine's Day card for Mary, their first as new parents; X's eighth anniversary card to Mary from 1953; An apron featuring one of X's designs; Judianne, Tori, and X barbecuing, with X wearing one of the aprons he designed; OPPOSITE (CLOCKWISE FROM TOP LEFT): X and Mary strike a pose and Mary breaks ground for their new home in the Woodland Hills section of Los Angeles; Tori and Judianne photographed in the family's upstairs addition as it was being built; The exterior of the finished Woodland Hills home that X designed for the Atencio family; Interior photo of the Atencio home's new living room.

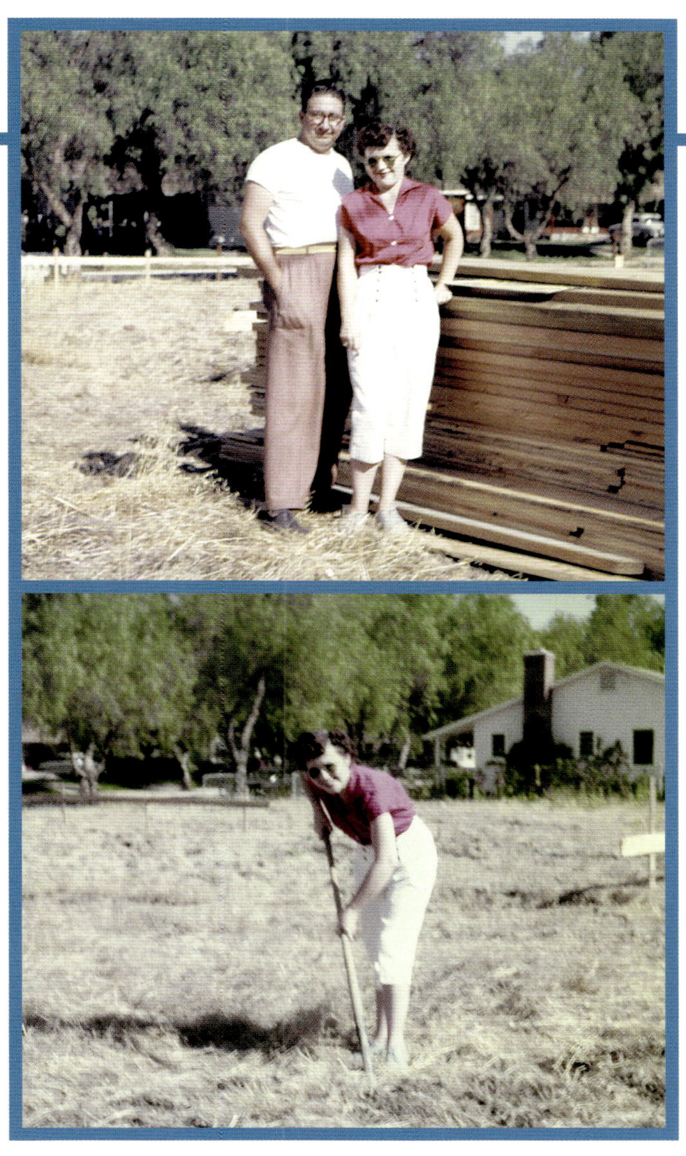

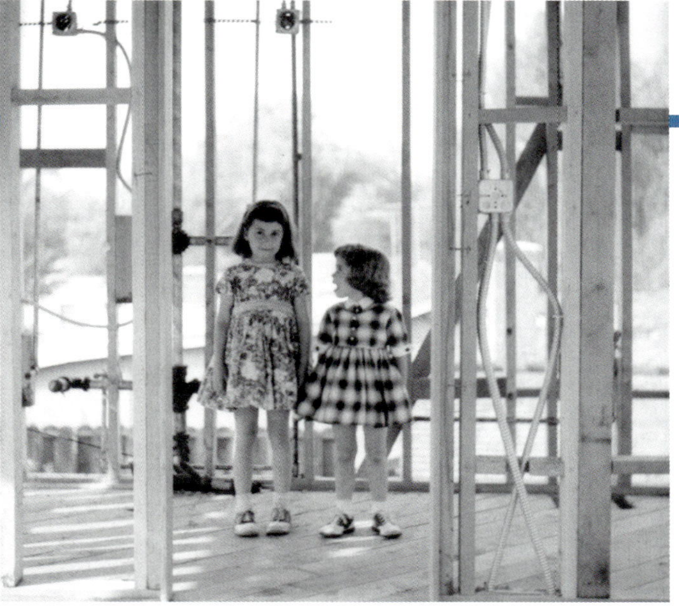

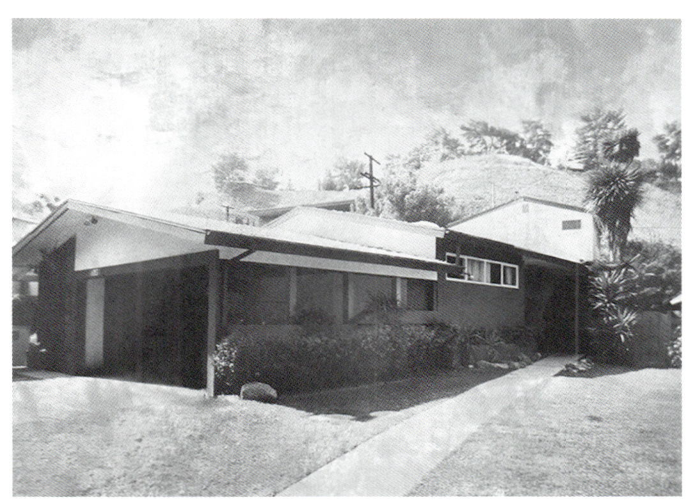

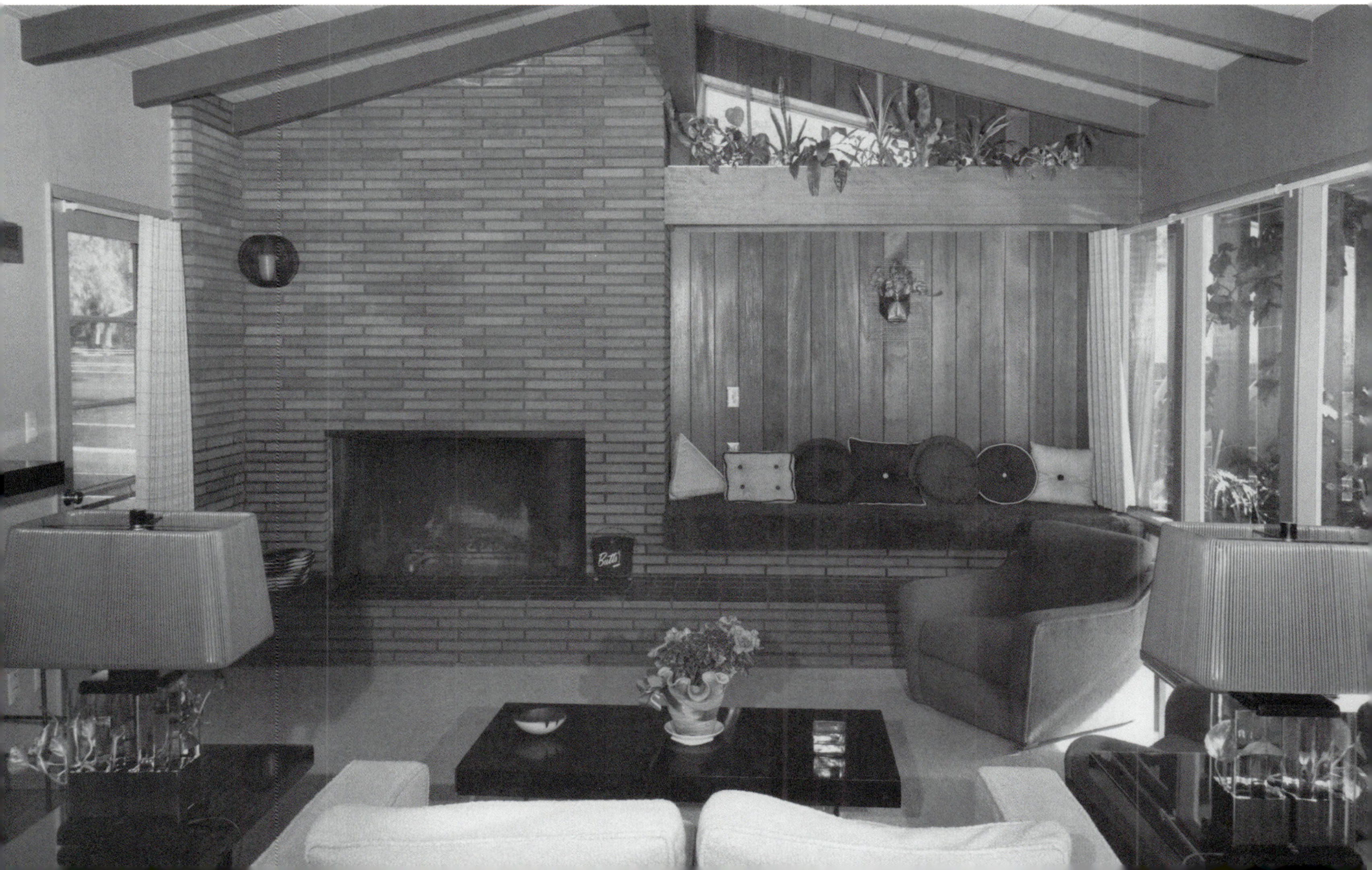

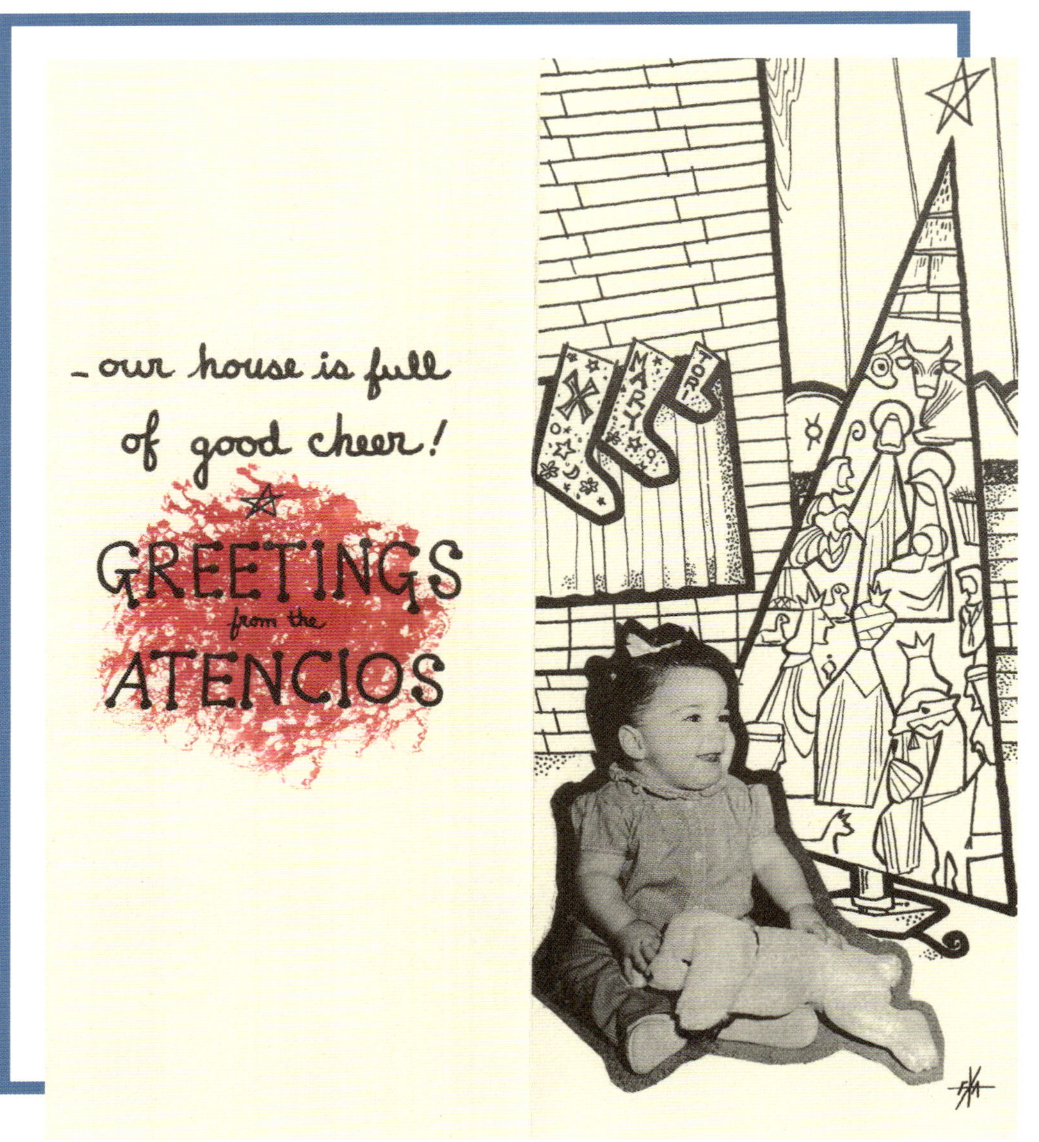

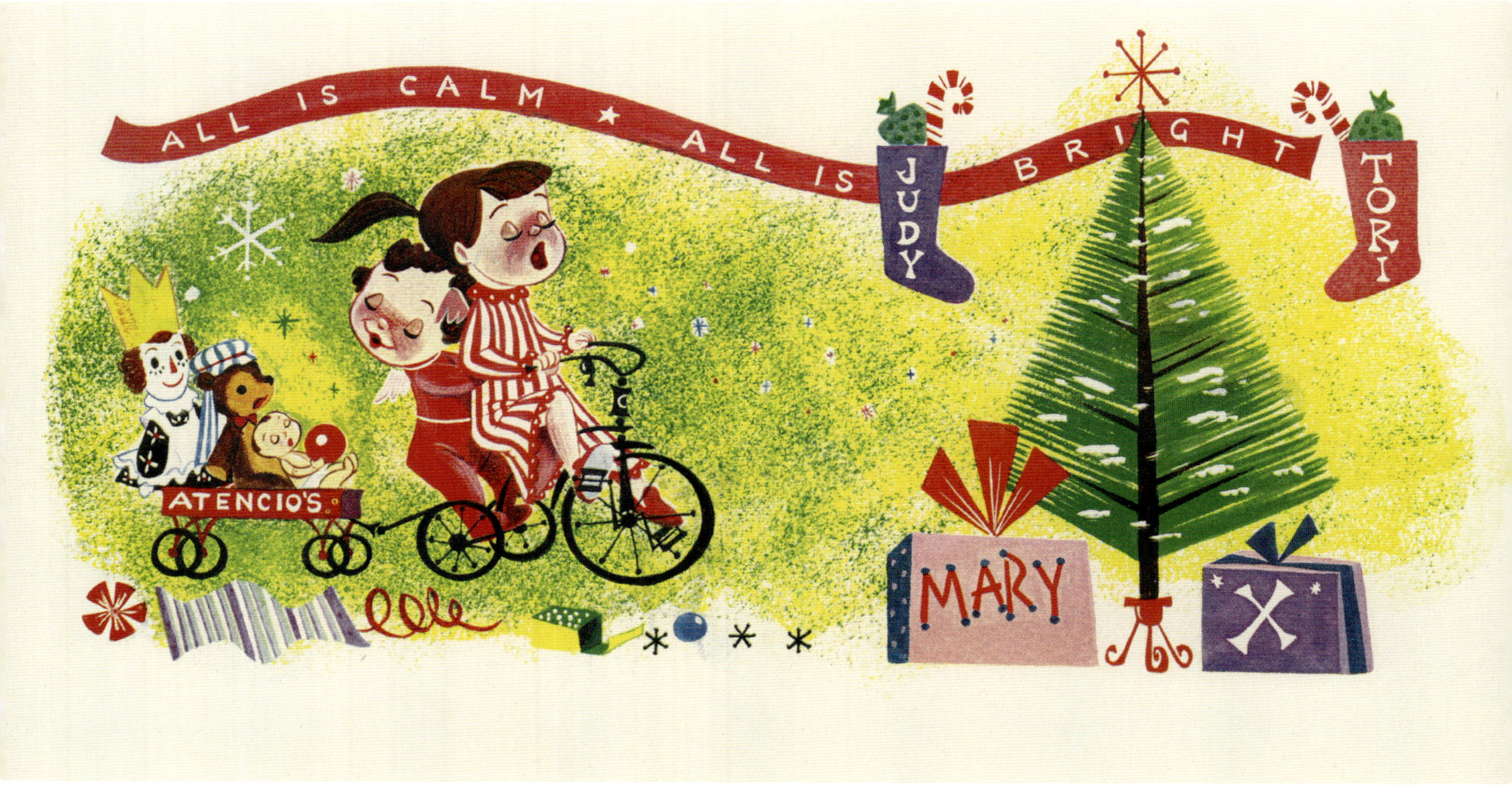

ALL IS CALM ★ ALL IS BRIGHT

JUDY

TORI

ATENCIO'S

MARY

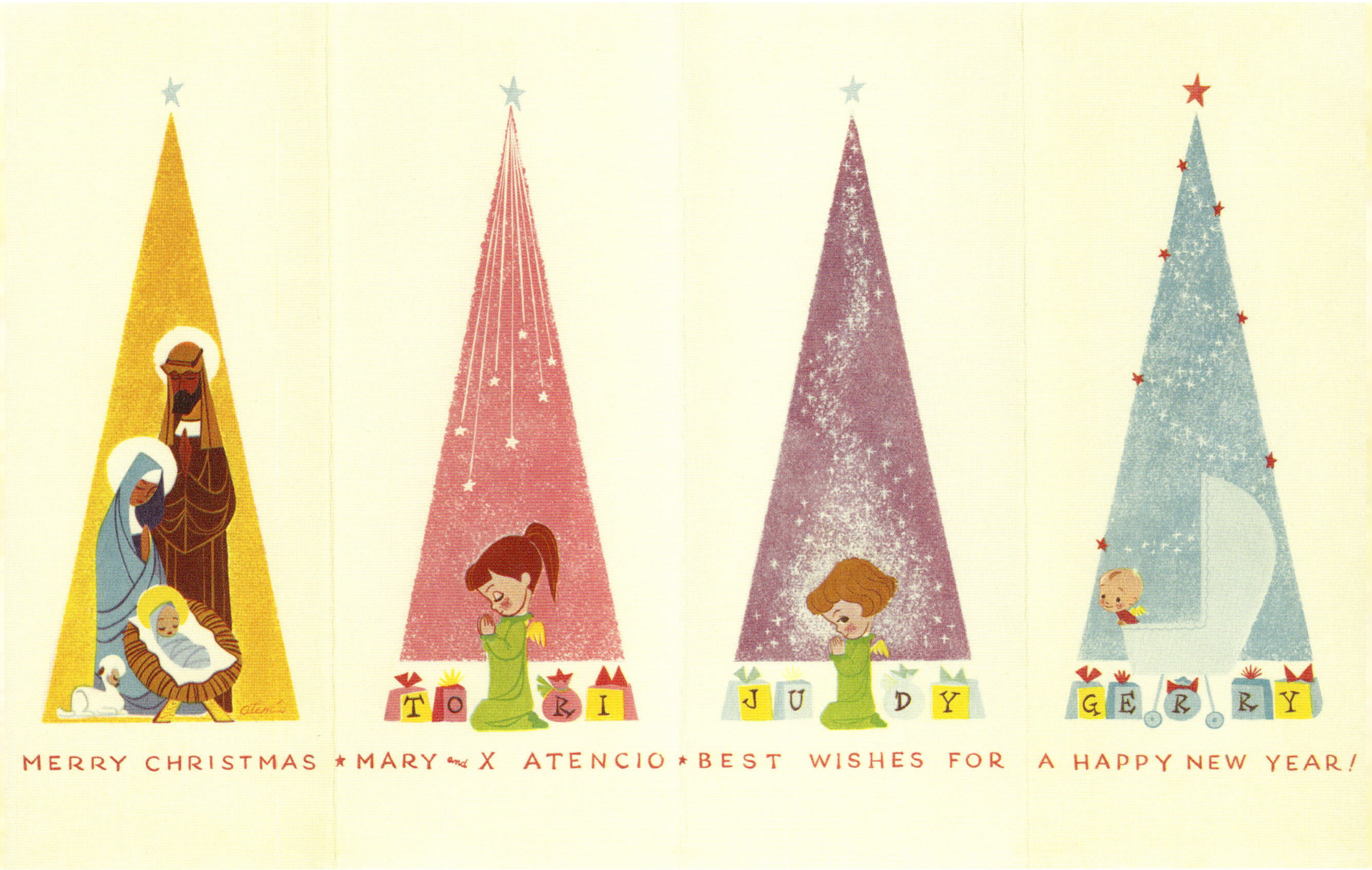

TO RI JU DY GE RR Y

MERRY CHRISTMAS ★ MARY and X ATENCIO ★ BEST WISHES FOR A HAPPY NEW YEAR!

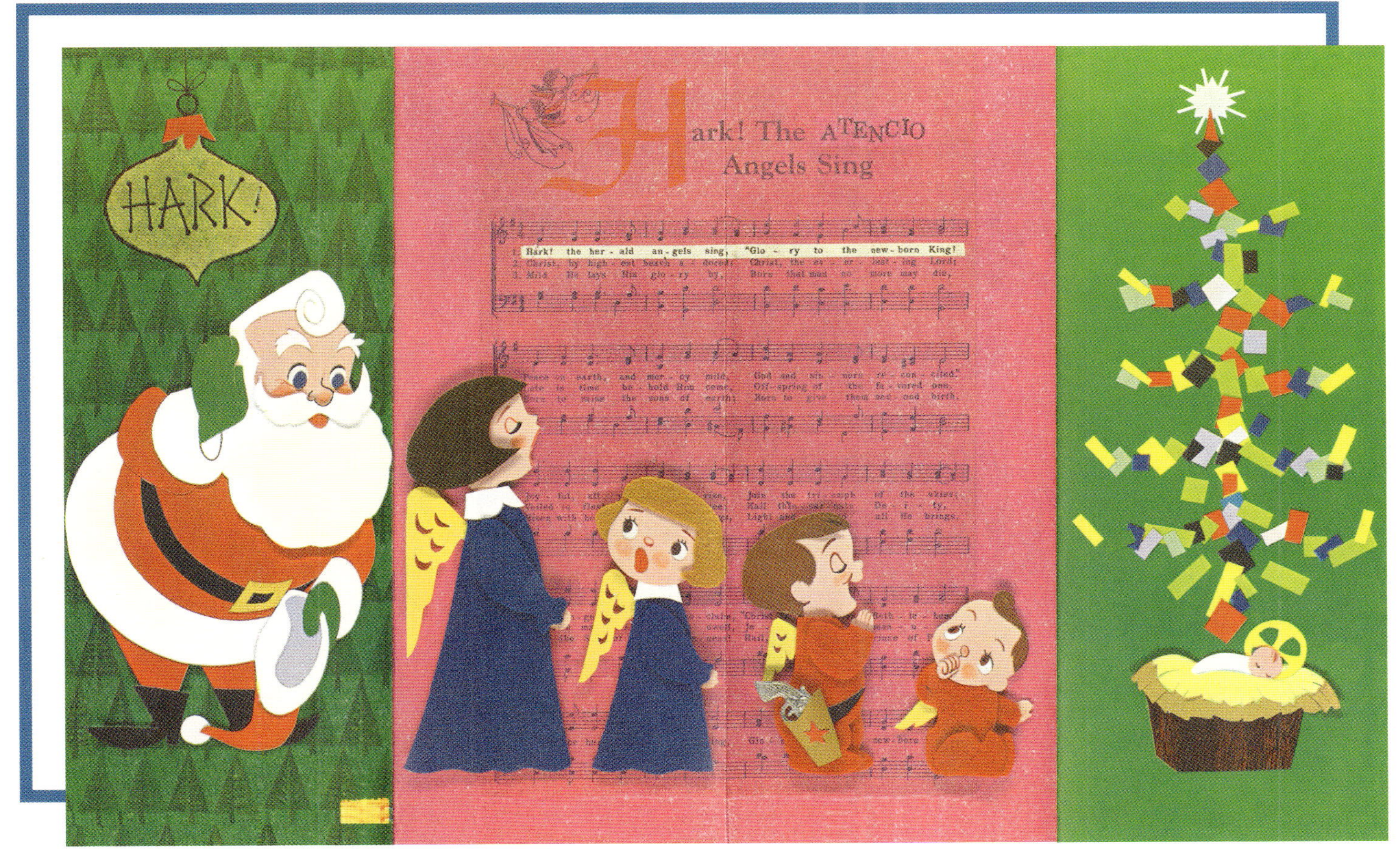

OPPOSITE AND ABOVE: Christmas cards from 1954, 1956, 1957, and 1959 illustrating the growing Atencio family.

with each passing year you grow lovelier....
AND LOVELIER
and lovelier
AND LOVELIER......

....until sometimes I wish you weren't quite so lovely!

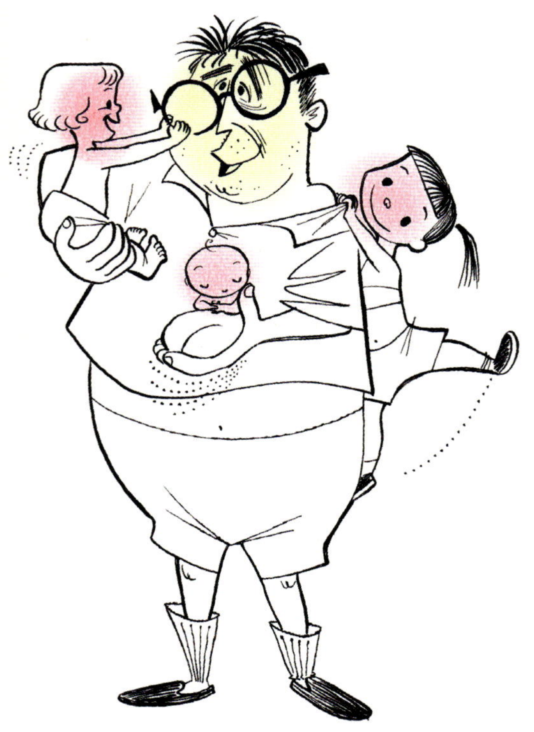

HAPPY BIRTHDAY... YOU LOVELY DOLL!

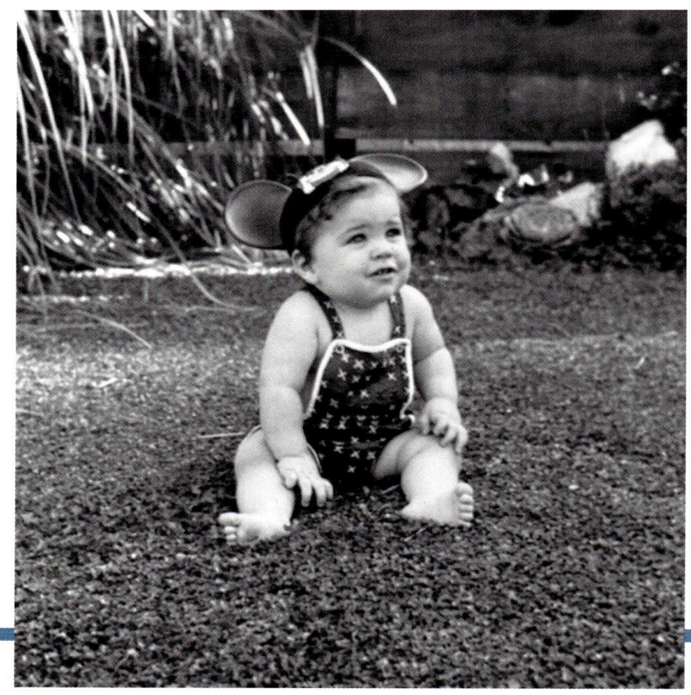

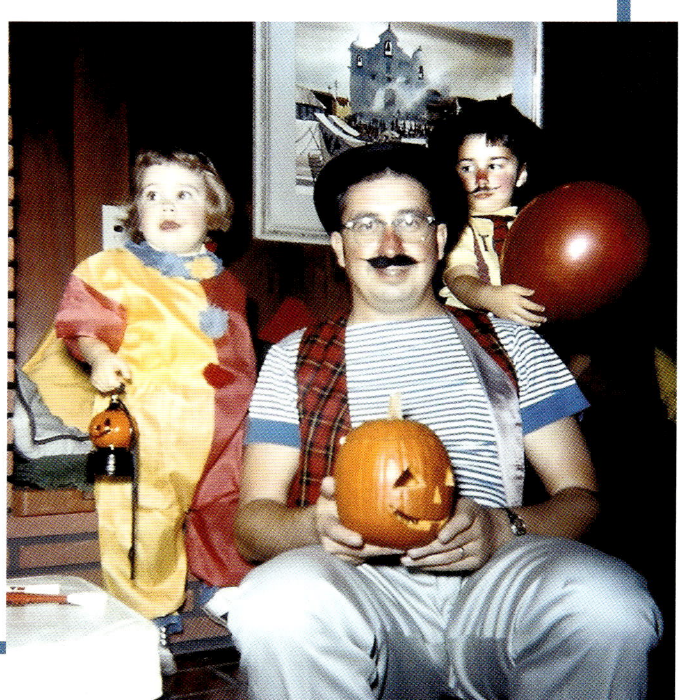

TOP: X's birthday card to Mary, who at this point was now a mother of three, depicting their loving, busy lives as parents; ABOVE (LEFT): Judianne on the lawn donning a classic pair of Mickey ears; ABOVE (RIGHT): Judianne, X, and Tori on Halloween; OPPOSITE (CLOCKWISE FROM TOP LEFT): Tori and Judianne, with Mickey hats, lounging outside; X outside with Tori, Judianne, Gerry, and Joe; X's card announcing the arrival of their fourth and final child, Joe; Tori, Gerry, and Judianne in bed with X.

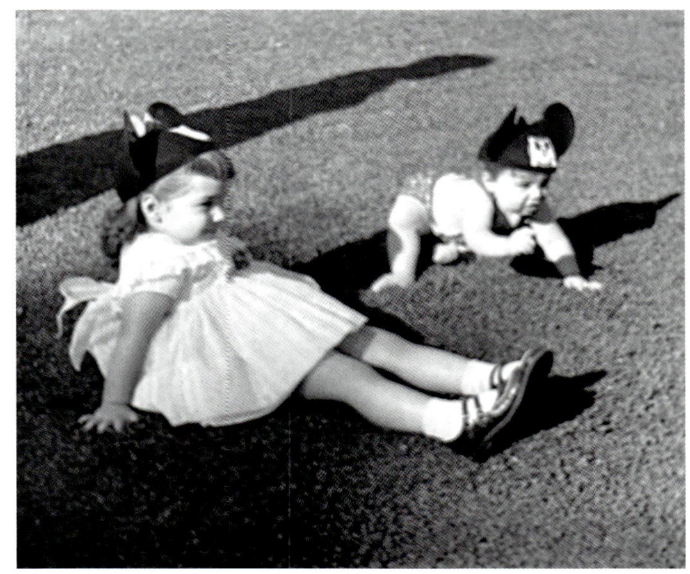

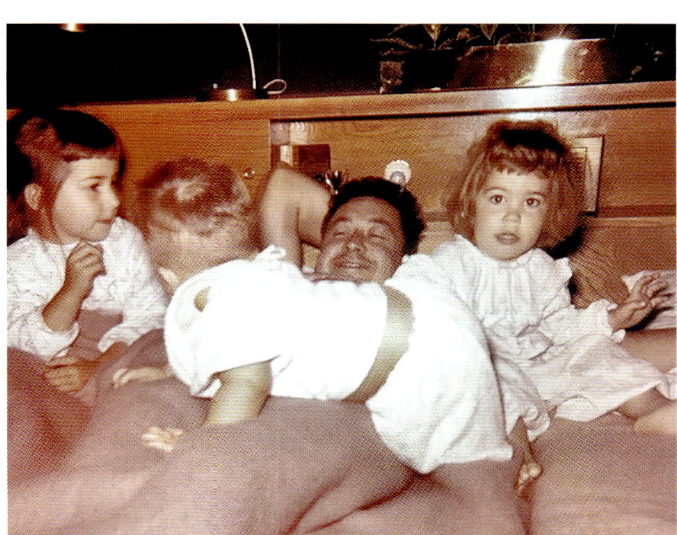

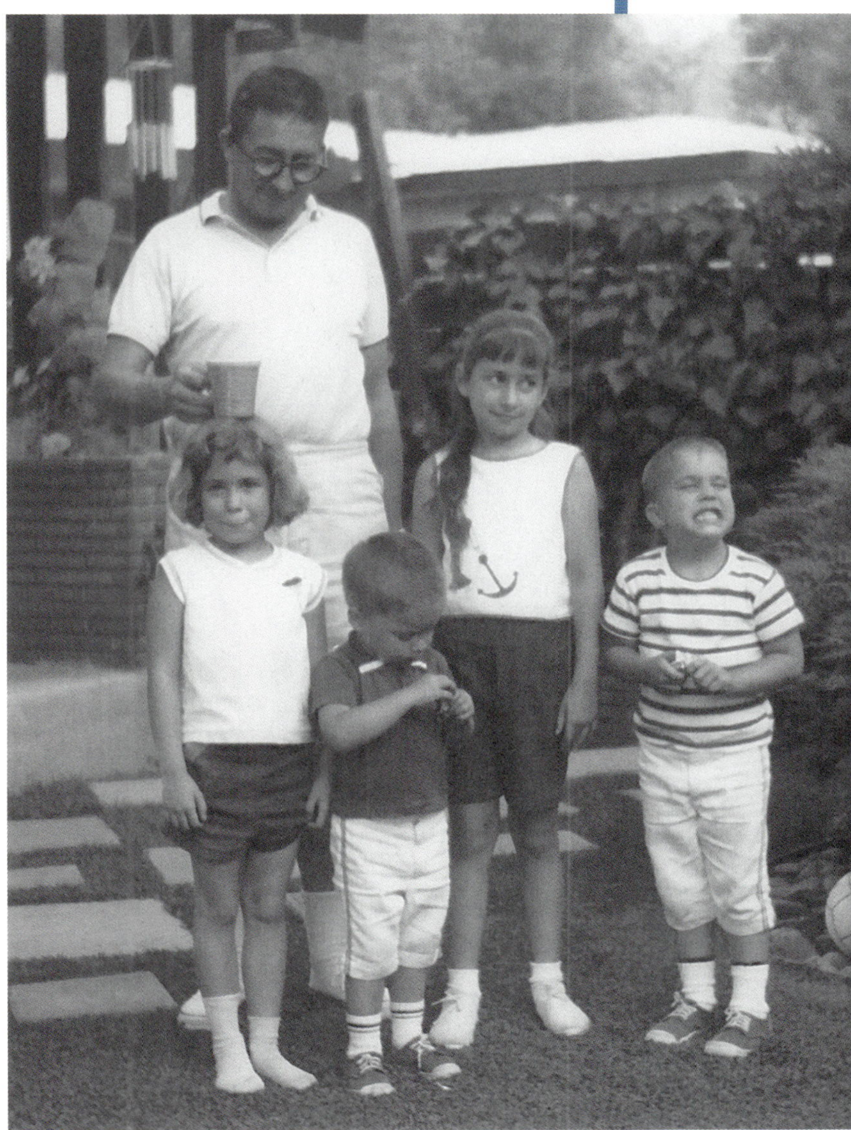

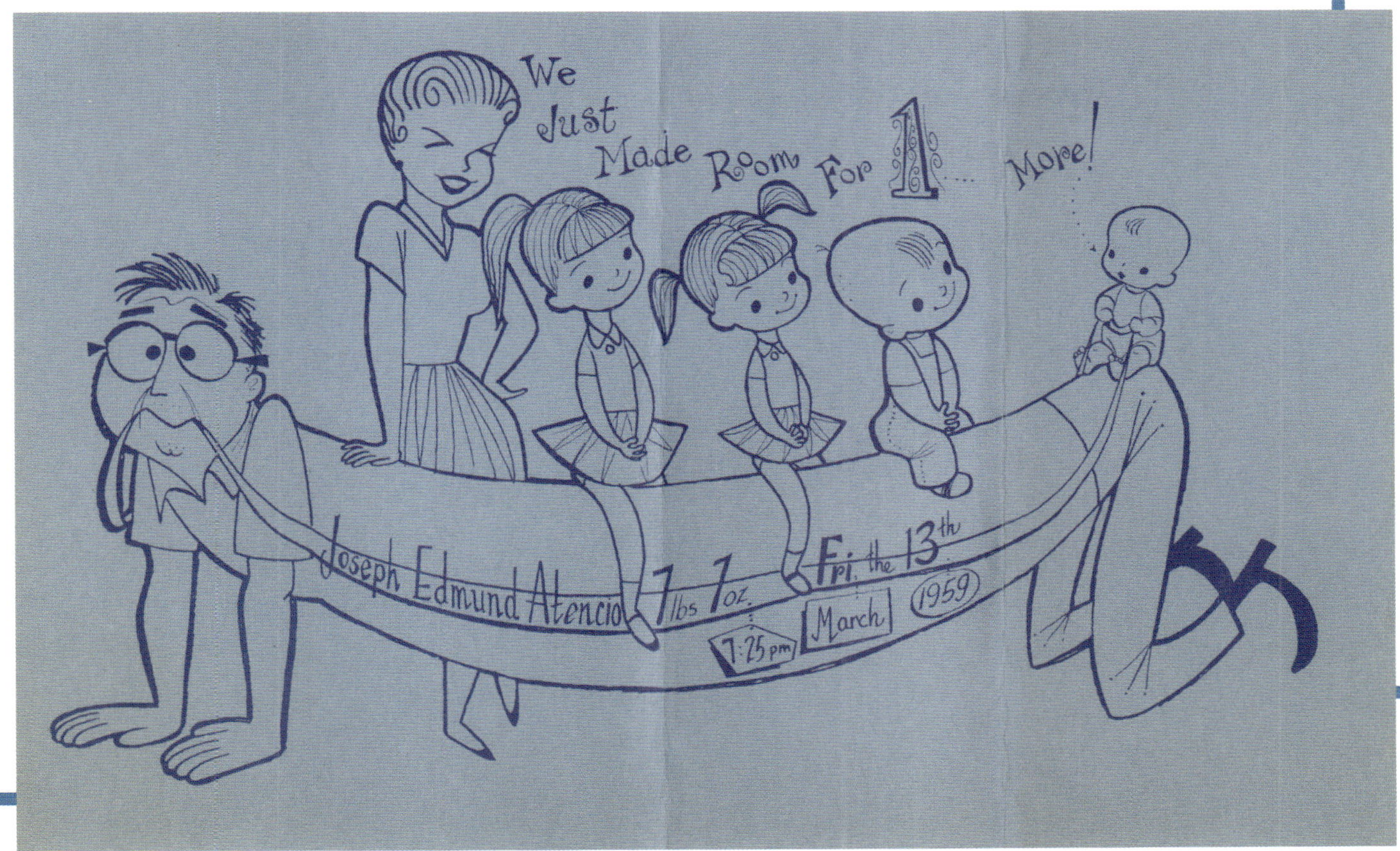
We Just Made Room For 1 ... More!
Joseph Edmund Atencio
7 lbs 7 oz.
Fri. the 13th
March
1959
7:25 pm

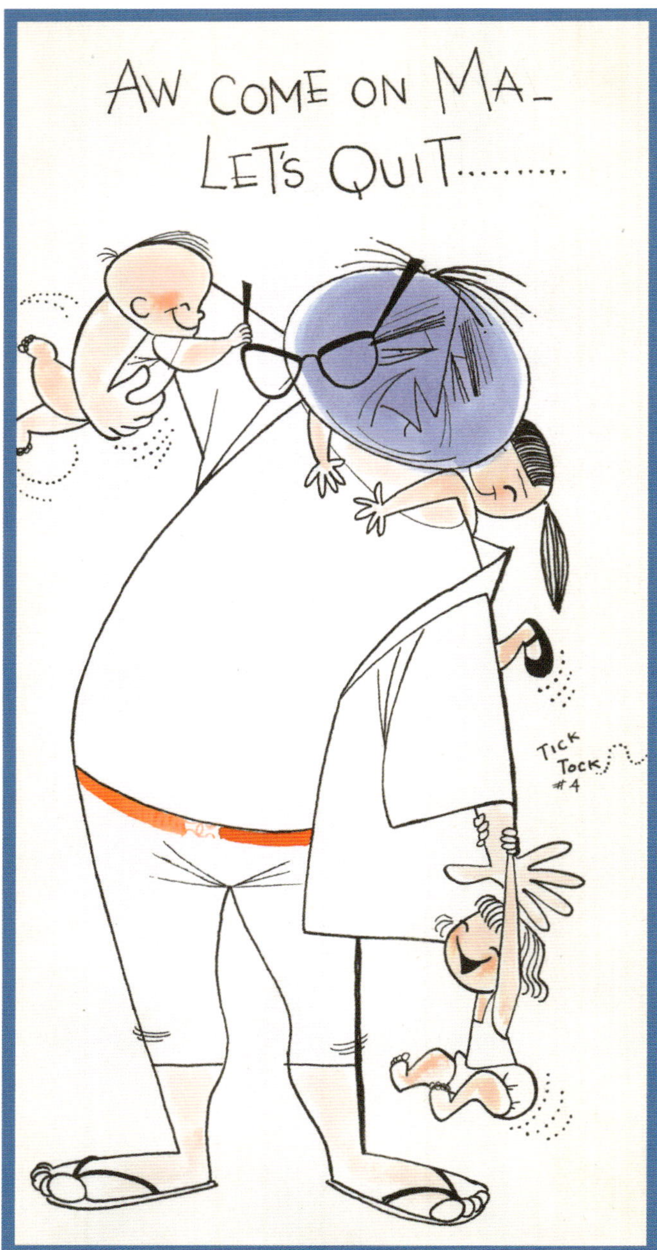

divisions, outside his official job, illustrating children's books and creating album covers for Disneyland Records. One extensive freelance assignment X had was with the Little Golden Book series, published since 1942. It had quickly become a popular children's book brand and was an early synergistic companion to other media brands like Disney. In 1947, *Dumbo* became Disney's first title in the Little Golden Book family. And by 1956 the Disney series of Little Golden Books had appeared in seventeen countries and had been translated into thirteen languages.

Today, Little Golden Books is a division of Penguin Random House and still works with Disney, on titles for various films and park attractions. Dating back to the 1950s and throughout the years, book illustrators on the Disney-specific Little Golden Books have included such Disney artists and luminaries as Eyvind Earle and X himself. Combining all of his favorite things into one endeavor (Disney, Mickey, and Christmas), X painted Disney studio publicity artist Bob Moore's pencil art on the 1953 Little Golden Book *Walt Disney's Mickey Mouse Goes Christmas Shopping*.

X also designed mail-order beach towels and aprons for Barth and Dreyfuss, a Los Angeles–based home goods maker and a "Beach Towels of California" series for Royal Terry's 1958 catalog alongside fellow Disney artists such as Bill Justice, Ralph Hewitt, and T. Hee. As the series was specifically designed to highlight local California artists, they each signed their works. All of the artists used their preferred Disney styles at the time in their side work, with X's freelance projects heavily influenced by those modernist stylings of *Melody* and *Toot, Whistle, Plunk and Boom*. At times, X experimented far beyond the bounds of his usual Disney productions with different visual styles and materials. His personal work covered a broad range of mediums, including gouache, ink, alcohol-based markers, colored pencils, and collage, though they always started with his instrument of choice: a Blackwing pencil. Nearly all his work, even many years after his animation days, was done on animation paper. While it was not uncommon for X's Disney styles and techniques to reappear in his per-

LEFT: X's 1958 birthday card to Mary; OPPOSITE: The 1960 St. Patrick's Day card X drew for Mary.

sonal work, his freelance work stylings also slowly made their way into his professional art, and eventually on-screen.

Another small revenue stream, which the family did not learn of until they cleaned out X's studio after his death, was his cartoon submissions and correspondences with various magazines like *Town & Country*. For years X had been submitting "funnies," little cartoons with wry comments, echoing his original art school career goal of creating cartoon content for newspapers and other publications. Within the letters and submissions were the responses from the magazines, telling X the reasons why his drawing was either being rejected or accepted. Countless lines of "It's not funny" or "Doesn't align with our audience" were kept in his files. These rejections show that while X's creativity, animation, and writing talents led to a prosperous career at Disney, he only found middling success as a cartoon artist.

Nevertheless, the discovery of the "funnies" also reaffirmed that X had ended up in the right place, and more deeply reflected how X never gave up. His art was his passion, and he found ways to feel fulfilled in all forms of those artistic drives. Successful or not, X continued creating and submitting funnies, following his creative inspirations as they arose.

And yet, in all honesty, the Atencios' favorite client was the local Chinese restaurant in Woodland Hills, the House of Kwong. X designed the restaurant's drink menu, strongly influenced by the popular tiki culture's influences and styles sweeping the nation in the 1950s and 1960s, and the annual New Year's card that the restaurant sent out to its loyal patrons. The family loved X's work with the House of Kwong because he bartered for food in return. As a family of six at that time in America, going out to dinner was a rarity. However, with their House of Kwong connection, it was the one place X could take his

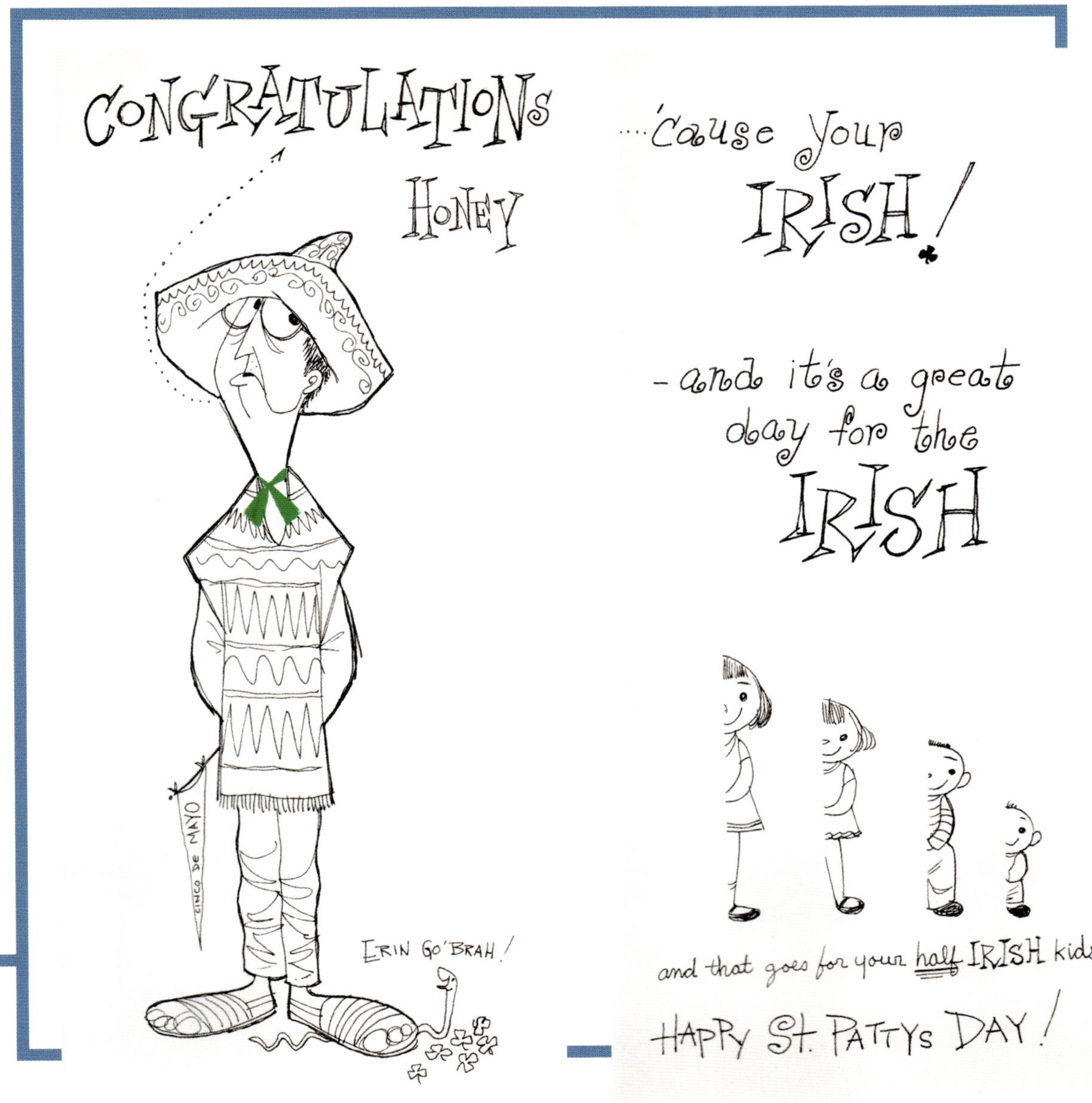

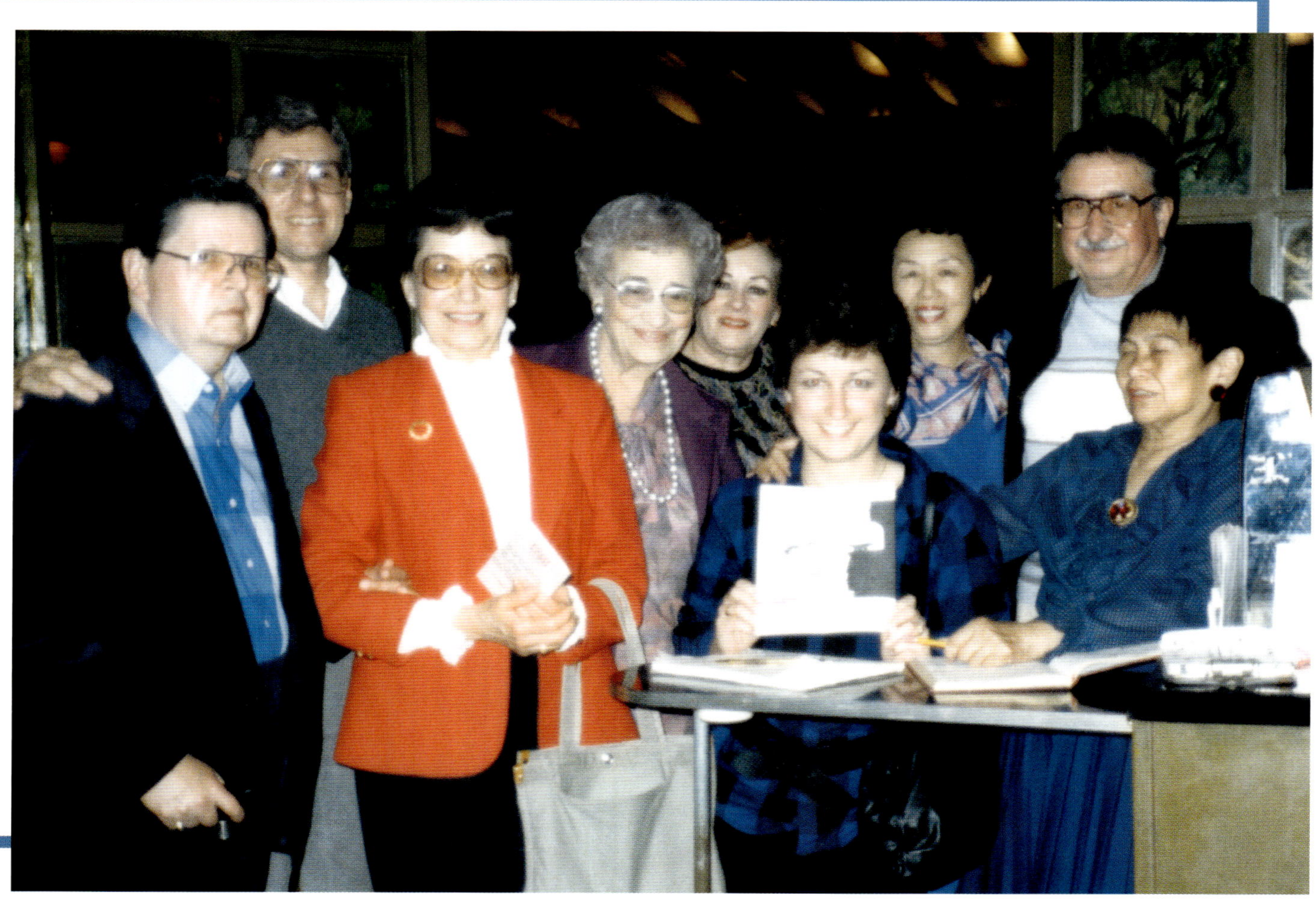

family out for nice dinners and drinks on special occasions. The House of Kwong was also a rite of passage in the Atencio household, as this was where X took each of his children on their twenty-first birthdays to buy them their first drinks. This almost thirty-year period of outside work with this establishment continued until 1986, when the restaurant closed.

In addition, the freelance design work for the restaurant most likely outlasted X's actual need for the side income, given that X seemed to perform his artistic services well into retirement. Most likely, his reason for continuing this specific work was his loyalty to the owners, his love of the tradition they had established, and as an ode and remembrance to the fond memories he and his entire family had made at the restaurant along the way.

Overall, the postwar period of the mid-1940s through the 1950s for X was one of personal and professional growth. He kept busy building a home, starting a family, and expanding his talents both out of financial necessity and creative ambition. While much of this postwar era, during which X's attention was focused on short-film animation, was often glossed over in later years in his retelling of his life story, it was a pivotal time of development.

For X, moving away from working on larger feature films was the catalyst he needed for his talents to really shine and gain recognition. In a way, he became a bigger fish in a smaller pond. However, equally, if not more important, was that X transitioned to working on smaller-scale, more experimental projects that gave him the opportunity to demonstrate his creative vision, versatility, and project leadership, putting his personal stamp on his assignments and finally receiving screen credit for his work while also gaining the freedom to take risks and ultimately to pioneer new techniques in animation.

ABOVE: X with family and friends as they gathered at the House of Kwong on its closing night; OPPOSITE: X's design for one of many House of Kwong's annual holiday cards.

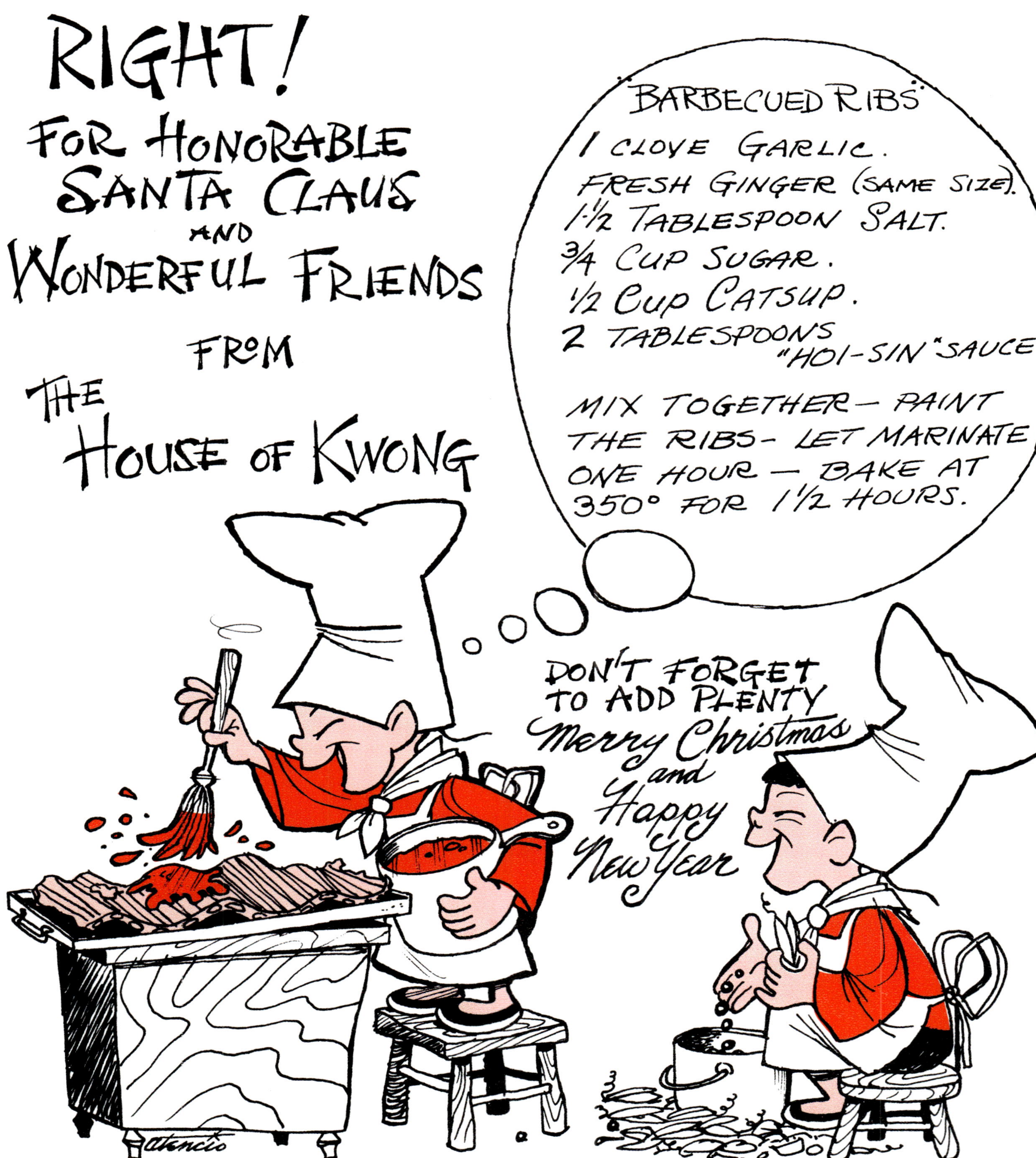
RIGHT!
FOR HONORABLE SANTA CLAUS AND WONDERFUL FRIENDS
FROM
THE HOUSE OF KWONG
BARBECUED RIBS
1 CLOVE GARLIC.
FRESH GINGER (SAME SIZE).
1½ TABLESPOON SALT.
¾ CUP SUGAR.
½ CUP CATSUP.
2 TABLESPOONS "HOI-SIN" SAUCE.
MIX TOGETHER — PAINT THE RIBS — LET MARINATE ONE HOUR — BAKE AT 350° FOR 1½ HOURS.
DON'T FORGET TO ADD PLENTY
Merry Christmas and Happy New Year
Atencio

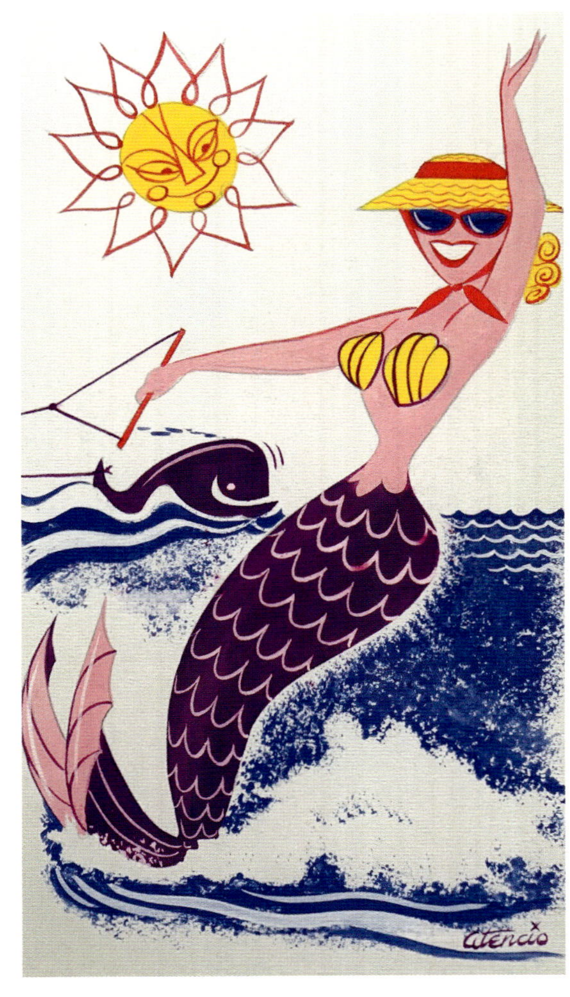
atencio

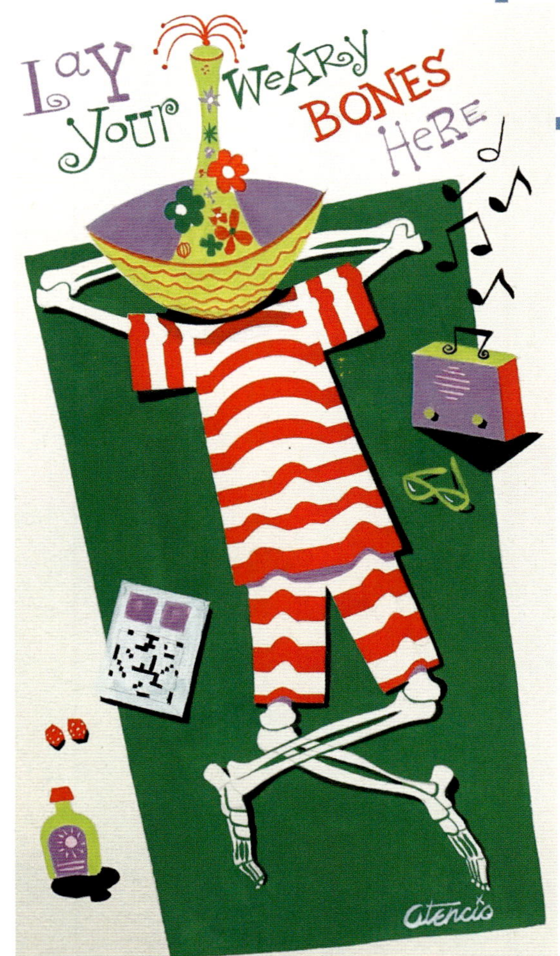
LAY YOUR WEARY BONES HERE
atencio

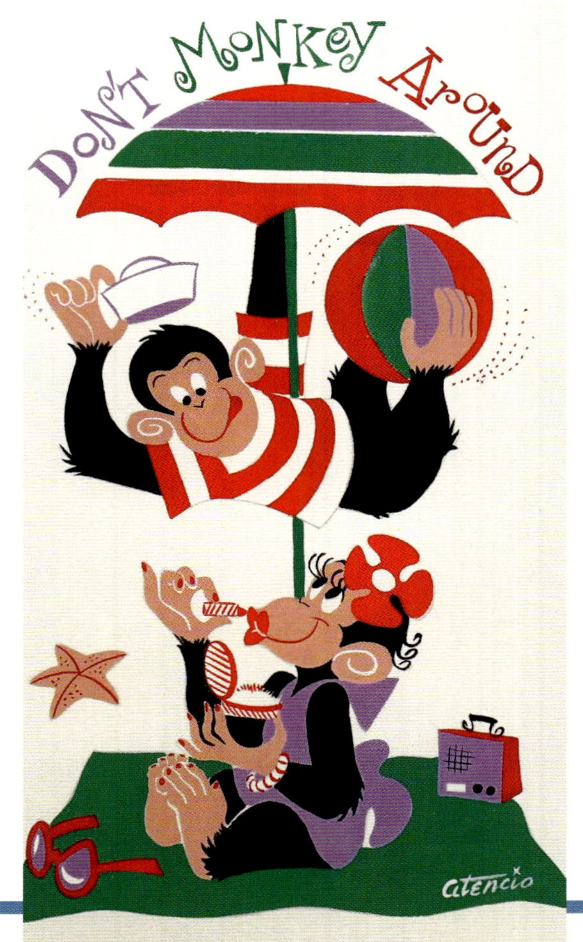
DON'T MONKEY AROUND
atencio

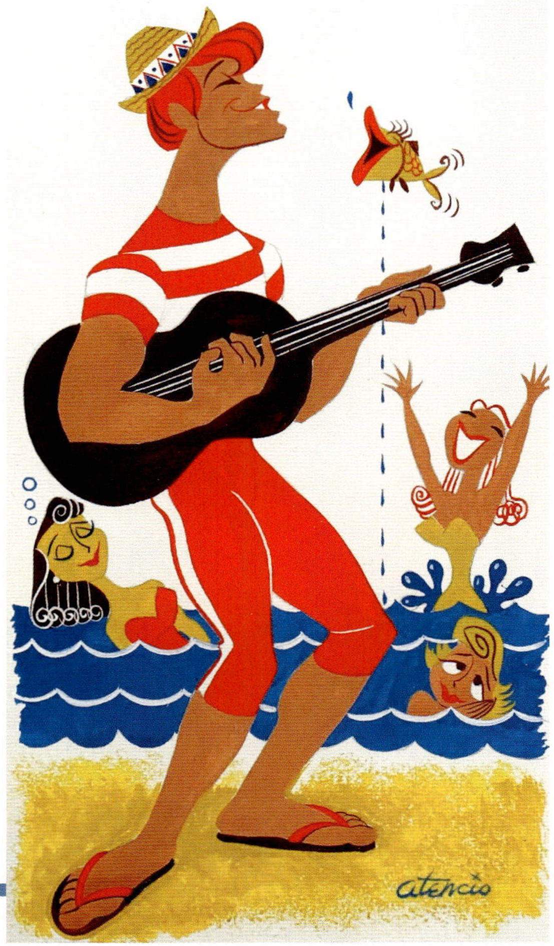
atencio

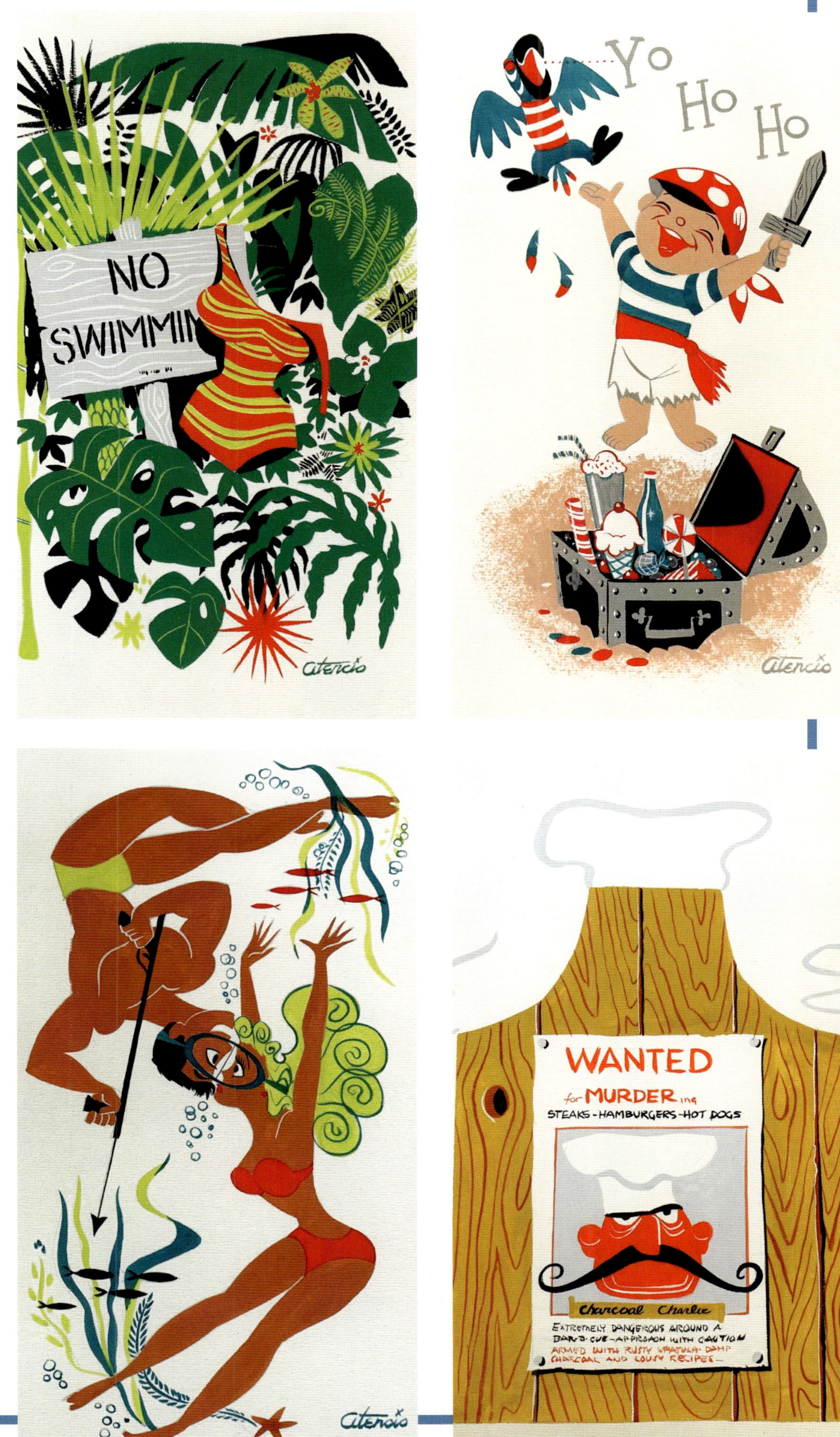

OPPOSITE AND ABOVE: A selection of X's gouache painting designs for home products such as towels and aprons for Barth and Dreyfuss.

5

Moving Beyond Animation

VENTURING BEYOND HIS CHARACTER credit under Bill Justice for the seven-minute short film *Jack and Old Mac*, X continued partnering with Bill, further exploring the boundaries of creativity and innovation with the use of stop-motion animation. Stop-motion animation captured images in succession while moving the physical objects between frames to create the illusion of movement when played back rapidly in sequence. Although the first known uses of stop-motion occurred in a now lost film from 1898 called *The Humpty Dumpty Circus*, and then in the still-accessible 1902 short film produced by Thomas A. Edison entitled *Fun in a Bakery Shop*, it wasn't until 1959, amidst continuing changing tastes, mandates, and supply-and-demand structures on the audience end that the Walt Disney Studio officially released any form of stop-motion animation in film.

But finally, on November 10, 1959, *Noah's Ark*, a twenty-minute short film, was released alongside the main-title feature *Third Man of the Mountain*, ultimately making it Disney's first film to use stop-motion animation. This retelling of the biblical story of Noah and the ark again teamed X with Bill Justice, alongside X's closest pairing to date with T. Hee, an established story artist and designer, and narrator Paul Frees, a noted vocal talent.

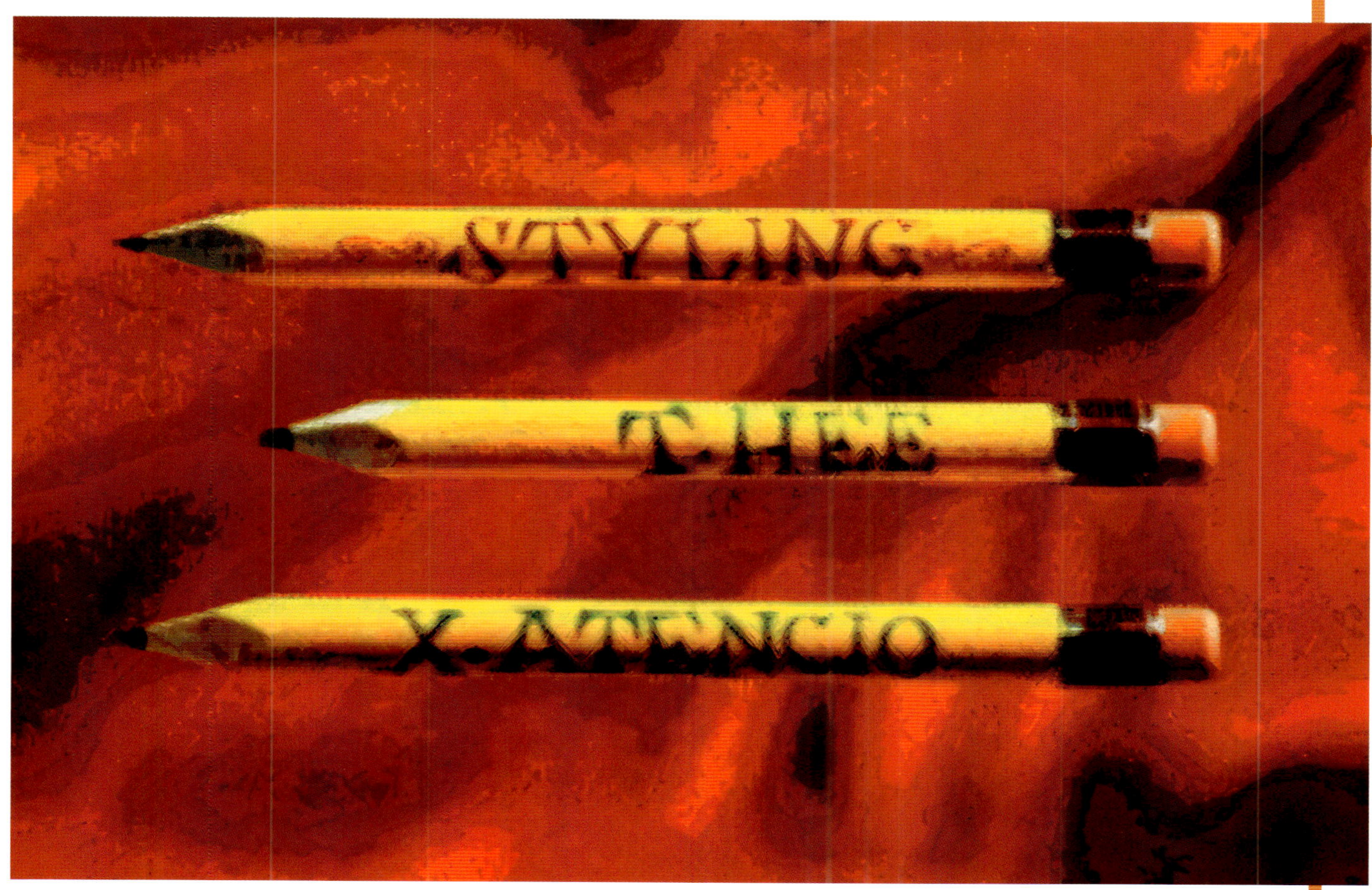

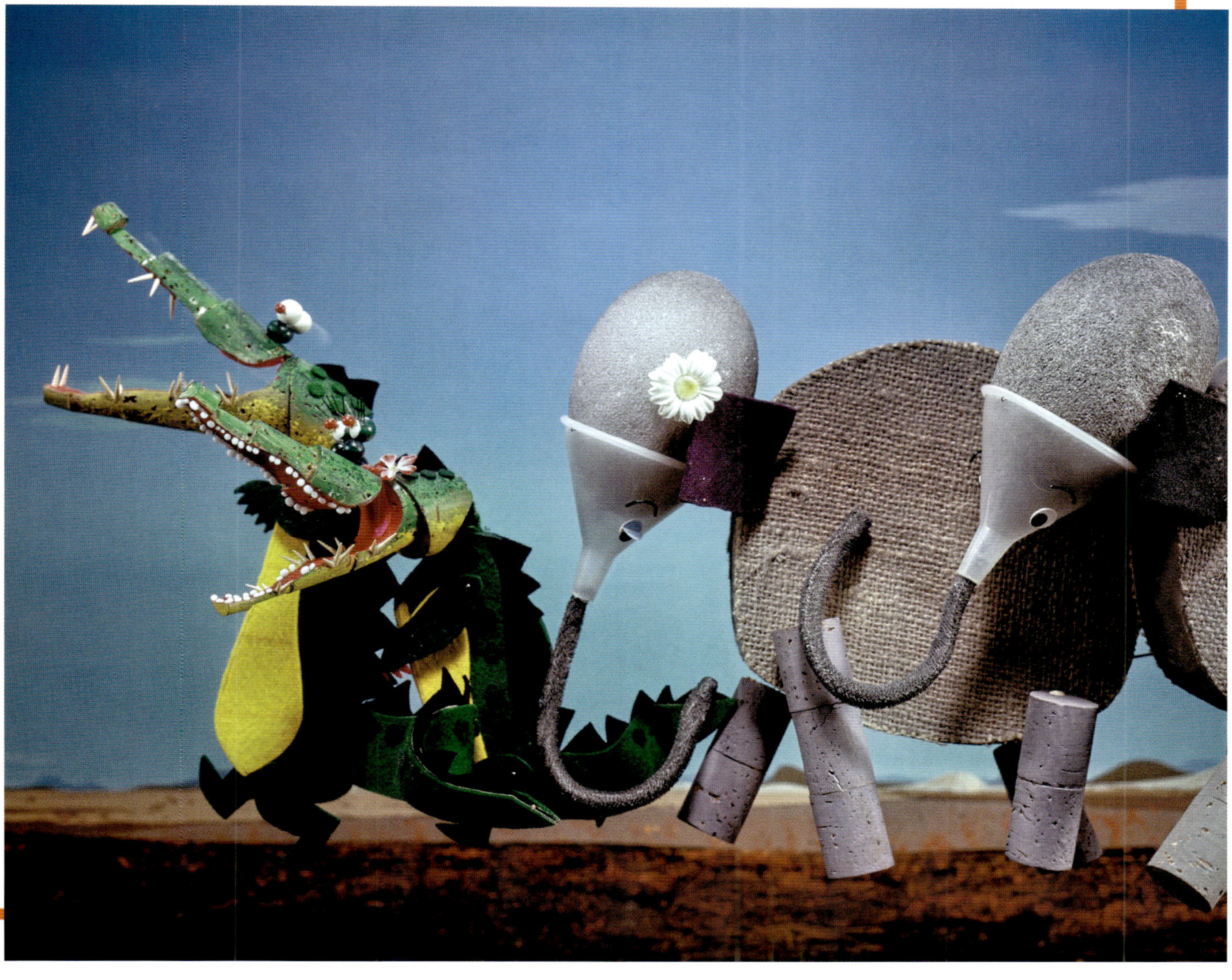

ABOVE (TOP): X's styling credit in *Noah's Ark*; BOTTOM: A still from *Noah's Ark*.

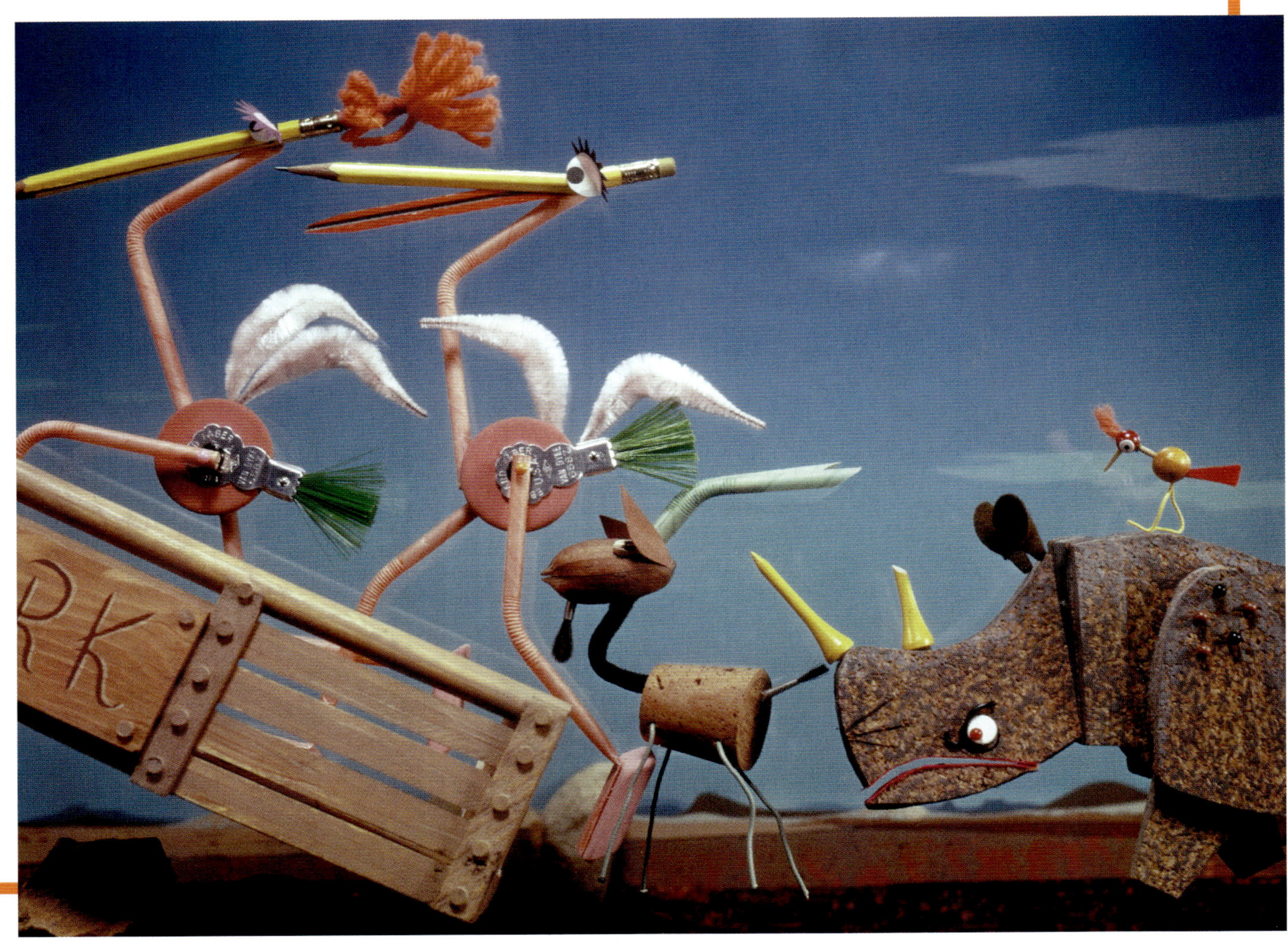

Having been tasked by Harry Tytle, the cartoon production manager, with figuring out ideas on how to deliver Disney-quality films for less money, all while up against the ever-increasing need for more and quicker animation to fill the widening television landscape, Bill looked for any and all original concepts. Turning to his right-hand man, X, they started discussing the potential of stop-motion animation and how making malleable characters they could adjust for each frame would be quicker and cheaper than the process of animating individual cel drawings. Knowing Walt had been receptive to the little shorts and experimental cost-saving projects they had worked on, and that Walt had dabbled with stop-motion in his early animation days, Bill approached Walt with the idea. He readily agreed to the proposal, granting X and Bill the freedom to experiment in another new direction.

So, armed with Walt's blessing, X and Bill set out to test what that new direction might look like. A few days later they brought their creations to the Camera Department for some visual and lighting tests. Walt seemed content with their results, but X and Bill needed a story to go along with their new animations. T. Hee appeared as their storywriter and became the third member of their stop-motion team. T. Hee also brought in a songwriter friend of his, Mel Leven, to write a song for the short, and the rest of the music was done by George Bruns. While T. Hee had been working at Disney before X started there, he left to go to United Productions of America, only to return in 1958 and enmesh himself in the world of stop-motion animation. T. Hee had a story about Noah's ark, and given X's affinity for designing animals with heart and character, it seemed like a perfect match. However, it took two years before Walt gave them the official green light to get to work on the project. After that, X, Bill, and T. Hee gathered vast amounts of materials, even up to the point where the frequent trips to the hobby store started arousing the suspicions of the cashiers, who began to wonder if these supposed customers were going to open their own shop. Sometimes the men joked that the store clerks must have thought they were crazy, given all the absurd and random little junk items they bought in bulk every visit.

For *Noah's Ark*, Bill Justice once again directed, and T. Hee received a "story by" credit. But this time X also shared double credits for "character movement" and "styling" with Bill and T. Hee, respectively. Bill Justice asserted that while the film's credits acknowledged each of them for specific roles, they really functioned as a team and helped each other with any issues that cropped up during production.

And yet the sign of a great team is knowing how to support each other's strengths and weaknesses. T. Hee was an established designer, so X helped him stylistically design all the characters and animals in the film. X found the imaginative possibilities and realities of the stop-motion short to be fun and freeing; getting to make characters out of drinking straws, string, erasers, nuts, pieces of fruit, and eggs (among other easily sourced everyday materials) had its rewards. And for this short, character movement and style went hand in hand, since the shape of the animal or character had to match or be enhanced by the items chosen for design; simultaneously, those items also had to be functional for character movement— i.e., using string for the elephant's trunk so that it could bend and wave like a real elephant's, or using plastic forks for bird wings to give shape and structure.

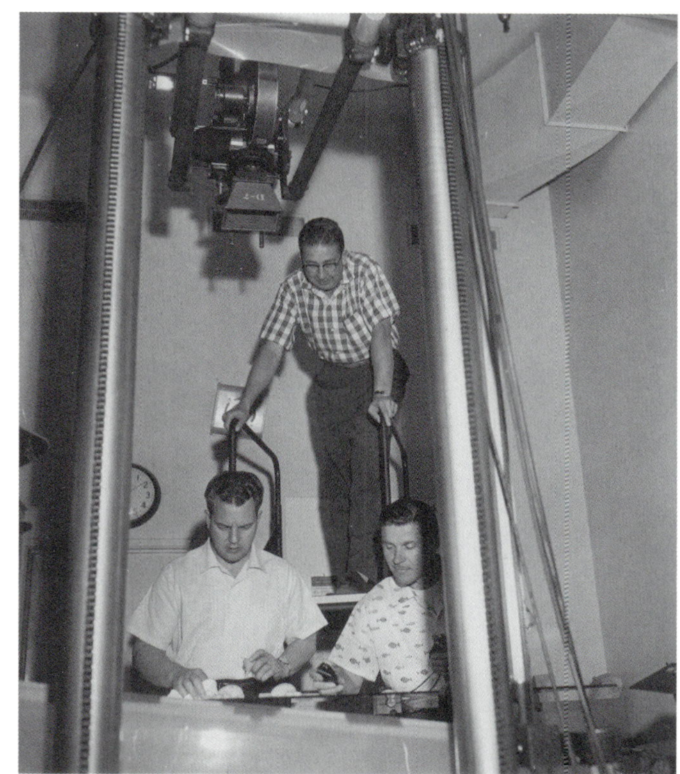

As trained two-dimensional animation artists, they had a natural inclination to sketch the characters on the page. However, they quickly found that this approach did not match with the characters' three-dimensional form. X and T. Hee then tried

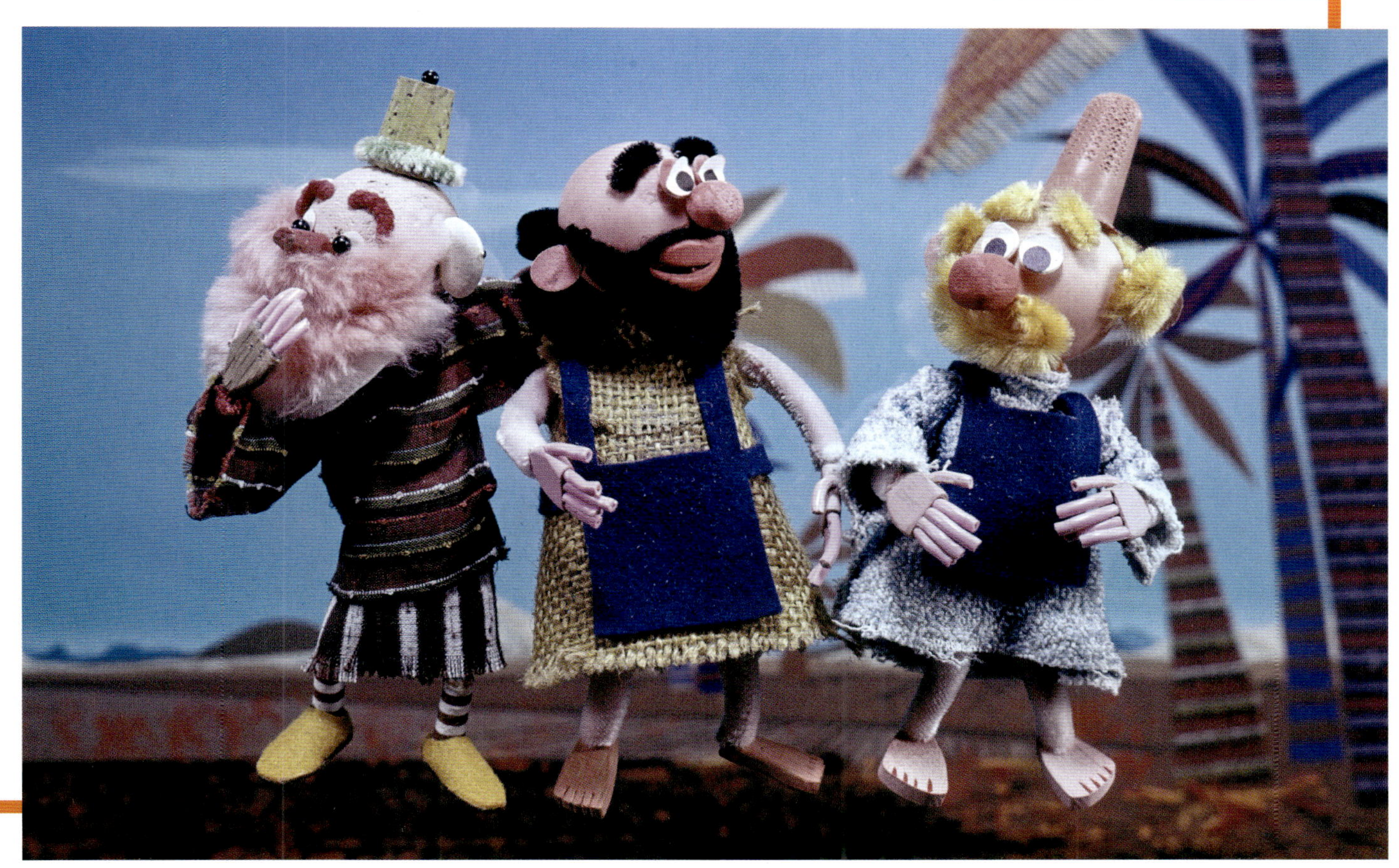

OPPOSITE AND ABOVE: Design stills of X and Bill Justice's *Noah's Ark* characters; TOP: X (STANDING), Bill, and artist Ed Sekac working on their stop-motion creations.

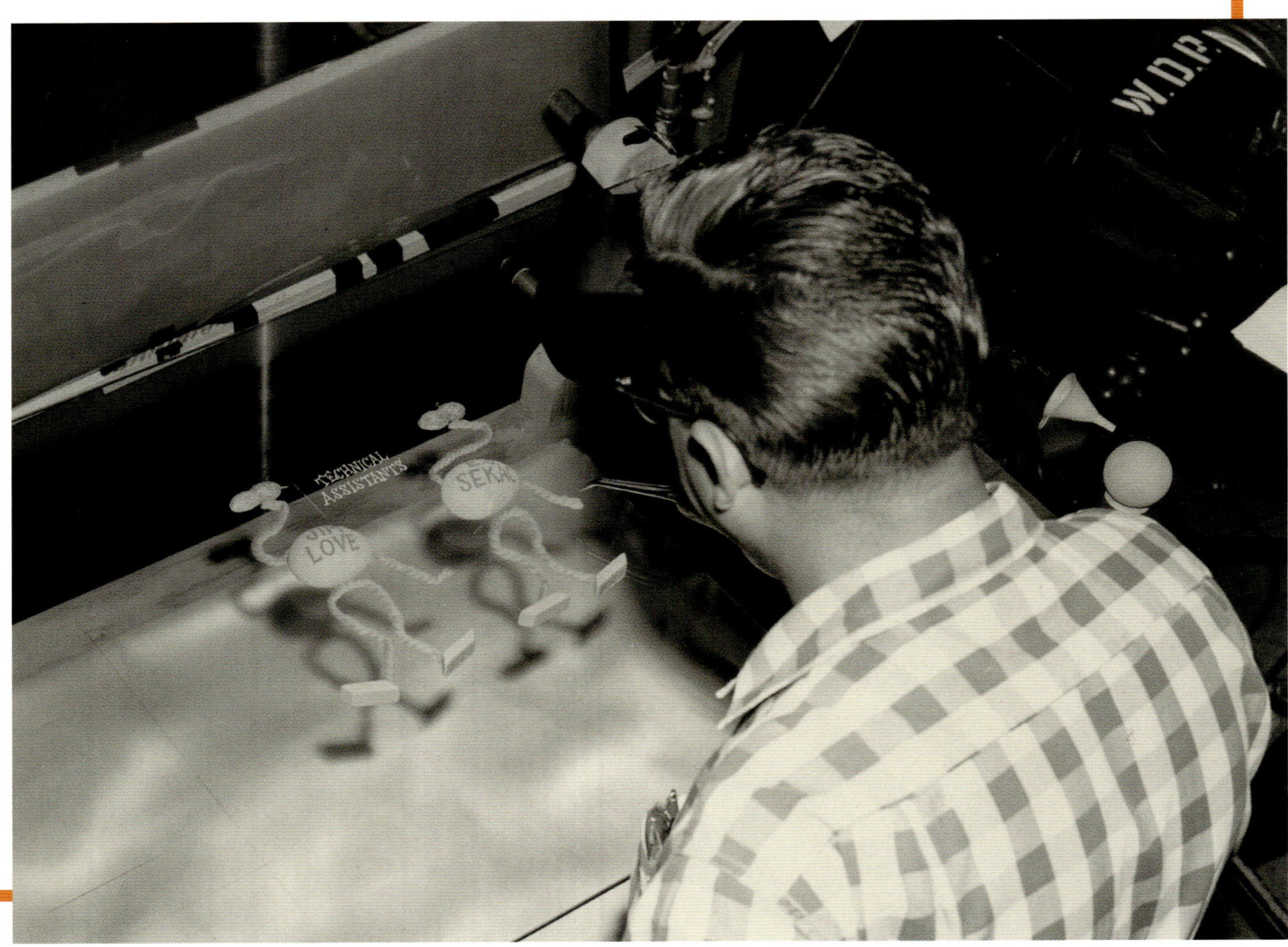

different items to see which materials best suited which silhouettes, animals, and proportions, resulting in many trips for the two to the five-and-dime and hobby stores, where they would fill up baskets with any items they could find. Likewise, one of the most rigorous points the trio had to constantly check and be aware of was that the figures they created could move properly throughout their changing roles in the narrative.

X pointed out that they originally planned for their characters to be flat, "based on the Necco Wafer test," but the more they shopped, the more they fixated on the idea of using recognizable objects, adding dimension and weight. Round, three-dimensional characters meant that they could move the characters' heads, though it also added issues when dealing with the glass and cameras. So they tried to make the characters flat on one side so they would rest easily on the glass. During their trial-and-error phases, they experimented with textured paper and a real coconut, both of which ultimately failed. It was only when they sliced off part of the same coconut (so that it could rest flatly against the glass but still retain its three-dimensional shape) that they found the test to be successful. Another major issue was the sheer number of characters required in a story about Noah's ark. In this twenty-minute short, they had approximately 150 characters. No matter how much screen time a character received, be it five seconds or the full twenty minutes, it still required the same amount of time and effort to create the character.

Knowing the large undertaking ahead, they constructed all 150 stop-motion characters, even ensuring that the "two by two" of the same breed of

ABOVE: X staging his creations for the camera; OPPOSITE: Walt, Bill Justice, X, and T. Hee on an episode of *Walt Disney Presents* called "The Title Makers," welcoming audiences into their workshop.

animals had enough small defining differences to stand out as individuals—whether it was hair, fur, nose color, or some other such variation. According to X, the only character they didn't have to make from scratch was a fly, which Bill was able to find for free floating in his swimming pool.

As every inventor or experimenter knows, the promise of freedom to try to create goes hand in hand with the inherent problem of limited time and money. For X, Bill, and T. Hee, this meant often learning or discovering new twists or complications to their experimenting as they progressed. Sometimes, the knowledge came too late, and they couldn't go back and reshoot the corresponding scene. Other times, to be consistent across the entire film, they had to refrain from taking certain risks or making certain choices for fear of compromising the whole project. They laid out their purchased dime-store items on a long table, examining each and choosing what they believed would work best for the character's head, body, et cetera. If it didn't work or provide the proper movement or look, they would go back to their "assembly line" and see what else they had purchased that might prove better for the desired look and movement. X said that it reached a point where they would be photographing one set of characters while T. Hee was still downstairs manufacturing others. With the work feeling at times more like a toy factory than an animation studio, X described how they'd "go running up to the office to say, 'Don't make any more with legs like this—they don't work!'"

One of the things that they loved about working in the stop-motion medium was that once the characters were constructed, they could take them to camera, photograph them, and get their film back the next day in Technicolor—a far cry from the usual monthslong process for turnaround on traditional cel animation. X, Bill, and T. Hee also liked the limitations of early stop-motion (and the time/budget constraints) and used those to their advantage to create a certain charm and keep the characters from looking too much like puppets. They were also clear that they were not trying to compete with animated cartoons but instead were creating another genre that expanded and pushed the boundaries of animation's abilities, just as Disney had always been at the forefront of doing in other mediums. And like with past Disney achievements, X, Bill, and T. Hee knew that *Noah's Ark* was a test.

Walt granted those he trusted the chance to prove that a new direction was worth further investment and exploration. And for X, Bill, and T. Hee, the

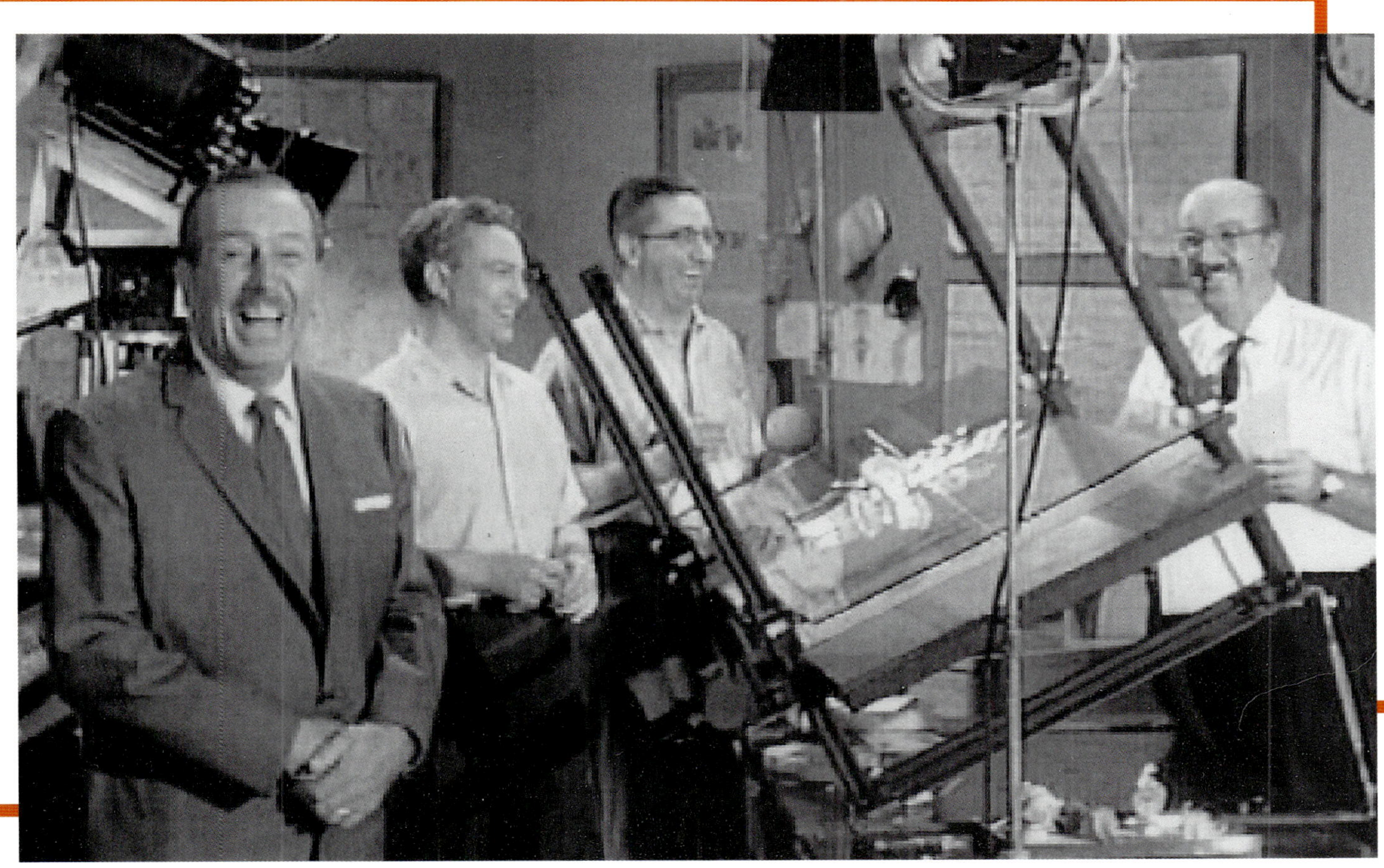

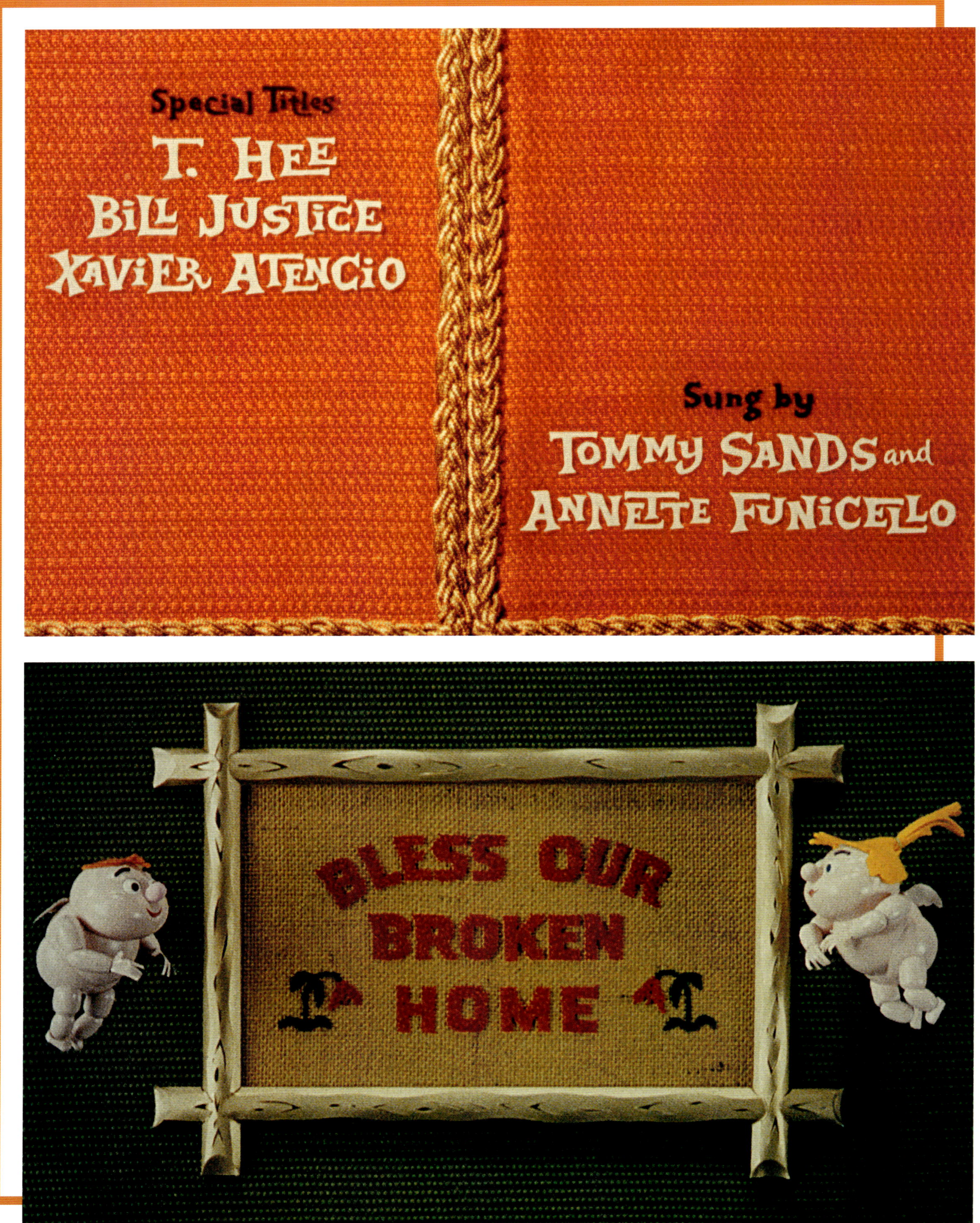

TOP: X's credit for the title sequence in *The Parent Trap*, which he designed; ABOVE AND OPPOSITE: Stills from the opening stop-motion animation sequence from *The Parent Trap* (1961).

project was successful enough that Walt gave them other projects to work on in stop-motion animation. For X personally, *Noah's Ark* continued to expand his collaborations and relationships at Disney and allowed him the opportunity to really begin to leave his artistic mark on the projects he took on.

In an interview conducted at Chouinard, X, Bill, and T. Hee discussed the process of creating *Noah's Ark*. During the interview, they made mention of other projects Walt had now given them to work on in the stop-motion animation space. Referencing their next project, they discussed how they were adapting the Hans Christian Andersen stories through the lens and style of "ani-motion," their coined term for stop-motion animation. Being true to artists pushing form, they went on to describe how they would take their learnings from *Noah's Ark* and their understandings of what they felt would creatively work for the new story they were telling to "create backgrounds, characters, and settings which are indigenous to the story itself." They further described their vision and highlighted how for this Hans Christian Andersen story they would not use recognizable household objects for the characters, and instead would opt for an abstract film that would leave much more up to the interpretation of the audience.

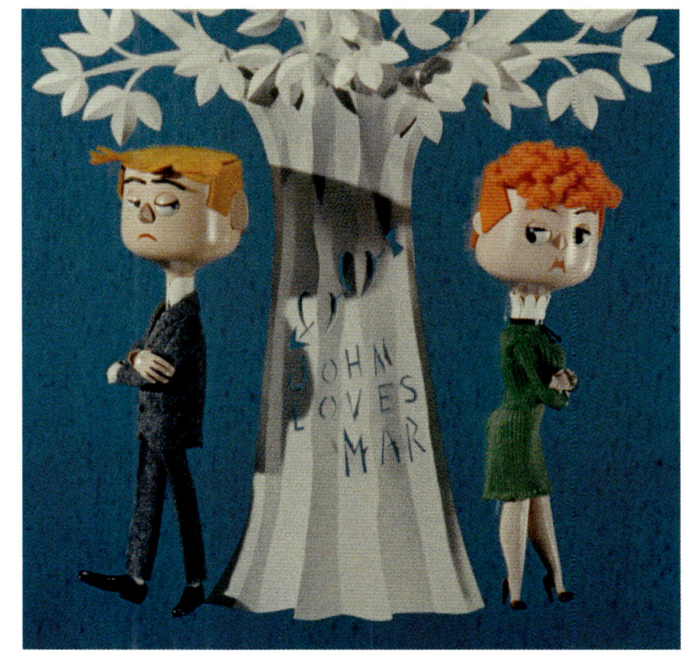

Their collective creative ideologies about the areas open for exploration within stop-motion animation were clear: it was not a substitute for animation but instead showed there could be unique branches within the larger realm of animation. They even went so far as to suggest perhaps doing a Western with just horseshoes, an inventive dea that never came to fruition. Likewise, while Disney had

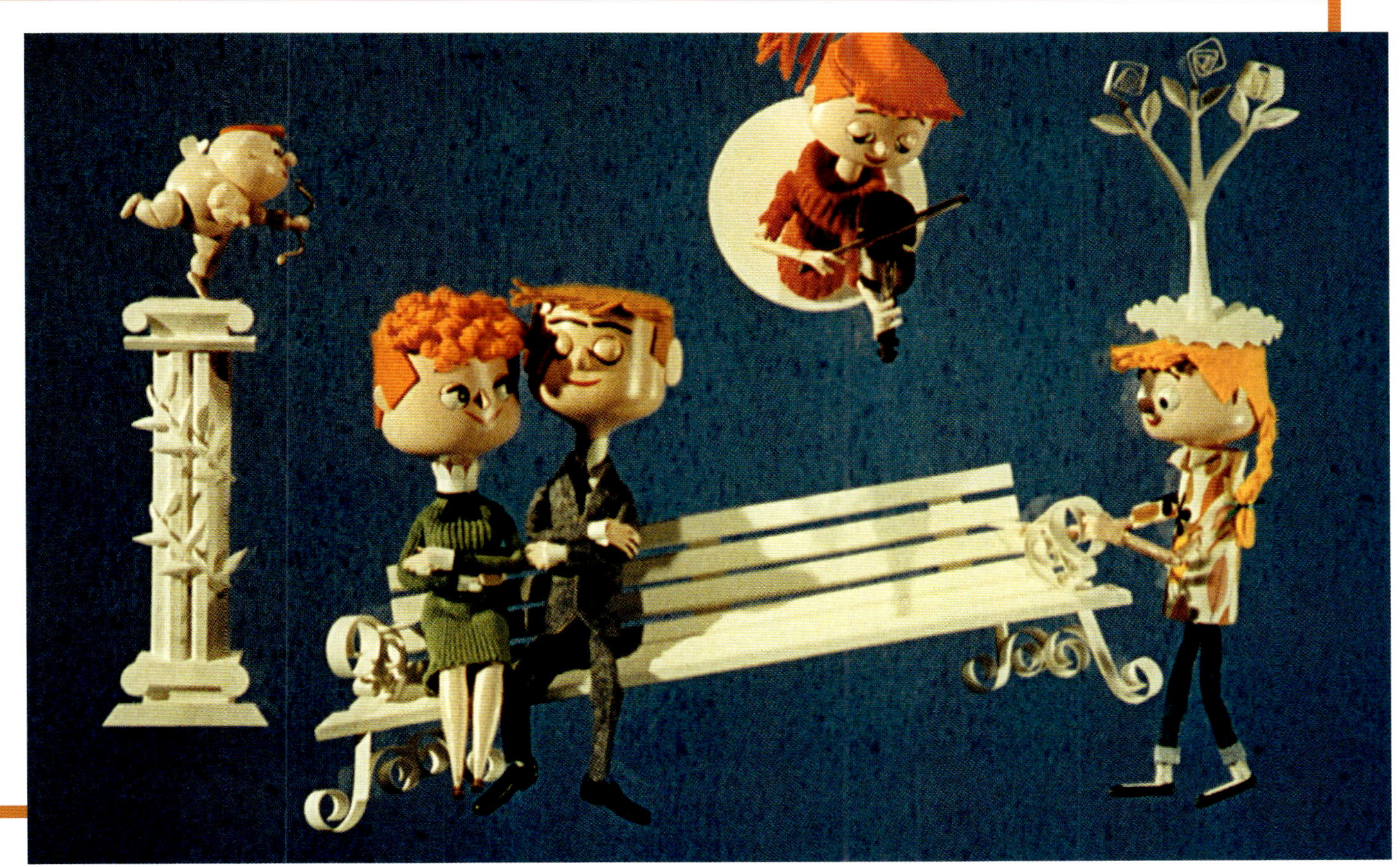

WALT DISNEY PRODUCTIONS

WALT DISNEY

INTER-OFFICE COMMUNICATION

To	Bill Justice/X. Atencio	Date	March 17, 1959
From	Walt Disney	Subject	Assignment

While we are getting the Hans Christian Anderson material in shape, there is a sequence in BABES IN TOYLAND - "March of the Toys" that I would like you to work on -- it would be puppet type animation.

Ward Kimball is handling the over-all picture, so if you will get in touch with him, he will explain it to you.

Walt

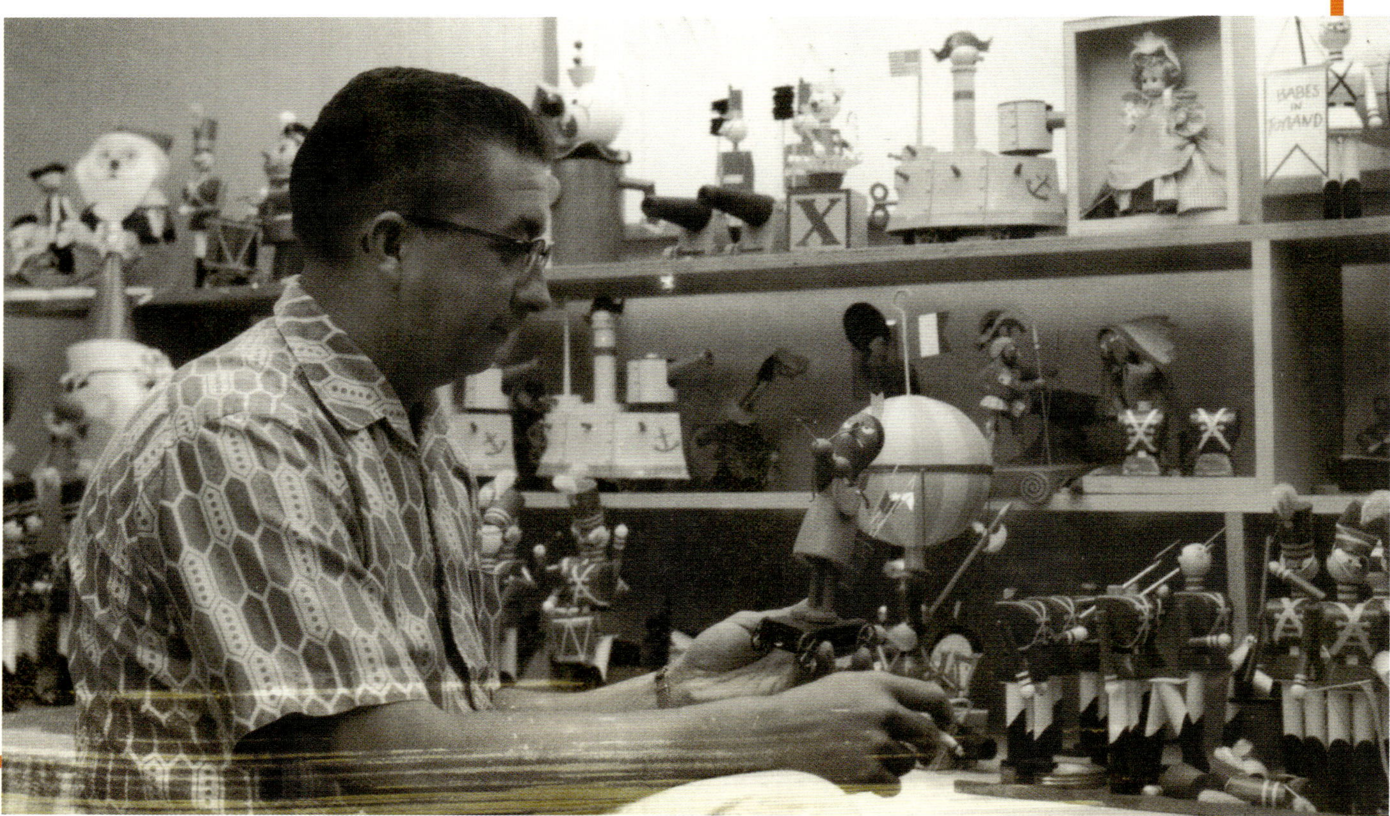

successfully and unsuccessfully attempted to adapt Hans Christian Andersen stories over the course of the company's history, X, Bill, and T. Hee's adaptation was never released nor finished, though it did make it far enough to get a studio production file, a not uncommon fate for projects to become stuck in development and never reach the production phase.

By the late 1950s, though the more experimental short films had found critical success (and Disneyland itself was a huge success, helping to bring in additional revenue), production on animated features was still troubled. *Sleeping Beauty* (1959), while a classic film that has stood the test of time, was an expensive and difficult production, taking almost ten years to make. Further complications arose with Walt's seemingly waning attention to his animated features and the other artists' struggles to match Eyvind Earle's style, which Walt was a strong supporter of. At the time, *Sleeping Beauty* was the most expensive Disney animated feature ever made, exceeding $6 million to produce, and consequentially resulting in a mass layoff at Disney soon after its completion. Viewing this as another marker of changing tastes and audience demands, Walt continued turning to live-action features, both to diversify studio output and to establish Disney as a stronger and more serious contender in Hollywood.

One such successful feature was *The Shaggy Dog* (1959), a family comedy that followed a teenage boy who was turned into a Bratislavan sheepdog by the power of an enchanted ring. For X and Bill, *The Shaggy Dog* was their first experience doing stop-motion opening titles. X and Bill created a shaggy dog out of an old mop. Against a gray backdrop and a catchy opening song, the titles set the tone for the film. In screwball comedic style, every time the dog ran across the screen, a new list of credits appeared. In one instance, the dog's leash dragged the credits in; in another, he chased his ball across the screen. While X and Bill were proud of their completed work, their buoyant feelings were dashed when they then received the dreaded call that the cameraperson had underexposed the film.

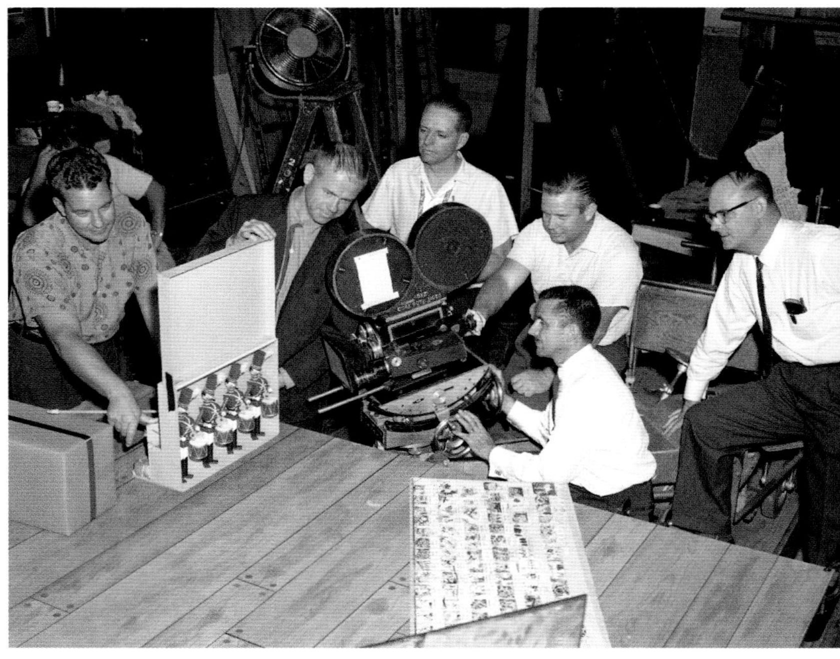

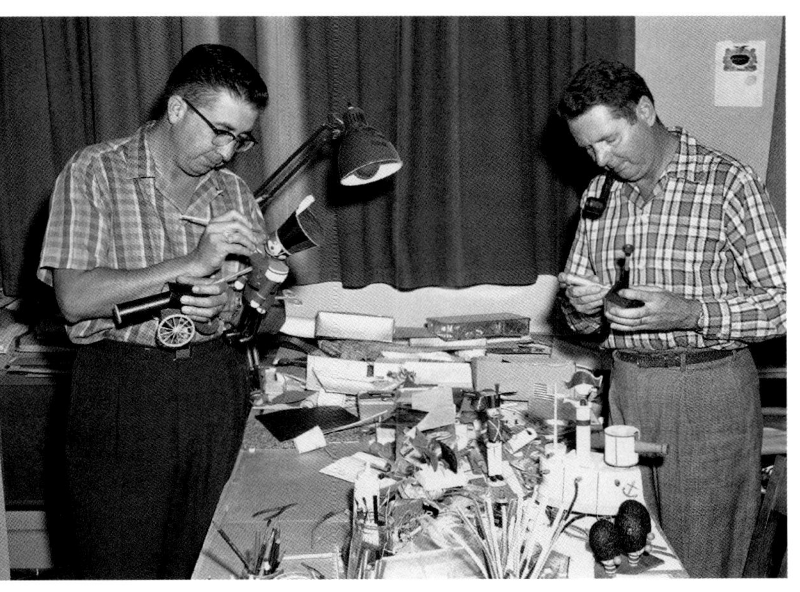

OPPOSITE (TOP): Memo from Walt requesting that X and Bill Justice work on the "March of the Toys" sequence in *Babes in Toyland*; OPPOSITE (BOTTOM): X designing toys for *Babes in Toyland*; TOP: Filming another angle of the "March of the Toys" scene in *Babes in Toyland*; ABOVE: X (LEFT) and Yale Gracey designing characters for *Babes in Toyland*.

Knowing that the title work needed to be redone, Bill dutifully reported the problem to Walt, promising that while it had taken five days to shoot the first time, they could complete the reshoots in three days and do an even better job. Walt permitted the work and offered X and Bill an added nod of approval, telling them to give themselves screen credit for "special titles," a first for the duo. X and Bill reshot the opening titles, perhaps even better prepared from their first five-day shoot in a way that ultimately made them prouder of the work and received "special titles" credit in their opening alongside their fellow collaborator T. Hee.

Impressed by their work on *The Shaggy Dog*, Walt had X and Bill use stop-motion to create the opening titles for *The Parent Trap* (1961). Double the length at almost four minutes, the *Parent Trap* opening titles proved to be almost a mini stop-motion version of the movie. The titles started with the curtain lifting on the stage, lightning, and then flashing. The scene then cut to a sign with wilted flowers that read BLESS OUR BROKEN HOME. Cherub-looking "cupids" then appeared as the "Parent Trap" song began to play, outlining how one needed to rig a parent trap when their family tree was falling apart. This led to public adulation—from Walt himself. Making their on-screen television debut, X, Bill, and T. Hee appeared briefly with Walt on Season 7, Episode 31 of *Walt Disney Presents* in an episode titled "The Title Makers," which detailed the making of the title sequence for *The Parent Trap*. The episode aired on June 11, 1961.

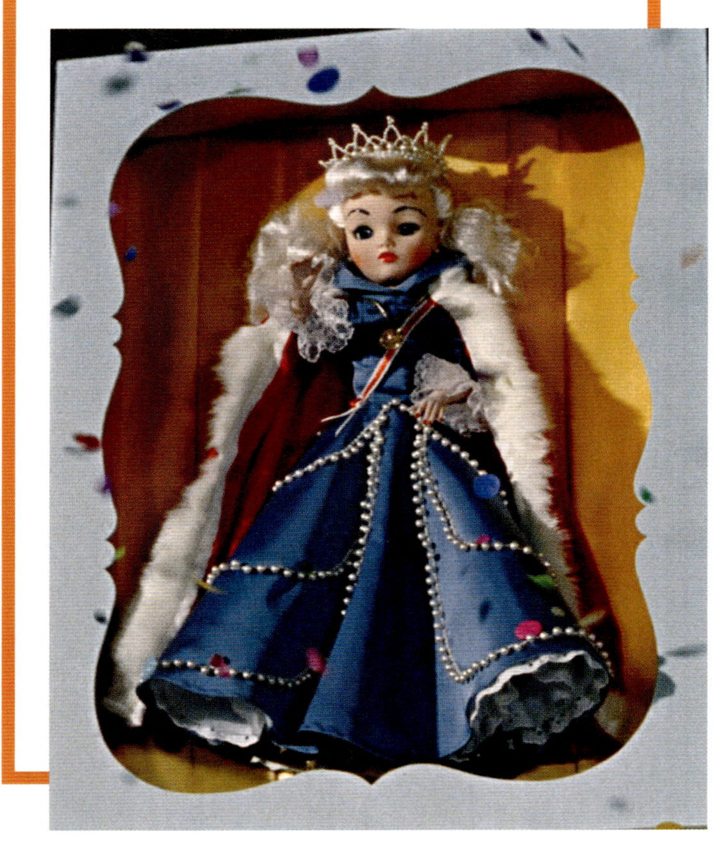

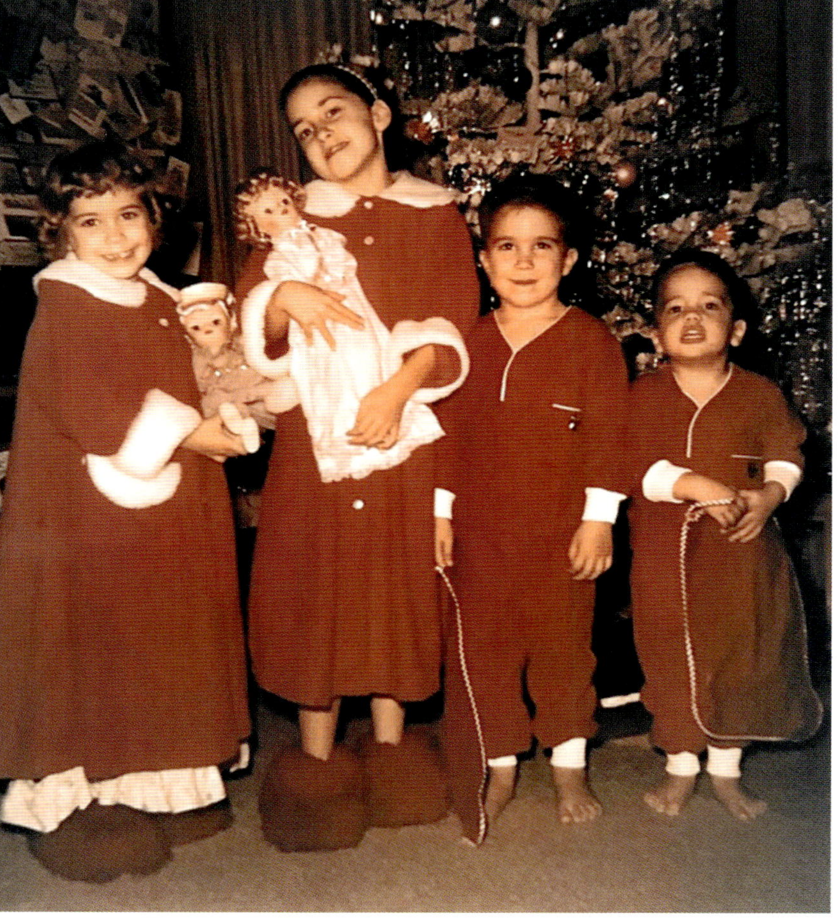

X, Bill, and T. Hee again earned their "special titles" credits in the opening, with X and T. functioning in similar roles as designers and animators (though T. was a seasoned story artist and designer, and X assisted, getting to learn from the best). However, as X described, T. had more of an ego and felt he was as talented as Walt, perhaps accounting for one of the reasons that T. continued to change studios, while X loved Disney and was content to stay and work under Walt's expert leadership.

Meanwhile, Bill channeled his vast patience and adeptness into animating the sequences, willing to take the time and energy necessary to work on tediously moving each item slowly, to capture the image, slightly adjust the item, and continually repeat the process—often for days on end. X even went so far as to call him the "evil genius of stop-motion animation." Unlike Bill, X preferred to focus on the character design and save his limited patience for other, more trying endeavors. Overall, X loved working with Bill and T. Hee and found their collaboration and creative combination to be enjoyable, producing legendary works that still resonate with current audiences while always making sure to have fun along the way. Furthermore, after X and Bill's stop-motion work, Disney as a company used stop-motion animation sporadically until *Tim Burton's The Nightmare Before Christmas* (1993), meaning that for more than two decades, X and Bill's work was the main reference for all those accessing Disney stop-motion animation.

X at this point was handling numerous assignments at the studio. When the live-action feature *Babes in Toyland* (1961) went into production, the team heading it realized they needed some toys designed and animated, so they called in X and Bill to accomplish this task. X and Bill, who were officially working as a team by that time, brought T. Hee onto the project with them again and set out to create the necessary stop-motion animation. They were assigned three of the toy sequences: "March of the Toys," the battle against the film's villain, and the sequence in which the Toymaker prepares the toys for Christmas with the children's assistance. Reviewing

TOP: The prop dolls that were later given to X's daughters from *Babes in Toyland*; ABOVE: X's children on Christmas, with his two daughters holding their dolls from *Babes in Toyland*; OPPOSITE (LEFT): X holding one of his original soldiers from *Babes in Toyland* nearly sixty years after the film was released; OPPOSITE (FAR RIGHT TOP): The filming of the "March of the Toys" scene; OPPOSITE (MIDDLE AND BOTTOM): X's toy soldiers marching in the Christmas Day Disneyland Parade.

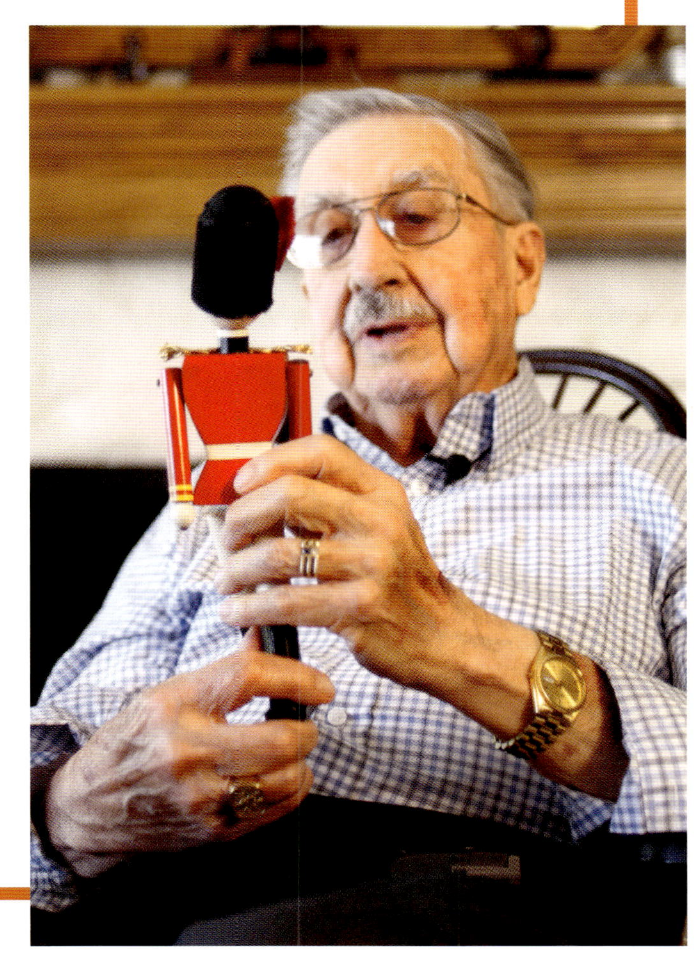

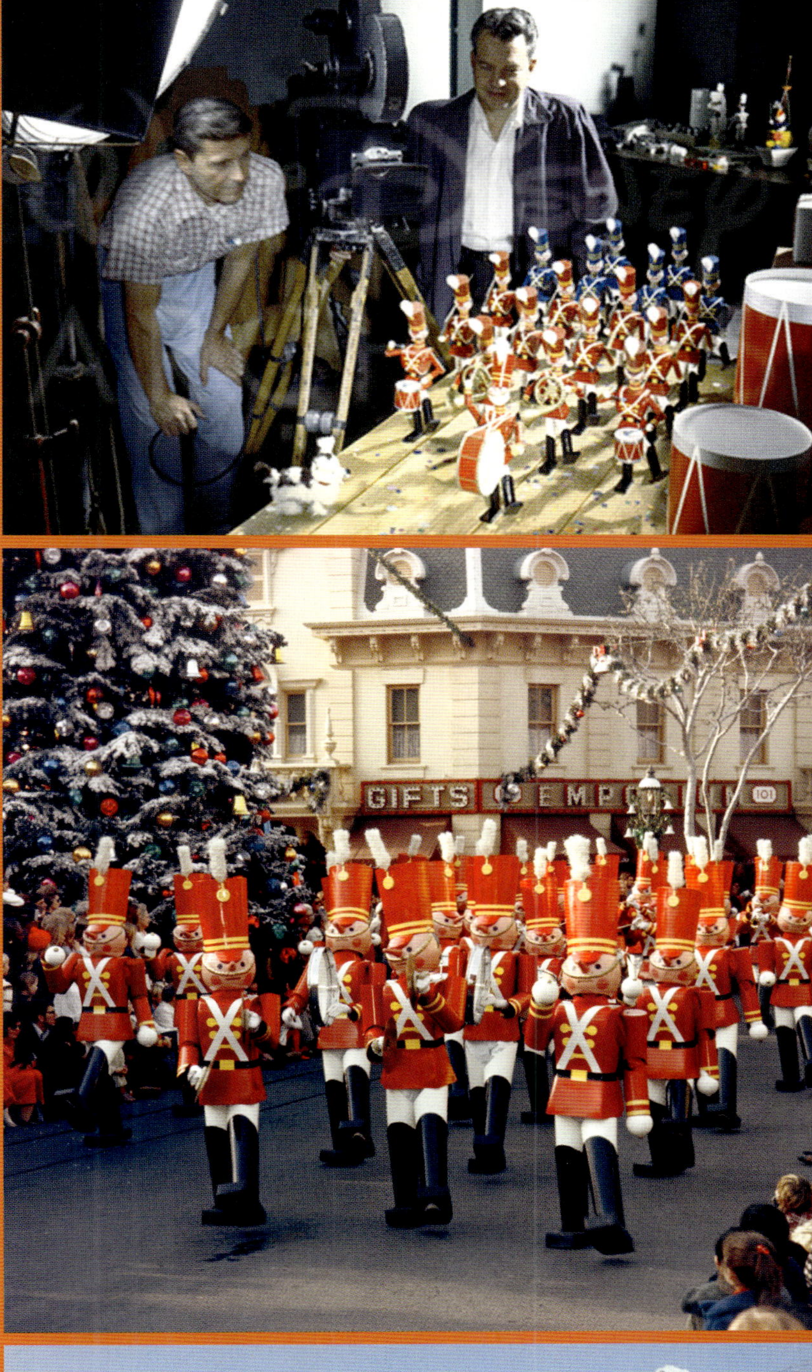

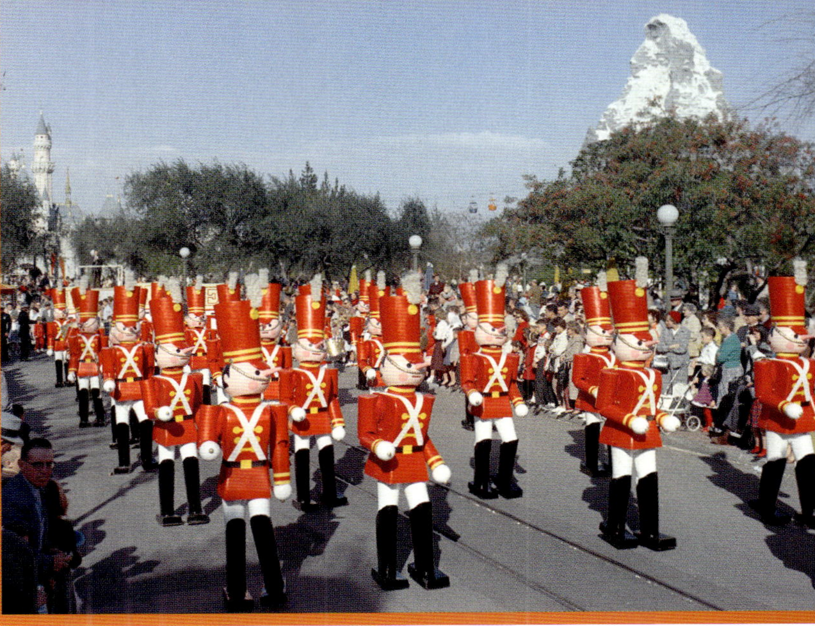

the storyboards, they discovered that their previous stop-motion animation tools wouldn't work on this project. Unlike the *Noah's Ark* flat animation against the plate glass, the toys in *Babes in Toyland* were upright characters that were moved throughout the scene. Likewise, with so many toy soldiers needing to march in straight lines, they knew they needed to, literally and figuratively, go back to the drawing board.

They drew traditional animation sketches of the soldiers marching, and selected the best from each, picking and choosing in this manner: arm movements from one pencil test, soldier height from another, leg movements from yet another test, et cetera. The team knew they needed to re-create complete marching cycles of the soldiers—thus the legs of the toys would need to move through every different position over the course of the sequence. Once the movements were chosen from their designs, they had to determine the best practical way to get the

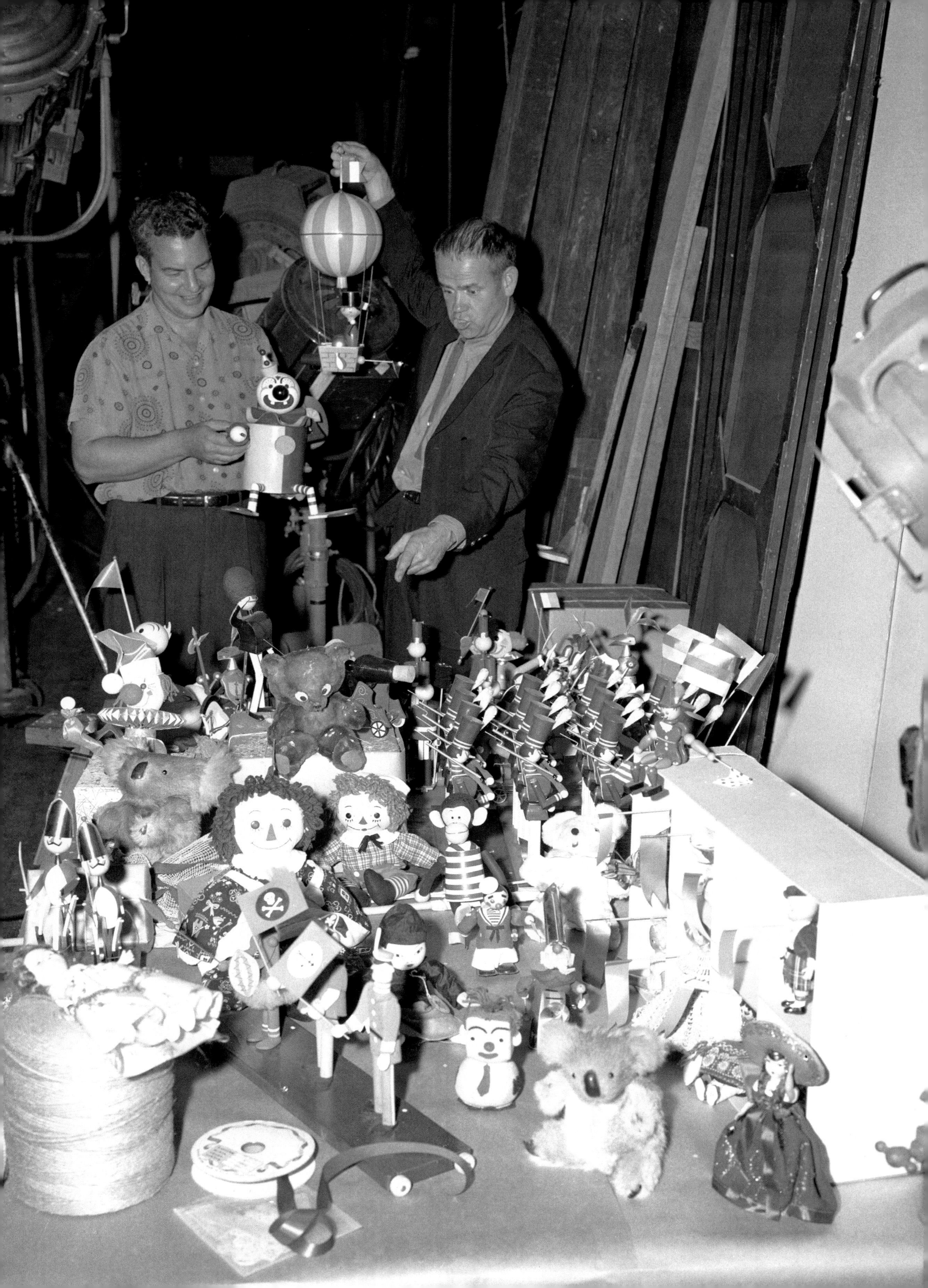

NY 1739
TO CARD WALKER
FROM IRVING LUDWIG

NOVEMBER 7,1962
12.00 EST

JUST SCREENED CASTAWAY TRAILER AND SYMPOSIUM. CONSENSUS HERE THAT SYMPOSIUM ONE OF THE ALL TIME GREAT SUBJECTS. SPECIAL PUSH IS GOING TO BE GIVEN TO IT AS WE FEEL THAT IT HAS DEFINITE PROGRAM VALUES. AN EQUALLY ENTHUSTIASTIC REACTION WAS GIVEN TO THE CASTAWAY TRAILER. REGARDS.

soldiers to stand up properly during filming. These regular toys, running about eight or nine inches high, were again designed by X and T. Hee. Ingeniously, according to Bill Justice, they decided to lay a steel plate covered with wood-textured paper over the toy shop floor and then put a magnet in the foot of each soldier to hold the toy securely upright in the correct position. To successfully film the marching sequence, each foot had to be changed out on the toy every two frames to clearly depict the marching movement pattern when the footage was played in succession.

While this brilliant creative fix was laudatory, X was particularly proud of the design of "his" soldiers. X crafted each of his soldiers to have their straps on their chests and backs, each in the shape of an X, a subtle Easter egg for the true aficionados. However, contrary to what one might imagine, X's favorite characters to work on in the film were not the soldiers, but instead the reindeer he designed in the Christmas scene that went with the Santa Claus float, again indicating his lifelong preference toward his animal characters.

After the production of *Babes in Toyland* wrapped, X took home the cannon soldier but returned it to the the Walt Disney Archives a decade later. In addition, X was gifted two of the dolls from the set—the princess and the pink ballerina, which he immediately brought home for his daughters, Tori and Judianne. Each doll came with a trunk full of custom costumes made by the seamstresses at the studio, as X had asked the costume department to make each daughter's doll a special wardrobe. The girls treasured their presents so deeply that over sixty years later both still have their dolls.

Shortly before the release of *Babes in Toyland* in December 1961, Walt called a meeting with Bill. He told Bill that he wanted a giant toy parade at Disneyland to drum up publicity for *Babes in Toyland*'s release; X and Bill went to work on making Walt's dream a reality. Their biggest challenge was to make the toys large enough to create the effect of a giant toy parade without becoming too big or ridiculous. In looking at the movie toys they had created, both felt the soldiers stood out as perfect models of effective life-sized toys that they could scale up for the toy parade. They also developed snowmen and snow-women, revisited X's favorite reindeer, and invented a few other ideas that still run in today's Disneyland's A Christmas Fantasy Parade. X so loved the soldiers and reindeer he had created and the memories they evoked that even in his later years, well after his retirement, X would often watch the parade on Christmas morning just to see his creations.

X and Bill's next collaboration was *A Symposium on Popular Songs* (1962), a twenty-minute animated featurette film that was again directed by Bill Justice. *A Symposium on Popular Songs* starred Donald Duck's uncle, Professor Ludwig Von Drake, as he directly

OPPOSITE: Bill Justice (LEFT) and Ward Kimball filming the "March of the Toys" scene in *Babes in Toyland*; ABOVE: Memo from distribution executive Irving Ludwig to studio executive Card Walker expressing his excitement about *A Symposium on Popular Songs*.

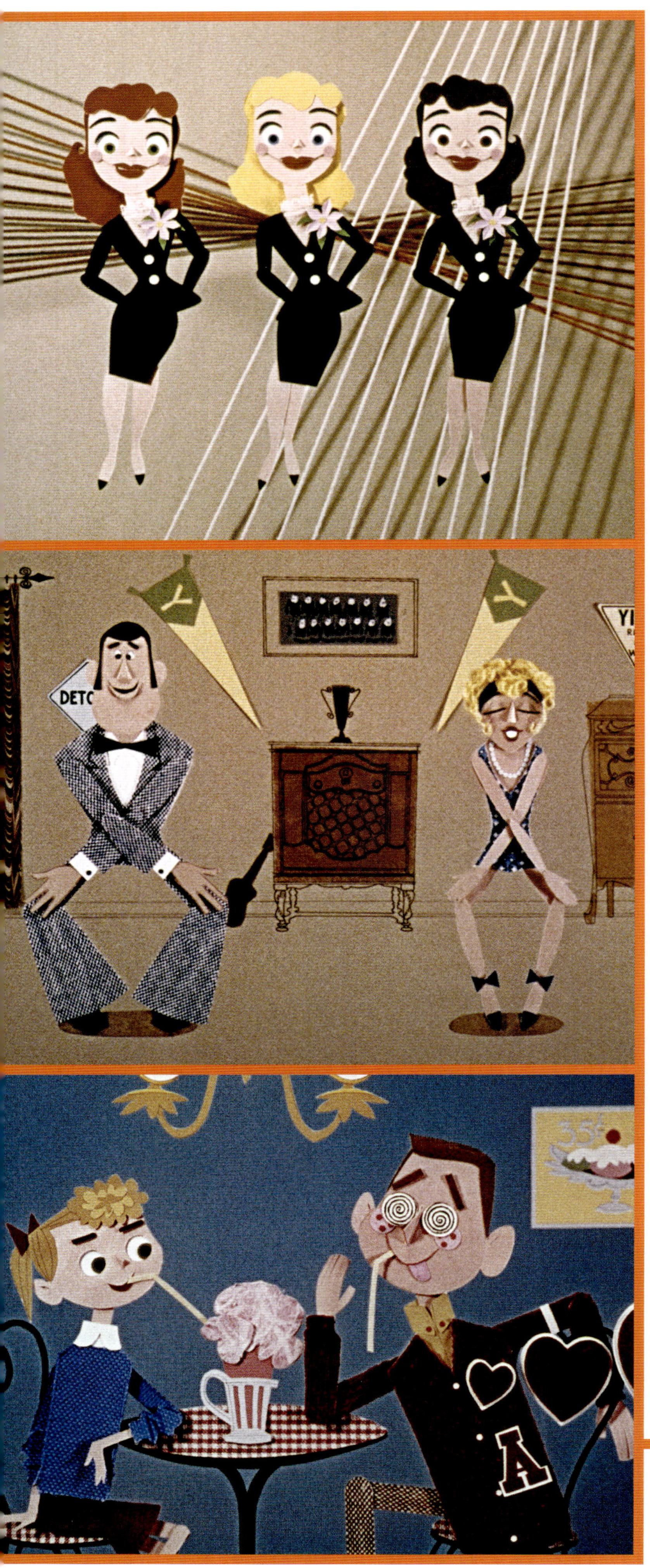

addressed his audience with his lecture on the history of popular music. In traditional humorous Disney fashion, Ludwig claimed to have invented every genre of music that was popular in the twentieth century. The film used songs from several modern genres—from ragtime to 1950s rock—to depict songs Ludwig asserted that he wrote. While the scenes with Ludwig lecturing in his mansion featured more traditional animation, several of the song interludes used stop-motion photography.

X received the opening credit in the title sequence for "story and styling," and Bill was granted credit for directing and for "stop motion." Paul Frees, whom X would later collaborate with as the voice of the Haunted Mansion's Ghost Host, was one of their vocal talents in the film. Paul was an impressive (and expensive) talent whose stylistic work voicing Von Drake gave the character its life force. X believed Paul became Von Drake, taking the script and running with it, infusing the character with additional dialogue and tones that X never imagined.

A new addition to X and Bill's collaboration on *A Symposium on Popular Songs* was the Sherman brothers, who would later go on to write perhaps their best-known song, "It's a Small World," for the 1964–65 World's Fair as well as the songs for *Mary Poppins* (1964). The Sherman brothers were brought on to handle the music but also collaborated with X and Bill on the story development, since they all felt that the music and the story went hand in hand for this film. X's work with Bob and Richard Sherman would end up influencing him greatly in his later career. However, at this point in the early 1960s, he was just pleased to partner with two talented songwriters who also understood how to weave story and music together into an inventive Disney film. They used vegetables and paper cutouts for the stop-motion animation set against original songs that parodied classic genre songs, like "Boogie Woogie Bakery Man" (instead of "Boogie Woogie Bugle Boy") and "Rock, Rumble and Roar" (instead of "Shake, Rattle and Roll").

Although the film earned an Academy Award nomination for Best Cartoon Short Subject, the

LEFT: A series of stop-motion stills from *A Symposium on Popular Songs*; OPPOSITE: X (RIGHT) and Bill posing with their vegetable characters from *A Symposium on Popular Songs*.

market for film shorts had started to shrink. Even with stop-motion, the shorts were becoming too expensive to produce and offered less return on investment, especially as buying and programming strategies from the theaters shifted to cater to the changing demands of audiences and the drive for larger profits. Previously, theatrical programming was set up so that theater owners would pay for a feature film, a newsreel, and a shorter cartoon film. However, the trends had changed, and the focus became turning over the theater for the next feature or double feature, as tickets were sold per feature showing and didn't charge extra for the cartoon or newsreel that went alongside the main film.

But as ticket sales and audience turnover became the focus, largely due to the added competition from television, which remained as strong as ever, theater owners no longer wanted to spend twenty minutes showing a short film every screening. And much like many of the other experimental short films that X had worked on, *A Symposium on Popular Songs* was a test to see if the electrostatic process could transfer animation drawing to cels. Its successful ability to do so meant a quicker and cheaper process of xerography that replicated the art, but also meant an end to many of the traditional inkers' responsibilities in the Ink and Paint Department as animation continued adapting to advancing technologies.

For X, this stop-motion animation trend also marked the point in his career in which he was officially classified as an animator. And yet X didn't feel like an animator, given the limited animation he was actually doing. Instead, he spent most of his remaining career at the studio working on story and layout work, leaving him to always feel throughout his whole career more like an artist than an animator. However, X's work was influenced by the time he spent in animation, and regardless of whether he would directly classify himself as an animator, Walt Disney did. When looking at X's personal work, one sees the stop-motion influence, starting around 1958 and 1959, where more drastic changes are quite apparent. X's holiday cards from those years included paper cutouts and dimensionality, a direct link to his stop-motion work at Disney. And by 1961, X was even mixing photos with artwork, again paralleling his Disney work, when he ventured into live-action films mixed with stop-motion animation. And in

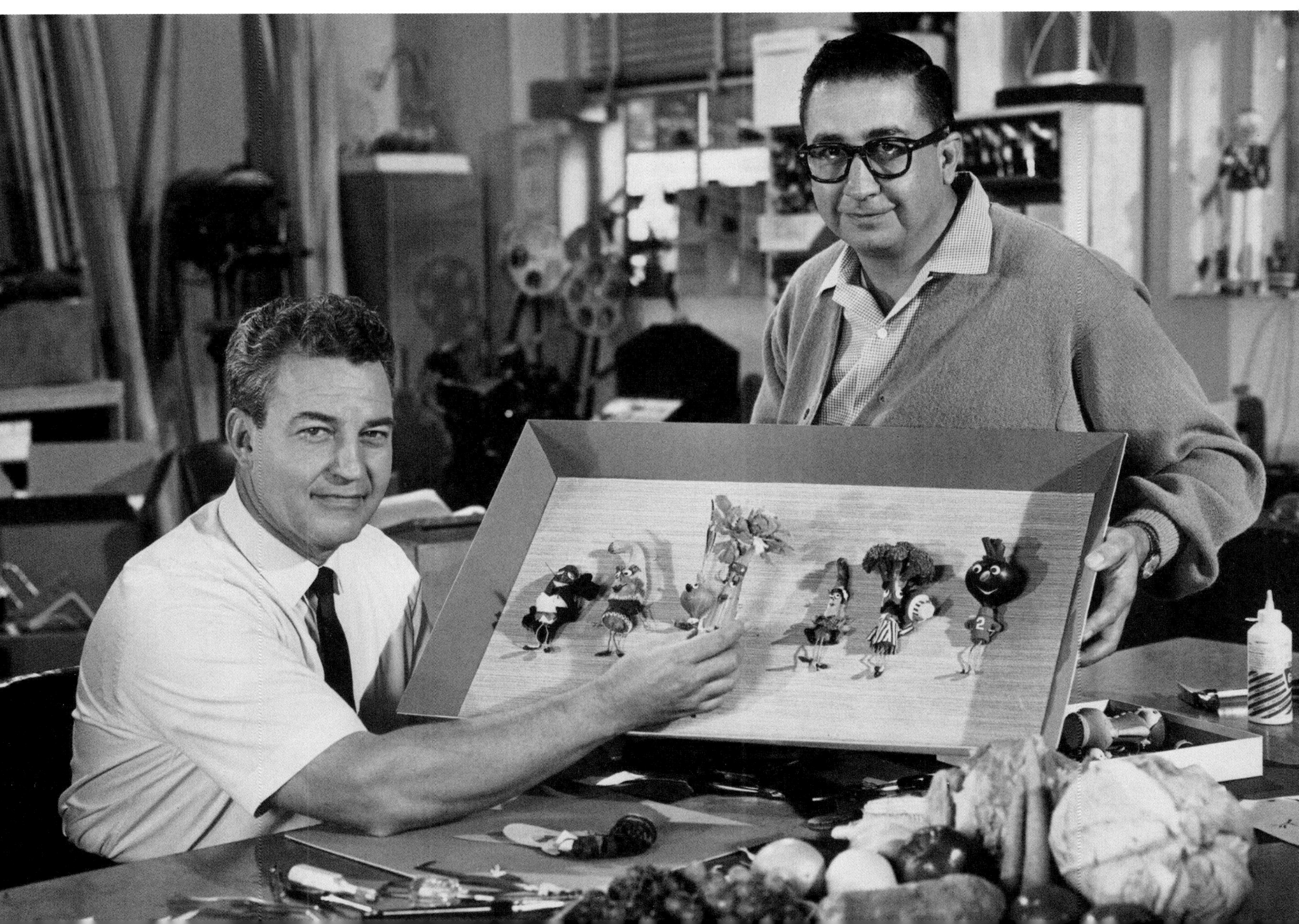

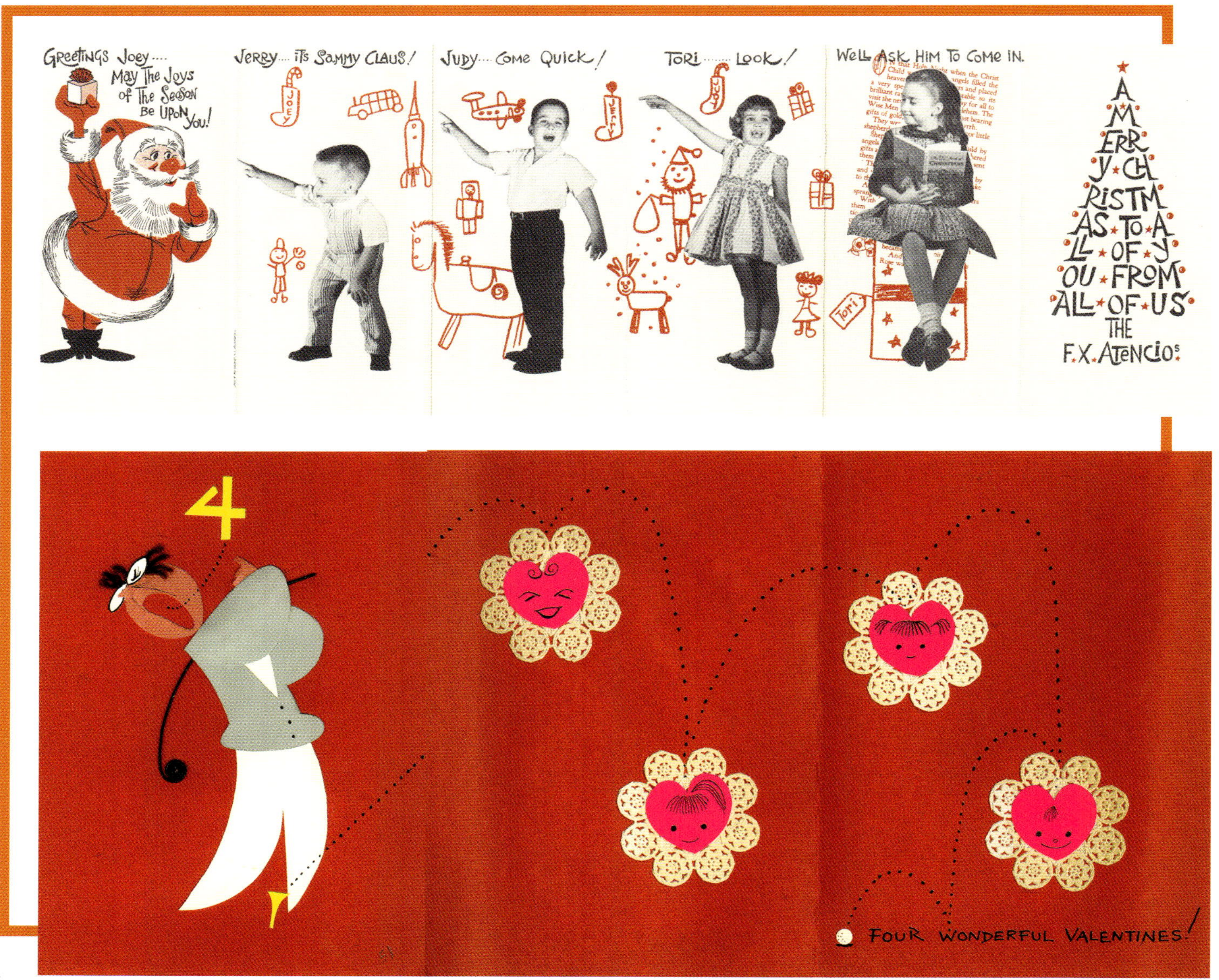

1963, he started writing elaborate letters along with the stories depicted in the cards, foreshadowing some untapped narrative talents that Walt would soon discover.

But before that, in the fall of 1962, Walt called X and Bill to his office and introduced them to Carlos Amador and his movie star wife, Marga López, with whom he had been meeting. Carlos was preparing the live-action movie *Cri-Crí, the Little Singing Cricket* (1963), about the life of famous Mexican children's author Francisco Gabilondo Soler. Carlos was meeting with Walt to request permission to include a four-minute animated segment on "The Three Little Pigs," using Walt's three little pigs. Walt agreed and had brought X and Bill into his office to officially assign them to the project, saying, according to X, "I want you to meet these people and do what they would like." Knowing that half the film's profits would go to help provide underprivileged Mexican children with a free daily school lunch and that it was the first lady of the Republic of Mexico's favorite charity, Walt decided to donate the animation and assign two of his most-trusted creatives, with Bill again directing the segment. Moreover, production was set to begin as soon as possible. As X, Bill, Carlos, and Marga left Walt's office, Bill joked that they would love to deliver the finished cartoon to Carlos personally, humorously hinting at a desire to travel to Mexico, far away from

TOP: X's 1961 Christmas card combining photos and hand-drawn artwork; ABOVE: X's 1958 Valentine's Day card to Mary, which used paper cutouts of hearts and flowers to depict Mary and their three children; OPPOSITE: X's 1959 Mother's Day card to Mary, featuring a 3D miniature saltshaker, shortly after the birth of their youngest son.

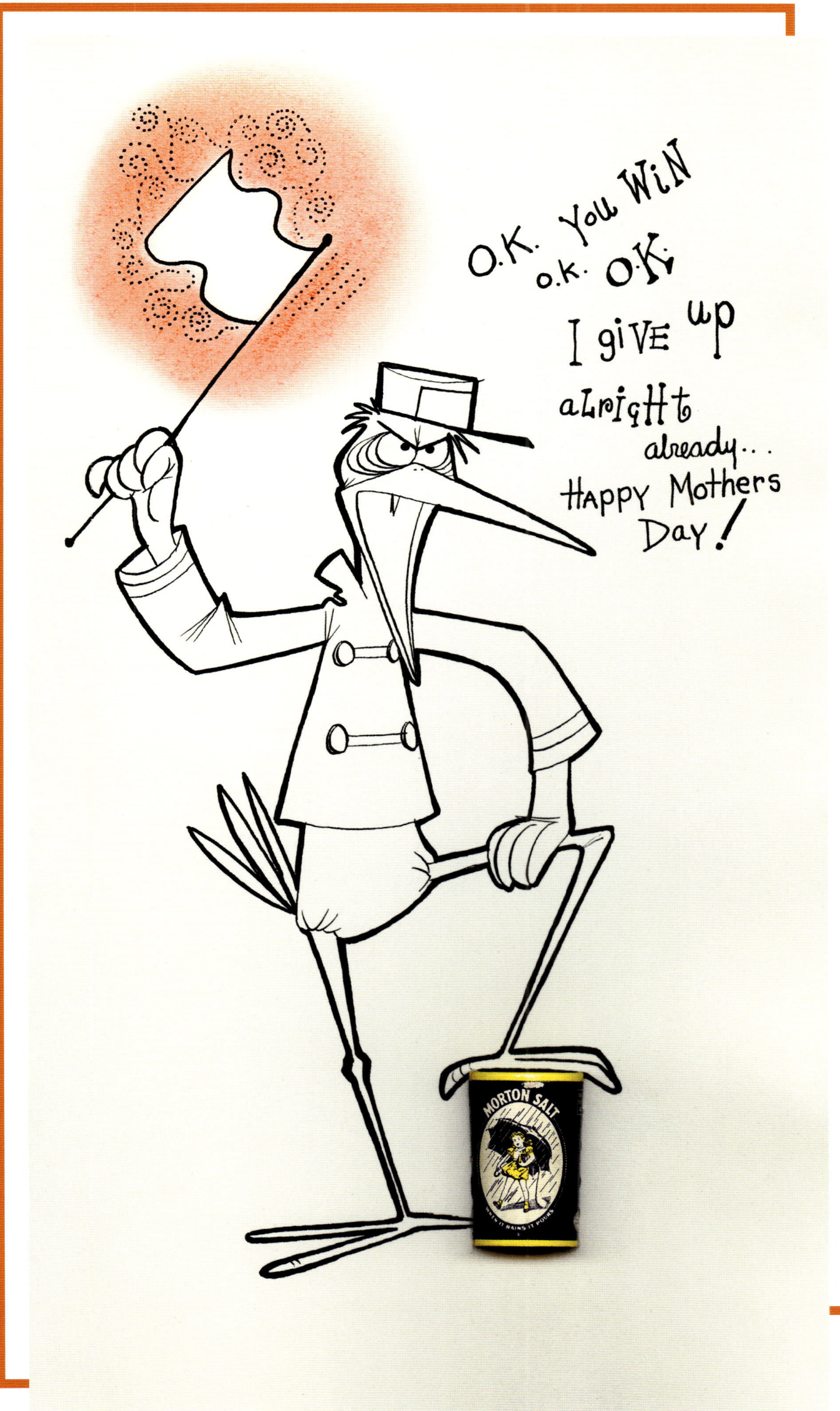
O.K. You WiN
o.k. O.K.
I give up
alright
already...
Happy Mothers
Day!
MORTON SALT
WHEN IT RAINS IT POURS

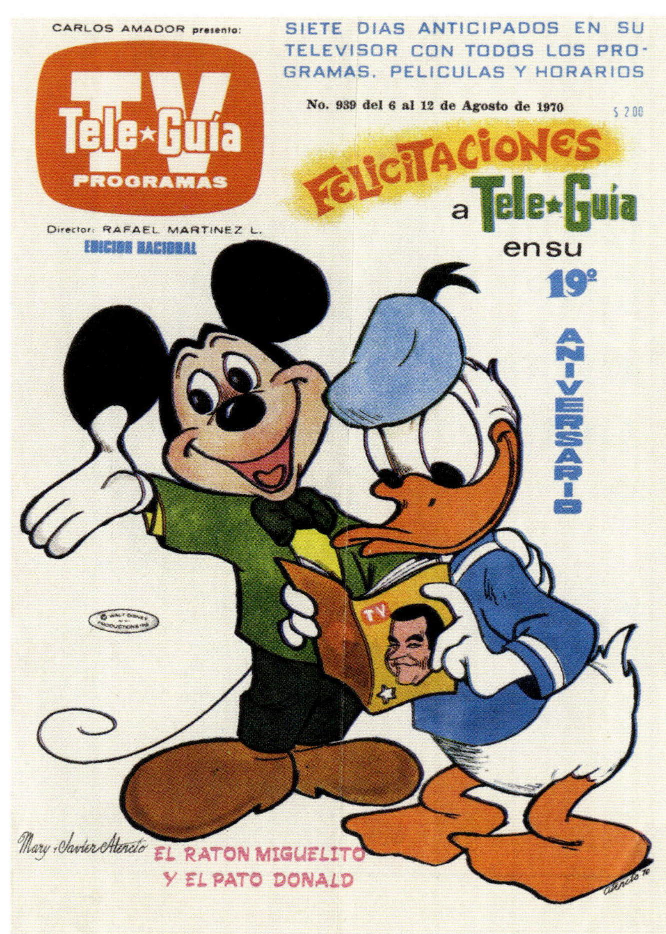
CARLOS AMADOR presenta:
TV
Tele★Guía
PROGRAMAS
SIETE DIAS ANTICIPADOS EN SU TELEVISOR CON TODOS LOS PROGRAMAS, PELICULAS Y HORARIOS
No. 939 del 6 al 12 de Agosto de 1970
$ 2.00
FELICITACIONES
a Tele★Guía
en su
19º
ANIVERSARIO
Director: RAFAEL MARTINEZ L.
EDICION NACIONAL
TV
Mary y Javier Atencio
EL RATON MIGUELITO
Y EL PATO DONALD

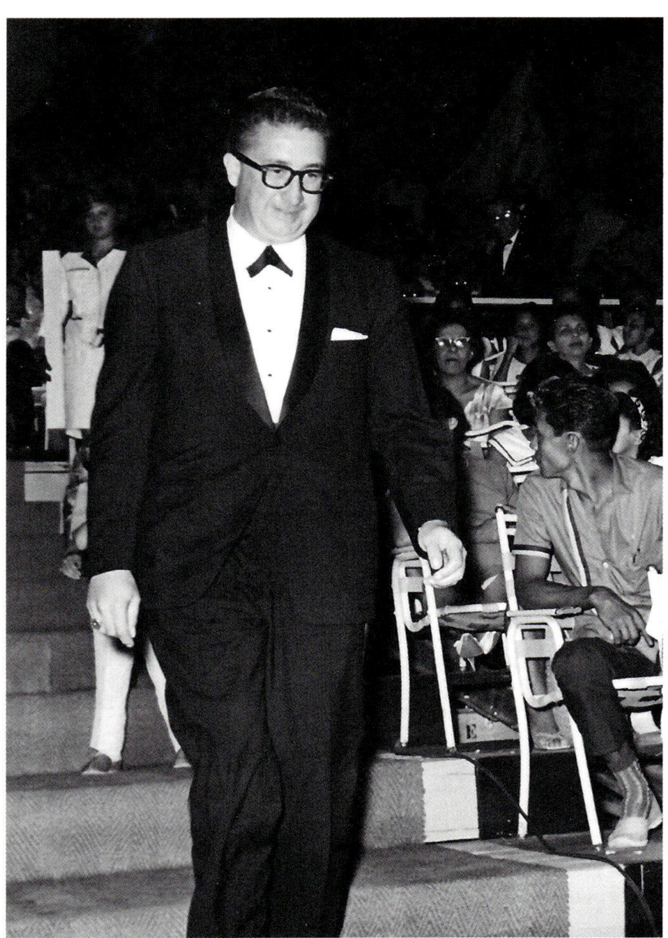

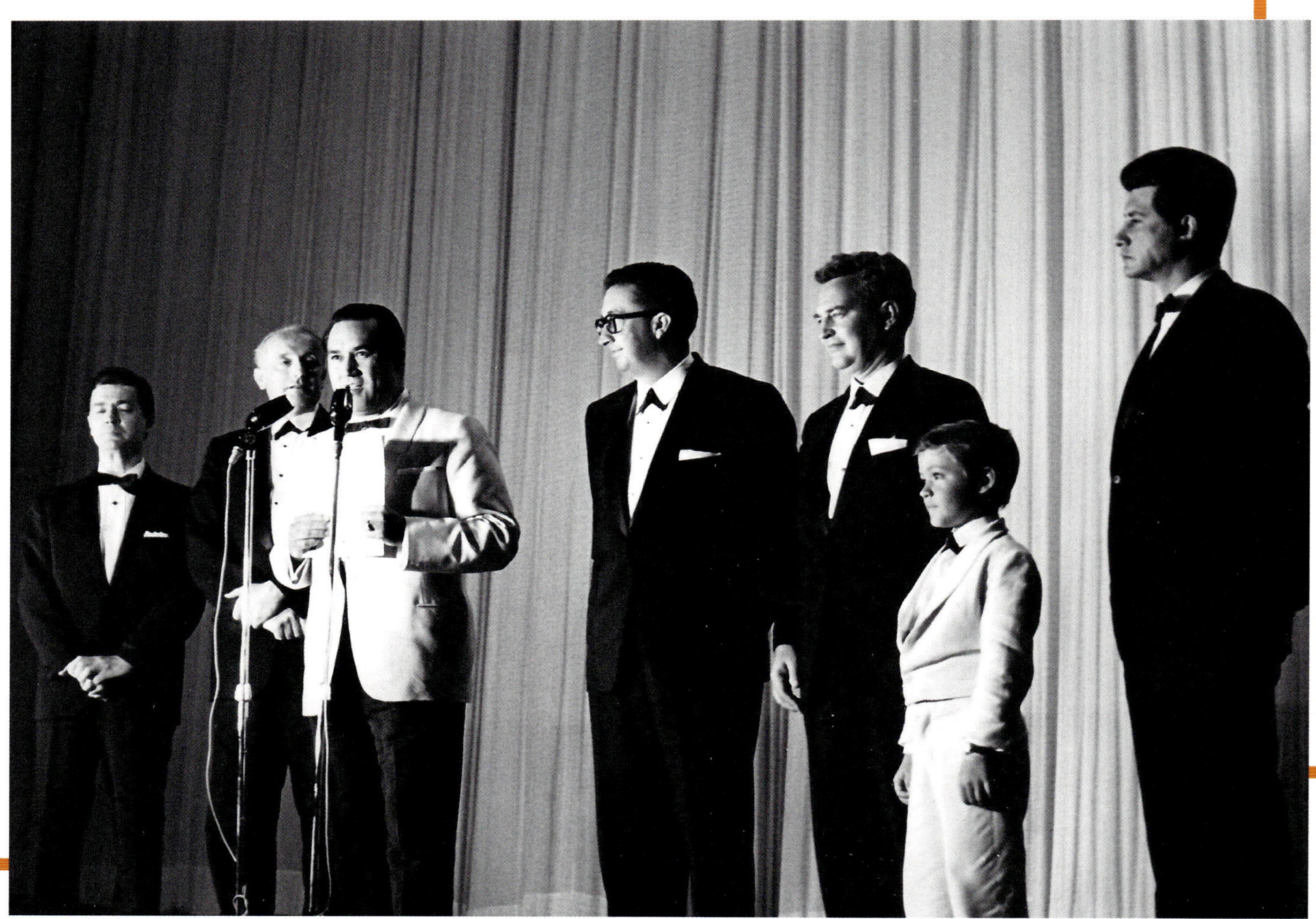

their offices in Burbank. Carlos took it at face value, graciously and immediately extending an invitation for X and Bill to come and stay with them as guests.

Once work started, Carlos wrote the four-minute adaptation while X and Bill focused on the storyboards and the production animation. The animation was simpler stylistically than what X and Bill had worked on in the recent past, but the comical complications and narrative style were reminiscent to X of his earlier Pacheco cartoon drawings, which had helped him land the job at Disney back in the late 1930s.

A few months later, X and Bill showed Walt the finished film for his approval. Once Walt signed off, the men notified Carlos of the final authorization, at which point Carlos responded with an invitation to express his gratitude for their efforts to X, Bill, and Gene Armstrong, an employee from the studio's foreign department, to come visit Mexico City for ten days with their wives. All three readily accepted and headed out on VARIG airlines, which Carlos was part owner of, being treated on the flight like visiting dignitaries. They were then welcomed by a mariachi band at the airport, and the spouses were each given a bouquet of roses. Each free day they awoke to a waiting taxi and were whisked off to various sightseeing excursions. During their stay in Mexico, a special dinner was held in which the finished film *Cri-Crí, the Little Singing Cricket*, or, as it was known in Spanish, *Cri-Crí, El Grillito Cantor*, was presented to the first lady of Mexico. In return, she gave the guests of honor, X and Bill, gold medals for their contributions and wonderful work on the movie.

As a 1963 letter soliciting Walt Disney's participation in the film noted:

> Knowing your great humanitarian gifts and affection that through your inspired work you have always shown on behalf of the children of the world, we are soliciting from you for the first time your esteemed cooperation that would be of tremendous assistance to the Mexican motion picture and especially to the children of our Republic.

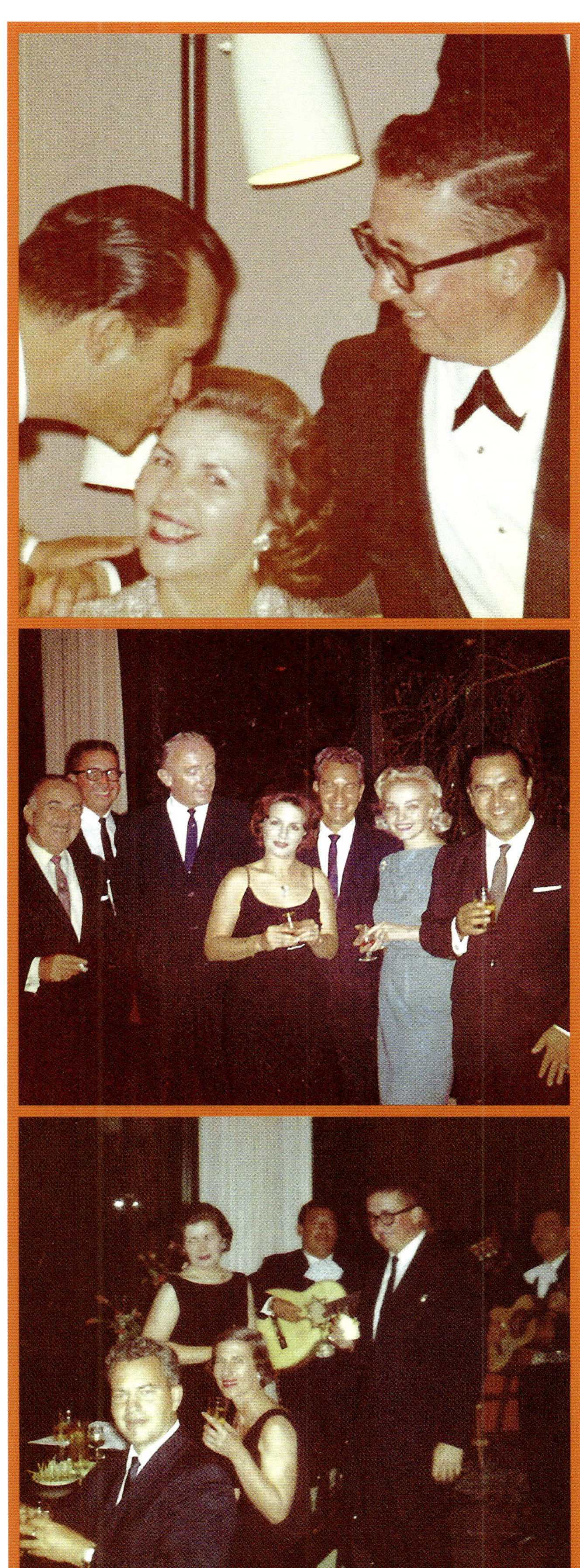

OPPOSITE (TOP LEFT): The *Tele-Guia* (the Mexican edition of *TV Guide*) cover using a drawing from a card that X had sent to Carlos Amador; OPPOSITE (TOP RIGHT): X walking to the stage to accept his award for *Cri-Crí, El Grillito Cantor*; OPPOSITE (BOTTOM): X, Bill, Gene Armstrong, and other Disney colleagues onstage with Carlos Amador receiving their award; RIGHT: X, Mary, Bill and Marie Justice, Carlos Amador, and others celebrating in Mexico.

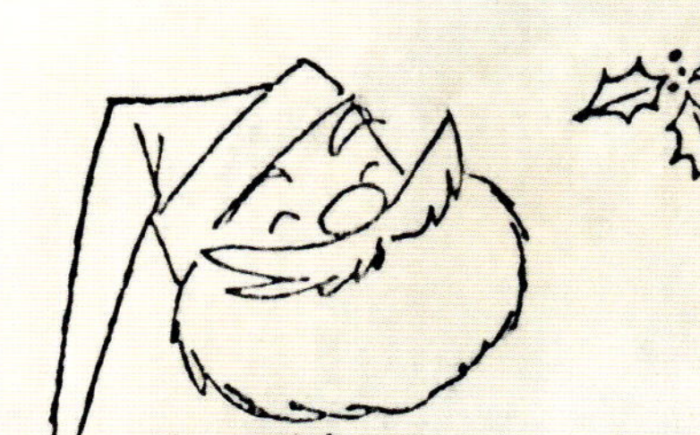

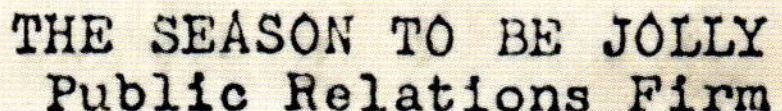

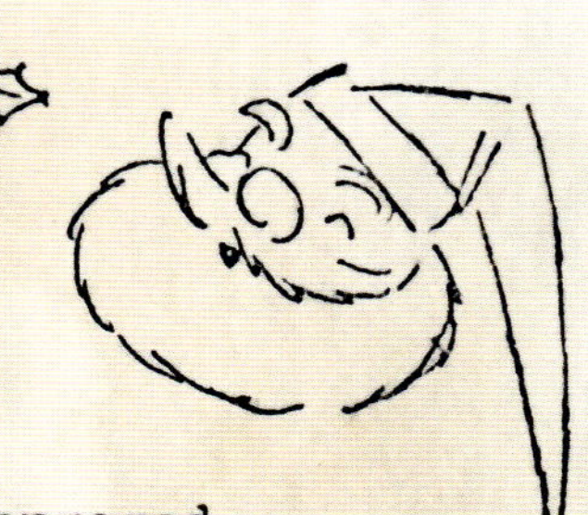

THE SEASON TO BE JOLLY
Public Relations Firm

Greetings;

It is our pleasure to announce that we have been engaged to represent the F. X. Atencio family of Woodland Hills, Calif. It will be our responsiblilty to inform the world at large and their friends in particular of the many exciting things that have happened to them in the past year.

To begin. The enclosed brochure indicates rather subtly that the past year was high-lighted by two glorious trips to Mexico. Our client, Mr. Atencio, was commissioned by his employer of the past twenty five years to prepare and produce, with his partner, a film for the Mexican Government. The National Institute for the Protection of the Children of Mexico had asked Mr. Disney to donate to the Mexican children a cartoon sequence to a film which the Institute was co-producing. The Title of the film is "CRI CRI the SINGING CRICKET". Mr. Disney who is always ready to help the children of the world was glad to cooperate considering that the proceeds of this film would go toward feeding millions of children in Mexico.

When the cartoon sequence was completed Mr. and Mrs. Atencio together with his partners and their wives were invited to Mexico as quests of the Mexican Government to present the Film to Sr. Eva Samano de Lopez Mateos, the wife of the President who is the patroness of the Institute. They were wined and dined for ten glorious days and they departed thoroughly impressed with the delightful hospitality of the Mexican people.

A few days ago the same group was invited back this time as guests of the Producer of the picture "CRI CRI " which was selected as the Mexican entry at the International Film Festival in Acapulco. This trip unfortunately coincided with the assassination of our beloved President and an air of sadness prevailed throughout the trip. However, it was interesting to our clients to be in a foriegn country at that time to see first hand the reaction of the Mexican people who held Mr. Kennedy in such high esteem.

By comparison every thing else that happened in the past year seemed dull and unexciting to our clients.

The Children, apparently, are growing and developing in a normal manner. Victoria, the eldest, is almost ten years old. She is in the Fourth grade and the highlight in her past year was her "Fly-up" from Blue Bird to Camp Fire Girl. Judy is in the Third grade and enjoying just being a Blue Bird. Jerry is in the First grade and the high-light of his past year was being rushed to the emergency hospital after falling off the stairs and putting a fair size dent in his cranium. Joey is four and a half and wont go to school until next year. He just enjoys bugging his brother and sisters.

This then is the Atencio story for 1963 and their wish for you is A VERY MERRY CHRISTMAS and A VERY HAPPY NEW YEAR.

ABOVE: X's 1963 Christmas letter, written in the style of a press release, recapping X and Mary's wonderful time in Mexico; OPPOSITE: Closed and open views of X's 1963 Christmas card, featuring the family coming out of a piñata that Santa had broken open.

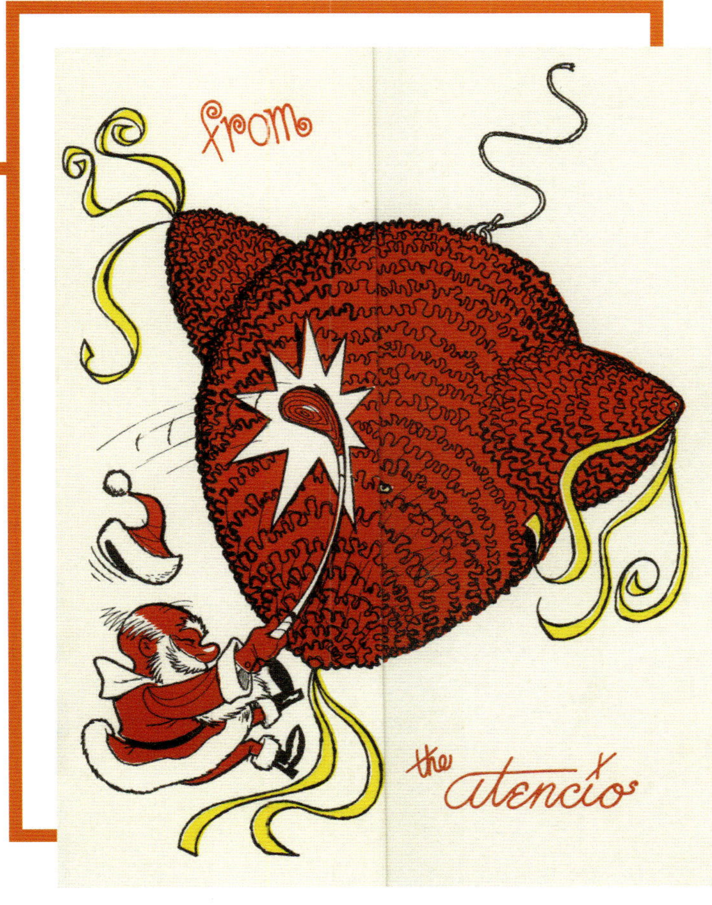

The National Institute for the Protection of Children, whose principal work consists of bringing the benefits of free daily school breakfasts to a million children, plans to produce in collaboration with the company Organizations Carlos Amador S.A. a feature length picture in color entitled *Cri Cri, The Little Singing Cricket*, based on the life and songs of a famous Mexican composer who has sung to three generations.

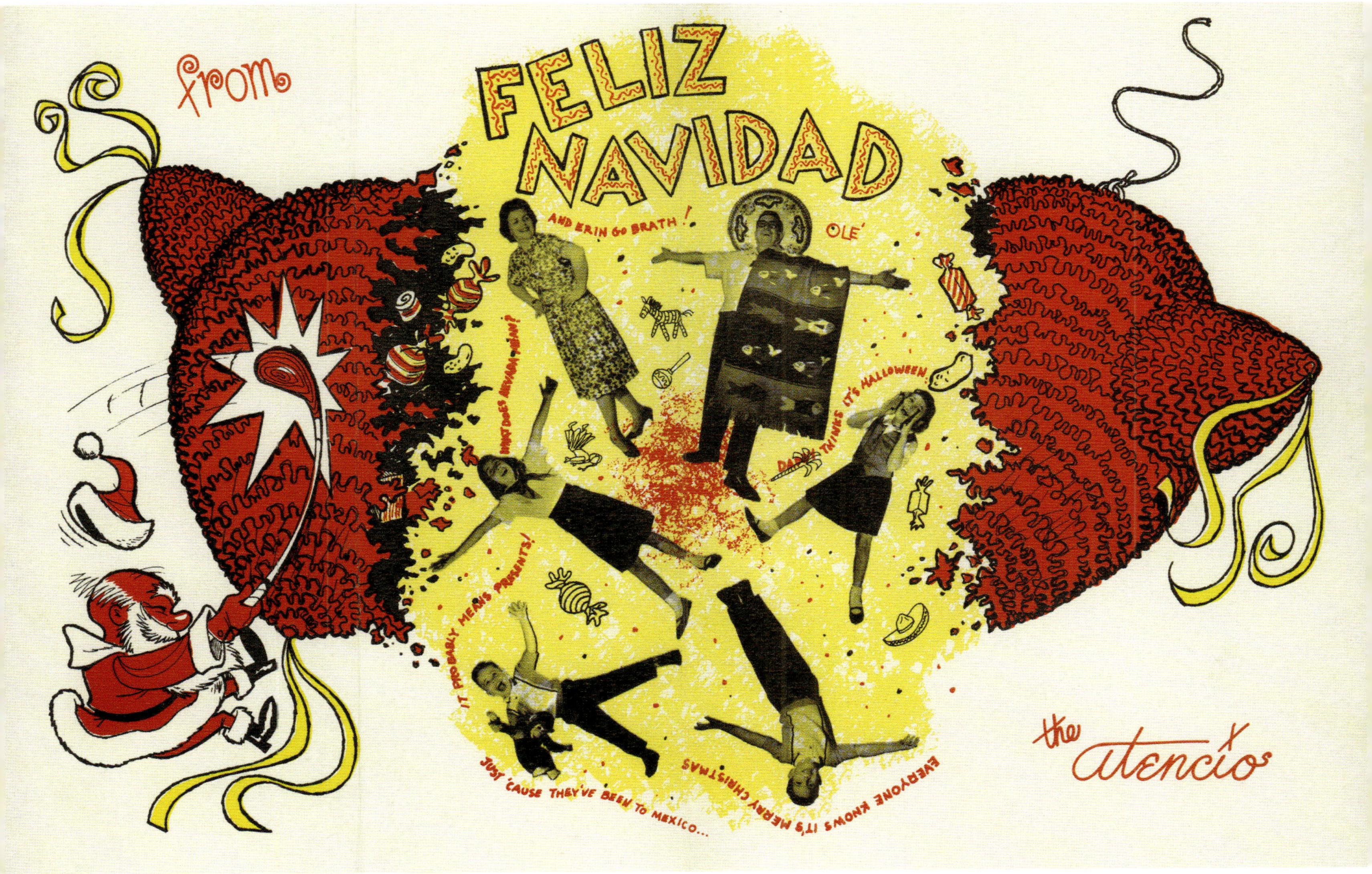

X, Bill, Gene, and their wives returned to Mexico in November 1963 at the invitation of Carlos to attend an international film festival in Acapulco in order to see *Cri-Crí, the Little Singing Cricket* receive an award. The men and their wives had just arrived when they heard the announcement about the assassination of President John F. Kennedy. Although the tragic news event dampened the tone of the evening, Bill always remembered how gracious everyone was, especially expressing their sympathies when they found out that X and Bill were U.S. citizens. In addition to the warm receptions in Mexico, X forged another friendship through a trusted work collaboration with none other than Carlos Amador. X's family Christmas card from 1963 reflected the influence from his trip to Mexico. The card even went so far as to depict X wearing a serape and sombrero while he, Mary, and their four children emerged from a piñata.

X and Bill's next project was *Mary Poppins* (1964). After their work with the toys on *Babes in Toyland*, Walt assigned them to animate the scene in which Mary Poppins and the children, Jane and Michael Banks, cleaned up the very messy nursery while Mary sang "A Spoonful of Sugar." Mary snapped her fingers, and magically the mess and chaos of the nursery was put back into place, item by item, turning the usual chore of cleaning up into a game, one that was especially fun when set against a catchy song. In awe, the children tried to replicate her snapping, eventually succeeding. While the story was well established before X and Bill were brought onto the project, their responsibilities included adding the details to the nursery scene and figuring out how to make the special effects of Mary's magic happen on camera via a combination of live action and stop-motion animation. X worked on the storyline for their nursery scene, and Bill again focused on bringing the animation to life. X said it was a fairly simple project as it comprised just that one four-minute scene in the nursery, and their main efforts were getting the magic of tidying up the items to appear effortlessly and magically on-screen.

They used a few different tricks to accomplish this depending on what the items were that were being filmed. The first tool at their disposal was "reverse animation," or filming things backward. When Mary, and eventually Jane and Michael, snapped their fingers, the knocked over tea set and table righted themselves. For this "clean up," the table was set upright, nicely, and neatly, and then when the cameras started rolling, it was knocked over. Later in post, they would print the film backward frame by frame to create the "reverse animation" effect so that it looked as though the items were going back to their proper positions. The second effect that went hand in hand with accomplishing the reverse animation was clear fishing wire, which they attached to all items needing to be animated in reverse: the unmade bed, the tea table, the scattered hats, the disarrayed pictures on the wall, et cetera. Then when filming started, the made bed, set table, hats on a rack, perfectly aligned photos, et cetera would be pulled by off-camera propmen to create a sense of disorder, which when printed backward instead actually seemed to create order.

Another key nursery scene piece was the toy soldiers that had to, when a character snapped their

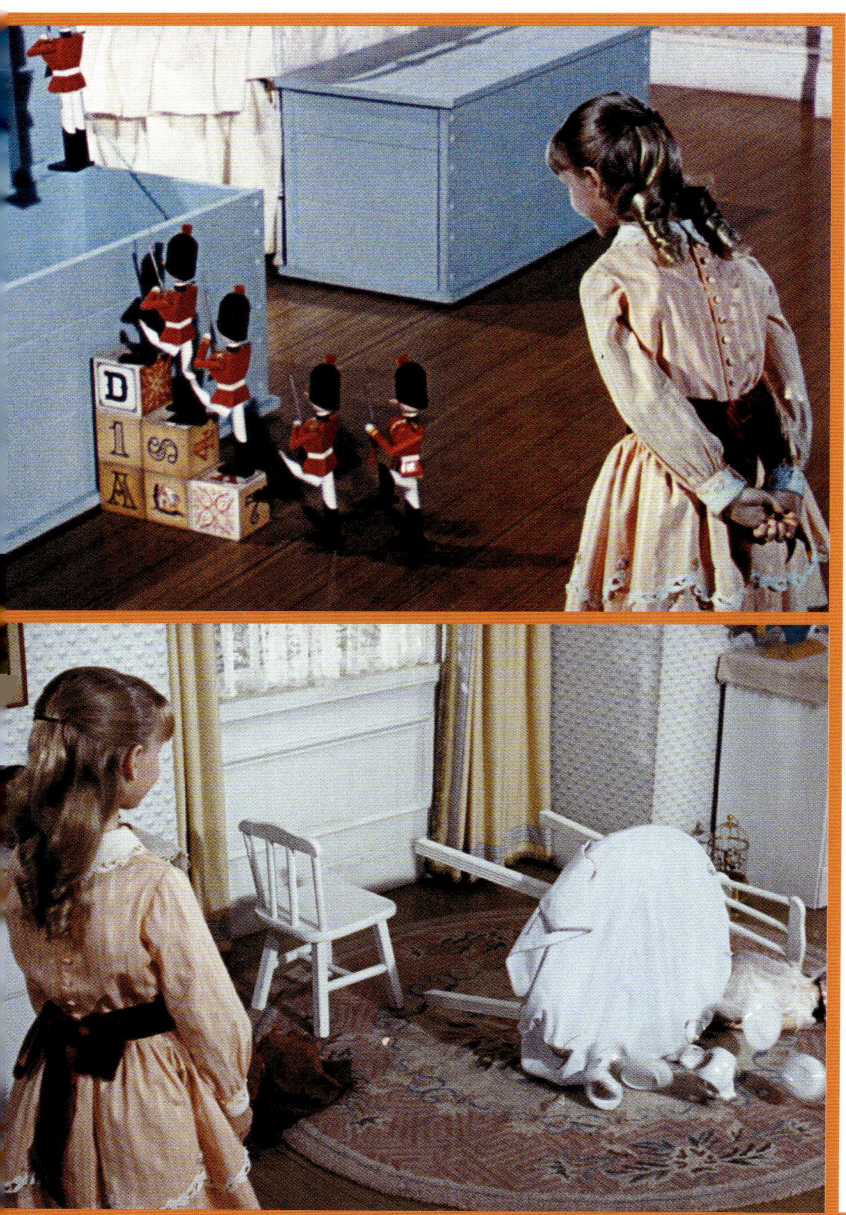

LEFT (TOP): A still from the nursery scene that X animated in *Mary Poppins* using the toy soldiers from *Babes in Toyland*; LEFT (BOTTOM): Another still from the nursery scene in *Mary Poppins* that shows X's animation effects, which were accomplished by running the film in reverse; OPPOSITE: X's invitation to the *Mary Poppins* premiere.

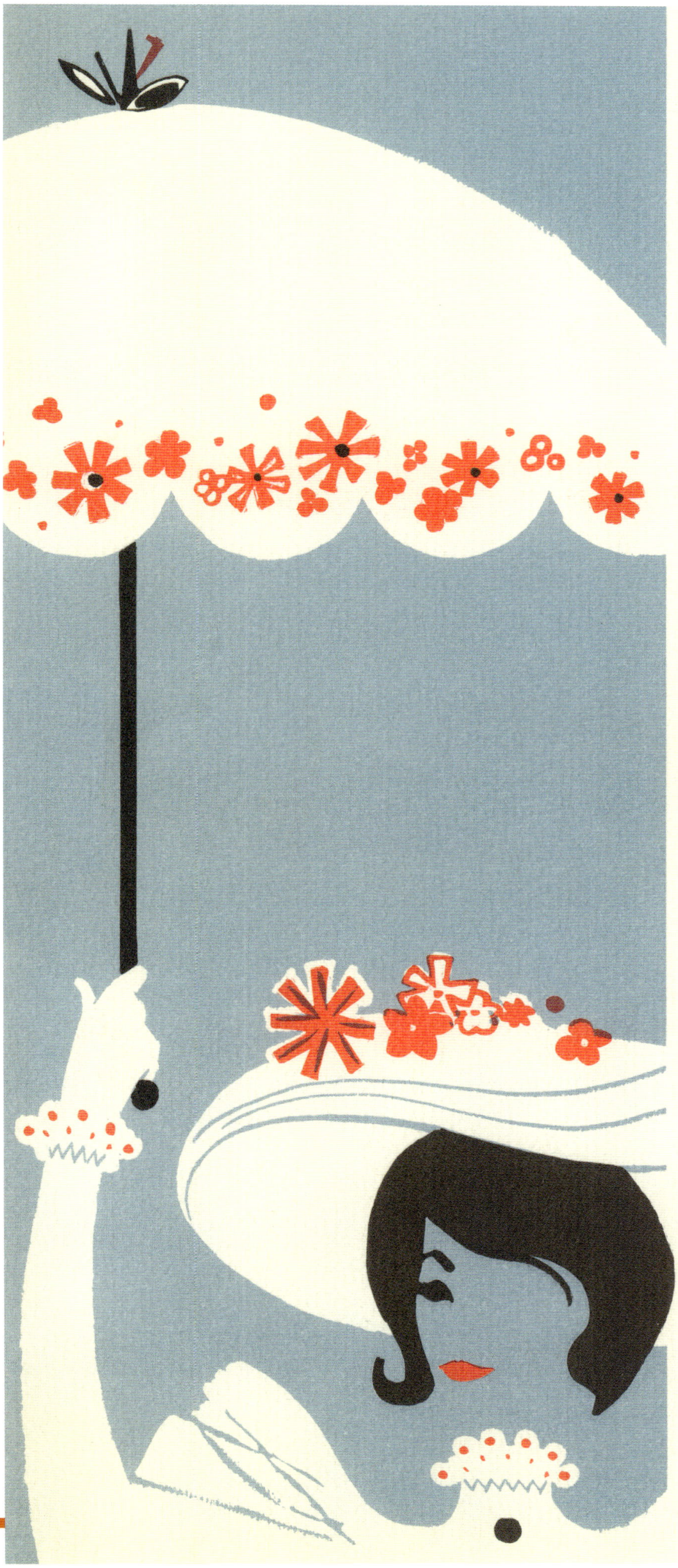

Mrs. Richard Von Hagen
and
Mr. Walt Disney

on behalf of the
Board of Trustees of
The California Institute
of the Arts

cordially invite you to attend
the World Premiere of

"MARY POPPINS"

starring
Julie Andrews
and
Dick Van Dyke

and a presentation of

"THE CAL ARTS STORY"

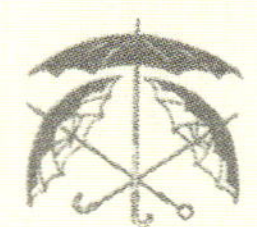

GRAUMAN'S CHINESE
THEATRE
6925 Hollywood Blvd.
Thursday, August 27, 1964
8:30 P. M.

R. S. V. P. *BLACK TIE*

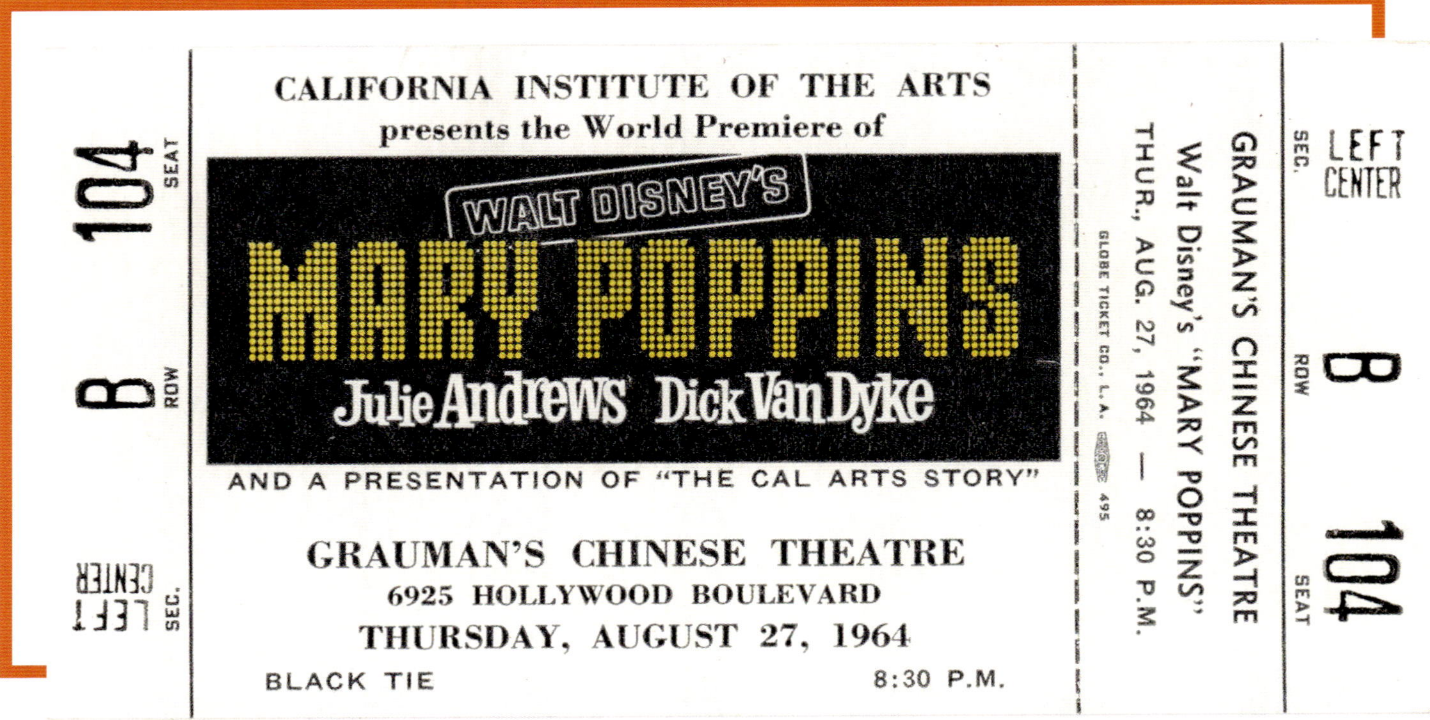

fingers, march back into their toy box. For this, X and Bill used the same stop-motion animation process that they had for the soldiers in *Babes in Toyland*. They even went a step further and reused some of the same little soldiers from *Babes in Toyland*. For another prop, the robin that sat on Mary's finger while she sang, they used an Audio-Animatronics bird similar to those present in Walt Disney's Enchanted Tiki Room attraction at Disneyland. In addition, they decided to hide the wires to control the bird up Julie Andrews's shirtsleeve to create the appearance of a live, magical bird.

X was partially correct in saying "this was a simple scene" buried within a magical and aspirational family film that imagined what happens when a "practically perfect" nanny appears to create magic through the unexpected and bring a family closer together. However, this nursery scene was also vital in establishing the tone of the movie and building the entire relationship between Mary and the children. Before this point in the film, viewers had seen Jane and Michael's latest nanny in a long line of dull, strict-rule-following characters quit, unable to put up with the children's antics. When Mary Poppins arrived, the children were at first skeptical and distant, until the nursery scene, which served both as the confirmation and proof of Mary's magic, and as evidence that she was the nanny Jane and Michael needed (and wanted).

It was this scene that blended the realities of being a nanny with Mary's magical games, wry wit, and ability to understand the children, consequentially finally opening their hearts and minds to what Mary could provide to them. The film went on to garner five Academy Awards, including for Special Visual Effects, in 1965.

While the award was not presented to X and Bill, their stop-motion work was a pivotal part of this inventive, groundbreaking, cultural touchstone feature classic. Though not at the Oscars, X and Mary were invited to attend the *Mary Poppins* premiere alongside Bill and his wife. It was at this premiere evening event that Mary, after years of hearing X speak so fondly of Walt, officially was introduced to him in person.

Capturing the essence of what that scene in *Mary Poppins* should solidify and accomplish was not an easy feat; yet X and Bill had again and repeatedly proven that they could do exactly that with their work. Blending pathos and humor in even the most

ABOVE: X's ticket to the *Mary Poppins* premiere; OPPOSITE (LEFT): Mary and X before the *Mary Poppins* premiere; OPPOSITE (RIGHT): Marie Justice, Bill Justice (holding his daughter Melissa), Mary, and X before the *Mary Poppins* premiere.

technical of creative tasks, they had captured the hearts and minds of audiences for years with their work, particularly in the stop-motion characters they created. Due to Bill's partnership and trust, X had been able to stand out in his work, add his own personal touch to the projects, and take risks. Through X's storylines and stop-motion work, he was able to encapsulate what Mary Poppins had said at the beginning of the nursery scene: "You see, in every job that must be done, there is an element of fun. You find the fun and—*snap!*—the job's a game."

X and Bill's stop-motion work on *Mary Poppins* also led to the opportunity to be featured on national television for a second time. On an episode of *Walt Disney's Wonderful World of Color*, airing in 1964 as "A Rag, a Bone, a Box of Junk," X and Bill moved in front of the camera alongside Walt to show TV viewers their experiments and craft to make everyday objects talk.

Walt liked to keep the episodes relaxed, unrehearsed, and as spontaneously unscripted as possible, to appear honest, natural, and more relatable to viewers at home. In this fourth episode of season eleven of *Walt Disney's Wonderful World of Color*, Walt took viewers behind the scenes to experience the movie magic. The episode began with Walt using a magic wand to tidy up his own desk with the stop-motion animation "snapping" effects, reminiscent of Mary Poppins. Walt explained to the audience that when they set up this highly unusual department, "At first, I wasn't sure if they were junk collectors or artists." He then snapped his fingers and took the audience with him on a behind-the-scenes look at how the magic happened.

Appearing in the hallway with a giant "box of junk," he led viewers to the sign posted outside this special department's door. The sign stated, NOTICE TO FELLOW EMPLOYEES: WHEN YOU CLEAN OUT THE ATTIC, BASEMENT, OR YOUR GARAGE, CALL US BEFORE YOU CALL THE JUNK MAN. YOU MAY BE HARBORING A HIDDEN MOVIE ACTOR. YOUR COOPERATION WILL BE APPRECIATED. P.S. WE CAN USE ANYTHING. As animators, they also included designs on the sign, illustrating each description of their humorous, desperate, but deeply serious appeal. Adding in more hilarity to the television episode, Walt then found out that his wife had also sent X and Bill a box of junk, filled with all of Walt's favorite items. He implored them to put a hold on that box, to which they reluctantly agreed.

Getting to work, Bill joked that the assembly of items was easy, it was the gathering of junk that took time. The three men then sat down together at the workstation and used Mary Poppins's snapping-fingers action to build cute characters like two talking hippos made of cork. X then demonstrated how they used an air hose to make the "floating" globe that appeared at the end of *Noah's Ark* spin. In the televised episode, they also showed the complete *Noah's Ark* and *A Symposium on Popular Songs* featurettes, minus the title sequences.

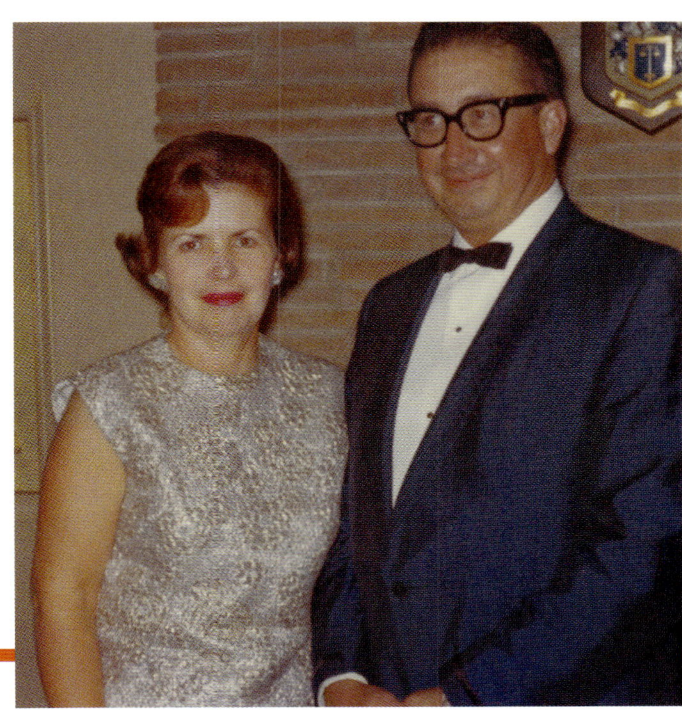

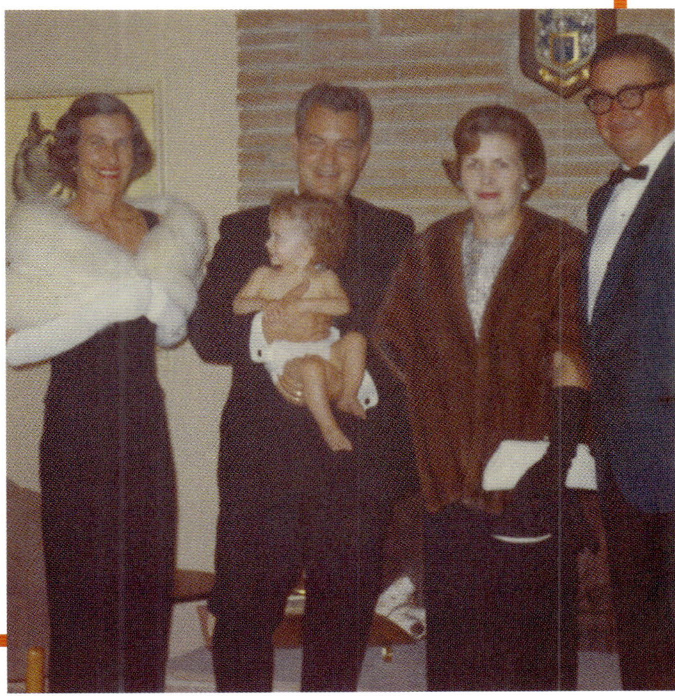

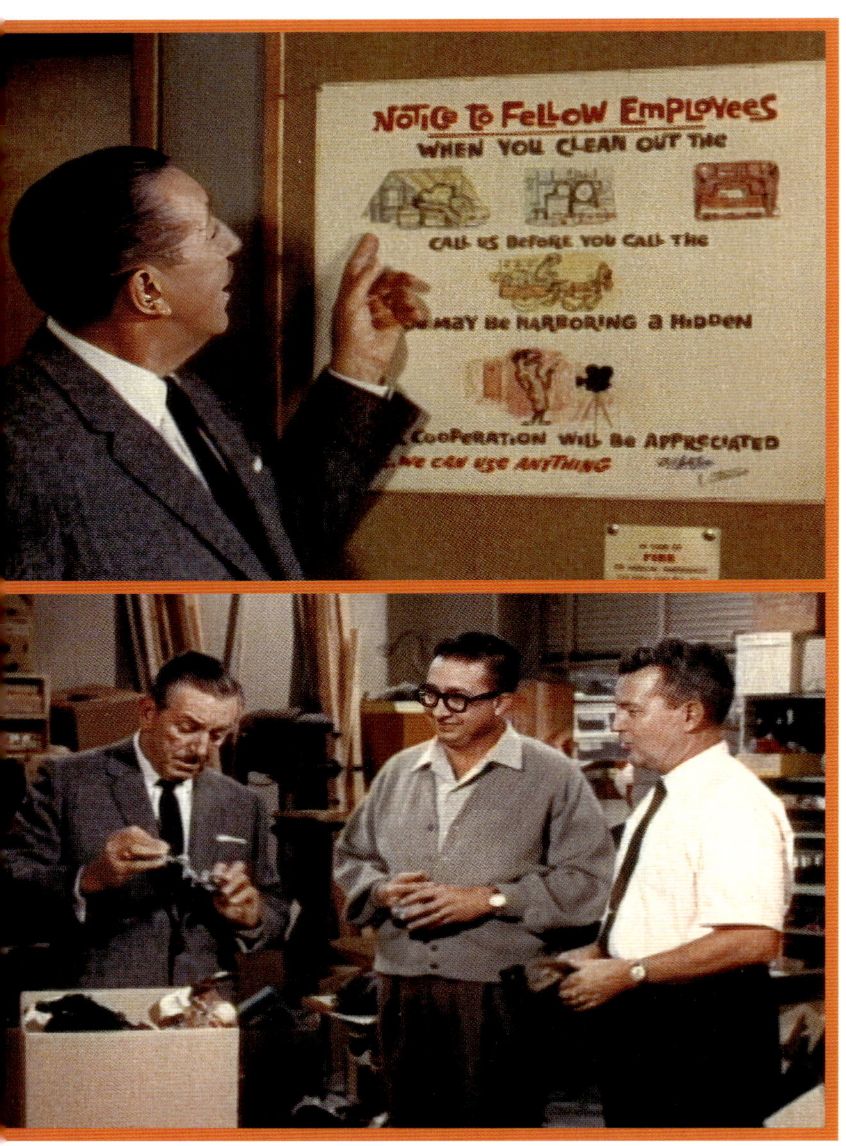

Between the featurettes, Walt appeared back in the studio to set the scene for *A Symposium on Popular Songs*. He explained, "To change the format slightly, we have decided to combine the stop-motion photography with the standard type of animation. Now we've called on our old friend here"—he gestured to a portrait of Ludwig Von Drake, which hung framed on the wall behind him—"the universal authority on popular music, Ludwig Von Drake, who will be drawn in the standard way to act as master of ceremonies. Bill and X have come up with a fresh approach to character styling using paper sculptures and vegetables. Any questions?" Bill then showed the real vegetables they used for the "Rutabaga Rag" song, and X modeled the paper cutout dolls they used for the rest of the sequence, with both explaining that making the dolls out of paper made them very flexible and easy to move from position to position. They used wire or thread to connect each "pivot point" of the doll, or what on humans would be called "joints." Showing a larger close-up face, Bill demonstrated how the eyes opened and moved in all directions. Its eyebrows also moved, plus the mouth opened and closed to give the illusion that the character was talking when adjusted by Bill between frames. The paper doll said, "But first, let's warm up the band," and a series of paper dolls then played instruments.

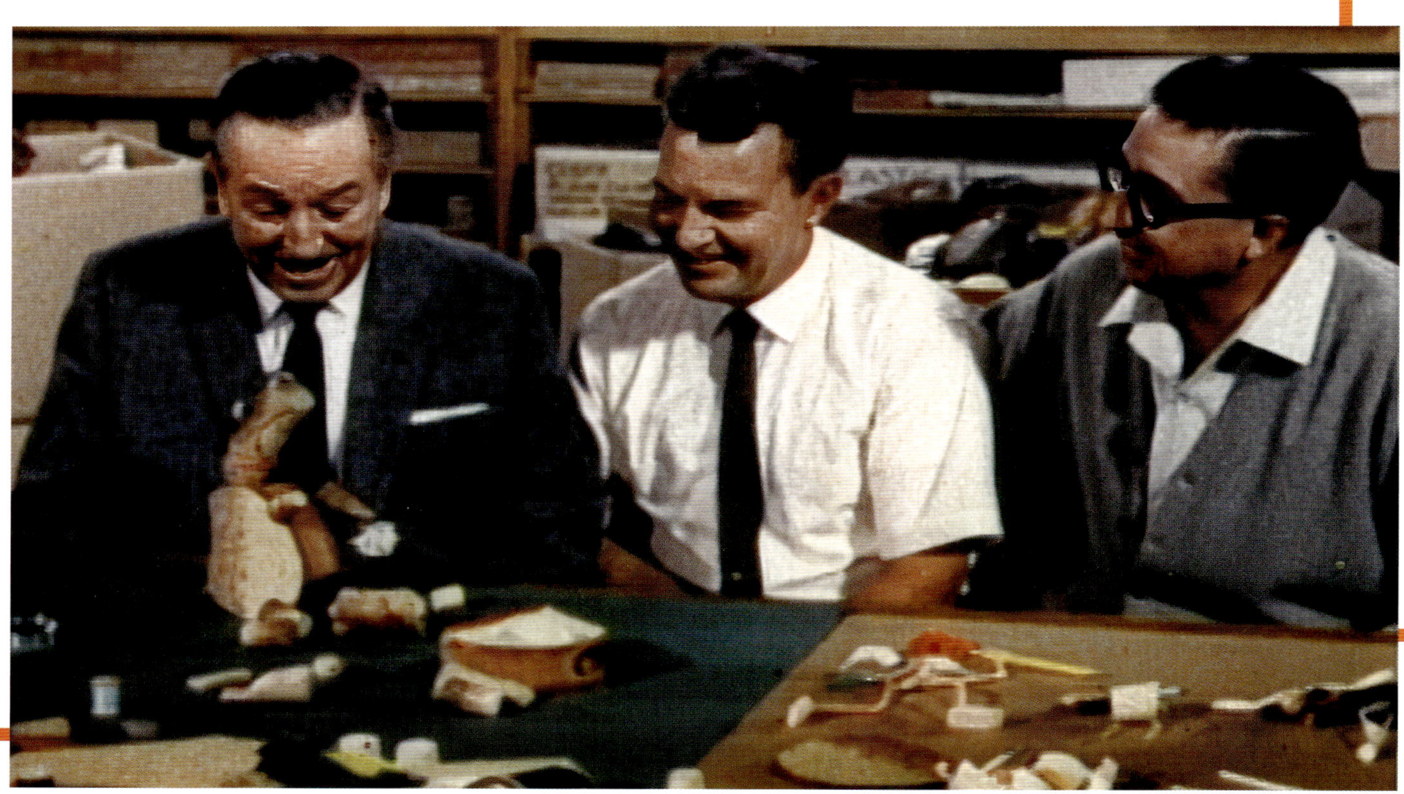

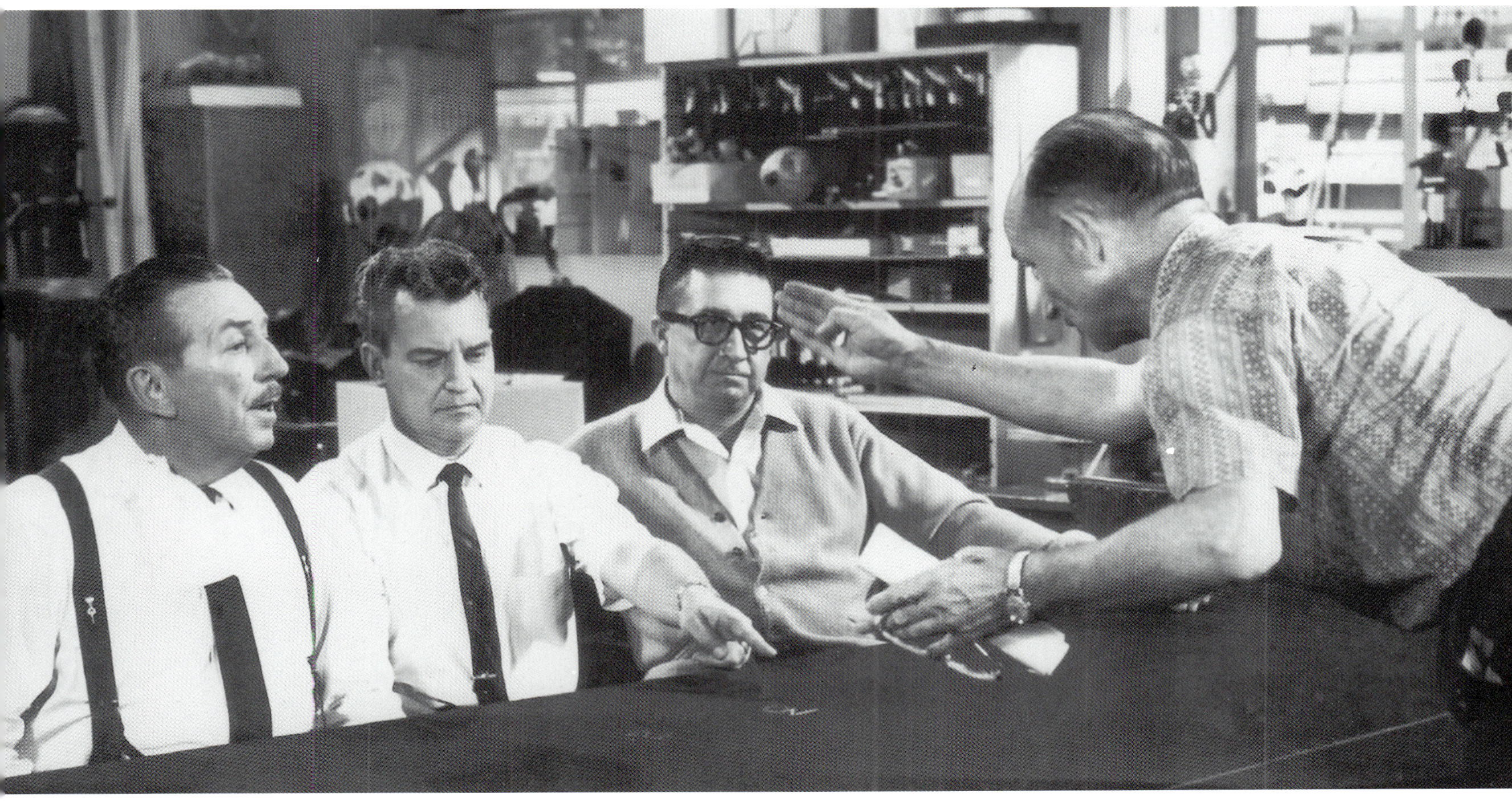

Revealing this behind-the-scenes work to the home-viewing audience welcomed them inside the magic and connected them more deeply to the stories that Disney was telling. For X and Bill, this program gave them a chance to show off their work on-screen with Walt, demonstrating how they had done the "impossible" and given life to all materials by way of creativity, art, and stop-motion photography. Furthermore, they had managed to hold their own on-screen, looking smart, witty, and natural even when juxtaposed against the master of ceremonies—Walt Disney.

From there, X worked on the cartoon featurette *Winnie the Pooh and the Honey Tree* (1966). X enjoyed being on this project, as he had first heard the stories of Winnie the Pooh when he was over in England during World War II. At that point in the 1940s, X had heard from the British how popular and famous Pooh was in England, but he had never heard about the character back in the United States until Walt Disney Productions licensed certain film and other rights to the Winnie the Pooh stories from author A. A. Milne's estate in 1961. Then, that year, he bought copies of Milne's book as gifts for his daughters, Tori and Judianne, and they, like many other American children, became enraptured with the "new" character. Furthermore, the subsequent release of multiple Disney featurettes in the 1960s and 1970s helped to put Winnie the Pooh into an international cultural stratosphere.

Walt had talked about doing a Winnie the Pooh feature, and that was originally the assignment X and his unit started to work on. But they found it difficult after months of trying to successfully craft a full two-hour narrative film. They worried the concept of Winnie the Pooh would not sustain a full-length movie because of "the sweetness" of Milne's stories. Delving further into the matter, X explained that there were no real villains or adversaries or darkness in the Pooh stories. Instead, it was just pleasant

OPPOSITE (TOP): Walt pointing to the illustrated sign asking employees to bring in junk from their homes for X and Bill's stop-motion projects; OPPOSITE (MIDDLE): Walt, Bill, and X going through the "box of junk" Walt's wife sent in, conveniently filled with Walt's least desirable possessions; OPPOSITE (BOTTOM): Walt, Bill, and X looking at one of the characters X designed for *The Wonderful World of Disney*; ABOVE: Walt, Bill, and X getting direction while filming the episode "A Rag, a Bone, a Box of Junk."

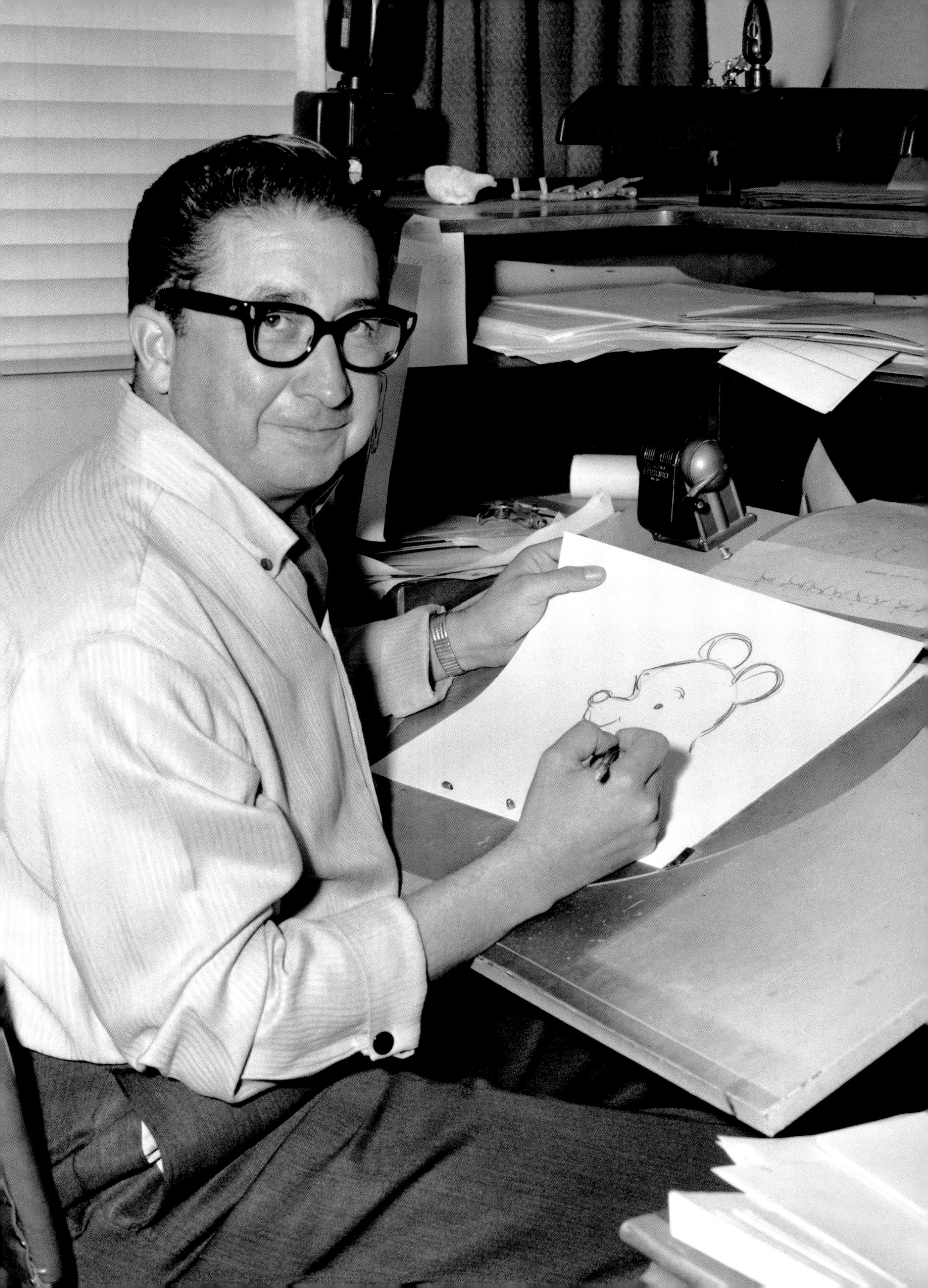
ENDURO

stuffed toy animals and Christopher Robin going about their little lives. In making the featurette, X and his unit added a few liberties to the Disney adaptation of the Milne stories to Americanize it, including the new character of Gopher, whose injected humor they felt enhanced the story. While it worked for Disney, X said that he thought, "The British have never forgiven us for fooling around with the stories. I think we took certain liberties that the average British thought was a little bit of heresy in there on our part." Given that it was then the British children who grew up on the Winnie the Pooh stories, straying from their childhood memories could indeed sometimes add a harsher judgment, as all renowned series are known to face some possible "tampering," even with modern-day examples like those in the Harry Potter and Twilight series.

X received the "story by" credit on *Winnie the Pooh and the Honey Tree* (1966) with Larry Clemmons, Ralph Wright, Ken Anderson, Vance Gerry, and Dick Lucas. X and his unit worked on the project before turning their work over to Woolie Reitherman's unit, since Woolie was directing. After that, X continued working on the featurette with his fellow "story by" colleagues and doing the story sketches. X explained that for storyboarding you can either build your story from scratch on a storyboard and do the dialogue or narration as you draw, or you can narrate the action and then match the storyboard images to those lines of dialogue. Given X and many of his fellow colleagues' visual and artistic abilities, they often would work with images and words at once. However, on *Winnie the Pooh and the Honey Tree*, X worked with Larry Clemmons, who was not an artist but was a very clever writer. Larry would write out just the lines of dialogue—clever lines from Eeyore or Owl or whomever—directly or paraphrased from Milne's story, and then everyone would take those words and illustrate. Given the textual adaptation, using the story first as structure and building the images around Milne's original creation made sense but caused X and his unit to be more faithful to the text than their creative imaginations might have otherwise led them to be.

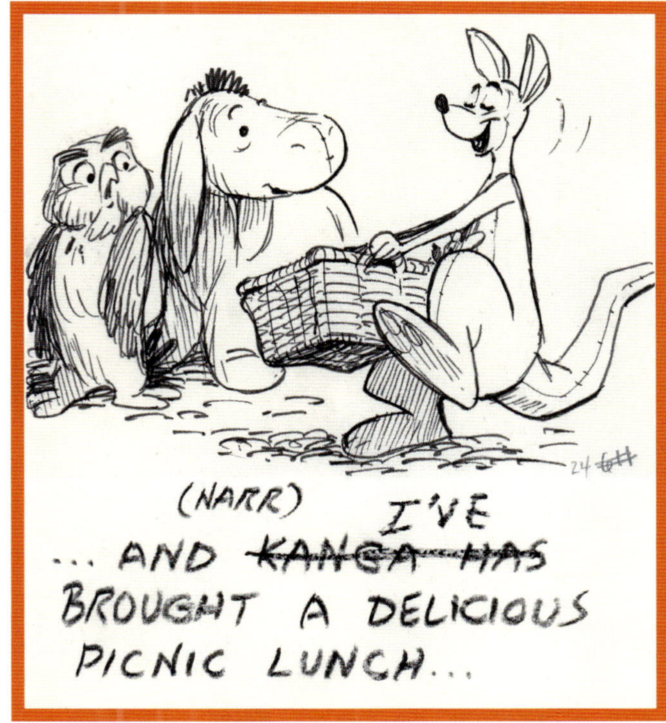

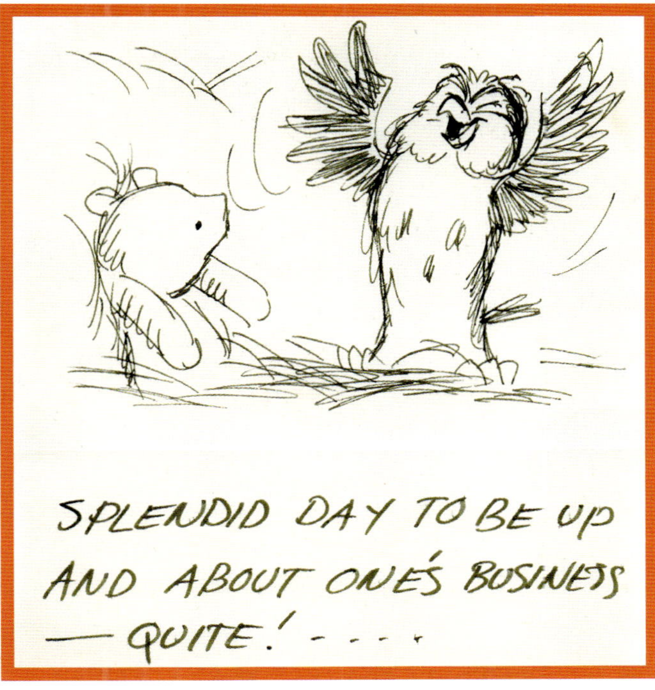

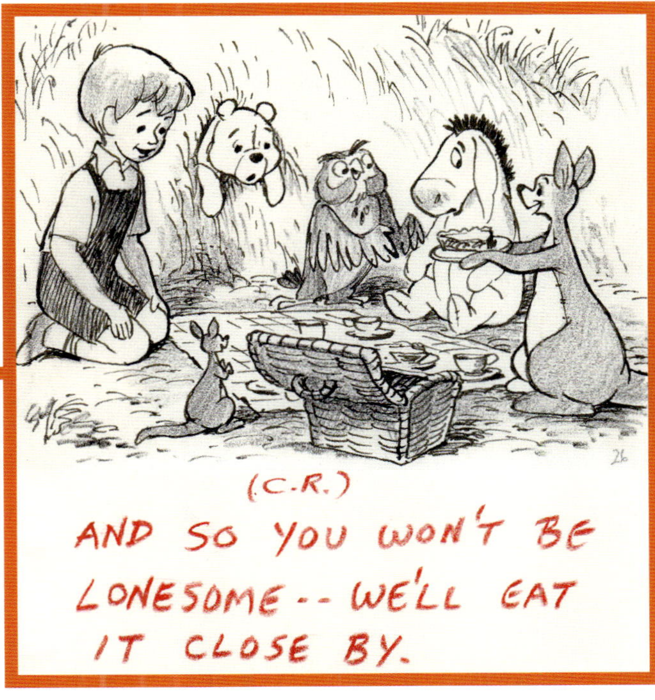

OPPOSITE: X drawing Winnie the Pooh at his desk; RIGHT: A selection of Winnie the Pooh drawings.

While X was still working at the studio, he was asked to help with setting up the Enchanted Tiki Room at Disneyland around 1962 to 1963 and with the process of animating the first sophisticated Audio-Animatronics figures, or as they were more commonly known, "the birds that populated the Tiki Room." X's stop-motion experience was most likely the reasoning for this cross-divisional assignment. Wathel Rogers oversaw animating the Audio-Animatronics figures, so X accepted Walt's request and went to assist.

X had correctly perceived that he didn't have the patience for actually animating stop-motion animation, but then he found himself even more exasperated when stuck working on the Audio-Animatronics figure animation. In one interview, X described it as "the most frustrating thing in the world" and said, "I just went crazy. I couldn't get the damn bird to open its mouth." Knowing his own limits, X understood that patience was a virtue he didn't have. That was Bill Justice's territory, and X's strengths were in many other pursuits. Wathel, X, and the team would put strips of foil, silver paper, or tape on the soundtrack that was activated by a light to trip the action and enable parts of the bird to move up, down, left, and right; its head to lift; et cetera. If the bird didn't do exactly what they wanted the way they wanted it done, the animator used a razor blade and cut a little piece off the material until the desired effect was created. X used the Moviola machine, the razor blade, and the tape, but if the desired effect was achieved properly once, the next time the bird would turn quickly, and then slowly, and so on. X's frustration mounted until finally he felt like the bird would never do what he wanted and visualized it to do, and for an artist used to conquering and mastering his materials, this added an even deeper level of annoyance.

X eventually lost patience with the Audio-Animatronics birds completely, and when the Tiki Room job was done, he put it behind him. When it was later suggested X do some Audio-Animatronics figures animation back at the studio, X replied, "No, thanks. I don't want to be involved in it at all." He knew he would go "completely bonkers," so he "voluntarily" stepped away, saving himself and his colleagues a lot of aggravation. And yet even in his most frustrated moments, X persevered through his assignment, recognized his limits and talents, showed a willingness to try anything once, and was rewarded with an incredible picture of himself in *National Geographic* animating his archnemesis, an Enchanted Tiki Room Audio-Animatronics bird.

In 1964 the biggest thing happening at WED Enterprises was the finalizing of the four Disney attractions in development for the 1964–65 New York World's Fair. X was invited to go to the fair on two separate occasions, and both times on the Disney company plane. The first trip was with his wife, Mary; Marc Davis and his wife, Alice; Bill and Marie Justice; and Ward Kimball and his wife, Betty. The second time, the trip included Walt Disney. After her flight, Mary sent a postcard with the company plane on the front home to the children to update them on their journey. At the top of the card she wrote, *Good food and drinks aboard (SAVE THIS CARD).* On the second trip, X flew to Detroit from New York with Walt, Card Walker, and others to make a pitch to Ford, asking them to consider sponsoring The Magic Skyway—a major draw at the fair—as an attraction at Disneyland. From Detroit, the group flew on to New York for another visit to the world's fair. On that flight, X remembered receiving his best compliment ever from Walt. Upon boarding, Walt went to the back of the plane and took a nap. When he awoke, he said it was time to "open the bar." Following Walt's order, they all went to drink in the back of the plane. Walt came up behind X, put his hand on his shoulder, and said, as X remembered, "You know, you did a good job, X, but don't let it go to your head!" X loved this compliment, as it embodied who Walt was—someone who "complimented you with one hand, but with the other hand, challenged you to keep it to yourself."

Walt pushed people to be the best they could be, gaining a reputation for being stingy with compliments. Thus, when someone received praise from Walt, it immediately was burned into the recesses of their memory. Walt was tough, and expected the

OPPOSITE: This image of X animating a tiki bird was featured in the August 1963 edition of *National Geographic*.

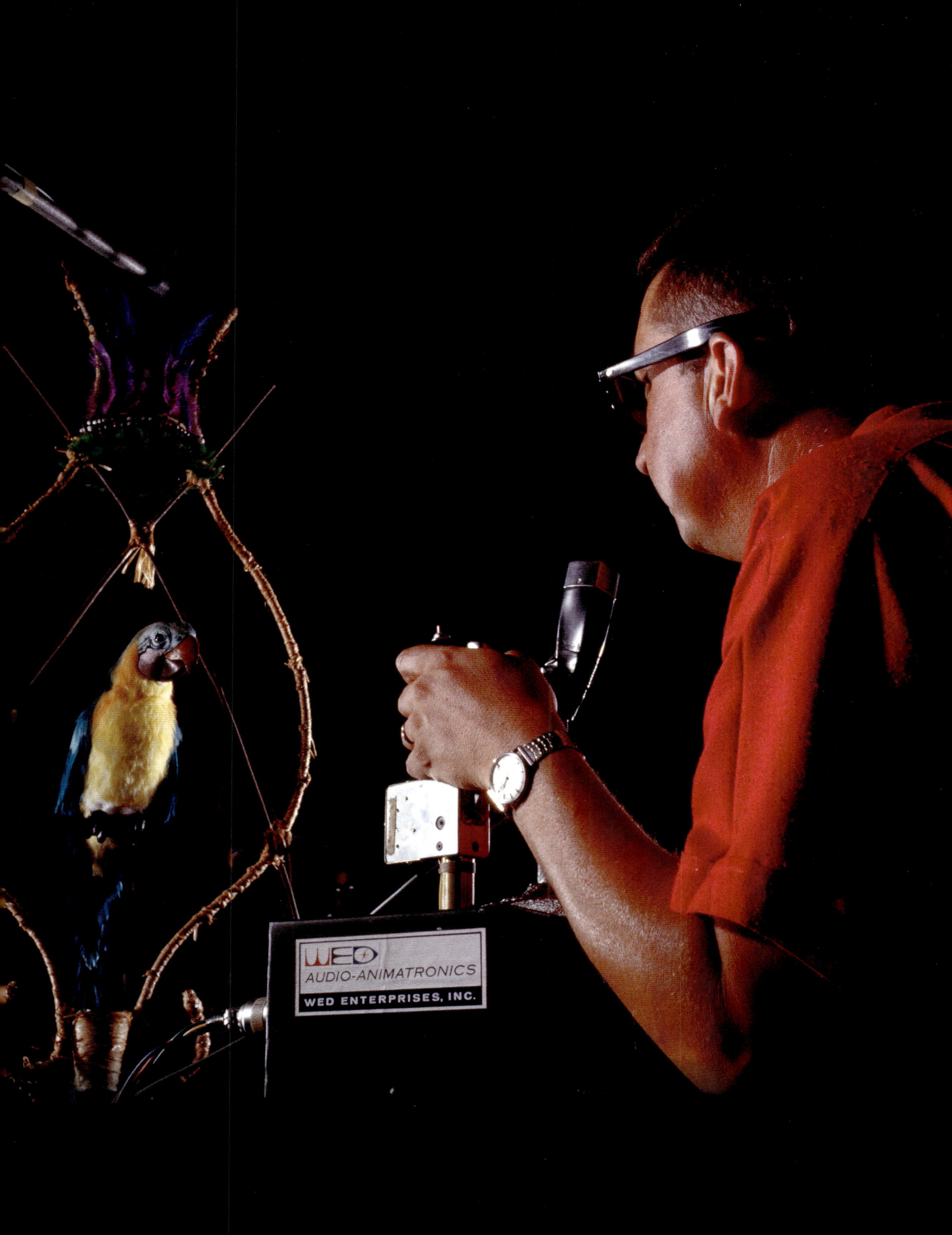
AUDIO-ANIMATRONICS
WED ENTERPRISES, INC.

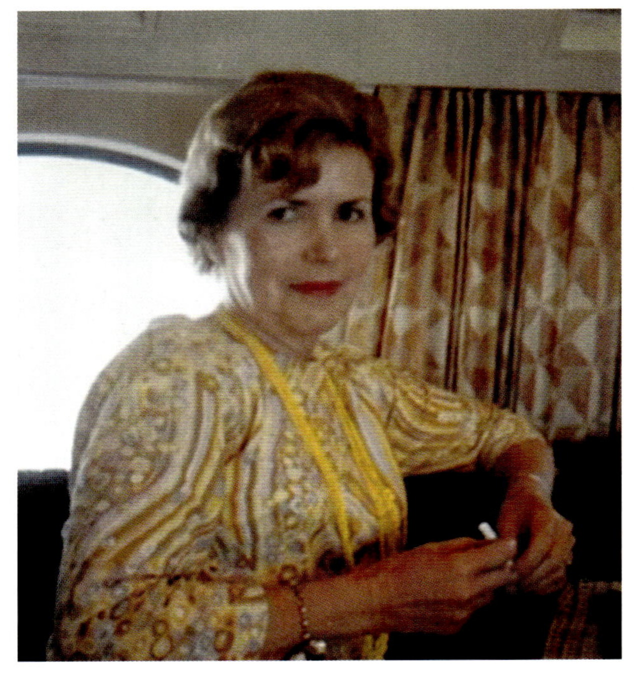

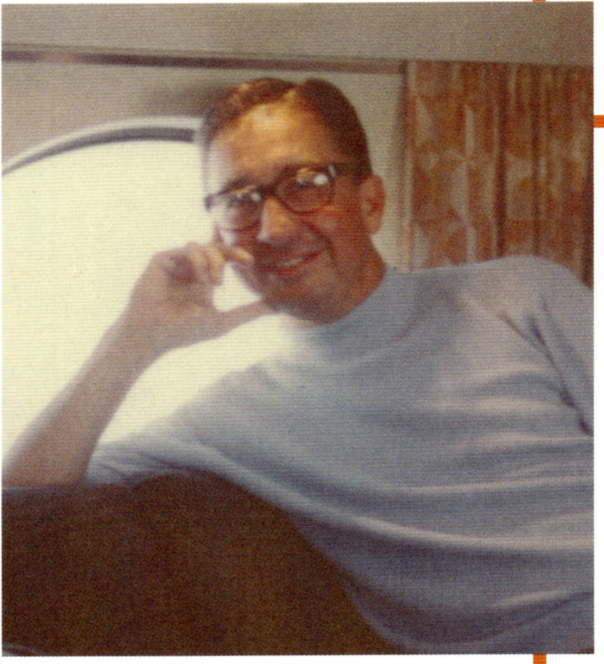

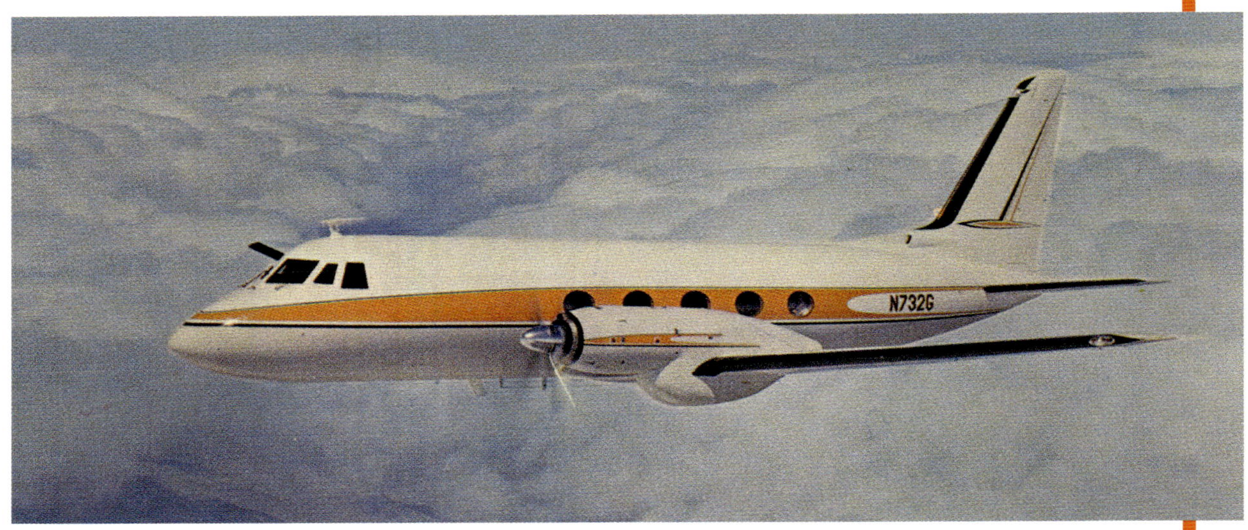

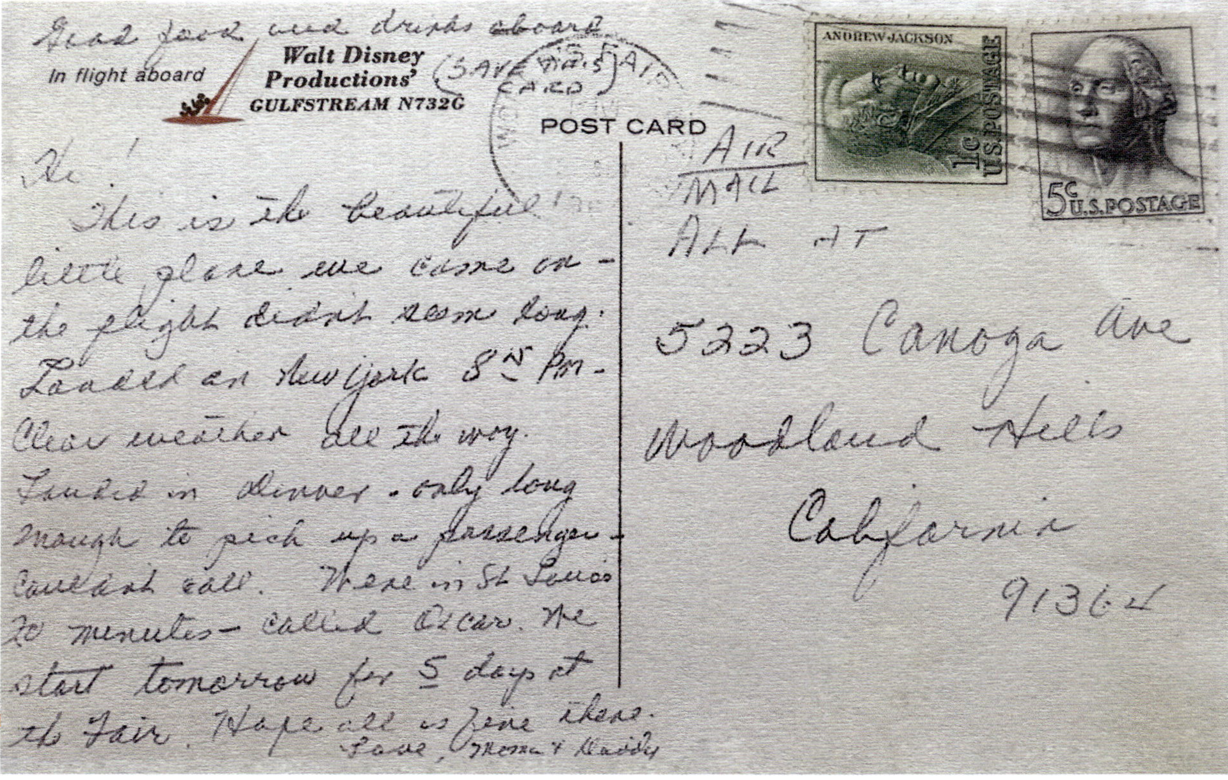
Good food and drinks aboard

In flight aboard Walt Disney Productions' GULFSTREAM N732G

(SAVE THIS CARD)

POST CARD

ANDREW JACKSON 1c U.S. POSTAGE

5c U.S. POSTAGE

Hi!

This is the beautiful little plane we came on - the flight didn't seem long. Landed in New York 8⁵ PM. Clear weather all the way. Landed in Denver - only long enough to pick up a passenger - couldn't call. Were in St Louis 20 minutes - called Oscar. We start tomorrow for 5 days at the Fair. Hope all is fine there.

Love, Mom & Daddy

AIR MAIL

ALL AT
5323 Canoga Ave
Woodland Hills
California
91364

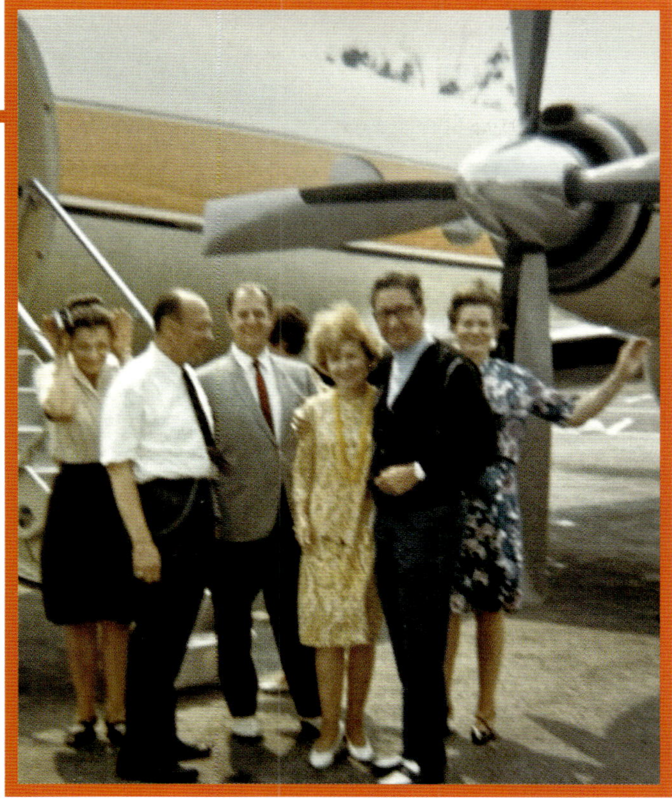

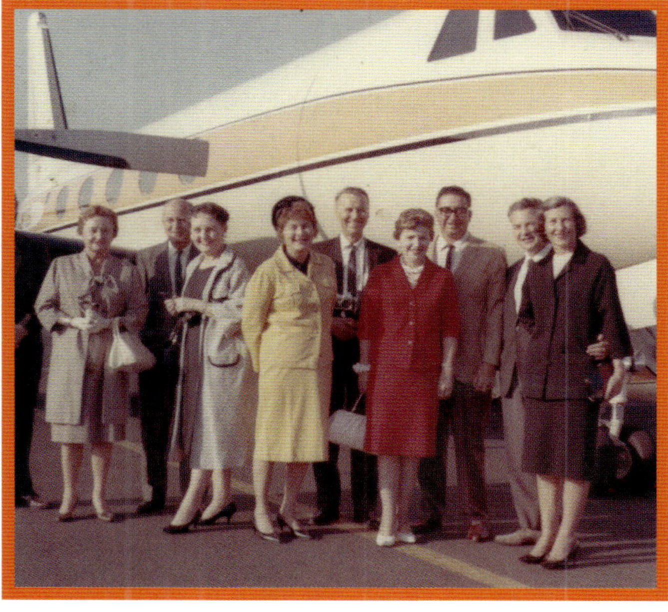

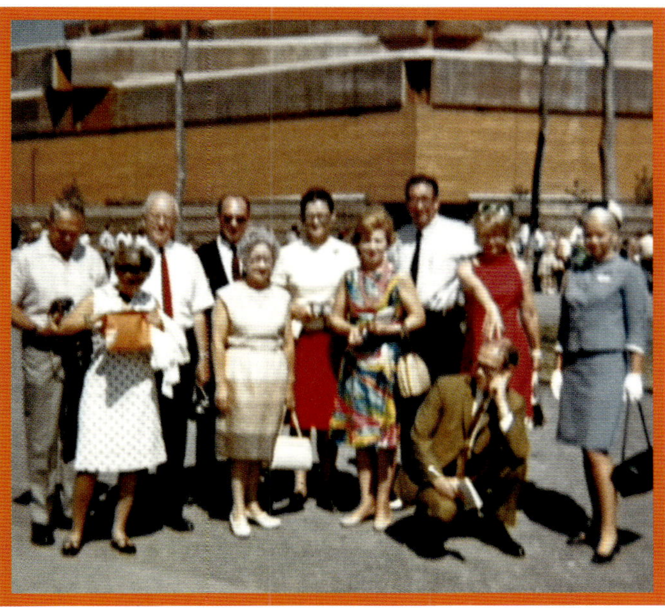

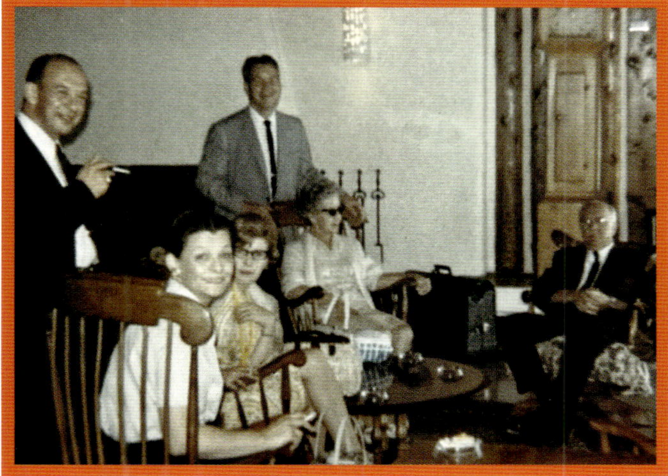

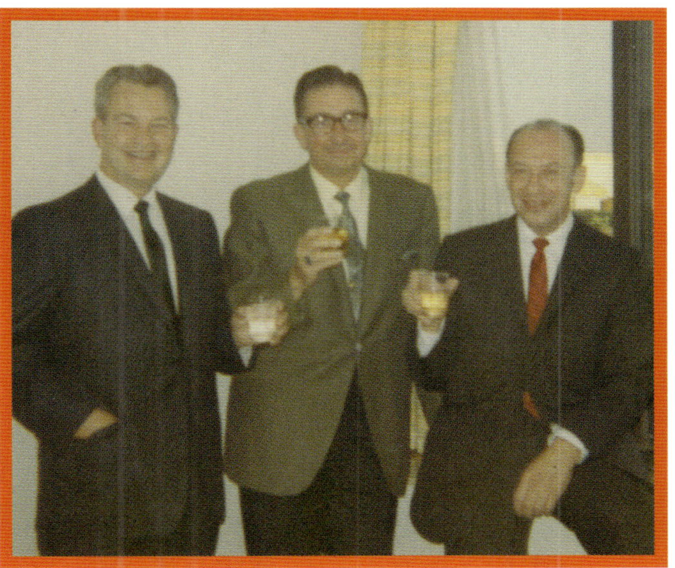

OPPOSITE (TOP LEFT): Mary on the Disney jet flying to Montreal's 1967 world's fair, Expo 67; OPPOSITE (TOP RIGHT): X on the Disney jet flying to Montreal's world's fair, Expo 67; OPPOSITE (CENTER AND BOTTOM): A postcard of the Disney corporate plane that Mary sent home with a note to the kids from their visit to the 1964–65 New York World's Fair; CLOCKWISE FROM TOP LEFT (THIS PAGE): Alice and Marc Davis, Mary and X, and others outside the Disney jet going to Expo 67; Al Taliaferro and his wife, Al and Kay Dempster, Mary and X, Bill and Marie Justice, and others in front of the company jet before they headed off to the New York World's Fair; Marc and Alice Davis, Mary, Bill Justice, and others take a break at Expo 67; Bill Justice, X, and Marc Davis enjoying drinks at Montreal's Expo 67 (also known as the 1967 International and Universal Exposition); Marc and Alice Davis, Mary and X, Betty and Ward Kimball, and others at Expo 67.

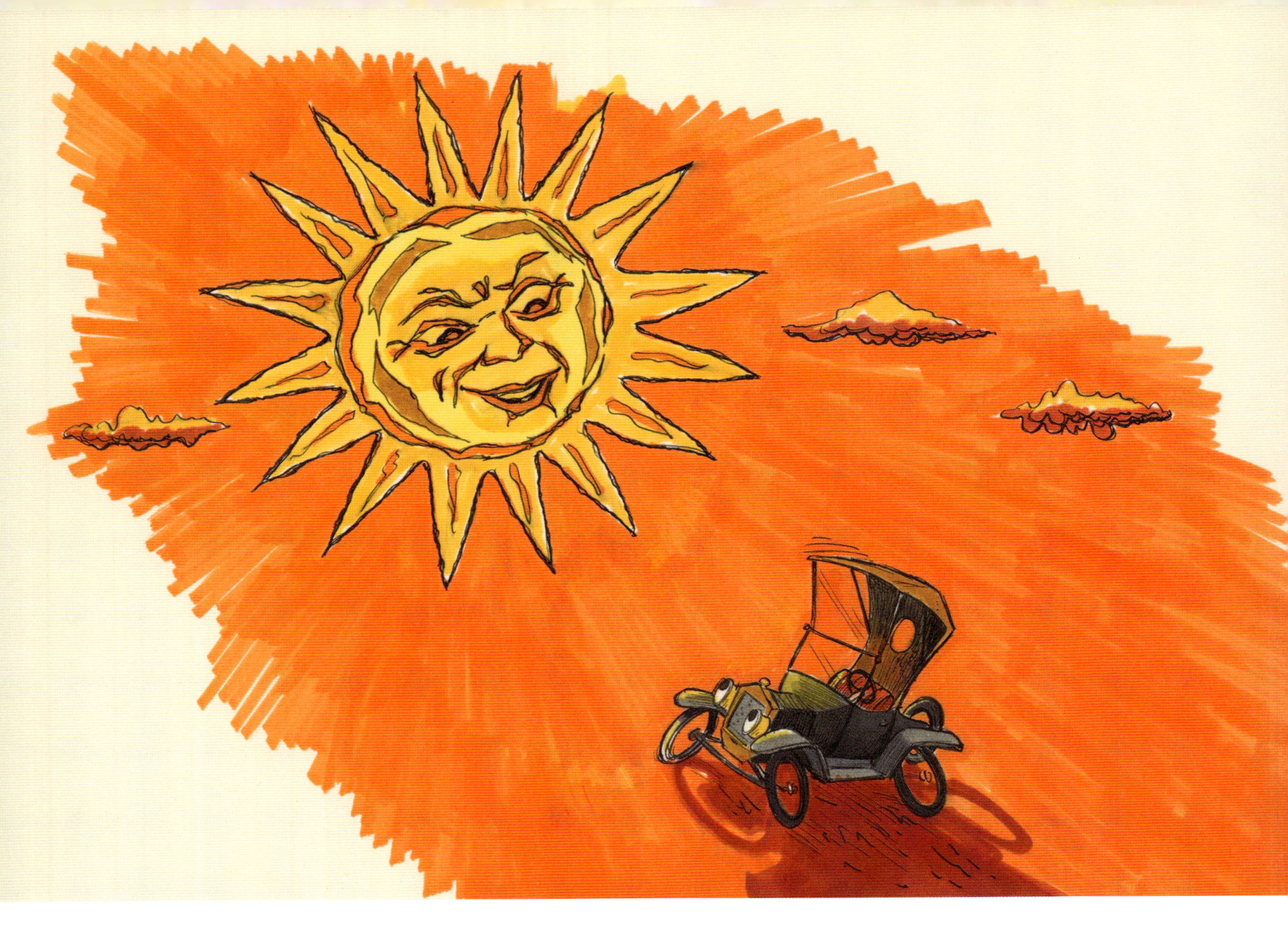

best from his employees, just as he expected the best from himself. For people like X who appreciated his style and rose to the occasion, their working relationship was more than amiable.

Another perk at the time for those core Disney employees was use of the the WED Enterprises house at the Palm Canyon Country Club in Palm Springs, a few hours east of the Los Angeles area, which key personnel could rent for use for themselves and their families, paying only two dollars per person per night. X would often take Mary and the kids out there to use the house, allowing for a close-by desert escape. While this was a nice perk for select employees, they always ran the risk of being outranked by noted Disney talent, like the time X's family was asked to reschedule due to a visit from Mary Poppins herself, Julie Andrews.

Overall, X had been thoroughly loving his time at the Disney Studio. He had grown from an eighteen-year-old apprentice animator to an official Disney animator. He continued to pick up design and art projects from various clients, which helped him financially support his family. His children loved the ability he had to turn any piece of junk into a creative masterpiece. The lasting impressions of X transforming any household item into a character beyond a child's wildest dreams still live in the family lore. At Halloween, X would even turn plastic produce bags into little ghosts, adding to the mystery and possibilities of the holiday for his children and then grandchildren. Even after his death, his children found boxes of little trinkets and "building materials" when cleaning out his home studio. X viewed everything as a treasure with endless possibilities and each person as an individual worthy of telling their story. With this mindset, X's respect and admiration for every item and human shined through.

By 1965, X's creativity and affable personality had allowed him to reap numerous rewards that afforded him the opportunity for over a decade to take on creative experimentation projects, travel to Mexico, build an eleven-year partnership and friendship with Bill Justice, and given him the chance to grow a diverse portfolio of pioneering projects that

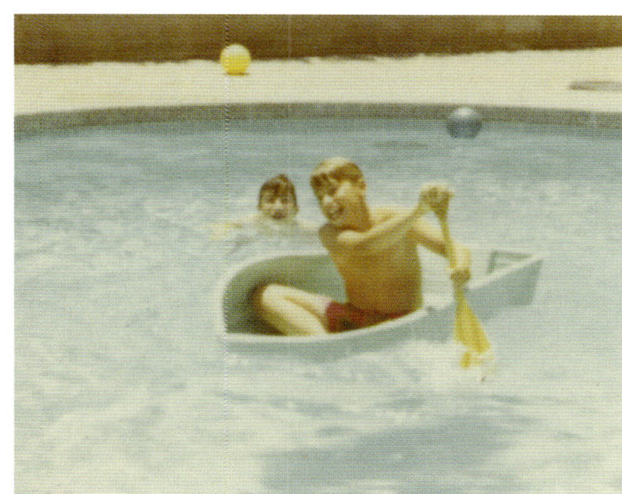

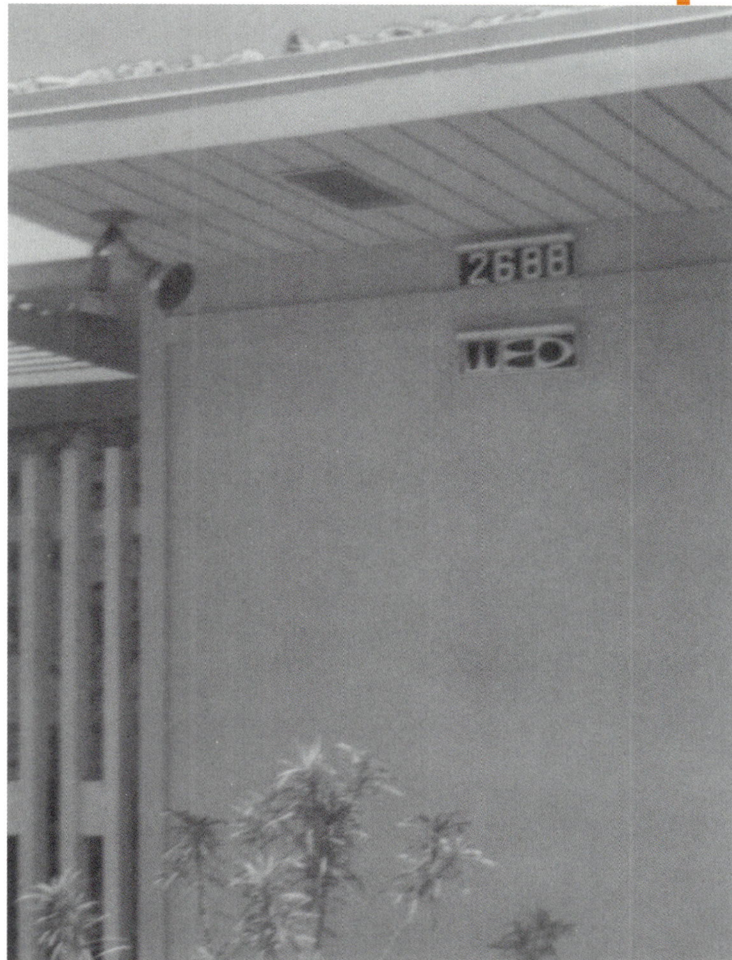

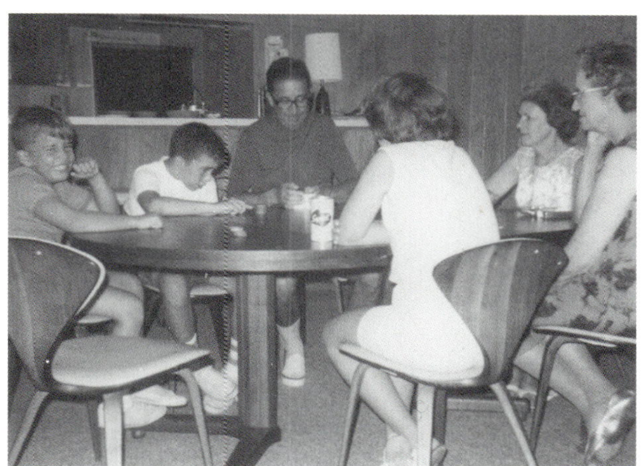

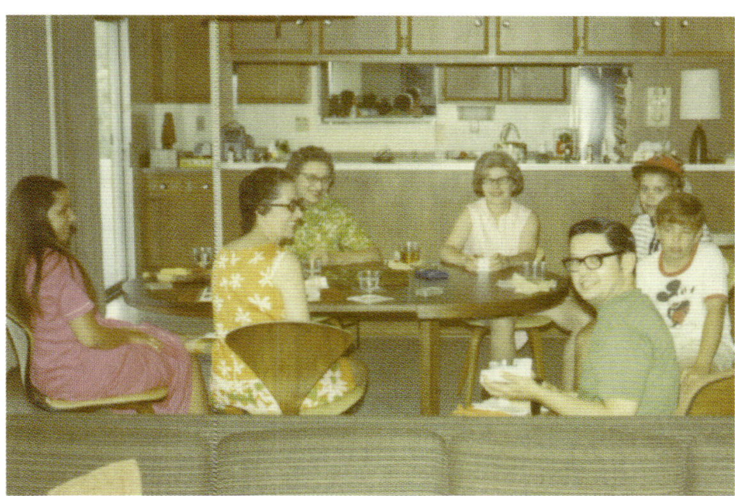

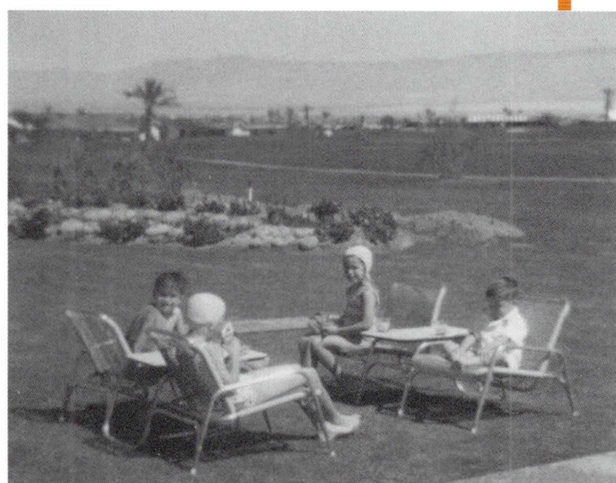

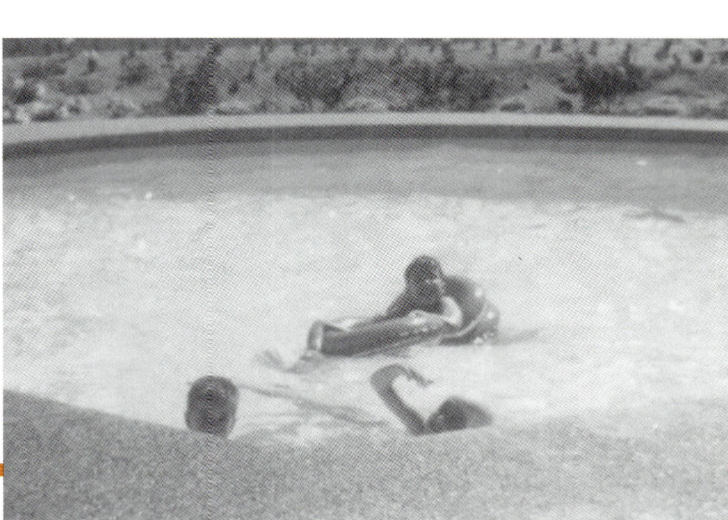

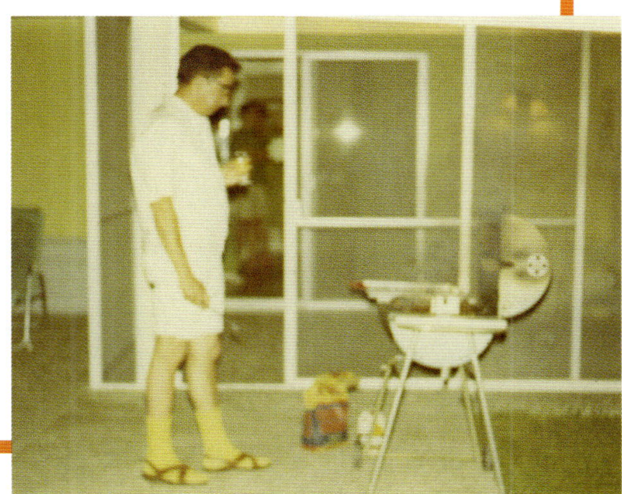

OPPOSITE: X's concept art for the Ford pavilion at the New York World's Fair; ABOVE: Photographs from the Atencio family's vacations at the WED Palm Springs house a few hours from Los Angeles.

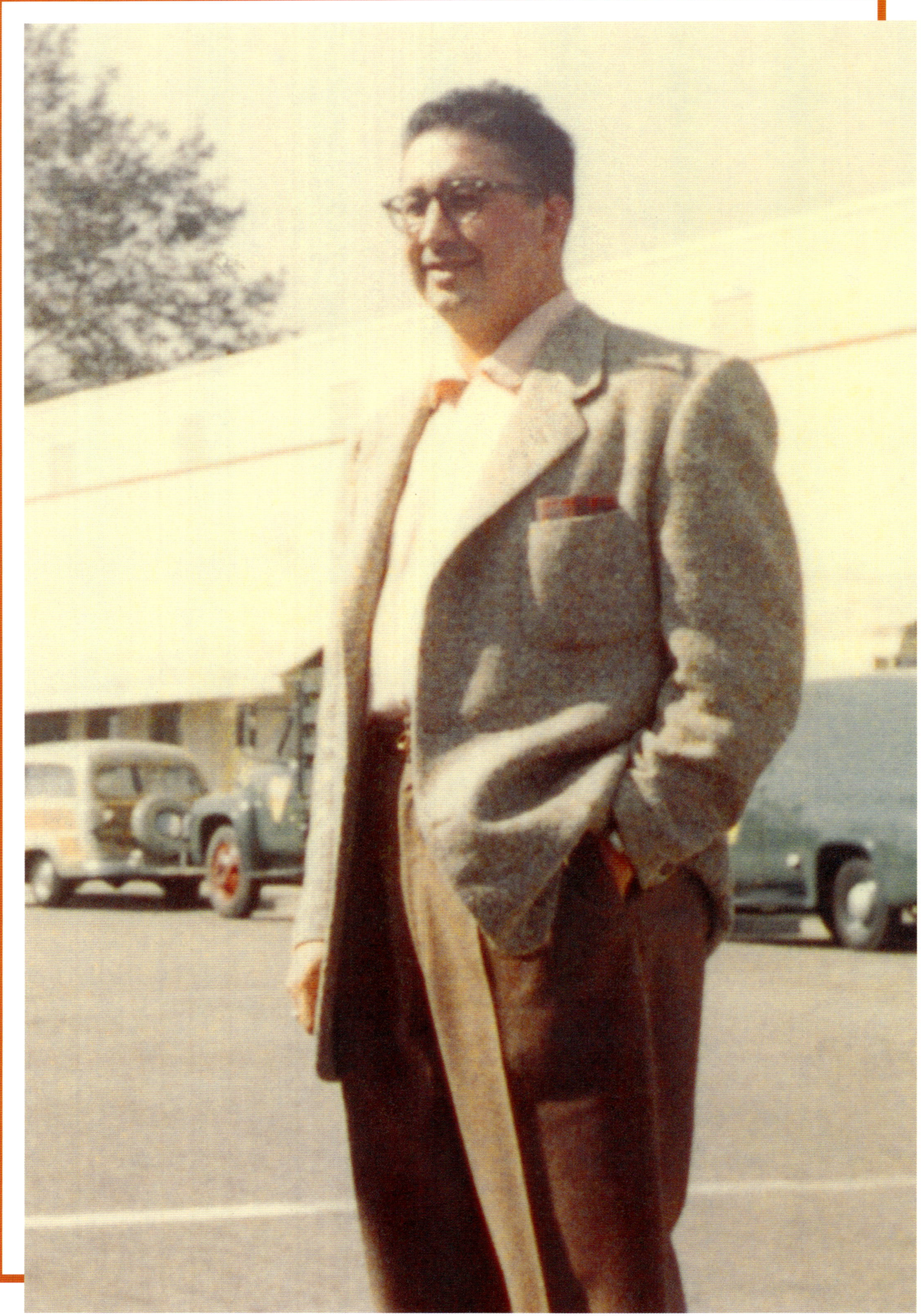

would give millions of children memories and experiences for generations to come. Walt Disney knew his name and trusted X's talents and abilities. X and Bill had helped the studio garner four Academy Award nominations and worked with everything from cork to vegetables to create an array of Disney fun.

And for X, just when he thought he would be continuing his creative pursuits with Bill Justice, "Somethin' was brewin', about to begin," to quote Mary Poppins again. Specifically, it was the point when X, in his latest project, was attempting to develop a short based on the idea of doodling, an avid hobby of Walt's. Walt and X were on their third story meeting, striving to turn his vague doodle idea into a short, when X, without mincing words, admitted to Walt, "I don't think we know what the hell we're doing here." Walt regarded him with a severely arched eyebrow (an occurrence known among his staff as "The Look"). X waited, unsure how Walt would take this admission. Walt then grasped X's hand and replied, as X remembered, with "I appreciate an honest man. I think now is the time to scrap the whole thing."

While X's honesty had again impressed Walt in the moment, X went back to his other projects, but Walt had other ideas. The next day Walt called X to his office, but this time Walt was the one with a surprising but frank statement for X. Walt said, "I've been wanting to get you over to WED for some time, and now would be a good time for you to go."

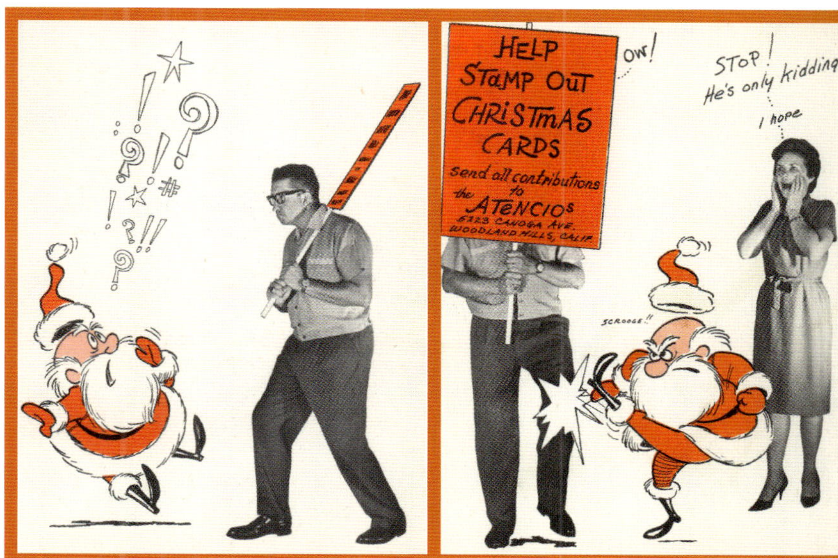

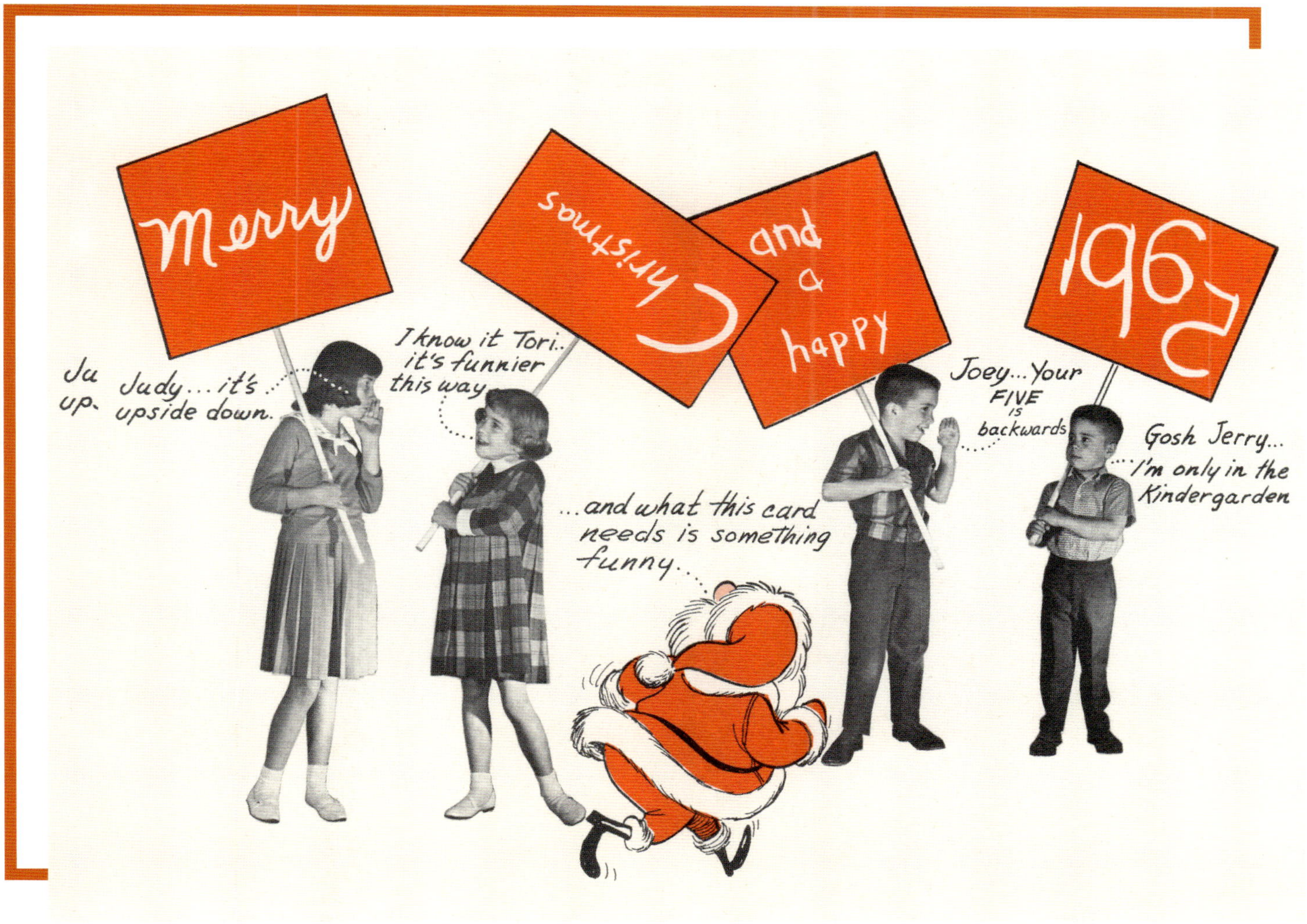

OPPOSITE: X on the Disney Studios lot; ABOVE: X's Christmas card from 1965, the year he moved to WED. At this time, X started the "Stamp Out Christmas Cards" campaign, which featured funny jokes about no more Christmas cards for several years, showing that he was getting tired of making such elaborate cards each year.

6

Early Years at WED

DATED APRIL 6, 1965, X'S OFFICIAL transfer from the Disney Studio marked the end of an era and the start of an unfathomable new adventure at WED (now known as Imagineering). While X's heart was at the studio, he trusted Walt. Yet after accepting his new position at WED, just a few miles away from the Burbank campus, X felt a little unsure of what exactly he would be doing in this new role. Bill Justice would eventually follow, getting a similar summons from Walt, but the move from the studio officially ended their working partnership.

Walt's desire to bring over his most talented and trusted movie creatives could be traced back to his creation of Disneyland. When Walt's ideation of Disneyland was ready to become a reality, Walt needed to find a lead designer. He initially approached his friend and neighbor Welton Becket, a Los Angeles–based architect. After listening to Walt's vision, Becket encouraged Walt to rethink his decision to use a traditional architecture firm and instead to bring in accomplished art directors, production designers, story creators, et cetera (from within his studio and beyond) to design and build Disneyland. These filmmakers would need to translate their work in two-dimensional storytelling into three dimensions. Not only would this give Walt people whose work ethic and creativity he already trusted, but it also meant it would be easier to execute the aesthetic that Walt envisioned in the theme park. After all, these collaborators already knew the values and expectations—some could even go so far as to say "brand"—that Walt wanted and expected in his creations.

While WED Enterprises was officially created in 1952, X didn't move to it until 1965. Walt spent the years in between enacting his various plans, opening Disneyland and continuing to broaden its scale and scope, and viewing his studio staff in a new light—determining whether their talents in creating movie and television magic also held untapped potential beyond their current skills that might be right for the future of WED and Disneyland. X's abilities to work well with others, experiment but see projects through to fruition, and quickly and adeptly

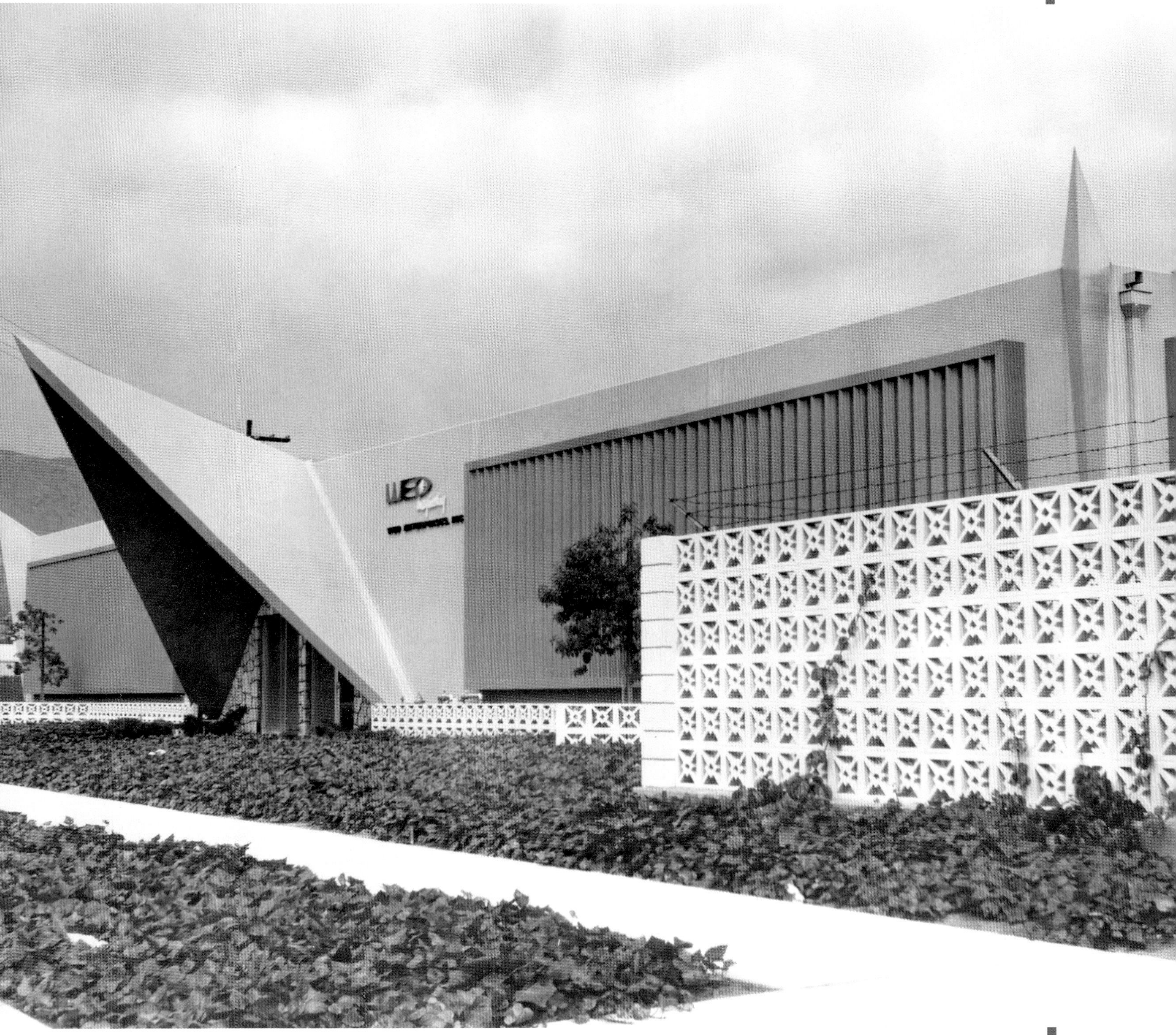

learn new aspects of the creative process made him a prime candidate for WED. In fact, the skill to operate dexterously as both a collaborator and an individual at WED became even more important in 1965, the year it officially became a wholly owned subsidiary of Walt Disney Productions. Walt had kept the companies separate to that point to build his vision without the pressures of being fully bound to the banks and shareholders and Wall Street, but with Disneyland's success and rapid growth, this acquisition and company alignment became a priority.

ABOVE: The exterior of WED's headquarters in Glendale, California, a few miles "down the street" from the studio lot in nearby Burbank.

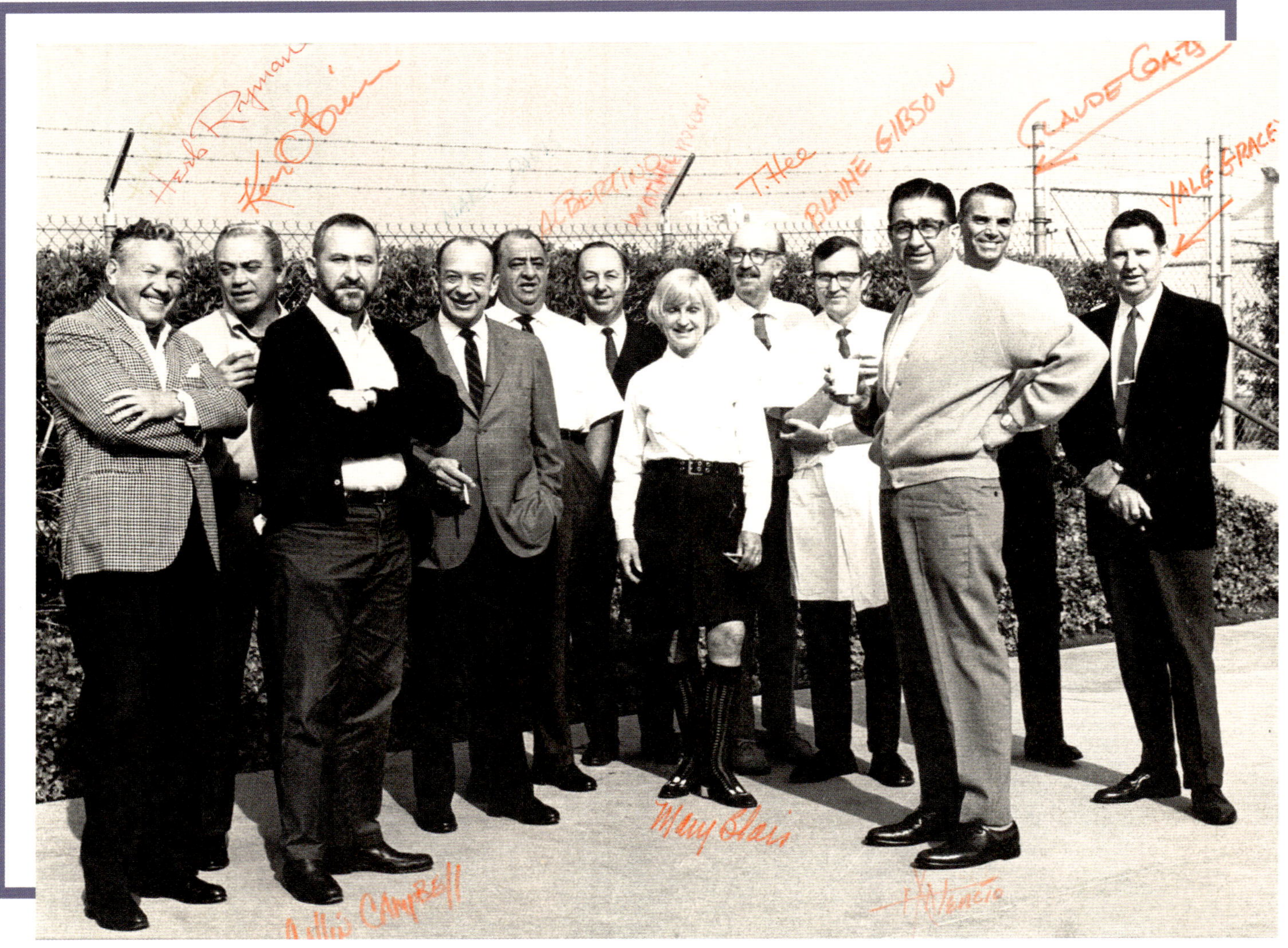

The importance of teams and creative leads who understood Walt's working style, professional ideologies, and temperament matched the need for standard engineers and architects to collaboratively and creatively achieve the Disney vision. The reliance on his own homegrown proven talent would form the foundation of shaping Disneyland from the ground up. Operating under the "story is story, design is design, and technology is technology" mindset, Walt took those ready for a new challenge and supported their growth and efforts as they learned together how to mold their talents to fit a new medium: that of live theme park attractions and entertainment. As renowned former Imagineer Kevin Rafferty wrote in his book *Magic Journey: My Fantastical Walt Disney Imagineering Career*, "That's why they were all so good at what they did at WED, creating the classic and timeless attractions everyone knows and loves. They were showmen and women, first and foremost."

When X arrived at WED, he reported to Dick Irvine, a feature art director who returned to Disney to head design and planning for all Disneyland attractions. WED was still a small operation at that point, and everyone knew everyone—reminding X of his early days at the studio. Walt seemed to have told Dick and John Hench, senior vice president of Imagineering (who had also started his career at the studio), that X would be joining their ranks, and Dick and John sent X to help Claude Coats. Claude had transitioned from animation to show designing at WED, and by the time X joined him ten years later, he was hard at work on the Primeval World, a diorama for the Disneyland Railroad inspired by an attraction based in part on the "Rite of Spring" sequence

ABOVE: Several of the original Imagineers who had started their careers in Animation, taken just two years after Walt's death; OPPOSITE: X and Claude Coats reviewing Claude's environment paintings for Pirates of the Caribbean.

from the Disney animated feature *Fantasia* (1940). In a "full circle" moment, X was back helping bring the same sequence to life for live audiences that he had brought to the screen at the beginning of his Disney career. X was in charge of putting trees and other items into the prehistoric diorama, which would be added to the Disneyland Railroad immediately after the Grand Canyon Diorama and directly between the stations for Tomorrowland and Main Street, U.S.A.

The diorama was an adaptation from a part of the Ford attraction at the 1964–65 New York World's Fair. The Ford Motor Company met with Walt in 1960 and asked him and his team to create a unique show for the upcoming gathering. The attraction that the WED team created for them was the Magic Skyway, a moving experience in which guests traveled in more than one hundred new Ford Mustang convertibles on a journey through time and transportation history to different scenes, from depictions of the early ages of the dinosaurs (who broke out of eggs to become fierce fighters) and cavemen (who invented the wheel) to futuristic cityscapes. The ride was introduced by Henry Ford II and, for the second year of the fair, was narrated by Walt Disney.

After the World's Fair ended, three of the four major Disney attractions introduced there—"it's a small world," Great Moments with Mr. Lincoln, and the Carousel of Progress—would find a new home at Disneyland. However, the Ford Magic Skyway took up too much space and, in Walt's opinion, needed a revamp to perfect the cavemen figures. Ford declined Walt's pitch to sponsor this altered version at Disneyland, so Walt went about taking bits and pieces of it and setting them up in various parts of the park. The Imagineers took the preserved dinosaurs from the World's Fair attraction, shipped them to Anaheim, and placed them into the new Primeval World diorama, which opened at Disneyland July 1, 1966. The following year, the Magic Skyway's innovative ride system would be adapted for the new PeopleMover attraction in Tomorrowland.

Ultimately, X spent only about four to six weeks working with Claude on Primeval World, but as he described it, he spent the whole time "flubbing around and latching onto Claude." X found Claude to be one of his favorites and seemed to innately understand him, describing to others how Claude "wasn't one to gab around the watercooler." While X yet again managed to blend in, forge trusted relationships with colleagues, and complete the work, he spent the whole time working with Claude wondering, "What the hell am I doing here?" Walt never officially answered that question for X, and while Dick Irvine and John Hench knew about X's transition to WED, they

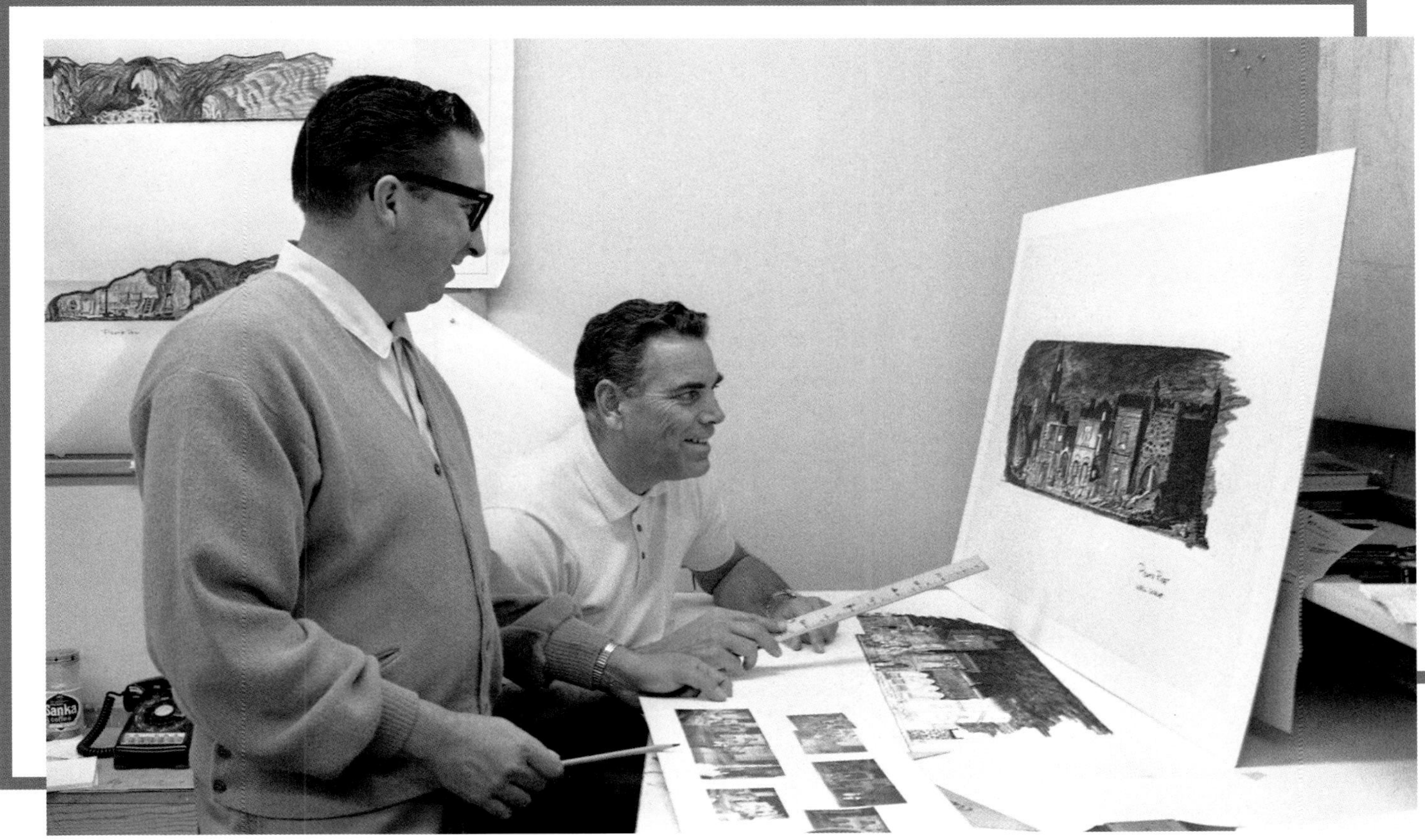

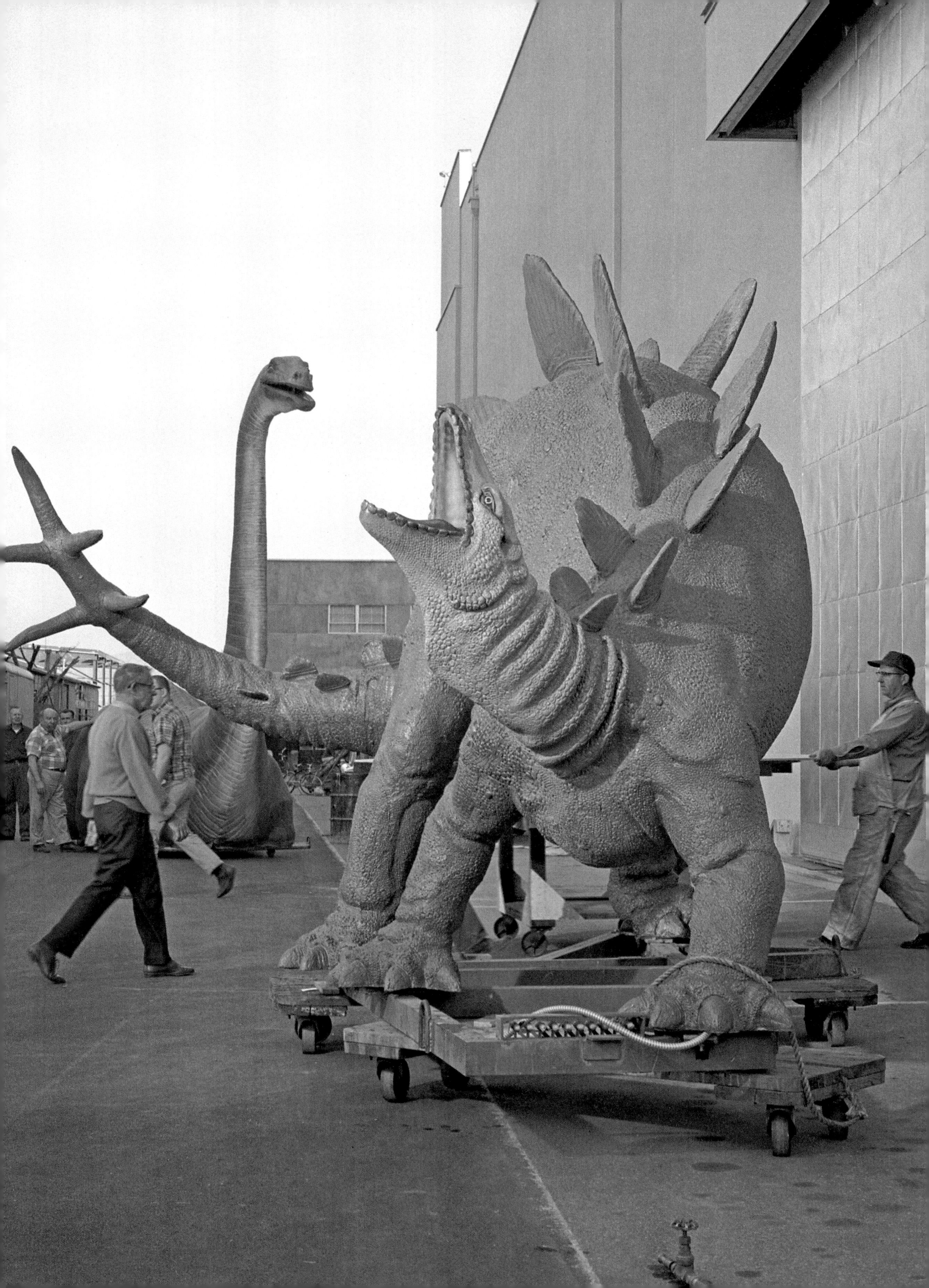

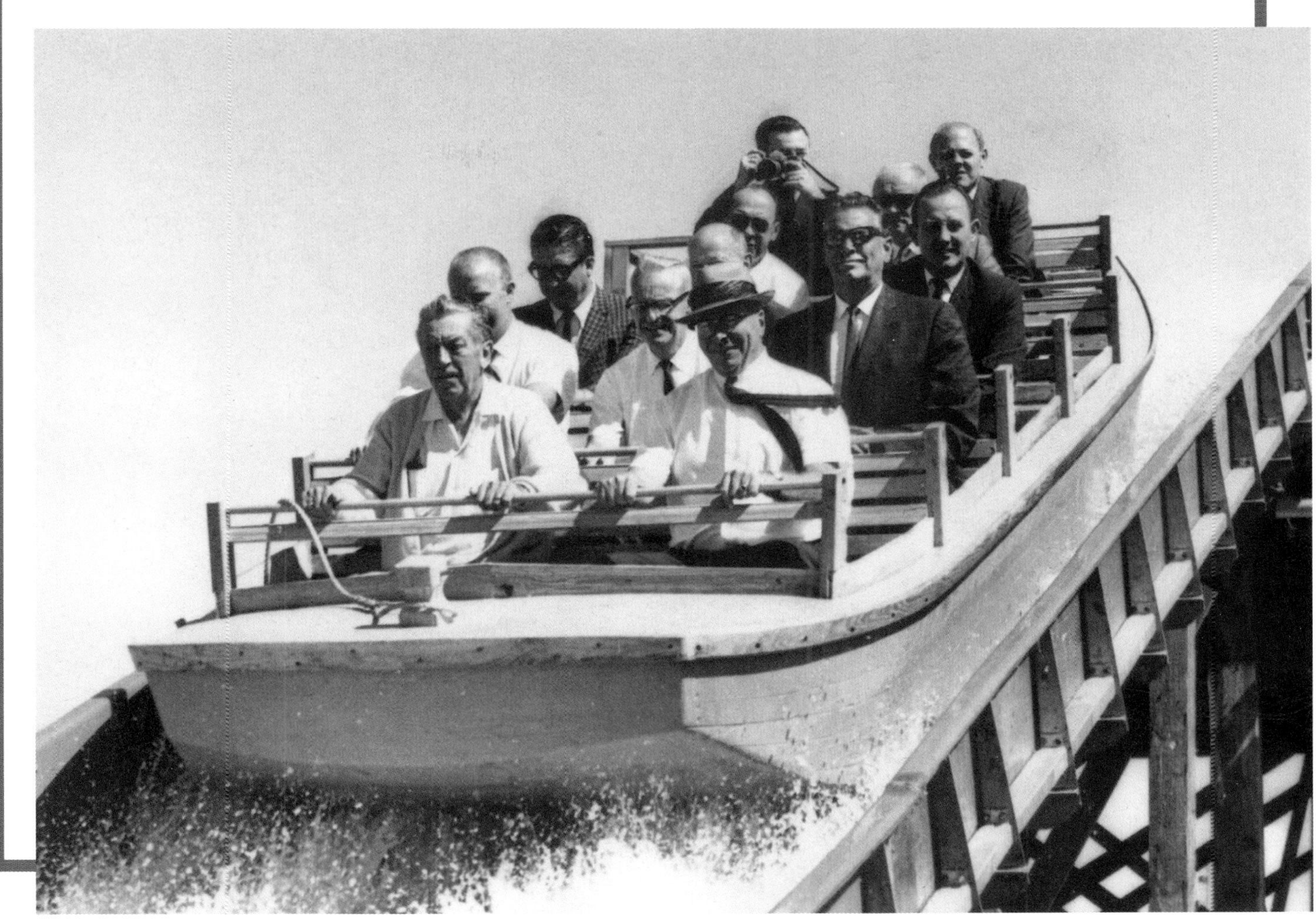

also seemed unsure of Walt's reasoning and plan for what X was actually supposed to do. At one point, Dick even asked X, "What are you doing here?" to which X replied, "I don't know," adding to X's existential questioning of Walt's intention. Yet Walt's loyal employees never asked that question directly of Walt.

X no longer had an office and was confused as to his role. He was still adjusting to life at WED and his now "long-distance" friendships with his studio pals when he received another Walt Disney–inspired plot twist. This time Walt called X and said he wanted him to start working on a script that would tie all of Marc Davis's ideas together for the Pirates of the Caribbean attraction being planned. While X had received "story by" credits on animation shorts at the studio, he had only ever done storyboards, not written official scripts. Moreover, live attractions were a new medium, and X was diving in alone, without Bill Justice or any other trusted partner.

Walt left X to it—giving no other guidance, ideas, or suggestions. There was already an early version of a script created by a more experienced writer, but it was filled with dry, straight narration, and evidently not what Walt was looking for. The pirate show had originally been planned as a "wax museum of piracy," a walk-through attraction that would showcase famous pirates and their historical artifacts. The development of realistic human figures for Great Moments with Mr. Lincoln and the Carousel of Progress attractions helped cement the change to an Audio-Animatronics-based experience for a stimulating and interactive boat-ride attraction.

Knowing what not to do, X set out to tackle this new project, aiming to tap into whatever it was inside him that Walt had seen. He put on his "pirate hat"

OPPOSITE: The dinosaurs for the Primeval World diorama on the studio lot in Burbank; ABOVE: Walt, X, and other Imagineers testing the Pirates of the Caribbean vehicles created by Arrow Development at their facility in Mountain View, California.

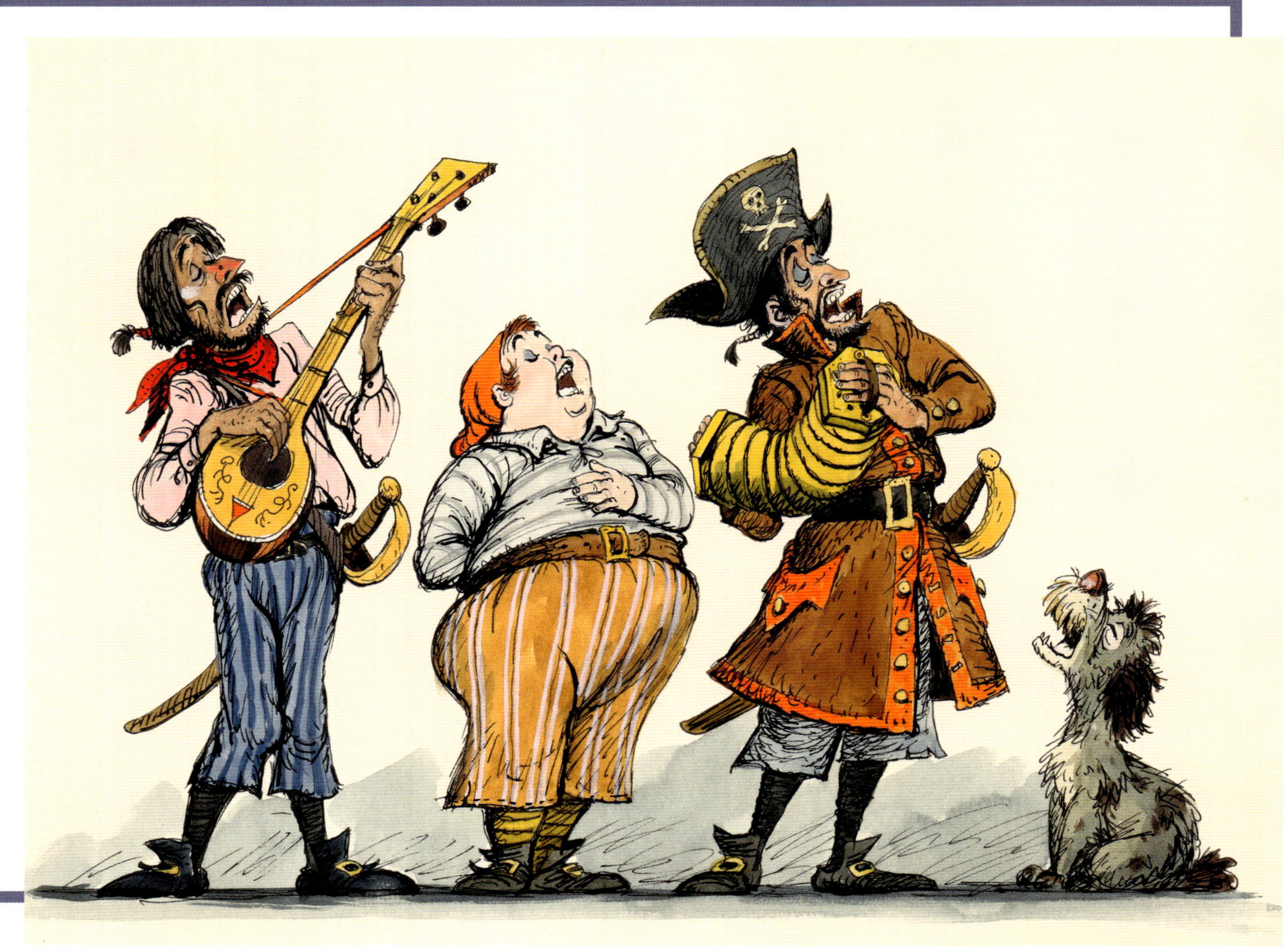

and researched anything he could on pirates—checking out books from the library and watching films such as *Walt Disney's Treasure Island* (1950) to learn the jargon, the culture, and the media depictions that formed the general population's perception of pirates. Marc, whom X had previously worked with on the animated shorts *Melody* and *Toot, Whistle, Plunk and Boom*, and Claude were already hard at work on the attraction, with Marc working on the pirates' designs, gags, and staging while Claude focused on the environment and how the ride would operate. They walked X through the layout and models of the attraction, and then X fully got to work on what the story would be, beginning with the auction scene. When he felt this portion of the script was ready, X sent it over to Walt for his feedback and revisions. All X received in return was Walt's reply: "Fine, keep going."

X built his pirate act from his research and his imagination, creating the pirate voice that would come to define the genre with vernacular and dialogue like "Avast there! Ye come seekin' adventure and salty old pirates, aye?" Marc and Claude's design inspired X, challenging him to figure out what the story would be in each scene, what would be said, and the narrative of the entire ride. Marc and Claude were very encouraging and open to X's vision and creative choices, working well as a team. The three brainstormed and came up with the idea that the pirates couldn't take the treasure with them because it was cursed. This small story point became a pivotal narrative influence in the franchise-spawning films of the same name, beginning with *Pirates of the Caribbean: The Curse of the Black Pearl* (2003).

In terms of the rest of the mood and influence for the attraction's story, X drew on the importance of the language to set the tone and specificity. He felt that his Spanish background helped him get the environment of his creation, understanding coming into a new land or defending a fort—creating the atmosphere as the guests are pulled in their boats through the darkness of the cave into the moonlight amidst chaos and cannon fire. Another personal touch and Easter egg in the attraction that X added was in the "well scene" where a woman yells, "Carlos, don't be chicken!" out the window to her husband, the town magistrate, who is being dunked in a water well and questioned on the location of the treasure. The name Carlos was a nod to his new friend Carlos Amador, the Mexican producer X had worked with on *Cri-Crí, the Little Singing Cricket*.

Eventually the three mocked up the auction scene of the ride at full scale in a warehouse to walk Walt through. When Walt would come over to WED, everyone was nervous, waiting for approval on their deeply personal creations. According to X, before you saw Walt, you heard his chronic cough. Walt traveled alone without an entourage so that he could sit

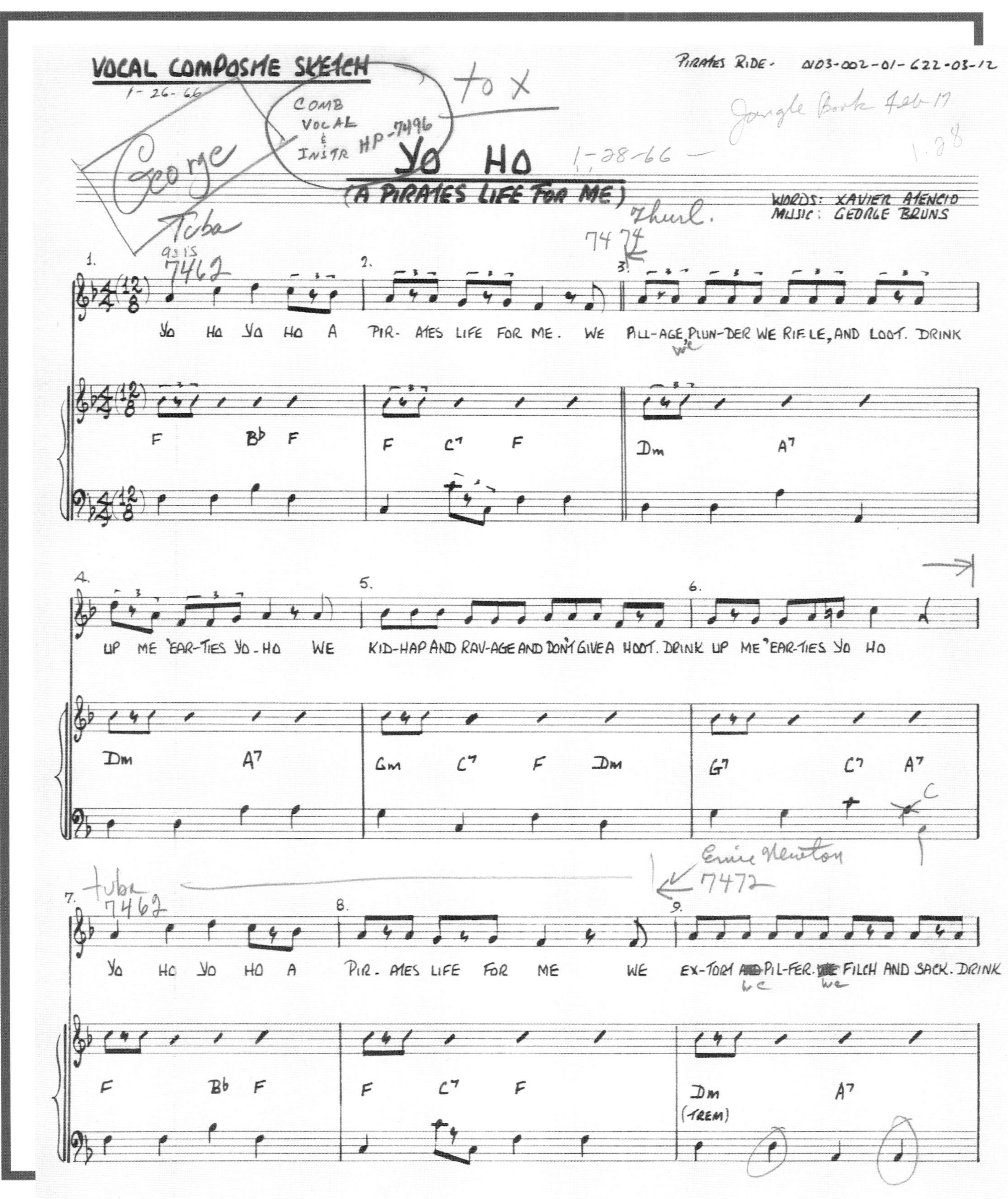

OPPOSITE: Marc Davis's illustration of pirates singing "Yo Ho"; ABOVE: An early version of the "Yo Ho" music and lyrics from X and George.

and brainstorm with the Imagineers. X recalled the process in an interview, stating, "You'd be at a storyboard, and you'd have your back to him. He would be in his wooden chair. And then you'd hear him tapping his fingers on the arm of the chair, and he was suddenly way ahead of you. He'd talk about a board further down in the sequence than where you were, and he'd say, 'Why don't we take that sequence down there and move it up here?'" Another reveal about Walt from X was that if Walt liked your vision, he'd be with you—dancing, enthralled, whatever the project called for—but if he didn't, he'd be "coughing with disappointment."

When the fateful day came to present the Pirates of the Caribbean auction scene to Walt, X, Marc, and Claude were ready. Ever the visionaries, they built a cart and pushed Walt through the experience at the same speed that the boats would be going, showing him the attraction from the eyes of the guest. During the test run of the auction scene, they realized that the noise from the Audio-Animatronics figures talking over one another rendered much of the dialogue inaudible. As the auctioneer called out to start his sale and the crowd of pirates shout back their bids, one drunk pirate's reply, "Six it be. Six bottles o' rum!," got lost in the overlap of dialogue. Apologizing, X told Walt, "I'm sorry. I don't think you are clearly hearing what these guys are saying." Understanding storytelling, human experience, and the potential of what this attraction could offer, Walt replied, as X remembered, "Hey, X, when you go to a cocktail party, you pick up a little conversation here, another conversation there. Each time people will go through, they'll find something new." X was impressed, thinking, *Why the heck didn't I think of that?* With the boss's blessing and this new inspiration, X, Marc, and Claude continued with their mission.

At the final story meeting with Walt, X suggested that it would perhaps be a good idea to add a song. He had an idea for the lyrics and delivered the tentative melody he had in mind, half singing, half reciting what eventually became the world-renowned song "Yo Ho (A Pirate's Life for Me)." X assumed that if Walt approved, he would send X to the Sherman brothers to take over the whole process, constructing the melody, fixing and building on the start of X's lyrics. Instead, Walt said, "Fine. Get George [Bruns] to do the music for it." Having no musical training except for his "unofficial school" of working on musical shorts at Disney with talented legends like the Sherman brothers, X's original lyric creation was all innately his. As for the song's melody, X hummed a few ideas to George, who was working on the score for *The Jungle Book* (1967) and Disney live-action films at the time, and then let George take it from there. While the music was now being handled by a professional, X found himself inexplicably adding "lyricist" to his resume.

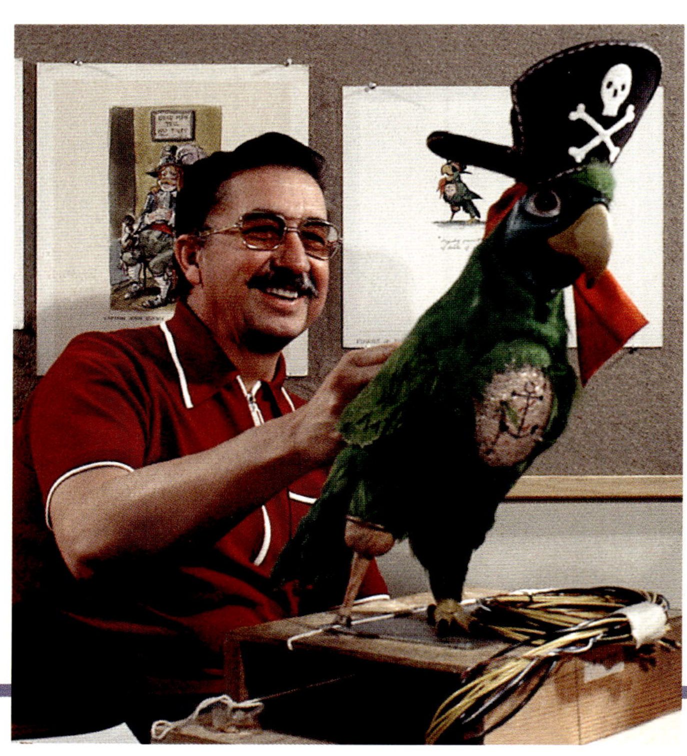

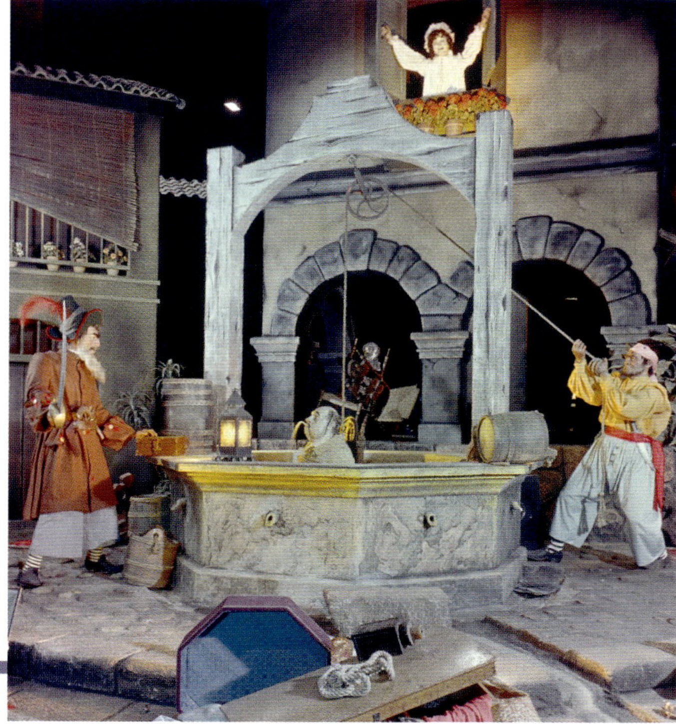

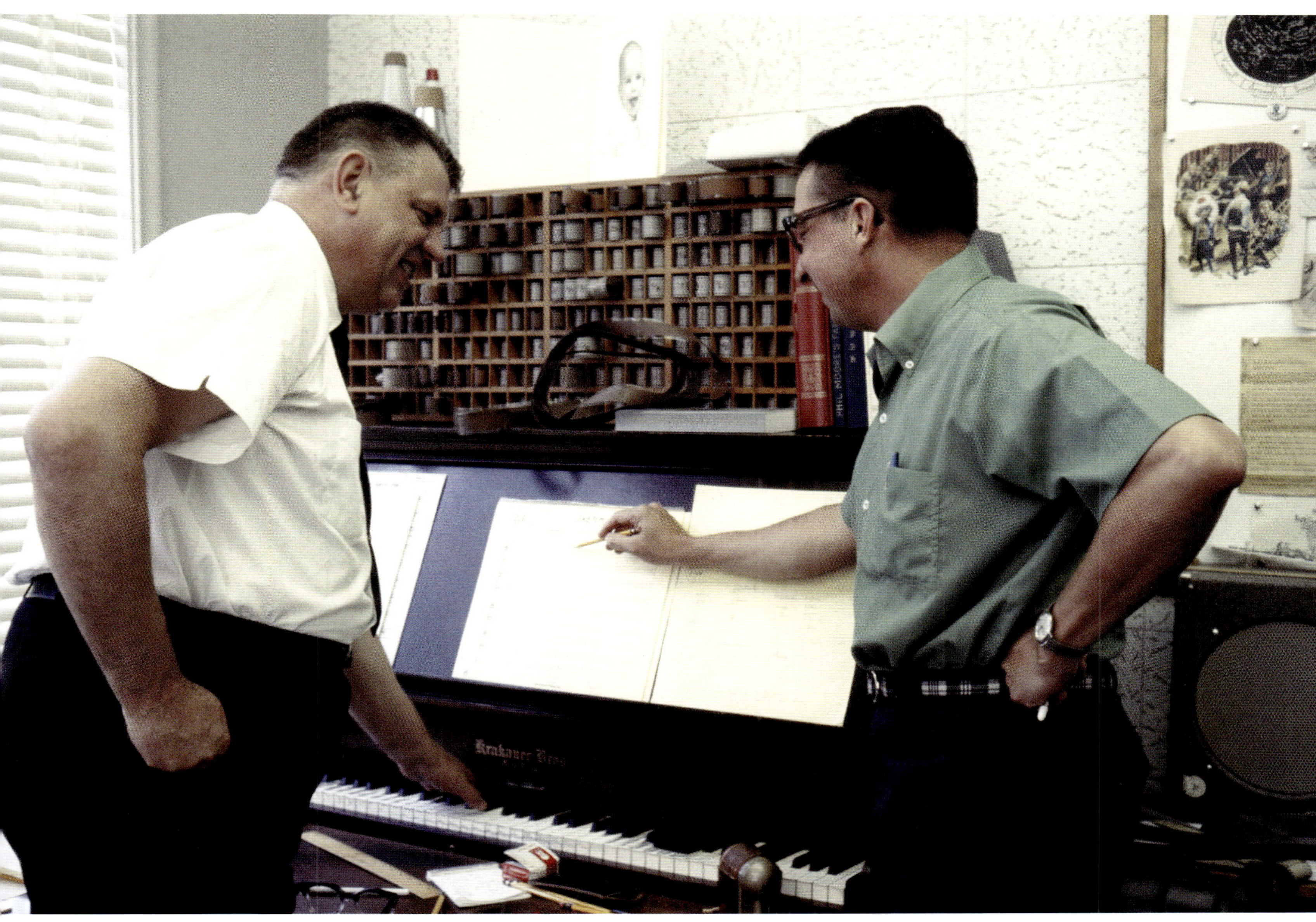

X's extensive pirate research had influenced his song creation sk lls. He got out his *Roget's Thesaurus* and made lists of all the traditional "pirating" words, resulting in lyrical phrasing such as "maraud and embezzle and even hijack, drink up, me hearties, yo ho." X pointed out the difficulty of writing a song for an attraction like Pirates, where there really wasn't a beginning or an end. Instead, one came into the middle of the life of a pirate and left in a similar state. As already established during the run-through for Walt, the guests drifted in and out of the story, hearing different pieces each time depending on seating and boat placement, and thus each verse had to stand on its own. Likewise, the verses couldn't be reliant on telling the story of the auction scene specifically, since some guests would watch it play out after a related lyric had ended or before it restarted.

In some ways, that added even more pressure on the song's refrain to be memorable and communicate the theme of the attraction: this show was a general statement about what "fun loving" pirates did in their adventurous daily lives. For them, every action and interaction involved drama and stakes, because they were the traditional villains/story antagonists. "Yo ho, yo ho, a pirate's life for me" and "Drink up, me hearties, yo ho," managed to humorously

OPPOSITE (LEFT): X with an Audio-Animatronics parrot from Pirates of the Caribbean; OPPOSITE (RIGHT): The "well scene," featuring Carlos, named after X's friend Carlos Amador; ABOVE: X and George Bruns hard at work on writing the lyrics/tune for "Yo Ho (A Pirate's Life for Me)."

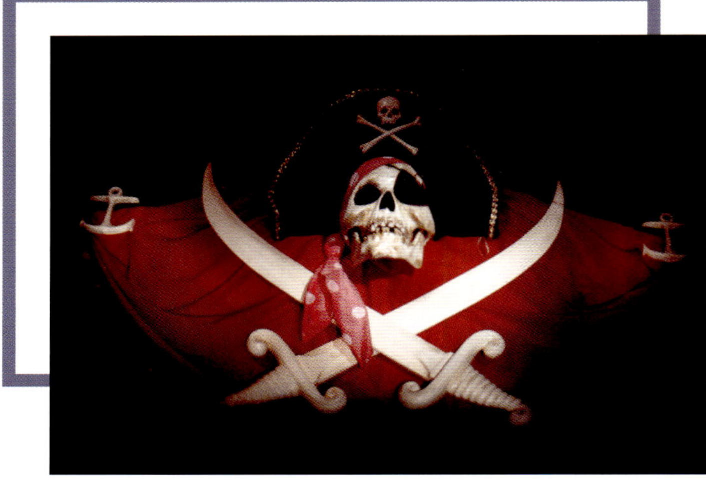

and hauntingly captivate and do exactly that, especially when set against George Bruns's melody.

Pirates of the Caribbean altered the trajectory of X's career for many reasons—the scope of the attraction, its status as a cultural phenomenon, the story writing, the songwriting. But it turned out that it was the songwriting that X ended up enjoying most of all. Though at first confused and out of his depth, X rose to every challenge Walt put in front of him, creating a Disney attraction that still ranks in the top three across many lists, including one from a 2023 *Los Angeles Times* ranking. While parts of the attraction have been updated to reflect more modern cultural, political, and social values (as well as the influence of the hit film franchise), Pirates of the Caribbean solidified its place as a cultural touchstone that elevated the standard for a Disneyland attraction and established a new basis for what it meant to be a pirate.

For X, the assignment wasn't something he had expected, yet it revealed new talents and advanced his status and role at Disney. To each attraction he worked on at the Disney parks from then on, he almost always added a song. In some ways, the musical transition made sense. In reflecting back on his career, nearly every short piece X had worked on with Ward Kimball and Bill Justice had been musically driven: *A Symposium of Popular Songs*, *Melody*, the *Mickey Mouse Club* title sequence, and more. All of them proved that a catchy melody could influence audiences far beyond what the story alone could accomplish; X's work to this point perhaps, either consciously or subconsciously, swayed his decision to include songs.

Another first for X on Pirates of the Caribbean was the voice work. While he had previous experience working with talent, it was here that X first became a voice talent himself. He played the pirate up on the bridge offering bottles of rum as a bid in the auction scene. And most famously, he voiced the Jolly Roger skull that guests heard before going down the first waterfall as the they entered the darkness of the Pirates of the Caribbean realm. Hiring exceptional voice talent, like Paul Frees, was very expensive. On Pirates of the Caribbean alone, Paul recorded voices for the ghost that ominously echoes "Dead men tell no tales," the Audio-Animatronics auctioneer pirate, Magistrate Carlos, and the "Pooped Pirate." After the Imagineers had recorded with talent like Paul at the helm, any additions or changes would be very costly, since bringing Paul back meant paying another day's salary. X and the other Imagineers then originated "No Dough Productions," their inside joke production company that signified using themselves and other "local Disney talent," all for the low cost of "free" and taking pride in a job well done.

After Paul had finished recording for Pirates of the Caribbean and gone home, and the ride had been officially installed, the Imagineers realized they needed some sort of introduction to the attraction to warn the guests to keep their hands and feet inside the boat and, equally if not more important, to prepare for the initial drop in the darkness and splash from the pooled water beneath. Adding in the warning through the voice of the skull, X volunteered to do the voice, telling guests to "keep your ruddy hands inboard . . . and mark well me words, mateys . . . dead men tell no tales." Disney sound designer Glenn Barker, who started his Disney career in May 1975, explained in a personal interview, "The earlier sound teams at the time on Pirates worked with X to jockey up the sound levels, adding reverb throughout to create the chilling but playful voice resonating a warning that all should heed. The voice, language X had written, and placement worked so well with the rest of the attraction that

ABOVE: The Jolly Roger in Pirates of the Caribbean, featuring X's voice; OPPOSITE: Illustrated lyrics of "Yo Ho (A Pirate's Life for Me)."

most guests never realized the addition was a required state regulation."

After X's own successful voice work on Pirates, No Dough Productions took off. Glenn recalled how later X was always listening to everyone's voices, picking up who might be right for which parts, or who among them might have their own untapped potential for voice recording. While relying on average Disney employees could pose a risk in quality, it saved money and boosted morale. They even started opening up auditions so they could hear more people's voices and see if there was anything generally available that they had to offer. At times it was hit or miss, with some overacting when called into the sound room, coming off as a hams, and others turning out to be far too shy. One Disney phone operator who X felt had a great voice accepted the request to record, but completely froze with stage fright once in front of the microphone. And yet overall, it was a total hit, with most of those who expressed interest willing to get over their nerves for the chance to happily proclaim to their families, "That's my voice!" when going through an attraction in the parks.

However, before Pirates of the Caribbean was finished and ready to be unveiled to the public, X and the entire Disney universe were in for a fateful twist. Walt's history of smoking, which likely triggered his notorious chronic cough, caught up with him. In November 1966, he was diagnosed with lung cancer. On November 30, 1966, Walt felt unwell and returned to Burbank's St. Joseph Hospital, where he remained until he died on December 15, 1966, at 9:35 a.m. from circulatory collapse caused by the cancer. When news broke at WED and across Walt Disney Productions, everyone was heartbroken and worried about the future of the company without Walt, the consummate creative visionary. What did this mean for their projects? And both professionally and personally, what would life be like at WED without him? John Hench came to X's new office at WED, and they both reminisced about their time with Walt, trading stories about their encounters during the projects they had worked closely with him on.

Everyone was dismissed at noon that day. Though X's tradition was always to buy the family Christmas tree on December 15, he ignored that

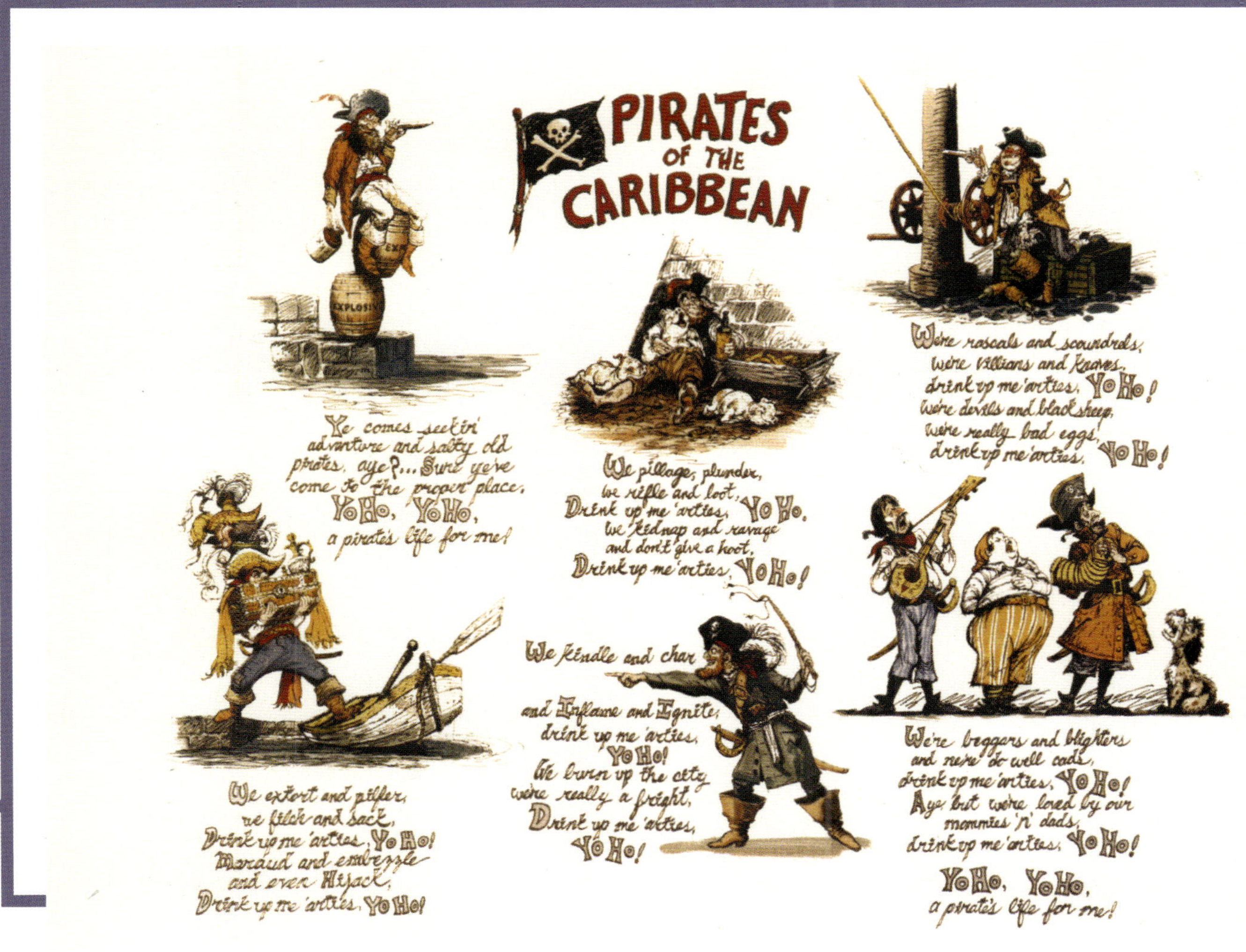

task and went home to continue reflecting on Walt's legacy and what he meant to X personally. However, at home alone with his thoughts, X found himself unable to just sit with his grief, so he went out to buy his tree. Given Walt's passing, Mary went to pick up the children early from school, knowing that they would also be upset. They returned home not only to their Christmas tree, but also to their father crying—the first time they had ever witnessed this sight. For X, and many others who had worked closely with Walt, it felt like they had lost a father. X recalled how the remainder of that holiday season was filled with the delivery of many Christmas cards from all over the world, and even from his friends in England, all including special condolence notes expressing their sympathies as if a member of X's family had died, which in a sense was what had happened. The patriarch of X's entire thirty-plus-year career had passed away, and the work family was grieving, unsure how to function without their leader, mentor, harshest critic, and greatest champion.

On the day of Walt's death, company employees received a letter from Roy O. Disney (drafted by Marty Sklar), which read in part:

> Much of Walt Disney's energies had been directed to preparing for this day. It was Walt's wish that when the time came he would have built an organization with the creative talents to carry on as he had established and directed it through the years. Today this organization has been built and we will carry out this wish.
>
> Walt Disney's preparation for the future has a solid, creative foundation. All of the plans for the future that Walt had begun—new motion pictures, the expansion of Disneyland, television production, and our Florida and Mineral King projects—will continue to move ahead. That is the way Walt wanted it to be.

The next project X undertook, which was already underway when Walt died, was a show featuring performing bears developed by Marc Davis, originally envisioned by Walt as part of an Alpine Village project in Sequoia National Forest. After Walt's death, the project stalled, but corporate decided to

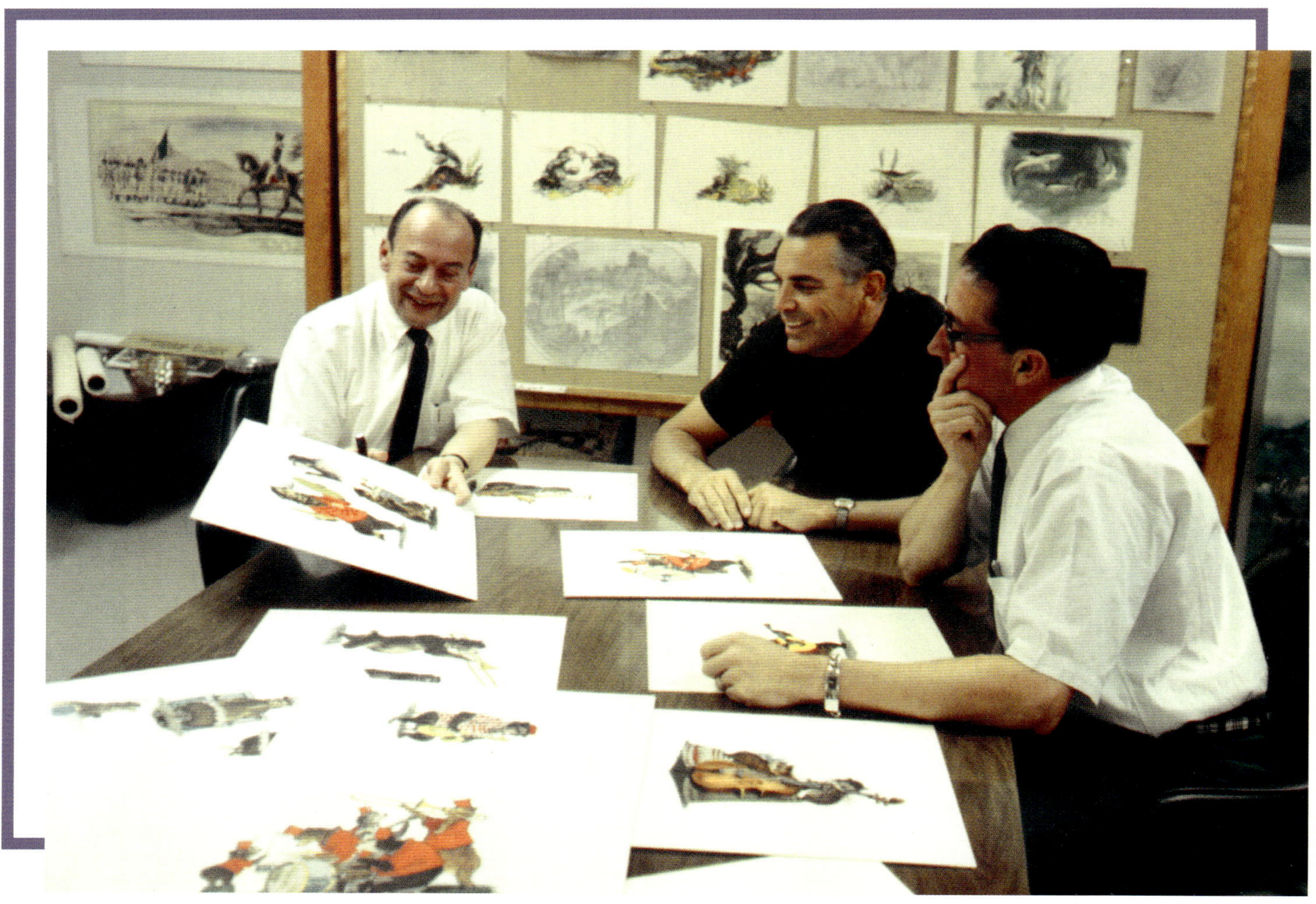

continue developing the bear band for the new Walt Disney World Resort in Florida. X constructed a loose script with a country theme and wrote the lyrics for a song in the newly named Country Bear Jamboree attraction. The song, "Bear Band Serenade," had original lyrics by X and music by George Bruns. X tried out a number of character names, ultimately landing on these: Henry, Ted, Zeb, Fred, Tennessee, Trixie, and Big Al. Ted was named after X's baby brother, adding another connection in the ever-growing list between Disney and the Atencio family. The setting resembled the Grand Ole Opry, and X and Marc imagined fun antics and Opry-like effects for the attraction, with X refining the script. After years of work, Country Bear Jamboree opened in Walt Disney World in 1971 and Disneyland in 1972. It eventually opened in Tokyo Disneyland as well, with X's song present and on rotation at all three park locations.

One of the final projects that Walt and X were involved in together was Adventure Thru Inner Space, the first attraction to use the Omnimover ride system. The attraction harnessed some of the technology developed for the Ford Magic Skyway from the New York World's Fair. Opening at Disneyland in 1967,

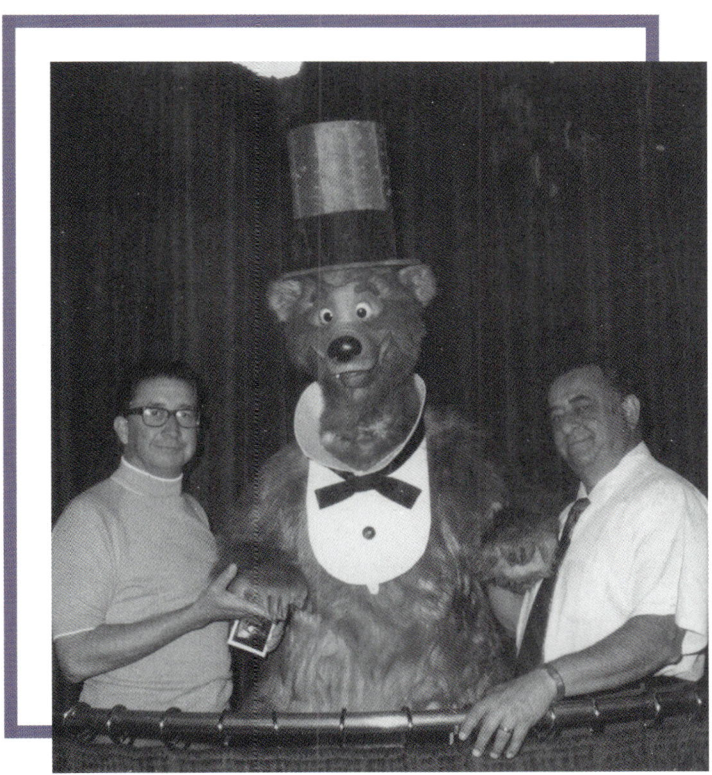

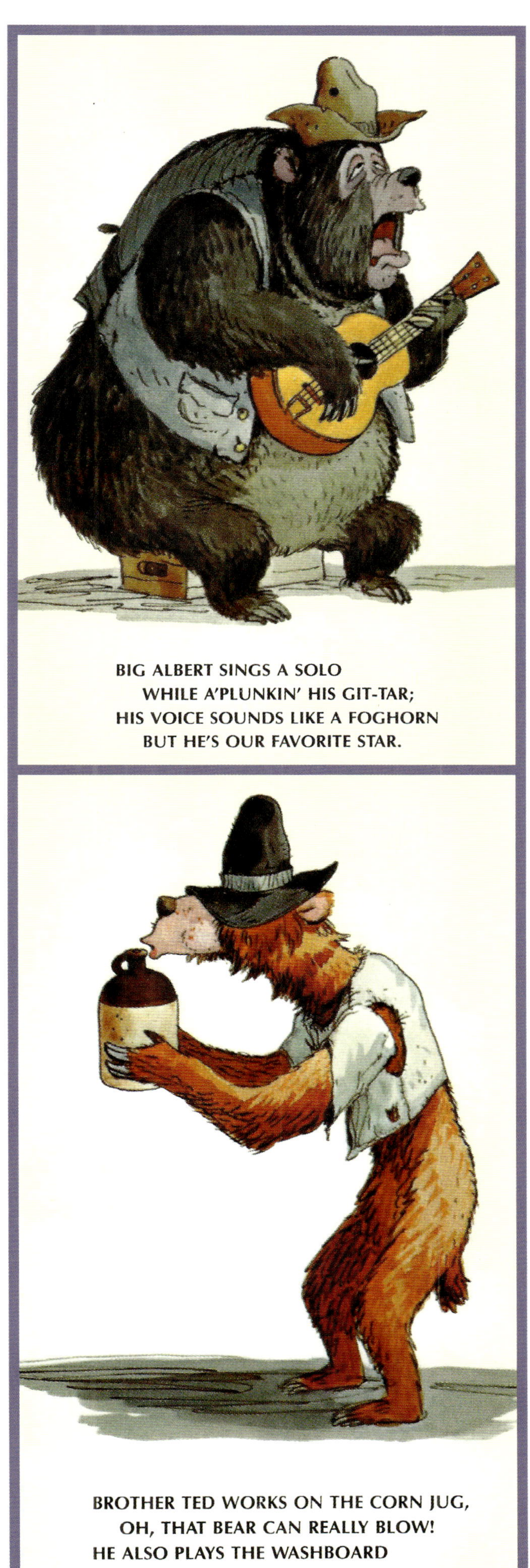

OPPOSITE: Marc Davis, Claude Coats, and X reviewing Country Bear Jamboree concept art; ABOVE: X and Al Bertino posing with one of the bears from Country Bear Jamboree; RIGHT: Two Country Bear postcards featuring Big Al (TOP), who is named after Al Bertino, and Ted, who is named after X's brother.

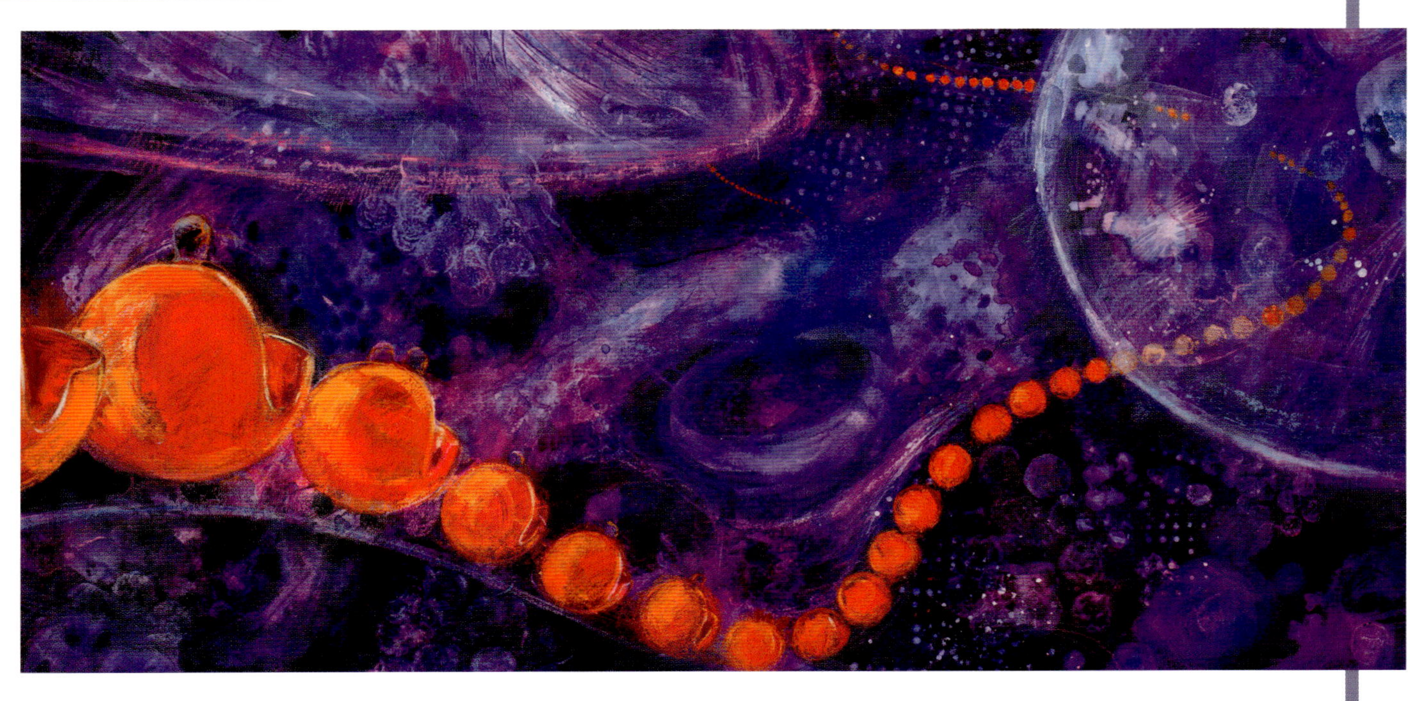

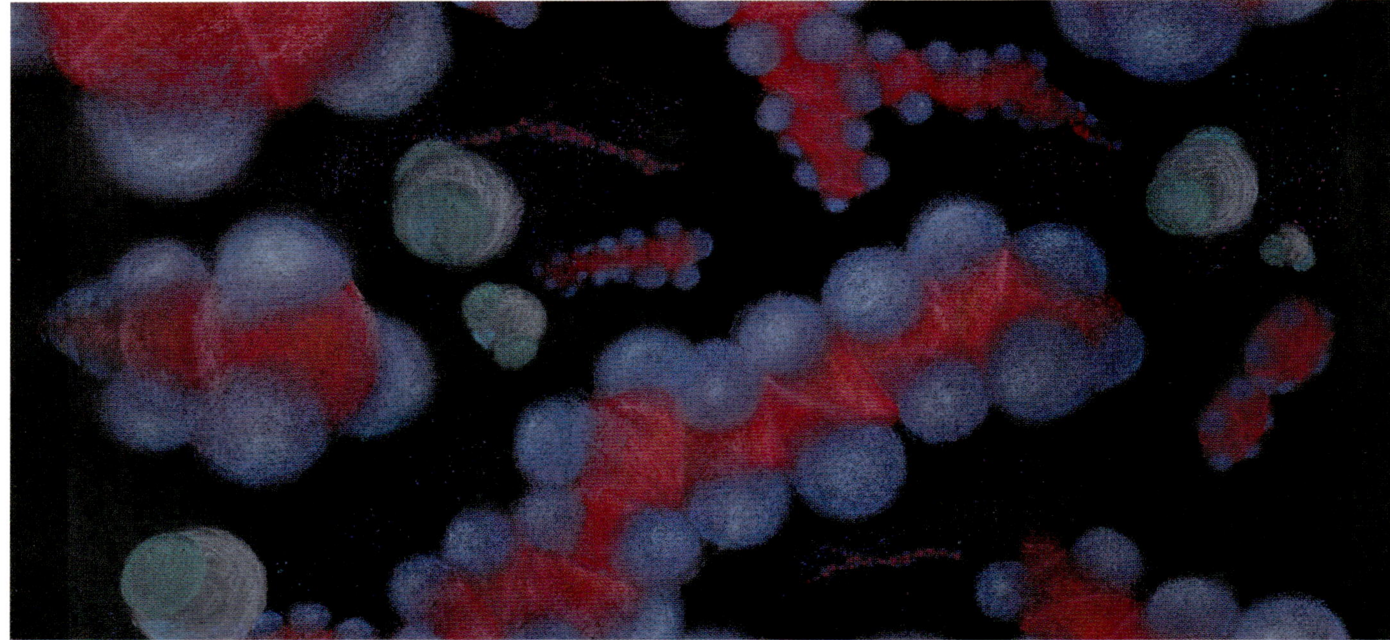

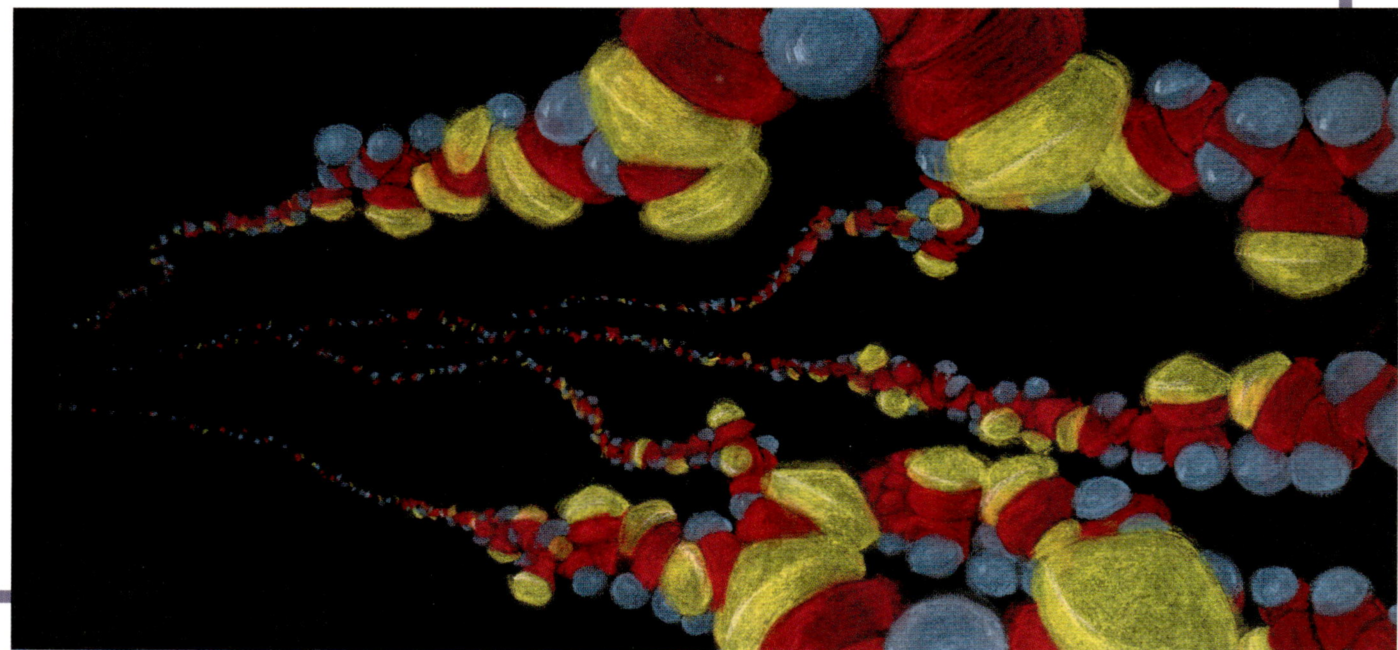

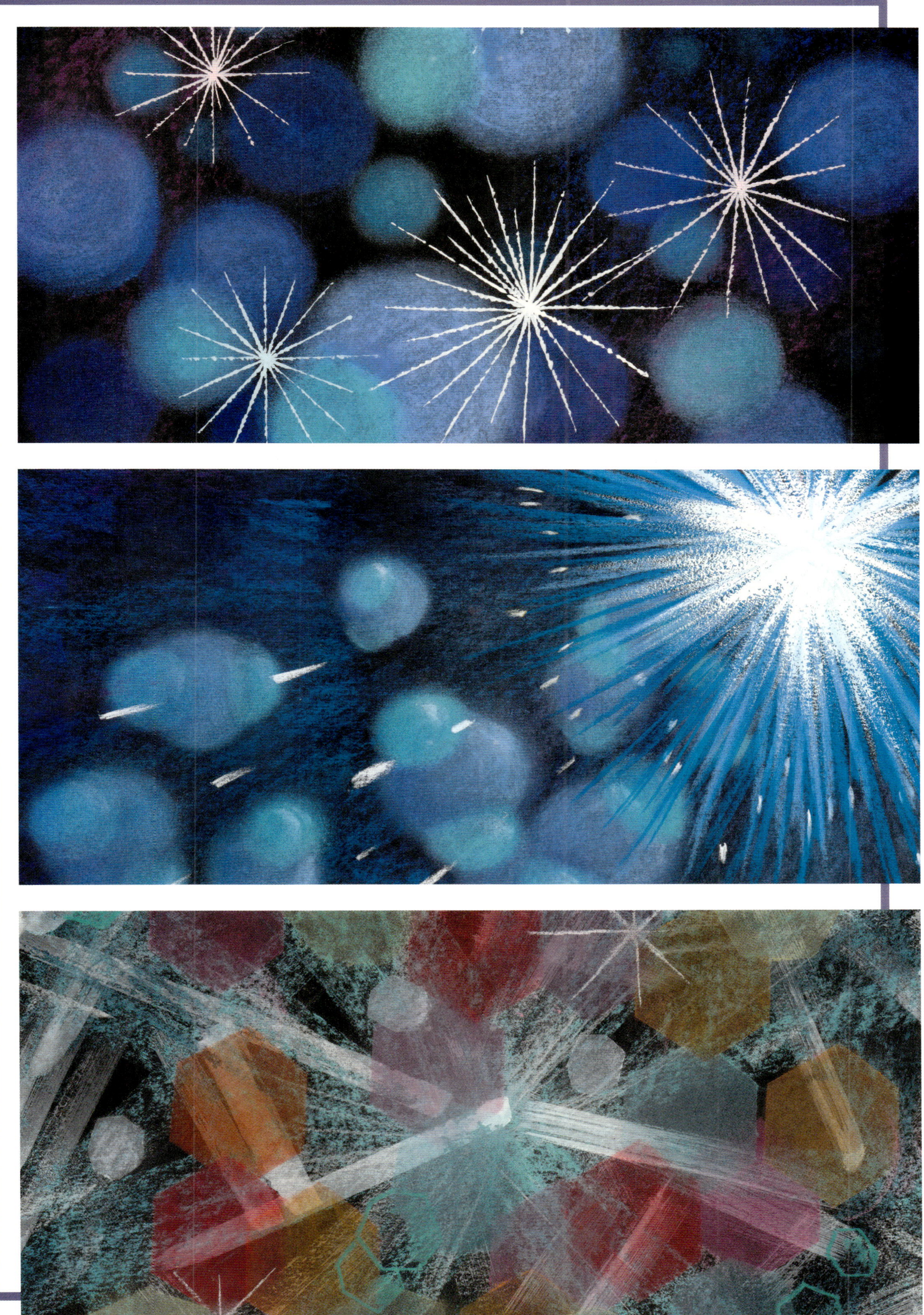

OPPOSITE AND ABOVE: X's concept art for Adventure Thru Inner Space, reflecting a more abstract type of art, done with pastels, which differed from X's usual works.

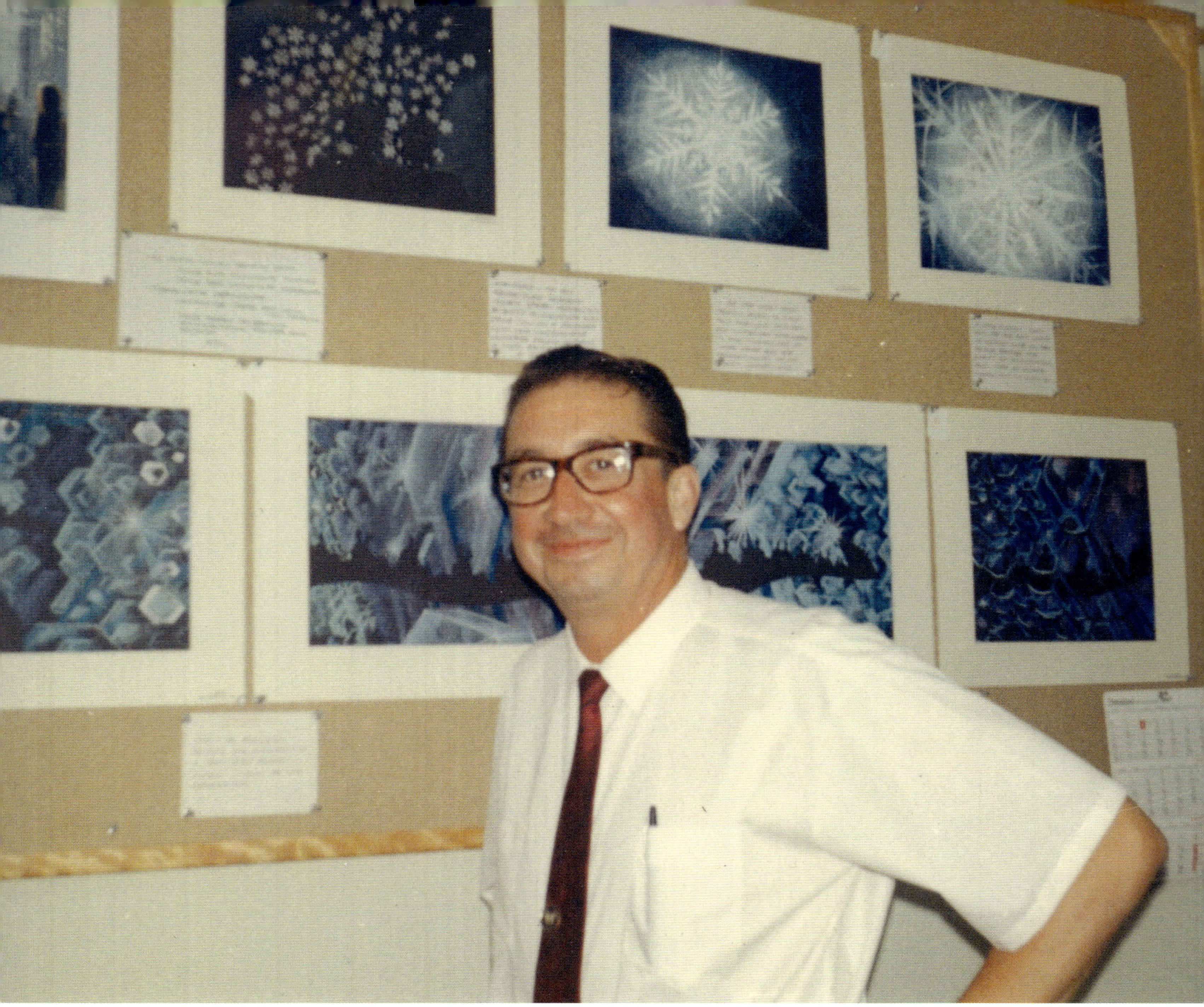

the same year as Pirates of the Caribbean, Adventure Thru Inner Space was Claude Coats's passion project, an ambitious attraction made even more ambitious by its ultimate goal—making molecular science and its inner workings interesting and understandable for the average park guest and child. Each guest boarded an Omnimover car, traveling with it through the "Mighty Microscope" and shrinking enough to fit inside the molecule of a snowflake. The attraction's success hinged on making the idea and experience interesting with a specific world that showed character, scale, and mood, and required guests to feel like they were truly being reduced in size, even though they were remaining the same size they'd always been.

X wrote the script and did some abstract concept art for Adventure Thru Inner Space, and Paul Frees was once again hired as the voice talent for this project. The sponsor of the attraction was the Monsanto Company, an agrochemical and agricultural biotechnology corporation headquartered in St. Louis. The president of Monsanto reviewed the project's storyboards for scientific accuracy, and X listened to the Monsanto team's ideas for the attraction. Understanding Disney and the average park guest, X told the Monsanto employees that one could not assume everyone knew as much chemistry as they did. X pointed out that he had never even taken chemistry in high school and that the knowledge needed to be reduced into easily comprehensible pieces of information for the audience to understand. One piece Monsanto and X agreed on was that whatever was written for the masses needed to

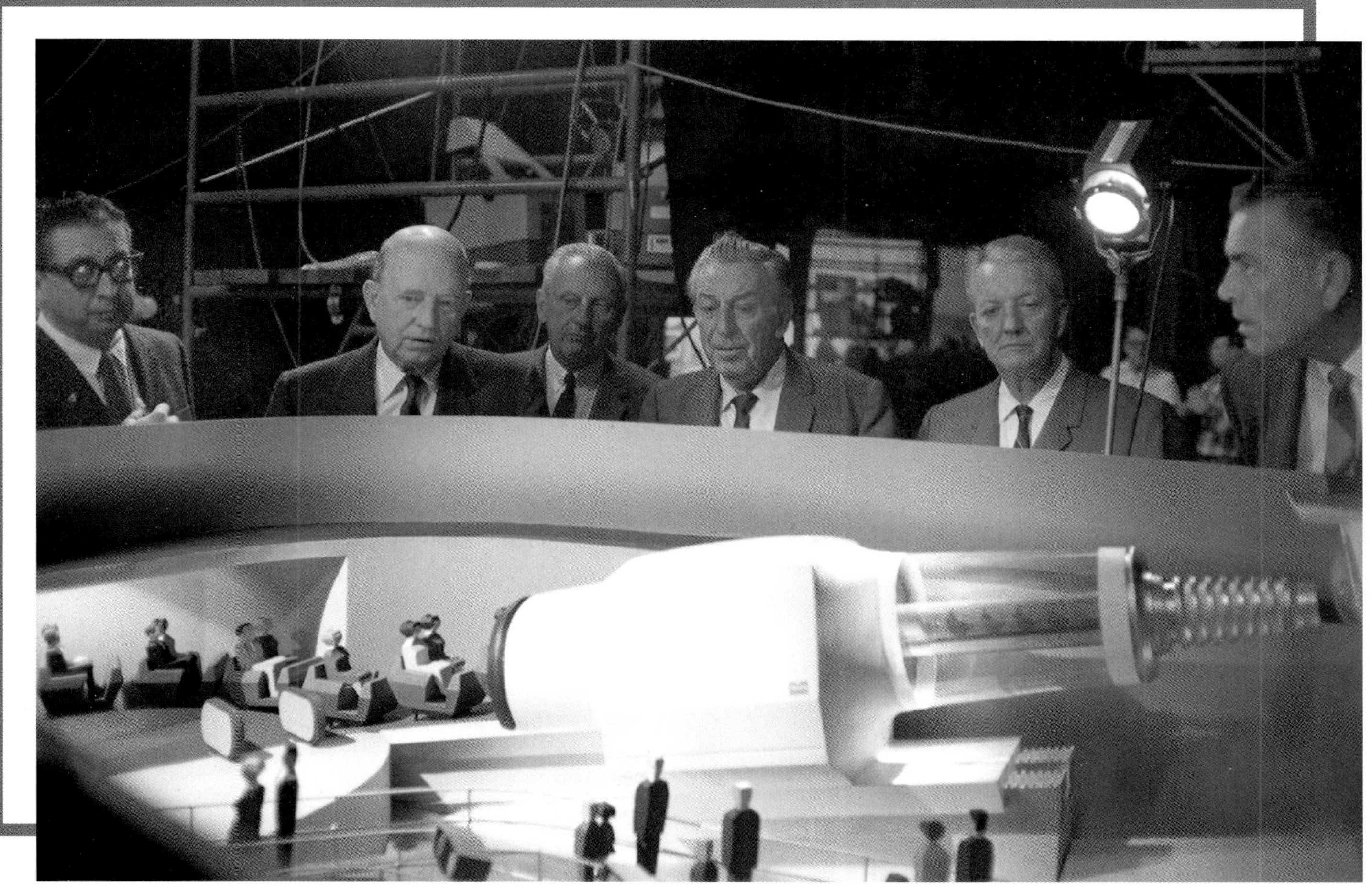

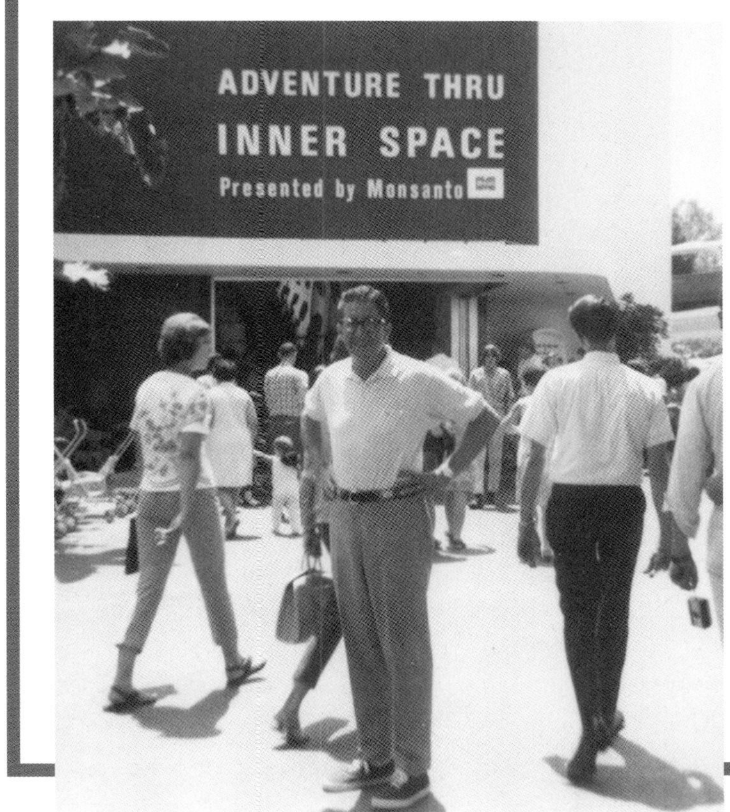

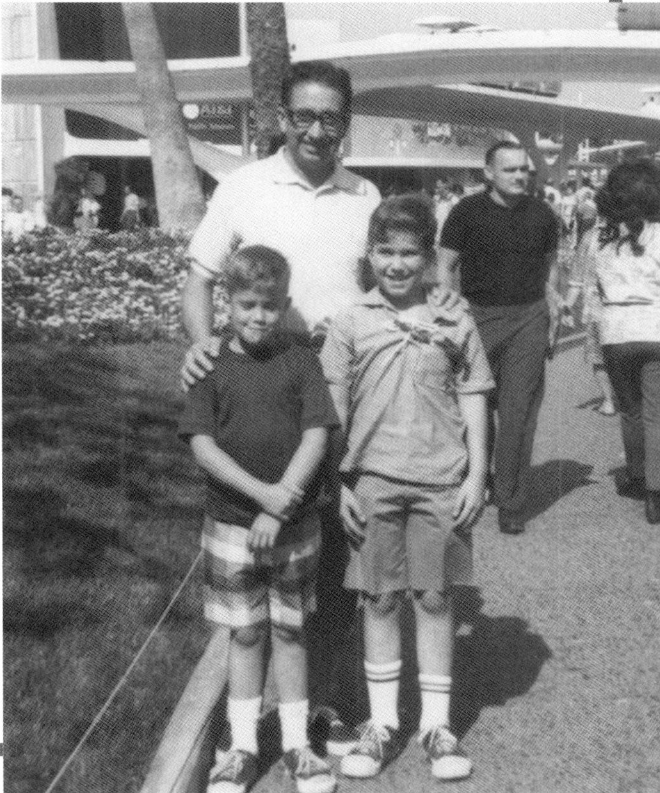

OPPOSITE: X posing in front of his concept art for Adventure Thru Inner Space; ABOVE (TOP): X, Walt, and other Imagineers looking at a model of the loading zone for Adventure Thru Inner Space; ABOVE: X on a visit with his family to see Adventure Thru Inner Space on its opening day.

be accurate. Whether for a budding young chemistry prodigy or just a typical child out for an enjoyable day of screaming in dark attractions with friends, they wanted whatever information was written and recorded to be entertaining, easy to process, and factually correct. All the parties involved managed to succeed in their mission, with a few teachers even writing to tell them that they liked the ride as well as its accuracy in depicting for their students how molecules work.

Imagineer George McGinnis designed select scenes in the attraction, working on the "Mighty Microscope" and the "Atomobiles" that shrank in the tube when in view on the microscope. He recalled how he would sketch and draw his designs at lunchtime while sitting with X. On the day George sketched the microscope and corresponding microscopic Atomobiles, X grabbed the drawing away from him and took it to the Model Shop, where he asked for a matching model to be constructed.

After the success of the Pirates of the Caribbean attraction, which seemingly coincided with the period when X's children were reaching the perfect age to appreciate all that Disneyland had to offer, the Atencios started to spend more time at the park, beginning with a family outing to the opening day of Adventure Thru Inner Space.

Mon. April 24/67
9:30 AM

Dear Mary –
I am praying for X's immediate recovery – and if I can be of assistance in any way – please do not hesitate to call me day or night. My home phone is. 805 WH 61834.
Your friend,
T. Hee

ABOVE: A letter to Mary from T. Hee after X's heart attack; OPPOSITE: A note from Emile Kuri, a colleague from *Mary Poppins*, after X's heart attack.

Another part of the Imagineer's job on an attraction, even long after it was open, was to go to Disneyland occasionally to check on the ride, to make sure everything was functioning properly, that the sound levels were behaving, and that guests continued to get a top-tier experience. While today Disney has an entire team within Imagineering responsible for upholding quality guest experience, aptly called the Show Quality Standards program, the responsibility at the time was left to individual Imagineers. X would always wait for a weekend, usually a Sunday, to do his check-ins so that his children could come as well. One weekend in May 1967, X and Mary decided to have a couple's getaway to Disneyland and combine the visit with a check-in on the Pirates of the Caribbean audio. They left the four children behind and enjoyed a lovely outing for just the two of them. That Saturday evening at dinner, X started to complain of indigestion but soon discovered that, just shy of fifty years old, he was suffering a heart attack. His stresses at work and unhealthy lifestyle choices had caught up with him.

X fortunately recovered from the heart attack and immediately changed several things and habits in his life. The memories of his father's death from a heart attack and Walt's lingering smoker's cough and early death influenced X's post–heart attack decisions to quit cigarettes cold turkey and start exercising daily. The greeting cards X drew at that time also reflected these changes, most specifically by humorously commenting on his new stationary bike workout regimen. To underscore the severity of his health issue, it is worth noting that X gave up his membership in the Academy of Motion Pictures Arts and Sciences in January 1968.

Despite the health scare, X wasn't slowing down at work. His next major project at WED was the Haunted Mansion. Dick Irvine and Marty Sklar knew that X had successfully scripted Pirates of the Caribbean and wanted him to accomplish similar feats on the troubled Haunted Mansion. The building for the Haunted Mansion had been present in the park for a long time as the Imagineers and Walt debated the attraction's concept. They originally envisioned a walk-through attraction in which a few dozen guests at a time would move through the house together, scene by scene, watching each setting's action unfold before moving on to the next. To that end, former Disney studio layout and background artist and WED special effects wizard Yale Gracey had already designed some incredible illusions with clear beginnings and endings. After the proven success of the Omnimovers at other attractions, the Imagineers took stock of their development to see which other sites this technology could be right for—and the Haunted Mansion, which needed a quick and efficient way to move large numbers of guests, proved the perfect fit. The Omnimovers were renamed "Doom Buggies," a play on the name of dune buggies, vehicles designed for driving across beaches. The show narration describes Doom Buggies for guests boarding the attraction: "The carriage that will carry you into the moldering sanctum of the spirit world will accommodate you and one or two . . . loved ones."

This technological addition helped the Haunted Mansion but set back many of Yale's ideations, since the use of the Doom Buggies meant the Imagineers were back to the basic problem that every car's entrance timing into a scene would differ. No longer would a guest be in the room for the entire scene, instead entering and exiting at differing points in the action. However, the technical evolutions on the Haunted Mansion allowed for an even more specific and curated experience than on Pirates of the Caribbean. In Pirates, guests were seated in a forward-moving boat along a flume. The action took place all around them: to the left, right, above, and straight ahead, and it was the guest's choice of where to look. The Doom Buggies, though, could rotate along their ride path—twisting the car to show one side of the room versus the other, tilting backward so guests would look up, and hiding certain angles by turning in the opposite direction—meaning guests experienced a visual treat that felt more like a three-dimensional simulation of a movie camera. At this point, X was called in to work on the story alongside the dynamic duo of Marc Davis and Claude Coats, a pairing that had already proven masterful during the creation of Pirates.

For nearly a decade prior to Walt's death, there were several concepts being explored for the Haunted Mansion, ranging from dark and terrifying to playful and silly. Research had been done into Japanese lore with the idea of applying some of its story tenets, but Walt had made it clear—no blood and guts, and the attraction should not be as gruesome as Japanese legends could get. There were two schools of thought on how to accomplish the right mood and tone, leading both sides to advocate strongly for their ideas of how Walt would want it—scary or funny, to what degree, et cetera. The ongoing debate amidst a void in creative direction was why the fully constructed Haunted Mansion facade sat empty at Disneyland for six years.

With tensions mounting, Marc and Claude had worked out most of the scenes of the attraction, and so it became X's herculean task to walk through each scene and to determine the tone of the script through what was said in each scene or vignette to enhance the experience. Along the way, they realized that the tone was even less spooky than expected; yet finding the right balance between humor and the macabre was vital. X said he always wanted to believe in ghosts and had found that most people either did or would like to believe in ghosts and in the idea of something beyond this earthly realm. Like Pirates, these traditional villains or antagonists

EMILE KURI

April
Twenty-sixth
1967

Dear X,

I was surprised and genuinely shocked to learn that you are in the hospital. With all the good care you are getting, I am sure the situation will be looking brighter very soon.

Don't worry about things - just concentrate on getting well.

My prayers and best wishes are with you for a speedy recovery.

Warmest regards,

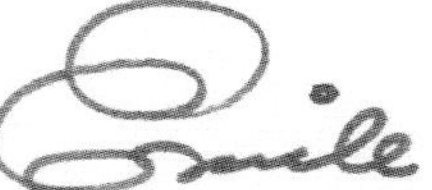

Mr. Francis Xavier Atencio
Saint Joseph's Memorial Hospital
Coronary Care Unit, Second Floor
Burbank, California

12/13/67

Dear Nickie Baby:

This week I'm enjoying a wonderful visit with the Atencios in Woodland Hills. California is delightful this time of year - smog or no smog.

You won't recognize X when you see him. He lost thirty-five pounds and looks years younger. (If you weren't so jolly and sweet just as you are, I'd suggest you go on a diet.) It seems that X had a Coronary Occlusion last April that laid him up for three months. His Doctor made him lose weight and quit smoking and so now he's as good as new - only more so. He's really taking care of himself. He exercises daily and rides a bicycle several miles. (Mary had to buy one - he couldn't wait 'til Christmas.) He's playing better golf and doing everything he did before, but with more zip. (Hmmmmm, maybe you had better go on a diet after all.)

Mary is well but looks a little thin. Just watching her cope with the demands of four kids wears me out. Chauffering them around is a full-time job in itself It's not like when we were kids. Her folks still live just around the corner and are doing well considering their advancing years.

The kids are all currently well. They've had their usual share of bumps and bruises this past year, but nothing serious.

Tori is quite the young lady - a good student and loaded with school spirit. She is currently on the St. Mel girls' Volley-ball team competing in the C.Y.O. finals for the diocesan championship. Next year it's high school.

Judy was just confirmed and is also quite a young lady. She had a little bicycle mishap just after Christmas last year and for a while it was feared that they would have to do a root-canal on her lower teeth. Fortunately, she mended nicely and is doing fine. She has one more year at St. Mels.

As you recall, Jerry was mending from a dislocation, last year, when you dropped in. Well, he's made it through this year with hardly more than a scratch. He and Joey are still occupied with the Cub Scouts and other typical boy projects.

Joey, the hustler, has made it through the year with a few miscellaneous stitches and black eyes. He made his First Communion while his Daddy was sick, but he got to visit him in the hospital on his big day. That boy's the leader of the gang, believe me.

They're all good kids, so remember them with a little something extra this year. They're a little embarrassed about writing, but you know how it is when you're almost 14 - 12 - 10½ and 9.

The kids are taking me to Disneyland to see all the wonderful new things. X wrote the dialogue and narration for two of the new attractions; "The Pirates of the Caribbean", and Monsanto's "Adventure Thru Inner Space." The children say they're great.

I'll let you know when and where the reindeer are to pick me up just as soon as I make my Jet reservations. Mary and X and all the kids send their love to old Santa. Take care of yourself and don't worry, I'll be home on time.

Your everlovin' wife,
Mamma Claus

P.S. - I think X is only kidding about stamping out Christmas cards ... I hope.

ABOVE: X's Christmas letter from 1967 mentioning his heart attack and his writing the scripts for the attractions Pirates of the Caribbean and Adventure Thru Inner Space; OPPOSITE (TOP LEFT): X's Valentine's Day card to Mary from 1968 following his heart attack; OPPOSITE (TOP RIGHT): X's twenty-fourth wedding anniversary card to Mary, from 1969, reflecting his newfound interest in exercise; OPPOSITE (BOTTOM): X's 1971 Valentine's Day card to Mary showcasing his new stationary bike workout regimen.

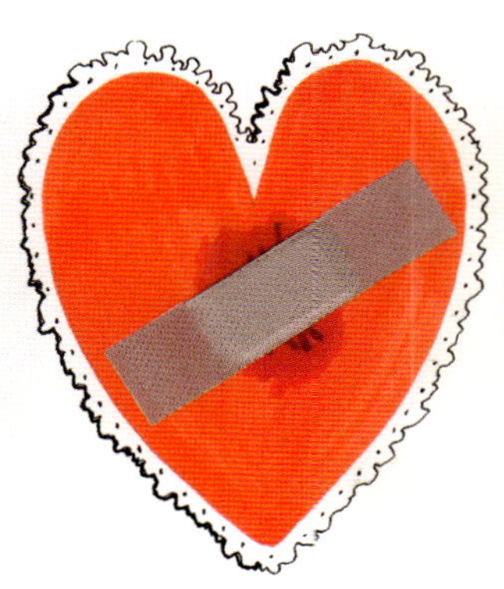

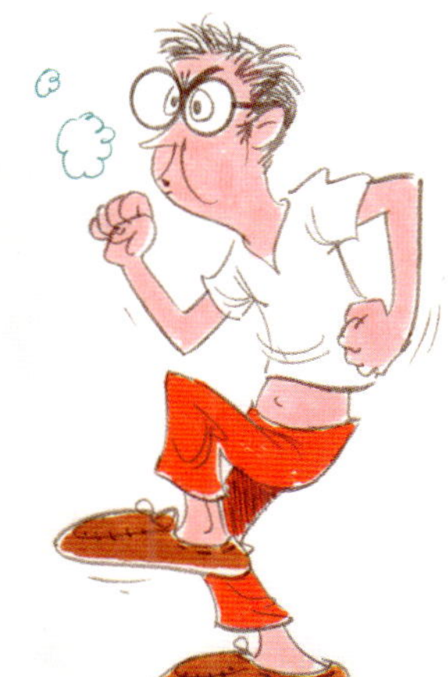

are like humans in that they need socialization and community; they just so happen to be spooky ghosts.

As X would go on to write in the attraction's song, "Grim Grinning Ghosts," the attraction's residents "come out to socialize." X pointed out that this lyric defined the theme and tone of the attraction—the ghosts terrorize, but not from a dark or mean intention. Instead, their goal was to socialize, not as benignly as Casper the Friendly Ghost, but in a well-intentioned manner, nonetheless. The words "welcome, foolish mortals" greeted the guests who entered the Mansion's Portrait Chamber, immediately hooking them in with the spooky yet still ominously friendly tone that clearly made the attraction a Disney tale. Nowhere was the dark humor that permeates the attraction more apparent than on the tombstones throughout the queue leading to the home's entrance. X penned the epitaphs, each one dedicated to the core contributors of the attraction, with his own reading, REQUIESCA FRANCIS XAVIER—NO TIME OFF FOR GOOD BEHAVIOR—R.I.P. When the attraction queue at Disneyland was updated years later and the original tombstones were removed, X was given his as a keepsake, and he displayed it proudly in his backyard for the rest of his life.

X, along with Marc and Claude, developed a story that worked with the Doom Buggies, a change that altered, in X's expert opinion, "the entire philosophy of the ride." However, this change meant that X was more involved in the show design and script than he had been for Pirates, even brushing the dust off his art supplies and doing some concept art for

HAPPINESS IS
LIVING.....

... with a bunch of
WEIRD VALENTINES!

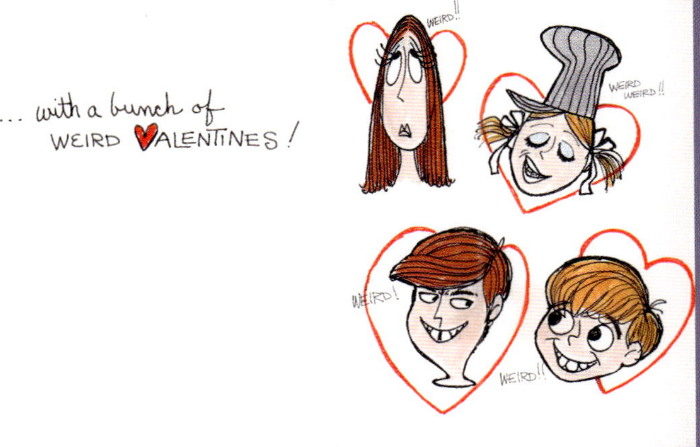

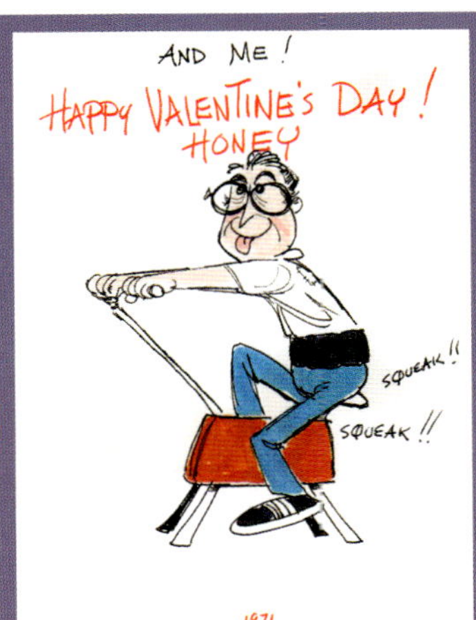

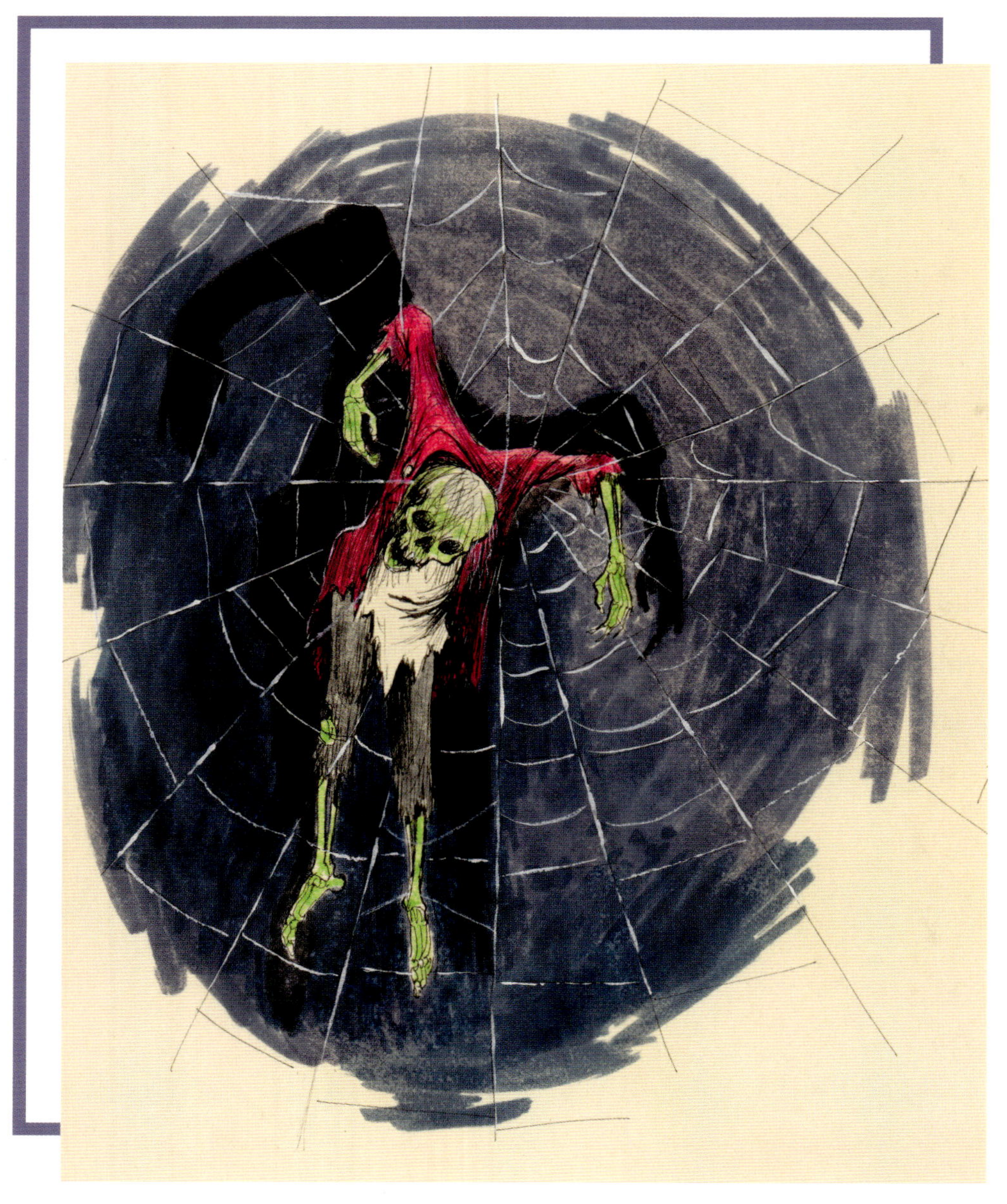

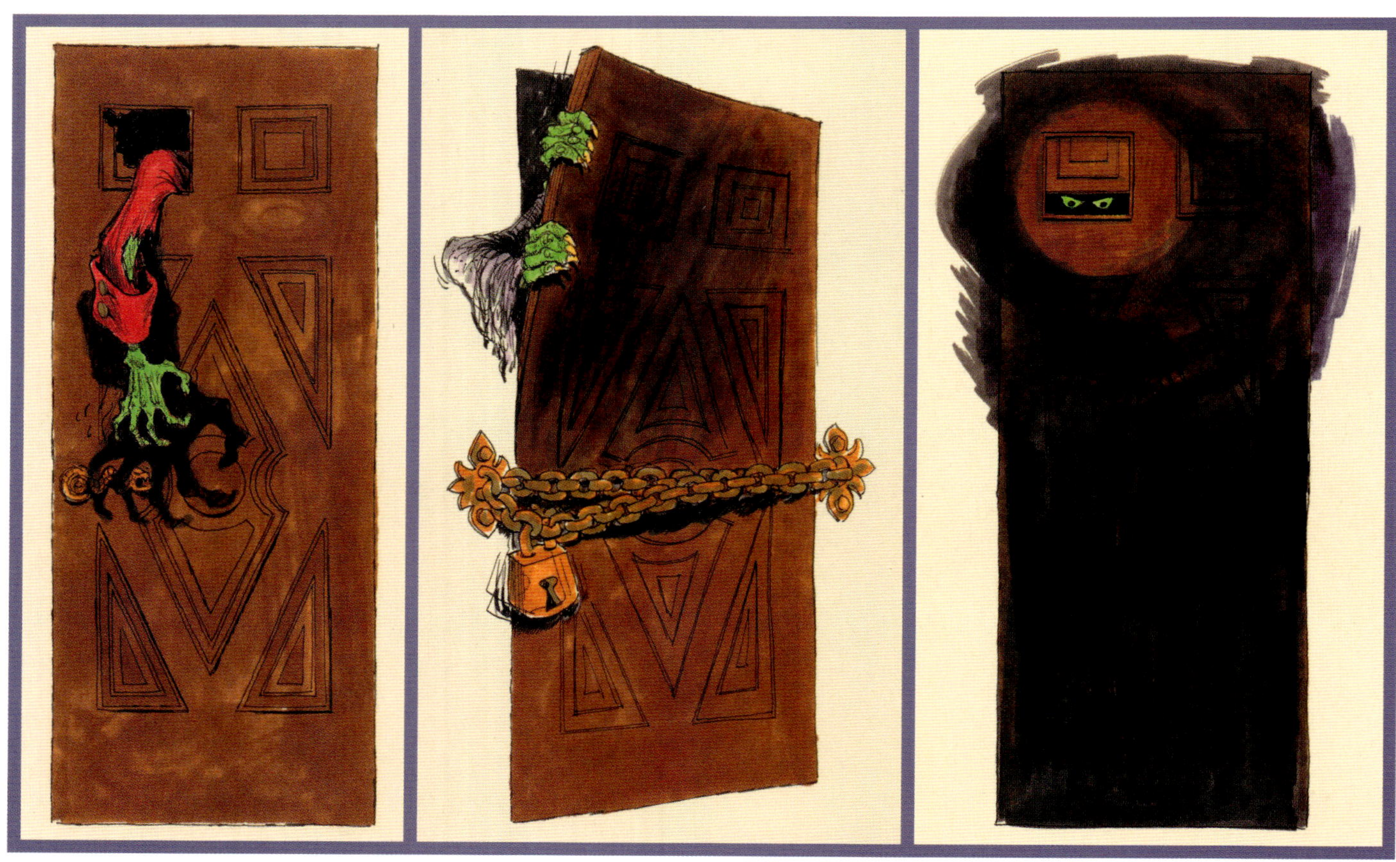

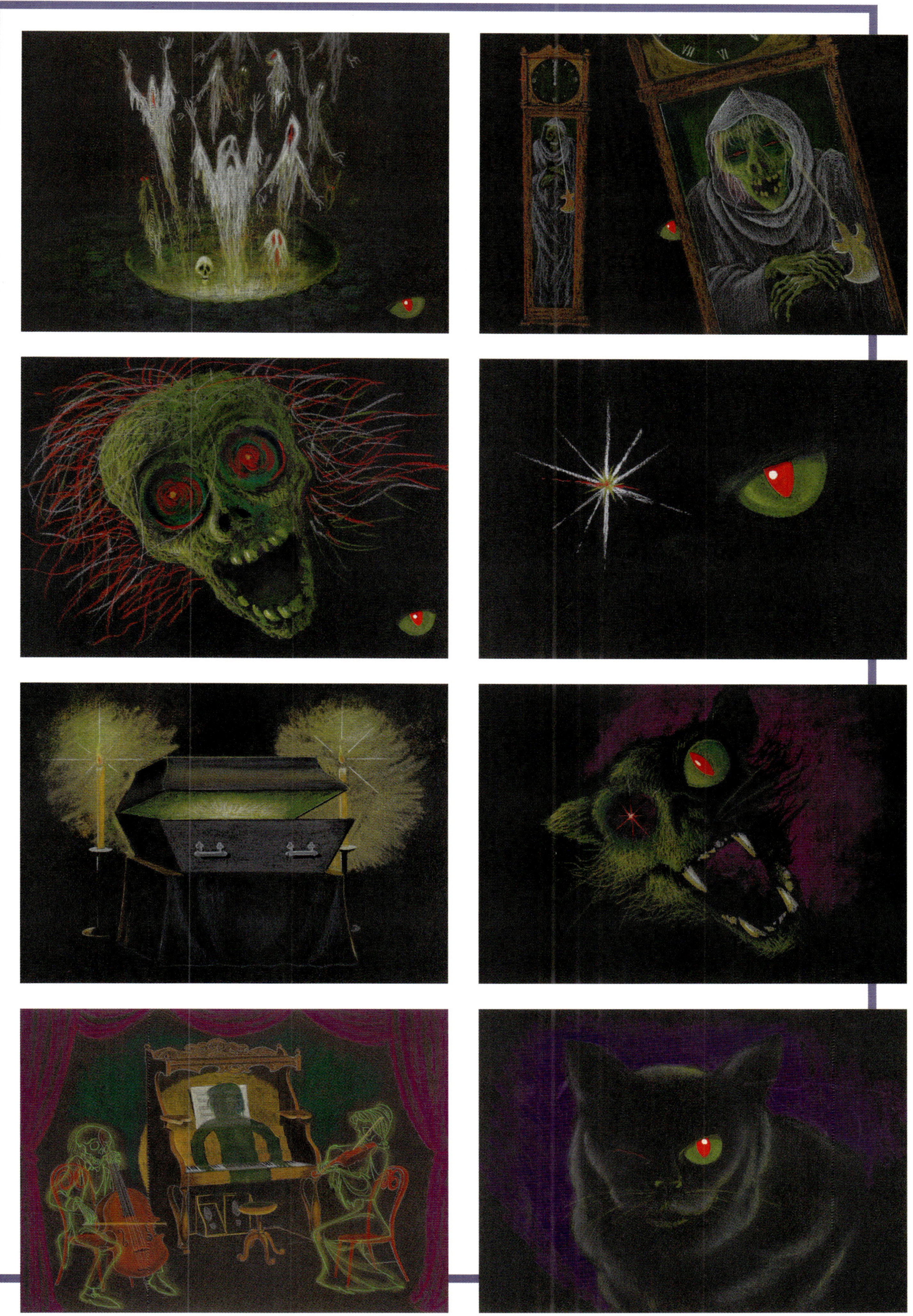

OPPOSITE: X's Haunted Mansion concept art for the Florida version of the attraction; ABOVE: X's concept art for Disneyland's Haunted Mansion, which shows a much darker tone than his other work.

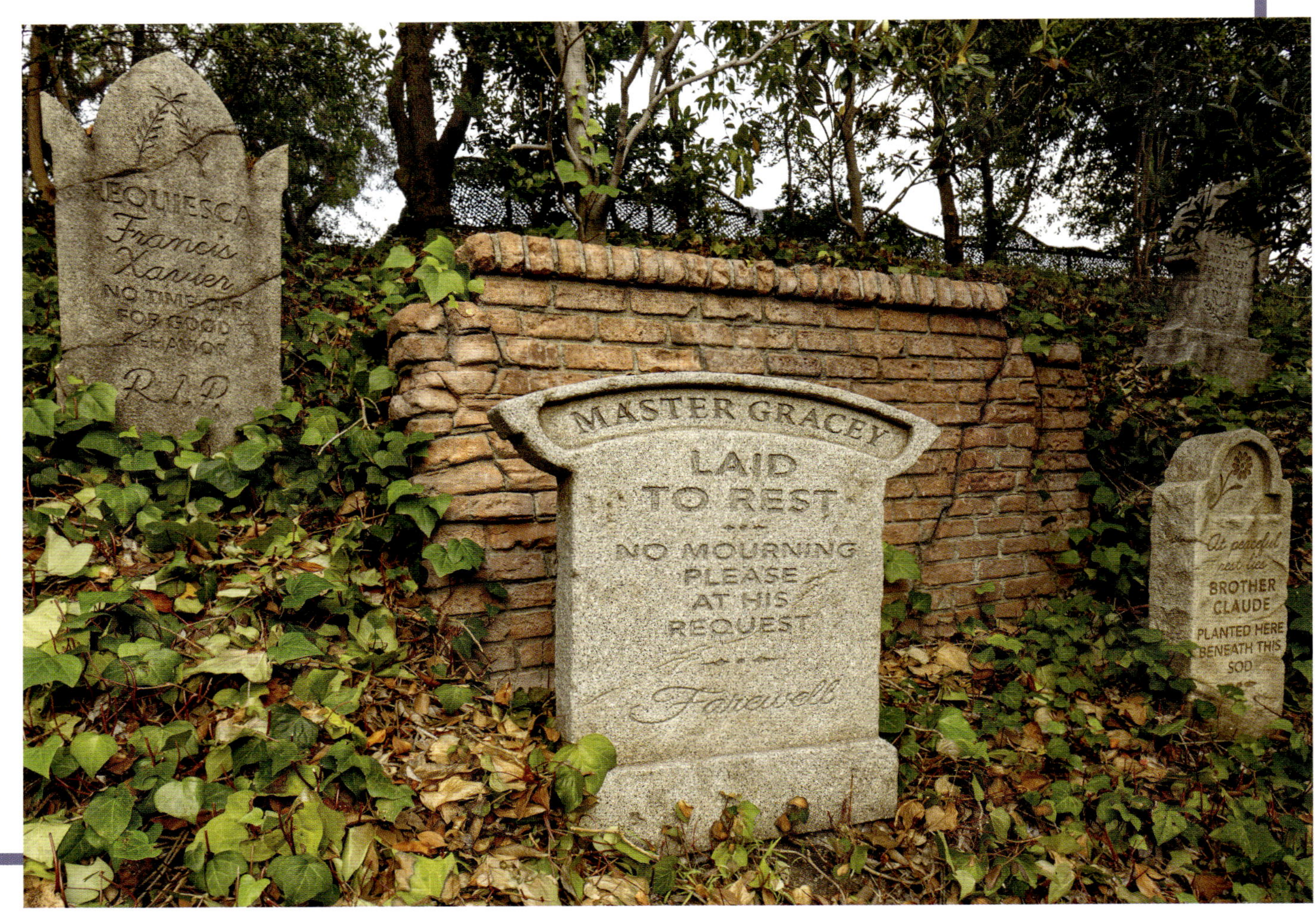

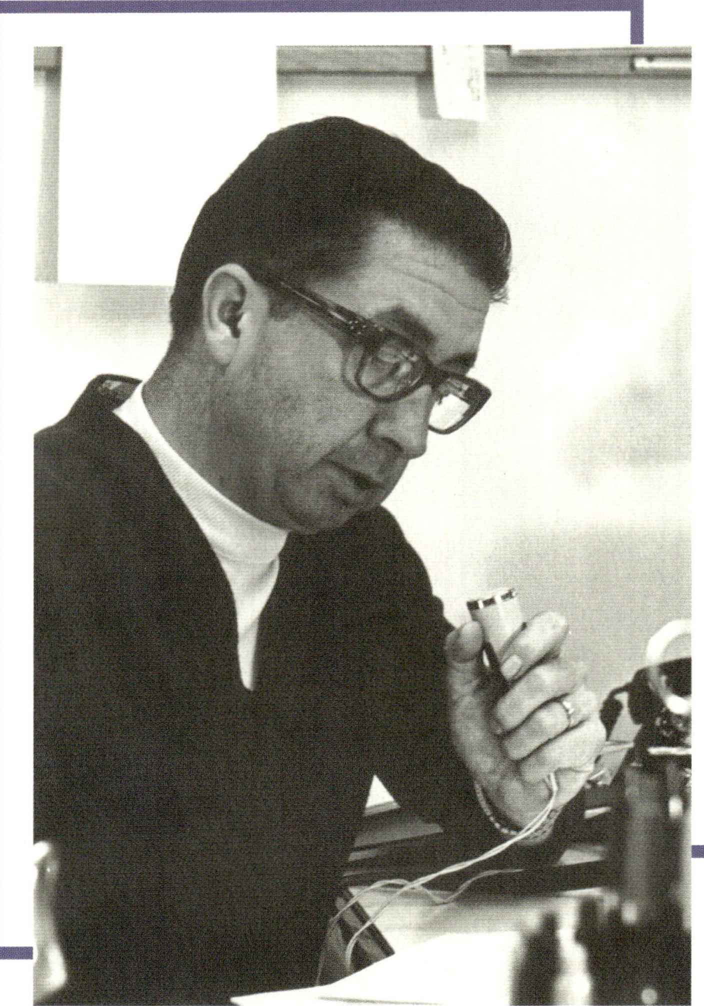

the attraction. They knew that the story needed to be generic and universal so that it didn't matter at which point guests' buggies entered and exited the room, and guests would—just as at a cocktail party, as Walt had pointed out on pirates—pick up different things every time they came through on the ride. This technological limitation was proving to be a creative bonus for Imagineers and park guests. As X had shown his home audience when working on the ending of the opening title sequence for the *Mickey Mouse Club*, different experiences kept the attraction feeling fresh and exciting, allowing one to continuously pick up on new moments, lines of dialogue, or hidden Easter eggs.

Originally, X had envisioned a cat as the recurring guide throughout Haunted Mansion. Reminiscent of the title character in Edgar Allan Poe's "The Black Cat," the guide would be a one-eyed cat with vampire-like

TOP: The tombstones in the Haunted Mansion queue, with the epithets X wrote, including the one for himself (LEFT); LEFT: Recording audio for the Haunted Mansion; OPPOSITE: X's concept art for Disneyland's Haunted Mansion.

fangs and an eerie redness to its sole eye; the hollow void of the second eye socket exhibited a starlike redness. As X pitched it, this cat would have served as the antagonist, prowling around, being predatory, and acting as a bridge between living animal and phantom spirit. The cat would search for spirits, popping in and out of the attraction like quiet, quickly moving cats often do, and appear sometimes simply as an eye in the ominous darkness. When the animal was altered into a raven, the creatives decided that the raven would be present at the beginning of the mansion and then, through the speakers in the Doom Buggies, provide consistent narration throughout.

Having either not learned his lesson or forgotten it from the Enchanted Tiki Room experience a few years before, X placed too much hope on the Audio-Animatronics bird and instead found his creative vision dashed when they couldn't get the raven synced properly. Altering his course of action, the team scaled back the number of appearances of the raven so that guests would meet it upon entering the mansion and then see it again only when the Doom Buggies went down the ramp into the graveyard, at which point the raven called out, "Ah, there you are." The raven then disappeared, and appeared one more time at the end, when guests were driven into the tomb. Despite the tinkering, it was still not working, so the raven was scrapped as host but would appear at several points throughout the attraction: first in the Conservatory, then in Madame Leota's Séance Room, then on a large tree in the descent to the Graveyard, and finally in the Mausoleum. A new narrator—the Ghost Host—would instead greet guests with the "ah, there you are" in the graveyard. Switching to a Ghost Host was brilliant for many reasons, the least of which being that ghosts can be ever present without being seen.

The raven represented one example of many in which artistic choices that read so well on the page or in the ideation phase must ultimately be scrapped in execution. Meanwhile, other ideas came in the heat of the moment or as an afterthought and sometimes ended up being so well received that one could not imagine the experience without them. In the case of the Haunted Mansion, the vital afterthought was the Hitchhiking Ghosts, a bandied-about gimmick that perfectly encapsulated the tone of the attraction and raised the level of guest experience.

Following the success of Pirates of the Caribbean and their more frequent visits to Disneyland, X's kids

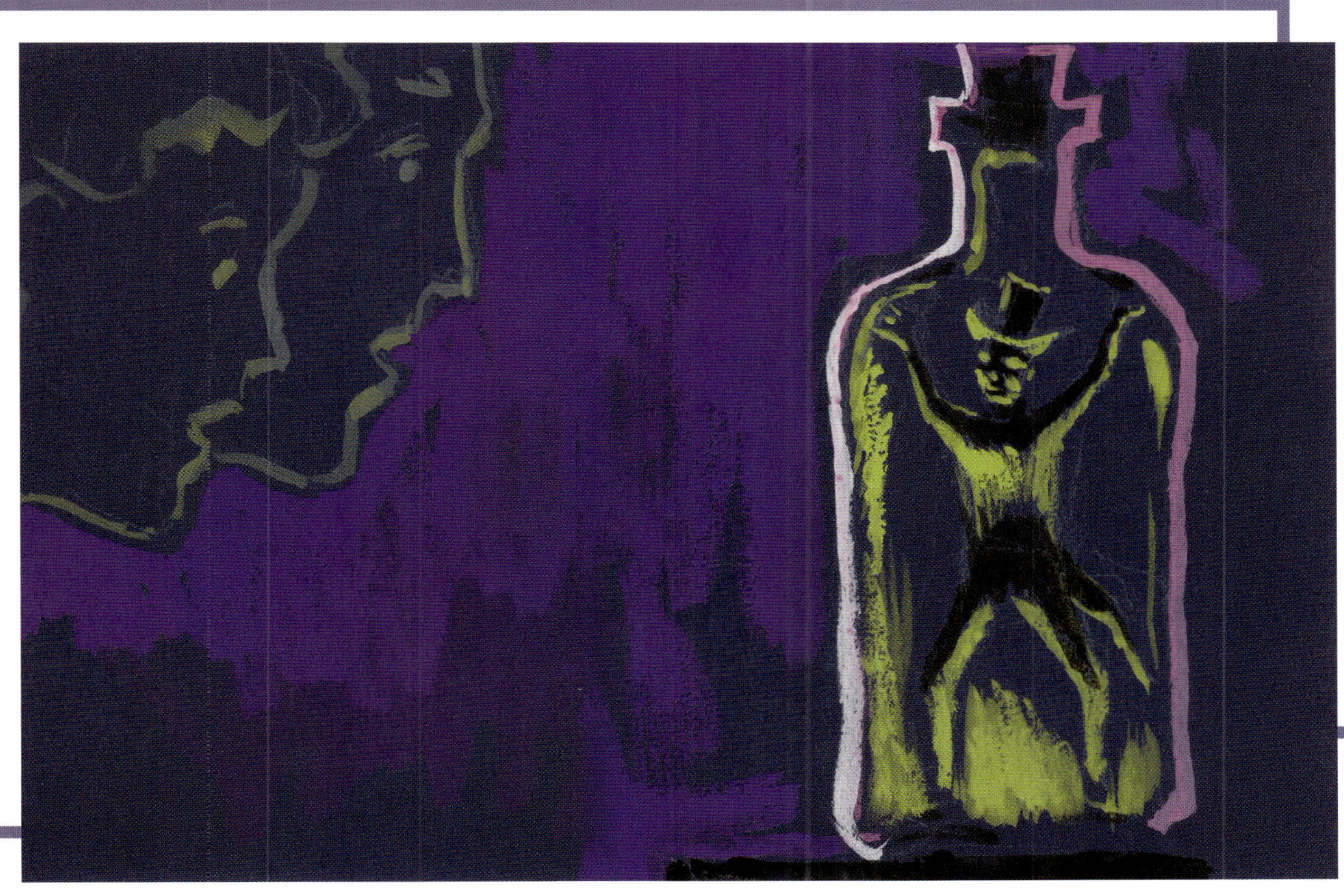

WED ENTERPRISES, INC.
MAY 13, 1969

THE HAUNTED MANSION [DISNEYLAND]
CONTINUITY AND NARRATION

"FINAL SCRIPT"

Sc. I - THE HAUNTED MANSION VESTIBULE

AN ATTENDANT OPENS THE LARGE FRONT DOORS TO ADMIT A GROUP OF APPROXIMATELY SIXTY [60] PRECOUNTED VISITORS TO THE HAUNTED MANSION WHO HAVE ASSEMBLED IN A DOUBLE QUEUE ALONG THE COVERED VERANDA. THE SPOOKY STRAINS OF A MORTUARY ORGAN SETS THE MOOD AS THEY ENTER THE DIMLY ILLUMINATED VESTIBULE OF THE HOUSE. A GHOSTLY VOICE ADDRESSES THE ASSEMBLING TOUR.

GHOST-VOICE

WHEN HINGES CREAK IN DOORLESS CHAMBERS - AND STRANGE AND FRIGHTNING SOUNDS ECHO THROUGH THE HALLS. - WHENEVER CANDLE-LIGHTS FLICKER WHERE THE AIR IS DEATHLY STILL.....THAT IS THE TIME WHEN GHOSTS ARE PRESENT, PRACTICING THEIR TERROR WITH GHOULISH DELIGHT.

Sc. II - THE PICTURE GALLERY [ELEVATOR]

THE TOUR PROCEEDS THROUGH THE VESTIBULE TO A WEIRDLY DECORATED, EERIE, CANDLE-LIT PICTURE GALLERY. THE HAUNTING VOICE OF THE GHOST-HOST IS NOW HEARD FROM THE FAR SIDE OF THE GALLERY BIDDING THE TOURISTS ENTER.

GHOST-HOST

WELCOME FOOLISH MORTALS - TO THE HAUNTED MANSION. I AM YOUR HOST - YOUR GHOST HOST.

[CHUCKLE]

KINDLY STEP ALL THE WAY IN, PLEASE - AND MAKE ROOM FOR EVERYONE....THERE'S NO TURNING BACK NOW!

OUR TOUR BEGINS HERE IN THIS GALLERY.... WHERE YOU SEE PAINTINGS OF SOME OF OUR GUESTS AS THEY APPEARED IN THEIR CORRUPTIBLE MORTAL STATE.

started to pay more attention to what their dad was working on, understanding that his job just might have been cooler than the "average" parental occupation was. Judianne and Tori knew that the Haunted Mansion was his current assignment, and so when they returned home from a friend's house where they had screened *The Haunting* (1963), they excitedly told X that he needed to watch it. Trusting his children's input, he organized a viewing for his fellow Haunted Mansion team of *The Haunting* at the office in one of the small "sweatbox" theaters traditionally used for viewing dailies. As his girls had promised, X and his team started pulling some inspiration from the film with things like the breathing and shaking doors and wallpaper making their way into the Haunted Mansion attraction.

For the attraction's script, X followed a creative process similar to what he had employed when working on Pirates of the Caribbean. He chose words that fit the story, theme, and tone, bringing to life welcoming, mischievous ghosts who seemed as though they had lived for hundreds of years. X respected his audience, never dumbing down the writing to attempt to make it mass marketable. Instead, it was smart and elevated and depicted how X expected his audience to rise to the occasion of the theme and the story's language. He never wrote for the lowest common denominator, proving that if entertaining, the attraction could thrill and educate. He also showed that if the guests understood the story's essence, they would take the words, even those vocabulary words they were unfamiliar with, and comprehend them on a subliminal level.

X's inventive and original phrases were lyrical, with statements like "your cadaverous pallor betrays an aura of foreboding, almost as though you sense a disquieting metamorphosis" encapsulating everything the attraction set out to bring to life. For the Haunted Mansion, though the song is beloved, it was the script that gained the most attention and public discourse. Even today, the Haunted Mansion script continues to make the attraction a must-see for returning and first-time visitors. Guests still stand in the attraction's Portrait Chamber and recite the script word by word, watching the room stretch and having their own individual connections in a collective communal setting.

By this point, X understood that while the script was important, the visuals needed to stand on their own. For X, the barometer of knowing that the attraction would be strong enough was that if the sound failed or was too low, or if one missed intimate little details, the visuals of the attraction still gave the sense and feel without the sound or other quality issues detracting from the guest experience. Likewise, as the attraction developed, it became a mix of building those little moments into each scene—Madame Leota leading a séance in a Séance Room, the ghostly party in the Grand Hall, and so on—with a consistent mood and tone: some darker visuals with humor that added levity to the situations. Locking the guests in the dark Portrait Chamber as the ceiling started to stretch higher and higher played into the fright, but the higher the ceiling stretched, the more comical gags were revealed, including a gentleman in a derby who is revealed to be seated on the shoulders of another well-dressed gentlemen, who sits on the shoulders of still another. All of them are sinking into quicksand. Often it was a bait and switch, scaring them and then quickly bringing them back with humor.

In other instances, X knew that in setting the scene of each of these rooms and the general experience, one often didn't have time to tell the full story of an individual character. For example, the Bride in the Haunted Mansion was just an illusion that guests traveled by and saw, but her story could either be

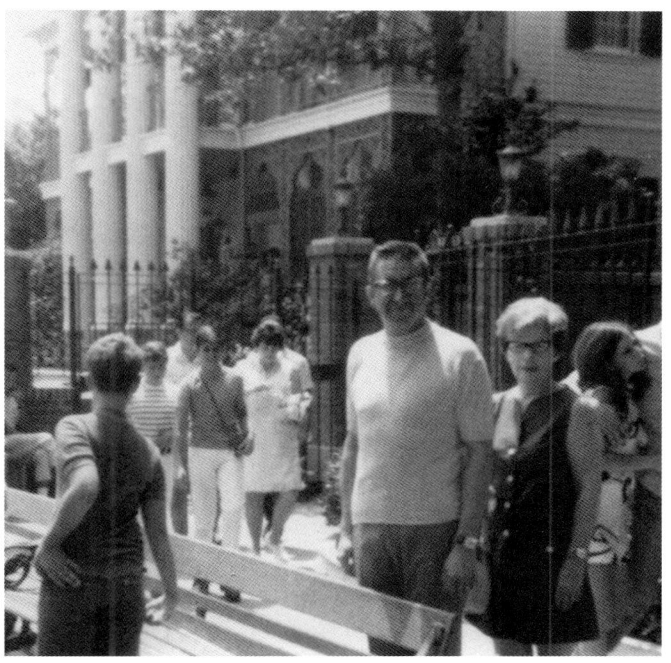

OPPOSITE: X's final script for the Haunted Mansion; ABOVE: X and Mary standing outside of Disneyland's Haunted Mansion, six days after its opening in 1969.

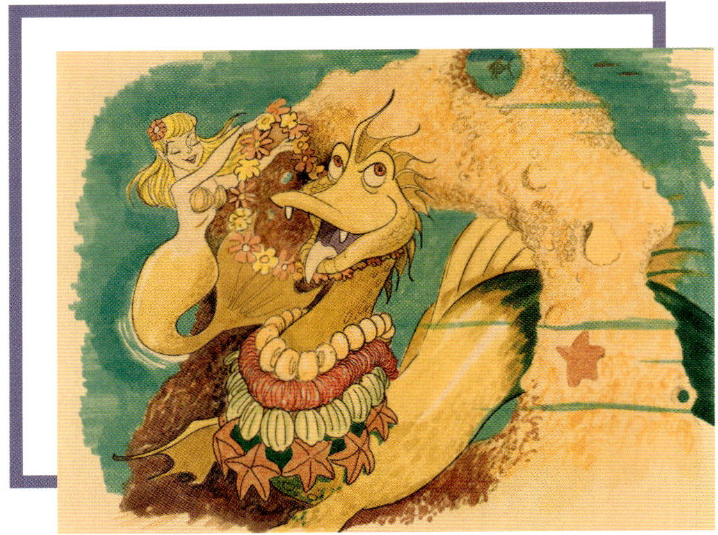

missed or interpreted to reflect a Miss Havisham–like quality.

In keeping with the new themes and traditions that occurred in X's later work, X's voice again appeared in Haunted Mansion both as a ghost in the coffin in the conservatory shouting, "Let me out of here!" and as the voice when the ride vehicles stop, imploring guests, "Please remain seated in your Doom Buggies." Outside of his own vocal talents and those Disney employees tapped by No Dough Productions, X again worked with Paul Frees, whom X hired to voice the Ghost Host. X remembered how Paul was an interesting talent and remarkable man, always coming in, spending the first half hour of a session just talking, allowing them to get a sense of how terrific he was while he would tell them about his previous work and how great he was (just to hammer home what *they'd* already noticed). Then, once Paul finally got to work, his talent resonated even clearer. He'd take the script X or another scriptwriter had created and "just run with it. Man, he was a genius," X observed. "One take! Other people would try doing it all sorts of ways. Not Paul. He ran with it, and he'd put things in and ad-lib it at exactly the right place. I couldn't think of it, but it was always a great addition."

Having worked across multiple projects with Paul, X could even see within his talents and range which projects had in fact sparked Paul's greatest "one take" and "ad-lib" abilities—the attraction Pirates of the Caribbean and the character Professor Ludwig Von Drake. Paul could become the characters, imbuing each one with an individual essence. X wouldn't correct him, instead telling him, "Keep going."

As important as the script in setting the tone of the attraction, if not more so, was the music. X once again suggested a song after finishing the script, and the Disney powers that be readily agreed. X's "Grim Grinning Ghosts" perfectly encapsulated the humor and upbeat philosophy within the otherworldly. Buddy Baker composed the score, with X again writing the lyrics. X got to know Buddy just after he finished his work on Pirates of the Caribbean. They became close friends, professionally and socially, and managed to seamlessly blend their skills to create a great working partnership. When working with Buddy, X always wrote the lyrics first. For Buddy, the lyrics inspired the composition. At times, he would have to make small changes to fit the music, but for the most part X's words remained unchanged. The Haunted Mansion marked their first collaboration and set the tone for their working style.

In reflecting on X's early work, Glenn Barker was amazed at X's ability to work with voice talent—whether professional or amateur. One of the hardest parts of working with the talent was getting the performance one wanted (and needed) without giving line readings or pre-hearing it in one's head. Instead, X was laid-back, and "let the talent be themselves." X would say, "Let's do one more for protection," but more often than not only had the talent do one or two takes, a stark contrast to some directors who would have the talent repeat and repeat the dialogue until all sides were frustrated.

Glenn Barker also recalled an earlier Haunted Mansion video that showed X directing the recording sessions and listening to Paul record the voices. At the end of the take, X instructed Paul to "try it again and kind of whisper." That specific but open feedback helped Paul nail the next take, and with that they moved on to the next piece of recording. X also loved entertaining all the talent and sound technicians by declaring after particularly fruitful performances or recordings, "It's too good for them. Ship it!" It was his favorite thing to say and showed X's ability to incorporate humor and "charm and disarm," even in the most stressful and important of circumstances.

Buddy worked over at the studio, so he would compose the music over there and then come to WED for work sessions with X. On Haunted Mansion, X and Buddy knew that the music should build along the way to match the various points at which guests arrived in the song. They saved the lyrics for the Graveyard near the end. Originally, they had assigned each vignette throughout the mansion its own lyric, but the amount of noise coming from all angles kept the listener from being able to decipher who sang what and when. Realizing the issue, X and Buddy went through and started paring back the soundtracks, leaving one main track with all the ghosts singing "Grim Grinning Ghosts." The cacophony had been distracting, and a more streamlined soundtrack let the words, ghosts, and visuals set the tone. Along with the singing busts, the mummy, opera-singing ghosts, and tea-sipping Victorian couple got their own identifiable song moments, since the guests were close enough to view and hear who was singing, and because they added another moment of levity. The score confirmed the mood. While ominous, the Haunted Mansion was a lively and fun place, a party that never ended, going on for generations. The organ heard in the Foyer might have included dark, heavier chords, but the music nonetheless built to an upbeat party tone that stayed consistent with a rollicking, swinging wake. For the Graveyard, they switched the notes to feel jazzier and more Southern, solidifying the outdoor location's Gothic Southern–mansion setting.

X also happily returned to the studio for music recording sessions, where he delighted in watching Buddy bring together twenty-five to fifty musicians to record the music they had created. When the musicians, some of whom had never played together previously, would gather, the music sheets were handed out, and they set out to bring the composition to life. Buddy would conduct, using his pencil as a baton to deftly mimic what he was saying: "Oboe. Bar 26. Do this or that." While the entire process sounded incredibly beautiful to X's untrained ear, Buddy could pick up even the smallest deviation, conducting the musicians to perfect his creation.

During the late 1960s, around 1968, X also worked on a revised script for the Submarine Voyage attraction. By this point, X was familiar with the inner workings of crafting the best experience for the guests for live theme park attractions. The original script lacked the type of playful humor that had made Pirates of the Caribbean and then Haunted Mansion such big hits. He knew he couldn't narrate the specific action with phrases like "Look, there's a mermaid!" because the ride vehicle was so long that while those seated in the front of the submarine would perhaps get a perfectly timed experience matching the dialogue, those seated toward the middle would not yet have seen her, and those guests all the way in the back would have a good few seconds before they even came close to being able to spot the mermaid. Thus, as for Pirates of the Caribbean and the Haunted Mansion, X was back to writing pithy and humorous general statements about mermaids, sea monsters, and other exciting sea creatures, capturing the audience's attention with spectacle, heart, humor, and mystery, ultimately allowing viewers to draw their own conclusions.

Within just a few years, X had weathered an entirely new Disney landscape. He went from the safety of his secure partnership making experimental shorts and putting his creative stamp on larger hybrid live-action/animated features at the studio with Bill Justice to WED, now part of Walt Disney Productions, where he forged a completely new path led only by the small, unexplained glimmer of light from Walt's trust in his talents. X frequently said, "Walt had an uncanny ability to see talents in people that they didn't see in themselves." Yet again, Walt's correct bet on X and other like-minded Disney artists proved that he was indeed the person who understood story—in a growing and unmatched number of mediums—perhaps better than anyone else. And while X was less sure, he didn't want to let Walt down, and he found the strength and abilities within himself to outshine Walt's expectations.

While Walt didn't see the official opening of Pirates of the Caribbean or the reception to its enduring legacy, he trusted X to take on not only the new task of script-writing, but lyric-writing as well. Pirates of the Caribbean marked a dramatic pivot in X's career, officially shifting him away from animation, design, and story development to a larger central creative role as a scriptwriter and lyricist for some of the most globally known and enduring Disney theme park attractions. X's successful foundation at the studio in these vital elements—including his involvements with musically driven experimental stop-motion short films—formed the basis of his own understanding of story and audience reactions, giving him the building blocks to craft witty, emotionally moving, thrilling experiences for generations of guests.

OPPOSITE: X's drawing of the Sea Monster for 20,000 Leagues Under the Sea: Submarine Voyage.

7

Final Years at Imagineering

ASCENDING TO A NEW ECHELON AT WED, X found himself under the direct oversight of John Hench and Marty Sklar, the principal creative executive at WED, along with a host of other talents.

Following the success of Disneyland, Walt's dream of building a larger resort destination was finally realized with the 1971 opening of the Magic Kingdom near Orlando, Florida. Walt Disney World, unlike Disneyland, was envisioned and constructed on enough land that there was room left for continued growth, both inside and outside the park berm. As Walt Disney World's development became the top priority, X began working on some new attractions for Magic Kingdom. The first, If You Had Wings (1972), was an Omnimover ride in Tomorrowland. Sponsored by Eastern Air Lines, one of the four big domestic airlines at the time, the attraction was structured similarly to Adventure Thru Inner Space but took guests on a leisurely journey to destinations serviced by the airline, such as Mexico, Puerto Rico, Bermuda, Jamaica, and New Orleans.

That If You Had Wings resembled Adventure Thru Inner Space shouldn't have been a surprise, given both were designed by the same creative team–Claude Coats and X, who now was writing the song lyrics (set against music by Buddy Baker). X's theme song of the same name, "If You Had Wings," clearly stated the attraction's message and Eastern Air Lines' advertisement: that "If you had wings, you could do many things, you could widen your world." With the repeated chorus of "if you had wings" set against wanderlust-inspiring, nostalgia-inducing music, guests experienced the dioramas of far-flung locations to which they may or may not have ever traveled, and left the attraction perhaps longing to book a trip of their own. As riders exited the attraction, disembarking into an area complete with an Eastern Air Lines travel desk, actor/director Orson Welles's voice floated up, guiding guests with a final mantra: "You do have wings. You can do all these things. You can widen your world. Eastern: the wings of man."

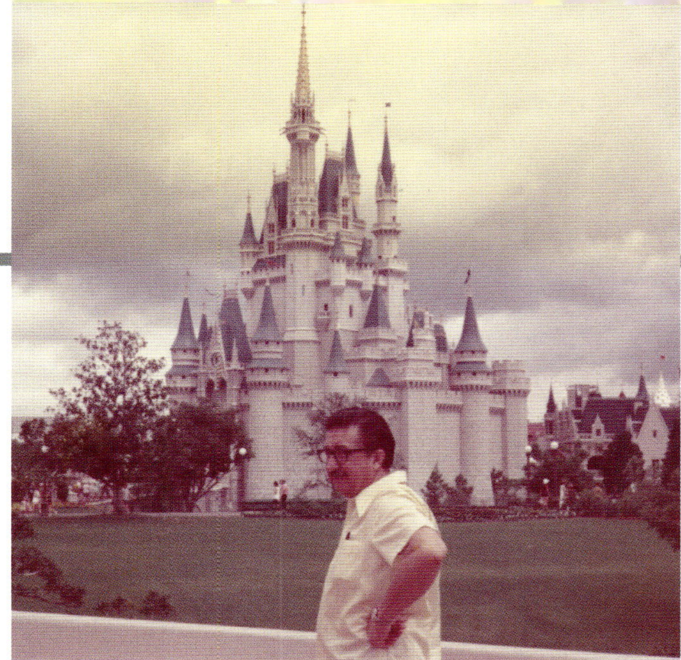

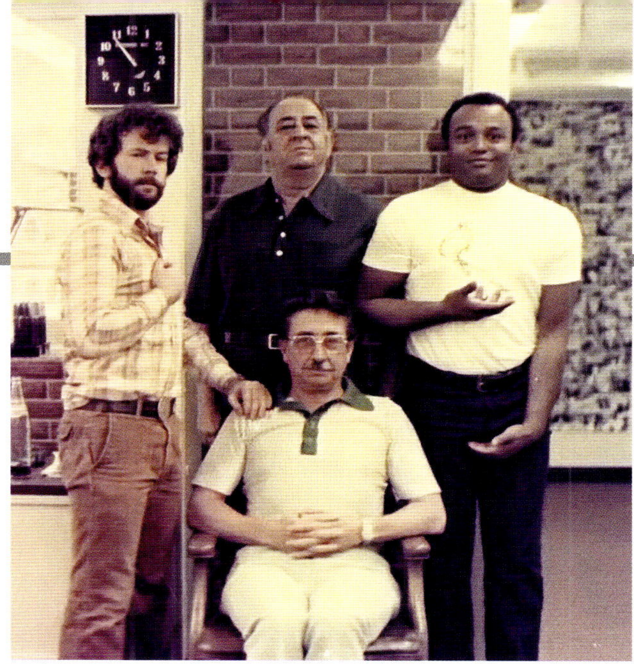

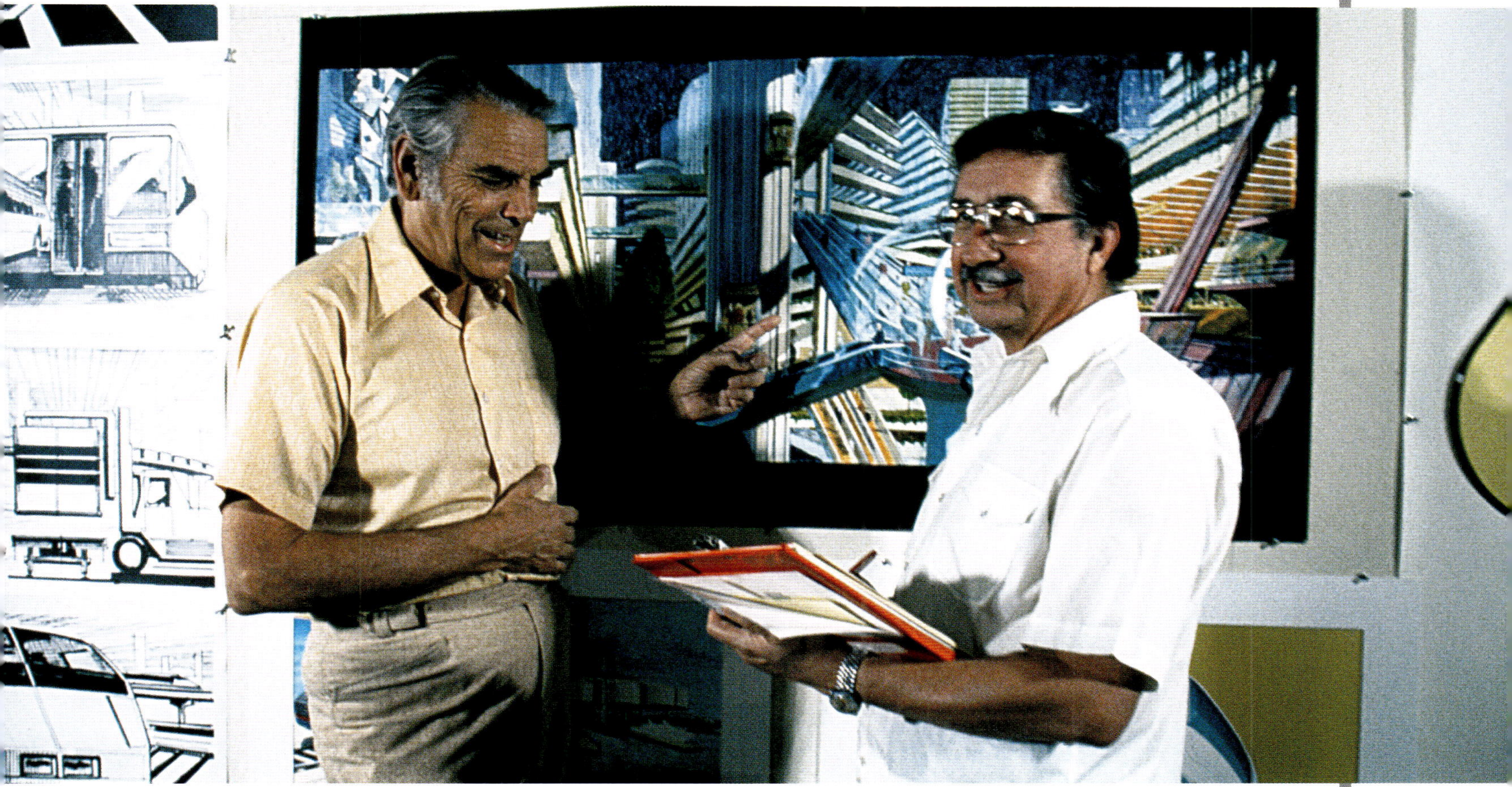

X's lyrics again needed to set the tone of each room's setting, giving guests a general sense of the specifics of each diverse place shown without narrating the events. Likewise, X and Buddy needed to create a warm and catchy tune that was timeless and aspirational while keeping the attraction from feeling too commercialized, a feat they managed to accomplish. Ultimately, If You Had Wings remained in Magic Kingdom for fifteen years, until it closed on June 1, 1987, when Eastern Air Lines withdrew its sponsorship of the attraction, just four years before the carrier went out of business.

TOP (LEFT): X standing in front of Cinderella Castle at Florida's Magic Kingdom; TOP (RIGHT): X (SEATED) with (LEFT TO RIGHT) Gary Goddard, Al Bertino, and Phil Mendez goofing around at WED; ABOVE: Claude Coats and X working on EPCOT's World of Motion.

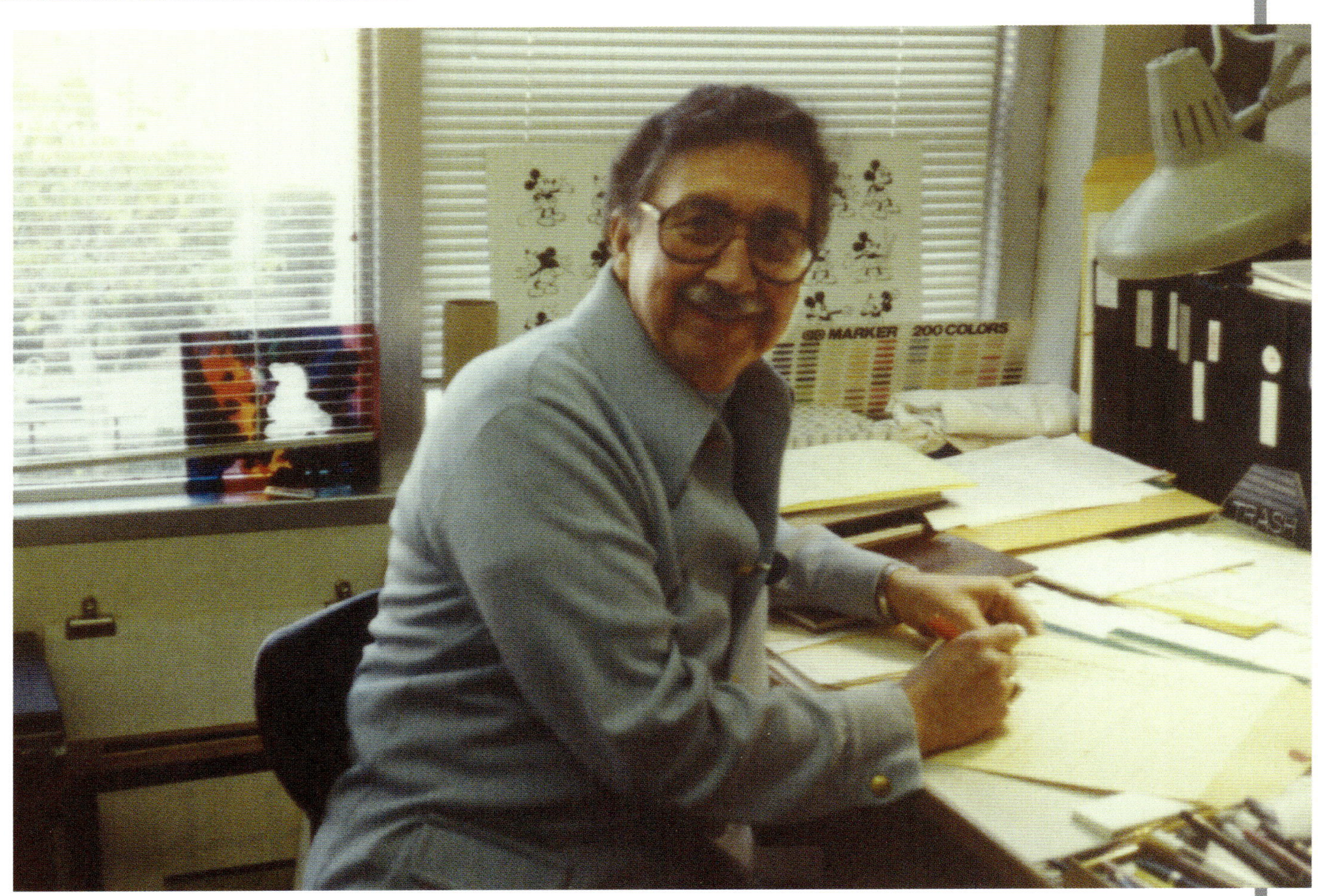
MARKER 200 COLORS
TRASH

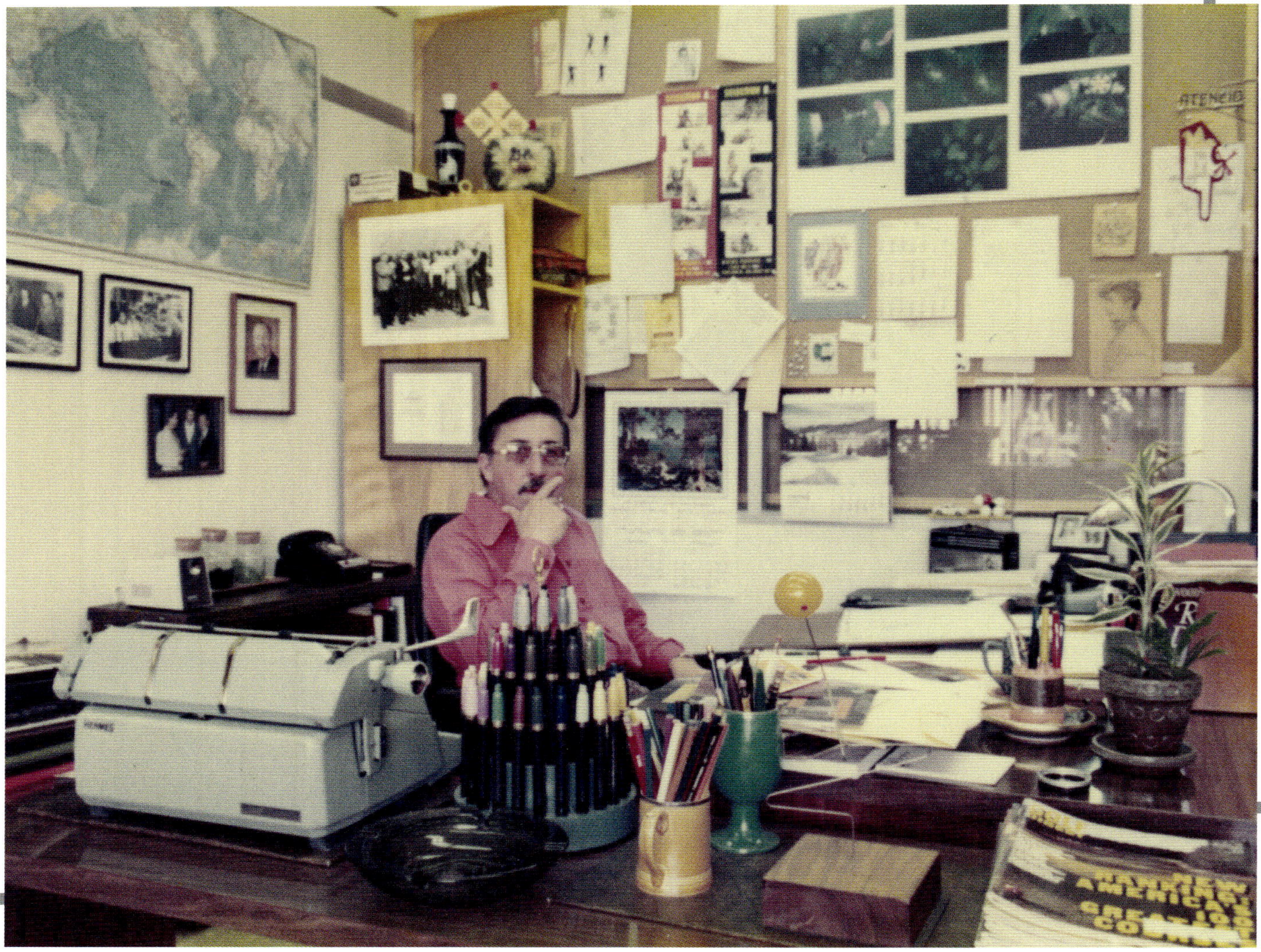

From there, X and Buddy went to work on Space Mountain, which was set to open in 1975 at the Magic Kingdom. Buddy composed the music and X wrote the lyrics for "Here's to the Future and You." RCA sponsored the attraction, helping with some of the funding. An instrumental version of "Here's to the Future and You" played at the entrance of the attraction. After guests disembarked from the attraction, they again heard the tune, this time with lyrics, as scenes were shown of a family interacting with new and futuristic technologies. The upbeat and catchy lyrics promoted hope for the future and in society, encouraging guests to be the best version of themselves with the help of new technological innovations: "Here's to the future! Here's to the future! Here's to the future! Here's to the future and you! It's a world full of color, of perfect harmony. A world full of music, a living melody. The dreams of tomorrow are beginning today. It's a world of discovery, the world of RCA . . . so here's to the future that's coming into view . . . RCA leads the way." Encapsulating the full scope into another pithy song, X established RCA as the leader of innovation, ushering the average family into the future, a future that very much relied on the achievements and actions of the present moment.

By this time, X wasn't the only Atencio employed at WED. As was common then, many of the animators and Imagineers would get summer jobs at Disney for their growing children, mostly in what were deemed "rite of passage" roles in the model shop, research library, and mail room. In 1972, X's eldest child, Tori, started her first summer job at Disney, and she came back for each of her four summers during college. She worked in accounting and at the research library, and she filled in for the executive assistants when they went on vacation. During one such short-term assignment, Tori served as John Hench's temporary assistant, when his usual assistant, Edie Flynn, went on vacation. In 1976, upon graduating from Loyola Marymount University (where she studied interior design), Tori applied for a job in the Interiors Department at WED, inspired by her experiences interning there. Having found her own niche in the company that was becoming the "family business," she was officially hired and never looked back.

Judianne came next, interning for one summer in the library and filling in as Marty Sklar's assistant when Marty's assistant Irene was home sick. Judianne was sent to the executive office area known as the "Gold Coast" to fill in for her and was told that all she had to do was answer the phones and take messages. As is always the universe's way, however, when one is told it'll be easy and "all there is to do is . . . ," there's usually more to it. Judianne looked up to find esteemed author Ray Bradbury walking through the door with some papers. He was looking for Marty, who wasn't in the office. Bradbury then handed

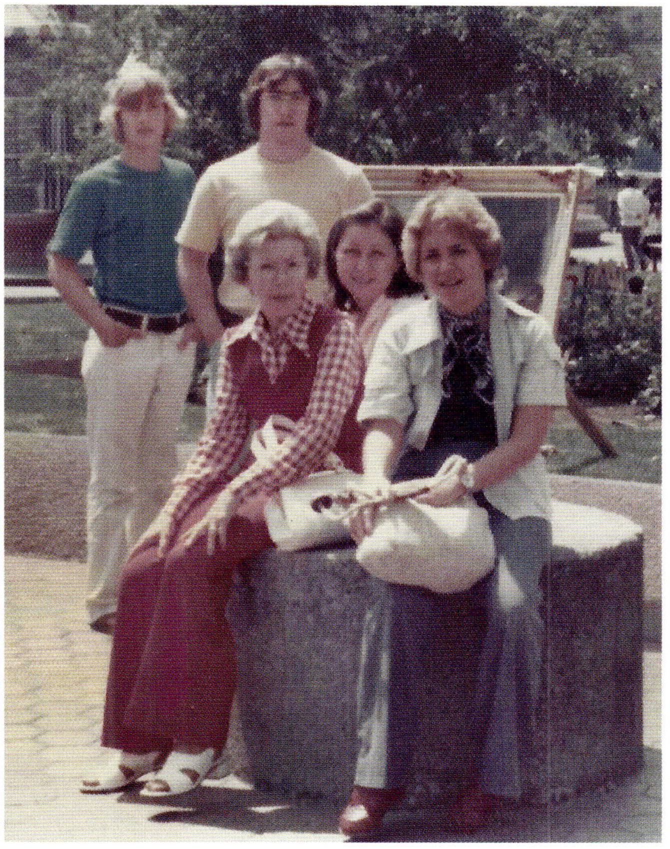

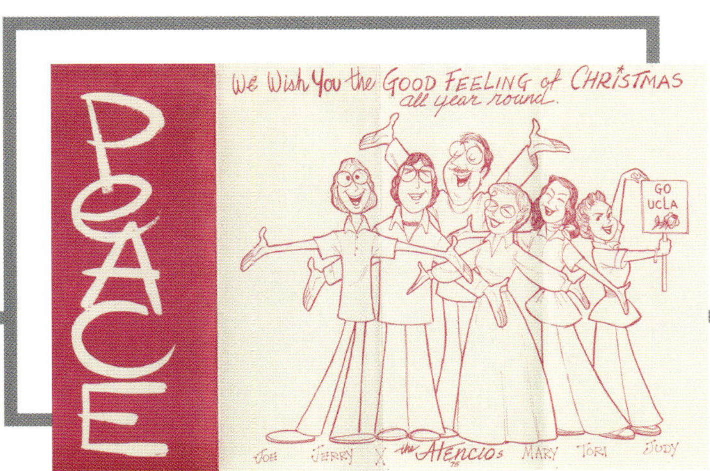

OPPOSITE: X at work in his WED office; LEFT: X's Christmas card featuring the family, 1975; ABOVE: Joe and Jerry (BACK ROW), with Mary, Tori, and Judianne (IN FRONT), from around the time all the kids were working at Disney.

Judianne the papers, marked up with his loopy penmanship, and asked her to type up his revised treatment for Spaceship Earth, the icon attraction of the next park project underway: EPCOT. Awestruck, Judianne readily agreed, and she used more correction tape than typewriter ribbon to properly retype his draft. While her secretarial days were short-lived, Judianne went on to spend three additional years reigning full-time over the WED library's front check-out desk, from 1976 to 1979.

In the meantime, Joe worked at Disney in 1978 in the studio's Riverside warehouse with the accounting department and then with the fixed asset accounting division when he returned to intern in 1979. Not to be left out, Jerry also worked at Disney in 1978, covering traffic (aka mail) at the studio. The number of Atencios working at Disney in the late 1970s was consistently evolving as the children forged their own careers and went in and out of internships, but during the summer of 1978, X and all four of his children worked at Disney.

Family members would often carpool to work with X. X would put two of the children with him in his Porsche—one child in the front seat and one child (always Judianne) in the back, stuck in the jump seat. Forever one to know the importance of details, X had a vanity license plate on his Porsche that read C X GO, making his car a Disney celebrity sighting in its own right.

While each child spent time working at X's beloved Disney, only Tori remained for her post-college profession, having used her open door to prove her talents and abilities and recognizing the WED Interiors Department as the perfect place to foster her career and creative pursuits. For the others, while they treasured their time at Disney and the memories they had made, they realized that their careers and futures lay elsewhere, far from the soundstages and theme parks.

Walt's final dream for Florida's "Vacation Kingdom" was now underway: building his Experimental Prototype Community of Tomorrow, more commonly known as EPCOT. This was to be the first Disney park without a castle, steering into an entirely new concept, different from any park Disney had ever built before, and thus requiring an entire slate of new attractions. X was one of the people entrusted to this new area in Walt Disney World. His first assignment was for the EPCOT attraction Spaceship Earth, originally sponsored by the

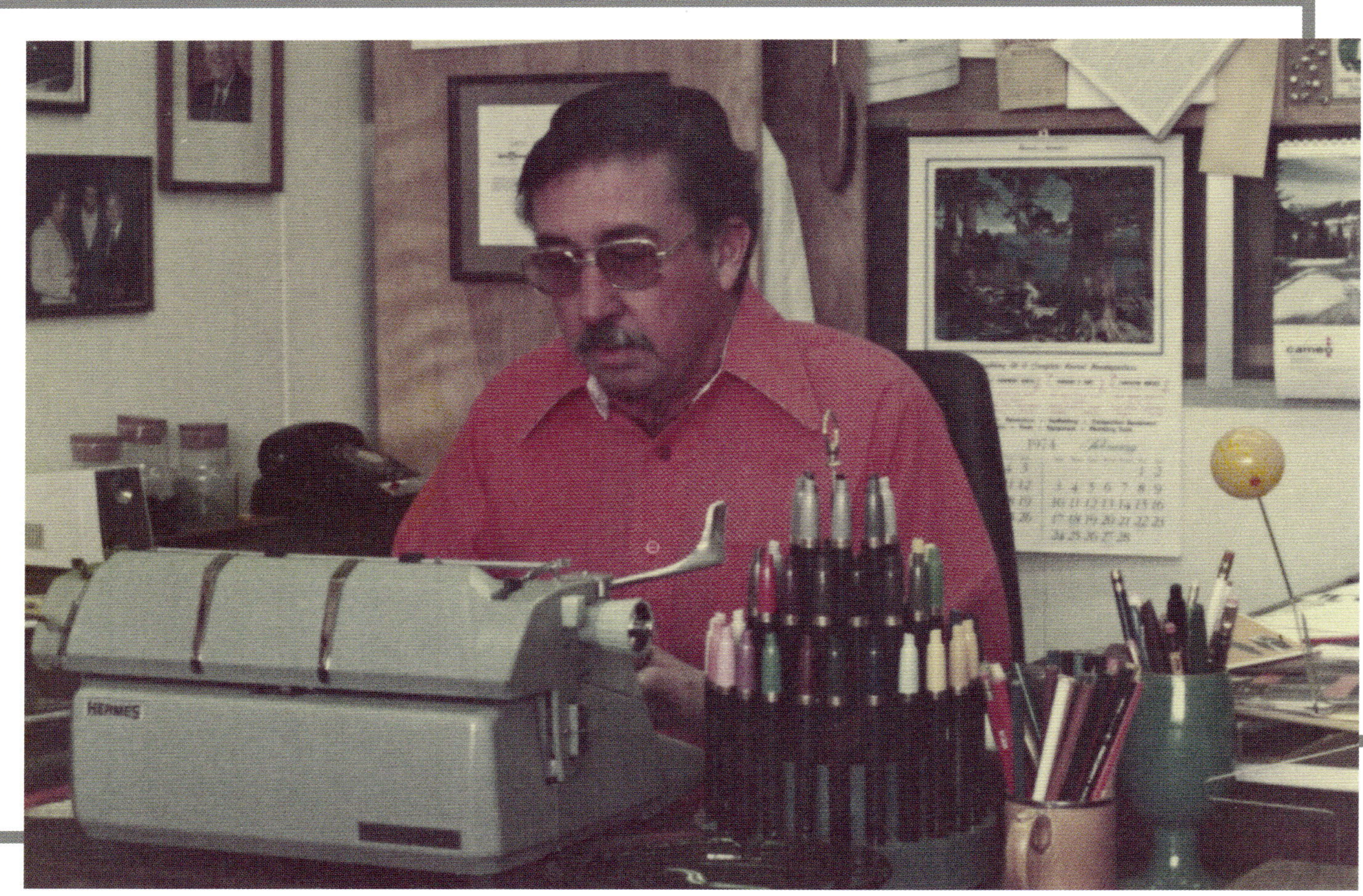

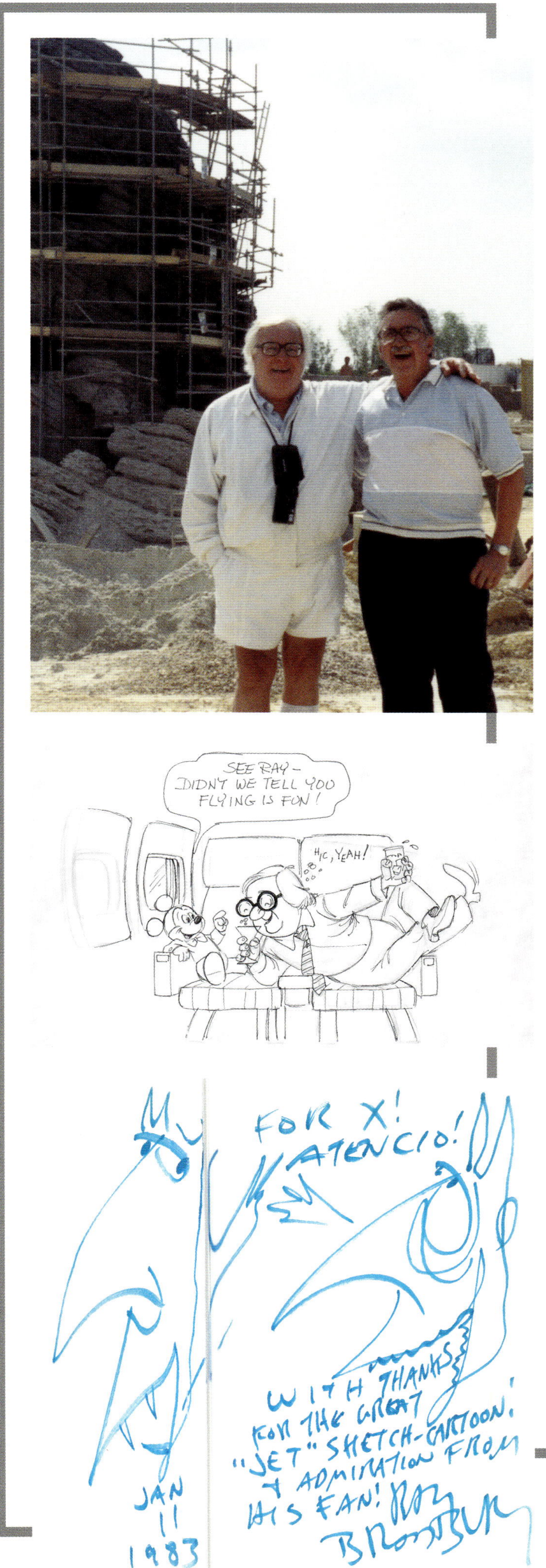

Bell System, whose parent company was AT&T. As the park icon, Spaceship Earth was planned to open with EPCOT on October 1, 1982. The fifteen-minute attraction would use an Omnimover ride system to take guests on a time machine journey through different breakthroughs in human communication. To successfully establish the differing tone for EPCOT, renowned science fiction writer Ray Bradbury was hired to write the story treatment for the attraction, as noted earlier. X took Ray's treatment and wrote the script for the attraction, making sure to enhance the design and properly reflect the history that was present in the attraction. X found Ray Bradbury to be "a very fascinating man, an intellectual fellow, very interesting to work with." X also was again working with those recording the voices, including Vic Perrin, a radio man, who did the narration for Spaceship Earth. With his great ear for talent, X noted that Vic's voice was "resonant, good, and rich." While they had him do the recording a few times, X knew that even the last one didn't live up to Vic's first take. Vic's innate talents, plus the spontaneity on his first take's delivery, infused with a radio man's skill of doing it live, meant X knew the first take was the best take for the attraction—narratively and emotionally.

At the opening of EPCOT, X and Ray Bradbury were among the attendees. Despite being one of the most famous science fiction writers of the time, Ray was afraid of flying and had never been on an airplane. After a canceled train, and with no other way to get home, Ray was out of options and said to X and the other Disney people, "Put three double martinis in me and put me on a plane." To calm his nerves, X drew a card of Ray with Mickey on a plane drinking a martini to commemorate the occasion. Ray loved the illustration, which perfectly embodied his getting over his fear of flying, and as a token of his gratitude, he signed a copy of his book *Long After Midnight*, complete with a few sketches of his own. In a correspondence with WED show designer and executive Pat Scanlon, Ray wrote, *Dear Pat, Thanks for your letter and the enclosure. Wonderful! Super! Great! I have written to X. Atencio to thank him personally, and to send him one of mybooks* [sic] *in which I have*

OPPOSITE: X with his favorite typewriter; LEFT (TOP): Ray Bradbury and X on the construction site of Disneyland Paris; LEFT (MIDDLE): The underdrawing of the card X drew for Ray Bradbury to commemorate his first flight; LEFT (BOTTOM): A 1983 inscription from Ray Bradbury in his book thanking X for the kind card.

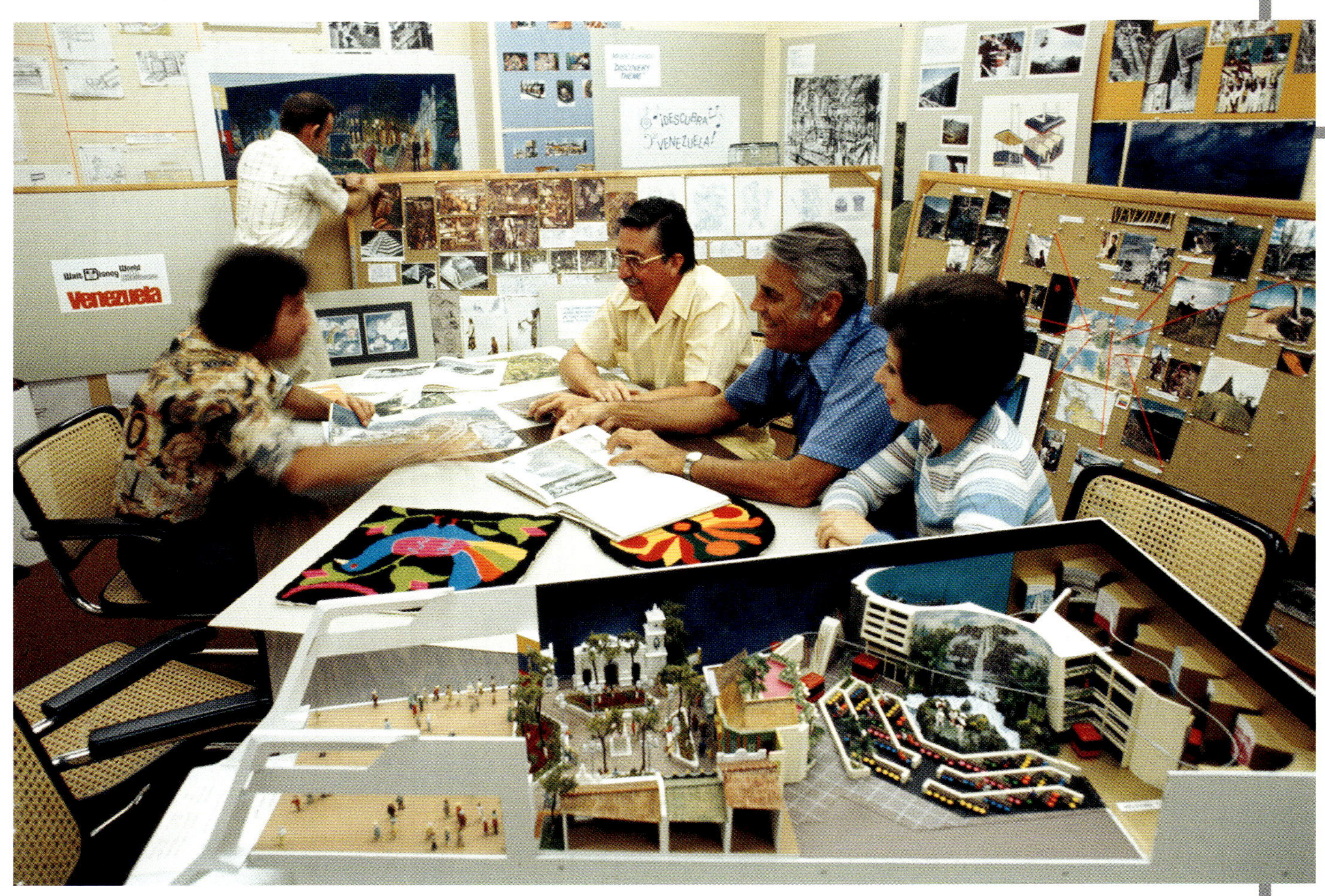
Walt Disney World
Venezuela
¡DESCUBRA VENEZUELA!

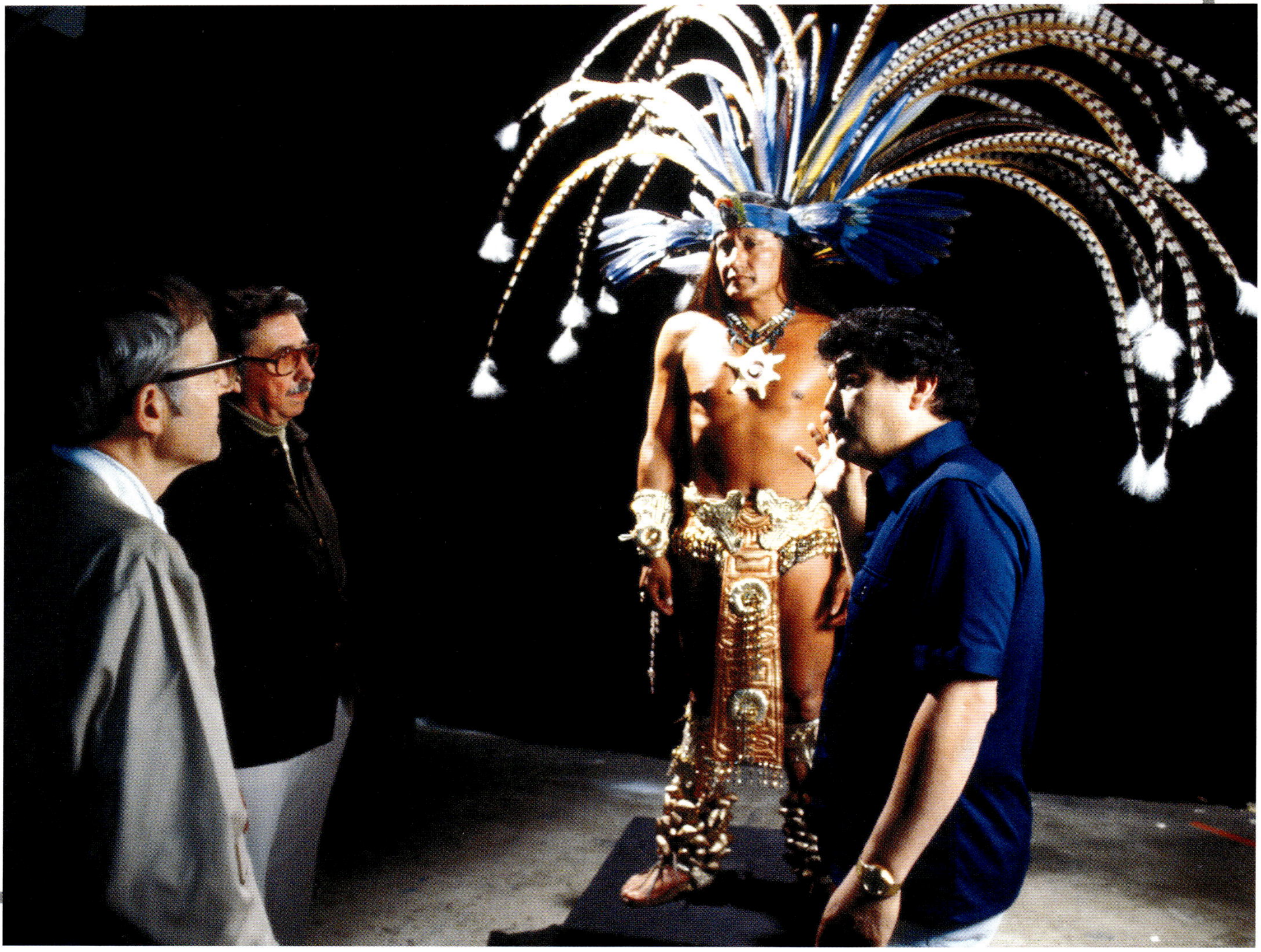

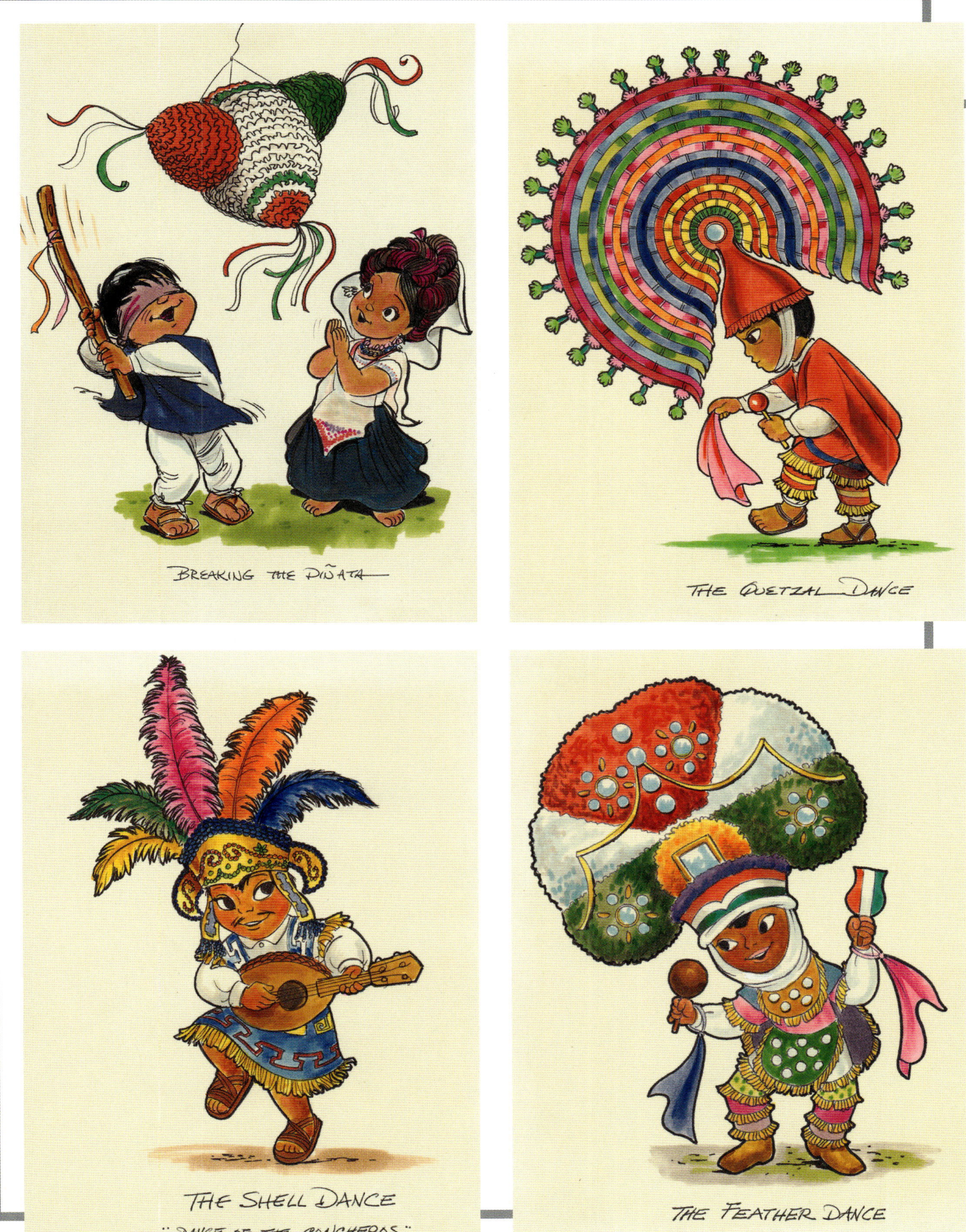

OPPOSITE (TOP): X, Claude Coats, and other team members designing EPCOT's Mexico pavilion; OPPOSITE (BOTTOM): X, Blaine Gibson, and Eddie Martinez reviewing a model for EPCOT's Mexico pavilion; ABOVE: A selection of X's drawings for EPCOT's Mexico pavilion.

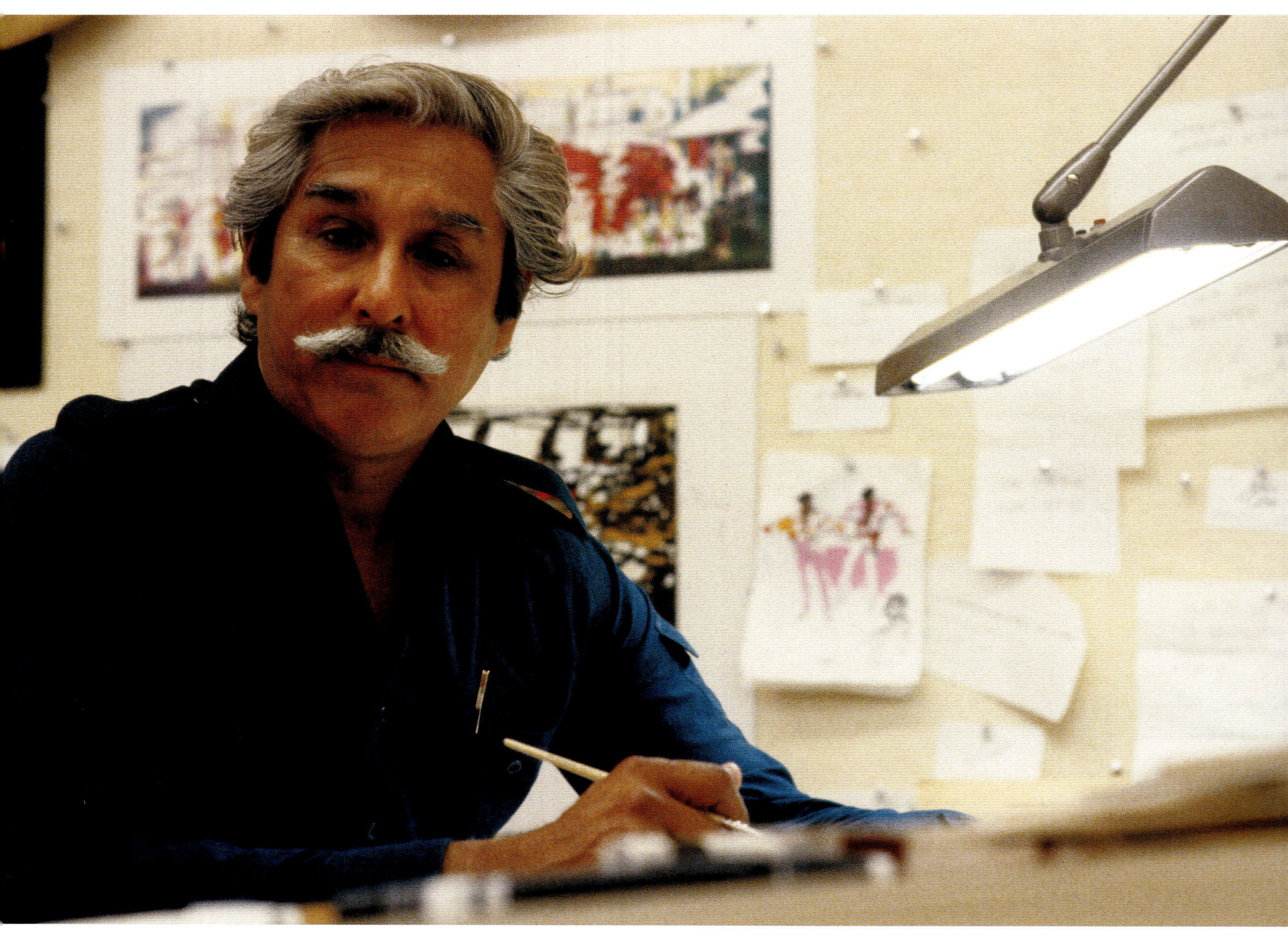

sketched one of my own – rather bad – cartoons! What an experience! not [sic] *only to fly, but to wind up flying with – the Mouse! Affectionate best to one and all, Ray.* Pat sent this around via an interoffice communication memo for all relevant parties, including X. Meanwhile, X received his direct gift from Ray, the autographed book, complete with cartoon drawings that read *FOR X! ATENCIO! WITH THANKS FOR THE GREAT JET SKETCH CARTOON + ADMIRATION FROM HIS FAN! RAY BRADBURY.* In an interview years later, Ray said, "I discovered along the way, I wasn't afraid of flying, I was just afraid of me . . . so I learned that lesson and then I flew to Paris and to London and to all the other places in the world . . . by flying. Thank God for that." Ray's conquering his fear of flying led him not only around the world, but also, almost as if out of a storybook, to another meeting with X years later, when X was visiting his daughter Tori. She was living and working in Paris at the time, and X and Ray were reunited at the construction site of what is now Disneyland Paris.

X's next original show-concept creation was the Mexico pavilion at the World Showcase in EPCOT. The main attraction in the Mexico pavilion was El Rio

ABOVE: Artist Ray Aragon drawing at his desk; OPPOSITE: A portrait of X drawn by colleague Ray Aragon.

Del Tiempo, a boat ride that included films projected onto small screens and set against elaborate sets with dancing Audio-Animatronics figures and music, echoing X's earlier work on If You Had Wings. X had been envisioning the original concept of the pavilion and then building the best possible team to help bring the idea to life. To that end, he had reached out to Eddie Martinez, an artist who had done work for WED over the years and had previously gotten to know X through colleagues when Eddie worked on the Hall of Presidents attraction for the Magic Kingdom at Walt Disney World. Eddie wasn't working at Disney at the time; instead he owned a little gallery in East Los Angeles and was focused on his own art. Eddie agreed to meet with X, and when they got together, X explained his current plight on the Mexico pavilion. Collin Campbell, working wherever Claude needed him, had been collaborating with X on the design and presentation for the Mexico pavilion. They decided to present to a group of UCLA exchange students from Mexico to get some fresh but culturally relevant eyes on their work. They gave the students the presentation and a questionnaire, using their responses as early audience testing, and unfortunately, they had failed. The responses of the queried students were largely consistent: the artifice was apparent, and they urged them to go to Mexico to actually see the cultures they were attempting to re-create.

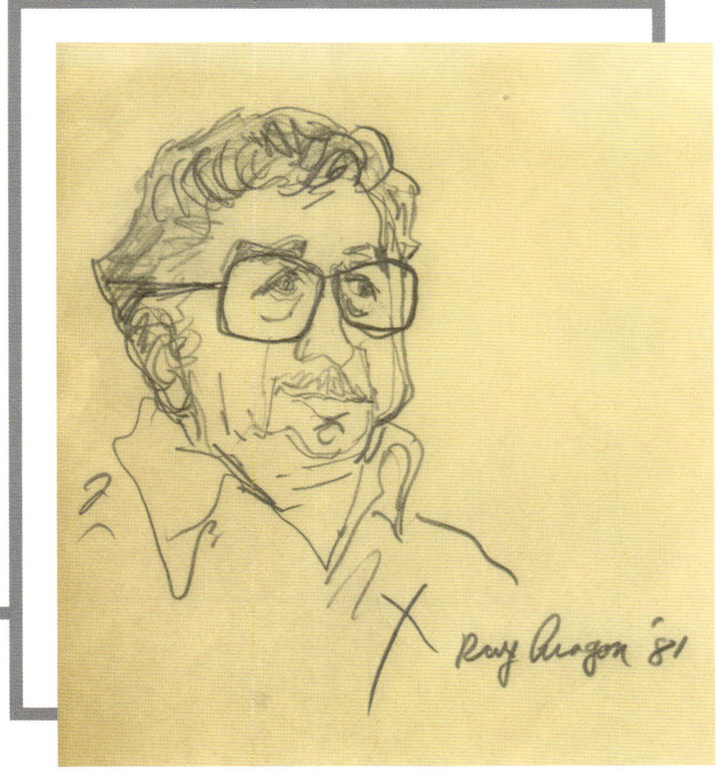

As with most forms of problem-solving and kismet, X knew he needed another set of fresh eyes and vision within Disney to help authentically shape the Mexico pavilion. Recently, Eddie had been in between jobs, struggling to find his next gig. His wife, Jessie, urged him to go to Mexico instead of wallowing or letting the stress of securing employment consume him. She said that she knew he had wanted to go all his life, and now was the time. Eddie went with a friend, driving their station wagon, complete with sleeping bags for their car "hotel," and toured Mexico for about a month, learning the ins and outs of the culture. After arriving back in California, Eddie invited friends and family to his one-man art show at Goa Studios to exhibit his art that had been creatively and culturally influenced by his trip. X and other friends and former colleagues from Disney came out to support him. For X, his attendance at his friend's art show turned out to be serendipity, giving him the trusted Disney voice in the room to elevate the project to the level at which X and the UCLA exchange students knew it needed to be to stand the test of time and hold itself up as a beacon of the Disney brand.

X officially brought Eddie onto the project as an art director, and the first thing Eddie did in his new role was hire Ray Aragon, a friend who also hung out in East Los Angeles and knew a lot of the same people, works, and influences in Chicano art, their own culture that inspired them and their creations. Eddie and X, also a friend of Ray's, called Ray in 1980 and asked him to leave the smaller studio he was working at and join them on this project. Ray accepted and came on as costume designer and art director for certain parts of the attraction.

One reason for emphasizing the importance of the mission and coming in on time and on budget was that during the design phases of EPCOT, Disney was still exploring different ideas for EPCOT's World Showcase, namely what exactly each pavilion would look like and how they would fund it. Coming off the success of the New York World's Fair and corporate sponsorships for various attractions, the Disney executives creatively pitched the idea of seeing if the countries they were depicting would be interested in synergistically partnering on the pavilions, sharing or covering the production and construction costs and ensuring the cultural legitimacy of their "World Showcase." To properly present their pitches and solicit these countries, the executives and WED project designers met with a select delegation from Mexico at Walt Disney World. Given his role on the creative end of the project, X wound up on the Disney company plane with Marty, John Hench, Orlando Ferrante, and many other WED executives headed for Orlando.

After an initial all-hands meeting with the Mexico contingent, they split off into two separate groups: a business group and a creative group. In the creative one, Disney was represented by X and Eddie, both of whom spoke Spanish and were able to converse with their creative Mexican counterparts in their native tongue. That was until X and Eddie quickly realized that their Spanish wasn't nearly good enough to effectively communicate the aesthetic nuance of their World Showcase vision and ensure a partnership with Disney. Appreciating X and Eddie's efforts and speaking some English themselves, the Mexico team and the Disney team cordially agreed that they could flip back and forth between English and Spanish as needed to all understand each other and the finer details of the project at hand.

Afterward, the two groups reunited to discuss potential collaboration. The Mexico group said that they knew WED was designing Tokyo Disneyland in Japan while simultaneously constructing EPCOT. They pitched the idea that if Disney also built a theme park in Mexico City, they would then sponsor the EPCOT Mexico pavilion. One person in the Disney contingent smiled, shirtsleeves rolled up, and expressed their interest but then said with Tokyo and Florida, they just didn't have the bandwidth to consider it. With disappointment lingering on all sides, it was decided that WED would have to foot the bill for the Mexico pavilion or find other means of financing. Consequently, X, Eddie, and the rest of their team knew it was now more important than ever to stick to schedule and budget, as there would be no extra money coming from an outside benefactor in the foreseeable future.

After that, Disney cautiously scaled back on the costs of the World Showcase, deciding that only certain countries could have rides and shows as attractions. For the rest, the country's atmospheric pavilion would serve as the main attraction. To fairly choose countries, each group had to pitch their presentation for their attraction. Mexico was one of the few chosen to get an attraction, and at that point X called Eddie, and they were back to work on bringing their concepts to life.

While X was always in line and working with Eddie on all phases of the projects, sharing artwork, talking story, et cetera, he trusted Eddie to handle conversations with Marty and others to bring the project to life on time and on budget with the best team. According to Eddie, "X was everywhere. He was all over. When we were filming the Mexican dancers and all of that at the studio stages, X was there. He was helping with the casting on the scenes." X also worked to script all the smaller pieces of narration and interacted with the writers on the show. X was the one who came up with the storyline and walk-through of the attraction and envisioned the presentation of how it would all fuse together. They

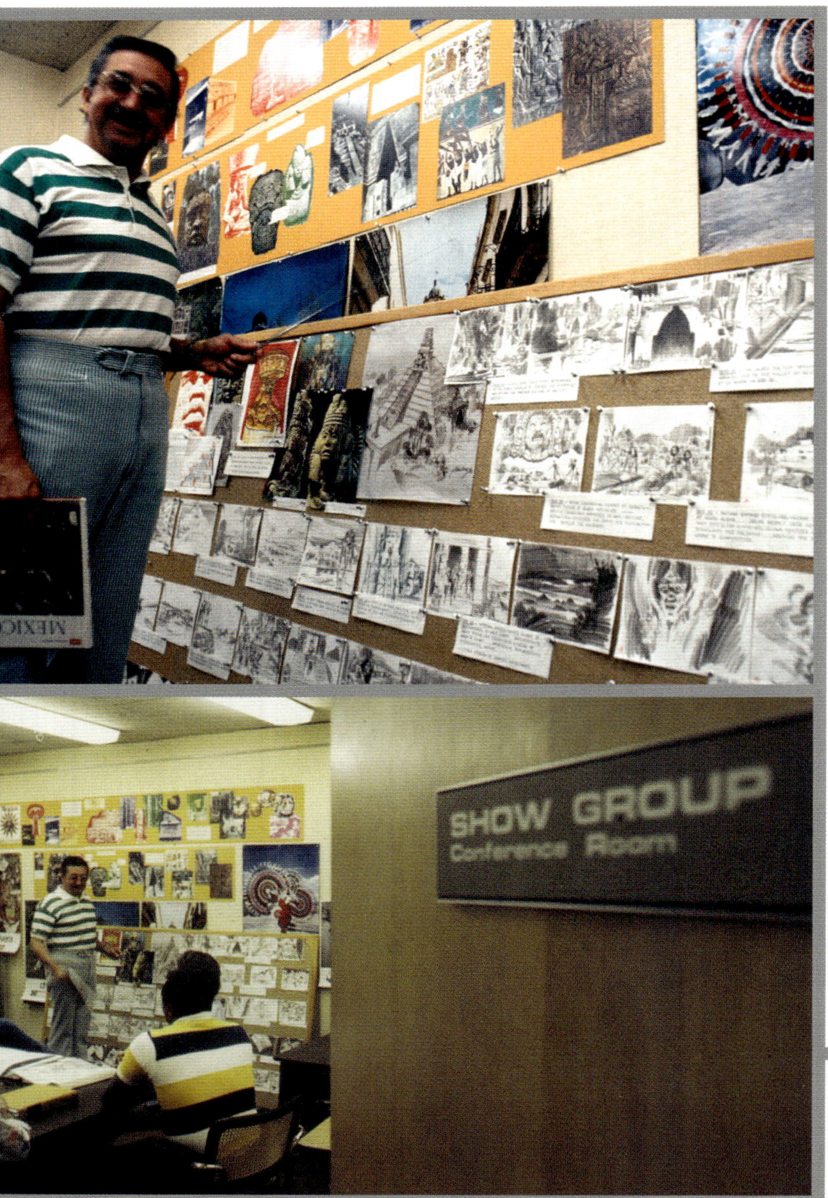

LEFT: X reviewing storyboards with the Show Group for the Mexico pavilion; OPPOSITE: X at the Mexico pavilion in EPCOT.

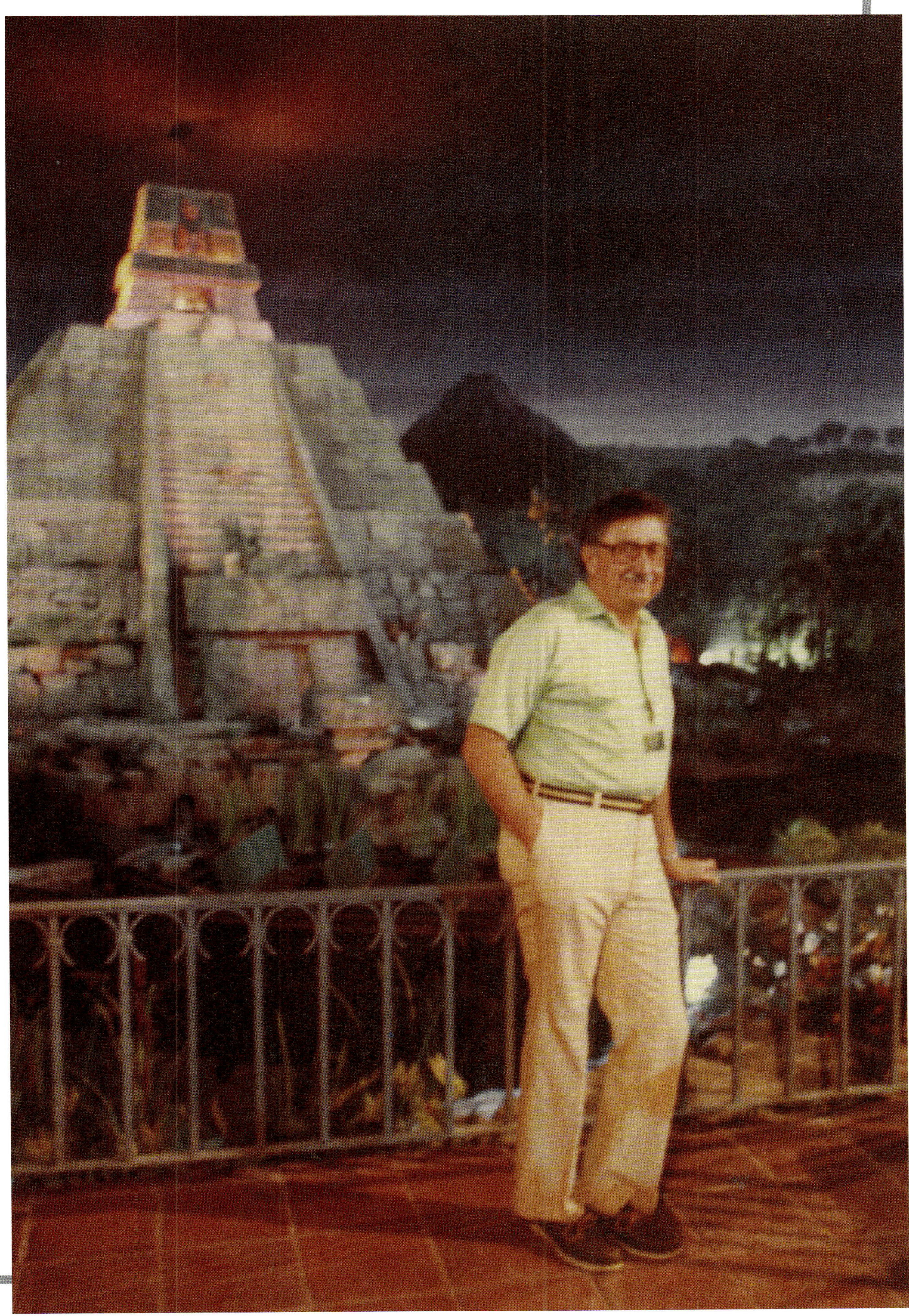

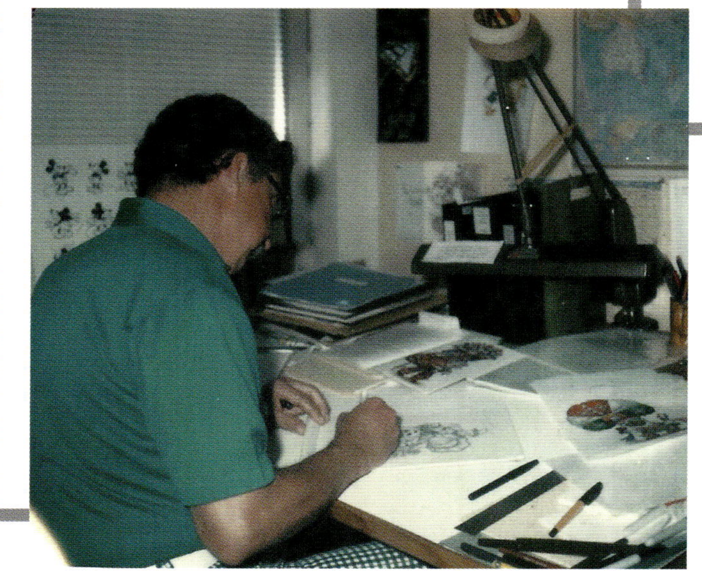

had a big team, working together to design set pieces. There would be a beautiful restaurant like Blue Bayou at Disneyland's Pirates of the Caribbean, but even more elevated. They were designing a sixty-by-forty-foot backdrop that they painted at MGM Studios, and they wanted to have smoke come out of the painting of the volcano. Eddie told Marty that he needed space in the warehouse to build the model of the show. Marty said they had never done

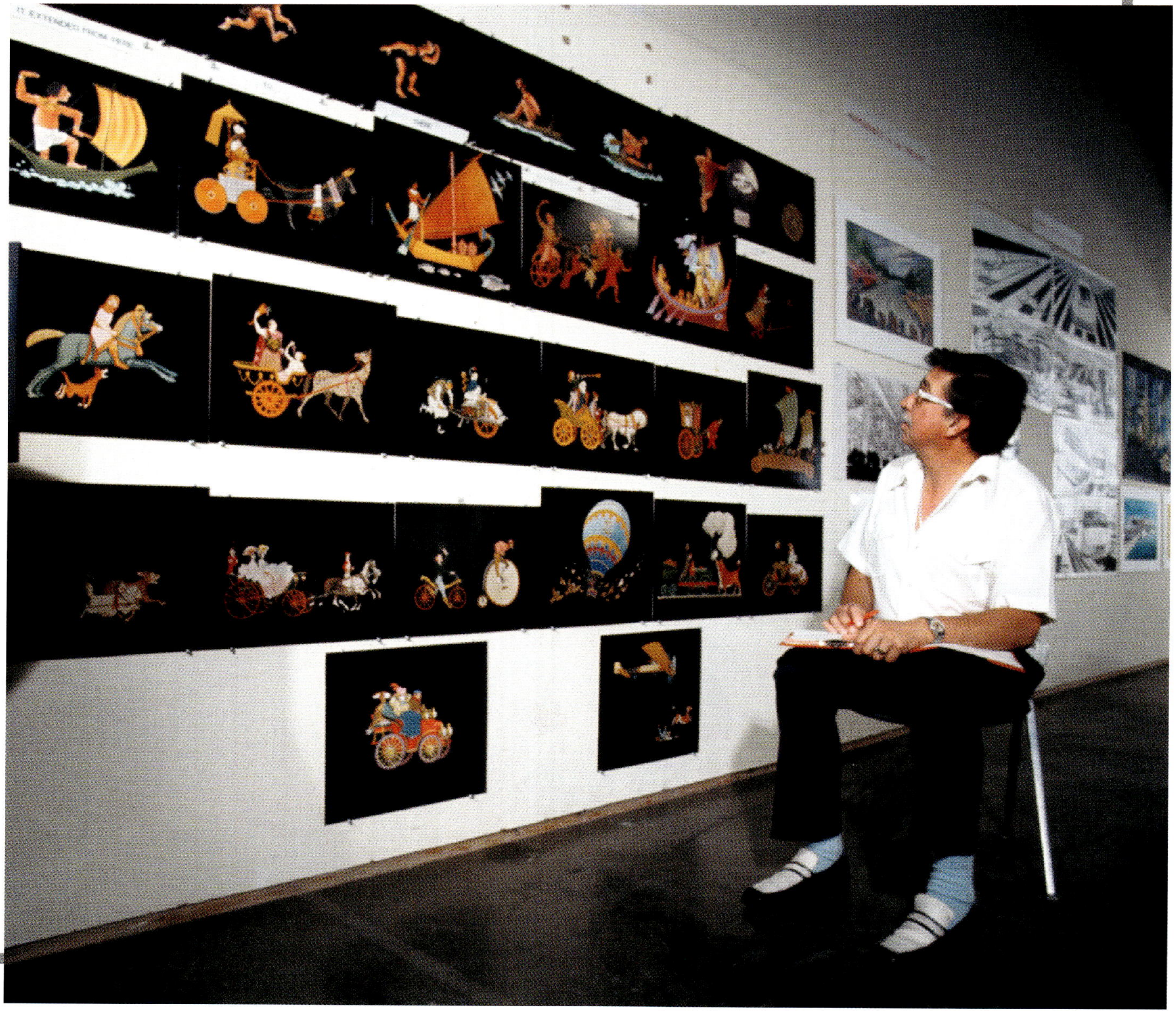

ABOVE (TOP): X at the drawing board working on concept art for the Mexico pavilion; ABOVE (BOTTOM): X sitting in front of concept art for World of Motion at EPCOT; OPPOSITE: X and Glenn Barker working on a sound recording for EPCOT.

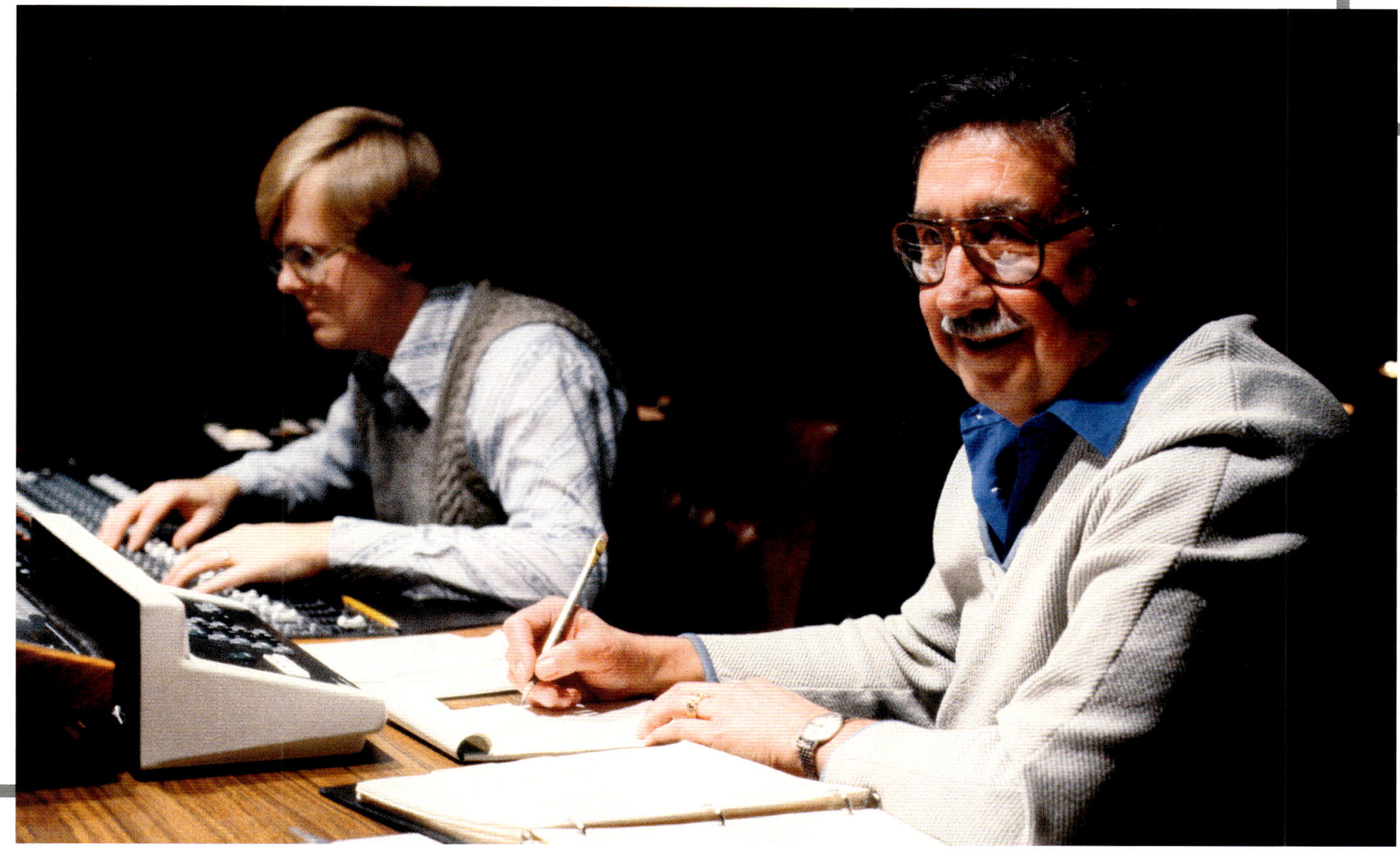

that before, but he ultimately gave Eddie everything he needed: the space, drafting tables, worktables, his team—all present and accounted for in the warehouse, with X involved in every phase. X knew they didn't have the budget that Pirates of the Caribbean had and they were still actively wooing the Mexico delegation to see if they would receive any financial contribution, so he told Eddie to do movie projections on screens like they did in If You Had Wings. Eddie was unsure what that meant and how to accomplish it, so X sent him to talk to the expert: Claude Coats. Claude walked Eddie through the process, reminiscing on his work with X along the way. For certain parts, Claude said Eddie should go see for himself, so Marty sent Eddie to visit the attraction in Florida. From there, Eddie just had to make it work, even when locked into the attraction's square footage well before he and his team would have preferred. Eddie, under X's guidance, hit the required time and budget targets, proving himself to be adaptable against all constraints.

X wrote another song for the attraction, bringing in Armando Corral, a consultant to Buddy Baker, to compose the musical score. Together X and Armando collaborated on a song about the cultural touchstones of Mexico: the fiestas, the music, and the history.

Disney was by this point pioneering digital technology for sound, which they could use for the Mexico pavilion. While CDs were not commercially available in the United States until 1983, Disney started using them in 1980, according to Glenn Barker. WED started after the studio had already been using them for some time. Everyone wanted the EPCOT sound to be the best that it could be, so they advocated for digital even though the digital master would then have to be played back on analog. Recording on a digital master allowed for a quicker mix of the music, dialogue, and sound effects. In addition, the digital quality didn't degrade over time the same way that analog copies did. Sometimes with the recordings a little noise would pop or show up, like a record pop, which Glenn, X, and the team jokingly called a "snat." Whenever a "snat" was heard, they had to go back and rerecord. Glenn said that they also all joked how they were "not only on the leading edge of technology, but the bleeding edge." On opening day, X came in with a "snat" drawing that said "We did it!" The drawing still hangs in Studio F at Walt Disney Imagineering.

The Mexico pavilion and eight of the other eventual eleven World Showcase countries opened October 1, 1982. Only one of the eleven, Morocco, managed to secure funding and sponsorship from

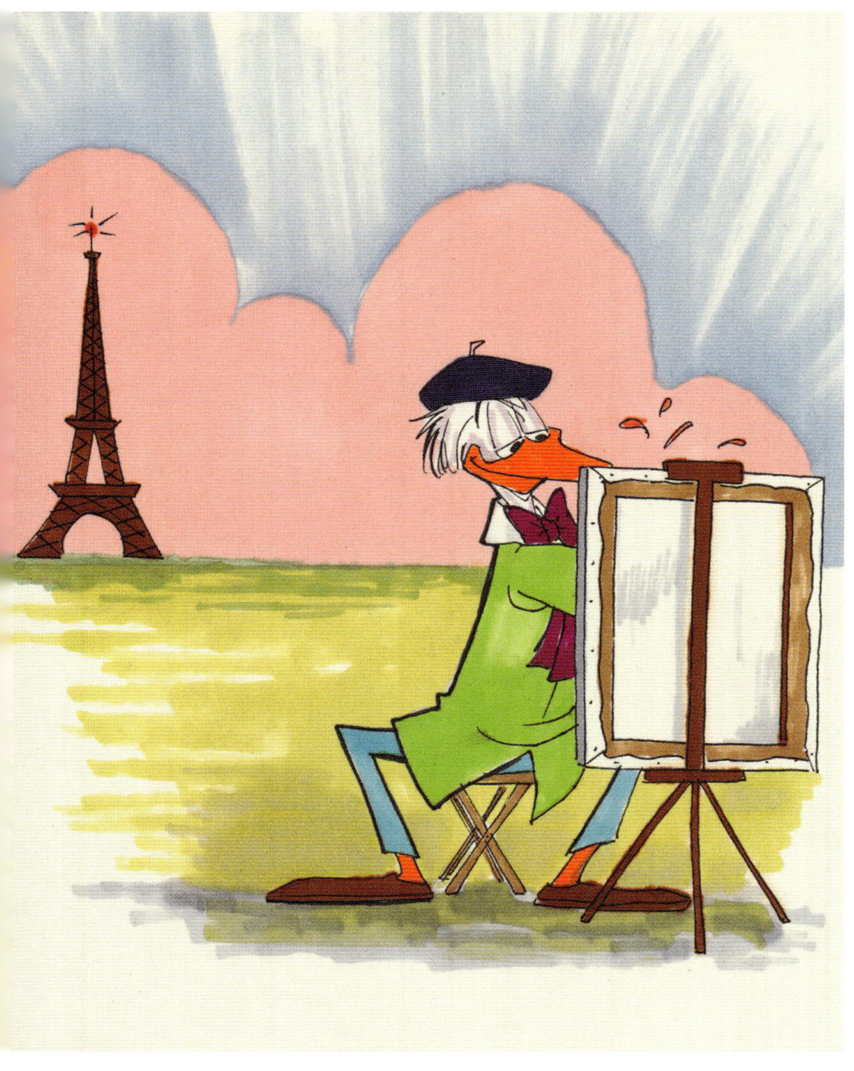

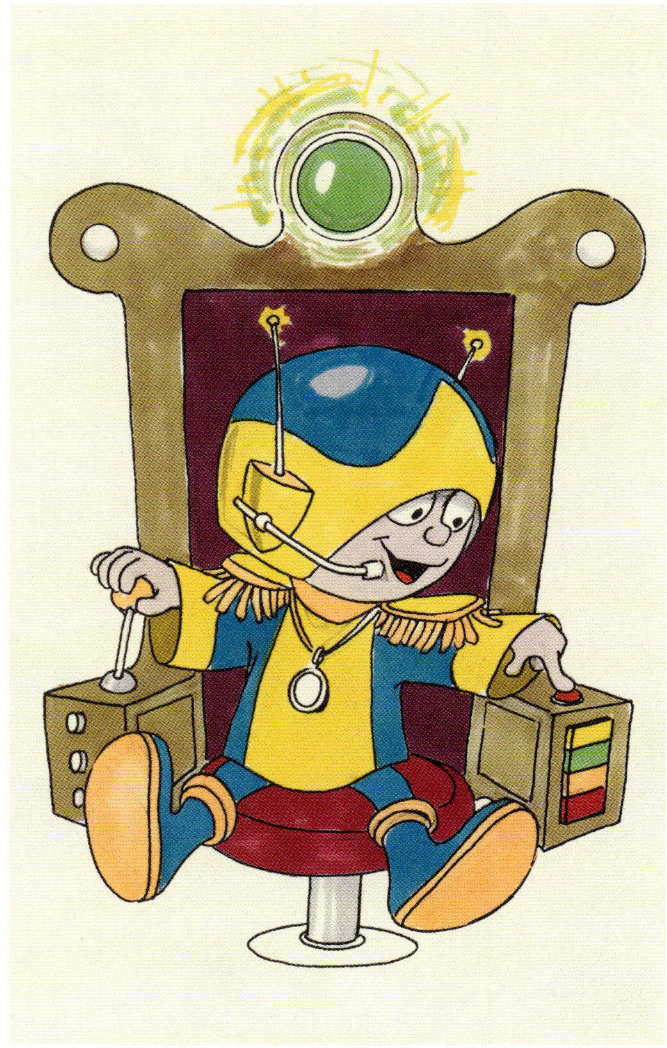

the country's government, though it was one of the two countries to open at later dates. The king of the North African nation not only fully sponsored his country's showcase, but also sent his own artisans to do the tile work and carve the plasterwork for their pavilion to ensure it accurately represented the culture of the country. For the other countries, they found private corporate sponsorship, often from companies affiliated with the corresponding local country. The Mexico pavilion ended up looking to sponsorship from the San Angel Inn and Cuauhtémoc Moctezuma Brewery, a major Mexican brewery established in 1890.

For X and Eddie, the experience was a positive one. They had produced a pavilion culturally and emotionally inspired by their heritage. Likewise, they had pitched a strong enough vision to secure one of the few attractions within the World Showcase. They had delivered on time and on budget and had built a lasting friendship and working relationship along the way.

X also teamed up again with Buddy on the theme song for EPCOT's World of Motion pavilion, presented by General Motors, which used Omnimovers and Audio-Animatronics figures to give a humorous look at the history of transportation. X and Buddy's song "It's Fun to Be Free" had an RCA quality and was an earworm, getting stuck in the heads of guests long after the visit to the attraction had ended. The song played on a loop, with distinctive harmonies and arrangements added for different locations and time periods to reflect the changing eras. Those in the

ABOVE: X's concept art for various EPCOT attractions; OPPOSITE: X with friends Mickey Mouse, Herb Ryman, and Dick Grills after his heart procedure.

queue for the ride and around the World of Motion pavilion heard various interpretations of "It's Fun to Be Free," which played repeatedly as a Broadway show tune, a jazz piece, a ragtime piano piece, and even a kazoo tune. All were interspersed with vehicle noises that added to the infectious quality of the theme song.

X once again worked with George McGinnis, as well, this time on SMRT-1, the talking robot for EPCOT's CommuniCore. Like Siri and Alexa, SMRT-1 used voice-recognition technology to engage in simple question-and-answer conversations with guests via telephone. SMRT-1 would use the screen behind him for his answers. X's decision to give SMRT-1 "friendly cartoon proportions" made the robot a favorite among visiting children.

With the large-scale EPCOT construction and maxed bandwidth of the art directors, each covering their own shows, Marty Sklar and Randy Bright decided that it might be wise to have one person supervise all talent-recording sessions. That person was none other than X. For each show, the team would reach out to X and tell him what they needed for the voices: number of performers, genders, desired voice quality, et cetera. X would then go through Bill Shepard, the studio's casting director, to get a few people to audition or to request their favorite talent, depending on the role. X enjoyed this work and was good at it, having had much experience on this end. One project that tested his patience, however, was The American Adventure. In addition to its having the largest cast of any show, there were a few complications with voice talent. While the art directors thought they had the voices they had wanted to read as the characters, they found with a few roles that the completed recordings just didn't measure up to their original visions and hopes. They called X and told him they needed another talent—although they seemingly preferred the well-known celebrity voices, at least until they ran into issues getting the desired recordings. X felt the opposite. To him, a well-known voice talent was chosen for the voice they were already known for, and this "take-it-or-leave-it thing," as X said, could cause problems. With lost time and money, they turned instead to X's tried-and-true voice-over talents. To X's point, while well-known talent had specific, recognizable voices that could often distract

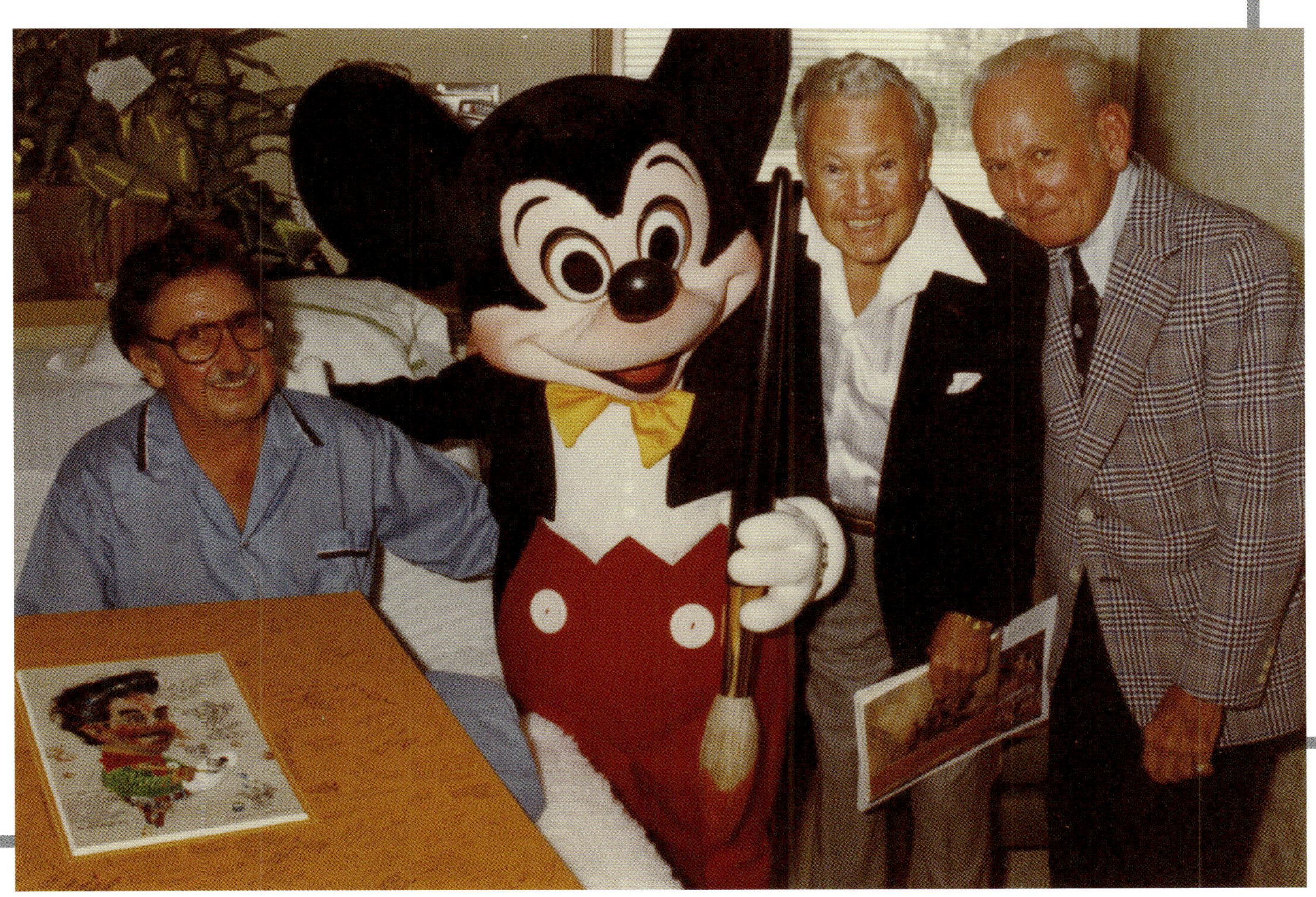

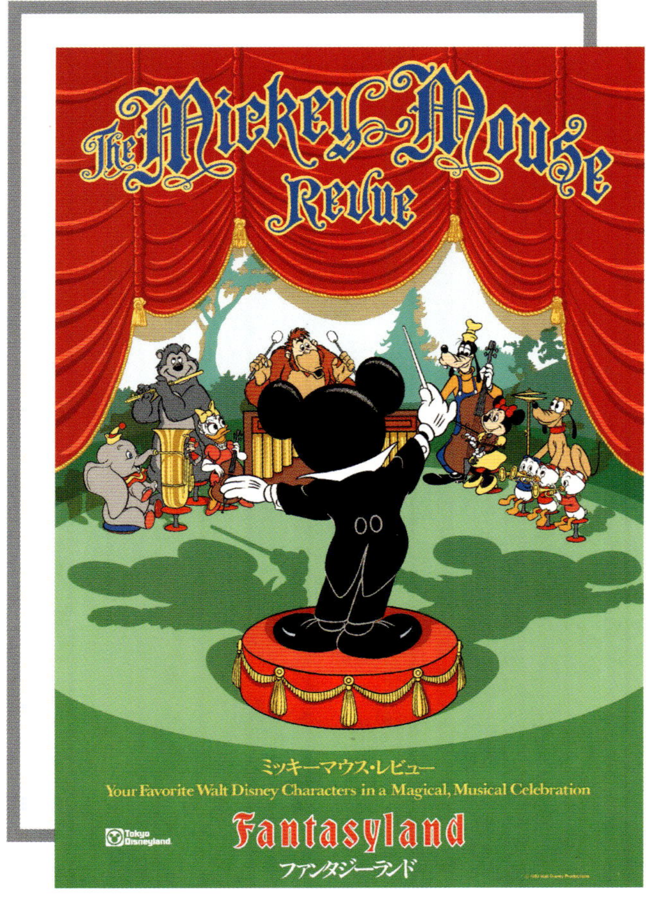

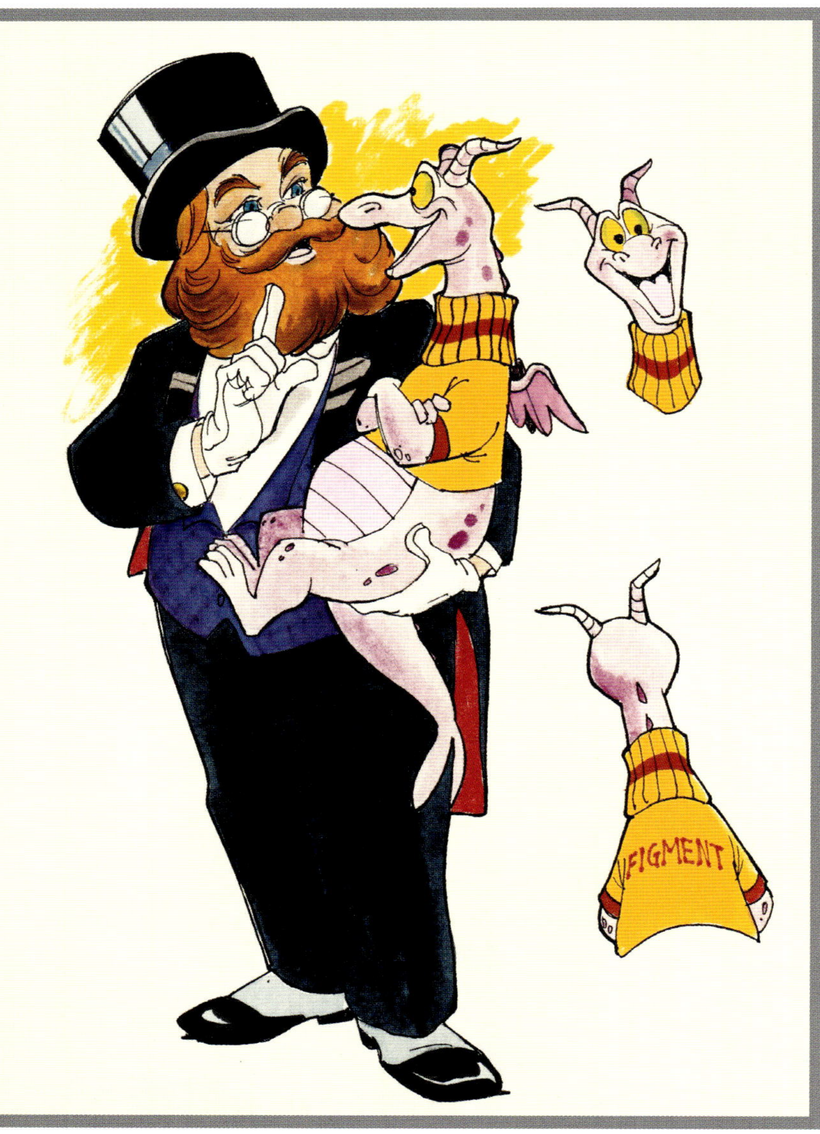

from the experience, quality voice-over talent (like Paul Frees) had a range of voices, ultimately allowing the performer to disappear within a character, and sometimes within multiple characters in the same show.

While X was heavily involved with all things EPCOT—Spaceship Earth, the Mexico pavilion, World of Motion, SMRT-1, and overseeing talent-recording sessions—he found out he needed heart bypass surgery. After the surgery, X awoke in the recovery room and found his family waiting for him, worried and supportive. Always one to find humor even in the scariest of circumstances, X opened his eyes very wide in response to Judianne's telling him the Dodgers had won the World Series, causing his family to laugh, landing the joke, and simultaneously assuring his family he'd be all right.

Back on his feet, X next helped design the character of Figment for the Journey Into Imagination pavilion, which was sponsored by Kodak. Tony Baxter came up with the name and idea, and then Imagineers Steve Kirk, Andy Gaskill, and X brought him to life. Formed from imaginary elements, the concept of "figment" was wide open for interpretation. Steve did the initial drawings, and true to form, X made this imaginary dragon lovably relatable to children, finalizing the character who went on to become one of the most popular at Walt Disney World. The Journey into Imagination pavilion debuted October 1, 1982, with its memorable ride-through attraction officially opening March 5 the following year.

In 1983, X made several trips to Tokyo Disneyland in Japan to supervise the recordings for the Haunted Mansion and Pirates of the Caribbean attractions. In the United States, Marty Sklar and Randy Bright had appointed X, Claude, and longtime Disneyland entertainer Wally Boag art directors for creative direction, review, and approval of the process. The Imagineers, through countless meetings, had come to the realization that these attractions should be recorded in audio studios in Japan and wanted Japanese artists to record the park attraction dialogue, since Japanese idioms changed the wonderfully crafted expressions quite a bit from X's original intentions.

LEFT (TOP): X's character artwork featured in the poster for The Mickey Mouse Revue at Tokyo Disneyland; LEFT (BOTTOM): X's drawing of Figment and Dreamfinder; OPPOSITE (TOP): The Figment model sheet signed by X; OPPOSITE (BOTTOM): X's concept art for the Country Bear Jamboree in Tokyo Disneyland.

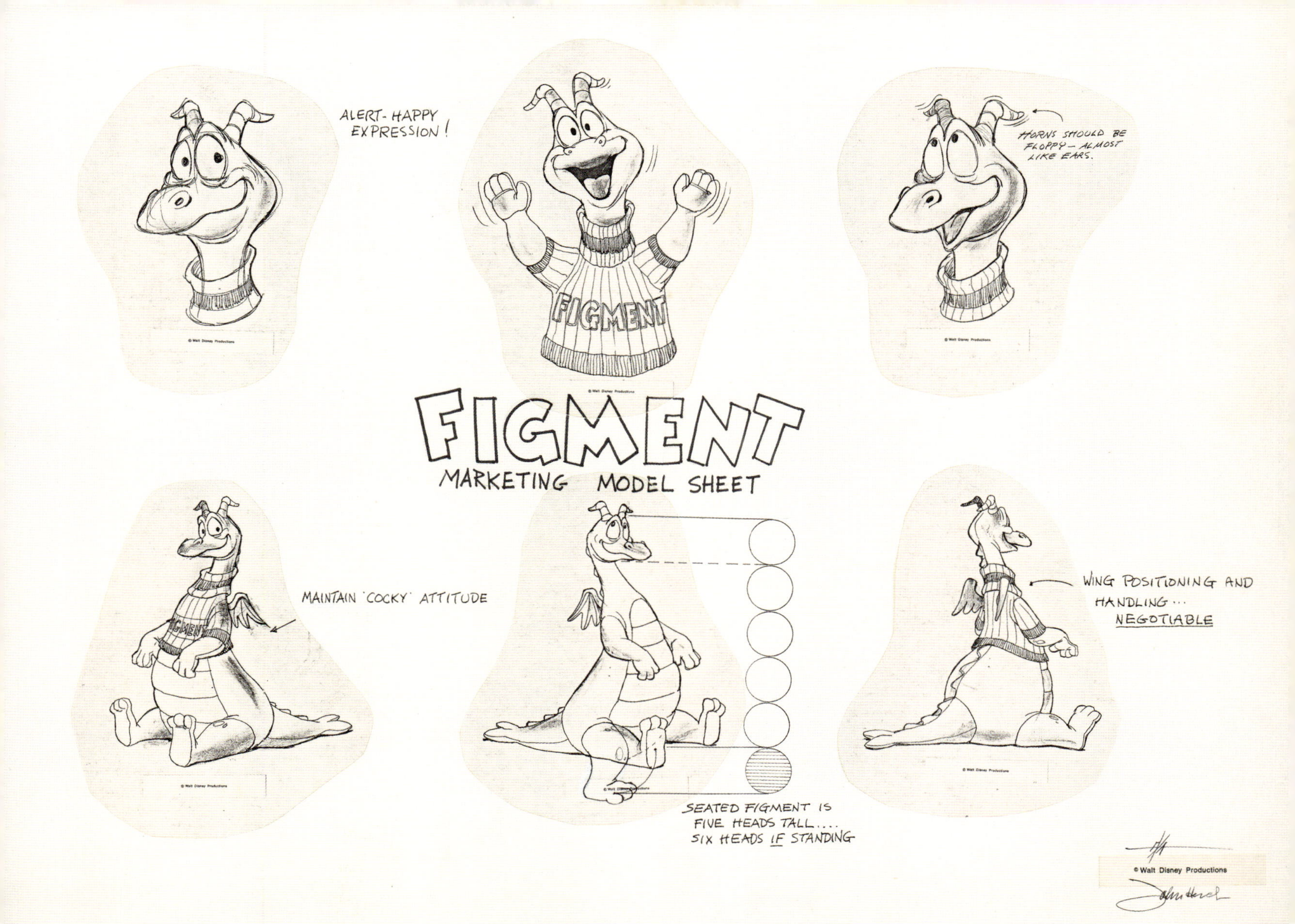

ALERT-HAPPY EXPRESSION!

HORNS SHOULD BE FLOPPY—ALMOST LIKE EARS.

FIGMENT

FIGMENT

MARKETING MODEL SHEET

MAINTAIN 'COCKY' ATTITUDE

WING POSITIONING AND HANDLING... NEGOTIABLE

SEATED FIGMENT IS FIVE HEADS TALL.... SIX HEADS IF STANDING

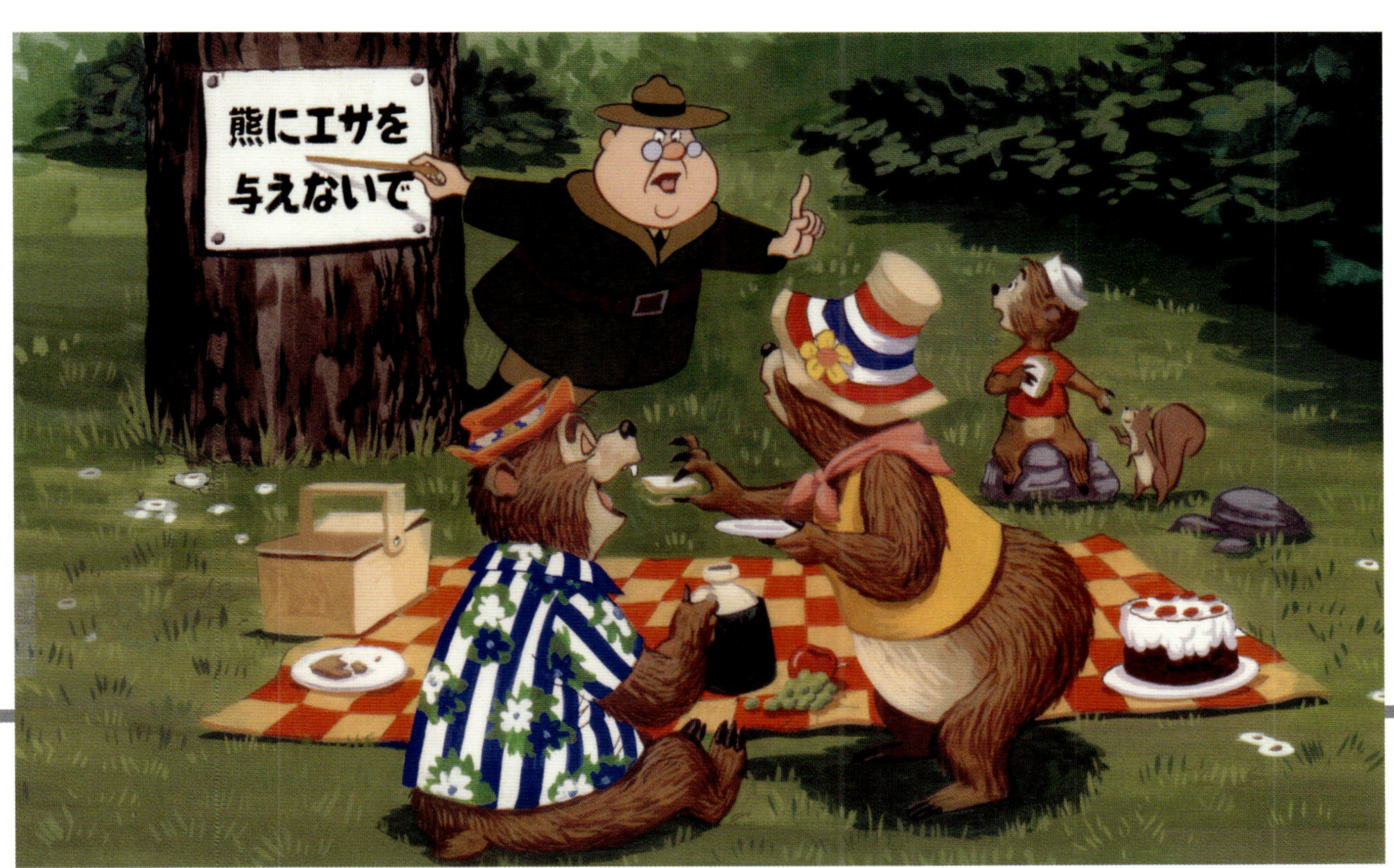

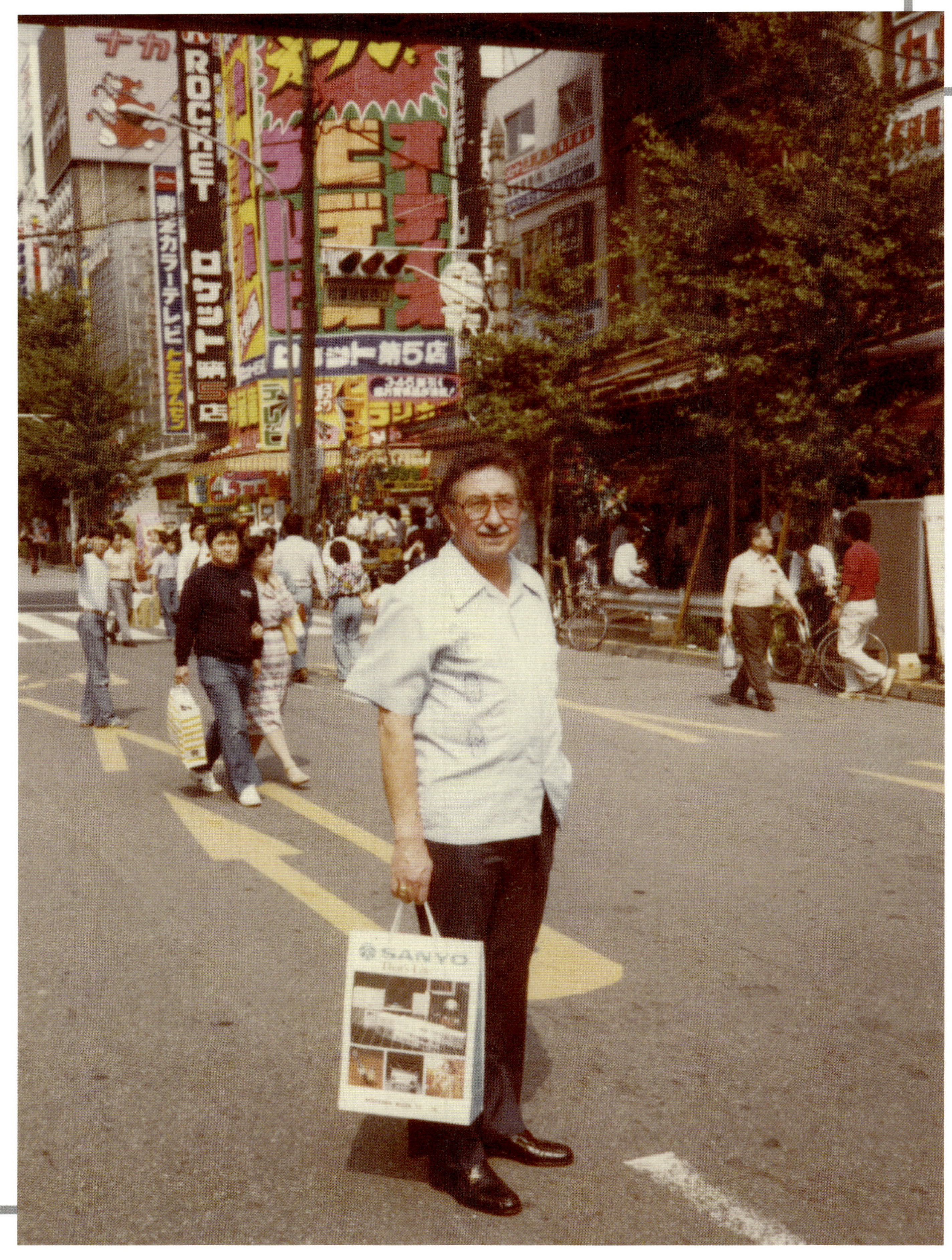

ABOVE: X got in some shopping time during one of his trips to Tokyo; OPPOSITE: X receiving his forty-fifth service anniversary award statue in 1983.

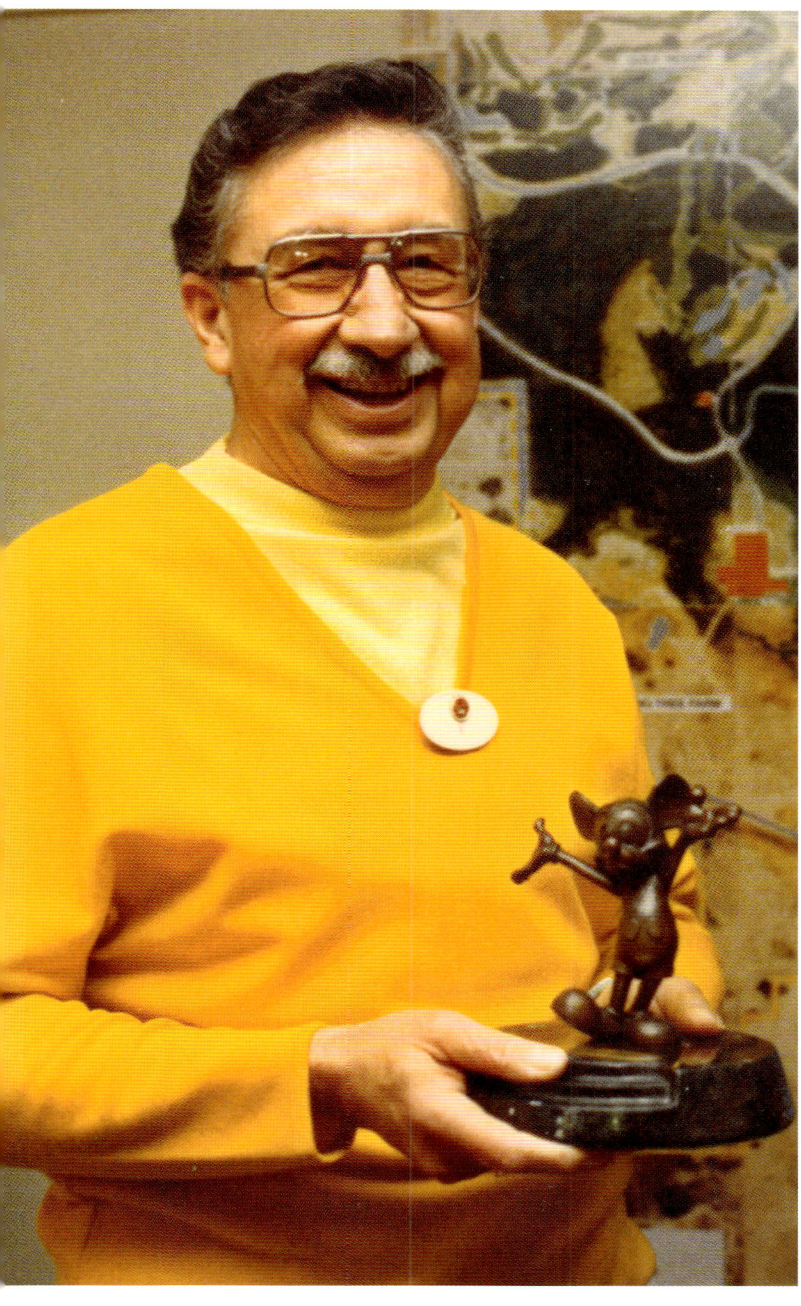

On Pirates, when attempting to record "Dead men tell no tales" for the Jolly Roger skull, the initial translation came back as "There is no mouth on a dead person." Because there was no comparable Japanese phrase, they opted for a new phrase, which translated to English as "If you're not careful, you'll not pass this way again." While this phrasing was a little less succinct, it still captured the ominous essence of the intended meaning.

While X was in Japan, he also worked on the script for their Jungle Cruise. X was present for the translation of the script but had no idea what they were saying. To be sure the spiel kept its humor and matched its American counterpart, X and his translator went to the park and rode the attraction. As X recounted in an interview, his translator laughed in all the right places, so he said, "Well, I guess it's okay!"

As Lee Lanselle, an assistant project manager on Tokyo Disneyland who also oversaw audio-based production, recounted in an email correspondence, for the Haunted Mansion, X couldn't get the lead voice actor to give the reading he wanted. Before recording, the Ghost Host voice actor was briefed on the attraction: its physical layout, its narrative and aesthetic essence, and the Ghost Host's personality and role in the story. While the voice actor tried various interpretations and attempted to incorporate X's and others' feedback into his takes, he couldn't capture what Paul Frees had created in the original. With the language barrier and X's expertise in knowing whether someone could properly capture a voice, he knew he needed to try something new. And with his keen ear for voices, X turned to Teiichiro Hori, a board member from Disney's partner for the Tokyo park, Oriental Land Company. Hori-san happened to be in attendance that day and was very familiar with the attraction from visits to Walt Disney World and Disneyland. X liked his voice. Lee stated that Hori-san "had a deep, resonant, commanding voice—and much experience as a master of ceremonies and presenter." X suggested that perhaps Hori-san should read it. In his deep voice, Hori-san repeatedly said no, but X said, "Read it," and then he did. The tape rolled, Hori-san spoke, and all were pleased. Hori-san's delivery was exactly what X had envisioned. X congratulated him, saying, "Hori-san, you are now the Ghost-o Host-o!"

Throughout the 1970s and early 1980s, X's influence grew. X had guaranteed his legacy in WED history, and his work at EPCOT allowed the power of his many talents to shine, whether he was writing attraction scripts filled with heart, humor, and thrills; crafting unforgettable song lyrics; overseeing all the vocal recordings for shows; or still adding his design and animation expertise whenever needed among his trusted creative collaborators and friends. His reach had expanded far beyond Southern California, accruing a global audience with the opening of EPCOT in 1982 and Tokyo Disneyland in 1983. And yet another change was on the horizon, perhaps inspired by Walt's own ability to recognize new and untapped talents, the importance of change to keep creativity fresh, and the growing legacy of Disney. However, unlike in 1965, this time the surprising change was announced by X, completely of his own volition.

8

Retirement and Life as a Disney Legend

AS X'S SON JOE WROTE IN HIS 2017 eulogy for his dad, "X's life may have seemed magical based on his professional accomplishments, but one must remember that he endured the tragic loss of his son Jerry and his wife, Mary, within the span of a few years. His deep faith gave him a resiliency that was inspirational to his family and friends who were also grieving." Mary passed away in 1983, and though X had intended to retire the next year, her death caused him to question those plans. After some soul-searching, X decided it was still time to retire.

Upon hearing of X's impending departure, John Hench asked him, "Why are you going to retire?" The question slightly irked X, who felt he had contributed a lot to Disney over his time at the studio and WED. He believed it was time to "leave while the party was still fun." X felt pride for the work he had done and trusted its enduring legacy, remaining humble as he said, "I was glad that I had contributed what I did contribute, and now in my late years, people still say thank you for what I've done, like the Pirates ride. I think it will go on for many years. After thirty-six years, it's still going strong, and I'm sure it will last longer than I will. It's very rewarding, and I have it all in my heart."

So in 1984, X officially retired from WED Enterprises after forty-six years of employment at the company. A few weeks before his retirement, X met Disney president Frank Wells and chief executive officer Michael Eisner, who had just started in their new roles at Disney and came to WED to introduce themselves. Straight to the point, X shook their hands, and wryly said, "Now, don't screw up. I hope to live comfortably on my stock!" X was "bullish on the company," and on the next generation of talent that he had helped nurture and mentor during his career, symbolically passing the torch of Mickey ears and Disney badges to them. He also knew the value of life outside of work, and at age sixty-five, felt it was time to go out and have fun. Again, John Hench needled him about retirement, saying, "Why are you retiring? You're going to get tired of playing golf. You can only play so much golf." Of course, there are countless country clubs and golf courses in Los Angeles full of men disproving John's theory, and X never regretted his retirement, saying years later in an interview, "I'm not bored. I still haven't cleaned out the garage!"

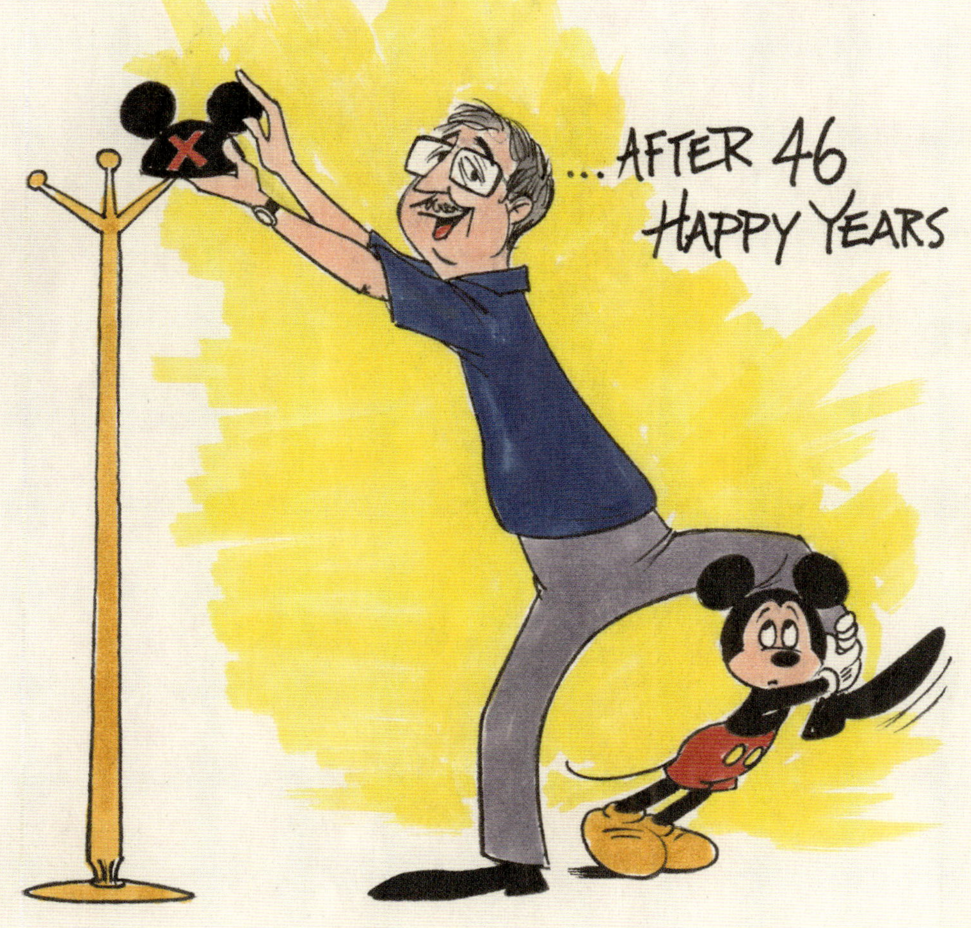

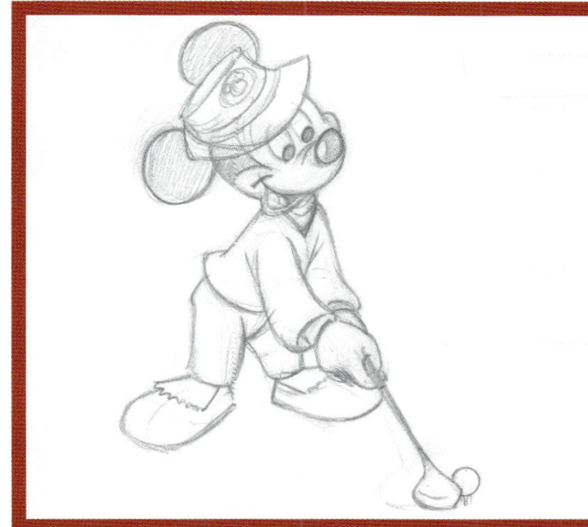

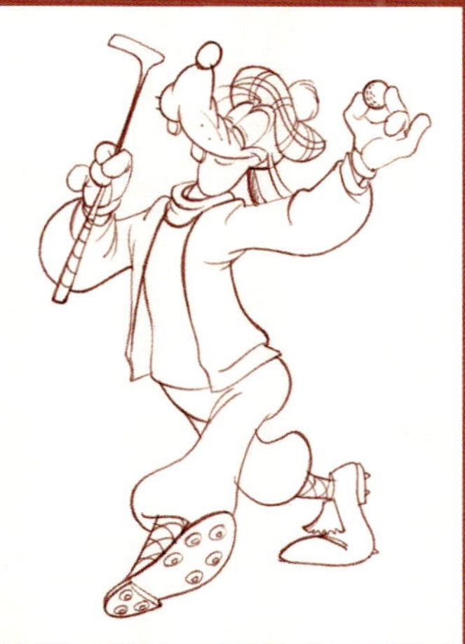

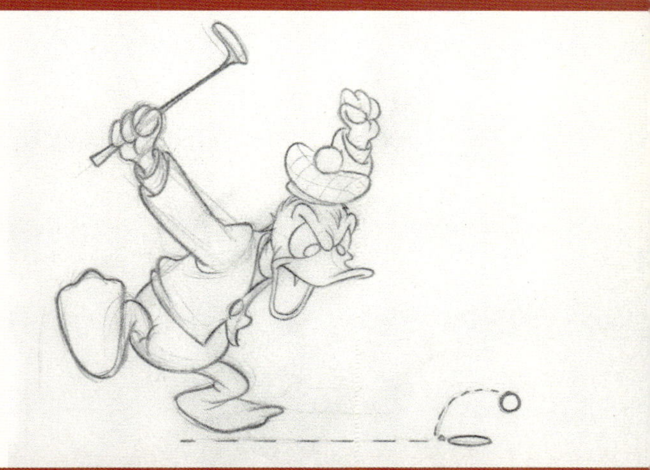

ABOVE (TOP): X drew his own retirement announcement; ABOVE (BOTTOM): X's illustrations of his favorite Disney characters golfing.

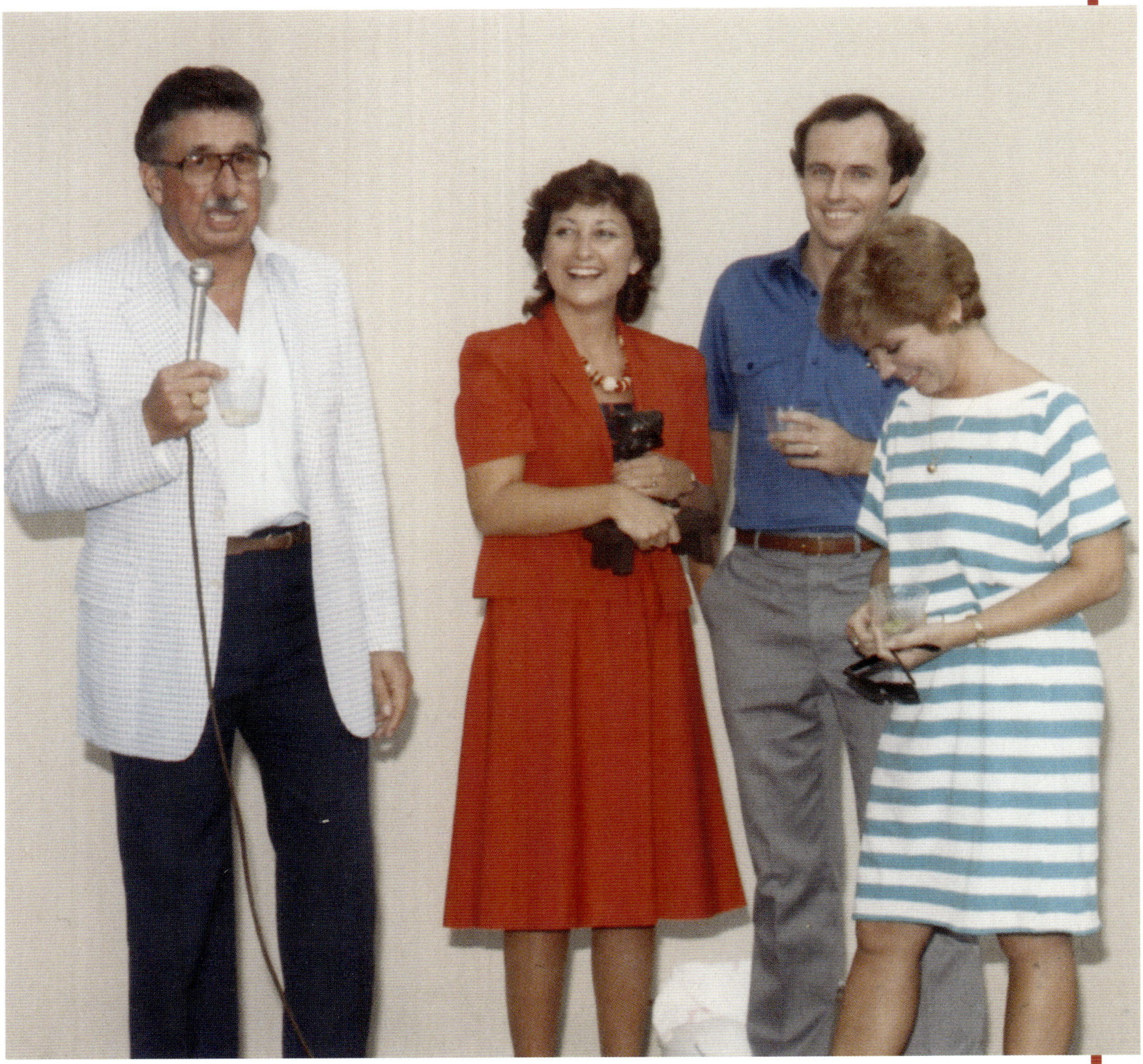

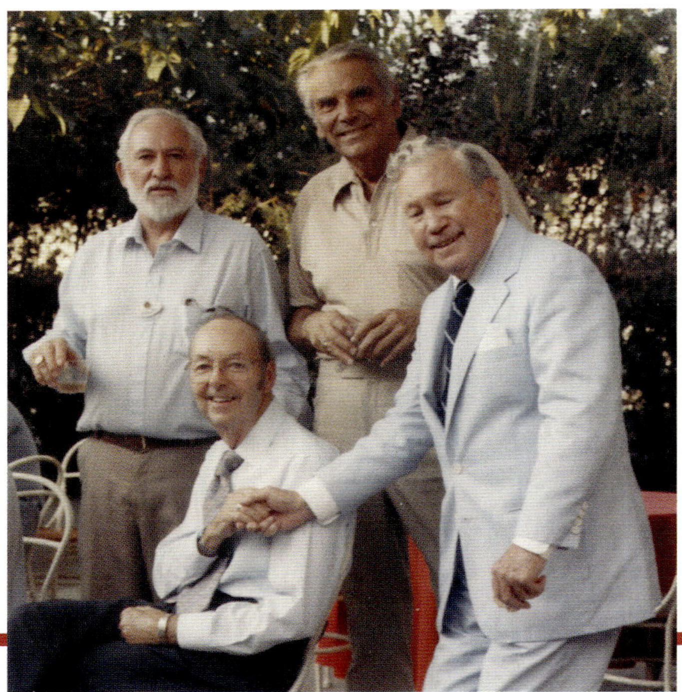

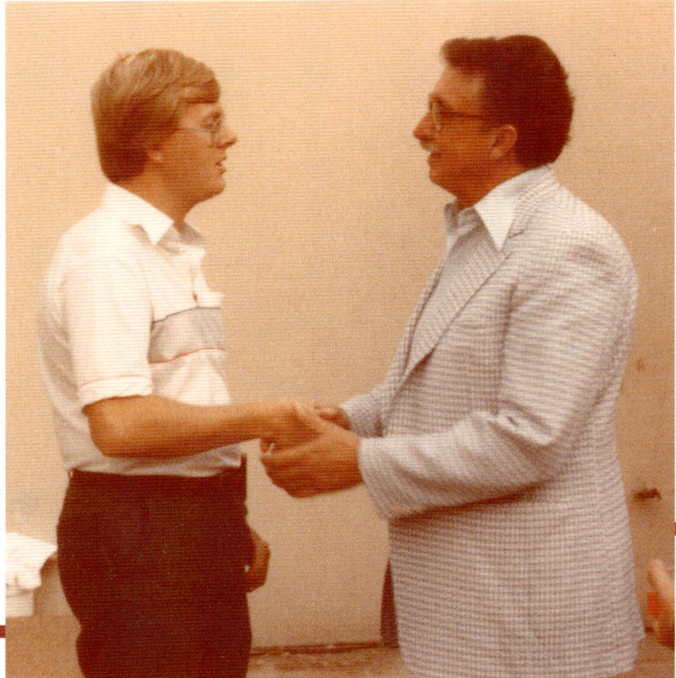

X remained busy and creatively fulfilled. He signed a consulting contract with Disney every year, but with the return of his signed contract, he told them, "Don't bother me; if I'd wanted to work, I would have stayed here. And I'm enjoying retirement, too!" All joking aside, X enjoyed his consulting work for Disney, which for the most part consisted of answering a call every few months to come in and speak about what it had been like to work with Walt. Sometimes, especially at the beginning of his retirement, he was also called back to do character drawings, most often of Mickey Mouse. X found it strange that he had become somewhat of an authority on drawing Mickey, given that his time at the studio had mainly been spent becoming an expert on Goofy (not so much as an animator but as a clean-up man, knowing Goofy's proportions and how to make him look uniform).

X had done a little work on Mickey, animating one scene from the "Mickey Mouse March" opening of the *Mickey Mouse Club* program and providing some illustrations for a book about Mickey. But X quickly established a "feel for the mouse," with Mickey appearing often in his world-renowned cards, earning him the status of "Mickey Mouse specialist." In the *Behind the Attraction* docuseries for Disney+, retired Imagineering colleague Rolly Crump even went so far as to say that "X was the best Mickey Mouse artist who ever worked for the Disney studio." X's working theory was that some animators' talents were more aligned with illustrating Goofy, who required a more slapstick type of animation; some were better at Donald Duck, who needed a rapid, crazy "yakety-yak" type of animation; and others were meant for drawing Mickey, who necessitated the keen eyes and steady hands of more subtle personality-type animators. While X's early work at the studio was spent cleaning up Goofy, his own style seemed to align the closest with his description of a talent for drawing Mickey, given that he established from a young age his ability to bring life and personality to each animal and character he drew.

X found it odd that there was no standardized Mickey Mouse drawing. Instead, Disney relied on the

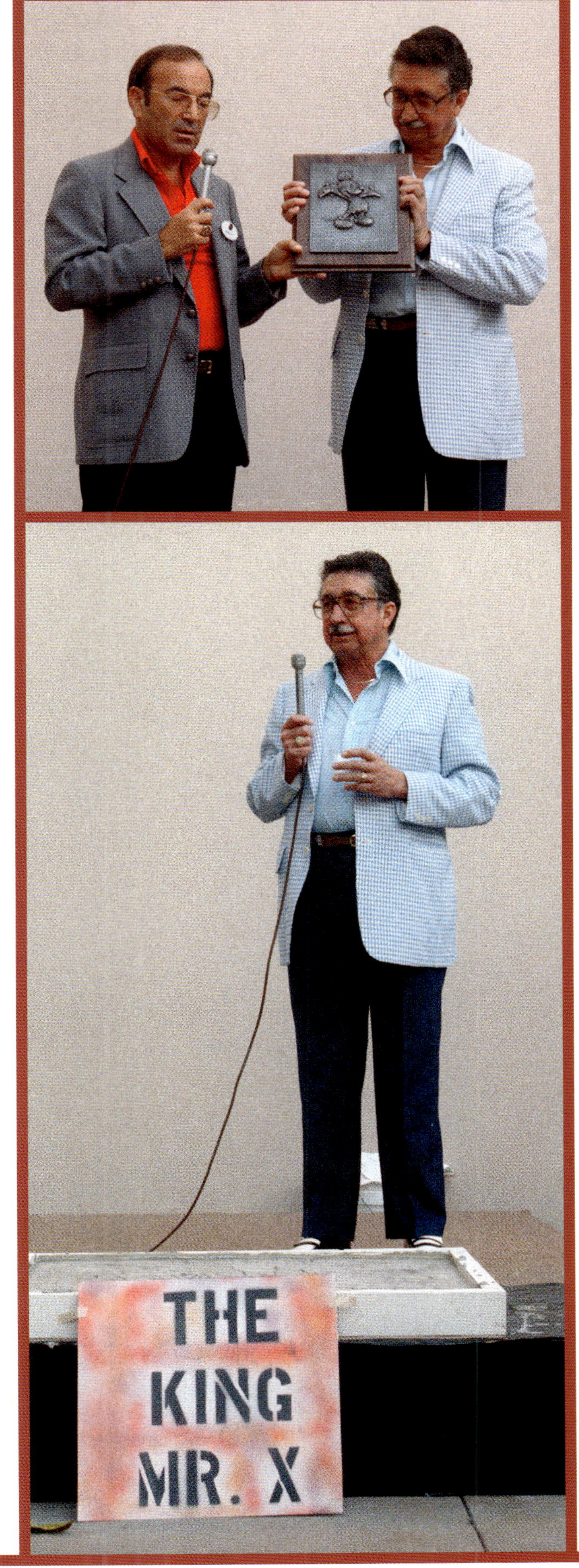

OPPOSITE (TOP): X at his retirement party with daughters Tori and Judianne, and Tori's husband, Mike; OPPOSITE (BOTTOM LEFT): X's old friends and colleagues Collin Campbell, Claude Coats, Herb Ryman, and Wathel Rogers (SEATED) celebrating his retirement; OPPOSITE (BOTTOM RIGHT): X shaking hands with Glenn Barker at his retirement party; ABOVE (TOP): Marty Sklar presenting X with a commemorative plaque for his years of service; ABOVE (BOTTOM): X making a heartfelt speech.

few who had proven capable to continue illustrating Mickey. He claimed that the younger animators didn't even know Donald, Mickey, or Goofy since the opportunities to draw them had dwindled. Meanwhile, some of the tried-and-true Disney legends disagreed with what constituted a proper Mickey Mouse. X and John Hench, for example, had very different ideas of how to draw Mickey. The lack of uniformity seemed even more unusual given the fact that Mickey Mouse was their corporate logo.

Ever the honest but humorous realist, X even went so far as to speak to this point at John Hench's memorial service. As recounted by Eddie Sotto, a former Imagineering concept designer, X said at the event, "I never agreed with the way John drew Mickey Mouse . . . but if it was good enough for Walt . . . ," earning him laughs from the mourning audience. He riffed further on some of the variations of Mickey he found to be hilarious, asking John to forgive him and acknowledging their deep bond that stemmed from their joint mourning over Walt's death, recognizing in each other the same love, respect, passion, and lifelong dedication to Walt and his vision. All in all, X enjoyed the opportunities to draw Mickey, even long after he was retired. It gave him a reason to pick up his pencil, and he viewed it as a form of therapy or creative practice—so long as it came without the usual rushed "due tomorrow" animation deadline.

His phone continued to ring anytime anyone at WED was planning to retire. WED would call to tell X that the only thing the employee was requesting for their retirement was an original X Atencio card. And with that wish relayed, X would get to work, crafting the perfect card for that specific person. Outside

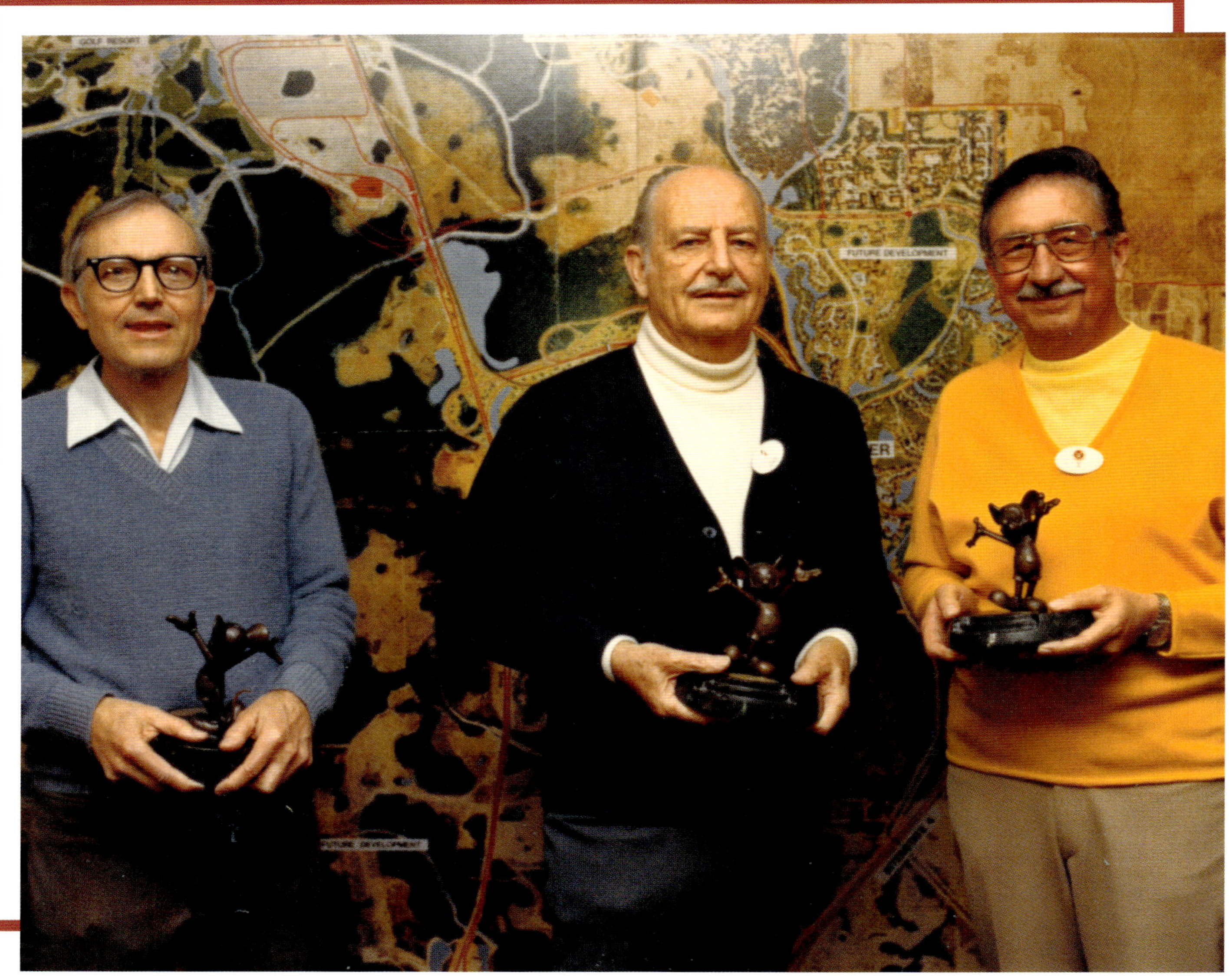

ABOVE: Blaine Gibson, John Hench, and X celebrating forty-five years with The Walt Disney Company; OPPOSITE: X and the mouse who started it all.

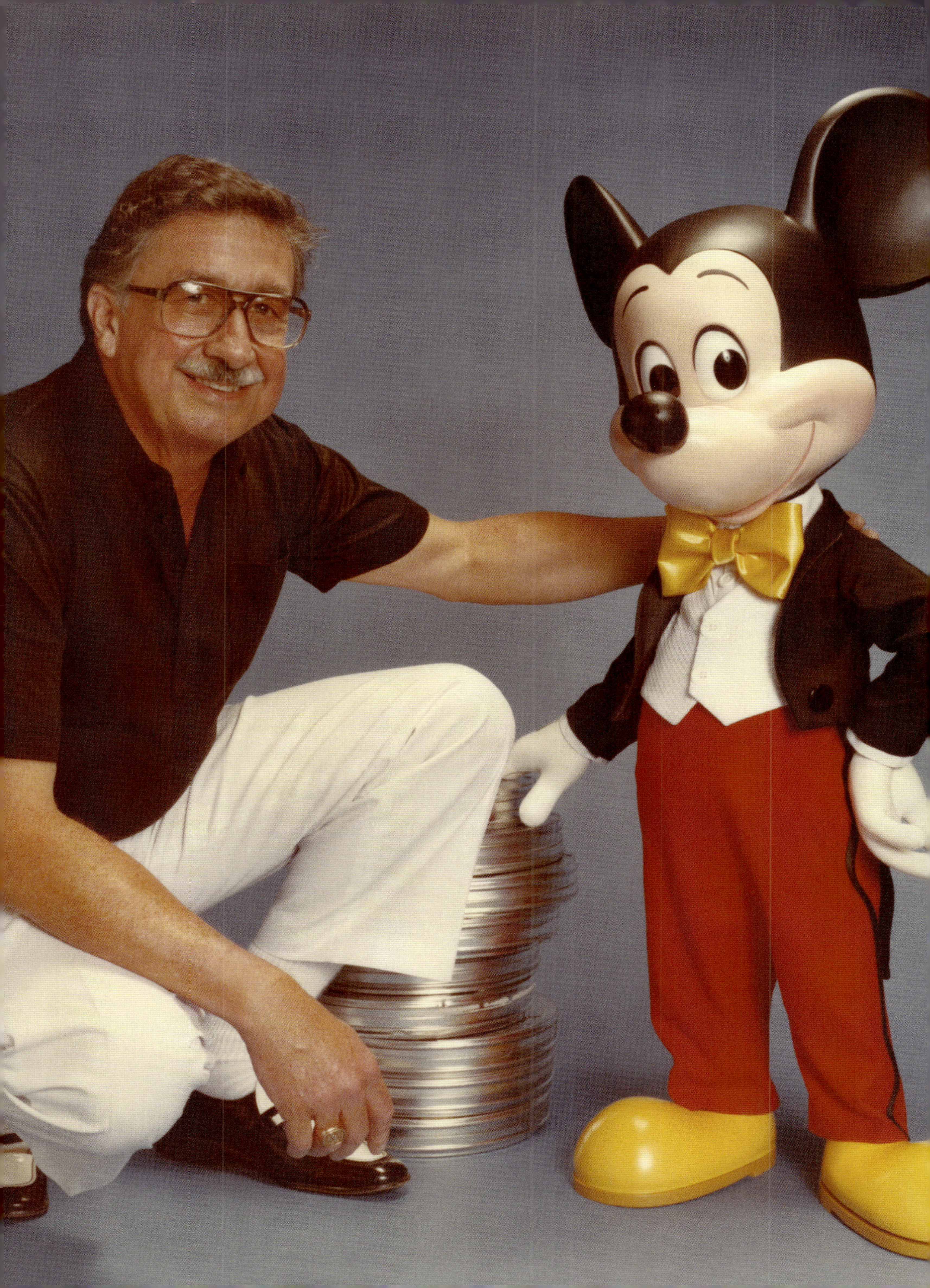

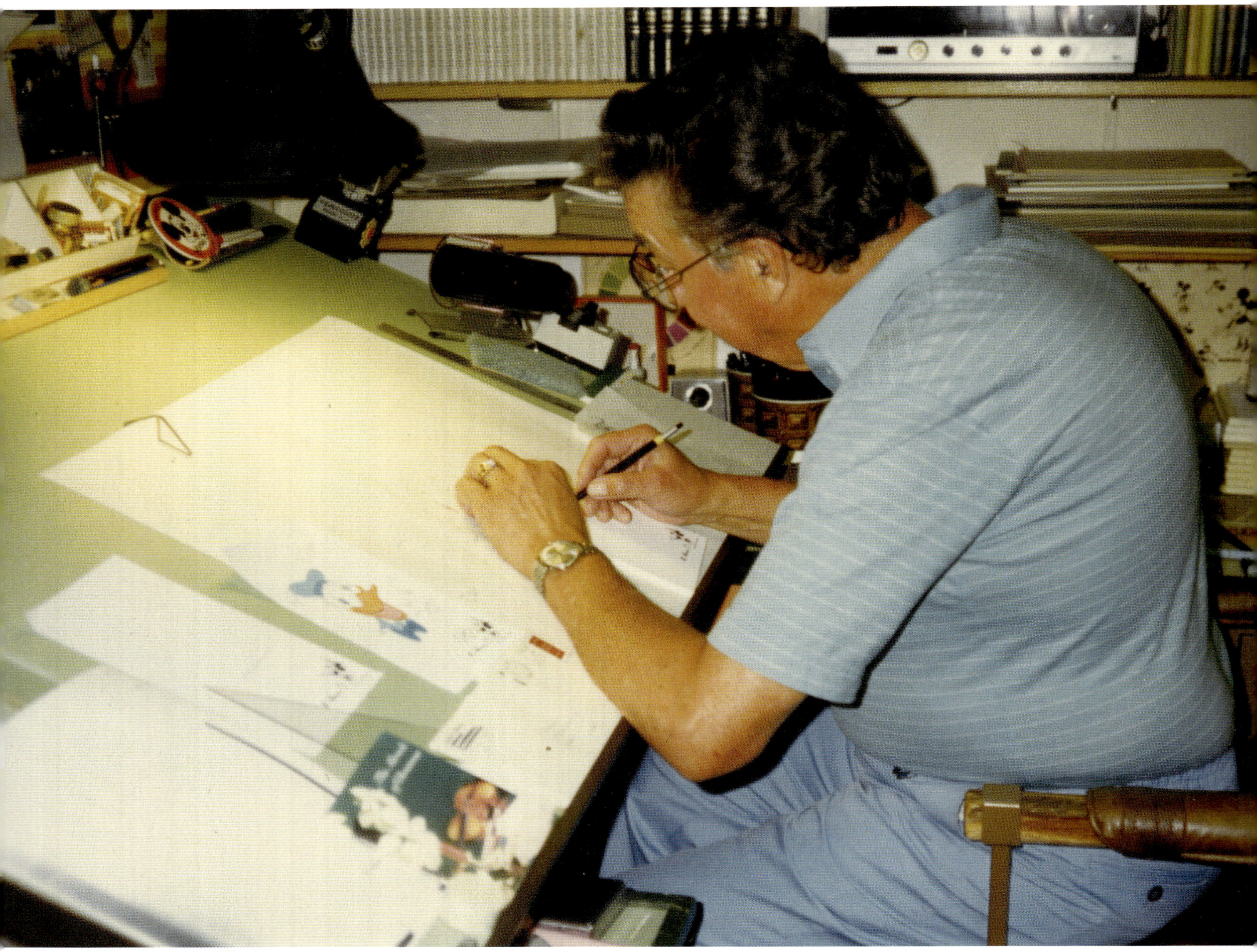

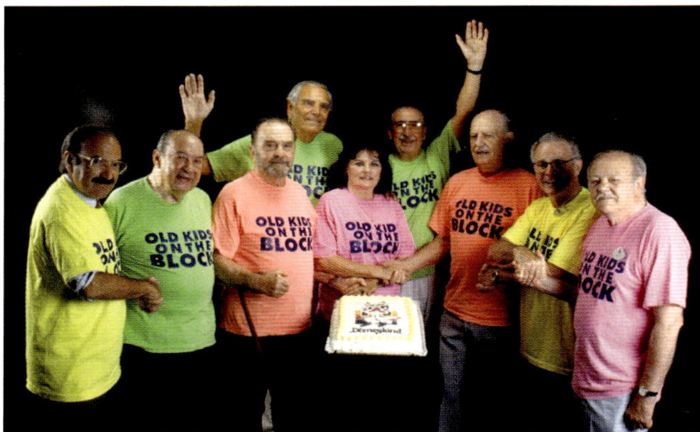

of his retirement card commissions, he continued his busy regimen of drawing holiday cards, birthday cards, and many other well-wishes for major milestones. X knew he was fortunate to have worked in a creative field where, even in retirement, he could be called back for brief commissions and could continue creating art on his own, making it easier for him to adjust to life outside of an office. X stated, "There'll be calls on my talents whether it be WED or the communications people or the publications people to get

ABOVE: X at his drawing board at home in retirement; LEFT: X alongside many of the original Imagineers reuniting at Walt Disney Imagineering (LEFT TO RIGHT) Marty Sklar, Marc Davis, Ken Andersen, Claude Coats, Leota Toombs, X Atencio, John Hench, Sam McKim, Bill Martin; OPPOSITE: X and Maureen aboard the *Disney Wonder* with (BACK ROW) Richard Sherman, Bob Lane, Marty Sklar, Alice Davis, and Roberta Brubaker, and (FRONT ROW) Elizabeth Sherman and Jeff Hoffman.

little jobs done to keep me busy, to keep me in 'martini money.'"

And work for his "martini money" he did. X was repeatedly asked to speak about working with Walt, an easy task for a self-described "Walt Worshiper." He had viewed Walt as a father figure and valued him as a boss and the consummate storyteller, or as X said, "The Storyteller of the Century." However, being the honest man he was, X did also acknowledge his belief that while Walt's storytelling was unmatched, his talent as an artist would have never gotten him hired as an animator at his own studio. Regardless, he knew that Walt was an unrivaled talent, and X was amazed that he had forged a career where Walt knew his name, respected his abilities, and pushed his aptitudes in directions beyond X's own wildest dreams. The first time the two met, X was waiting for an elevator. Walt appeared and was also waiting for the lift. Cheerfully greeting the boss, X said, "Hi, Walt," and Walt replied, "Hi, X, how are you doing?" X was flabbergasted that Walt knew who he was, and Walt's attention to detail and personal address showed signs of a good boss who knows that it's the little things that boost employee morale. That mere interaction, small though it was, meant the world to X. In looking back on his entire career, he knew that having risen high enough through the ranks at Disney to receive calls and assignments directly from Walt was an astonishing feat.

X reflected on working with Walt in animation at the studio, explaining how no one ever worried about budgets. Walt was concerned first and foremost about delivering the best product possible. The only way someone would hear about things from Walt was if they brought a project in under budget and then it tanked. On the reverse, if someone did something great but it went over budget, Walt never worried. His brother Roy and the accounting people might be upset, but Walt Disney looked at all values, including the nonmonetary, in the finished product.

Outside the Disney realm, X stayed engaged. In 1986, he met Maureen Sheedy, introduced by Father

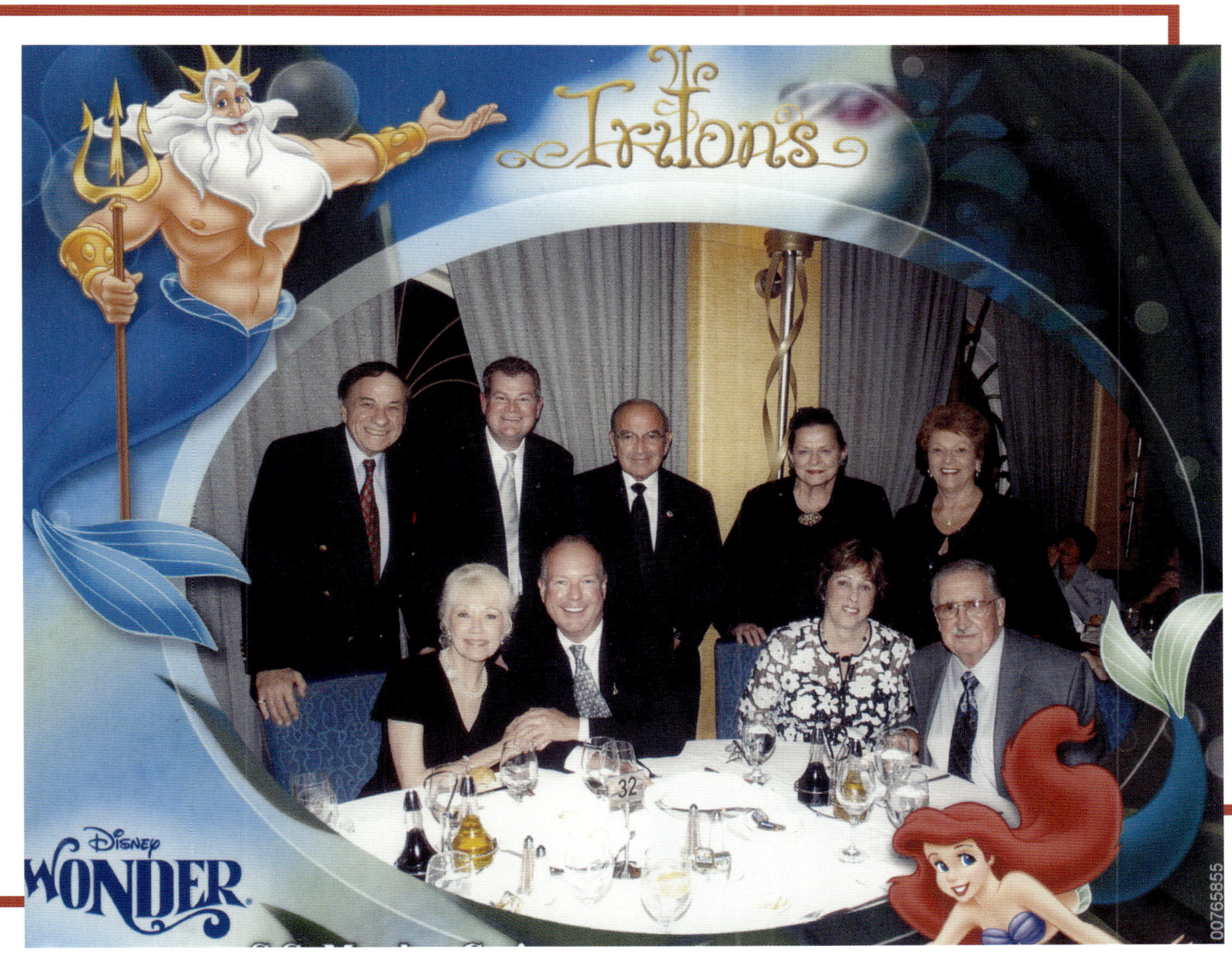

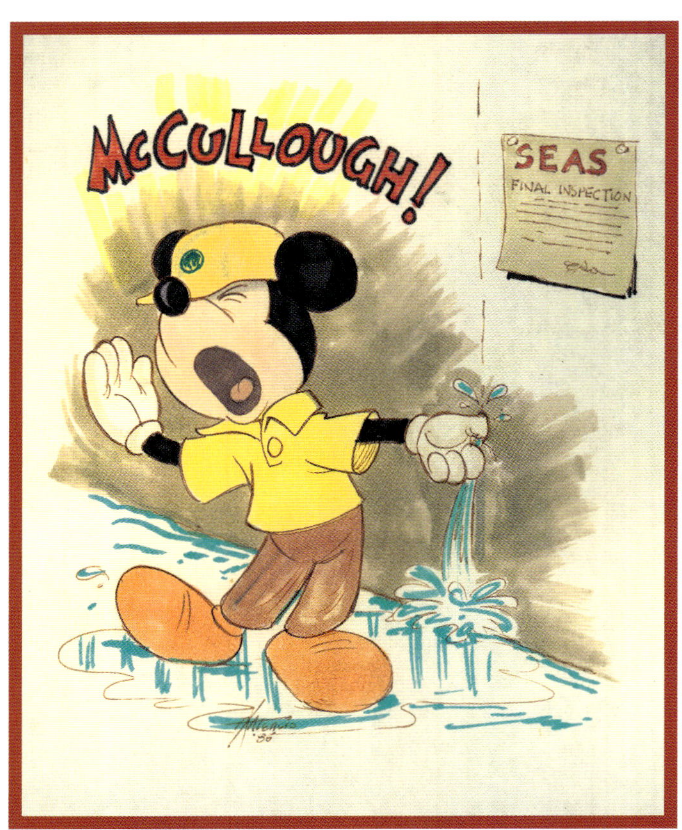

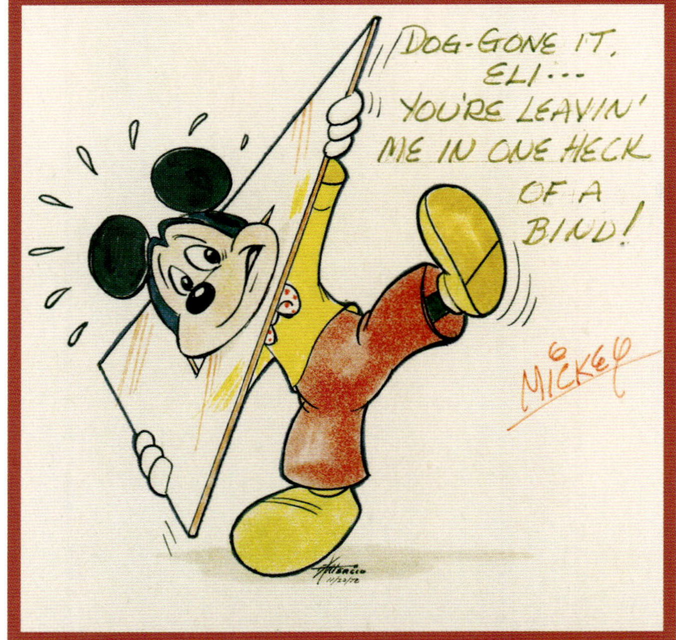

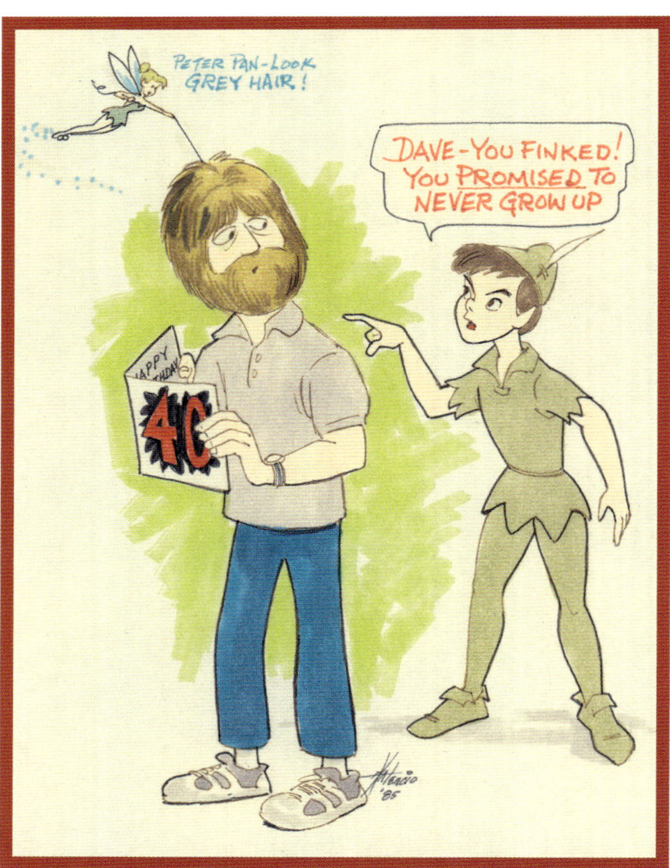

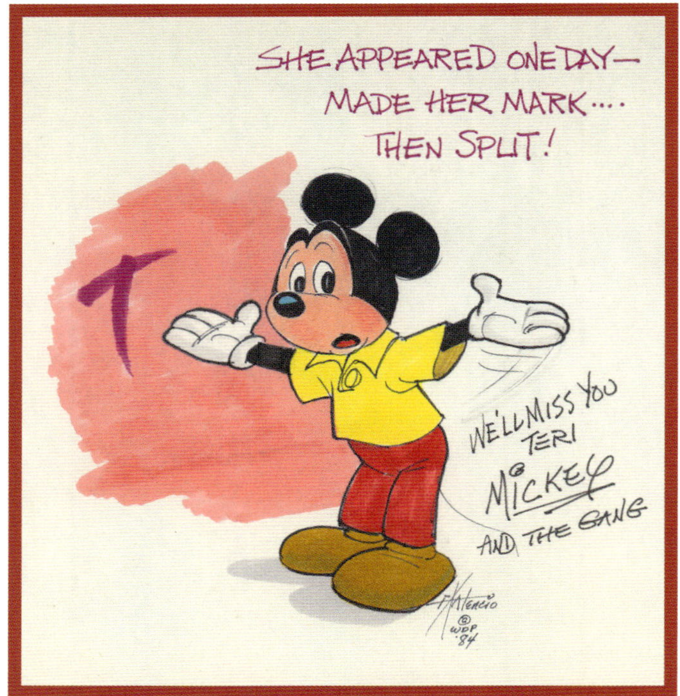

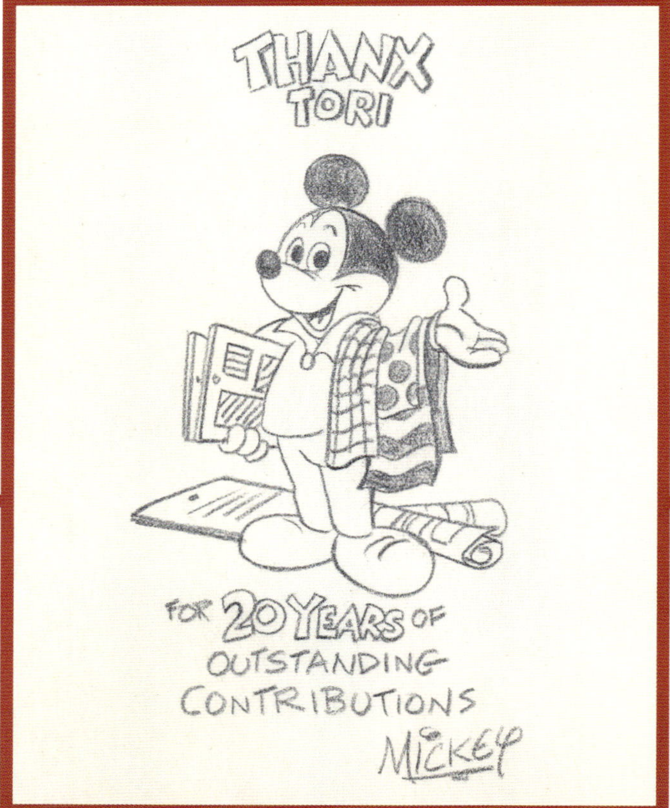

ABOVE AND OPPOSITE: An assortment of cards that X drew for coworkers and family celebrating various milestones and events.

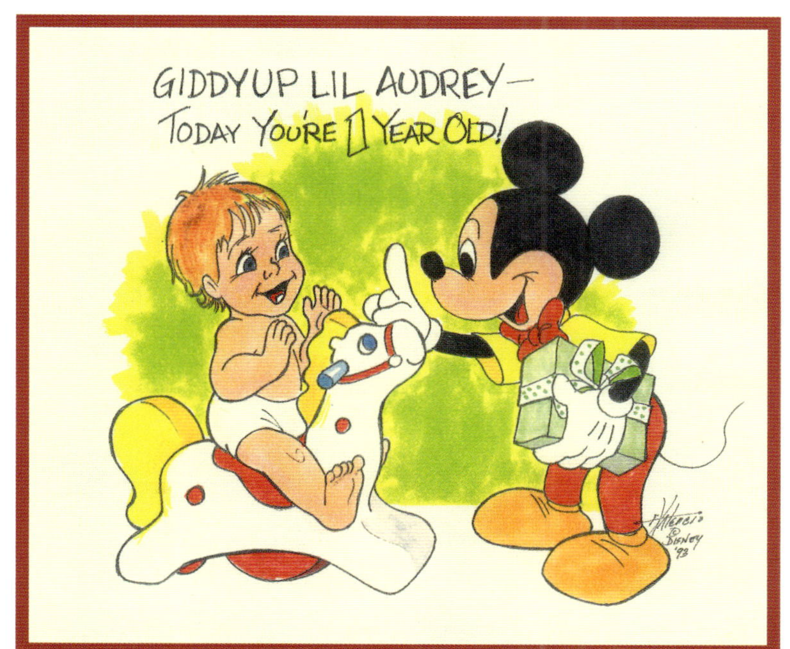
GIDDYUP LIL AUDREY—
TODAY YOU'RE 1 YEAR OLD!

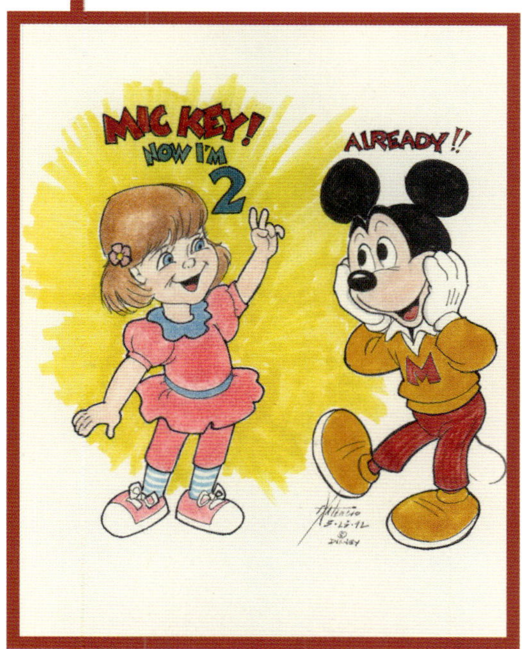
MIC KEY! NOW I'M 2
ALREADY!!

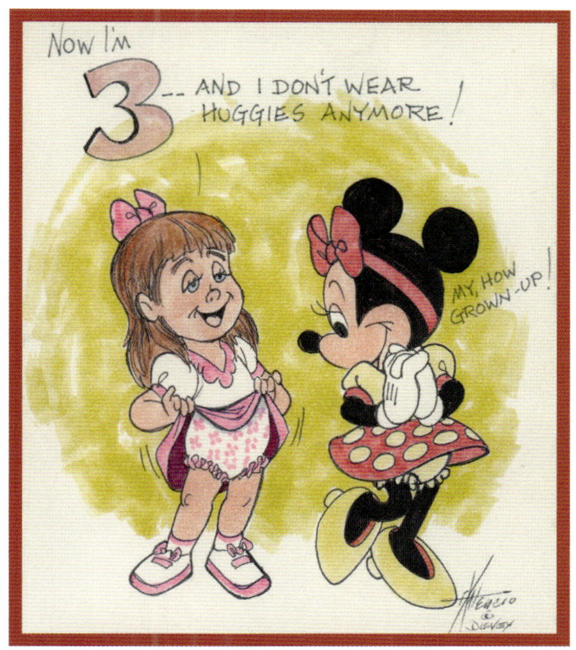
NOW I'M 3 -- AND I DON'T WEAR HUGGIES ANYMORE!
MY, HOW GROWN-UP!

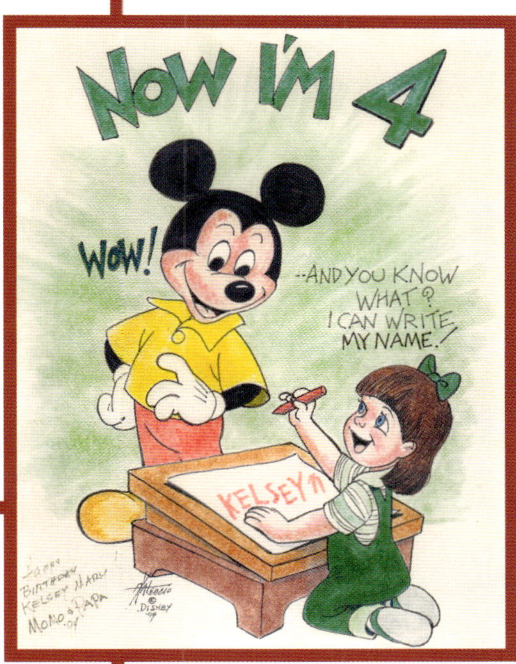
NOW I'M 4
WOW!
--AND YOU KNOW WHAT? I CAN WRITE MY NAME!
KELSEY

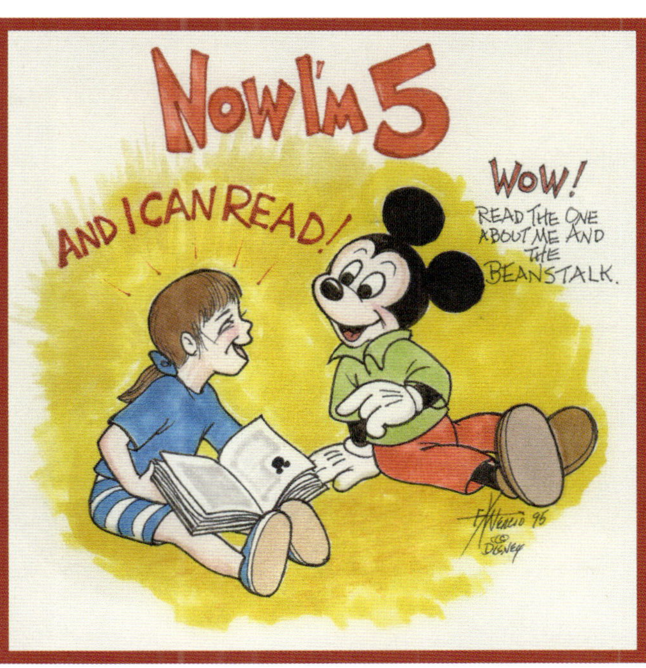
NOW I'M 5
AND I CAN READ!
WOW!
READ THE ONE ABOUT ME AND THE BEANSTALK.

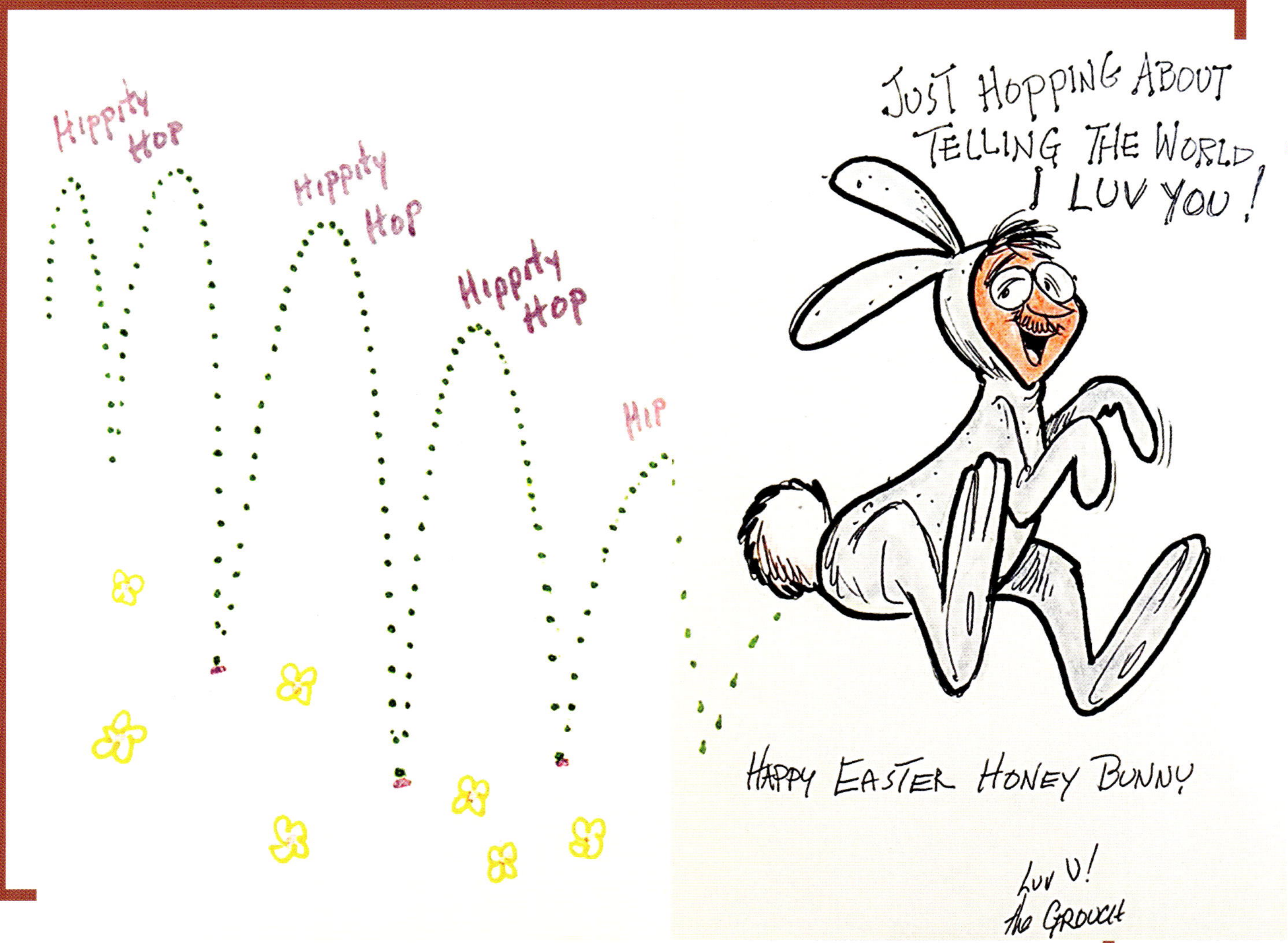

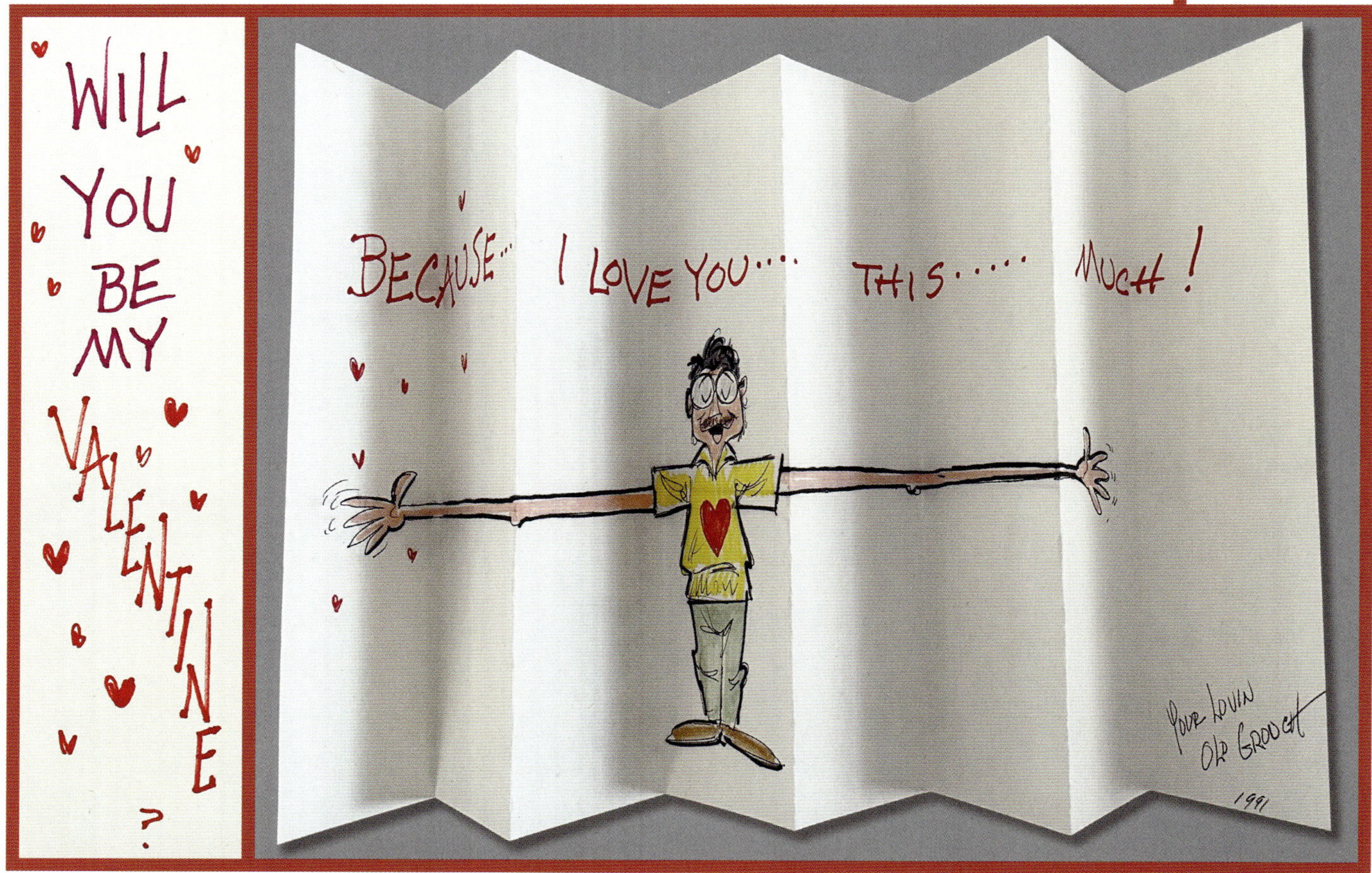

ABOVE AND OPPOSITE: A collection of cards X drew for his second wife, Maureen.

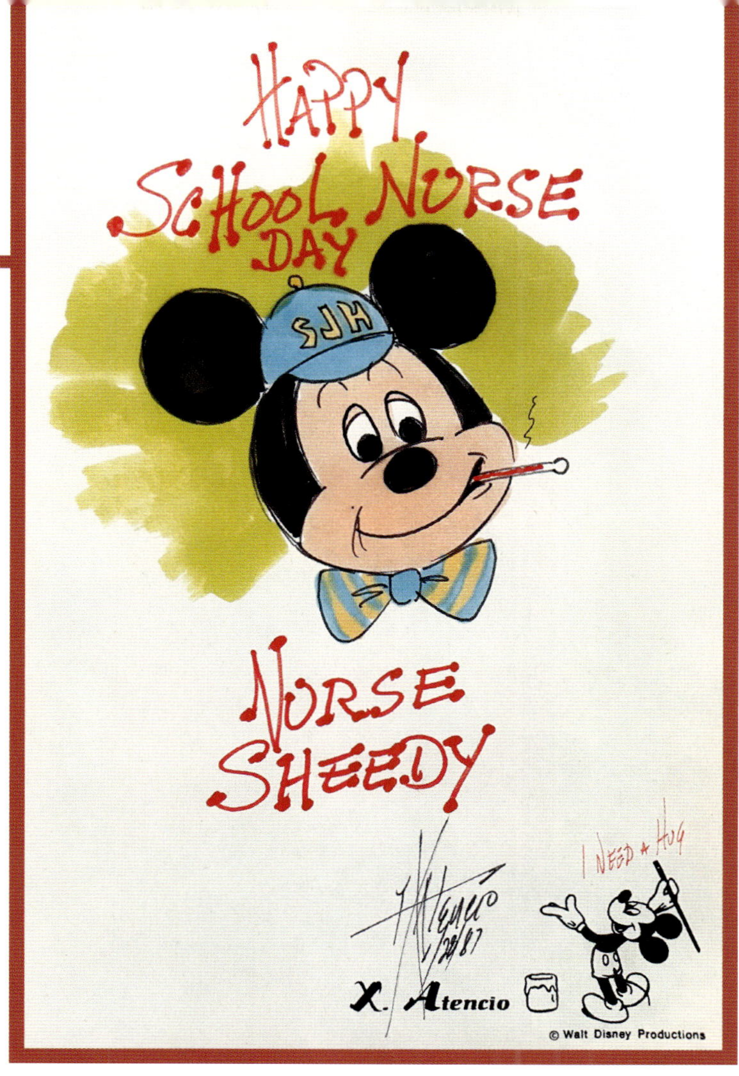

KNOW WHAT?

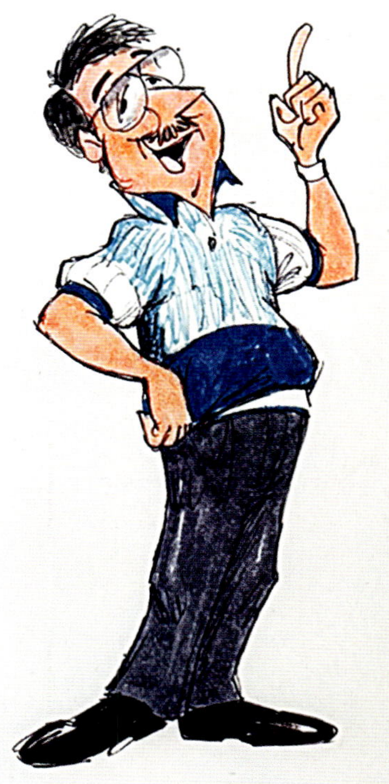

IM GLAD YOU HAPPENED A YEAR AGO!

HAPPY FIRST ANNIVERSARY HONEY.

LUV U
X

Tom Batsis, who knew them both through the high school their sons attended. As throughout his lasting relationship with Mary, X wooed Maureen with his signature style: drawing her cards featuring his forever wingman, Mickey Mouse, and a revolving cast of side characters. Disney illustrations, plus the presence of a priest at a first meeting, spelled success for X's courtships. X and Maureen dated for two years before marrying in 1988. They were welcomed by each other's families, having three children each from their previous marriages in true (adult) *Brady Bunch* fashion. X and Maureen remained happily married until X's passing in 2017. Together they traveled, hosted holiday and other gatherings at their Woodland Hills home, and became grandparents to nine grandchildren beginning in 1990. X loved being a grandfather, teaching his young charges how to draw Disney characters, and ensuring that they had the best birthday cards in town, complete with hand-drawn Mickey and friends.

While X received many Disney honors in his lifetime, receiving the Disney Legends Award, an honor

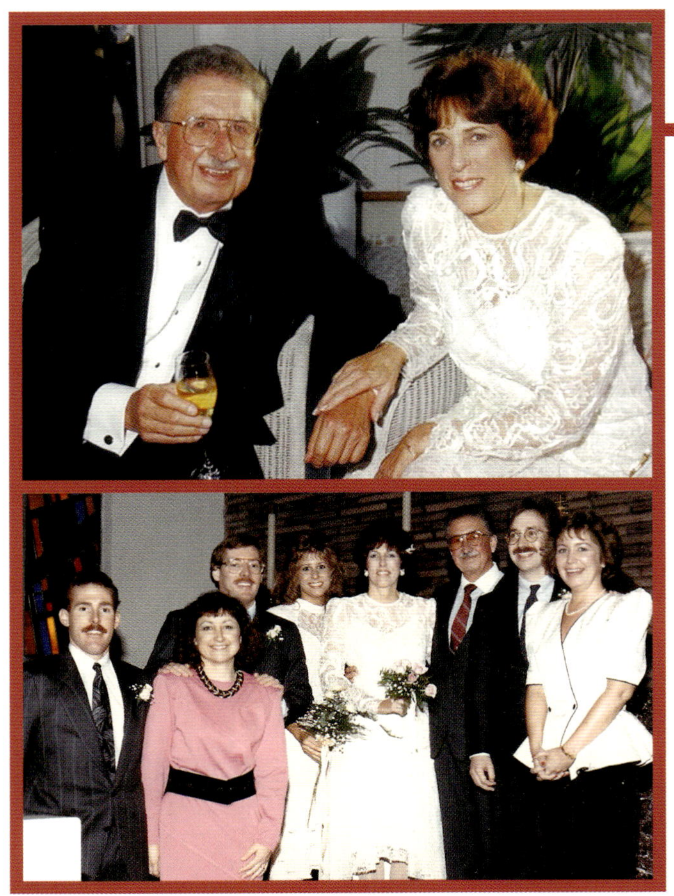

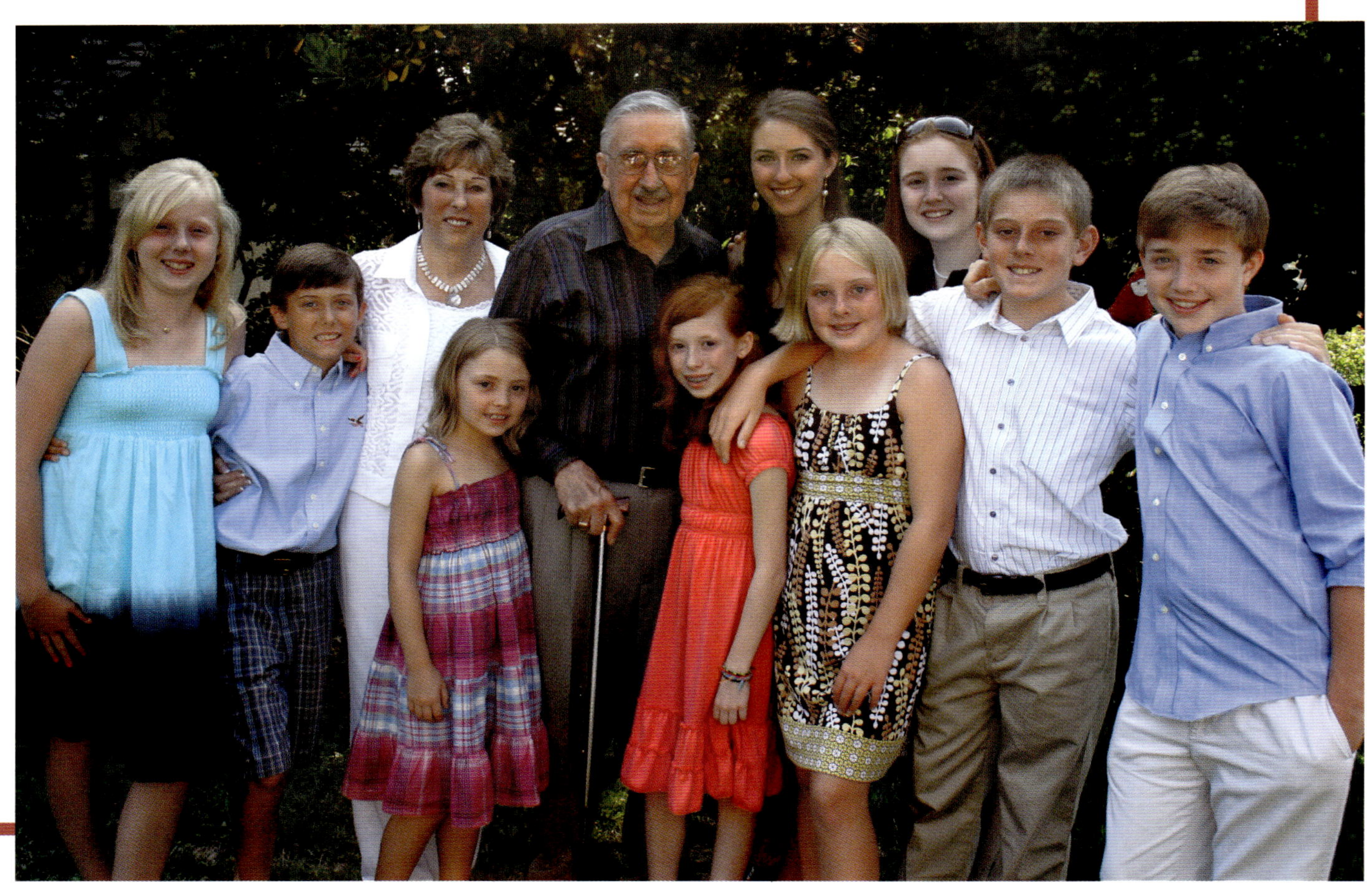

ABOVE (TOP): X and Maureen on their wedding day; ABOVE (MIDDLE): X and Maureen and their children on their wedding day; ABOVE: X, Maureen, and their nine grandchildren at X's ninetieth birthday party; OPPOSITE (TOP LEFT): X receiving his Disney Legends Award from Roy E. Disney; OPPOSITE (TOP RIGHT): X and Bill Justice at the Disney Legends ceremony in 1996 on the Disney studio lot in Burbank; OPPOSITE (BOTTOM): X with his handprints in Disney Legends Plaza on the Disney studio lot.

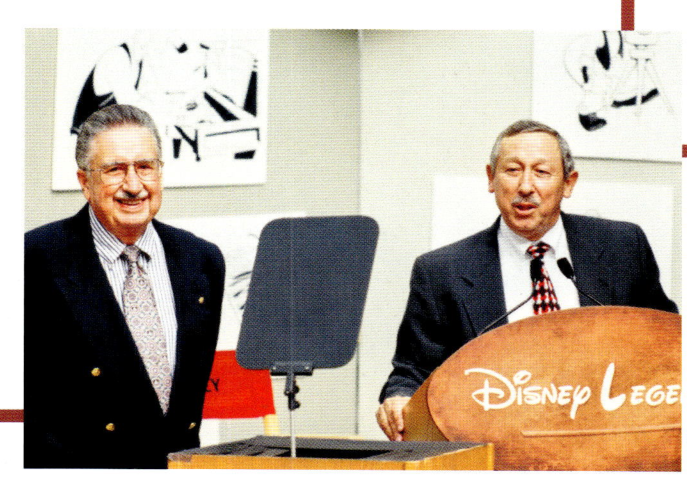

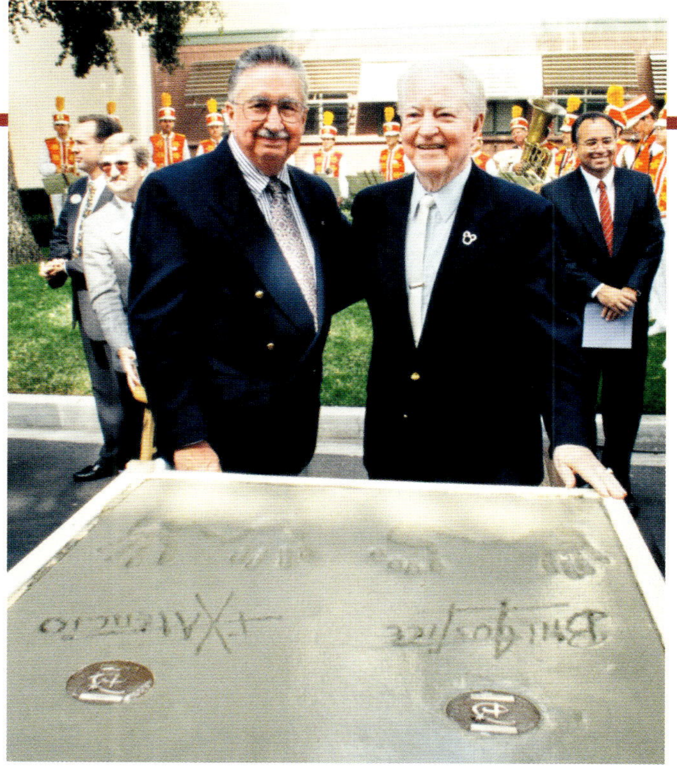

bestowed on a small number of individuals who have made a significant impact on the Disney legacy, elevated him to a new category. At the 1996 Legends ceremony, company vice chairman Roy E. Disney said that when he was a child, "There were two guys my dad [Roy] used to refer to who seemed rather mysterious to me. One was T. Hee, and the other was X. . . . Yo Ho Ho, it's a legend's life for you." X's handprinted Legends plaque hangs in Disney Legends Plaza at The Walt Disney Studios in Burbank, forever near the *Partners* statue of Walt holding hands with Mickey Mouse. X also received two Main Street, U.S.A. windows in dedication to his work. The one at Disneyland is on the second level above the Mad Hatter shop, while in Walt Disney World, his window rests above the Main Street Confectionery. The Disneyland window reads, THE MUSICAL QUILL—LYRICS AND LIBRETTOS BY X. ATENCIO. The Walt Disney World window reads, HOLLYWOOD PUBLISHING COMPANY—MANUSCRIPTS AND MELODRAMAS—F. X. ATENCIO—AL BERTINO—MARTY SKLAR. Joining an even smaller, more selective group, X has his own tombstone at the Haunted Mansion, which reads, REQUIESCAT FRANCIS XAVIER—NO TIME OFF FOR GOOD BEHAVIOR—R.I.P.

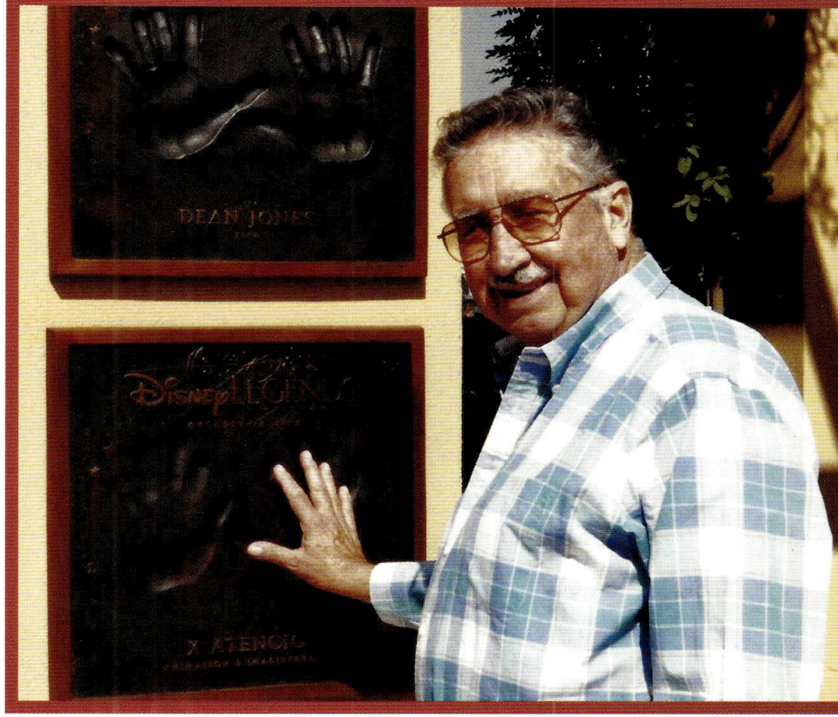

After reaching Disney Legends status, X received more calls asking him to come discuss his own career in addition to his time with Walt. He spoke at the D23 Expo in 2013. He was always surprised at how interested people were to talk to him and his old colleagues, or, as X called them all, "the old dinosaurs." X found himself at one Disney event in the Haunted Mansion until two o'clock in the morning, shaking hands and conversing with all the visiting guests, shocked and honored at how many fans and admirers had come.

X's career encompassed a broad scope of versatile roles, each filled with its own highs and lows. However, X personally found his time at WED to have been his favorite. Although storyboarding at both the studio for film and WED for theme park attractions shared similarities, his early time at WED gave him direct access to Walt through the assignments Walt gave him. While X worked at WED with Walt for only about two years, until Walt's death, the leap of faith X and Walt had both taken in X's transition to WED stuck with X and emotionally guided him for the rest of his career. Originally unsure as to why he had been

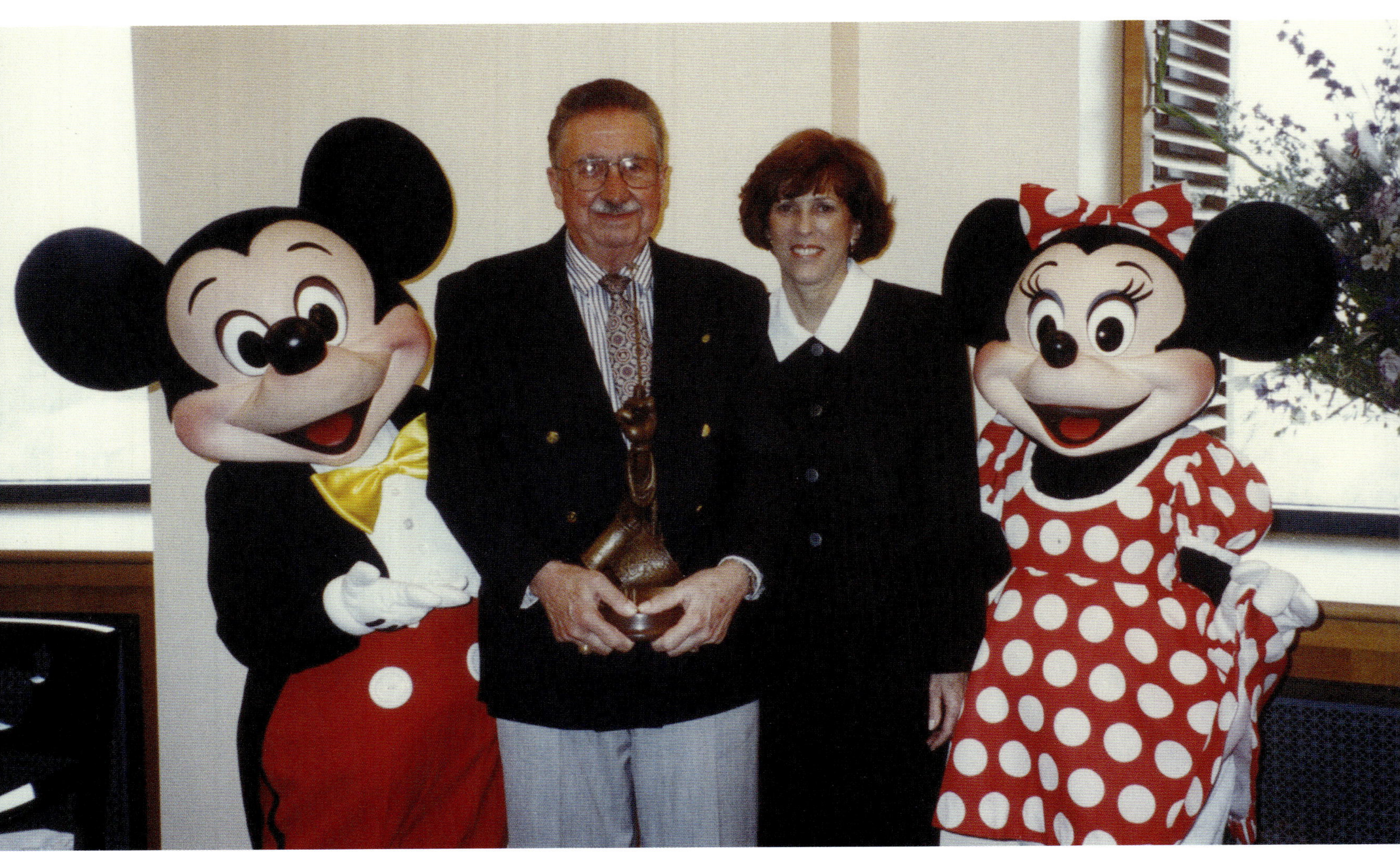

sent from the studio to WED, X soon found his footing and prospered, at first under the expert purview of Walt Disney, and then with those left in charge, like Marty Sklar and John Hench. X learned that the power of taking a risk and saying yes could pay off in spades. Furthermore, X valued finally getting to write, both believing that the writing had done more for his career than his earlier work in animation and feeling personally fulfilled given his youthful experiences working in and around newspapers and aspiring to live like those very same reporters. This love first appeared with his father and their *El Clarin* newspaper and then grew with X's own work on his high school paper.

While his first childhood dream of writing for a newspaper was thwarted when Denver University rejected his application, in hindsight X realized his dream of becoming a writer had come true, just not in the way he had expected—after twenty-seven years of work at the studio, it was when he was called to WED and officially became a writer. X loved both jobs, always saying, "What better life could you have?" The writing challenged him—both script writing and songwriting. He felt that those were his, coming from deep within his imagination and psyche, created on his own, with the help of talented composers and other wonderful Imagineers bringing his work to life.

Disney Imagineering creative director and show writer Kevin Rafferty described how X's work influenced his own career and raised the bar of incredible work, saying, "X did his homework before thinking long and hard about the story he wanted to tell through lyrics, narration, and dialogue. While

ABOVE: X and Maureen at his Disney Legends ceremony; OPPOSITE (TOP): X's dedicated window on Main Street, U.S.A. at Disneyland (TOP LEFT) and on Main Street, U.S.A. at the Magic Kingdom (TOP RIGHT); OPPOSITE (MIDDLE): The concrete mold created at X's retirement and formerly displayed on the WDI patio space; OPPOSITE (BOTTOM): X with his family at the Disney Legends ceremony.

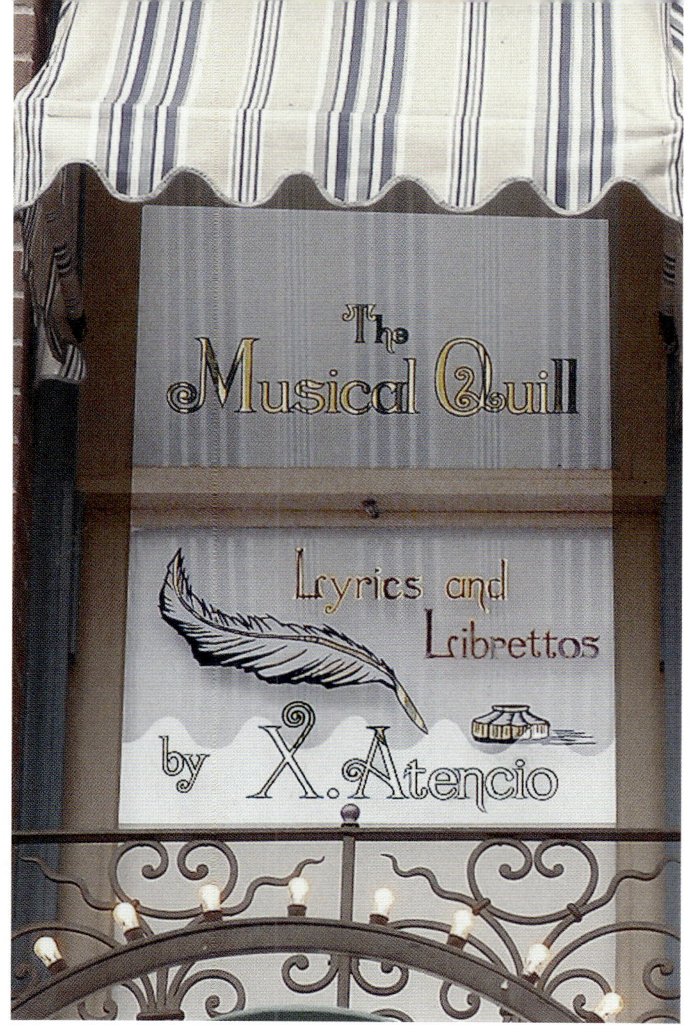
The
Musical Quill
Lyrics and
Librettos
by X. Atencio

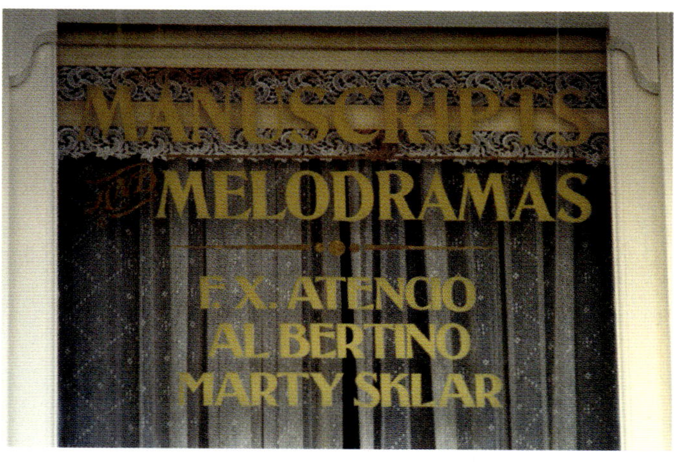
MANUSCRIPTS
MELODRAMAS
F.X. ATENCIO
AL BERTINO
MARTY SKLAR

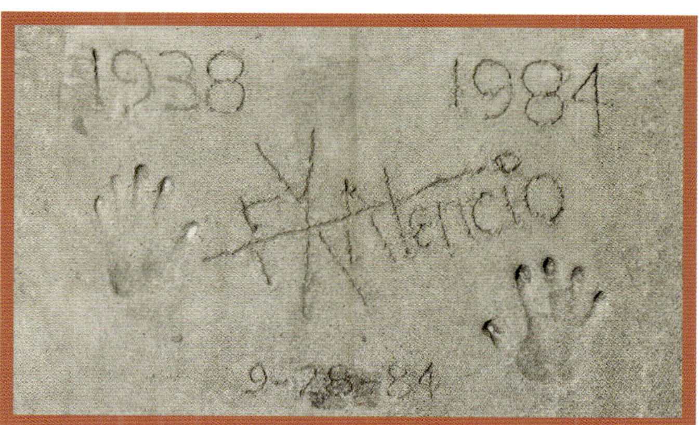
1938
1984
9-28-84

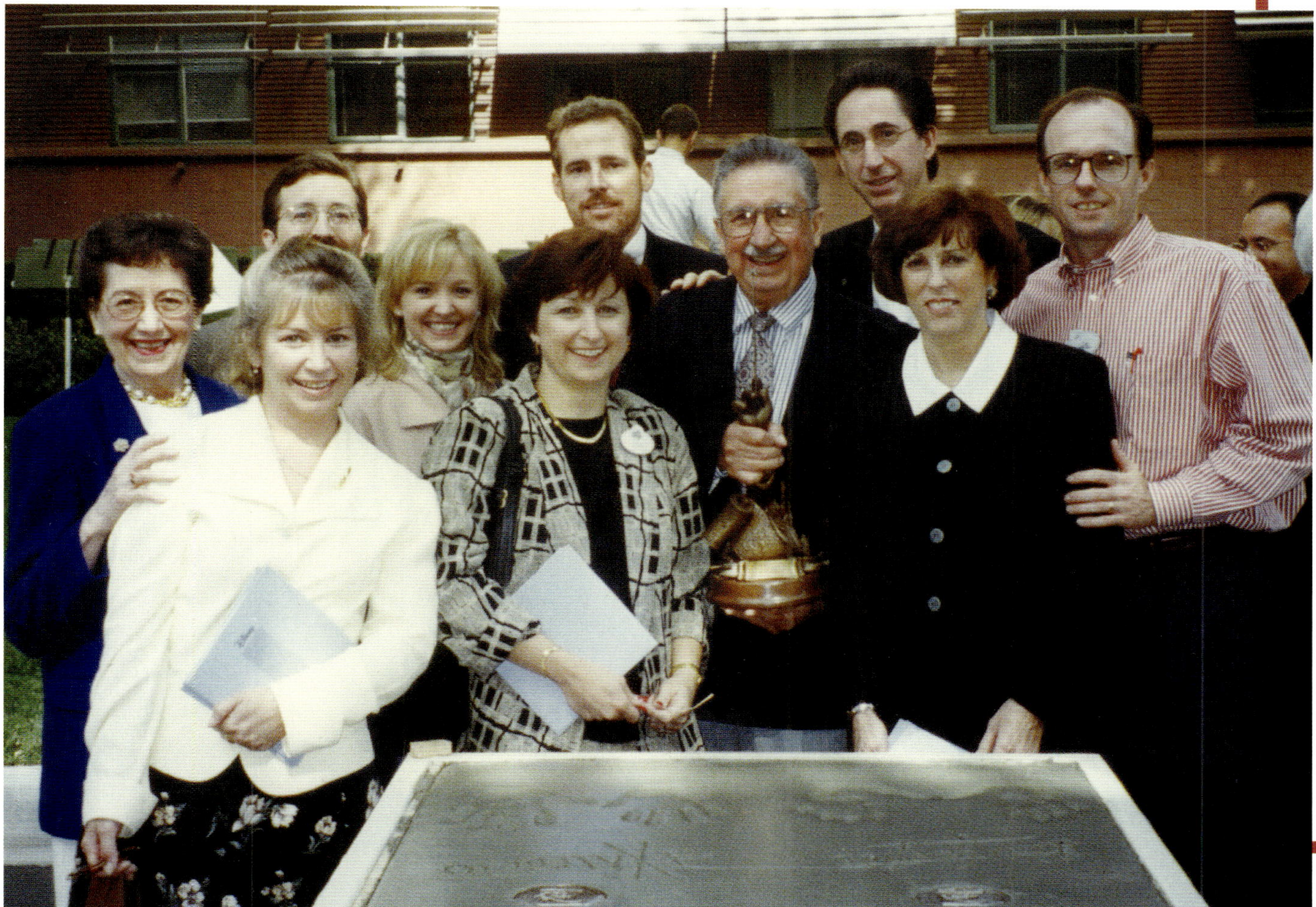

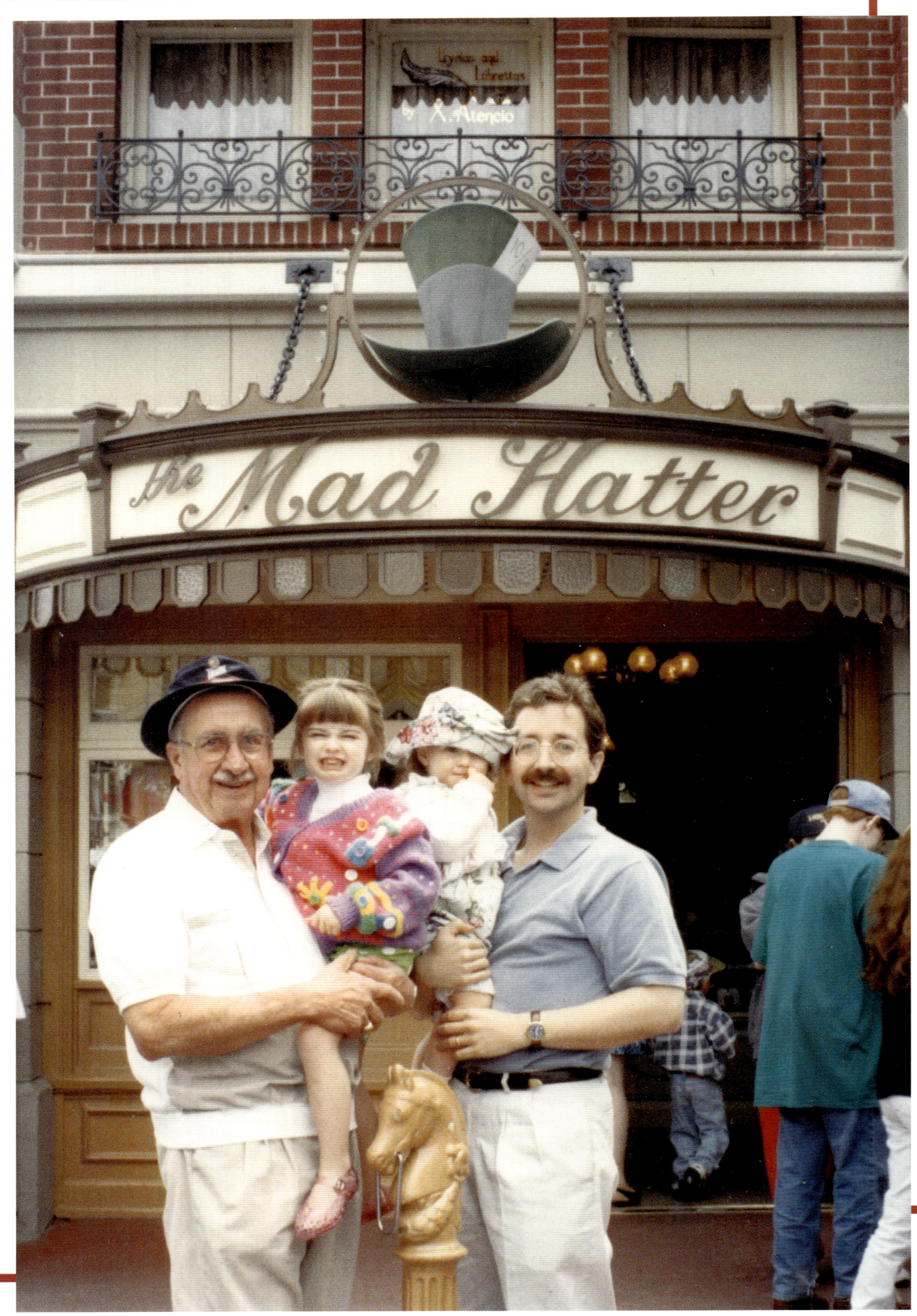

The Mad Hatter
by X. Atencio

carefully crafting each line, he strung an unusual collection of words together like perfect pearls to say what he wanted to say in a most uncommon way. . . . As both a fan and a dedicated student of X's work I can tell you the true treasure of this gifted storyteller is he took his clever and humorous approach to show writing quite seriously." Going further, Kevin detailed how when he was a young Imagineer, he found a section of the research library filled with old books on pirates. Looking inside at the checkout library card, he found the names X Atencio, Claude Coats, and Marc Davis scrawled across it. Kevin was awed that the tools his idols had used were now available for his own use. Inspired by their work and their dedication to ample research, collaborative creativity, and pushing the bounds of imagination, Kevin, and many other like-minded Imagineers of the next generations, continued pushing boundaries and striving to create work that would have made their predecessors and mentors proud.

Although unpretentious, X did realize that he had a part in the Disney legacy. He never let it inflate his ego, but instead took seriously his important role as part of that larger history. From his hiring at age eighteen for his dream job as an apprentice animator at Disney to his 1996 Disney Legends Award, X worked tirelessly to bring to life globally impactful entertainment for generations. While he spent more time than he had hoped as an assistant animator, the work he put in there—learning the craft, navigating different personalities and styles, and slowly adding his own influence—built the foundation of how X would operate throughout his career.

Ironically, X never felt like an animator. Though he left the studio having earned the official job title qualification of "animator," he personally felt more like an illustrator and wished he'd had a "better talent for animation." X backed up his argument by saying, "For being classified as an animator, I did very little animation. Mostly character development, layout, and story. So when people ask me about animation, I have to admit that I don't know a hell of a lot about animation. I think animators are a born talent."

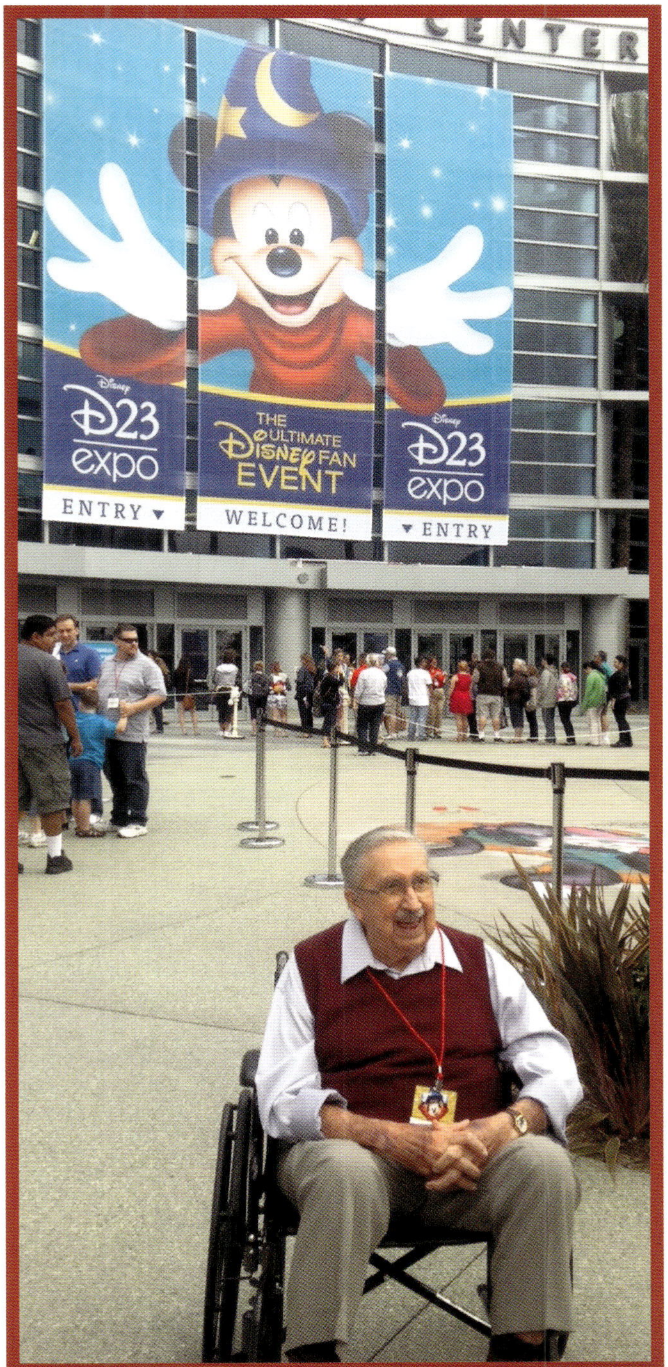

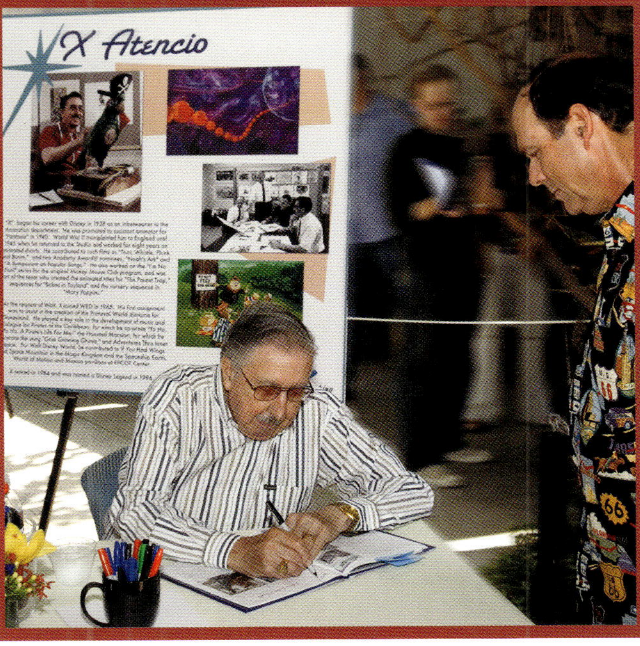

OPPOSITE: X, his granddaughters Kelsey and Audrey, and his son Joe standing underneath his window at Disneyland; RIGHT (TOP): X outside D23 before going onstage in 2013; RIGHT (BOTTOM): X signing a book for Kevin Rafferty at Walt Disney Imagineering.

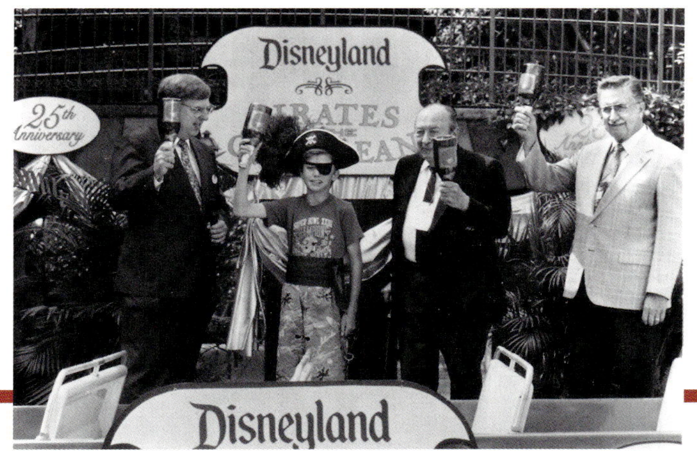

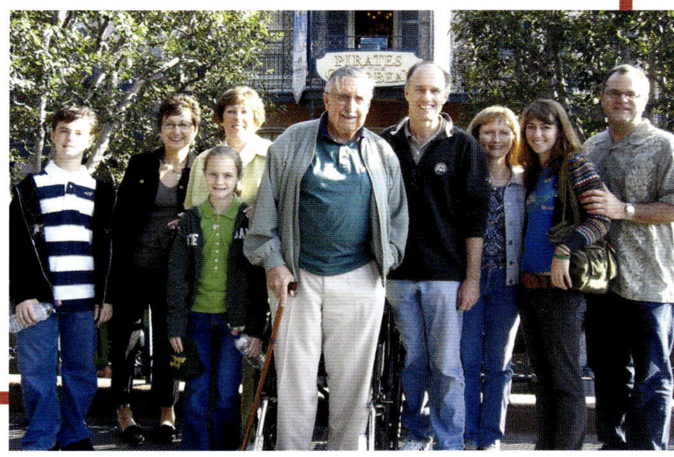

X knew that everyone's individual contributions were important but that the most fruitful and lasting successes at Disney came from working as a team, elevating the creativity through collaboration, experimentation, and trust in the Disney vision and in one another. X said when asked, "That's the way I was brought up in this organization, to be in a team. A team effort. No one took credit for specifics. *We* did it. It always bothered me when I heard someone say, 'I did it.' That word makes me so mad. I just don't like the pronoun 'I.' Everything we do is with the help of somebody else . . . somebody else puts their ideas in with it. . . . I don't care who gets credit as long as the end product is good for the company. That's the main thing."

Moving over into his experimental short animation and stop-motion animation phases gave X the creative freedom to take risks and take on bigger roles on the projects, allowing his talents in humor and narrative to shine. While the postwar, pre-WED period tended to be the biggest mystery and gap in X's career, especially when he would later tell his friends and family about his life, this timing and oversight makes sense. For one, X was balancing his growing family with his career and side freelance work, meaning he was always busy. Secondly, the style of recordkeeping at Disney in the 1940s and 1950s, especially given the team mindset, made it difficult to officially keep track of who worked on which projects and when. And lastly, because X had so many huge successes at WED (from Pirates of the Caribbean, Haunted Mansion, and all his work for EPCOT to eventually reaching "Legends" status), the earlier stepping stones in his career tended to get glossed over, especially since most of the true retellings happened in one- to two-hour official interviews or brief chats with family and friends. "Giving the highlights" proved insufficient to fully encapsulate the entire breadth and scope of X's professional career, considering how many highlights he had.

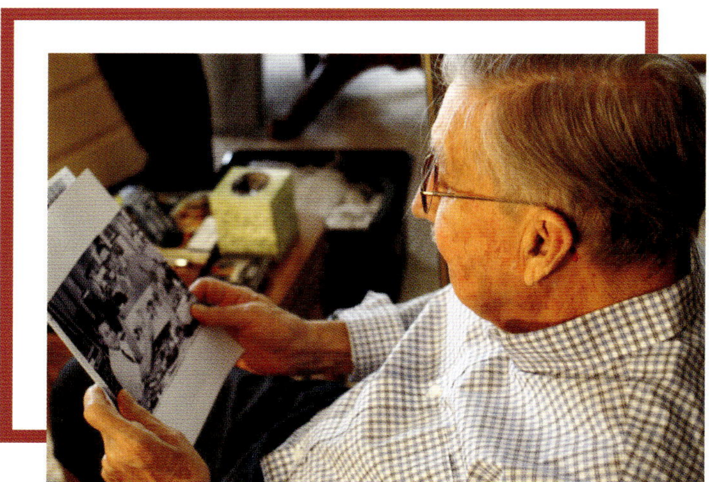

While the movies, television, and short films he worked on at the studio could quickly reach a broader audience, filling theaters and broadcasting live into people's homes, his later interactive work at WED offered the opportunity for slower, continued global reach. Each guest, sitting in the dark in an Omnimover vehicle, journeying through one of X's fantastical creations, went on their own personal

TOP (LEFT): X at the twenty-fifth anniversary of Pirates of the Caribbean; TOP (RIGHT): X and his family celebrating the fortieth anniversary of Pirates of the Caribbean at Disneyland; ABOVE: X looking at photos from *Babes in Toyland* during an interview for D23; OPPOSITE (TOP): X photographed at his home for a D23 profile; OPPOSITE (BOTTOM): X and Johnny Depp on the set of *Pirates of the Caribbean: Dead Man's Chest* in 2005.

emotional adventure. So X never knew when he'd be confronted with a random but meaningful interaction demonstrating the impact of his work. One time, X went to Balboa Island, a part of Newport Beach (just south of Anaheim), for a day trip and saw some children out on the bay, rowing around in a boat. Slowly, over the water, X heard them singing, "Yo ho, yo ho, a pirate's life for me." It was those unexpected moments that reminded X about all that his work had accomplished, even long after he created it.

He wrote with big words, making the dialogue or lyrics entertaining and true to the project, but with a respect for audiences' ability to understand. He knew how to craft without overly explaining, balancing narration with room for audience interpretation. X invested himself deeply into his work, throwing his full heart and mind into every project he worked on. He was beloved by talent because he understood and supported their gifts, treating everyone with respect and keeping the humor up even when the stress of large projects could very easily lead to patience running low.

His humility and honesty set him apart, making him someone that everyone from Walt Disney to the up-and-coming generation of Imagineers, like his

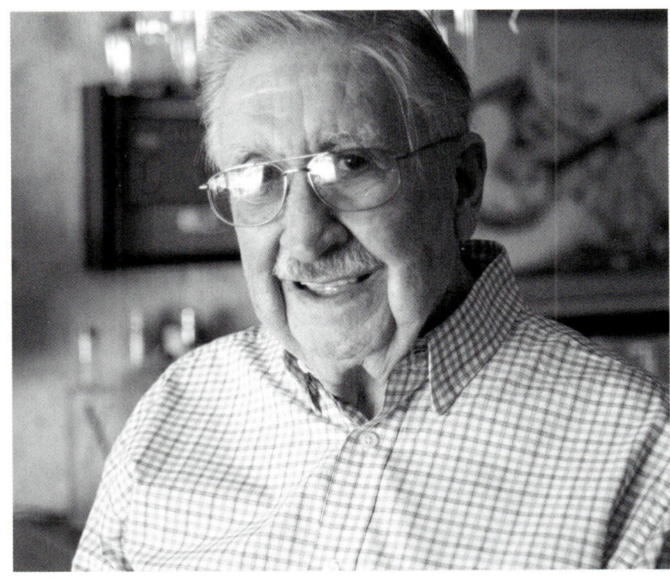

mentee Tom Fitzgerald, could admire. When Tom and X were on the plane coming back from a hundredth-anniversary celebration of Walt Disney's life, Tom asked him about the things he had created, saying, "Where'd you get those ideas?" X thought carefully before replying, "I'll be damned if I know! They just work out, you know? I think some of the things I wrote in the holding area of the Haunted Mansion . . . rereading or listening to them, I think they hold up

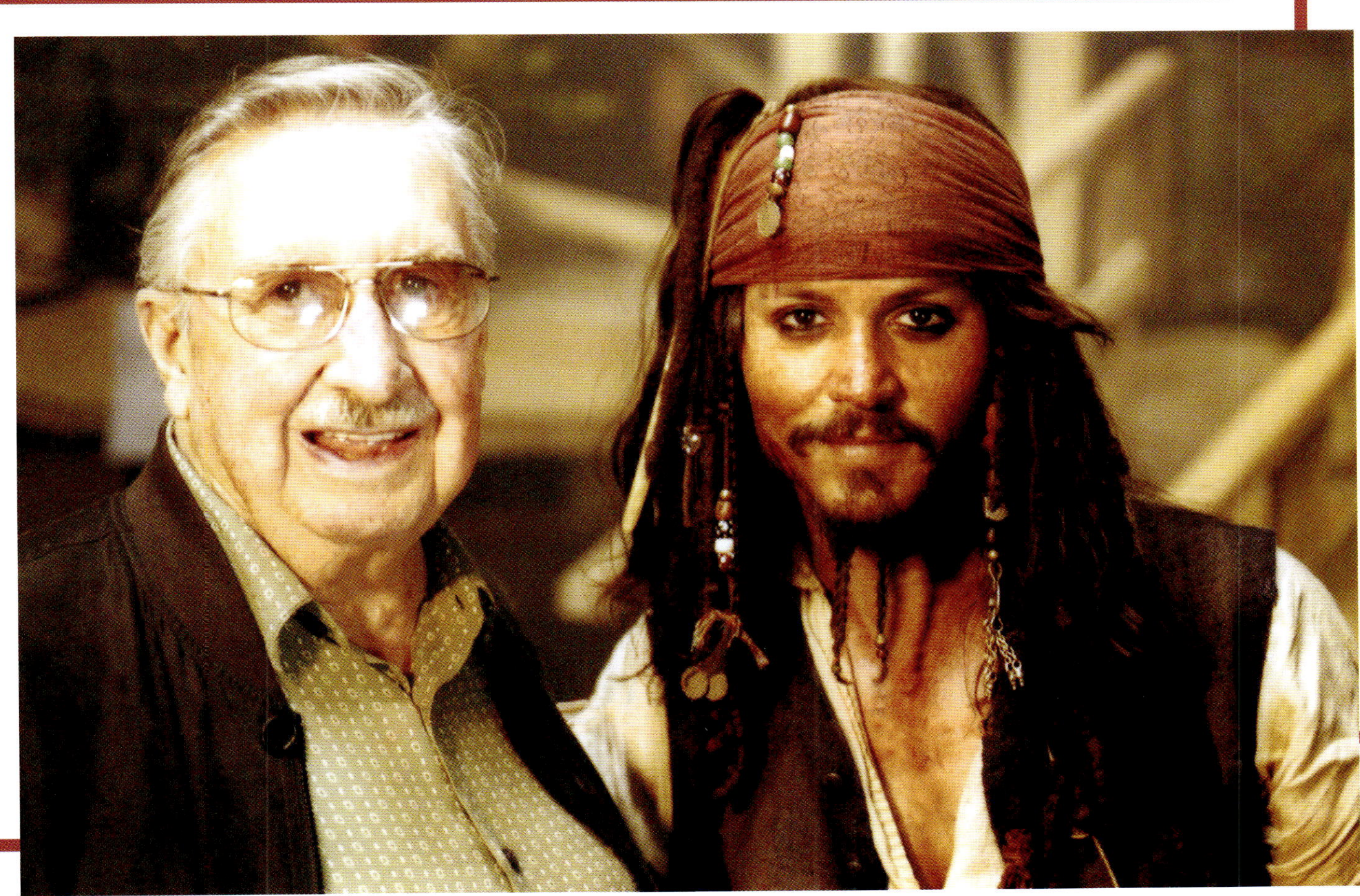

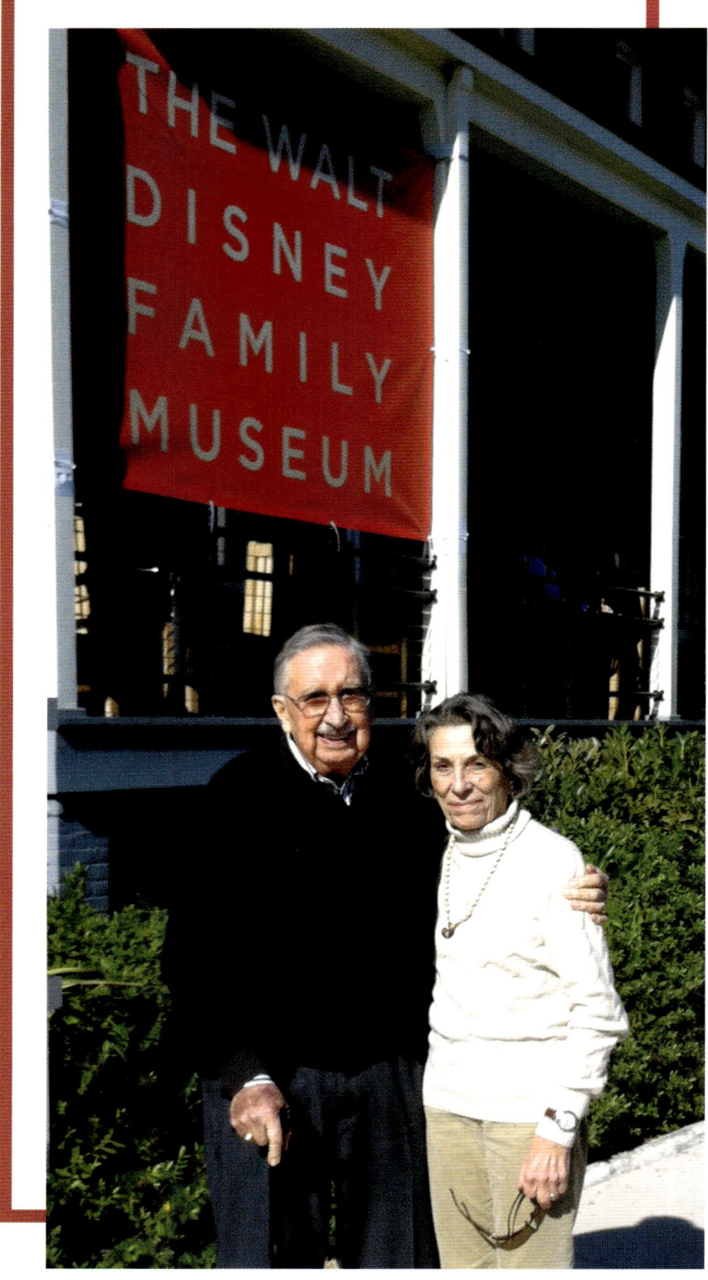

pretty good, if I must say so myself!" X found his work, especially the lyric writing, to be a highlight, but admitted that he was sure there were several people who could do everything he had done, perhaps better. Many people with far fewer accomplishments than X would be reluctant to acknowledge anyone could do what they do, and few would be inspired by the fact that the lasting creative work would continue long after their own had ended. X was secure enough in himself and his accomplishments that the next generation of young minds gave him hope instead of making him feel threatened. Always a team player, X wished them well in building their own legacies, hoping that their work would eclipse others' as technological innovation continued to expand the potential of what the Imagineers and Disney as a global brand could accomplish.

X passed away at the age of ninety-eight on Sunday, September 10, 2017. Even more than thirty years after his retirement, news of his death was picked up by all the major entertainment publications—*Variety*, the *Hollywood Reporter*, the *Los Angeles Times*, et cetera—and by massive talents on social media, like Neil Patrick Harris and Pirates of the Caribbean film series producer Jerry Bruckheimer, who sent their thoughts and admiration for X and his indelible career. From around the world, people continually reached out to his family to express their sympathies and memories of X. What struck his family most was that many of those people, whether former colleagues or brief acquaintances, acknowledged that they were touched most by X's kindness. And with that, X's legacy was secure—he was incredibly talented, successful, and fulfilled in his work, all while being a great person. He took the work seriously but never took himself seriously. He was humble, generous, kind, creative, funny, a devoted family man, and a great listener. He made anyone he met feel at ease and had taken the hardships and losses he had faced in life and channeled them into showing people that darkness and light existed on a spectrum. He understood emotions and how to create, even subconsciously, in a way that entertained but provided hope of a happily ever after. Yet he never shied away from the "dead men" or ghostly ending that awaits us all. Whether animals, pirates, ghosts, cartoons, toys, or robots, he found the spirit and humanity in each, instilling them with individuality but also a universal desire for community and search for meaning in their own worlds. As X said in an interview, "When I go to the big cartoon studio in the sky, I can say I was part of this."

X's legacy continues through his family, his lasting work, and the millions of Disney fans across the globe experiencing the unceasing life-changing thrills and memories that X created. While his daughter Tori McCullough (née Atencio) is now retired from her own forty-year career with Disney, the third generation, his granddaughter Kelsey, walks the hallowed studio halls every day at Disney, continuing the Atencio tradition of a family history that is deeply entwined with the history of Disney. For X, whose greatest sources of happiness were his family and his career, this important link and achievement would make him proud and confirm that he is still "bullishly" and forever betting on the creative vision of the next generation of Disney talent.

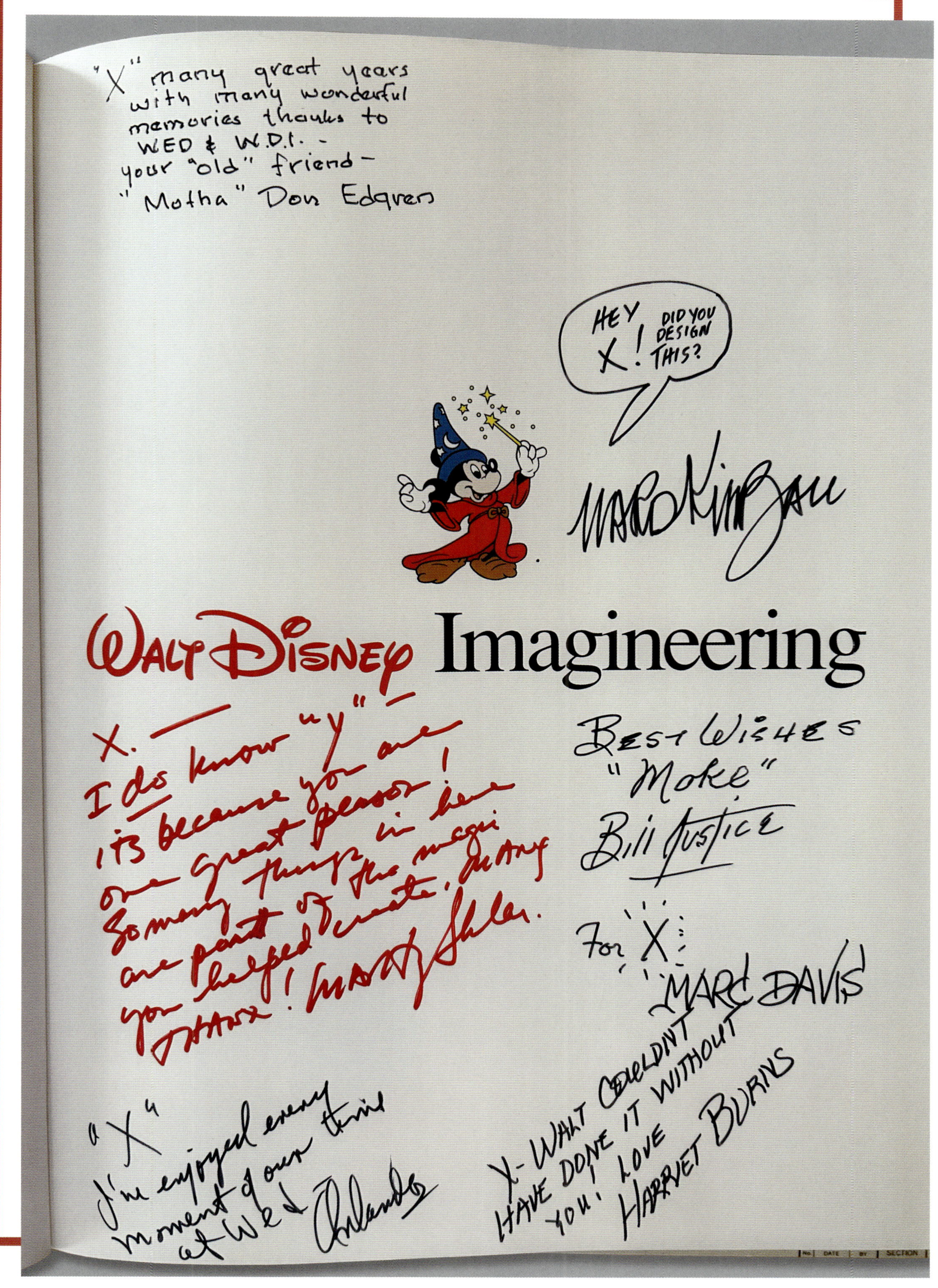

OPPOSITE: X and Diane Disney Miller outside The Walt Disney Family Museum in 2011; ABOVE: X's copy of the *Walt Disney Imagineering* book, inscribed by some of his fellow Disney Legends.

Acknowledgments

WE ARE FOREVER GRATEFUL to the many knowledgeable collaborators here who have shared their time, insights, expertise, and fond memories of X with us, and without whom the successful completion of this book would not have been possible.

Tom Fitzgerald: Thank you so much for your beautiful introduction to this book and your continued advocacy of X's legacy. The student has truly become the master, and X would be so proud.

Dr. Allan Williams and the Medmenham Collection: We owe you a debt of gratitude for responding to a cold message from a stranger on LinkedIn. Your incredible book and research so intelligently and vividly opened our eyes to the period in X's life we originally knew the least about. Your writings gave us a deeper understanding of his time in war and clarified the broader context within which X and his fellow servicemen contributed to the eventual Allied victory and end of World War II.

The Walt Disney Archives: Thank you for aiding us with your knowledge and keeping us honest in our quest to accurately tell X's life story, for allowing us to use your vast array of resources, and for your ongoing commitment to preserve the histories and legends of a company that means so much to so many people. Kevin Kern, Steven Vagnini, Mike Buckhoff, and Matt Moryc—thank you for your tireless efforts.

Walt Disney Imagineering Art Collections and Information Resource Center: As the home of the first Disney job for Tori, Judianne, and Kelsey, these teams hold a very special place in our hearts. Aileen Kutaka, Denise Brown, Mike Jusko, and Dave Stern—thank you for your support in bringing X's story to life.

Eddie Martinez: We are incredibly grateful and wildly impressed by your vivid memory in sharing the colorful stories of working with X on the creation of the Mexico pavilion.

Glenn Barker: We were fortunate enough to interview Glenn before his passing in 2023. Glenn was an expert in his field, and we appreciated hearing his memories, his precise understanding of his craft, and the humorous anecdotes of his time working with X. Both he and his wife, Sandy, were a joy and the best hosts we could have asked for!

Tom Morris: To the ultimate historian of Walt Disney Imagineering, thank you for always being able to solve any mystery that came our way. You are a legend in your own right.

Dave Fink: Thank you for sharing all your stories about X's involvement with General Electric through the years and sharing the unique card he drew for you, the only time he actually drew a caricature of the recipient!

Wendy Lefkon and the team at Disney Editions: Thank you to the incredible team and our editor, Wendy Lefkon, for championing this book and allowing us the freedom to honestly tell the story of X's life and career. Through your unwavering dedication and support, we were able to bring to life a book beyond our wildest dreams.

Mary O'Byrne Atencio and Maureen Sheedy Atencio: Last but certainly not least, thank you to the women who loved, supported, and inspired X.

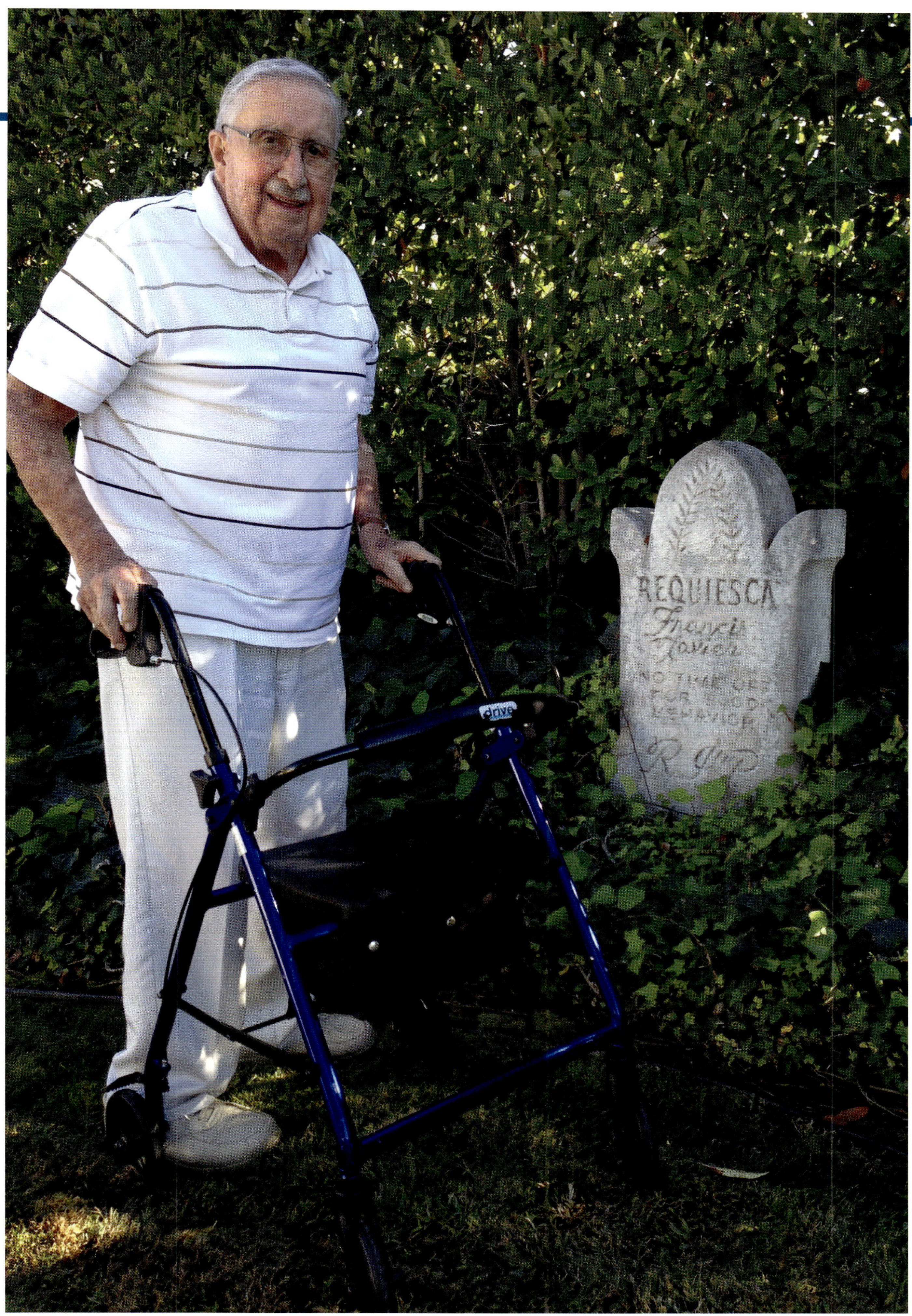

ABOVE: X standing beside his Haunted Mansion tombstone in 2013.

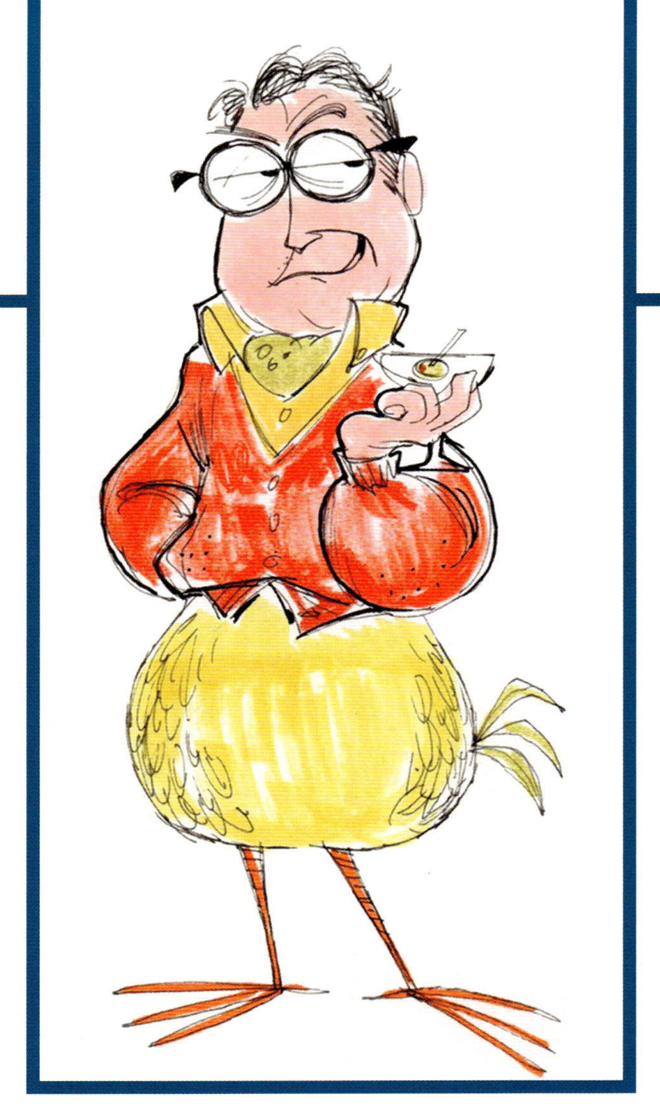

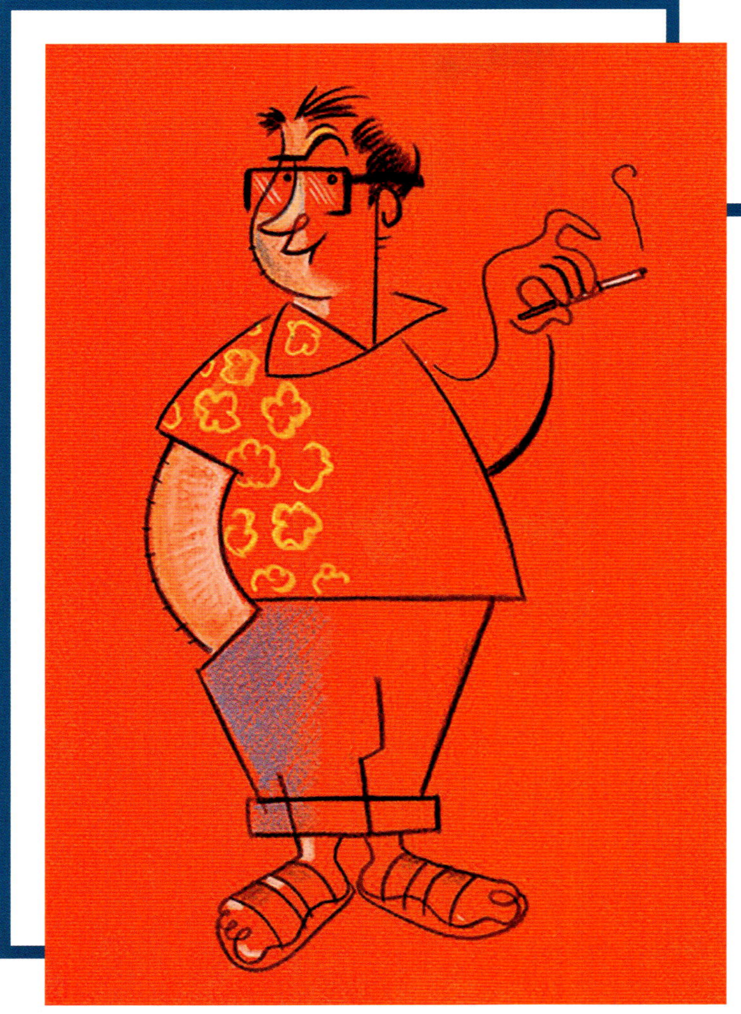

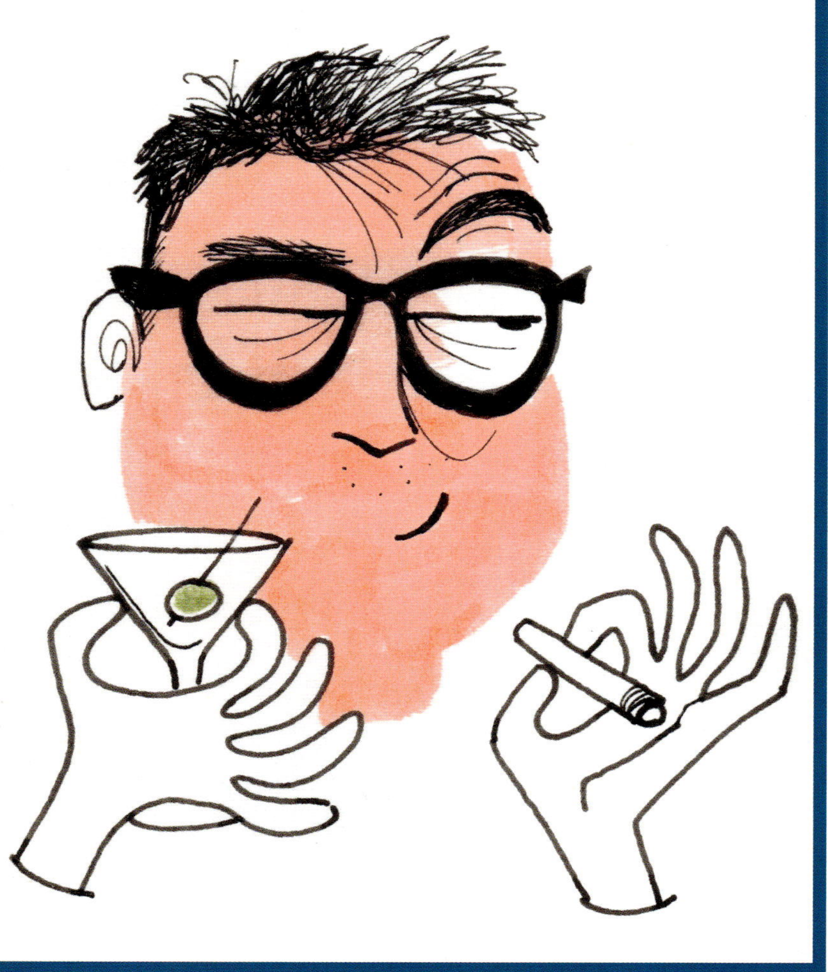

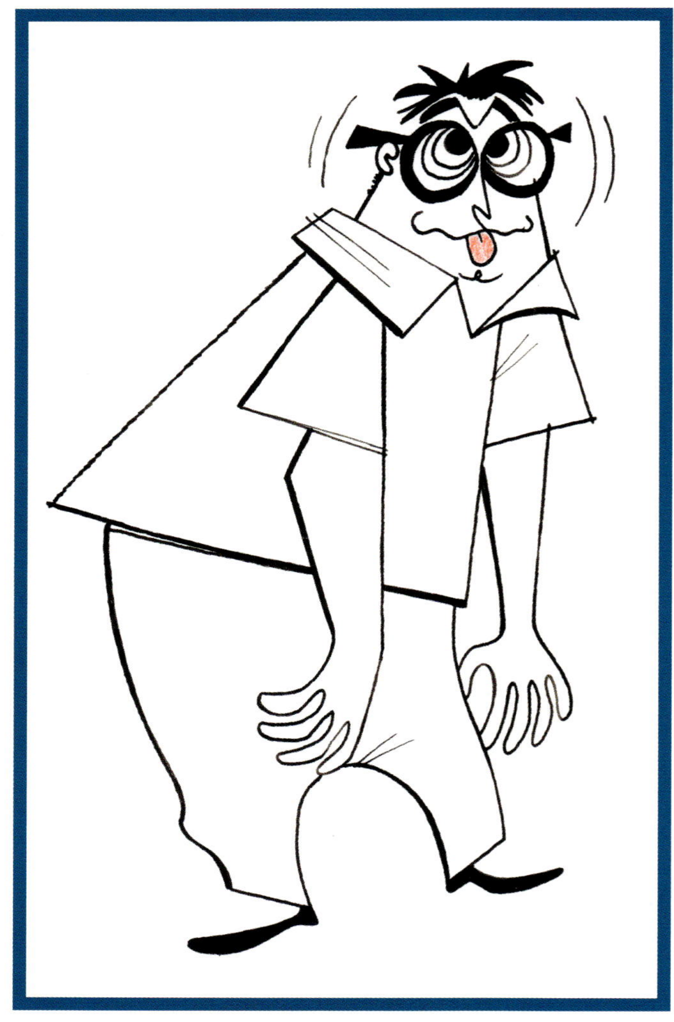

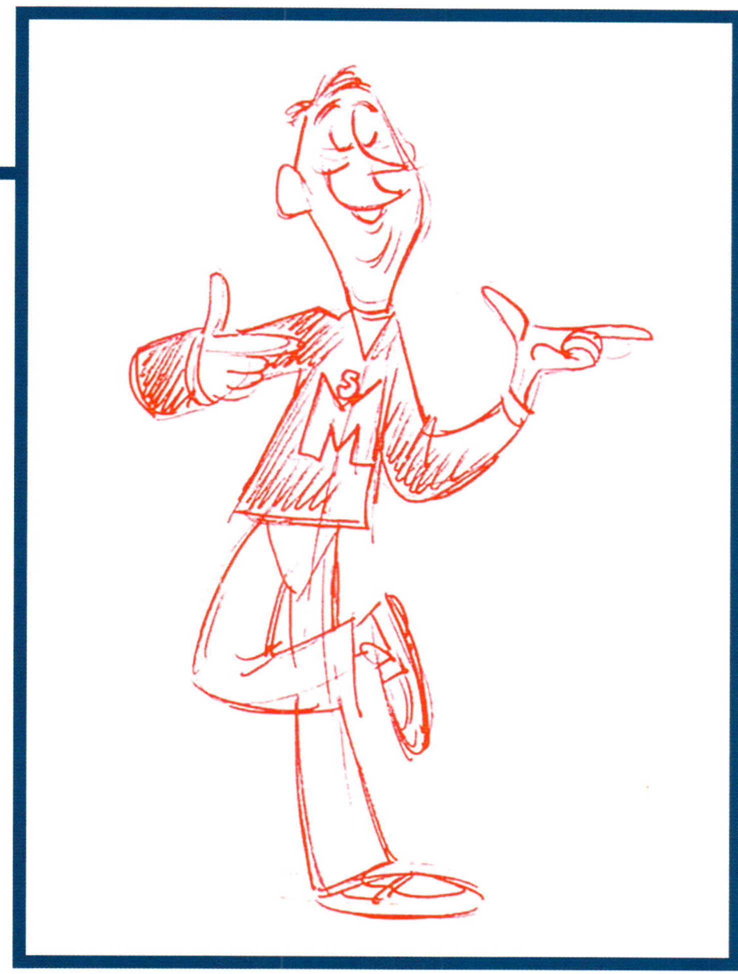

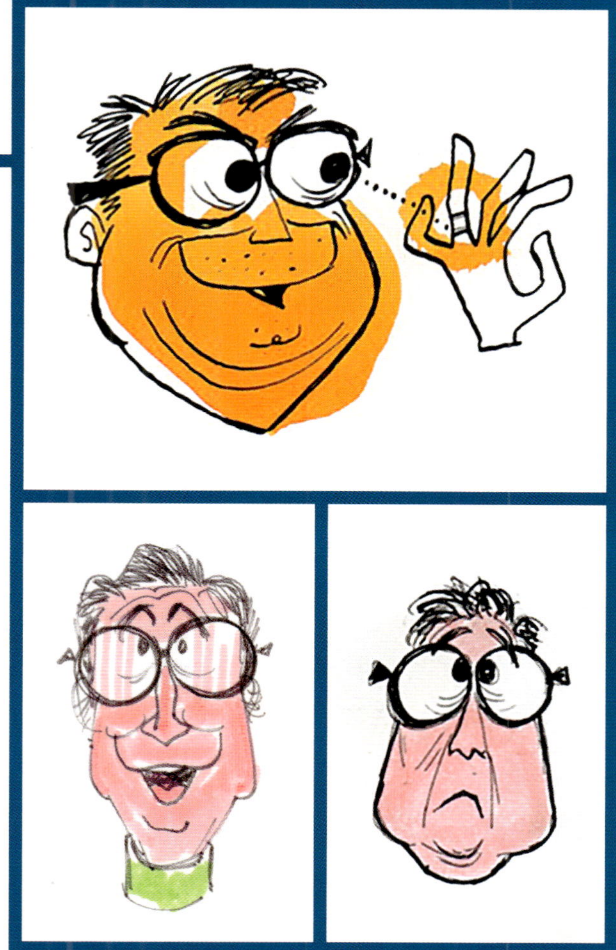

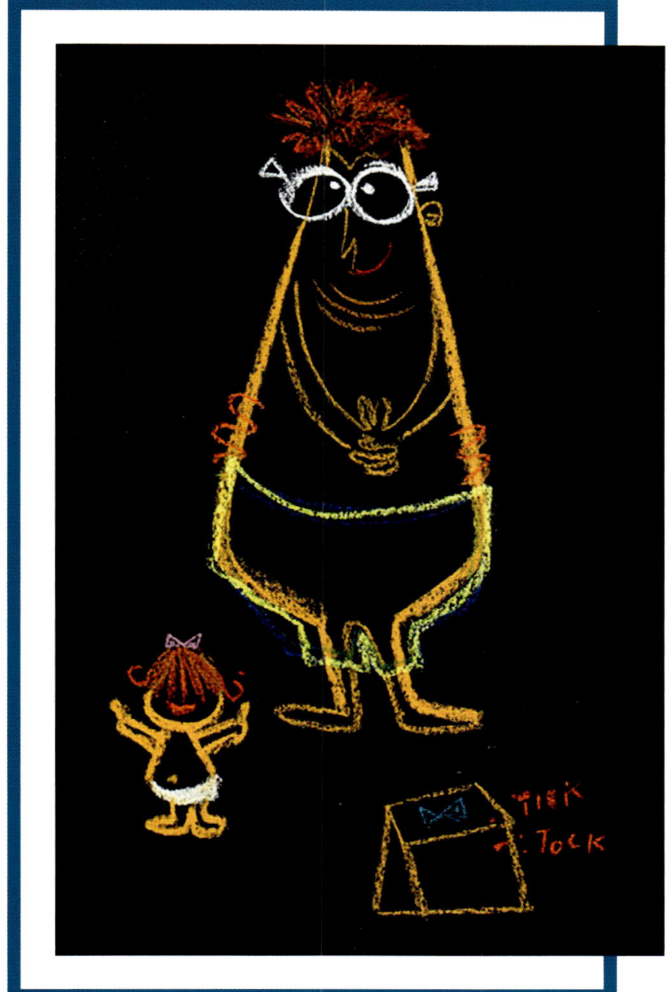

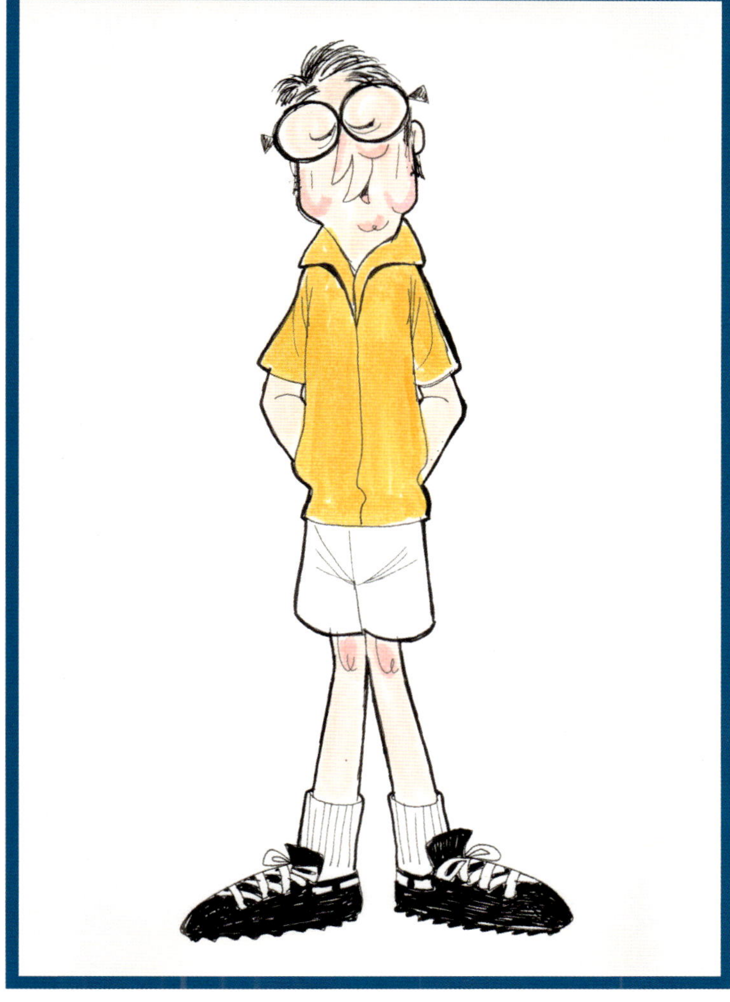

OPPOSITE AND ABOVE: An assortment of self-portraits X did throughout the years as part of Christmas, birthday, and anniversary cards.

Illustration Credits

Tim Delaney: 165

Elisabete Erlandson: 188

Dave Fink: 188

Gary Goddard: 161

Huerfano Heritage Center: 6, 7

Indiana University Libraries Moving Image Archive: 69

The Medmenham Collection: 50, 52, 55

Dana Morgan: 135

National Geographic: 123

Teri Roseman: 188

Walt Disney Animation Research Library: 76, 121

Walt Disney Archives Photo Library: 24, 29, 34, 40, 70, 76, 77, 79, 93, 103, 104, 106, 107, 119, 134, 137, 138, 140, 147, 156, 158, 161, 193, 198, 199, 208

Walt Disney Film Library: 68, 70, 93, 94, 95, 96, 98, 99, 101, 102, 118, 120

Walt Disney Imagineering Art Collections: 126, 131, 132, 133, 136, 138, 141, 142, 143, 144, 145, 152, 153, 154, 155, 166, 167, 168, 170, 172, 173, 174, 176, 177, 179, 183, 184, 186, 195, 197

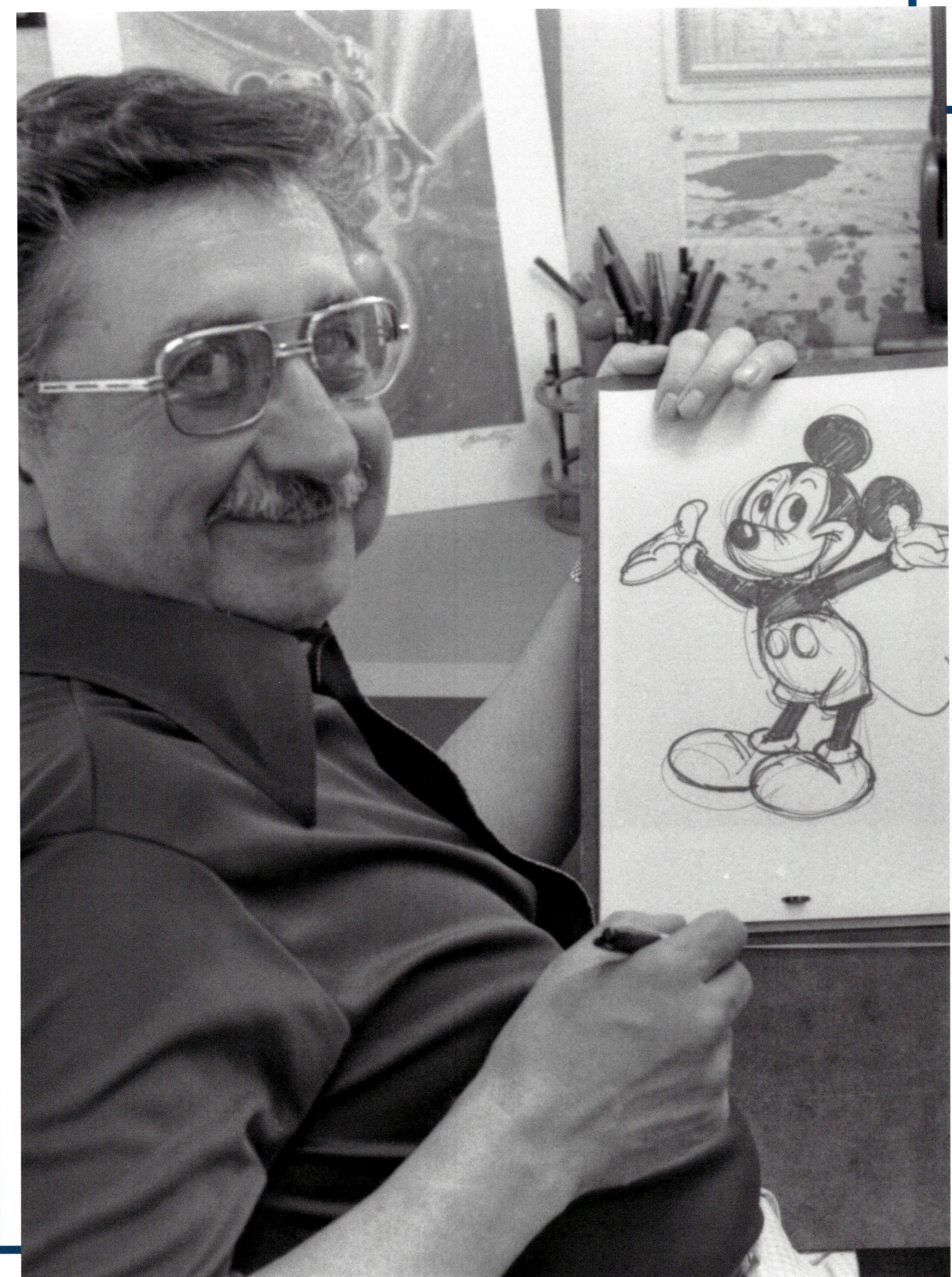